CONTENTS

THE KENNETH WILLIAMS DIARIES

Edited by Russell Davies

HarperCollins*Publishers*

HarperCollins*Publishers*
77–85 Fulham Palace Road,
Hammersmith, London W6 8JB

This paperback edition 1994
3 5 7 9 8 6 4

First published in Great Britain by
HarperCollins*Publishers* 1993

ISBN 0 00 638090 5

Set in Linotron Meridien

Printed in Great Britain by
HarperCollinsManufacturing Glasgow

The Kenneth Williams Diaries

Russell Davies, editor of *The Kenneth Williams Diaries*, became a freelance writer and broadcaster soon after leaving Cambridge University in 1969. He has been film and television critic of the *Observer* and television critic of the *Sunday Times*, and lately has been writing a column about sport for the *Sunday Telegraph*. For television and radio, he has presented many literary and political features, a history of radio comedy, more than fifty editions of 'What the Papers Say', sundry jazz documentaries and a number of arts documentaries (some of them watched by Kenneth Williams); but in spite of his involvement with Light Entertainment, particularly in radio, he never quite collided with Williams himself – except in print. ('Sounds like a nasty piece of work' was Williams's verdict in the *Diaries*. If only they had met!)

Russell Davies is also the editor of *The Kenneth Williams Letters*.

Have a Cool Jule
Love
Gela '94

ILLUSTRATIONS

ACKNOWLEDGEMENTS

I should like to thank the Estate of Kenneth Williams for giving me the opportunity to produce this selection from his diaries. No doubt it could have been done, here and there, with different emphases. I can only say that, while welcome advice was offered as to KW's storytelling propensities (including his occasional penchant for exaggeration and misattribution), no pressure was ever put on me to give any particular slant to the choice of material. The representative of the Estate with whom I dealt was Paul Richardson, KW's near neighbour through the last years of his life. Paul was a thoroughly welcoming presence from the beginning, and not only saved me from many an error of interpretation and tact, but also demonstrated those qualities of liveliness and appreciation which endeared him to Kenneth Williams himself.

The process of inspecting the diaries in the early days was curious, as they skipped capriciously from vault to vault, but I was grateful for the amiable assistance of Mr Spanton, of the Midland Bank Trust, in catching up with the documents. I took it as a good sign that as I finally waited to take possession of the diaries, outside the Midland's premises in Enfield, a BBC comedy archive tape of Kenneth Williams was playing on Radio 4.

The diaries record the events of five decades, and cover a very large area of cultural reference, from the poems of Rilke to the nude shows at the Collins Music Hall. Libraries and archives, in these circumstances, are almost one's only friend. I should like to thank the staffs of the Cambridge University Library, the BBC Radio Reference Library, the BBC Sound Archive, the BBC Gramophone Library and the Corporation's Left Staff Registry for their help with a large number of strange and perhaps trivial-sounding enquiries.

Many BBC staff and contributors supplied important anecdotal details. I am particularly grateful to David Hatch, Simon Brett, Jonathan James-Moore, Pete Atkin, Richard Willcox, John Whitehall, Anne Theroux, Denis Norden, Jimmy Perry, Denise Coffey, Delia Corrie and Ned Sherrin. Particular points were addressed with great good humour by Sheila Hancock, Mavis Nicholson, Tony Palmer and Alistair Cooke.

Ms Joyce Greenham of Newquay, a well-known historian of the area, settled several points concerning KW's early career in Cornwall. A chance meeting with Michael Branwell of British Actors' Equity proved invaluable. It is surprising how many actors – even quite prominent film and West End performers – are liable to become untraceable once their heyday is past. Equity itself does not readily release details, but Mr Branwell went to the limits of the permissible to help me. I apologise to any actor (alive or dead) whose dates are wrongly given; but, as the reader will realise, it is sometimes in the interests of senior professionals to be less than straightforward on the matter of age. Having consulted all the sources, one may have to take a plausible-looking guess.

Some of the quotations, asides and topographical references in the text defeated me. But I was in the lucky position of being able to throw them open to consideration by the readers of the *Telegraph* (Saturday) *Magazine*. They solved every problem put to them. I am grateful to Thomas Grout, L.A. Hemming, Jean Sheridan and Mrs O.J. Clarke for particularly enlightening replies, though all were helpful. Those few questions still remaining I submitted to my old friend John Gross. That a couple of problems defeated even him indicated to me that they were indeed insoluble.

Caroline Dawnay of Peters, Fraser & Dunlop first introduced me to the possibility of taking on this work, and at once made me feel suited to it. I have been continually grateful for her enthusiasm and encouragement throughout its progress. Her colleague, Pat Kavanagh, knows of my gratitude for her continuing support over the years. At HarperCollins, Richard Johnson presided over the arduous production process with astonishingly relaxed suavity, and Robert Lacey edited the enormous text with the kind of patience I had thought incompatible with such perfectionism.

As one bends to a task such as this, one's family bends a little too, and I salute mine for their heroic pliability. My parents, Gladys and John Davies, are used to being treated like ambulant archives. I thank them for all their help with this book, and indeed for everything they have given me through all the decades it covers. My son, Steffan, has coped wonderfully well with the sight of the unavailable father slaving over a computer which he, the son, understands so much better than I do. I hope he will be able to look at this book in later years and feel a part of it. The story it tells is one of solitariness, and of unfulfilled longing for partnership. With every page, I have felt more grateful for the tender and inspiring company of Judy, my wife.

INTRODUCTION

Kenneth Williams, who died in 1988, kept a journal for more than forty years, and made no secret of it. Indeed, he advertised the existence of the big black Desk Diaries he came to prefer, by having himself photographed in front of a shelved row of them for the cover of his 1985 autobiography, *Just Williams*. There is a hint of menace in these looming volumes, and in the little ceramic figure who shares their shelf, a cloven-footed faun with devilish elongated ears. The effect is not out of place. Colleagues who displeased Williams sometimes found themselves threatened with inclusion in the daily log; and some say that the threat ('I'll put you in my diary!'), made only half in jest, could sound intimidating, even though there was no immediate prospect of the diaries' getting into print. When his agent, Peter Eade, enquired, in that pointedly offhand way agents have, 'Will they ever get published?', Williams resisted the notion. 'Some sides of my character,' he explained, 'aren't presentable.'[1]

More than half aware of that, his public was fascinated by the hidden possibilities. So much of Williams was loudly on show that he could scarcely help leaving you wondering what he was 'really like'. His working life presented contradictions, for he seemed to be a man with intellectual hankerings, if not actual attainments, and yet much of the material he took on, during the years of his fame, paddled around among life's baser ribaldries. Even his voice suggested unreconciled duality, swooping as it did, often within a single phrase, from a sort of professorial woofle, patronising and urbane, to an acidulous, jeering Cockney.

His vocal agility was Williams's outstanding gift, and so dominant that it almost unbalanced him as a performer. In his early days as a concert-party artist for Combined Services Entertainments,[2] he specialised in imitations of voices, both male and female. When he progressed to the 'legitimate' stage, the question 'Which voice shall I

---

[1] *Just Williams*, p.191.

[2] The Forces' own theatrical organisation, staffed by serving men and women; the successor to ENSA.

use?' continued to determine his approach to each new role. But once he hit on a vocal register, he did not necessarily stick to it. He might shift from tone to tone, and from a languorous delivery to an agitated jabber, much as he did in conversation. While still a beginner in repertory, he felt he should be given the licence to let his own qualities as an entertainer show through the allotted part: he called it 'personality playing'. It clearly unnerved some directors, who were apt to take him aside and question him as to the seriousness of his commitment to the theatre. Later on, in his West End roles, Williams would become a notorious ad-libber. As his autobiography shows, he remained proud of his exercise of this privilege, even when it ruined a scene or a sketch or a working relationship. Naturally he raged at anyone else who departed from the script, arguing, probably rightly in many cases, that they were simply no good at it. Williams had many of the instincts of the music-hall comedian. He knew about laughs. When there were no laughs, or when a director aimed for a straight-faced reading of a scene where laughs would otherwise have been available, he became troubled, and troublesome.

His own view of his professional capacities varied wildly according to the needs of his morale on a given day. What most of us, coming home from work, pour out to our spouse or partner by way of self-justification, Williams could confide only to the page. (Late in life, he refers to the diary as taking the place of a 'mentor', which was the sort of fantasy-companion he truly desired.) So there are moments, even early on in his career, when he expresses a downright bumptious confidence in his talent, at the expense of everyone else's; but such self-sustaining bluster did not prevent his recognising his technical limitations. With props, for example, he simply could not cope at all. He dreaded being called upon to speak and manipulate objects at the same time. Over the years sympathetic directors sheltered him so well from this disability – a serious one for an otherwise versatile actor – that it is now quite surprising to see a film sequence like the inn-scene in the Peter Brook/Laurence Olivier *Beggar's Opera* (1952), where a young Williams, playing Jack the Potboy, comes swinging through the throng, spilling bottles from a high-held tray. So enjoyably physical an entrance is hard to connect with the Williams we later knew from the Carry On films. The physical dimension of the Carry Ons was slapstick, a genre Williams abhorred. He underwent it painfully, with many complaints and frequent visits to the first-aid room. Somewhere in the script of each new film, he feared, a tank of foul gunge would be waiting for him, and he was very often right. His feeling that he in particular had been chosen to suffer these discomforts may not have been entirely mistaken, either. These disorderly scenes always feel, to me, like the filmmakers' half-conscious revenge on Williams for his physical primness.

Films and broadcasting did not figure in his ambitions at the outset. He had dedicated himself to the stage, the first place he had felt himself to be at home, and among fellow-spirits. The young Kenneth Williams took the social role of the theatre seriously. Like many returning soldiers, he remained for some years avowedly radical in his political outlook – he made up for that later – and in the early years of his career agonised intermittently over where the English-language drama was going, and what his role in it might turn out to be. Some of these reflections may strike the young actors of today as pompous or inflated, just the sort of thing they have been warned against by the satirists who pose as breast-beating ac-tors or gushing 'luvvies'. But it is worth bearing in mind that without this kind of questioning and discussion, post-war British actors, from whose ranks many playwrights sprang, might have had to go on forever purveying the kind of worthy, familiar fare – Priestley for the box-office, Shaw for far-out intellectual challenge – which Williams found himself tackling in weekly repertory at Newquay and Margate and Salisbury.

Of course, when the social outlook of the drama did begin to broaden in the mid-fifties, taking in territories beyond the vicarage garden wall, Kenneth Williams played no part in the process. There was nothing in the kitchen-sink world for him (although he did help later, through his involvement in the work of Joe Orton, to make a final mockery of the old, rep-standard drawing-room play). But high theatrical artifice was no longer fashionable either, once the vogue for Eliot, Fry and Anouilh had passed; so it looked as though there might be nowhere for Williams to practise his own version of what he called the 'self-send-up sophistication' of his true master, Noël Coward. In the end, he was rescued by revue, at the very moment of its transition from campy, naughty, night-clubby 'intimacy' to the new knowingness of the University generation.

But first, there was time for just one sizeable, 'legitimate' West End hit: Shaw's *Saint Joan* (first performed in London in 1924), with Siobhan McKenna in the title role and Kenneth Williams as the Dauphin. It was Miss McKenna who brought in the crowds. Her Dauphin compensated by dismembering her performance in his diaries, thus beginning a long personal tradition of vexed relations with leading ladies. But Williams was noticed, not least for the strikingly convincing vocal change he brought to his portrayal of the character in the last scene, when the Dauphin, twenty-five years on, has become the prematurely aged Charles the Seventh. This performance certainly did Williams's career lasting good, but he did not feel it had really put him 'on the theatrical map'.

What it did, paradoxically, was to propel him into broadcast comedy. The BBC producer Dennis Main Wilson, impressed by Williams's evident vocal range, invited him to join the cast of a new radio series, 'Hancock's Half Hour', as a bits-and-pieces character man. In the first episode he came on right at the end, as 'Lord Bayswater', a querulous ancient (much older than the Dauphin) whose flat has been vandalised by a partying Hancock and his cronies. It is a tiny part – a few lines of senile indignation – but the tone of lost love and infinite sorrow that enters Williams's voice on the line 'Who threw jelly over the Rembrandt?' must have convinced Main Wilson that he had chosen the right man. After an uncertain start, the series grew into a much-loved success, transferring to television and taking Kenneth Williams, for a time, along with it. There was a period when he and Hancock were quite close. They shared an interest in philosophy and political theory, which they discussed for hours – generally unsocial ones. When Hancock was in the London Clinic on a slimming course, Williams would visit him there and continue their debates. At Hancock's flat, discussions could take all night, and in accordance with the habits of the host (and indeed the guest), drink was enthusiastically taken. Only a handful of Williams's diary entries could be characterised as incoherently scrawled: and most of these follow some all-night session at Tony's. The result is, alas, that while the topic of their debate is sometimes recorded ('long chat about anarchy'), the substance of it is not.

The two men eventually fell out; and it was at that point, when Williams was angry with Hancock, that he began to write articulately about him. It follows that a very negative view of Hancock emerges from the diaries, for there was no reconciliation. The cause of the quarrel was the very facility with voices that Williams had originally been hired for. In his search for a comedy based on some kind of authenticity or human truth more available to philosophers than to professional funny-men, Hancock had begun to try to strip out of his shows everything he felt was designed to produce ready-made or formula laughs. One of the early targets of this campaign was the most gleefully applauded of Williams's voices, known to the team as the 'snide' character (whose nasal catch-phrase was 'Stop messin' about'). The scriptwriters, Ray Galton and Alan Simpson, struggled against this prohibition, for the character and its voice were too good to throw away; but from that moment on, all Williams's instant characterisations came under threat. Gradually, his appearances in the weekly Hancock gallery were squeezed down until only fragments remained. Virtually the last of them was the part of a 'half-deaf dodderer with an ear-trumpet', giving Williams's career in the Hancock entourage a kind of circularity, if nothing else.

This is an oft-told tale from Tony Hancock's point of view, but looking at it from Williams's, you can see why he had few good words to say for 'the lad 'imself' in later years (and not many more for Sidney James, a survivor of the Hancock purge and a perennial Carry On colleague). Williams acknowledged the genuineness of Hancock's quest for comedy-in-life, but he knew that it was doomed, and it must have been galling to be sacrificed along the road to obvious failure. But in other ways he was not sorry to go. The Hancock bunch suffered badly in social terms, he felt, by comparison with the jolly team he had joined in the rival radio show 'Beyond Our Ken'. Fatherly, impeccable, encouraging and organised, Kenneth Horne was everything Hancock could not be as a working colleague. Through the follow-up series 'Round the Horne', right up to Horne's death, this partnership remained harmonious, and again produced work for which there is still an audience thirty years later.

Kenneth Williams underestimated the impact of these programmes on their contemporary public. Radio work for him was very much a sideshow, and not 'important'. The money it paid came in handy, but it was not enough to be a determining factor in career decisions. Still concentrating on his destiny in the theatre, Williams appeared not to notice what fame was being built up for him by these agreeable weekly meetings at the BBC's variety theatres. He was surprised by the size of the crowds who turned up to see the recordings made. The truth was that he was becoming a 'radio star', quite effortlessly, and in supporting roles, while pinning his real ambitions to his stage work. But every medium had suddenly discovered a taste for him. There was an astonishing period in 1957 when Williams was a member of both the Hancock and the Horne companies, spent his days filming a television-comedy series ('Dick and the Duchess') and, after dark, enjoyed real theatrical stardom for the first time with *Share My Lettuce*, the first of his three celebrated revues.

It had been Tony Hancock's opinion, when Williams complained of the difficulty of finding good parts in the theatre, that his best plan would be to devise an act and go out as a comedian in his own right, on what remained of the variety stage. Williams did well to ignore this advice at the time (though it was not many years later that he found himself writing and performing stand-up 'spots' in television variety). Revue, for an actor so tricky to cast in conventional drama, represented the ideal compromise. 'Personality playing' was not discouraged; questions of the 'integrity of the role' tended not to arise within the brief space of a sketch. As a revue artist, Williams was able to be 'outrageous'. All the critics used the term, and so did many of his friends. For years, he professed to be mystified and even angered by it. They trotted it out, he sensed, in order to register both enjoyment and some sort of disapproval at the same time. 'Outrageous'. Was it a veiled accusation of irresponsibility towards his own talent, or the talents with whom he shared the stage? Or perhaps a way of referring to his seeming sexual orientation without having to define it? No doubt some commentators did have some such implication in mind. Others probably meant only that he overdid things in a relishable way. For him, the matter remained irritatingly unresolved until, one night in 1971, in a theatre dressing room, the visiting Noël Coward remarked how much-loved Kenneth was on account of his outrageousness. He never complained about the word again. It must be the *mot juste* after all, since his idol had seen fit to use it.

In Williams's private pantheon of artists who could do no wrong, Coward held the most honoured place. If Maggie Smith was less revered, it was only because he knew her better. He co-starred with her in *Share My Lettuce*, and in the Peter Shaffer double-bill *The Private Ear* and *The Public Eye* (1962), and they were theatrical neighbours more than once during long runs on Shaftesbury Avenue. She fascinated him, both on and off stage. He delighted in her success, quite selflessly for the most part, though fancying that in certain of her performances he glimpsed a little of his own manner and method, reflected back. Of all his leading ladies, he found Maggie Smith the most immediately compatible, but he also worked happily with the unlikely figure of Ingrid Bergman, despite her inconsistency in performance and the ricketiness of the production (of Shaw's *Captain Brassbound's Conversion*) that surrounded them. In the last of the revues, *One Over the Eight*, in 1961, Sheila Hancock was the co-star. This was a fascinating pairing, which fought an honourable draw and became a friendship. Ms Hancock stood less nonsense than most, won Williams's respect, and retained the right to put him in his place. Nobody else who worked with him seems to have learned, by experience, to deal with him so firmly.

Other leading ladies – Fenella Fielding, Caroline Mortimer, Jennie Linden – had a hard time. Williams felt himself to be senior to all of them in one sense or another, which did not get any of the partnerships off to the best of starts. The rehearsal process also irked him increasingly – nobody conducted rehearsals to his satisfaction (except, belatedly, himself) – and not even a critical and commercial hit could keep him happy after the first few weeks of a run. The comedy *My Fat Friend* (1972–73), in particular, was a victim of his growing neurosis about the nightly trap that was West End success. As the weeks went by, Williams seemed to work himself into an obsession over his fellow-players' fluctuating standards of delivery; but it is clear even from his own account that he himself was hardly a beacon of stability and reassurance. His illness, which brought the run to a premature close, was genuine in the sense that symptoms were observable; but they had arguably been psychosomatic in the first place, and their physical impact was exacerbated, in its turn, by his anguish and exhaustion – a downward spiral. A similar fugue, more spectacular diagnostically, had characterised Williams's exit in 1965 from a failed comedy called *The Platinum Cat*. His recovery, once it had been established that he was not expected to return to the cast, proved rapid.

Having experienced a string of hits in the revue days, Williams found a sequence of West End flops doubly depressing, and he grew extremely wary of accepting any theatre work at all. His reputation as a difficult presence within a company – a 'stirrer', some said, and he did not particularly deny it – may have put some attractive offers out of his reach. Low farce he generally spurned. This caused puzzlement, since he remained obstinately attached to the Carry On films, which had never traded in any other idiom; but Williams had his own reasons for continuing to turn up at Pinewood long after the series had gone stale. He enjoyed the family atmosphere of the group, its trading of insults and japes; here again, he enjoyed a special licence to be the bad boy of the outfit, performing his favourite mimes of masturbation and urination off-camera while others staggered through their scenes. When it came to his own turn to deliver the much-despised script, a single merciful take would often suffice. To perform the same sort of stuff night after night in the theatre would have been torture. (When the Carry On team eventually put on a London stage show, Williams did not take part.) He enjoyed the company of several of the regulars – Bernard Bresslaw, Peter Butterworth, Kenneth Connor, Hattie Jacques, Barbara Windsor – and on viewing the finished films was usually critical of himself and generous towards even those of the troupe he did not particularly care for. Connor in particular always delighted him, on screen and off.

None of them made much money out of the Carry Ons. Moreover, their basic rates seem scarcely to have changed from the first film to the last. As explained by the production team, the idea was that instead of paying out big money to a star, they would share that sum among a team in which no member predominated. It is not a particularly persuasive notion (even on a big-name picture, the support players have to be realistically paid); but the work was regular, and nobody in the cast carried individual responsibility for a flop. Williams budgeted to expect five thousand pounds from each picture. For a good fifteen years, the Carry On money guaranteed him a healthy annual income in spite of vicissitudes elsewhere, and he was grateful for it. At the same time, as he told his diary with gathering anguish, his Elstree experience was symptomatic of a career that had brought him 'star status without star money'.

This was a fair complaint. Kenneth Williams had to suffer most of the inconveniences of stardom, while wielding none of the power. On a low day, he found it intolerable to be recognised, however politely, in the street; and sometimes people were quite stunningly rude to him. The number of random folk Williams met in public places who felt entitled to insult him gratuitously – impelled at some level, presumably, by a frightened aversion to his 'camp' persona – does not seem to have struck him as remarkable; but he did grumble that the work that made him famous enough to be slighted never paid sufficiently well to buy him a sheltered existence. Invitations to appear in America, where he might easily have been a great commercial success (playing caricatural parts, no doubt, but what else were the Carry On roles?), always drew from him a brusque refusal. Fond though he was of Hollywood heroes, from John Wayne to Elvis Presley, Williams never even visited the United States.

In the late fifties, when he certainly was a high earner, working hard in several media, he devoted a good deal of the profit to setting up his parents in their own dwellings. Like many comedians, Williams enjoyed spreading the idea that he was mean; he made the expected jokes about the burglar alarm on his dustbin. But although he did have his stingy moments in the matter of small-scale tipping, he was more than averagely generous where larger sums came into play, bankrolling friends in business ventures, keeping unemployed chums in funds, fulfilling requests for loans by return of post. During a theatre run, he would be the first to think of organising a commemorative gift or presentation to a fellow-player – even on one occasion a management – and would pay for the inscribed ashtrays or engraved salvers himself, refusing contributions. This was not the behaviour of a miser. Perhaps it would be truest to say that Williams was 'careful' with money in the most literal sense. He kept neat and scrupulous accounts, in proper books. When asked for a payment by the Inland Revenue, he would send it off immediately, without waiting for the due date; and he must be one of the few artists who has not only protested to the BBC that his fee was too high, but has persuaded the Corporation to moderate its munificence.

Kenneth Williams lived in a succession of small flats in the St Pancras/Marylebone area of London, never far from the scenes of his childhood in Marchmont Street, Bloomsbury. Apart from a very brief period spent sharing a friend's apartment in 1959, he was always alone. His last rooms, near the southern edge of Regent's Park, shared a landing with his mother's. They tended to spend their evenings together, since Louie, as he called her, owned a television set. Her son never bought one (and if he had, he would have used the term 'purchased', for which he seems to have had a lifelong preference). He pondered his solitariness frequently, concluding for the most part that in spite of its trials, it was the right state for him. He may have proposed marriage to, or at least discussed the possibility with, as many as four women; but each very sensibly judged the idea inappropriate – one offering the well-chosen and completely convincing argument that the sight of her smalls drying over the bath would be bound to drive Kenneth into a fury. His personality was indeed a strange one, designed by him for self-sufficiency but kept only very precariously in that state. A monk, visiting the Carry On set, once dismayed Williams considerably by remarking on the 'desperation' he had deduced to be at work in some of the actor's radio performances. This was by no means a revelation to Williams – he often talked of stand-up comedians in terms of despair and desperation, and favoured those who flirted most openly with the depressive background of the trade – but in his own case, he did not like his emotional neediness to be so obvious as to attract the sympathy of a stranger (especially not at break-time in the Pinewood studios). But as the years went by, and his unscripted appearances began to outnumber his actorly roles, Williams was obliged to excavate more and more of himself for our amusement.

One did not have to be a monk to be alarmed by the spectacle on occasion, if one took it literally. In the radio show 'Just a Minute', where panel-members (still) have to speak for sixty seconds without hesitating, deviating from the subject or repeating themselves, withstanding 'challenges' from their fellows as they go, Williams sometimes revealed an uncontrollably demanding personality, issuing insults, corrections and high-pitched protests in a terrible crescendo which might momentarily endanger the playfulness of the game. But if his rage were punctured by a remark he perceived to be witty, he could subside into a comical, even touching, contrition. One knew it was all a performance – and even if it wasn't, it could be safely taken as one, because of the trivial nature of the show in which it occurred; and yet it seemed to erupt from a part of Kenneth Williams that did not need to be 'acted'. His own attitude to these outbursts was interesting. He often professed to have shocked himself, but though he knew self-disgust was the appropriate emotion, he could not register it in a completely disapproving way. 'I behaved disgracefully,' he would note in the diary, his would-be remorse sounding an unmistakable note of satisfaction. Privately, Williams railed against himself year after year for lacking the courage to 'join in' with life. To 'behave disgracefully' was one brief, unsatisfactory, but necessary way of making that missing contact. Some of his most disgraceful behaviour occurred in restaurants, for he had a low tolerance of both alcohol and other diners, but managements at his favourite eating-houses valued his custom too much to be censorious.

Many rumours circulated, in and around showbusiness, about his mode of living. The best-known, and most widely corroborated, concerned his reluctance to make his lavatory available to visitors, who were directed to a nearby public convenience instead. At one point it was whispered that he kept his kitchen stove wrapped in cellophane; this was true. Again, Williams did not go out of his way to disguise these obsessive tendencies. In the chat-show appearances which were the starring roles of his late middle-age, he became his own material. His own foibles were part of what he had to sell; so he was as frank as the airwaves permitted about his solitariness, his celibacy, and his bouts of despair, though the briskness required by the entertainment format obliged him to make light of his problems. Sometimes a journalist, catching him on a bleak day, would be disconcerted by the depth of his misery (and Williams himself, looking back on the interview, would be further depressed by his own compulsion to 'confess'); but this kind of material seldom got into print. Reporters came to Williams not for such doomy stuff – which in general they tried to ignore – but for upbeat and eccentric quotes, or perhaps a display of his famous erudition.

He was in fact almost completely self-educated, while healthily open to the influence of friends, who passed on their enthusiasms to him. At odd moments of gratitude in the diaries, he thanks them individually. If there was any systematising influence on his thought at all, it was the German scholar Erich Heller, with whom Williams struck up an improbable but lasting friendship in 1950, when Heller headed the German Department at University College, Swansea, and Kenneth was playing in the local repertory company. Letters suggest that Heller would have liked the relationship to become physically intimate, but Williams, as he generally did, backed off. They met now and then over the years, Heller always hoping that his friend would finally tackle something in the theatre that was worthy of his talent. When Heller later moved to Northwestern University, in Illinois, Williams kept in touch with his critical output. It had introduced him to, among other things, the pessimism of Schopenhauer, which he found all too congenial, and the novels of Thomas Mann, in which he delighted.

Williams read thrillers when he felt bad, and sizeable novels, at a sitting, in periods of recovery. He was a rather acute critic of fiction, and at all times a very decided one, having learnt the virtue of trenchancy from his great favourite, Dr Johnson. Oddly, for a player so easily imagined moving among the Copperfields and Nicklebys in the costume of their day, he had no feeling for Dickens at all. Just too verbose and sprawling, perhaps; for it was the well-tended garden of

English poetry which (along with music) gave Williams the purest pleasure. His excellent memory, further trained by long experience of rapid line-learning in repertory, enabled him to file away extensive quotations from all manner of poets. From 1953, he was much taken with the poems of T.S. Eliot, phrases from whose work recur, more or less disguised, throughout the diaries. They even had townscapes in common: for in his first years as a poet, as his work attests, Eliot himself hovered around that Bloomsbury/St Pancras area which was Williams's lifelong territory.

Kenneth Williams was a devoted Londoner, fond of long, nostalgic walks along favourite routes. New friends were often invited to pause at the National Gallery, to inspect Guercino's 'The Incredulity of Thomas', a painting whose fascination he found inexhaustible. He had no time for the church and its orders of service, still less for the history of religious schism, which merely exasperated him; he preferred to argue out his need for faith in private. Most religious imagery he found too sentimental; yet this single pictorial moment seemed to satisfy him. As he admitted, a believably strong Christ was one of its attractions. For Williams, visions of personal redemption, whether religious or emotional, involved his being gathered up and made safe by muscular arms. It seems never to have happened to him in life.

His self-proclaimed celibacy, as the diary shows, was not complete; he arrived at it, eventually, by default. Reading of the tortured history of his sexuality, one must bear in mind that homosexual liaisons were not decriminalised until 1967. Before that, Williams tried to maintain two points of view on the subject, on the one hand expressing society's own lofty contempt for the 'queer' world, from which he stood apart, but at the same time betraying his own fascination with it and his familiarity with its modes and customs. His own way of flirting with it, in his days as an armed forces entertainer, had been to adopt the sort of theatrically 'camp' persona he would later reproduce in the Kenneth Horne radio programmes. The extent to which he used camp catch-phrases and the homosexual argot called 'polari'[3] in those early days became a matter of dispute when the dramatist Peter Nichols, in his memoirs *Feeling You're Behind* (1984), reproduced the conversational effect as he remembered it. Williams was distressed by what he felt to be an exaggerated picture of himself, and he was sustained in his opinion by his friend Stanley Baxter; yet the 1947 diary, with its exclamatory sing-song, tends on the whole to vindicate Nichols. Some references to homosexuality were lightly encoded, and continued to be

---

[3] Or variations on the term, e.g. 'parlyaree'.

('traditional' stood for 'homoerotic' or 'masturbatory' for many years). Some readers may be surprised to learn that 'gay bars' were called by that name as early as 1947, and to see the diarist mention 'obviously gay' airmen the following year.

All in all, there seems to have been much more talk than physical contact – an enduring imbalance in Williams's life. Yet, back in Britain, some brief, ecstatic affairs with men of his own age did ensue (one of them terminated, as a late verse of Williams's bizarrely recalls, by his fastidiousness over body-odour). Later in life he tended to run away from the offer of a loving intimacy, preferring – or needing – to settle instead for the masturbatory mechanics of 'the tradiola', as he called it. Even that, since it entailed inviting strangers into his impeccable flat, was reserved for direst emergency. He felt freer abroad, though his adventures in Morocco must be judged timorous when compared with those recorded by his friend Joe Orton. Williams seems to have fought shy of full penetrative intercourse in all circumstances, though he would permit a controlled violence. His fantasies, as he records, were sado-masochistic, and it seems likely that his masturbatory routines, alias 'the barclays' ('bank', rhyming slang for 'wank'), partook of this element too.

Certainly he seems to have treated masturbation as a considerable play-acting performance, and often a lengthy one (he provides occasional timings). In the imaginative passion of the moment he even caused himself superficial injuries on more than one occasion. His moments of extreme narcissism, too, will surprise and enlighten those who have always found difficulty in understanding why a synonym for masturbation should be 'self-love'. In Williams we see someone who – and this in middle-age – is capable of being so captivated by his own image in the mirror that he must resort at once to 'the barclays'. This is self-regard of a rare order; but the strangeness and the charm of it, within the diaries, is that Williams can be overcome by a sense of his own beauty one day, and disgusted the next by his bad complexion, erupting pustules, baggy eyes, and so forth. The aesthetic sensitivity worked both ways. In the story of another life, such details of bedroom and bathroom life might seem crass and unnecessary, but Williams was an exceptionally solitary being, who day by day sustained a whole inner industry of compensation and sublimation. He would not have regarded these as 'presentable' sides to his nature, but they were essential to his survival. A version of the diaries that failed to give some idea of their workings would have left too much unexplained.

Explanation seems most necessary in the matter of Kenneth Williams's death. No aspect of his life has puzzled his friends and admirers so much as the manner in which it ended. The open verdict of the

Coroner cannot be set aside, nor would one wish to overturn what is always a kindly judgment in these cases; but if the court had studied all the diary volumes, and not just the single concluding one which was taken away to be examined for signs of suicidal intent,[4] it might have been pressed to a different conclusion. As far back as 1947, Williams described himself as a 'suicidalist', who did not 'believe in existence at all'; and this is a theme to which he returns countless times. On several occasions he considers, in what feels a more than merely rhetorical way, the idea of putting an end to his sufferings – only to be saved by a failure of nerve, or a realisation that all necessary dispositions have not been made, or by a dramatic improvement in circumstances. It is the latter which in one serious instance rescues him when he has got as far as writing letters of farewell to his family and friends. Many practical details, besides, conspire to insist that Williams himself decided the moment of his death. The most obvious is his reference to his hoard of 'poison' (a barbiturate he was not in the habit of taking medicinally), set aside for the purpose. This was the drug which, swilled down with alcohol, did indeed terminate his life. And the last words of the diary – though it was not the first time he had closed a day's entry with such a phrase – suggest depths of exhaustion and resignation to which he had not been brought before. He was sixty-two years old.

As to the causes of his hopelessness, the most immediate was clearly pain. He had always supported pain very badly, and now found himself assailed by several varieties at once. The idea that his body could enclose such self-destroying sensations appeared to bewilder him. And this was the end of a long road. Both Kenneth and his mother had been in intermittent medical trouble for two years. Louie's powers had suddenly begun to fail, leaving the twinned households beset by an unaccustomed atmosphere of rancour and disintegration. Mother and son had come almost to resemble the decrepit married couple Louie and her husband would have been, if Charlie had survived (instead of finding his own controversial way out of bewilderment with a strangely mislabelled bottle of carbon tetrachloride). Kenneth had often found himself tearfully unable to contemplate life after Louie's death. What he had now was almost worse: a living Louie, but no longer reliably like herself, imprisoning him in her needs. Reading these late diary entries, one sees a man facing the collapse of what has been, for so long, a fragile truce with existence. The logical consequences of his loneliness, bravely defied for years, seem to press

---

[4] This fact emerged when a Coroner's officer was accused of stealing a book, *Back Drops*, from KW's flat on the day his body was discovered (*Daily Telegraph*, 15 January 1992).

in on him all at once. Yet on the last day, he is still himself, haggling combatively with a watchmender, and recording his small triumph.

Whether the earlier, still viable Williams is a lovable character, or, as one acquaintance declares him in a moment of semi-serious exasperation, not even *likeable*, is a judgment over which the reader is liable to vacillate from page to page. Kenneth Williams was a difficult presence in many social contexts, from the Equity committee meeting to the private dinner party. Sometimes one can join in the feeling that there is something liberating about his disruptive behaviour; sometimes it is just nasty. He prided himself on giving 'good value', but could not bear any attempt to top him in the telling of tales. His social world, as he saw it, was peopled with comedic incompetents, all reciting inconclusive anecdotes badly. His holidays were almost invariably purgatorial (he chose them unimaginatively, but then he often had Louie in tow); and yet they brought him into contact with 'normal' families, which he liked. Some of his most tranquil moments were spent in the company of the actors Gordon Jackson and Richard Pearson and their wives and children: he approved of 'straight' domesticity and basked in it (though as his trip to Wales to stay with the Jacksons in 1966 showed, he had horribly old-fashioned expectations when it came to the role of the woman of the house and her catering arrangements). He enjoyed the company of children, and they enjoyed him; something of his spiky directness must have reminded them of themselves. 'Jackanory', the story-telling programme on BBC Television, happily exploited this compatibility for years.

Williams always had a quite exceptional ability – perhaps it was even a compulsion – to face the unattractive sides of himself with a curiosity bordering on eagerness. His honesty is often exhilarating, and equally often quite hard to deal with. It might be said of him that he is destructively honest at times. He sets down things about himself which it might have seemed more 'natural' to tone down, or camouflage, or omit. Even *Just Williams*, his carefully neutralised autobiography, made one reviewer, George Melly, feel baffled by some of the anecdotes he was being offered. 'The point here,' Melly wrote, 'is that most of us have behaved this badly, but not only does Williams include the anecdote (and how many people would do that?); he leaves it without comment or explanation despite the fact it's the kind of story most of us tell about other people to prove how unpleasant they are.' The whole performance amazed Melly. 'Someone who disliked him intensely couldn't have done a better hatchet job.'[5]

Exactly so: a part of Kenneth Williams (as Melly's piece went on

[5] *Sunday Times*, 13 October 1985.

to recognise) surely did dislike himself intensely. A deeply Puritan, 'right-thinking' – latterly Right-thinking – part of him had set itself against his sexual instincts, which were powerful, from the very first: thus the war between right and wrong within him became a war between indulging the sexual impulse, or not. By and large, right/abstinence prevailed, but at great cost. The censorious self allowed Williams a good deal of latitude in return for his continence. While adhering in matters of principle to a stern morality, he began to 'behave disgracefully', and secretly to admire himself for it. I believe he rather enjoyed seeing the raw London boy within him – the son of his outspoken father – emerge again to impose himself upon the world. The worst consequence of this was an ugly racism which surfaced, rarely but horribly, in the diaries of his later years. It was a generalised hatred whose vocabulary of abuse belonged to a low-life London; it seemed to correspond to nothing else in his existence except a need to be momentarily evil, and it melted away when confronted by the realities of social living. The neighbour whom Williams odiously greets as one of a 'pack of chimps' on their arrival in the Osnaburgh Street apartment block is mourned, on his departure some weeks later, as 'the best one who's ever occupied the furnished flat'. Did Williams realise he had recorded such violently contrasting judgments of the same people? There is no sign that he did. The malevolence of the one moment had been released: the sociable regret of another moment likewise.

This is how the diaries work: their moral balance has to be averaged out over long periods. A randomly chosen day may feature a Williams of exemplary sensibility and conscience, or a hobgoblin, or both; for both he assuredly was. But he was never afraid of himself, or of what he had thought. Looking back on his daily reflections, sometimes years afterwards, he might sometimes enter a correction, or a comment, but nothing was ever deleted.[6] He was prepared to let it all stand.

THE DIARIES

Kenneth Williams left forty-three years' worth of diaries. The first, for 1942, is a little pocket edition, begun when he was fifteen years of age. Its content is necessarily terse and boyish, but there are things in it that do contribute to the later picture of the man. There followed a gap of four years, during which Williams joined the Army, graduating eventually to a Combined Services Entertainments troupe touring the

[6] And only once does he tear out a page and start again, the better to rhapsodise over a performance of Maggie Smith's.

Far East. He resumed his journal there with a 1947 volume, pocket-sized and leather-bound, into whose tiny spaces he was able to squeeze, with his fine nib, as many as fifty words or more per day.

One of the hobbies he later listed for *Who's Who* was calligraphy. In the eyes of an editor, no skill could have been more welcome. It enabled Williams to make many of the diary pages attractive as well as enlightening, for his facility with different styles of handwriting led him to experiment; a single page might be written in three or four different scripts. A change of mood, or a switch of pen (he kept several), could change him from a devotee of wispy copperplate to an exponent of fat italic. Whatever his choice of lettering, the diaries remain heroically legible throughout, even when their content makes it plain that Williams must have written them under the influence of a considerable intake of alcohol. Some clarifications were made by him during his re-readings of the volumes (he occasionally read them aloud, for the entertainment of close friends or family). The upshot is that among all the words these journals contain – there must be more than four million – there are perhaps just half a dozen over which I have had to puzzle. Where these have survived into the edited version, I have indicated the fact.

To accommodate the events of 1948, the year in which he became a working actor, Williams 'purchased' for the first time a desk diary – one of the smaller sort, about eight inches by five – with the result that we have an unexpectedly full picture of his beginnings in the profession. Then came two more years of pocket diaries, after which he returned to the page-a-day desk diary format and stuck with it until 1965, by which time he was living alone and filling each page with reflections. For most of the fifties, however, he was either living at his parents' home, where confidentiality was threatened, or working too busily to need the solace of the written word. The diary, in consequence, is sometimes sparsely written – though few days are left completely blank – and the edited version you see here represents quite a high proportion of what Williams actually recorded during these years. The entry dated 2 June 1953, for example, is reproduced in full; this is all he had to say about Coronation Day.

In 1966, he took to the Standard Edition desk diary,[7] a squarish format (ten inches by eight) which contented him for five more years until, in 1972, he accepted the challenge of the full A4-sized Executive version. Only a love of the act of writing itself could account for the diligence with which he continued to fill these large volumes year after year. Nothing but a black binding would content him. His diary

---

7 Not altogether voluntarily: it was a gift from Gordon Jackson.

routine by now included, at the top of the page, a one-word summary of the weather, and a report on the bowel movement of the day, an important indicator for one of Williams's temperament. One year, he assessed the trouble he was suffering from 'the bum' by mapping its severity neatly along a five-week graph: what could be more anal?[8] Later, observations about his health were recorded in red ink, a sign of the importance he attached to them. An actor needs good health, of course, and an untroubled countenance; but Williams took vigilance to a fierce extreme, monitoring the progress of every tiny eruption and irritation with an accusing horror. On the whole, I have suppressed these red-ink contributions except where they help to explain Williams's mood of the day – and, sadly, towards the end, where questions of health begin to dominate his existence. In the last weeks of his life, I have allowed as much of the diary as possible to stand uncut, in order to give the reader the evidence from which to draw an independent conclusion as to Williams's state of mind at the last.

Otherwise, my guiding principle has been to attempt to let the diary tell its own story with minimal narrative interference from me. Having read Williams's complete original text now three times through sequentially, I will admit that the full version, for all that it teems with trifling detail, momentary irritations and inconsequential asides, does exercise a kind of hypnotic, diurnal fascination. The boring bits are somehow not boring, because they are part of the completeness of a life. My concern, therefore, has been to retain something of this throb of day-to-day existence, while giving a sense of a life that was, in many other ways, highly productive and at least potentially glamorous. I have included, I believe, all important ruminations in which Williams attempts to understand, instruct or chastise himself.

I have tried to preserve his developing views on the main events of his working life. Some of his jobbing appearances – in one-off TV shows, commercial voice-overs, unremarkable editions of his many radio series, book-signing sessions – go unrecorded here, but are represented by others of the same type. Where his comments on fellow-actors, directors, broadcasting colleagues and friends are concerned, discretion had sometimes to prevail. I have usually disguised the names (or omitted the surnames, or supplied only the initial) of living persons whose sexual activities, homosexual or otherwise, are no business of any of us, except in so far as they affected or interested Kenneth Williams. Certain of his personal observations, even though it is clear they are exaggerations prompted by frustration or an evil mood,

---

[8] 1968, 'Chart showing progress of the bum from the 22nd February which was the first day out of hospital.'

might amount to libels under English law. In a few instances, remarks I would like to have included (if only as prize examples of malice, written with gusto by a connoisseur of the genre) I have been obliged by conscience to omit, judging them to be unreasonably offensive to persons still living, and in many cases still working in the performing arts and elsewhere. I doubt, however, whether collectors of hilarious abuse will feel seriously deprived by the text that is left. Williams took against most strangers instinctively until proved wrong. But I urge those who, reading these pages, feel insulted by their earliest appearances in them: please read on. It is more than likely that your reputation will recover later. Those who start out in high esteem tend to come a cropper later; and there are some unfortunates, of course, who never escape from Kenneth Williams's bad books. To emphasise my sympathetic solidarity with them, I have included every reference he made in his diaries to me. They are all to some extent hostile. I take comfort from the fact that he did not actually turn off his mother's TV set when I was on; and I naturally like to think that had we met, I could have persuaded him that I was not, as he suspected, 'a nasty piece of work'. Alas, though we were together in the same room several times – BBC parties, mostly – that meeting never occurred. I could easily have told him (what everyone told him, till he was sick of it) that his work had given me enormous pleasure. What would have been harder to say would have been how fascinating and unusual he seemed as a personality. I hope my work on these diaries will say that for me now.

THE TEXT

Williams's spelling and grammar improved steadily throughout his life. I have retained a few examples of his eccentricities to indicate the sort of thing that tripped him up. (Much later, he would enjoy correcting the same mistakes when others made them.) The odd confusion persisted – for example, he often uses 'aesthetic' when he seems to mean 'ascetic' – but I have let these instances stand, the unusual flavour of the resulting phrase seeming more useful than a silent correction. Williams's general preference for oddities like the poetic form of the exclamation 'O!' has been respected, as has his fondness for the biblical 'straightway' and other curiosities. When writing in haste, he also showed a liking for the clerkly form 'fr.', meaning both 'for' and 'from', according to need, but it did not seem helpful to retain this and thereby risk confusion. Williams spelt proper names unreliably, and sometimes inconsistently. I have researched where I can and taken the likeliest form of names that have proved untraceable. The punctuation of the diaries required a good deal of rationalising in the earlier years, where a breathless style is held together much of the time by dashes. I have not deleted all of them, but tried to minimise the gulping effect by putting in conventional stops. Where a phrase fades out into three dots (. . .), it is invariably because Williams's text does so; I have not used the effect to denote editorial cuts or elisions. (There are many such, of course, but I have not indicated where they occur.)

A more persistent problem, throughout the diaries, is Williams's habit of putting key words into capital letters – for clarity in the case of names, but more often for emphasis. It so happens that this works poorly in print, where the sight of capitals randomly booming out from the page is very distracting. I have substituted italics in many cases. Where even they became wearisome, I have trusted to the reader's unaided sense of emphasis. After all, most of what Williams writes 'reads itself', in the sense that his voice is so easily imagined speaking it. Round brackets are his own, as are asterisked notes. My small annotations or alterations appear in square brackets, and my footnotes are the numbered ones.

A bonus disclosed by the diaries, and the ancillary boxes of correspondence and memorabilia, was the amount of illustrative material Williams kept in them. All but a few of the photographs appearing in this volume are drawn from this most private of archives.

Found this today, in the book – it's lovely.

'We do not know our own souls, let alone the souls of others. Human beings do not go hand in hand the whole stretch of the way. There is a virgin forest in each; a snowfield where even the print of birds' feet is unknown. Here we go alone and like it better.'

Virginia Woolf, 'On Being Ill'

Kenneth Williams, Diary, 24 March 1948

Diaries are written so that one has a record of events, and because there are certain events one *wants* to remember. There is perhaps also the element of the confessional in them, and that isn't a bad thing in my eyes. It has certainly eased my loneliness. The accusation of falsity comes because they say one isn't really objective, and only puts down what *one* wants, not what *others* want. Of course one does. That's what is so delightful about the diary: it is what the self wants to say.

Kenneth Williams, Diary, 18 March 1972

I am sick and tired of wondering whether people are offended or not. My crimes are nothing compared with those of Genghis Khan.

Kenneth Williams, Diary, 15 April 1972

1942

Kenneth Charles Williams was born on 22 February 1926, at an address in Bingfield Street, directly north of King's Cross Station. His father, Charlie, had been a railway van boy, but later managed a hairdresser's shop at 57 Marchmont Street, St Pancras (still a hairdresser's at the time of writing), whose upper rooms became the family's home. In 1940, aged fourteen, Kenneth was sent – in search of the trade Charlie had conventionally insisted he learned – to Bolt Court, the School of Lithography off Fleet Street; but the war was now under way. Under the threat of the Blitz, Bolt Court evacuated its juniors to Bicester in Oxfordshire. Billeted in Sheep Street with 'old Mr Chisholm', a retired vet and a bachelor, KW was impressed by his host's love of poetry, and his florid way with a recitation. It is imaginable – and indeed some friends of Kenneth's did imagine – that Mr Chisholm seduced the boy; but if advances were made, KW does not seem to have experienced them as unwelcome, for his memories of Chisholm were always respectfully expressed. The idyll soon ended, and late in 1941 Kenneth returned to complete his lithography studies in central London – at which point we join him.

Kenneth Williams's first surviving diary, begun when he was fifteen years of age, is a slim pocket volume ('Collins Emerald Diary') whose 'Personal Memoranda' page records his weight, at 20 February, as seven stone, his height as five feet three inches, his collar size 14 and his hat size 7. The number of his identity card, a wartime essential, is given as D.P.L.X.28.4. One reason for the seeming emptiness of the Marchmont Street home was the absence of Kenneth's older sister Pat, who had joined the Women's Auxiliary Air Force.

Thursday, 1 January

Christmas was as expected very quiet, without so many it seemed almost melancholy, and brushed over with false gaiety. Have smashing overcoat. Went to the Dominion, saw especially good program, [*It*] *Started With Eve*, and *Bombay Clipper*.[1] Those stairs!

---

[1] A list of films seen or mentioned by KW appears on page 803. Plays are dealt with in footnotes.

Tuesday, 6 January
Went to Bolt Court, 10, worked with Cheeseman. Etching. Made one metal print. Scrubbed both off.

Wednesday, 7 January
I made a carbon tissue print. In litho I watched Brown make a print on zinc.

Thursday, 29 January
Finished the litho map work– room for improvement. Levy to go to the RAF. Stan came. Saw *Citizen Kane* – boshey rot.

Saturday, 14 February
Went to Art – rather a long wait for an 18. Rather on the boring side – patriotic windbag.

Sunday, 15 February
Pat left today – as usual uneventful. Singapore lost.

Sunday, 22 February [KW's birthday]
What does it feel like to be sixteen? Daisy 5/- and Edie, Aunt Mary, Meg, Mum D.= £1 more. Capture of Bali by Japs. Am getting attaché case.

Saturday, 28 February
Registered at Islington today expected questions etc. Fire watching met the Mah-Rajah and Henderson. OK. The cash will come in handy.

Sunday, 15 March
Nothing doing. As usual uneventful – three job applications sent out.

Tuesday, 31 March
Letters for appointment two!! Do hope I will be successful. Please God, I shall be!!

Wednesday, 1 April
Went for interview to Stanford's[2] very satisfactory – to the point!! Went to Hubner's – very vague and uncertain – will let me know.

Friday, 3 April
I start on Tuesday at Stanford's.

---

[2] Edward Stanford, cartographer, of Long Acre, London WC2.

Easter Monday, 6 April
Had glorious ride in car, bump!! fun! Came back by car. Prayer: Please God! make me worthy of the post.

Tuesday, 7 April
Started – felt very nervous! everything OK, those I saw jolly decent lot. Other fellow a conchie!! objector

Wednesday, 8 April
Started smaller lettering make me worthy oh God!

Thursday, 16 April
Tea fund taken over – by KCW. Marvellous map!

Wednesday, 29 April
Started and finished the World Outline map. Started making a tracing on small stone. Feel very proud!! Please God it will be good!!

Thursday, 28 May
Indenture signed. Nothing to report.

Tuesday, Wednesday, June 2, 3 (across two days)
The reading of *1649*, and *London Bridge Is Falling* cause these gaps. Am I a communist?

Friday, 19 June
Practise byke – can certainly ride it.

Monday, 22 June
Rode to work on byke.

Wednesday, 1 July
Lost sunglasses. Nothing to report. Tobruk fallen!

Saturday, 4 July
One seldom sees such talent as I saw yesterday – *Musical Boys* – splendid performance, wonderful show. Received my badge for three years' service.[3]

Monday to Thursday, 20–23 July [across four dates]
Did little. Went on Tues to the Cadet Corps learnt about torpedoes. Very interesting. Went again Thursday got membership forms learn about signals and mines – signals appeals to me most.

---

[3] As a firewatcher?

Friday, 24 July
Went to the offices of the War Cabinet, very impressive, also to Faber and Faber and Geog. Magazine.

Saturday, 25 July
Went to see *The Maltese Falcon* and *Bedtime Story*. Not up to par.

Sunday, 9 August
Read *She*[4] balderdash! tripe! eyewash! blah! etcetera.

Thursday, 13 August
Did Compass – and had Drill. Saw Granma Williams fell off chair – so assinine!

Saturday, Sunday, 29–30 August
Read *Jew Süss*.[5] Very Good.

Wednesday, 9 September
Went with Orford to see *Doctor's Dilemma*,[6] it was grand! a wonderful evening.

Tuesday, 15 September
Stone job proved today! terrible!!! almost makes one feel ashamed. Cadets – knots – terribly uninteresting.

Sunday, 20 September
No need to get up early! hols start tomorrow.

Monday, 21 September
Uneventfull. Stamps perused, got a good few mounted.

Thursday, 24 September
Cadets – no uniforms of course, am resigned to fate now! Painted bathroom.

---

[4] By H. Rider Haggard (1887).
[5] Translation of *Jud Süss*, by Lion Feuchtwanger (1925). A historical novel by a Jewish writer, and a worldwide success in the twenties, perverted by the Nazis in 1940 into an anti-Semitic film.
[6] By George Bernard Shaw, at the Haymarket. The outing, remembered by KW as 'my first memorable visit to the theatre', was arranged by his older colleague Valentine Orford, from the Ordnance Survey section of Stanford's, who remained a loyal, if keenly critical, friend to KW.

Wednesday, 30 September
Cadets, passed medical – measured for uniform.

Thursday, 8 October
Got my uniform tonight! terrible hat too small, tunic too big!!! most unsatisfactory. Barrow jealous as hell!!

Friday, 9 October
Clifford showed me how to wear uniform! fine chap! explained everything! what a job!!

Saturday, 10 October
Got Belt. Took uniform in to Cohen, have to go for it on Saturday. Saw *Secret Agent For Japan*. Firewatched etc. got three weeks' money.

Saturday, 17 October
Got Sweet Ration. Uniform seems to fit all right it was 5/-.

Sunday, 18 October
Football. We lost to ATC, 5–1, an entertaining afternoon. Will order the book *All The World's Fighting Fleets*.

Tuesday, 20 October
Sea cadets tonight with uniform for first time!! Working on job for Ministry of Aircraft Production.

Saturday, 31 October
Went for suit Mr Orford lent me. *Rebecca*! marvellous!

Sunday, 1 November
Uneventfull – wandered mentally through Manderley.

Wednesday, 4 November
Started at work a map of the Philippines, news of the war in Libya is extremely good!!

Sunday, 8 November
Uneventful except for parade, not so good service best of all – would not have missed it for worlds. It seems rather small to me to think of the thousands that gave their lives for the peace, yet some can't even turn up at Church because of a uniform, to remember them.

Friday, 13 November
Pat came home this evening few hours after Dot went!! Went to pub in uniform met Canadian!!!

Tuesday to Thursday, 24–26 November
Keeping a diary is a fine idea, so long as it is in such a place that access to it is only possible by the right people.

Friday, 27 November
Cheap music is so potent – Coward.[7]

Monday to Thursday, 7–10 December [across dates]
So near to another 25th. When I think of 1942, it all seems so plaintive and makes me rather feel like crying – another measurement of time gone – crying into the wintry night with a pathetic helplessness, where will I be 2 years hence

Monday to Thursday, 14–17 December (across dates)
J. Johnson, having somewhat taken advantage and overstayed his welcome announced Frid. 18th he was going to live with Fred at Tufnell Park. The suggestion was greeted with enthusiasm all round I think. He will be sorry, he exploited a damn fine home, but he will never get the chance again. (moral – casting pearls.)

Friday, 25 December
Pat could not come. Tom S. ill in bed –! Christmas rather disappointing. Finished 7*am*

MEMORANDA
Now that we are in October, this year, '42, seems to have flown by on silver wings, not that it has witnessed much triumph for *our* cause! Hmph!

On the Cash Account page for April appears a sketch for a poem, as follows:

The empty headed idle rich
That drive in poshest cars of which
The very like will ne'er be seen
Upon the streets but on the screen
Dazzle us like sedative
And radiate imaginative

---

[7] 'Extraordinary how potent cheap music is.' (*Private Lives*)

1947

No diaries survive from the years 1943–46. KW's autobiography Just Williams *(1985) records little in the way of new developments during 1943, except his brief experience with an amateur dramatic troupe, the Tavistock Players. In his early years as a repertory actor, he would carefully plant a mention of this in the potted life-story he supplied to theatrical programmes, to establish his long-standing commitment to theatre.*

The process of KW's induction into the armed forces began in February 1944. Sea Cadet experience counting for nothing, he was medically graded B2 and sent to the Border Regiment in Cumbria to be 'built up'. In spite of the physical rigours of the course, 'Casey' ('KC') Williams seems almost to have enjoyed it. Regraded A1, he was posted to the Survey Section of the Royal Engineers, a destination for which his training at Stanford's fitted him perfectly. He left Greenock on a troopship in April 1945, and arrived in Bombay as the war in Europe was ending. After the surrender of Japan in August 1945 he was sent on to a Map Reproduction unit in Ceylon (Sri Lanka). Here, at Kurunegala, occurred an incident which KW regarded as his first step towards spiritual maturity. Finding the British Other Ranks' Mess full of Indians listening to the radio, Lance Corporal Williams officiously ordered them out. It later emerged that they had been waiting for an announcement concerning India's imminent independence, and that Williams had insulted them at the most sensitive of moments. The experience of delivering a formal and public apology to an Indian officer on the barrack square taught KW much, he said, about the religious dimension of tolerance and 'reciprocity'.

Shortly afterwards, he secured a transfer to 'Combined Services Entertainments', the drama and variety organisation that had lately supplanted ENSA*. His audition brought that most dreaded of rejections, 'Return to Unit', but KW's skill in drawing posters bought him time to try again. After his debut as the detective in* Seven Keys to Baldpate*, at the Victoria Theatre, Singapore, he was accepted. It was at this point that he took up again the journal that would carry through his story until the day of his death.*

Williams's leather-bound pocket diary for 1947 is coy with personal information ('Weight: ha! Date: ha!') *and the legend 'Memoranda from 1946' is scratched out with the comment* 'There just wasn't anything worth remembering!' *But addresses for Combined Services Entertainments (Welfare) in Hong Kong, Rangoon and Colombo define the corners of KW's territory as a touring entertainer in uniform. The diary helpfully starts in the last days of 1946 at Singapore, where C.S.E. had their Production Centre (No. 1 British Transit Camp, Nee Soon). Already he is signalling unease at the sexual imperatives he feels, through the private phrase 'traditional worries'.*

Christmas Eve, 1946

Going Gay at R.E. camp Ayer Raja, Singapore – terrific success – 3 cheers from the audience, and delightful reception after at the Officers' Mess. Ray played, and Alma sang my 'The Stranger'[1] very beautifully. Roy cut his head open on the gharry returning.

Christmas, 1946

Splendid party in Green Room at Nee Soon. Send-up of *7 Keys to Baldpate*[2] called *7 Stops to Aldgate*, tore the place up! I did impersonations. Hilarious days – great fun.

Wednesday, 1 January 1947

Stan Baxter[3] moved into my room. Just been vacated by Alfred Kirby, he's en route Ceylon for U.K. Went to Singapore with Stan – very camp evening, was followed, but tatty types so didn't bother to make overtures. No. Traditional worries.

Saturday, 4 January

Another walky talky evening. Frustration predominant. Stood on And[erson] Br[idge] and looked at the lighting on the water. Fine effect.

Thursday, 16 January

Went round to the gay bar which wasn't in the least gay and saw K. and Co.

Thursday, 23 January

Our first night at Nee Soon. Place full of VIPs. Terrific reception –

---

[1] 'Dark night with hidden sky,/No friend when I draw nigh/To meet me;/No moon to shine above,/No waiting call of love/To greet me;/Save for the wind to sigh,/Save for a bird to cry/So lonely;/Only the rustling trees/And whispers of dying leaves/Are with me.'

[2] The 'melodramatic farce' by George M. Cohan (based on a novel by Earl Derr Biggers) in which KW had made his C.S.E. debut, as 'Jigs Kennedy, a police Inspector'.

[3] Stanley Baxter, the Scottish actor, comedian and writer, who remained KW's lifelong friend: part mentor, part rival.

wonderful applause. Reception afterward at the Officers' Mess. Classic example of military snobbery. Couldn't care less myself, intend to stay away from it tomorrow.

Saturday, 25 January
Went along to Radio Malaya for broadcast on the Blue Network. Adza Vincent – a really charming woman. Wants me to have an audition for children's educational programme. Await developments.

Tuesday, 28 January
Lazed on charpoy all day. Show went down dreadfully at the Victoria last night. Half the audience walked out during the interval.

Thursday, 30 January
The Lincolns Boy said Goodnight Ken! *familiarzeitung!! Ich weiz nicht was sollez bedeuten! Schöne Knabe!*[4]

Friday, January 31
His name is Ronny! and so I returned the goodnight compliment as he left tonight. The show went down very badly. I dried up in the middle of the Brigadier and actually started repeating myself. Thoroughly ashamed!

Monday, 3 February
The Brigadier went down lousy! Ronny giving me lovely smiles – couldn't get a bloody seat in the café at Nee Soon so I didn't say goodnight!

Friday, 7 February
Bought myself a Swan Pen today in the village for $9, can't really afford it but still! Ronny beamed at me tonight from the orchestra pit! awfully nice chappy

Sunday, 9 February
Lazed about during the day. Harry M. came round during the evening and Stan and Geoff; he and I went into the village – so gay it wasn't true! coffees and things in cafés, bought myself a cigarette holder! camp!

---

[4] A comment coded in approximate German: 'What familiarity! I don't know what it can mean! Nice-looking boy!'

Monday, 10 February
Coffees in Nee Soon with Harry M., details of affaires. Gory. 69 etc. Cut head open in morning – fainted. Visited M.O.

Monday, 17 February
Letter from Jock! – damn and blast! he arrives in Singapore on Mar. 3. I wonder whether or not it is best that we should meet again. As he says – who knows – who indeed. Am all packed and ready for move tomorrow. Went for long walk with Stan and Roy – bags of psycho-analysis.

Tuesday, 18 February
Ship S.S. *Empire Pride*, lousy troopdeck accommodation. Left Singapore at 4.15, food pretty filthy. Slept in hammock for the first time, shocking!

Saturday, 22 February
Landed in Rangoon at approx. lunch time today. No room at the Hostel so had to come to Burma Comd. Lousy. Frank B. reported 5 of us to Elms for being late out of the canteen. We have to report to him on Monday. Fine bloody tour.

Thursday, 27 February
Went into Rangoon with Peter B. Awfully nice chap. He took several snaps. I bought some camp initial stationery, $2. Show went down OK at the Garrison. Good reception. Found that Peter was sermo huni obrepens![5] never thought so before! We live and learn! Shocking.

Friday, 7 March
Rehearsal in morning. I am to do impersonations in place of Cat's Cradle!!

Tuesday, 11 March
Played at Mingaladon RAF station tonight! The best audience we've had so far!! My impersonations – Suzette Tarri, Hutch, Felix Aylmer, Bette Davis, Nellie Wallace[6] – tore the place up – shouts of more! It

---

[5] A code phrase perhaps preserving the rhythm of the word 'homosexuality'. Note variant form in entry for 2 April.

[6] Respectively, a radio comedienne and monologuist (1881–1955); a suave singer-pianist of cabaret fame (Leslie Hutchinson, d.1969); a distinguished veteran actor (1889–1979) whose voice remained a favourite of KW's in his interpretation of elderly roles; the Hollywood actress (see entry for 27 March 1969, p. 347); and a heroine of the music-halls (1882–1948). The name, omitted here, which KW always mentioned when recalling his days as an impressionist was that of Mabel Constanduros

really was wonderful, never felt so bucked!! Grand reception afterwards in Officers' Mess – me on gin.

Monday, 24 March
Walked into Maymyo with Miguel and bought odds and ends. Show went down very feebly – went to supper at an awfully tatty restaurant– turned out to be a brothel. Most embarrassing for the two girls with us! I cracked the ah! soles in season gag and everyone roared. Bed at 10.45. Happy days, what a laugh! oh! life!!

Wednesday, 2 April
Long talk with Lees about hermo sumi obrepens in a philosophical vein.

Tuesday, 8 April
Wrote to Val [Orford], after receiving two of my letters from him! Says I am exaggerating about my health.

Friday, 11 April
Letter from Val. Replied clearing up the hypochondria business – so wearing.

Monday, 14 April
Went with David Rippon tonight, and did announcing for the 'Blighty Calling' programme over the Forces Network of Radio Rangoon. Grand experience. Went to Chinese rest. after for coffee. Ken Rimmer listened in, and said I sounded very serious!!

Thursday, 17 April
Long talk with Ken Moseley about the theatre. No hopes according to him – unless I have a private income!!

Sunday, 20 April
3rd Anniversary – joined Army 20.4.44.

Thursday, 24 April
Saw *Chinese Crackers* in the evening, quite jolly! Leo Conriche played piano[7] and one of the notes fell out!! he placed it on top and carried on.

(1897–1957), an actress famous as 'Grandma Buggins' in the early years of BBC radio. Army audiences, KW claimed, 'had never heard of her'.

[7] As he did for revues in which KW appeared, e.g. *At Your Service*. He was a civilian.

Friday, 25 April
Boarded the *Empire Pride* at 8 this morning. Sleeping on deck tonight! Weighed anchor at 2.30 this afternoon. Can't wait for Singapore.

Saturday, 26 April
Nothing to see but sea, am reading *Time Will Knit* by F. Urquhart[8] – very good. Hermo sumi obrepens enters into it. Special code of course.

Tuesday, 29 April
Disembarked this morning at 9 o'clock, met at docks by Major Woodings. Quite a load of bull in the Production Centre. Went into Singapore with Stanley to change Rupees to $.

Wednesday, 30 April
Met John Schlesinger[9] – charming fellow.

Sunday, 11 May
Stan and I went into Singapore, came back on the bus, and two nautics became quite friendly. Made overtures as we were getting off !! Laugh!

Tuesday, 27 May
Told by O.C. am to join *Over To You* doing my own impersonation spot. Am to live at Union Jack Club in Singapore.

Saturday, 31 May
Gay evening in S'pore Restaurant – so many gins wasn't true! Bath and bed at 11.30. Saw dreadful accident on Nee Soon road, one matelot killed

Friday, 6 June
Played Sembawang Naval Station. Best audience I've ever had in my life – they practically raised the roof. Entertained afterwards in the P.O.'s mess, terribly gay.

Saturday, 7 June
Went with Roy into Singapore, met Harry N. in the Singapore Restaurant Bar – terribly gay type. I became quite drunk. Went to Monico's and vomited.

Wednesday, 11 June
Holiday. Did no work, lazed about all day. Feeling thoroughly fed up.

---

[8] Scottish novel published in 1938.
[9] b. 1926. First an actor, later a film director.

Realise now, I'm a suicidalist – don't believe in existence at all. [initialled 'KCW']

Thursday, 12 June. King's Birthday
Holiday all day in celebration of above. Geoff and I went into Singapore, so gay it wasn't true! Got sent through the roof twice by the S.S.!! Quite the end. Came back to Nee Soon – sent up in café too!

Thursday, 19 June
Met Dudley and Bill in the Pegasus as arranged! Wonderful seeing him again, but I realise now that the thing is impossible – he's not really 'me' at all, am seeing him on Sat. and will conclude things in some way.

Friday, 20 June
Stayed in – had long talk with Stan about my sex life – he advised seeing a psychiatrist?

Saturday, 21 June
Went into Singapore – Dudley and Bill never turned up. Met John, a sailor from *Belfast* and asked him to give Dudley a message from me. Have I done the right thing? I wonder? – everything is so difficult for me – God! wish I were quite dead. Anyway, their not turning up has really made it a lot easier for me, because now I'm under no obligations either way, and can wholly ignore them in future. Thank goodness I never committed myself – ever.

Monday, 23 June
Stan suggested I do an impersonation of Cyril Fletcher?[10] Bit hackneyed?

Tuesday, 24 June
Hank Marriott the ex-Sgt. Major committed suicide in afternoon, drank prussic acid.[11] Rae Hammond saw whole thing and heard his dying words.

---

[10] b.1913. Comedian, verse-monologuist, pantomime dame and, later, part of the TV entourage of Esther Rantzen.

[11] Marriott had been facing charges of theft and extortion. A very full account of this event (and of this period in general) appears in *Feeling You're Behind*, by Peter Nichols (1984), which names the poison as cyanide. KW later elaborated the embarrassments of Marriott's funeral into an extended anecdote, some of whose exaggerations Nichols dismantles.

Sunday, 29 June
Went with Stan to the social in the mess, very tatty affair, only four guests! Went with Ray Ashley to the village and bought some ointment for testicles, very strong.

Saturday, 12 July
Impersonation of Arthur Marshall,[12] which I first tried on Wed. show, and 2nd at Changi, has been amazingly successful at both places. Have substituted it for Bette Davis for time being.

Saturday, 16 August
Arr. Kuala Lumpur at 3.30. Drew mattresses & sheets. Stayed in during evening. Had lucid argument with Rae Hammond, Pete Postlethwaite, Dave Perton, Stan, ref. camp embarrass in public. Very sensible discussion.

Tuesday, 19 August
Went to the theatre to do the show but nobody turned up except Norman Compton! (Show cancelled). He has been R.T.U.[13] by Woodings! Blue joke in script!

Friday, 22 August
This camp has ordered us all to parade!

Saturday, 23 August
Colin saw Adj. of this camp and squashed parade business.

Monday, 1 September
Rehearsal today – in the evening I am to go to H. Kong with Coy. and be demob. from there! Marvellous idea.

Thursday, 4 September
Maj. Hills gave me special demob letter to show in H.K., if no good am to return with Coy. Embarked S.S. *Empress of Scotland* at 3 o'clock.

Wednesday, 10 September. Hong Kong
Went to see Garrison Adj. ref. release from here – am to go again tomorrow afternoon. Met some P.O.'s in the bar tonight – sods opera! laugh! became quite tight!

---

[12] Monologuist and writer (1910–89), famous on radio in the character of 'Nurse Dugdale'; later known as a columnist and team-captain on the TV parlour-game 'Call My Bluff'.

[13] Return[ed] to Unit: what every C.S.E. performer dreaded to hear. It meant the resumption of a conventional military career.

Thursday, 11 September
Was able to draw my U.K. clothing today. Only got to have the medical now. Went with Geoff and Leo, to see *The Egg and I*, dreadful thing. Sent up silly by seaweed outside the building – gay place this.

Sunday, 5 October
Visited Pete Nichols up at the hospital.[14]

Tuesday, 7 October
Stan and I went to radio rehearsal – I am to take 2 parts!

Saturday, 11 October
David Whitfield,[15] the sailor from *Black Swan*, came to see me – we went to see the film *Notorious* together and had dinner afterwards. Then went to a café and drank lager till 2.45 in morning! Really delightful chap.

Wednesday, 15 October
Lazy day as usual. Met Arthur in the evening. He had dinner with Stan, Geoff and myself. He's very charming. Went to see *Here Come The Co-Eds* after – I'd seen it before actually. Drinks after in the bar! so gay mar dear!

Sunday, 19 October
Saw the film *Gilda* with Stan and Geoffrey, about gangsterism etc – obviously a film for sadists – shocking thing.

Tuesday, 21 October
Did the broadcast *Nelson at Trafalgar* at 9.30 tonight – seems to have been very well received.

Thursday, 23 October
Pay today at Kowloon. Met David [Whitfield] at about 11 this evening. Told him all about my phobias and philos – delightful fellow. We drank until 3 in the morning. Said goodbye to David.

Friday, 24 October
Very tired today. Did my packing, went to the matelots' bar – met 2 marines – very charming. Bonar shamshes.[16]

---

14 The future playwright was suffering from amoebic dysentery.

15 1925–80. Star vocalist of the fifties, reputedly the first British singer to have a million-seller in the USA, with 'Cara Mia' (1954).

16 In discussing Peter Nichols' book (see entry for 7 August 1984, p. 701), Stanley Baxter agreed with KW that the latter had not used 'polari', the macaronic

Saturday, 25 October
C.S.E. launch conveyed us to the *Devonshire* docked at Kowloon. Troopdeck accommodation.

Wednesday, 29 October
At sea. Paid today – £1. Did a 1 and a half hours' show. Very successful.

Friday, 31 October
Departed Singapore early this morning. Met three sailors whom Geoff knew – Soapy, Sandy & Wiggy – a very jolly crowd. I shall see more of them! (S.* equals bonar!)

*Sandy (films!)

Thursday, 13 November
Arr. Aden, 6.30. 3rd night of show. Everyone drunk. Sick in hammock, lost gold watch! Am livid over the whole thing!!

Tuesday, 18 November
Entered Suez Canal at 5 this morning. Very similar to what it was in '45 – plenty of catcalls from those on the bank – it is very cold now and B.D. is being worn.

Thursday, 20 November
Marriage of Princess Elizabeth. Listened in to wedding broadcast at sea – Mediterranean Sea! Very choppy. Reception quite good over the air – sounded most impressive.

Friday, 28 November
Weather extremely rough, ship rocking all over the place – everyone sick – terribly cold and I'm freezing in battledress. Oh to be in England!! roll on!!

Tuesday, 2 December. Liverpool
Came alongside landing stage at 09.30 – very cold. Sent a wire to 57, informing them of our arrival. Feeling terribly strung-up and nervy – long to get off.

Thursday, 4 December
Demob etc., and arrived home at 2.30 midday! Everything

---

code-language, in Singapore, but it is certainly present in the diaries before his return to England. 'Bonar' is a general term of approval (sexual and otherwise), while 'shamshes' might be an item of backslang ('smashers').

just wonderful. Went to Henekey's with M & D and Ladies – all tight!

Monday, 8 December
Went to Food Office and got ration books etc.

Wednesday, 17 December
Went to Met. Water Board. Salary is apparently v. modest. Don't know what to think really.

Saturday, 27 December
Letter from the Water Board and have been expecting it too! Their offer is 260 a year, and the condition that I pass one of their examinations, all of which is really quite ridiculous.

Sunday, 28 December
Drinks in Ward's Irish House. Left there for Henekey's – shared cab with two chaps* who we invited to Henekey's for drinks, and we all joined M & D at their table. Very gay evening.

*Cedric, and Socrates. Position is this – Socrates & Terry both bonar for Cedric, who's really rather naive? However, will await developments.

Monday, 29 December
Interview at Stanford's ref. future job – am to go to see Philips' tomorrow.[17]

Tuesday, 30 December
Went to Acton to Philips'. I start on Feb. 2nd at £6.5.0.

---

[17] Stanford's had been taken over by George Philip & Son, Ltd.

1948

Thursday, 1 January

Met Terry, and the two girls – Toni & Vicky (who were S.I.B.,[1] show at Singapore) at Piccadilly last night at 8'ish, and we all joined Mum and Dad at Henekey's, very gay party. Continued afterwards here at 57 doing the hokey-cokey and all that.

Went with Mum to buy records, 'We'll Gather Lilacs' and 'London Fantasia',[2] and to Regent St for a diamante clip she wanted to get. Stayed in during the evening and played gramophone, wrote off to Whitfield King's for some stamps of Aden, Antigua and Ascension. Finished reading *Brideshead Revisited* – some very amusing references to the queer side and so forth etc!

Saturday, 3 January

Cedric phoned – wants me to meet him at Piccadilly at 6, we might do a film or something? Wonder if I should ask Terry? or would gaiety spoil it? So enigmatic really!

Sunday, 4 January

Played gramophone and read during the afternoon, listened at random to the radio, and the tripe which the BBC puts over on the Home & Light programmes, is it being done in an effort to force one on to the Third?[3] Thinking more and more about my forthcoming return to work (litho) in the near future.

Monday, 5 January

Went with Mother to see *Starlight Roof* at the Hippodrome and we both enjoyed it very much. Vic Oliver[4] still as good as ever, and it was dressed very well – good choral singing – in fact they revived

---

[1] *Stars in Battledress*.

[2] Written by Ivor Novello and Clive Richardson respectively. The Richardson orchestral piece included a realistic instrumental imitation of air-raid sirens, which distressed some post-war radio listeners.

[3] The Third Programme, predecessor of Radio 3, had begun on 29 September 1946.

[4] V. von Samek (1898–1964), violin-playing comedian.

good old 'Pedro the Fisherman' and I couldn't help thinking of *High and Low* and *At Your Service*, shades of C.S.E. and so forth.

Wednesday, 7 January

Had a coffee in Forte's. The place was positively full of queens! never seen anything quite like it in my life before – it's positively frightening. How many future tradgedy's were present tonight? – god! it's horrible to even think of it! Sang all the way home and jumped on a traffic light bumper for sheer devilment and changed it from red to green!

Saturday, 10 January

Should hear from Marie Earley[5] soon about our seeing *Annie Get Your Gun* together – and I must return those evening clothes to her too!

Friday, 16 January

[Under a cutting from The Times *including 'a recent view of Singapore showing the Victoria Memorial Hall, the Supreme Court, and the tall Cathay Building'.]*

Just to remind me of 1946–7!! How many times have Stan and I walked over the Anderson Bridge together? How many times have we stood outside the 'Vic' waiting for that last 'gharry' back to Nee Soon? How many memories does this picture hold for me?

Monday, 19 January

Bless the Bride at the Adelphi Theatre tonight – bloody awful! – terrible acting, mediocre singing, and the only girl worth speaking of was Anona Winn as Nanny. The music by Vivian Ellis was very everybody – there are no song 'hits'[6] from the show, and the chorus, male and female, is so ancient they might all have come out of the 3rd programme. I was bored throughout. Still feeling lousy with dysentery.

Wednesday, 21 January

Took my gold (Hong Kong) watch to a nice old jew in Marchmont St., who says to call for it on Friday about 4'ish.

Thursday, 22 January

Went to the Regent in the evening and saw *Cottage to Let* and *Bel Ami* – both were reasonably well done. I came out of the cinema, and standing there, on the steps, confronting that ugly hulk of St Pancras

---

5 A friend who worked on the publicity side of the film industry.

6 This is perhaps uncharitable: 'La Belle Marguerite' and 'This is my Lovely Day' were very popular.

station, suddenly seemed to feel the realisation of a great truth. The necessity for 'belief' – faith, if you will, in this life of ours. I suddenly felt completely awed by the absolutely temporary nature of everything – and the memory of Stanley on the balcony in Singapore came crashing back to me – vivid. The memory of him telling me all about the 'suicidal theory' – of how utterly futile human existence was, without a real and lasting belief. He said 'I believe in art and sex' (and it is worthwhile remembering the order, for I believe he was quite sincere). I think that I have more affection and liking and respect for him than any other man I know. I hope I do not lose contact with him. I have that horrible feeling tonight that I just can't cope with the future – it all seems so dreadful in prospect! Will I ever meet that 'real love' in another which Marie spoke of at our last meeting? – although I feel it hopeless – yet I shall go on hoping and looking for it.

Friday, 23 January
Saw the new Korda film, directed by Duvivier, *Anna Karenina* – a superb performance by Vivien Leigh & Ralph Richardson – but Kieron Moore was really mediocre. I think he looks a little American? – those full sensual lips do wear one out rather – almost negro'ish – really quite revolting.

Monday, 26 January
I asked Ced. if he knew Socrates and Terry were q. and he said he did! and that I was *not*, he hoped?? – (mar dear!) I replied that my upbringing forbade such things and he said, believe it or not, so did his. Of course he just isn't true, and not a little unlike a gorm [*sic*], but I'll toy with the acquaintanceship.

Wednesday, 28 January
To His Majesty's to see *Anna Lucasta*,[7] a marvellous play about American negroes, with entire negro cast, about a prostitute making good! Really beautiful performance. They took 8 curtains at the finish and really deserved them all.

Friday, 30 January
Taxi to the Palladium – curtain up at 8.30. It was a rotten variety bill, with far too many acrobatic affairs – some of which were positively

---

[7] By Philip Yordan.

obscene. Sid Field[8] was marvellous, and received terrific and well-merited applause – what camping! I simply roared!

Saturday, 31 January
Toni & Vicky came to tea, and we went on to the Boltons Revue to see Reg Varney do his stuff. It was a very good show – quite gay in parts, with some lovely, oh luvly camping and drag! – producer Billy Milton who was clever, and very good throughout. Lovely numbers included 'I'm the only Fakir on the Pier', 'No Orchids for My Lady' and lots of other lovely numbers by Jack Strachey. Went backstage after in order to congrat. Reg, who hasn't changed a bit since I saw him in Singapore with *Jamboree* (S.I.B. show).

Sunday, 1 February
Excerpt from my diary of 1942: 'Easter Monday, April 6th. Had glorious ride in car (Hickmans) – prayer: Please God! make me worthy of the post.' Which sounds like I was a very earnest fellow of sixteen then! But everything worked out well enough! and my brief two years at Long Acre were quite happy really. Let's hope it will turn out as well for me at Philips' (though I must say I don't particularly go a bundle on the journey to North Acton every day!) Have packed my instruments in readiness. Oh! how I wish my employment were theatre work of some sort!!

Monday, 2 February
Rose at 6.30, left the house at 7.05, tube station at 7.10, and arr. at Philips' at Acton at precisely 10 minutes to 8. Miles, the head litho, gave me a neg. which required duffing – no lettering. I dread to think of what my work is going to be like when I am called upon to do something really hard!!

Tuesday, 3 February
David Whitfield – that delightful boy with *such* a voice whom I got boozy with upon two distinctly memorable occasions! – such a likeable fellow, and he writes such a charming letter! It really was terribly happy-making, so I typed him two airmails in reply. Is this what Marie once spoke of to me? I sincerely hope so – for it would certainly add something to this existence.

Thursday, 5 February
Did my first bit of lettering at Philips' today! – on the Stanford's USA,

---

[8] 1904–50, one of the most influential comedians of his time.

corrections in stump style[9] – and it didn't look at all bad, considering how long I have been away from it!

Friday, 6 February

In a short chat with Mr Coleman today, I was informed that Mr Miles thinks my work shows great promise and that I am worth the standard journeyman salary. I'm very glad to hear that. Arrived home to find Val awaiting me! We had tea together, and went on to the Odeon to see *Saigon*, a tolerable picture with Alan Ladd, and that fascinating woman Veronica Lake who always attracts and revolts me terribly. Left Val at Charing X. Was followed home, *all* the way by a strange man! mar deah! However, in the end, he just didn't have the courage!

Friday, 13 February

Everyone is raving about Danny Kaye at the Palladium – Marie says he's an education to watch – such eloquent hands! But it's hopeless to book for.

Saturday, 14 February

Met Geoffrey at 12.20. We both went over to Marie's for tea, and then on to the Ambassadors for *Sweetest and Lowest*, really *the* gayest revue, intimate or otherwise, I have ever seen! Gingold was superb – 'how queer, deah! may I pe–er?' – absolutely priceless. Back to Marie's for drinks and brought Geoff back to 57 for the night – we slept in M & D's bed 'cos Dad went into hospital today for the hernia operation. And long talk with Geoff in bed. Have decided to cut with Litho, and learn hairdressing with Dad, must write to Labour Exch. to see if this is possible.

Thursday, 19 February

Can't wait to hear from Labour people about changing my occupation. Geoffrey arrived tonight for a short visit, en route to St Pancras for Luton. We had a gay interlude of camping all the way to the station, and agreed that he would phone me tomorrow evening about arriving on Sunday for the day with us. He makes me feel curiously elated, in this otherwise 'drab' environment.

Friday, 20 February

No heating at Philips today, which made me resolve to hand in my

---

[9] 'Stumping Ink: a stick of writing ink or a very soft litho crayon, which is rubbed on to the finger or a piece of rag. These are gently rubbed on to the plate, so that some of the grease is transferred. The technique produces a very fine tint, akin to a wash.' Richard Vicary, *The Thames and Hudson Manual of Lithography*, 1976.

notice as soon as possible. Tony G. came over for drinks about 9'ish. In the course of conversation I made it clear to him about my own tendencies – daisy's chain and etc., and we generally left with mutual feelings of knowing one another better.

Saturday, 21 February
Visited Labour Exchange, in spite of the fact that it was snowing in ghastly fashion and learned that I can change my profession just as I please. They were very charming and expressed regret at having to drag me from my home on such a filthy day. There were numerous hangdogish fellows strewn and huddled about, waiting, I assume, either for 'dole' or work.

Sunday, 22 February
Geoffrey arrived at 12 from Luton for lunch with us. We had long talk, and have decided to get a flat together somewhere as soon as our financial conditions permit. He has a small part in the play *The Shop at Sly Corner*[10] with Luton Rep. but it's poor pay apparently.

Monday, 23 February
That hearty little horror, Hayden,[11] started work at Philips' today, looking terribly maritime in some naval overalls. Made lots of innuendos about actors being hatters and so forth, but I didn't bite the bait. Handed in my notice via Mr Coleman (about the only man in that Dept. I've any time for). He expressed surprise, but not great surprise. I think he half suspected it. Letters from David Whitfield (the dream!), Rae Hammond, Stanley Baxter (Glasgow) and birthday greetings from Mrs Duncombe and the Kaufmanns, and Hickmans and the Ladies. Most welcome was Dave's of course, and he was so sweet about everything. Oh! solace thou art dear . . . etc.

Thursday, 26 February
I was fearfully tired at work all day, and did practically nothing. I find the crowd *there* become more repulsive to my sensitive mind every day. Loads of 'queer' sex innuendos and so forth, which remind me of my schooldays.

Sunday, 29 February
Visited Dad in the Homœopathic – he expects to be out in 14 days or so. We discussed again the question of whether I should attend a school for hairdressing, but he waved it aside, maintaining that I

---

[10] By Edward Percy.
[11] A cousin of KW's.

should do better to learn entirely with him. Stanley Baxter tells me he is entering for the Old Vic in the spring. I wonder if I stand an earthly in this? – it might be worth trying. I shall never really be happy anywhere else but on a stage – of that I am quite sure!

Friday, 5 March

Camp conversation with Marie – she says Cyril Ritchard[12] is queue!!! I was really amazed!

Sunday, 7 March

Listened to that delightful reader Dylan Thomas on radio, reading *The Autobiography of a Super-Tramp*[13] – a most charming voice, so easy to listen to.

Tuesday, 9 March

Interview with Eric Croall, of the British Theatre Group (Director, Basil Dean) and had particulars taken. It appears they are casting four plays shortly, including *School For Scandal* to be produced at Bath, and Margate or somewhere. Auditions in 10 days' time, *if* B.D. likes one! I await with fear and trepidation! Posted another letter to The Stage because I found my original one was returned by the G.P.O. with postage due amount demanded! I must have forgot about stamp!

Wednesday, 10 March

Letter by the afternoon post from Alan Dent,[14] saying that if I ring him up, he will tell me whether or not I am an actor, and what parts I can play!

Thursday, 11 March

Visited Dad in hospital this afternoon. It was singularly boring – though I am glad in a way that I went, for it strengthened my resolution to get into the theatre as soon as possible – for in the course of an argument, he revealed to me how much we were poles apart in so many different ways, and that we should never really get on together in business.

Friday, 12 March

Phoned Mr Dent, and it seems my voice proves that I *am* an actor!

---

[12] 1898–1978, Australian-born actor, married Madge Elliott (d.1955).

[13] By W.H. Davies.

[14] 'Jock' Dent (d.1978), theatre critic of the *News Chronicle* 1945–60, formerly secretary to the critic James Agate.

A.D.: Are ye broke?
SELF: Good God No!!
A.D.: Good God No??
SELF: I should never allow myself to arrive in straits such as those!
A.D.: Look – right now I'm busy, but ring me at 12 on Monday.
SELF: Very well – 12 on Monday. Thank you and goodbye!

Wonder if he thinks I'm trying to get money out of him or something?

Tuesday, 16 March
Met Alan Dent at the Arts Theatre Club today. He was most charming, and gave me tea. It was a wonderful experience. He advised me to try hard for British Theatre Group and offers to help me into Wycombe or Colchester Reps if it doesn't come off. Met Michael Berry today (the brother of my school friend, Frederic) and he is a female impersonator! The whole thing seems to be a conspiracy! Is the whole of London going queue-ing?

Thursday, 18 March
Went with Marie in the evening, and Mum & Dad (who met her for the first time) to see *Edward, My Son*[15] at the Lyric. A faultless and beautiful production, in which Morley excelled himself. Conversation with Marie:

Self: I say, that woman in the third row looks quite naked, doesn't she?

M: Why – yes, she does.

Self: Be rather charming if some woman were to turn up naked in a theatre, wouldn't it?

M: Yes. I haven't done it myself for quite some time.

Sunday, 21 March
British Theatre Group informed me that they are fully cast – no hope in that direction then! Sod bloody Basil Dean, and his Hitlerian chairs from the Chancellery.[16]

---

[15] By Robert Morley and Noel Langley.

[16] Dean (1888–1978), organiser of ENSA, the entertainment organisation for the forces, reached Berlin shortly after the fall of the city and Hitler's death. Inspecting the Führer's Chancellery, he took a fancy to the furniture ('We ought to rescue some of those chairs'). Three chairs were 'rescued', but two were too badly burned to be restored and used as props. After the war, when ENSA was wound up in an atmosphere spiced by allegations of corruption, the press took a lively interest in the surviving chair, which ultimately found a home at the Theatre Royal, Drury Lane (see Dean's *The Theatre at War*). He was not a popular figure among actors.

Tuesday, 23 March

Letter from Alan Dent saying he has written to Wycombe Rep. and now it's up to me!

Friday, 26 March

Phone call from Toni Marks. Says she is feeling horribly bored & frustrated. I retorted that those were commonplace symptoms today, and told her she needed a lover. Reply: 'Yes, I know, but they all bore me so – men, I mean – though not you!' 'I can understand that,' I said – and we drifted into generalities. So gay.

Tuesday, 30 March

Wrote to The Stage asking them to insert the following advertisement – 'Rep. work required by experienced male actor. Age 22, height 5'9, ex-C.S.E. – Retentive Memory etc.' and now I await results of that too!

Wednesday, 31 March

If only I could get away from everything! get away from all this bloody austerity, and form-filling, and die, quietly and peacefully, reading Keats or something. Oh, this all-hating world! Can't anyone find a little happiness? But no one can tell me why I was born.

Saturday, 3 April

Played Grieg's *March of Homage*[17] which fascinates me as much as it ever did – bring[s] back those memories of Hong Kong, and Leo, and David and *At Your Service* . . . these things come back so vividly stark, and I feel the pain – playing it is like twisting the knife in my wound. I don't think it will ever heal anyway. O! what the hell, what's the good? what's the bloody use of it all?

Monday, 5 April

Just another bloody, stinking, disappointing day. Seriously thinking about taking my own life. I think it should be easiest by drowning – say to project one's body into the river from Westminster Bridge – nice to be linked up with sonnets in death – '. . . dear God, the very houses seem asleep, and all that mighty heart is lying still.'

Tuesday, 6 April

Lots of letters of a 'regrets' nature. Charmingly executed, on charming notepaper, and presumably written by a hell of a charming lot of

---

[17] From 'Sigurd Jorsalfar Suite', Op. 56. Also known as 'Triumphal March'.

people. I'm feeling more desperate than ever now, for I can't hold out much longer, or I'll go out of my mind.

Friday, 9 April
Stanley Baxter!! of all people, arrived here this afternoon, on a surprise visit. It was really lovely seeing him again. He is at present with the Celtic Ballet, at the Pendragon, in Reading. Bottom, he is playing, in *Midsummer Night's Dream*. So him.

Tuesday, 13 April
Two letters in reply to my adv. One from the Newquay Repertory Players, asking for particulars and photograph. And the other from a man in Felixstowe who is apparently opening a rep. season at Clacton on May 3rd, and wants to know all about me.

Thursday, 15 April
I'm probably daft, but have written again to David Whitfield asking why there has been no word from him of late.

Friday, 16 April
Reread *Omar Khayyam*, and felt quite moved when I came to the verse:

The worldly hope men set their hearts upon
Turns ashes, or it prospers and anon,
Like snow upon the desert's dusty face,
Lighting a little while or so, is gone.[18]

Robert Beazley wrote that in my guest book in 1940. He died soon afterward, in an air-crash. He was a pilot. I must write to his wife, Marguerite, again soon.

Tuesday, 20 April
Rang Anne Keble as asked. I am to travel [to Newquay] on Thursday – and start rehearsals Friday. Salary to begin at £4 a week. I have accepted. First play is *The Light of Heart* by Emlyn Williams.

Wednesday, 21 April
Lunched with Stanley, who caught the 1 o'clock train to Glasgow from Euston afterwards. We lunched at Fleming's in Oxford St, and he told me of the great success of the audition at the Old Vic Theatre School. I told him that I was not surprised – that I had great faith in

---

[18] The quatrain from Edward FitzGerald's translation actually concludes with the line: 'Lighting a little hour or two – was gone.'

his artistic ability. Apparently he feels that an academic background will remove the Glasgow inferiority complex which he has about himself!! He is curiously enigmatical this boy! – but oh! so brilliant. After seeing his train steam out of Euston I felt horribly empty and sad, and rather like crying. I suddenly felt that I was going away – and probably wouldn't be in London – dear London – again for ages! And Cornwall is so horribly uncertain. Oh! why have I made such a mess of everything? Or have I? If only I could have that affaire! If only I could meet the right one! How much longer have I got to wait?

Monday, 26 April

Rang Anne Keble again. Her letter, she says, is in the post confirming my job, and she expects me Thursday. That's a load off my mind. Went with Mum and Dad to Buckingham Palace and saw the flood-lighting on this occasion of the Silver Jubilee. All very exciting and mob hysteria-making.

Thursday, 29 April

Caught the Cornish Riviera Express to Newquay. Arrived at 6'ish. The accommodation is very good, and thoroughly satisfactory. Met the Rep. coy. here this evening, and watched their production of *The Light of Heart*[19] which was v.g. in parts. They all seem a decent set of people.

Friday, 30 April

My first rehearsal with the 'Company of Three' this morning. We went right thro' the play *The First Mrs Fraser*[20] in which I am to play Ninian. I read very badly, and didn't impress anybody at all I'm afraid. Fluffed myself silly. Conference called by Anne Keble (pronounced Keeble!! – ye gods!) about Stage Management in which we are expected to help!

Monday, 3 May

Rehearsed Act II of the play in the morning. Helped on the set in the afternoon. Miss Keble says my contract is ready for signing but I have made up my mind to sign nothing which mentions anything about ASM work, for I will not be a party to anything of that nature.

Thursday, 6 May

Dress Rehearsal at 3. Performance at 7.30. My first night with the Company of Three and I managed quite well – my lines got lots of laughs! and people seemed well pleased with me! After the show John

---

[19] By Emlyn Williams.

[20] By St John Ervine, KW as Ninian Fraser.

Field gave me my part for next week – the Doctor in *The Sacred Flame*,[21] think I shall use the Coleman voice for this.

Saturday, 8 May

Mrs Fraser went very badly. I dried in places, and so did everybody else. This must not occur again.

Monday, 10 May

Signed contract with the 'Coy. of Three' for one month at £4 a week. If they want me after that, I shall be more expensive.

Saturday, 15 May

Show [*The Sacred Flame*] was awful tonight. I'm sick of the Coy. of Three – the whole shoot of 'em – I'm sick of this bloody dead and alive hole they call Newquay, and I wish I was dead.

Whit Monday, 17 May

Performance of *The Sacred Flame* tonight to about 20 people, with feeble applause. More embarrassing for the audience than it was for us! Someone in the stalls shouted 'He's so stiff' as Peter [Ashby-]Bailey rendered a line, and it was really the end!

Wednesday, 19 May

Feeling curiously depressed again – fitfully, for I suddenly have bursts of terrific energy, and do mock ballet dances on the cliffs, *and* in the roadways.

Thursday, 20 May

Opening night of Emlyn Williams play *Night Must Fall*. I play the Lord Chief Justice!! Not very 'me' but still! Bad house tonight.

Saturday, 22 May

A letter today!! from David W., he is in Swatow, Japan,[22] and writes that whilst in Shanghai he was offered part in musical show in America. This boy is going to really go places!

Monday, 24 May

Letter from Equity. I am now a provisional member, with 40 weeks' probation before becoming entitled to full membership.

---

[21] By Somerset Maugham, KW as Dr Harvester.

[22] Actually on the southern coast of China (also known as Shantou).

Thursday, 27 May
First night of *Love In A Mist*[23] – I think I made a success as Howard – the house was rocking with laughter, anyway. Feeling moderately pleased with myself.

Friday, 28 May
Took four curtains tonight, after a very successful performance. I have never seen a better success here, since I arrived. The applause at the finish was terribly enthusiastic, and I felt greatly elated.

Saturday, 29 May
I have agreed to stay on for £5 a week. Will ask for a rise after a month or so.

Monday, 31 May
Rehearsed all day. Frightful cold, and terrible throat. Feeling dreadful.

Wednesday, 2 June
Feeling awful. Will probably die tonight at about eleven.

Thursday, 3 June
Didn't die after all. Though how I got through last night, I do not know.

Monday, 7 June
New Producer arrived this morning, and began rehearsals for his first play, which is *Fools Rush In*.[24] This producer chap is Richard West, son of Gladys Young (BBC Rep.) and looks as if he's going to get up everybody's nose! He has only been here for a few hours and has been babbling about 'discipline' to Annie Keble!

Saturday, 12 June
This was the biggest reception a play has ever had in this theatre, during my stay here! They stamped as well as clapped, and Inigo [Vaughan] had to stand for some minutes before he could make the curtain speech! It was all very happy making, and yet very sad, for Inigo leaves the 'Company of Three' on Monday. I felt that as the curtain came down on *George and Margaret*,[25] it also came down upon an 'era' in *my* history at any rate. I practically *ran* off the stage during the anthem, for I felt strangely moved.

---

[23] By Kenneth Horne.
[24] By Kenneth Horne, KW as Joe (The Bridegroom).
[25] By Gerald Savory, KW as Dudley.

Monday, 21 June
First night of *Breadwinner*.[26] I have never acted so badly in my life. I *hate* Somerset Maugham, and *all* his rotten plays. The dialogue is a positive barstard [*sic*] as far as weekly rep. is concerned.

Thursday, 24 June
Long talk with Richard West last night, whom I find very amusing. Very boyish type really, who maintains that one must have constant sex-intercourse to be really good at one's work.

Saturday, 26 June
Spent the afternoon on the cliffs with Sonia [Moray] and Gordon P., reading our parts. Quite fun-making. My suspicions about the latter are correct. Definitely q. he told me *all*. Ever so gay, reely.

Thursday, 1 July
Meeting tonight of the majority of the company, and decided to do what we could to get rid of certain members of the coy. whose work and behaviour has been outrageous. A petition was drawn up, signed, and presented to Richard West, the producer, as indicative of our feelings on the matter.

Friday, 2 July
Everything very electric in the company. Nasty atmosphere.

Saturday, 10 July
Anne gave the ultimatum to the [John] Field clan this morning, and he refused it – needless to say, she has not accepted our resignations. Obviously Field's intention now is to start a war of nerves. Both he and Linda [Hayward] deliberately cut all my lines and business in the show this evening: for this, I hate them. Some day they will get what they deserve. I hope I am here to see it.

Friday, 23 July
Missed five entrances at rehearsal of *Frieda*[27] today, and [Stanley] Hildebrandt didn't once lose his temper. I should apologise for this I know!! it's quite unforgivable. But then I've been doing things that are quite unforgivable *all* my life, and somehow enjoy doing them. Was introduced to our new member of the company – Frederick Treves – today. Seems a very decent chap – charming, ex-RADA. Very good actor. Trustworthy type, I should think.

---

[26] KW as Patrick.
[27] By Ronald Millar, KW as Tony Dawson.

Tuesday, 27 July
Missed another entrance tonight. If I go on like this, I shall soon get a reputation – 'good but quite unreliable'.

Monday, 9 August
Poor Fred Treves's brother has died in an accident, he went to Peterboro' over the w/e. God knows how he performed tonight! I *do* admire this chap! Find myself liking him more and more. Thoroughly honest, and decent. A damned fine actor, too. He's helped me a lot, in many ways.

Thursday, 12 August
Anne informs me that she has now got the theatre, and Field is well and truly *out*.

Sunday, 15 August
Peter & I saw Sonia off on the 12.14 from Newquay station. The poor lamb was in tears as the thing steamed out! I'm going to miss this sweet child of whom I have grown so fond, during the past few months. She has always been *such* a companion – so placid and tolerant with me.

Thursday, 19 August
Got a terrific hand on my exit tonight[28] – felt terribly bucked about it too. There's no doubt the Company of Three[29] have had their money's worth as far as I am concerned. If I left tomorrow there'd be nothing on my conscience.

Friday, 20 August
God!

Saturday, 21 August
Hell!

Sunday, 22 August
Went to Wolfe's home and sat for portrait – in 10 poses! Can't wait for the results. Met a charming young RAF fellow there obviously gay who played Debussy's *Bergamasque*[30] with more understanding than I've heard for many a day. We walked back as far as the Bristol together and talked Q. for hours. I left him at 1.15am!

---

[28] In *Grand National Night*, by Dorothy and Campbell Christie, KW as Morton.
[29] Billed as the Newquay Repertory Players, the group was contracted by the Company of Three (directors Anne Keble, John Field, Linda Hayward).
[30] 'Suite Bergamasque' for piano (includes No. 3: 'Clair de Lune').

Thursday, 16 September
Terrific crit. in the local rag about me! Quite the end! Very pleased. Performances going v. well.

Saturday, 18 September
Last night of *Importance*.[31] Great success. Bags of bouquets arriving over the footlights etc. They sent me up a toilet outfit from the Playgoers' Society, and book from Annie Keble.

Sunday, 19 September
Entrained from Newquay at 10.20 this morning for London, arriving at 5.30 with all luggage OK.

Monday, 20 September
Visited Richard at Thurloe Close today. Apparently Anne K. thinks she can go ahead in Newquay with a new company. Richard has got Giles Cooper[32] of Regent's Park to come in on it, as leading man.

Friday, 24 September
A.K. rang me tonight. All is fixed and we rehearse Oct. 5th.

Monday, 4 October
Caught the Cornish Riviera train, with Peter, at 10.30. Very comf. journey. Drinks with Giles Cooper, the leading man – and Richard and Peter.

Wednesday, 6 October
Rehearsal all day of *Candida*.[33] Richard and Giles came to my room tonight and asked me to read Eugene. I did. Now I have been asked to take it over from Richard!! I *am* !!

Thursday, 14 October
First night. Well, the Dolphin Players[34] got away with a flying start tonight and the show was a great success in every way. Gladys Young gave the most impressive curtain speech, praising a company of such integrity and everything went off remarkably smoothly. Party afterwards on stage was very gay. Everyone was very complimentary to

---

[31] *The Importance of Being Earnest*, by Oscar Wilde, KW as Algernon Moncrieff.
[32] 1918–66, better known later as a dramatist, chiefly for radio and television.
[33] By George Bernard Shaw, KW as Eugene Marchbanks.
[34] Reorganised under Richard West as Director of Productions, with an Advisory Council including Gladys Young, Mabel Constanduros, Belle Chrystal, Michel St Denis, Robert Harris and Frederick Valk.

me. As far as the locals are concerned, it was my own personal triumph tonight – no one else was even in the picture.

Saturday, 16 October

The afternoon matinée was a ghastly fiasco! I couldn't have cared less! and did not put very much into it! Ars gratia whatsit! Of course I'm *not* a sincere artist!! It's 'personality playing' that *I* am interested in – tell the others anything – couldn't care bloody less about any of 'em. But R. knows! There's no hiding much from *him* I'm afraid. Still, I think he regards me as talented – even though he does nothing but remind me that I have a long way to go etc. etc. Me and my Leslie Howard philosophy. The evening performance was the best I've ever given. Algernon West,[35] however, told Richard it was rotten. I think he rather disapproves of me!

Tuesday, 26 October

Letter from Stanley. He has joined the Citizens at Glasgow starting at £6 a week.

Monday, 1 November

Richard has got Michael Harald[36] down to take his place tomorrow.

Tuesday, 2 November

Met Michael Harald today. Charming man – and obviously very clever. I like him enormously. Very me.

Friday, 5 November

Performance in the evening of this stinking play[37] was f. awful. Bloody. Audience enjoyed it tho'. I sat on a bloody tomato in the second act!! – furious making.

Saturday, 6 November

General meeting in the office. Anne informs us all that we are getting 14 days' notice forthwith as the company can no longer remain solvent. It was suggested that a tour be arranged of surrounding villages etc., in an effort to make the thing sound financially.

Tuesday, 9 November

Our first one night stand tonight! The RAF at St Eval. It was a great success – they thoroughly enjoyed Lonsdale[38] (with purgatrations

---

[35] Veteran actor-director (b.1886), father of Richard, husband of Gladys Young.
[36] Actor/writer, né Cotton: d.1970.
[37] *Tobias and the Angel*, by James Bridie.
[38] *On Approval*, by Frederick Lonsdale.

[*sic*]!) and everything went very smoothly. They took 13 pounds profit. A small beginning, but not at all bad, considering all things. Dreary Offrs. Mess party after, which brought back C.S.E. so vividly to me! Ah me!

Wednesday, 10 November

Rehearsed in evening. Drinks in the New after, with Michael Harald. Somehow I feel very confident about the future now. I'm sure I'm going to get there – somehow.

Saturday, 27 November

Our last performance in Newquay.[39] It went down very well. Lot of silly speech stuff from Annie Keble after – *so* bad, but there one is!

Sunday, 28 November

Met Annie and the company at the Great Western – sort of farewell party. It was rather like the atmosphere in the Common Room for teachers in a rather tatty council school.

Monday, 29 November

Caught 10.10, and picked up the Riviera train at 11, at Par. Arr. Paddington 5 o'clock.

Friday, 3 December

Saw Ruth Draper at the Theatre Royal, Haymarket. She is very good. I was just a shade disappointed.

Sunday, 5 December

Richard rang in morning. Went over to Thurloe Close in afternoon. We had long discussions about future plans. His idea is either to get a coy. down at Newquay, or tour public schools.

Wednesday 8 December

Met Richard, who introduced me to Alec McCowen of Penge Rep. We spent the afternoon together. Saw Michael Harald on our way to the S.F. Grill for tea. Went with Richard to see *Paisà* at the Academy cinema. It was superb. Had supper with him after at the Corner House – it was full of queers and prosts.

Saturday, 11 December

My present capital is £24. Must try to improve on that very soon!!

---

[39] *Trespass*, by Emlyn Williams, KW as Bill.

Tuesday, 14 December
Saw *The Guinea Pig* at the Ritz. Quite well done. Best performance came from Robert Flemyng as Lorraine. Walked home feeling madly depressed and curiously detached. Don't want to go to Mabel Constanduros's party on the 17th at all.

Friday, 17 December
Met Margaret & Michael as arr. Richard found me at Margaret's flat later in the evening and was furious with me for not going to the Constanduros party. Said he could have got me a BBC job for 3 weeks on a serial. Says there is a poss. of getting me work at Stratford Rep. – it is all so vague.

Saturday, 18 December
GREAT DAY. Went to the Ashby-Bailey soirée at Phil Finch's flat. It was the most gay and amusing party I've ever been to before. Met Oliver Ford[40] – a charming fellow – scenic designer and obviously destined for greatness. Spoke to him for the greater part of the evening. V. naughty really for he was with a friend. Have arranged to see him tomorrow evening for a chat. Arrived home at 5.30am!! tight, tired, but elated. Life has taken on a wonderful design. I need never be morbid any more. A motive for working has been supplied. I feel *new*, and clean again.

Sunday, 19 December
Met Oliver at 3.30 in Portland Place. Went to his flat for tea, in De Walden St – he is the guest of Francis D. there, who was away. We had a most interesting discussion – I saw some of his work – terribly clever.

Tuesday, 21 December
Tea with Oliver and Francis. Saw Gielgud in *Return of the Prodigal*[41] at Globe Theatre with Oliver. Wrote to Stanley telling him everything! Whoopee!!!

Wednesday, 22 December
Went to see Alastair Scott-Johnston at the BBC. Says he might have something for me in the new year.

Saturday, 25 December
Michael Harald came in the evening. A quiet but very happy Xmas.

---

[40] 1925–92. Described by an obituarist as 'the doyen of the traditional decorators'.
[41] By St John Hankin.

Monday, 27 December
Oliver still staying with us.

Tuesday, 28 December
Went to see Francis – lots of drinks and the seduction scene from *Now Barabbas*.[42] God awful biz. Must stop this somehow. Home at 2'ish.

Wednesday, 29 December
Tatting around the agents. Oliver is still here – this boy is the personification of indecision, just doesn't know what to do with himself. Ye Gods! Wrote to Francis D. telling him it is best we don't see each other again for some time. Hope he realises the finality of that.

Thursday, 30 December
Grant Anderson rang – I went along to 199 Piccadilly to see them. I start on Tues. at two – Intimate Theatre, as Bellhop, in *Born Yesterday*.[43]

Friday, 31 December
My first year as a civilian again – just coming to an end. Well, it's been a doubtful year: full of hopes – and I've done as much work as I could under the circumstances. But it's been very miserable and frustrating too, in many ways – however, I must forget all that. I wonder what 1949 will be like? I feel on the threshold of something eventful.

---

[42] 1947 play by William Douglas-Home.

[43] By Garson Kanin. Intimate Theatre, Palmers Green, London N13.

1949

MEMORANDA
Watch out for Pisces types!

Sunday, 2 January
Phone call from Frankie D. telling me to contact BBC tomorrow.

Monday, 3 January
Am to play small part in the *Gordon Grantley K.C.*[1] recording on Sunday next for 5 guineas. Please God I'm successful. Spent evening at Francis's flat – took Maggie Lloyd along – it wasn't a success. Must keep Fran at arm's length.

Tuesday, 4 January
Rehearsing at the Intimate Theatre, Palmers Green. I have five lines or so as the Bellhop.

Monday, 24 January
First night at Stratford. Great success. I am the highspot of the show.

Tuesday, 25 January
The man from Midland Bank came in the evening to see the show – met me after for drinks. I thinks he's q.!!

Wednesday, 2 February
The Harbord office have given me an appointment at 10 on Friday morning. Kenneth Seale of Spotlight came to the matinée today – and Giles Cooper. We had tea together in Lyon's. First BBC cheque today for 5 guineas.

---

[1] A serial by John P. Wynn. KW as Edward Buttingham (Episode 2) and Patrick Dollard (Episode 6).

Friday, 4 February
Interview with the Harbord office. They're putting me up for Arts Council Rep at Swansea. I'm not keen but one never knows.

Sunday, 6 February
Good part in *Gordon Grantley* today. Very drama. Saw *Vote For Huggett* – terrible film. Really bad, in every way. Like a bloody documentary.

Friday, 18 February
Letter from Stanley – apparently I've hurt his feelings by writing carelessly – replied charmingly. He's a funny cove!

Monday, 21 February
Spotlight rang me about Newcastle Rep. Went along but didn't get it. I'm not a good rep type.

Thursday, 24 February
Met this film agent, Brophy. Queer as a coot – film is to be made in the Cocos Islands, obviously pornographic – I'm having nothing to do with it.

Tuesday, 1 March
Harbord office rang me, to play 2 small parts in *School for Scandal*[2] at New Theatre, Bromley – producer Ronnie Kerr. Gather the salary is to be £9. I accepted of course. This means I shan't be able to play the footman in *The Circle* with Richard at Stratford. Very glad I am too! Very bad to get all my work thro' or with him. This year is being good to me. Please God it will continue to be – I am so easily disheartened these days.

Wednesday, 2 March
Richard rang me – furious about my playing at Bromley. Said I should have rung him to let him know first! Apparently I did the wrong thing. Stratford has printed my name on the programmes etc.!! All very unfortunate and Hastings is livid over the whole biz – still, can't be helped and after all, if they want me enough, they'll get me eventually, won't they? eh?

Wednesday, 9 March
Rehearsal at Bromley – learning the Gavotte. It was absolutely bloody. I hate dancing. (My mood today has been very depressing – somehow

---

[2] By Sheridan, KW as Snake.

I'm back in that awful uncertainty of 1948! Wondering whether it's all worth it or not – and needing a real friend terribly.)

Monday, 21 March
Letter from Peter Ashby-Bailey – he's got the sack from Chesterfield Rep. Richard has offered me a job at Newquay at £10 a week – and Bailey has been offered character man too! So we may be meeting again.

Tuesday, 29 March
Rehearsed at Bromley – *We Proudly Present*,[3] small part to be played in my fat boy voice – rather interesting I think. Sonia came to see the show, and we had a drink after at Henekey's with Alastair and Nicholas Parsons.

Saturday, 2 April
Letter from Stanley Baxter. He has fallen in love. Silly boy. Nice tho'.

Tuesday, 5 April
Saw Alastair this morning and heard the Paul Temple records so that I may give an impression of his voice in the *Mannequin For Murder*[4] programme on the 18th. Alastair rang up Richard Stone the agent and asked him to see me! Am to go along at eleven tomorrow. So that's nice!

Played Bromley in the evening. The RADA students are in my dressing room – Brian someone and Jim Perry,[5] ex-C.S.E. – both good types and great fun.

Wednesday, 6 April
Saw Richard Stone[6] this morning. He was useless in a charming sort of way – asked me to tell him when I was playing a decent part anywhere and he would come and see me etc. etc. etc. the usual rubbish.

Thursday, 7 April
Jim Perry made the day bearable with his amusing company. I like this fellow more and more. Must remember to contact him in my own organisation in five years' time when I have my own theatre.

---

[3] By Noël Coward

[4] 'A Thriller in the Making' by Trevor Ross and Howard Bygrave. Light Programme. KW unbilled.

[5] Jimmy Perry, later known for devising nostalgic, troupe-based situation comedies, e.g. 'It Ain't Half Hot, Mum' and 'Dad's Army'.

[6] Influential agent, specialising in comedy performers.

Thursday, 14 April
Saw *Oranges and Lemons*[7] with Richard. Went to Max Adrian's room after, and chatted. All very pleasant – rather piqued that I wasn't the 'hit' I imagined I might be. Here is an ego every bit as strong as my own.

Tuesday, 19 April
Rehearsal at Stratford [*An Inspector Calls*] – routine stuff, moves etc. This play reminds me of so much which occurred at Newquay. Everyone in that company was so much better than this one!! The daughter in this is absolutely ghastly – really so bloody Roedean it just isn't decent! – gawd save us! – can't stand it meself.

Friday, 22 April
Went to Doctor about warts on my left hand. They are becoming unsightly. Have to go to University College Hosp. to see Skin Doctor on May 5th! – ghastly business this National Health Scheme! – one might be dead by then! Got home with a cloud of black depression over me – feeling near to the tears which don't ever come – absolutely suicidal feeling. Ghastly.

Monday, 25 April
Fair opening night [*An Inspector Calls*] – reasonable house – nothing exciting. Everyone in the production is bad, except me. I'm marvellous.

Saturday, 30 April
Got straps for trunk in preparation for Newquay, fixed them with rivets.

Sunday, 1 May
Went with Donald Morley to see *Passport To Pimlico* – wonderful laugh! Best thing I've seen so far this year.

Thursday, 5 May
Coffee – Derek came – at 11. Long chat. He is very worried, poor boy, about traditional overtures etc. I understand him so much. See myself asking the same question – and getting no reply.

Friday, 6 May
Tea with Hal at his flat. Very pleasant. He showed me pornographic book – v. exciting!

---

[7] A revue, with Adrian, Elizabeth Welch, etc.

Monday, 9 May
Saw *It's A Boy*[8] at Stratford in evening. Met Brian [Oulton] and Peggy Thorpe-Bates after the show. She is *wonderful*! I *love* her! What an artist!! Out of this world.

Friday, 13 May
Harold G. spent evening with me. Told me he was TBH v. gay!!!

Sunday, 15 May
Tony G. came in the evening. Long chat and drinks – he told me he was TBH etc. Never dreamed! Good.

Monday, 16 May
Entrained for Newquay at 10.30, arrived at 5.30. These digs at Crantock St are terrible!! I shall go raving mad if I stay here long. Madly working class'ish. Quite the end.

Friday, 20 May
Fixed new room at Tower Rd. Very nice – comfortable.

Monday, 23 May
Opening night – medium success. Nobody liked the Tchehov, at all, but *Destiny* seemed to be acceptable.[9] Ah well! I'm CCL[10] as far as that's concerned. Just another chance for me to show off and so all is justified. Party after on stage. Long chat with Ravilious.[11] Hope he says something good in the paper on Friday!

Friday, 3 June
Am really enjoying this week out! And taking it very easy. Have to frame Mr Naylin's photographs tomorrow. He told Richard I 'showed off' in public – and that it was a good thing for an actor to do!

Saturday 11 June
Went to the Bank and arranged to have my account transferred to Newquay. Deposited £7 – which means £3.10.0. a week saved, since I started on full salary, which is not so good. Must do better than this.

Richard came to my room and read this! – funny he's the only one I've ever allowed to read my private and so personal! diary. But I

---

[8] By Austin Melford. See entry for 20 June.
[9] Double bill: *The Proposal* by Chekhov, and *The Man of Destiny* by George Bernard Shaw, KW as Napoleon.
[10] Couldn't care less.
[11] Leslie J. Ravilious, known locally as 'Rav' or 'LJR'.

s'pose that apart from S., he's the only one I can really trust, who will never abuse my confidence.

Met some queers in the New, and got sent up by two young matelots – rotten! awful!

Monday, 20 June

Mrs Moonlight[12] quite a success. Owing to a 'dry' I gave the longest bit of gagging I've ever given in my life, just went on and on. Got a script for *It's A Boy* – Dudley is a whopping part!! I'll never know it!! ye gods!! – how I deplore weekly rep.

Tuesday, 21 June

After the performance Vere [Lorrimer] accused me of malingering on stage. I endeavoured to accept with good grace – for he was smarmy with it ('You're such a good actor if you want to be' etc etc).

Thursday, 30 June

Letter from Tony G. re his visit to Newquay with gay innuendo! must put him off – for I could never study at night. All this and repertory too!!

Wednesday, 6 July

This play *Letter Box Rattles*[13] we're rehearsing really gets on my nerves. So utterly puerile. C.C.L. myself. The part I've got is dreadful. The casting is completely wrong. Drears along in perfect Cinderella fashion. I *hate* everything. EVERYTHING.

Saturday, 9 July

Evening performance OK. Pinched Joan Dale's bot as she was going on! She sulked about it rest of evening. Pam Stamford livid too, and Vernon, so it's obvious she discussed it with them all, in the dressing room! She's a bitch but I'll fix her tomorrow.

Sunday, 10 July

Very pleasant afternoon swimming and sunbathing. I love Annette Kerr. She's quite the sweetest person I ever knew.

Thursday, 14 July

Very nearly slept too late before show! Housekeeper woke me at 9.30!! Good job I'm not 'on' till end of Act II.

---

12 By Benn W. Levy.

13 By James Bridie ('a sentimental comedy').

Tuesday, 19 July

Dreadful long day. Setting *Flat To Let* – just seemed interminable. I am completely miscast as a diplomat-lover of 30! back from bloody Vienna. Dated, rubbishy dialogue which makes you sick inside. I *hate* repertory in a week. Must try my damnedest to keep out of it after the finish of this season. It's too cruel for words. You can't have legitimate art churned out every week! It's not that I'm lazy, it's simply that I hate skimping everything. Must stick it out here till the end of the season. I feel as near to tears as those terrible months last March. If only I had the courage for suicide.

Monday, 25 July

Opening night of *Flat To Let.*[14] I have hateful part. Forgot to change into black socks for evening dress! Furious throughout show.

Friday, 29 July

Diana V[ernon] came out with this today – right out of the blue – 'If you left this company Ken, it would be finished' – she's an extraordinary mixture, this woman.

Friday, 5 August

Mum & Dad came to see rehearsal of *The Paragon*[15] in morning. Performance (6 lines) satisfactory.

Friday, 12 August

Performance in evening – terrible. Fight sequence quite terrible. I was shocking. What's the use?

Friday, 19 August

Performance in the evening – reasonable. A Miss Knight (customer at the shop, 57) called on me after the show, said she thoroughly enjoyed it. Said many patrons referred to me as 'Danny Kaye'ish'!!! Compliment. This after Jean-Louis Barrault! The end!!!

Wednesday, 24 August

Had long talk with R. who says his Father said he ought to fine me for making 'faces' on the stage. Of course that's the end. Apart from the fact that A. is now doddering theatrically I'm enlightened to realise that R. apparently agrees with him. Why don't the pair of them take a lesson from some of our best known comedy actors? Henson, Fields, Howes, etc. etc.! I'll get there – if necessary without either of them –

---

[14] By Arthur Macrae.

[15] By Roland and Michael Pertwee.

and make all the faces I want to. The dreadful thing is that I just don't care about anything now.

Thursday, 1 September
J. spent night with me because of mice in his room.

Thursday, 22 September
Sinking fund party on stage. Everyone very gay. Read poem. I got very drunk and was sick – staggered home at 1.30 (without assistance).

Sunday, 25 September
Train at 10.15. Arrived Paddington 5.20. Home at 5.45. Shared taxi with Joan Dale.

Monday, 26 September
Saw *The Lady's Not For Burning.*[16] Superb mechanics from Gielgud. Esmé Percy best.

Wednesday, 28 September
Mum & Dad brought me my new Invicta portable typewriter. It's lovely. They're wonderful.

Wednesday, 5 October
Paid my bill at Spotlight[17] for the next year's issue. Quarter page at £6.5.0.! Tears a hole in my savings this does!

Monday, 17 October
Played 'Briggs' [in *Thunder Rock*[18]] quite well in my opening night here at Wycombe.

Friday, 21 October
Long talk with Donald O'Malley, the producer, who wanted to know if my attitude to my work was sincere. He says there are going to be many changes in his coy. and he's only going to keep those who are sincere. Thinks I play a lot on technique.

Monday, 24 October
Tonight was probably one of the most important in my life. Playing 'Lachie'[19] is somehow rather thrilling. But oddly enough I don't think

---

[16] By Christopher Fry.
[17] The actors' directory.
[18] By Robert Ardrey.
[19] In *The Hasty Heart* by John Patrick, KW as Lachlan.

I am playing as well as I could. Peter Hawkins ('Yank') has been charming to me. I like him a hell of a lot. Wrote to Stanley.

Wednesday, 26 October
Performance in the evening very satisfying. I am *so* happy playing 'Lachie' – I don't think I've ever enjoyed a role *so* much in my life before. The company are so charming too. Life is very good.

Saturday, 29 October
Best performance of my life tonight, really sorry it is over. Something 'happened' to me as Lachie. Something exhilarating and wonderful.

Saturday, 12 November
At the matinée I played frivolously, O'Malley came backstage and reprimanded me. He ought to practise what he preaches. Wish I could get away from here.

Tuesday, 15 November
Performance in evening – terrible. Missed an entrance for a 2 minute space!

Saturday, 10 December
Reh. and did two shows of *Little Women*.[20] Richard came down to see the second house, and travelled back to Marylebone with me. We got a 30 bus, and I left my case on it, with my electric razor which I bought today and which cost £4 and M & D's Xmas presents in it!! Got a taxi to the bus depot and got it from the conductor who was checking out. Richard and I then took taxi to Piccadilly – and had dinner at the Chicken Inn. Talked about Eastbourne venture etc.

Friday, 16 December
Phone call from Williams and Woolley offering me fortnightly at Margate and Eastbourne, at 9 a week. I accepted. Annette is also going. We start off Feb. 16th.

Monday, 19 December
Dress reh. of *Treasure Island*[21] appalling. *Chaos*. Drear. Bed.

Tuesday, 20 December
Returned Wycombe on the 2.20. Perf. *awful*. Handed in my notice.

---

[20] Adapted by Marian de Forest from Louisa M. Alcott's novel, KW as Laurie.
[21] Adapted by Georg Sheldon from Robert Louis Stevenson's novel, KW as Dick Trym.

Saturday, 24 December
Drinks in dressing room. Drinks from Jack Stone on train to town. Sang rude songs and carols. Arr. home at 11.45.

Saturday, 31 December
The last day of the year. And I suppose it has been quite a progressive year for me. It has seen me broadcasting for the first time in this country, working at five different theatres, and meeting many new people. For really the most interesting part, I had Bonaparte at Newquay, for my fondest memory part, Lachie at Wycombe, and for my most hateful part Briggs!! in *Thunder Rock*. I suppose I've learned a lot too – certainly I have realised how much more there is to acting than just creating a character for oneself to enjoy & put over. I still think of Albert's[22] prophecy – 'I'll cut off my five fingers if you aren't established on the stage in 5 years' time', at the Vic. in Singapore in 1947. I wonder if 1952 will realise this for me? Still my life continues to be empty of the second most important thing. Perhaps 1950 will put that right.

22 Albert Arlen, a C.S.E. producer.

1950

Thursday, 5 January
Find myself getting really sick of *Treasure Island* which couldn't be more boring if it tried.

Saturday, 7 January
Last two performances of this dreary pantomime. Letter from Stanley who says his *Tintock Cup* is an enormous success.

Monday, 9 January
Harbord interview proved very disappointing. I may meet the director and may *not*. It's for the part of a 16-year-old in *Captain Hornblower*[1] (Warner Bros.)

Thursday, 12 January
Went to meet the Tonbridge boy, waited five minutes and then left. Very glad, for the whole thing was futile really, and he was too stupid for worlds.

Wednesday, 18 January
Peter Hawkins came to see the show. He said it was good! He is taking my job at Wycombe! Very funny after what he's said about Wycombe in the past!

Saturday, 21 January
2 shows at Wycombe. The last most successful. Val came to the matinée. Gay. Chatted for while. No one seemed sorry to see me go!

Monday, 23 January, Hayes
Dress rehearsal and evening performance a great success. Round of applause greeted my entrance to the stage!! very satisfying indeed.

---

[1] *Captain Horatio Hornblower* (1951), directed by Raoul Walsh, did not feature KW.

Saturday, 28 January
Ghastly contretemps at Hayes with a pansy s/director. Complained to Jean Shepheard who's just as barmy! Never again Hayes! Felt awfully upset all the way home. Did me packing for tomorrow.

Sunday, 29 January
Caught the 10.00 from Euston. The Royal Scot to Glasgow. Arr. at 9 o'clock. Missed Stanley on platform, got taxi, arrived at Wilton St, alone. He followed, with Laurie S. who had kindly brought his car along to the station to meet me! He is a very self assured young man, handsome, and I should think, clever. Am to see him again on Tuesday. I think it has happened.

Monday, 30 January
Saw Stanley's show. *The Tintock Cup*, at Citizens'. Very amusing and diverting. Stanley of course stands out like a beacon.

Tuesday, 31 January
Drove out into the snow-laden countryside with L. This is the dream from which there is no awakening. At last – no more worries now. Everything about it is honest and sincere. Feel uplifted.

Wednesday, 1 February
Lunched & tea with Moira, with whom Stanley is having a vague sort of thing. S. was on edge the whole time. Kept telling me not to camp. Really!

Thursday, 2 February
Coffee in La Scala with Laurie. The last time I shall see him for a number of months I s'pose. Miserable.

Friday, 3 February
Lunch with S. at the Royal. V.g. Played discs – nostalgia. S. left at 3.45 to see a friend. I said goodbye. Then like a rainbow! L. phoned. He came and drove me to the station. Then goodbye – au revoir? but of course. This must endure.

Sunday, 5 February
Arr. Eastbourne 12 o'clock. I am playing Danny in *Night Must Fall*! Terrible long part!

Tuesday, 7 February
John Hussey (another actor in the coy.) played piano in the evening very enjoyably.

Tuesday, 14 February

Reh. *Robert's Wife.*[2] ASM called Ash arr. v. late. J[ennifer] Sounes sacked her immediately. Q. right. Set most of it, in morning. Thankful that I have a small part, after the hectic of last week.

Wednesday, 22 February

Presents from Val and Aunt Edith. *The Symposium* and braces respectively. Rehearsed in morning. I play a Chinaman. Revolting. Of course the whole thing is quite ridiculous. However, I shall be brilliant. The show was well received. Jennifer Sounes in very frivolous mood, camping herself silly. Telegram arrived from Laurie, signed 'Leo'!! wishing me Happy Birthday.

Sunday, 5 March

Worried over Laurie's long silence. Drinks in evening with Jennifer.

Monday, 6 March

Opening night, *The Letter,*[3] Margate. Still no letter from L. Scribbled note during rehearsals and posted tonight.

Wednesday, 8 March

Wrote frantic note to L. re long silence. Must run the gauntlet.

Thursday, 9 March

Letter arrived from L. Read like an advt. for Frigidaire. Of course to read between the lines is to read finis. Shan't reply until the next. Shan't write for a long time. Must get out of this awful groove. Get back into proportion. Masses to learn in this play.

Monday, 13 March

Opening *The Letter*, Eastbourne. Letter from the bank. My credit now stands at approx. £80. Less than I expected.

Thursday, 30 March

Telegram from Richard. He has taken over production at Wycombe and wants me to join him there at £8 a week. They're on an economy drive. I can't do it. Must work for a better salary than this. Letter from Ted Shoesmith too. Officially asking me to return. Wired reply in the negative.

---

2 By St John Ervine, KW as Bob.

3 By Somerset Maugham, KW as the Chinese clerk.

Friday, 31 March
Letter from Jennifer imploring me to stay on here! I can't leave yet awhile. Thank God we're only with Morley for 2 productions. Can't wait to have Jennifer back again.

Tuesday, 4 April. Margate
Spent morning writing letters – one to Laurie breaking everything off rotten. Reh. in the afternoon. Performance in evening. Feeling really ill, mentally and otherwise. Wrote tormentedly to Stanley.

Saturday, 8 April
Letter from Laurie – let's say goodbye and leave it alone.

Wednesday, 12 April
All very tiring and drear. Mr Bell being insulting in the bar about my work. Cannot tolerate this.

Sunday, 23 April
Travelled by coach to Margate. New digs excellent. Jennifer Sounes now got the sack!! She leaves after *Fools Rush In*. This organisation is ghastly. Web after web of intrigue.

Monday, 24 April
Met Margaret Smith[4] from whom it appears that Jennifer has been very indiscreet. O dear! where will it end?

Tuesday, 25 April
Reh. *F.R.I.* Barbara Murray arrived. She appears quite charming. V. attractive. Jennifer bumming[?] to her madly. Tea with Margaret Smith.

Monday, 1 May
Letter from Laurie, he comes to Maidstone on July 16th!! Took my blue suit to tailor to make it single breasted.

Wednesday, 3 May
Reh. in morning. Critics describe my performance this week as 'outstanding'.

Thursday, 4 May
Had tea with Ronnie Kerr and discussed traditional worries. Saw queer

[4] Not Maggie Smith (whose career began in Oxford in 1952, and who later became a close friend of KW), but a theatre manageress.

drag show at the Royal. It was gay. Laugh. Met them all after, at our digs. They're charming.

Friday, 5 May
Performance in the evening went down well, I was 'off' for 1st act, and the 3rd!! fell asleep in the dressing room. It's the end. I feel so tired all the time– need a rest so badly. Gave the q's a photo of meself. Vanity tailor has buggered my coat completely.

Sunday, 7 May
Visited Margaret Smith, who's ill in bed this morning. Took some grapes.

Monday, 15 May
Letter from Winwoods – giving me 14 days notice w.e.f. June 3rd. *Gay*!

Friday, 19 May
Most thrilling experience of my life! *The Heiress* at the Haymarket Theatre. Received by Tearle[5] in his dressing room, with Rowena and John. Gins. It was magnificent. Terribly nervous. Walked and talked for long while after with John.

Saturday, 20 May
With L. to see *Cage aux Rossignols* with Noel-Noel. Lovely performances. Then to see *Soldiers in Skirts* which was disgustingly bad. Then back to town for traditional larks and bags of everything. Home at 12.30. Very frust.

Monday, 29 May
Richard rang in morning. We propose (R & I) to go to Paris on Wednesday.

Tuesday, 30 May
Trip will have to be put off till Friday now.

Friday, 2 June
Arrived Dieppe 3. Entrained for Paris at 3.35. Fixed accomm. at Hotel Dieppe, 22 Rue d'Amsterdam. Wonderful city, but stiflingly hot.

---

[5] Godfrey Tearle (1884–1953). Eminent actor, knighted in 1951. First president of Actors' Equity.

Saturday, 3 June
Left R. in bed and walked from Rue Amsterdam to Place de la Concorde, up thro' Avenue des Champs Elysées to Arc de Triomphe. Read the Daily Telegraph.

Sunday, 4 June
Paris is lousy hot. I want to go back to Londres.

Monday, 5 June
Spent the afternoon swimming at the De Lassigny pool. Choc a bloc with French bodies. Breath. B.O. Ugh. Drear. Queued for 20 minutes. Gendarme in charge. *Hell!!!*

Tuesday, 6 June
Went to Notre Dame & the Tuileries afternoon. Saw *Quartet* film (Maugham) in the evening. Très Bon. Excellent.

Wednesday, 7 June
Arrived Victoria at 6'ish. Taxi by luck! they're on strike. Very hot here, but so much better than France.

Friday, 23 June
Heard from R. that the Arts Council are casting for Swansea. Have to write Clifford Evans.

Sunday, 25 June
Met Hugh Manning in the evening at Piccadilly for drinks. Talked for long while on the Embankment about Existence. Left him at 11.30. Met a young spiv at 12. Gave him 5/- for a meal.

Monday, 26 June
Saw Clifford Evans. He wants actors who can speak Welsh. Obviously I've had it. R. was there.

Thursday, 29 June
Clifford Evans offers me job at £5 a week to start – on trial. I agreed. Think it's worth it.

Friday, 7 July
To Equity meeting where Miss Glasgow talked about the Arts Council. *Mad.* Lewis Casson in the chair – *terrible. Awful.* Dame Sybil[6] kept

---

[6] Dame Sybil Thorndike (1882–1976) and Sir Lewis Casson (1875–1969), the senior theatrical couple of their day.

jumping up to say equally *stupid* things and the whole thing was *laughable*.

Tuesday, 11 July. Swansea
First rehearsal with Swansea company. Most interesting. Everyone is obviously theatre – seems like it's going to be excellent.

Sunday, 23 July
Train to Swansea with Bill Moore – rather nice chap also in the company.

Tuesday, 1 August
Opening night.[7] Great, great success. Most exciting reception. We took 12 curtains. Thrilling.

Tuesday, 15 August
Read thro' *The Seagull* understudying for Burton who arrives on Thurs. It's dreary to say the least.

Thursday, 17 August
Entire cast now here for *Seagull*. I've only got 1 line as the cook. It's quite a gay rest really. Well reely.

Saturday, 19 August
Richard Burton is really charming.

Sunday, 20 August
Walked miles with R. madly talking and chatting about everything – theatre, sex, frustration, my career.

Monday, 28 August
Evening opening was personal triumph for Richard Burton. Colossal applause. V.G. He deserves every bit of it. I got his drinks for him between acts. Privileged. Fine actor – fine.

Tuesday, 29 August
R.B. unwell tonight. Performance successful however.

Wednesday, 30 August
Awful shock on arrival at theatre to find Richard B. was *ill*! Nearly died thinking I might have to go *on*! – alright however. He made it!

---

[7] Of *Family Portrait*, by Lenore Coffee and Joyce Cowen.

Thursday, 31 August
Find myself warming more and more to R.B. – a really charming actor. Beginning to *hate* this lousy Tchekhovian stuff. There is something about the thing which has frightening effects of melancholia.

Friday, 1 September
Feel myself becoming more and more imbued with morbidity. *Hate* the theatre. And the company. *Loathe* Church of England.[8] Complete drip *and a boor*. Wish I could get another job quickly from here.

Sunday, 3 September
Went with R, Lydia, Annette, Gilbert and Glyn to Rhossilly[9] – by car. It was really delightful. Had row after with Annette and R and walked off and left them.

Monday, 4 September
Went with Glyn by car all over the Rhondda and Afan valleys. Mist shrouded everything – purple heather, black slag heaps, disused pits, grim wet stone houses, uniform rows of drab streets. Occasional waterfalls cascading with pure music down the mountainside. Rain dripping steadily off of leaves bent with the pain of it. A brooding sadness.

Thursday, 7 September
Gay with B. in dressing room, and Sybil too. They are both delightful. Reading of *St Joan*.[10] I read 4 parts!!! – Dauphin among them. Cast to be announced later.

Friday, 8 September
I am to play Stogumber in *St Joan*. Livid of course. Should get Dauphin. Brambell[11] to play it instead. CCL anyway.

Saturday, 9 September
Said goodbye to Richard B. and his wife tonight. I shall miss them both very much.

Tuesday, 12 September
Given the part of Dauphin at today's rehearsal. Very glad – but too late in the day to be thrilling. The one part C.E. and I will *not* agree about.

---

[8] KW's name for Clifford Evans. He revised his opinion in retrospect.
[9] Now Rhossili.
[10] *Saint Joan* by George Bernard Shaw.
[11] Wilfrid Brambell (1912–85), later famous as Steptoe *père* in 'Steptoe and Son'.

Thursday, 21 September
Don't know what I am doing as Dauphin.

Friday, 22 September
R. returned from town with information via Fred Treves about letter I sent to Portman. Drear making. Bitter. Humiliation. However, my turn will come.

Sunday, 24 September
Feeling absolutely terrible. Raging cold, sneezing everywhere. Feeling at death's door. Couldn't care less about production. I am *terrible* as the Dauphin. Worse than I have ever been before.

Monday, 25 September
Got through rehearsal and opening despite malady! And managed to be competent.

Tuesday, 26 September
Wonderful notices about me in the local rag, *and* the Daily Herald. Quite gay making. God knows why, for I am *not* good in the play *at all!!*

Thursday, 28 September
C of E doesn't much care for my Dauphin, that's obvious from his attitude & from what he has said to others about it. I *loathe* him. Never again. Never the strange unthinking joy – never the pain.

Tuesday, 3 October
Dale says I am out of key in production, and that all I need is cap and bells. Bitch!

Saturday, 7 October
Went with the a/m to hear the Morriston Orpheus Choir. Most moving evening. Had to make speech thanking them for wonderful reception. Dear dear people.

Sunday, 15 October
Made it up with Joan Dale. She's sweet reely.

Friday, 10 November
John [Hussey] and Joan got 14 days' notice. John was told he was to be in *12 Night* by C of E!! *Naughty.* I feel I don't want to stay here, am handing in my own written notice of my desire to leave to C.E. tonight. Expect he will ask to see me. If he is charming he will be

able to get anything out of me. I am useless where flattery is concerned, let's face it. Chatt.

Saturday, 11 November
Interview with C of E. Persuaded me to stay. Says that our group (under R.) is Mutual Admiration Society. Half of that is dead right.

Wednesday, 15 November
Show in the evening lousy.[12] Bomb didn't go off. Colin (page in *St Joan*) came to see it. Thought it was excellent!! Coffee after with Rachel who was madly sexually analytical!

Thursday, 16 November
Session with Rachel who says she's got a big TBH with me. Tried to make her see the futility of it all.

Friday, 17 November
Letter from Dr Erich Heller,[13] head of German Dept. at the University. Says I really 'belong' to theatre. Shall ring him up, as he suggests tomorrow and meet him.

Sunday, 19 November
Visited Erich Heller. Dinner at the Osborne. Goose and Moselle. V.G. Long talk. Theatre. Gay of course. Charming and wholly delightful but I must [not] get too embroiled. No real hope there. But a very fascinating companion. Frightened and discreet. Arrived back in Swansea – very drunk.

Tuesday, 21 November
With Rachel in evening to see *Sunset Boulevard*. WONDERFUL. Superb. Stroheim. Holden. Swanson. Really exciting.

Sunday, 26 November
To Rachel's for tea in the afternoon. To her father's chapel in the evening, where he preached very well.[14]

---

[12] *Crime Passionel*, by Jean-Paul Sartre. KW as Hugo.

[13] Distinguished Bohemian-born Germanist, 1911–90, best known for his books *The Disinherited Mind* and *The Ironic German: A Study of Thomas Mann*.

[14] 'When I met Rachel's father, the minister [Rev. Richard Rees Roberts of York Place Baptist Chapel], we talked about the medieval Morality plays and the tradition of actors performing on the church steps. The next I knew, he'd invited all of us, the whole company, to Sunday service at the chapel and preached us a special sermon on the text, "In the Beginning was the Word". The congregation wasn't too pleased, if you ask me, to have a lot of raffish actors sitting in their nice respectable pews.' KW quoted in *No Bells on Sunday: The Journals of Rachel Roberts*, ed. by Alexander Walker.

Thursday, 30 November

Dinner at the Osborne, Langland Bay, in evening, with Erich. Delightful food & conversation, discussion after – over coffee and delicious cognac, at his flat, involving Goethe and Nietzsche. He gave me the text of his broadcast in the 3rd Programme last Sunday.[15] He ordered a car for me– got back 12.30. My flu makes me depressed.

Friday, 1 December

C of E informs me today that he wants me to play Feste with a hump back!! I *don't!!*

Saturday, 9 December

One show today – for a change. Charming letter from R. Burton. Wonderful. Row with Rachel whom I now feel CCL with.

Sunday, 10 December

Lunch with Prof. Heller.

Friday, 15 December

Champagne party on stage after show with everyone. Hermione [Hannen] madly neurotic. The end. V. frank talk with C of E.

Sunday, 17 December

Caught the 7 o'c. train arrived Padd. 20 to One. Home. Lovely. Restful. Unpacked and jawed.

Wednesday, 20 December

Tea at Regent Palace with Erich Heller. Then to the Equity Club for tea with Annette.

Saturday, 23 December

Stanley wrote to say he is going to marry Moira.

Wednesday, 27 December

Gladys Young rang up. She's giving me 4 tickets for the Equity Ball. Sweet. I shall take Annette and Joan.

Friday, 29 December

Attended first audition! – Tennent's at Globe Theatre. I was terrible. Nothing will happen from *that!!!*

---

[15] According to the *Radio Times*, Heller did not broadcast the previous Sunday. His Third Programme talk 'The Paradox of Nietzsche' had been printed, however, in the *Listener* dated 14 September 1950.

Sunday, 31 December

Had tea with Oliver Ford. Fantastic to meet him again, after all this time. He says I must visit him at B'mouth. Left him Waterloo at 6'ish and walked back over the dear bridge full of thoughts. So – the end of another year – all of them seem so full of false hopes. This has been a year of mediocrity really. When will something wonderful happen? – fool I am.

1951

NOTES

Financial capital amounts to about £25 in Midland Bank and £18 in post office. Outlook in the next few days: – A deep depression moving in a Piscerly direction. Rockall, Malin & Finisterre, fog patches, sleet, rain . . . oh dear.

Friday, 5 January

Tea with Rachel & Joan. Went to see Cécile Aubry in *Manon* – Studio One – with the Rachel. Afterwards walked along river and took her on the Kingsway subway. I like R. She's gay – but the trouble is, we both talk at the same time.

Friday, 12 January

Stayed in all day expecting to hear from Heller. No word. Rachel came for tea – no – I mean Joan Dale. I wrote 'Out of Work'.[1]

Wednesday, 17 January

Dreadful day with spirits at zero. Surely this unending drear cannot last much longer? These diaries of mine are becoming nothing better than moan books!

Saturday, 20 January

To Hyde Park for traditional fun with L. Supper in Corner House. Home. Bed.

Sunday, 28 January

Group met here at 57 today. Annette, Joan, Richard, John and I. R. says it is best to disband & individually seek work. The team idea to be shelved. I feel somehow that something has died tonight.

---

[1] Probably the poem surviving among KW's papers as 'Resting'. Concludes: 'Oh! Hecuba, Secuba, Gods of no age/Won't somebody ask me to walk on a stage?'

Thursday, 1 February
Richard suggested I meet agent – Peter Eade. Did so. He seems delightful person. Got me an audition with Laurence Olivier. Don't s'pose anything will come of it though. I never got anything out of an audition in my life.

Friday–Wednesday, 2–7 February [extended entry]
More and more troubled in my mind about myself. This heterodox knowledge seems to become more and more frightening – the whole nature of it being completely negative. I become increasingly obsessed with the feeling that I shall never be able to *create* my own background – give myself some kind of meaning in the world. Surely my existence cannot be so purposeless? In the past, it was always enough just to say that I felt I belonged to the world of theatre. Certainly this still applies, for I can think of no other sphere into which I can fit ideally. But *is* it enough? It seems that my work in the profession is not *harnessed* to anything. The first reason was pure vanity – and one can't build an existence on just that. There must be something more. The answer seems to be a theatre group of some kind, with a definite motive for presenting plays, but *must* the 'theatre' (as such) *have motive*? Isn't it enough that it *entertains*? I don't believe so. I think it must follow a line of intellectual enlightenment or commentary, through the dramatic medium. Authors like Priestley, and sometimes *Shaw* prove this to me. Certainly the Arts Council[2] doesn't provide an answer. Their Charter states that their object is to bring fine art into areas where it was formerly inaccessible. Yet they spend colossal sums on backing West End enterprises in the Metropolis. The last place surely? where this kind of thing is needed. Of course, like so much else which starts out nobly (viz. News of the World newspaper) it seems that the years lend corruption and lay a glazed meaning or interpretation over original motives. The real artists are the only purists and the middle man (who is absolutely necessary in the commercial set-up of today) provides – unwittingly or no – the corrupting influence.

Then of course the A.C. Charter, while it talks blithely about fine art, contains no definition of the term. Lewis Casson – stupid man that he is – says there is fine art in the antics of a superb farceur. Doubtless. But one can't help feeling that this is not what the Treasury Grant was intended for. Lewis Casson is, of course, a fool.

Thursday–Friday, 8–9 February
I hang on to the professional idea of landing a w[est]/e[nd] opportu-

---

[2] Incorporated by royal charter in 1946.

nity. Perhaps it is a ridiculous will o' the wisp. Each week drags itself by, and the depression spreads thro' my being like an evil cancer. Inside I am screaming and shouting. Inside. Outside everything is studied ordinariness. I find my books a great refuge and comfort. *Verdict of Twelve* by [Raymond] Postgate. And *That Immortal Sea* by Clifford Bax have influenced me very much.

Monday, 19 February
Met Russ – the boy I met up in Glasgow – with John as we were coming away from Odeon after seeing *Pandora and the Flying Dutchman*, which was terrible. Very TBH but I don't know whether to indulge in traditional games all over again. Still this old old worry persists, the same old arguments beating around in my brain.

Thursday, 22 February
My 25th birthday and still *unemployed*. This year is certainly proving a lousy one for me. Russ came round for coffee this evening. Erotic and gay – but I don't think it must go on. He is, I think, a quite unscrupulous young man, determined to make the theatre by hook or by crook. Emphasis on the latter.

Thursday, 1 March
Peter Nichols in town. Nice to see him again after so long. I like P. very much. He's amusing, clever, and enlightened. Altogether a charming fellow.

Monday, 2 April
Letters from Jennifer Sounes and Annette who opens tonight at York. Sent her telegram of good wishes. Received wire from John for my opening at Guildford tonight. Sweet of him to remember. 'So we cried vibrato – how is your old tomato.'

Friday, 6 April
Gordon Harbord's office. Met B.J. there, whom I shouldn't speak to really, 'cos he is too camp, but can't help adoring his company. Get me!!

Wednesday, 18 April
Labour Exchange. Went, collected my first 20/- from the government and felt incredibly smug about the whole thing.

Monday, 30 April
Dress rehearsal at Guildford. *Tonight At Eight Thirty*,[3] appallingly incompetent. Terrible mess everywhere. This is undoubtedly tat of the most menacing order. Sing hey for the end of my stay here! Peter E[ade] came to Guildford. Travel back with him. He said I was sibilant! – God! – the inane fool! How dare these people!

Sunday, 6 May
To Festival [of Britain] with John. It's all madly educative and very tiring. Beautifully cooked!!

Tuesday, 8 May
My going to York on June 3 is now *definite*. It's fixed – for better or worse. I have a terrible feeling that it's quite the wrong thing – but then what is *right* in this haphazard career? I am an actor because it is literally the only thing I can do well.

Tuesday, 15 May
Funny story from Peter about the Mayor of Bristol and Griller String Quartet – being so good they should be able to 'make the band bigger soon.' He's really very amusing but strangely bitter about Stanley of whom (I think) he is jealous. I'm sure I understand this, though I may be completely wrong.

Saturday, 19 May
2 shows today and roaring headaches. Feeling utterly broken physically and mentally. O where shall I hang a most unhappy head?

Tuesday, 22 May
Letter from Robert Sheaf, asking me to take part in a Shakespearean tour of villages. Sounds delightful. He saw me in *Bordeaux*,[4] obviously thinks I'm young and inexperienced and would be delighted to join him and a few intense young men, doing Romeo all over Oxfordshire. Very funny reely. This little chic stays single. Read *The City and the Pillar* by [Gore] Vidal. Wonderful book. Commended by Stanley in his last letter.

Wednesday, 23 May
Terrible people in the train to Guildford. Awful little men in striped trousers, their lives bursting out of their heads into fat, overstuffed

---

[3] By Noël Coward.
[4] At Guildford. *Richard of Bordeaux* by Gordon Daviot, KW as Maudelyn, Laurence Payne as Richard II. 'A Festival of Britain Production'.

briefcases as ugly as themselves. A sleeping clergyman with several chins – the end.

Thursday, 24 May

Wired York – I'm not going. Suddenly decided last night I just couldn't face it. Made up my mind in bed last night. Couldn't sleep. No use. R. will be furious. Clifford E. rang. Asks me to take part in pageant at Cardiff. D.V. and W.P. I *will.* Somehow it sounds a very pleasant idea.

Friday, 8 June

To E.P.'s[5] house first, with Peter for drinks, on by car to Hammersmith. Revue very clever, but I was far too drunk to notice. Terribly terribly tight. Back to E.P.'s house for aspirins and on to station to see him off.

Saturday, 16 June

Met P.E., told him about the unsettled nature of my particular frustration. E.P. was there. Traditional larks. Feel the complete 'naïf', consequently nothing happens. Begin to feel that I am utterly without any kind of courage morally or physically. O I am most abject and miserable. Back and back I seem to drift on the eddying flow. Undoubtedly *ebbtide.*

Monday, 25 June, Cardiff

Reh. all day. Met Donald Houston, looks same as all the other film stars.

Wednesday, 27 June

Letter from Erich saying he hates the Vidal novel. Disliked it intensely. This is rather foolish.

Sunday, 29 July

Morning of sunshine and cathedral bells . . . aeroplanes droning overhead . . . Sunday Times – in bed – cup of tea in one hand – cigarette in the other. Lav. occupied on every visit. Sick making. Reely.

Monday, 30 July

Opening night. *Chaos.*[6] Got through it somehow!

---

[5] Almost certainly Eric Portman (1903–69), the respected stage and film actor, a close friend of Peter Eade's.

[6] The production was *The Land of My Fathers: Pageant Play of Wales,* by Clifford Evans and six others, staged under the auspices of the Welsh Committee of the Festival of Britain. KW played several parts, including Edward the Black Prince and John Penry. Among his papers is a torn-off scrap on which is scribbled the following speech: 'It

Wednesday, 1 August
Notice in the Chronicle mentions only [David] Morrell and [Richard] Bebb, ignoring everyone else. There is corruption here.

Monday, 6 August
Tyrone Guthrie[7] out front tonight. No one knows how it went down with him. O dear. All in fear and trepidation.

Monday, 13 August
In evening to see film. *Sound of Fury*. T.U.[8] V. nice. But foolishly didn't react. Sorry after? But feel it's for the best.

Sunday, 2 September
Next year, if it seems that life must follow the same pattern, I shall leave the theatre entirely. If I go on like this I shall become mad.

Monday, 3 September
2.15, TV interview. Went v. well. They're letting me know. Rang R., he says can't let York down a third time. O dear. I don't know what to do.

Wednesday, 5 September
Obviously I died all day here.

Saturday, 8 September
Met Reg who didn't like talking about it. 'Would it surprise you to know I've never done it before?' 'No – not in the least. Is that the truth, then?' 'Yes.' Conversation enlightening, really! Home by 11.30.

Wednesday, 12 September
Worthing rang asking me to play Finch in *Whiteoaks*.[9] Refused of course. Dreadful place Worthing.

Monday, 17 September
Entrain York: King's Cross Station, 10.5. Arrived York 2 o'c. Freddy

---

hath been my purpose always to employ my small talent in my poor country of Wales, where I know that the people perish for want of knowledge. I trust that the time is come wherein He will show mercy by causing the true light of the gospel to shine among them.' KW's annotation reads: 'Speech for John Penry scene handed to me by Clifford Evans on the opening night.'

7 1900–71. Perhaps the most famous producer-director in British theatre at that time.

8 Touch-up.

9 By Mazo de la Roche, adapted from her cycle of 'Whiteoaks' novels.

Treves met my train. Charming. Went to visit York Minster. Saw film in the evening.

Monday, 1 October, York Rep.

Dress reh. *Wilderness of Monkeys.*[10] Opening night ditto – hope it augurs well for me as far as Y.R. is concerned. F– [*sic*] Y.R. for a start. Yes. Ho ho ho ho. To roll roll roll in a double bed oh. Performance went off and was mildly successful.

Monday, 8 October [but seemingly belonging to 1 October]

Performance evening went down well for my debut in York. Excellent exit round. Apparently M.[11] Staines is pleased with what he saw of me. [*Different ink*] Who the bloody hell cares whether he was or not?

Friday, 2 November

Peter Eade writes that I am to attend audition in town on Friday for Stratford-on-Avon. Perhaps this is my big chance.

Tuesday, 6 November

Learning Shakespeare rotten in readiness for Friday.

Wednesday, 7 November

More and more restless and excited about Friday. Praying hard.

Friday, 9 November

Audition was a failure and my heart is sick with disappointment & futile tears. Caught the 12.18 and arrived York at 4.15. Performance drear drear drear. I *hate* the awful company like hell.

Sunday, 18 November

Love scene played tonight – all very embarrassing. Slid out of it gracefully I felt. Hally Pally much too pally! At the same time, however, I must confess to a feeling of pleasure at being thought attractive to Hally Pally. It's so long since it occurred in my life. Perhaps I'm getting accustomed to doing without.

Tuesday, 20 November

Richard told me incredible story of his accommodating a strange young Scot in London at his mother's house and locking him up for the night. This is very revealing. We talked for some time about Army Life and early reactions to it. This has put me in retrospective mood

---

[10] By Peter Watling, KW as Miller.

[11] The Director of Productions at York Rep. was Geoffrey Staines.

and I long to begin the story of my life. To write it all down, and perhaps find, through the past, the reasonable future.

Saturday, 15 December
Finis. York Season. Caught the 10 o'clock train after show to London, with Fred Treves – arriving 3 o'c. this morning. Dead tired. Put Fred up for the night.

Tuesday, 18 December
Saw Peter Eade. Am to do a TV. *King John* on the 3rd January.

Saturday, 29 December
Broadcast on Home *Dunworthy 1313*,[12] seemed to go very well.

NOTES
York Rep. – 13 weeks. 2 weeks @ £6. 11 weeks @ £12. Equals £144. £144 = 13 weeks' work, more than I've ever been paid in the past . . .

---

[12] By John Pudney, KW as Peter Dorn (BBC Home Service, roughly equivalent to Radio 4).

1952

Tuesday, 1 January

Saw the old year literally 'go out' on the Northern Line tube, at East Finchley! Michael Harald, Hitchman, Susan, Rachel & me – all returning from the Kaufmanns' *gewöhnlich* parlour games party, all did our 'Auld Lang Syne' stuff in the carriage, and I invited the one other passenger (a ragged and befogged gentleman of 40 or so years) to join us in the crossed hands ritual. In the morning I collected my suit (grey lounge) from Hector Powe and then after lunch back home, went to Ealing to see Margaret Harper-Nelson[1] re part in *The Cruel Sea*. She was very kind.

So the old year of '51 has gone . . . not a very auspicious year and yet – I feel a certain sentimental affection for it . . . it was the first year I cried properly. Cried my eyes out on Boxing Night . . . in a sudden wave of utter futility . . . such a very silly young man.

Thursday, 3 January

Attended first rehearsal of TV production *King John* with Wolfit and Sonia Dresdel in the leads. Hated it all bitterly. Only ones I knew there were Judith Stott and Richard Bebb. What I really hated was having such a small part. One speech, as the Herald. Me! – that is so much better than half of the others. Wolfit so unutterably common. Terrible man. Such a vulgarian. In the lunch-hour, saw Wyndham Goldie and Douglas Allen at Lime Grove, and later learned that they want me to play in their forthcoming TV (lead) production. So got released from *King John* in the afternoon and bloody good riddance. Feeling very tired – vaguely elated at playing a lead in TV – but inwardly dead. As though things were all happening too late.

Monday, 7 January

Writing my diary in bed! the only occasion of its kind that I can remember. Really rather pleasant – cigarette and all. Getting the new bedroom (1st floor back) straight now, since I moved in, and M & D

---

[1] Casting director for Michael Balcon.

moved to 2nd floor front. Much nicer for me now I'm away from the upstairs tenants. We're to have a lodger next week – young waiter from Grosvenor House. Saw Peter Eade in the afternoon. I like this agent very much. Wish I could earn him some good money soon.[2]

Tuesday, 8 January
Feeling rather confused lately. I get the sudden feeling that I'm moving perilously fast, and my head seems to shriek aloud with action – yet my body is doing the slow normal things and part of my mind says 'slow down for God's sake – keep control – do things deliberately . . . careful . . . careful' – something like that. Awful sensation.

Saturday, 12 January
Day of preparation for party tonight, which was a great success. The room was crowded but comfortable. Coal fell out of the fire, and burned the carpet. Minor hiatus. Me doing my usual repertoire of anecdotes dramas and gay impersonations. Guests were: Peter Eade, Richard West, Michael Hitchman, Michael Harald, Susan Sylvester, Geoffrey Curtis, Pam Curtis, Edward Rutherford, Frances Rutherford, Donald Morley, Enid Irwin, Liz London, Hickmans, Annette Kerr, Rachel Roberts, James Rutherford.

Sunday, 13 January
Made a point of thanking Louie and Charles for a really excellent party which was a success entirely due to their own particular brilliance in warmheartedness as hosts. Everyone loves them. I know they are a wonderful couple of terribly human & lovable people. To the Morleys in the evening, a dreary little bedsit in Camden Town where I was made very welcome and given a delightful meal. I learned that Don was as Red as I am! madly Socialist in his outlook. Good.

Thursday, 17 January
Attended my first rehearsal for *Wonderful Visit*[3] with Barry Jones. Edie Martin, that wonderful little actress, is in it. She is a gorgeous person. Spoke to her. She sits quite alone at rehearsals. Somehow – pathetic. Great little actress. Must talk to her a bit more. Am to go tomorrow to see Emlyn Williams at Duchess Theatre. He has arranged a seat next to Mrs Emlyn Williams and I shall meet her before the show. This is delightful augury for my '52 year.

---

[2] KW remained his client until Eade's death in 1979. No contract was ever drawn up.
[3] 'A Fantasy by H.G. Wells'. KW as The Angel, Barry Jones as the vicar, Edie Martin as Mrs Gustick, Kathleen Boutall as the housekeeper, Wyndham Goldie as Dr Crump, Jean Cadell as Lady Hammergallow.

Friday, 18 January
Rehearsed drearily till 5.30. Went to see Emlyn Williams as Dickens – a wonderfully exciting evening. Went with Mrs Emlyn Williams, long talks in intervals. After we both went round for drinks with Emlyn. Delightful. Glen Byam Shaw was there. Drear creature. Also Wanda Rotha who is incredibly ugly. Nice seeing the show etc.

Monday, 21 January
Alexandra Palace all day rehearsing. Violent argument with the Boutall creature[4] who is revoltingly stupid. Heard her reviling me when she imagined I was out of earshot. Stupid woman. 2nd–3rd rate actress and mediocre person. Ugh!

Tuesday, 22 January
Rehearsing all day at Alex. Palace. Fitting at Wig Creations, where I looked exactly like a tarty lesbian. Should be gay.

Wednesday, 23 January
Filming all day at Alex. Palace. Novel experience for me in front of sound cameras. Finished at 5.30. Dresser was gay. Yes. Feeling very unreal and tired.

Saturday, 26 January
Rehearsed all morning at Alex. Palace. I am getting very bored with this entire business. That awful creature Jean Cadell who *never* knows her lines asked me to be serious in her scene! – said it put her off if I laughed at all!! Revolting old spinster! How I am repelled by these kind of people. They're like millions of ants, swarming all over the body of the theatre and stifling the rare legitimate actor.

Over Hampstead in the afternoon with dog. Called on Mike Hitchman for tea – saw Harry Davies who is living in the same house. Went with Mike in evening for drinks in gay bar of White Horse. After we met Laurence S. in Strand in a kilt! I introduced him to Michael. Laurie asked me to go along to the Regent Palace – he is off back to Scotland tomorrow. I declined of course. Regent Palace indeed! This little chick stays single.

Sunday, 3 February
TV Transmission – *Wonderful Visit*. Caught 9.30 bus at Langham Place. Worked all day. Transmission went over OK tonight at 8.30. I had no nerves of any kind and I couldn't even work-up to a utility tear.

---

[4] Kathleen Boutall. KW had already appeared with her in 1949 at the Theatre Royal, Stratford East.

Monday, 4 February
Good notice for my performance in Evening Standard and Evening News, Star, and Graphic. Very gratifying I must say. Reely. Also excellent notice in the Daily Mail.

Wednesday, 6 February
It was announced this morning that our King, George Sixth, had passed peacefully away during the night. The BBC then closed down for the rest of the day, save for gale-warnings and shipping news etc. Later in the day, Television Dept. rang me, to say that our transmission of *Wonderful Visit*[5] had been cancelled – with no instructions whatsoever. It was to have gone on the air at 8.30 tomorrow evening. The atmosphere in the city is heavy with grief, for the King was loved by so many.

Friday, 8 February
Got the Listener – terrible photograph of me, really appalling. Livid. Monica Cairns rang to say she was in *Moonraker*[6] with Jean Kent & Griffith Jones at Strand Theatre & would I like seats? Certainly not. Jean Kent indeed! Reely the profession becomes more and more bewildering each year.

Wednesday, 13 February
30 fan letters re *Wonderful Visit* to be answered! Nice reely.

Wednesday, 20 February
I shall be 26 years old on Friday next. O dear – I feel awful about it. The terrible waste of the young years. I shall be old so soon! To see Barri Chatt at Collins Music Hall, in a 5th rate variety show, which was appalling in every way. Saw Barri after in dressing room. Shocking really. Pathos here, covered in dusty gags.

Sunday, 24 February
John & I to Lyons for coffee at midnight. Met Søren Welling – Danish Bacon Company – brought him back to 57 to sleep on the put-u-up, as he had nowhere to go.

Monday, 25 February
Great schemozzle over Søren Welling. M & D both very obtuse over

---

[5] Since telecording was not yet available to the BBC Drama Department, plays were usually repeated 'live'.
[6] By Arthur Watkyn.

the entire business. I feel absolutely murderous inside. If only I could die painlessly and leave people behind for good and all.

Tuesday, 26 February

Lazed in the morning. Terrible boil coming up on my face. Feel so sick and depressed inside myself that I find I'm crying at odd intervals and *have* to literally pull myself together, lest I let go completely. I feel that if that actually happened, I should never recover. Tea over at Belsize Grove with Mike Hitchman. Opening night at Chepstow [Theatre, London W11]. Ghastly. Nobody came.

Wednesday, 27 February

Before You Die[7] reviewed in the Telegraph. John Hussey mentioned. No one else. Shock making. Pity reely. Would have been pleasant to have had a mention for my first London appearance per pro.

Thursday, 28 February

Went to see Herbert Wilcox. Interview lasted 2 mins. I am to play small part in his new film *Mr Trent's Last Case*[8] – Shepperton Studios. Monday starts. Tonight's performance attended by 20 Century Fox Films represent[ative]. Cannot understand it! Peter Eade didn't invite them! Incredible reely.

Saturday, 1 March

Nice notice for me in Times says I have an 'explosive emotion, rendered with sensibility & remarkable control' – also nice word for John. Rewarding at any rate.

Monday, 3 March

Caught the 8 a.m. to Shepperton from Waterloo. Am sharing dressing room with Sam Kydd with whom I got on so well in the TV show.[9] This is really delightful. Did my scene with the Coroner – Wilcox seemed very pleased. It's all rather drear.

Sunday, 9 March

Last performance at Chepstow. Thanks be to God. Cliff and Daisy drove us home. Never ever again.

---

[7] By Zygmunt Jablonski, translated by Andrew Wojiechowski, directed by Michael Harald. Three out of the cast of four – John Hussey, Michael Hitchman and KW (as Peter Neesen) – were close friends.

[8] Issued as *Trent's Last Case*.

[9] Kydd (1919–82), ever-present in British films of the fifties, had played a tramp in *The Wonderful Visit*.

Wednesday, 12 March
To Labour Exch. about unemployment. All quite disgusting. Purchased another 7 insurance stamps. *The end.*

Thursday, 13 March
To Labour Exch., told them I would not attend tomorrow. And shall not do so.

Monday, 17 March
Got gramophone from Lang's & got two records of *Gay's the Word.*[10]

Wednesday, 19 March
Up at 5. Filming *Trent's Last Case* on location. All very dreary. Met Bombardier Billy Wells.[11] He was sharing my dressing room. Charming fellow.

Friday, 28 March
Still madly decorating Mum's room – now almost finished.

Saturday, 29 March
To dinner with Erich Heller. Long talk about theatre etc. Taxi home at 2 in morning.

Thursday, 3 April
Went to see *Lear* at the Vic. Boy of 23 called Colicos[12] played title role as Stephen Murray is supposedly unwell after his awful first night notices. He was extremely good.

Friday, 4 April
Went to the Biograph in the hope of traditional entertainment but it was terribly desolait. No ventilation either. Walked home by Buckingham Palace & talked to myself all the way.

Sunday, 6 April
John and I went to Peter Nichols's flat & talked till one o'c. I walked all the way home. My feet were murder at the finish. Several prostitutes accosted me on the way. Charming. One of them said 'My feet are bleedin' frozen' and I felt a wave of compassion sweep over my tired body . . .

---

10 1951 musical by Ivor Novello and Alan Melville.
11 1888–1967. British Heavyweight Champion 1911–19, in films from 1918.
12 John Colicos, b.1928 in Canada. In spite of Colicos' success, William Devlin was brought in to play Lear on the tour which followed.

Monday, 7 April
Wrote my first short story today. No title for it as yet. A dissertation on a day at the Labour Exchange culled from recent events and local badinage.

Saturday, 19 April
Called on Peter E. & signed contract for Salisbury.

Sunday, 20 April
Thinking more and more in terms of a new method of earning my living. Just can't continue like this for ever. It's impractical and impossible & unhappy making in every way. There must be some kind of niche for me somewhere – where I'd be a benefit to my fellows, and doing some real kind of work. Would to God I could find it.

Monday, 21 April
Salisbury is madly *cathedral* and smug little self-conscious houses, freshly painted. All terribly disinfected and utterly *boring*. Huge notices asking for silence and telling dogs not to foul the paths because the church won't like it. It's all so *mock*. Pubs are *all* old-fashioned and quite unconvincing. The shops sell jockstraps à la Chaucer with a special 'musty smell' . . .

Tuesday, 22 April
First rehearsal with the Salisbury Arts Theatre Coy. as Bastien in *By Candlelight* by Siegfried Geyer.[13] This young man Denis Goacher seems very forward and self-assured and rather bitchy. I think I shall steer very clear of this one. O! I know this kind of entry means that we shall probably become the best of friends but one must register the initial impulses. No. Yes. Spent afternoon sleeping, and the evening trying to learn in a v. cold bedroom. Couldn't use the sitting room because a pest of a Scotsman with an incredible line in pedantry monopolises it, with drawings etc. *all over the place!!* Went out of the house at 9 and walked in pouring rain because I just couldn't face further emptiness. How long must I live in other people's houses?

Wednesday, 23 April
Rehearsed in morning. Seems terribly retrogressive to be playing *By Candlelight* now, just as I did at Newquay years ago, and writing in the same kind of diary. O! it's all so funny I'm almost hysterical.

---

[13] Adapted by Harry Graham.

Friday, 25 April
Denis Goacher is a really charming fellow and a very sweet person. An actor of quality. Obviously. Must say I was rather frightened of him at first, but he soon puts one at ease. This proves the truth of my entry of 22/4/52.

Saturday, 26 April
Letter – heartbreaking sad letter from Peter Nichols, asking me to help get him a job with Salisbury. What can I do? So little influence anyway. Must reply decently however. Perhaps he can get into a special week *School for Pisspots* or something. Yes. None of it really matters.

Sunday, 27 April
Hitchman phoned me in town but I was out of course. He is raving. Fancy waiting till noon to ring up. Reely doesn't matter though, does it? No. It doesn't. Life doesn't matter either. Don't care if that does sound daft, it's how I feel . . .

Monday, 28 April
Replied somewhat wretchedly to Peter Nichols, so tired I am. This boy* needs a rest of the world. This boy should kill himself. Yes. Should write to Peter E. but just haven't got any energy. None at all.

*(ME?) (No. Not me!)[14]

Tuesday, 29 April
Laid in the sun for a while during the afternoon, watching tennis with Michael Hitchman. We talked for a long while of the sadness of dying, before one could live.

Wednesday, 30 April
[*Enclosure: a cutting (probably from the* Salisbury Times*) containing a letter, clearly written by KW and signed with his father's name*]
To the Editor.

SIR, – Your drama critic complains about the 'mediocre' comedies at the Arts Theatre, and his melancholia on witnessing a production of *The Middle Watch*[15] there. Apparently, he abhors the fact that the audience were rocking with laughter, and indulges in pseudo-highbrowism about the policy of the theatre, without offering one really constructive piece of criticism.

From his column one learns nothing about the quality of individual

---

[14] Later annotations, made at two different times, by KW.
[15] By Ian Hay and Stephen King-Hall.

performances; the most he can do is to fall back on all the ancient clichés which one finds every week in The Stage, like 'competent' and 'smooth' – hackneyed and meaningless phrases, which are supposed to sum up a performance!

The gist of his argument about mediocrity is belied by the list of past productions at the Arts Theatre; and if he really desired to help, I suggest he print in his column the names of the plays he thinks should be performed – bearing in mind the extraordinary limitations of regional theatre – and that he tell us something more about acting, and less about play-synopsis, which we already know.

Yours faithfully,
CHARLES G. WILLIAMS,
26, Victoria-road, Salisbury.

Sunday, 4 May

Returned to Salisbury 8.10 train arriving 10 o'c. T[ouch].U[p]. on train with Soldier. V. gay.

Wednesday, 7 May

Peter E. came to see the show and said he thought I was camp. Oh God. Reely.

Saturday, 10 May

To Weymouth for matinée and evening performance of *Candlelight* – very good notice in local paper refers to me as actor of amazing vitality! and adds that I should go far!

Sunday, 11 May

In the Sunday papers today, there is a report of a 'well dressed & smart' Mrs Hillgrove, who is in court, because she refused to place her penny in slot at the Ladies' Lavatory – insisting that it was the Attendant's duty to do so!

Friday, 16 May

At rehearsals of [*School for*] *Scandal* today, Guy Verney terribly rude to me on stage, in front of company. 'You may ruin everyone's performance in *Candlelight* but you're not going to do it in my production.' Of course I had to reply from the stage, couldn't let it go at that – 'You may criticise my work in your own production,' I said, 'but don't indulge in cheap contumely about my work in *Candlelight*' – I was white with rage. In the evening he apologised and insisted on buying me a drink etc. O! I loathe and abhor the man.

Sunday, 25 May

To Goring to spend weekend with Lord Baldwin & Major Boyle. Quite delightful. Charming house. Charming people. Met a Keith Webster who was absolutely charming.

Saturday, 31 May

Two shows in evening. Death. Struck John Downing for pushing me. I will tolerate his kind of rudeness no longer.

Sunday, 1 June

Harald for lunch at 57 – also Mrs Williams. How dull and boring old people are! I felt quite furious at seeing her.

Thursday, 12 June

Dinner at L's flat with Peter E. there. All very charming and tradey.

Saturday, 14 June

To Goring to stay with Lord Baldwin and Johnny. All rather crushing. Naughty nights not a bit me. We sang ridiculous ballads.

Tuesday, 17 June

Interview by Lewis Gilbert for part in film *Cosh Boy*. I don't see much hope there. Walked all the way back to Chalk Farm with Michael, practically crippled myself. Had to sleep with him because I forgot my key.

Friday, 20 June

Went out with Henry W. & L. Drinks at a gay pub called 'Fitzroy' which really is the gayest pub I know. Charming. Full of sailors and queans with prying eyes and inquisitive nostrils – all searching for some new sensation – all empty vacuous faces devoid of anything, save sexual appetites. Long talk with Henry W. about Socialism. He is really very wrong-headed. Dear boy. O there is so much sorrow . . . Wrote begging letters to BBC fools and one mad one to Guthrie.

Saturday, 21 June

To Cuthbert Worsley's[16] party with Julien. It was utterly degenerate and frightfully depraved. Schocking.

Sunday, 22 June

Julien stayed at 57 for the night. Très embarrass. Never again. Too much. Much too much.

---

[16] T.C. Worsley, drama critic of the *New Statesman* 1948–52.

Thursday, 26 June
To see *Bicycle Thieves* which was superb, with John. After, we met Peter Nichols & talked at Marble Arch – listened to some amusing speakers. One said 'They say that unemployment is a problem. I regard it as an achievement.'

Friday, 27 June
Went to the park in afternoon with John, Don and Annette, who found our smutty jokes distasteful. She wrote me a letter explaining her attitude to all these sexual & sexually perverted anecdotes.

Monday, 30 June
It is increasingly obvious that my position in this profession is untenable. From the artistic point of view, I am continually frustrated, and from the economic point of view, I just cannot afford to keep myself. It's obviously high time for me to change my career. Only the choice of work is difficult. I hope that divinity* will give me a sign. Peter Eade being irritating the whole evening. Accused me of being a selfish entertainer! I pointed out the futility of personality comparison twixt myself and E.P.

*DIVINITY, not DRINKING[17]

Wednesday, 2 July
Saw Jack Benny at the Palladium. Excellent in a kind of second-rate way.

Thursday, 3 July
Reading *Quest For Corvo*[18] and finding it curiously magical.

Sunday, 6 July
Another ridiculous & wasted day. L & I trolled to Hyde Park très usual traditional worry. Ridicule. Socialist speaker was doing very well.

Monday, 7 July
Dinner with Erich Heller who invited me to go to the Continent with him. He is surely one of the kindest of the people I know, and I am full of admiration, respect and affection for him.

---

[17] KW's annotation of unclear handwriting.
[18] By A.J.A. Symons.

Sunday, 13 July
I read Perelman aloud, but without much heart, and got no laughs at all.

Wednesday, 16 July
Fruitless and ridiculous telephone conversation with Eade, who said 'I've found a play for you' as though he had secured me a job! It seems that Yvonne Arnaud has been asked to do it – a translation from the French by Alan Melville. Drawing room comedy about a group of bastards marrying another group of bastards. This highly original piece of nonsense to be produced by Murray McDonald. Of course it will be the old, old story – audition, and refusal. Looks young but too mature vocally, or some such rubbish. It's terrible to know so much beforehand: it is what always happens.

Wednesday, 23 July
Met Henry W. and John and all went to see Olivier in *Carrie* which was awful. Camped after in the Park.

Tuesday, 12 August
Frightful rude call from Oliver Baldwin saying I wasn't to go to Goring because I had asked if I could bring a friend.

Wednesday, 13 August
Telegram & letter from Johnny Boyle apologising for upsets.

Saturday, 16 August
Dinner with Erich Heller who goes to Greece on Thursday next. Lucky fellow. He seems sad at heart though. We walked along the Embankment.

Monday, 1 September
Richard West rang to say he was going to do this play by Noel Langley at the International Faculty of Arts and that there was no part for me in it. He wants a 'tough' juvenile, so I am out of that. Wrote for job in teaching children.

Tuesday, 2 September
To seek work in snack bar and typing etc.

Tuesday, 9 September
To see Trade Show of *Trent's Last Case* with Peter E. Horrified to see myself on the screen. Ghastly. Got laughs though.

Saturday, 13 September
Richard rang to ask if I would go to Thurloe Close. It was about ten at night. I went. He has the chance of producing a musical with black people. Most peculiar.

Tuesday, 16 September
To Elstree to play Window Dresser in film *Innocents in Paris* directed by Anatole de Grunwald.[19] Dreary business. Masses of q. degenerates.

Thursday, 18 September
With Donald Morley & John to see drag show *Morning Girls, Good Evening Boys* at the Queen's, Poplar. Barri Chatt was in it!!! Seemed absolutely incredible. We all laughed a lot.

Friday, 19 September
With Peter Nichols & John to the Queen's, Poplar once again. P. Nichols thought it extremely funny. He had never seen one of these shows before, and was amazed at the open depravity of it all. The management described it with delightful irony as 'good family entertainment'. It was riotous.

Wednesday, 24 September
Went to Shepperton to see about part in *Beggars' Opera*. Arrived at 1 o'c., and was seen by Brook and Olivier at 6, then I had to read for him, and afterwards was told I could play the part – Jack, the Potboy. 2 scenes with Olivier himself.

Saturday, 4 October
My first free day from the studios all this week. I haven't been on the set at all for shooting. Terrible waste of time really. Obviously I could have done the broadcast with Norman Wright after all! Got all the Insurance stamps which I owe, from the Post Office. Cost me £4.10!!! heavy price to pay for being out of work. In future I shall definitely go to Edgware Road. Never again shall I pay out these enormous sums. How frightened I am of bureaucracy.

Saturday, 11 October
Went over to Croydon with John but didn't like Croydon, so returned straightway.

---

[19] Written and produced by A. de Grunwald, directed by Gordon Parry.

Monday, 20 October
Cheque came from Wilcox[20] at last. Purchased chalet clock for kitchen, lovely. Purchased HMV 10" TV set for Louie.

Friday, 24 October
To Elstree for my one line in *Choir Practice*[21] directed by Gilbert Gunn. It was all over for me by 12 o'c. Very nice. My father was played by Kenneth Evans. Two Kenneths. Terribly funny really. Man came and took the TV away because it has been a bit faulty.

Tuesday, 28 October
To Shepperton for my 2 sequences with Sir L. in *Beggars' Opera* – got through all right, but wasn't an outrageous success.

Friday, 31 October
Am wanted at Shepperton tomorrow, a car will collect me 6.30 here and return me to BBC at 11.30 apparently.

Saturday, 1 November
Made up, dressed and on the set by 8.0 and the takes were over by 9.35. I thanked Pat Smith for laying everything on so beautifully, and the same car drove me back to the BBC in time for the broadcast rehearsal. I don't like this man who produces, David Godfrey. Everyone says he's a 'sweetie' etc. and I always distrust this kind of thing enormously. His criticism (which is *all* his production consists of) is entirely destructive – 'You sound rather like Noël Coward, dear boy' and etc etc. Ridiculous. But all true to the terrible BBC tradition of charming incompetence. Broadcasting is *easy* under good directors. These people make it difficult. Like Maggie Westbury's calling radio acting an *art* in order to justify their meagre middle-class existence. But they're all such 'sweeties'. Ho. Yes.

Sunday, 2 November
Dilys Powell mentions me in her crit. of *Trent's Last Case* !! Charming.

Thursday, 13 November
Had to go to see a man called Angus McLeod[22] about a part in *Peter Pan*! Audition tomorrow. Fantastic.

---

[20] Herbert Wilcox (1891–1977), producer-director of *Trent's Last Case*. Also co-producer (with Olivier) of *The Beggar's Opera*.
[21] Issued as *Valley of Song*. From Cliff Gordon's play *Choir Practice*. KW as Lloyd Haulage.
[22] W. Angus McLeod, 1874–1962. Producer.

Saturday, 15 November
Put 60 pounds into bank account. Mounted my Angel photograph[23] in large black frame and hung it in my room. Splendid. Went with John to Islington and purchased 38 piece dinner service for Lou. Charming – very simple maroon inside band.

Monday, 17 November
To Brighton Theatre Royal to see *We Have Company*[24] which is Rachel's first big part – tour prior to London. Rachel Roberts tended to stridency thro' nerves and erratic production, and the play needed some work done to it. Richard West was there when Peter Eade and I went backstage. Embarrassing 'cos he kept sending up PE which is silly. He is traditional (RW) with Rachel and all so obvious, Varda The Bonar etc. Nicht so schön.

Tuesday, 25 November
P. had such a cold, so I dosed myself with quinine and rather rashly took 25 grains! It's a wonder I'm not dead. My ears are singing like hell.

Friday, 28 November
Fred Treves came to tea and there was a furious argument – spiritual versus rational. Hell! Roman Catholicism from the foundation by Peter, Christ's meeting with John the Baptist, Individual Revelations – Church Antipathy to, etc. etc., the *end*. I was angry about getting worked up as I always do when discussing organised religion. I *hate* the aggressiveness which automatically follows its assumption of power.

Sunday, 30 November
Went with John to see *Pat and Mike*. Aldo Ray who plays a small part has that wonderful gaucherie which only the suave can acquire. A brilliant young man indeed. He gives an enchanting performance.

Monday, 1 December
First rehearsal of *Peter Pan*,[25] saw Brenda Bruce and James Donald who are the leads. It's all dangerously naice at the moment. And they've dug up Russell Thorndike for a pirate.[26] Disgusting.

---

[23] Photograph of KW as the Angel in *The Wonderful Visit* (February 1952).
[24] By Hubert Gregg.
[25] The Christmas institution by J.M. Barrie, directed (for the thirtieth time) by Cecil King. KW as Slightly.
[26] Russell Thorndike (1885–1972), brother of Sybil and author of the 'Dr Syn' stories, played Smee.

Wednesday, 10 December
Reh. all day. My tape recorder works very well. Annette came and we did Romeo & J. balcony scene. V.G. too. She is rather a darling.

Sunday, 14 December
Dinner with Erich Heller at Swiss Cottage. He gave me a copy of his new book *The Disinherited Mind* and inscribed it to me. There is a lot about this friendship that I love and there is something about it which irks. But it doesn't really matter. He is a dear sweet person. Arrived home at 2 o'c. v. tired.

Thursday, 18 December
Wish I'd never *seen Peter Pan*. Hate it bitterly

Tuesday, 23 December
Opening at the Scala of *Peter Pan*. I am Bad in this show and fearfully depressed over the whole thing.

Wednesday, 24 December
Two perf. This is *killing*!

Saturday, 27 December
2 perf. at Scala. Don't think I can last the run at this rate. I have never been so terribly sick at heart over anything before in my life.

Tuesday, 30 December
2 shows at Scala. Murder. Lots of trouble with these kids,[27] who are a gang of hooligans. No wonder juvenile delinquency is on the increase.

Wednesday, 31 December
2 shows as usual at Scala of this revolting play *Peter Pan*. So we come to end of 1952. It's been an eventful year – my first TV, my first film, my first new play at a theatre club. During '52, I suppose I have been reasonably happy. Certainly happier than other years. And now I go into the New Year, Coronation Year, with *Peter Pan*. This is sad but it is dictated by economics and I cannot bear inactivity.

---

[27] The Lost Boys.

1953

Thursday, 1 January
An excellent reference to my performance as Slightly in the dreadful Stage. It says I'm like Danny Kaye and all that stuff. This always seems to be happening.

Friday, 2 January
It's odd how my diaries always start off so prolifically and taper toward nothingness as the year grows old. There must be something very significant about this but I can't quite think what.

Sunday, 4 January
I think that people who manifest their love for you, physically, when they know your lack of reciprocation, are abominably selfish. Sooner or later, the relationship *must* suffer, however noble its beginnings. I must be comparatively under sexed or something for I have never particularly wanted to make physical love to anybody. All this touching and kissing which seems so popular among others passes me by. Denis Goacher knows I'm virgin, and is always saying that I make up for it by flirting continually. He says I should *do* something. He can't believe I could be abnormal. To him, everyone must do something, or die! Hm! Perhaps I am dead.

Monday, 5 January
It is always so easy for me to read what I have just written and find it vastly entertaining and well done. It seems that everything I accomplish is of enormous interest to me and I am full of admiration for myself. Is this a good thing? Or does it much matter whether it is or not? Enough of this self-analysis. Too fashionable by half in this day and age.

Tuesday, 6 January
How impossible it is for me to make regular entries in the diary. I suddenly remember how I used to puzzle over the world at school. Always wondering why diary was so like Dairy and what the connec-

tion was. Never found out. Like that label on the bottle of Daddies Sauce – it never stopped. The man on the label was holding a bottle of Daddies Sauce and on the bottle was a label with a man holding a bottle of Daddies Sauce . . . ad infinitum ad nauseam for me at any rate.

Thursday, 8 January

Met John Vere in lunch hour who invited me into a pub for a drink. I suddenly felt he was ashamed of me. He kept looking round the pub the whole time. I got quite confused and conversed wildly and stammered, and tore myself off to the matinée. How conscious queers are of persecution – and so gregarious.

Friday, 9 January

Genius is so inextricably bound up with taking pains, and meticulous detail, that I think I must be less than competent. But I enjoy myself so much that I would not have myself altered.

Sunday, 11 January

Annette K. came to visit me from Watford. She said – apropos of my saying that I'd like to share a flat with someone – 'My dear no. You know how you loathe people when you see them often.' And I suppose that is true of me.

Monday, 12 January

We went to Haralds. Sir Basil Bartlett[1] of TV script dept. came in for drinks. Obviously traditional but can't see what he is up to at Haralds. He seemed emotionally strung-up and talked a great deal. He was at Dunkirk and was at pains to seem heroic by saying that it wasn't at all heroic. These inverted boasters are tortuous for me. Still there were some very amusing anecdotes, including one about Isadora Duncan who died because her scarf caught in the wheel of her car, the car started, and she was dragged forward by the neck which broke. Sir Basil apparently cleared up the mess. This told by him with a maddening air of nonchalance and deprecation. I wanted to hoot with laughter. It was like some publicity story.

Tuesday, 13 January

Filming at Shepperton. Retakes on the *Beggars' Opera*. Sir Laurence and Peter Brook both awfully charming to me. Very gratifying after all the tat at the Scala. Sir L. gave a deliciously truthful impersonation

---

[1] b.1905. Dramatist and BBC TV drama script supervisor, 1952–55.

of Brenda Bruce and I fell about. The first shots were U.S. because the film buckled, so we had to shoot all over again.

Wednesday, 14 January

Called on Denis Goacher in the morning and we talked. I spoke about the 'obvious' potential profit which is scorned by the average intellectual purely *because* of its *obviousness*, which will be seized upon by the moron who later becomes important enough to merit the anger and hatred of the thinker. This is especially true of post-war periods & war periods when opportunities for easy profit making in taking advantage of national weaknesses are manifold. Denis agreed and pointed out that *now* there was no morality to counteract this. That whereas *once* there was real spiritual belief and a morality based upon it; and there was the continual surety of punishment from an omnipotent & wise paternal God, then people by nature acted differently. The fear of *hell* as such being a very real deterrent. Now God is replaced by Gold, and avarice becomes the order of the day. New values replace the old, and one wonders *what on earth* will replace *them*.

Friday, 16 January

I've really learned nothing about acting since I worked under Clifford Evans. With *all* his faults as a producer, he *is* theatre, and there is no denying the excitement produced in working under the impact of his personality.

Tuesday, 20 January

Cecil King (the producer of *Peter Pan*, who is married to Phyllis Neilson Terry) said to a stagehand (who is gay) 'There are only two queers I've ever liked – you, and Bryan Michie[2] . . .'

Friday, 23 January

Lunched with John Vere who was very amusing despite the fact that he's only just recovering from awful bout of flu. Delicious story about an Admiral coming across a case of traditional flagrante delicto twixt two matelots and saying 'If you chaps can't give this sort of thing a rest, I shall have it cut out altogether . . .'

Saturday, 24 January

There are two kinds of men on tubes. Those who blow their noses and then examine the results in a handkerchief, and those who blow their noses without exhibiting any such curiosity, and simply replace

---

[2] Talent-spotting impresario and compere (1905–71).

the handkerchief in the pocket. I, generally, come under the first category.

Monday, 26 January
Much talk at dinner of the boy Bentley who is to be hanged on Wednesday for aiding and abetting in the Craig murder of the policeman Miles. The papers announce the Home Secretary's (Maxwell-Fyfe) decision *not* to 'interfere in the course of the law' etc. etc. It all seems quite frightful – the terrible urbanity of all this – H.M. servants, H.M. Prison Governors, H.M. decisions – young 19-year-old mentally retarded boy helping a 16-year-old murderer.

Tuesday, 27 January
The jury's recommendation for mercy has been ignored and the Home Secretary will do nothing. There was a dramatic scene in the Commons tonight, when Mr Silverman M.P., Lab.,[3] was refused permission to discuss the case by the Speaker. It was out of order, he said! So a human life must go, because discussion of his death is 'out of order'!

Wednesday, 28 January
Realised today, after reading Calogero, that my particular faith in this life was a liberal faith. A strange kind of faith that (to quote him) 'seems to have no other content than the preparedness to admit doubt.' This is the kind of thing I've wanted to read for a long time.

Thursday, 29 January
Went to Streatham Hill, to find out how to get there from Bloomsbury, because this is the journey I shall have to do all next week, when we play *Peter Pan* at the Streatham Hill Theatre. It looks like a great cinema of a place. Oh! horror. I choose bus – though one can go by train from town – because I hate the smells on the Southern Railway, and the grimy smug suburban feeling of those dreary green stations. Hateful. And all those circumspect men with milk and sandwiches stuffed into important-looking briefcases.

Friday, 30 January
Went to Spotlight today, to read cues for Richard W. who was auditioning young men for the part he wanted me to play in *Dormouse Sings*[4] which he is putting on as his first venture in management. Tom

---

[3] Sydney Silverman (1895–1972), MP for Nelson and Colne from 1935. Author of 1964 bill to abolish the death penalty. Later Home Secretaries, most recently Kenneth Clarke in 1992, have refused to modify the Bentley verdict.

[4] *The Dormouse Sings* by Lawrence Storm. Later adapted by him into *I Hold You Prisoner*.

Fleming is one of the backers, and he was there. He behaves like a pseudo commanding officer & talks loudly in staccato barks and claps his hands & bangs his thighs. The entire personality has the effect of a machine gun, and is just about as interesting. I left him with R. in Cranbourn Street, he was exclaiming 'Rightie Ho! Lyons. Cups of tea. Rightie Ho . . .'

Monday, 2 February

Everything went wrong with the show. Brenda B. was banged everywhere by the Flying Ballet men, scenery crashed to the ground missing people by inches, and the new Lost Boys were terrible but *terrible*. To cap it all that squirt of a man with the waisted overcoat – McLeod or something – came round to say my make-up was pale!! Laugh. I assured him gravely that I would set it to rights, inwardly determined to do nothing about it whatsoever. How dare this dreadful creature discuss such a thing with me. What I do with my face is between my make-up and my maker. Harvey,[5] the negro pirate in the show, is a very good fellow. Socialist of course, like all sensible members of his race, and a good talker. All the 'pirates' rather deprecate him and refer to him as 'a bit of a red'. Har Ha. I am sharing digs with him in Edinburgh. Brenda Bruce tonight – on Ram Gopal: 'He smells of old spices and old dick . . .'

Tuesday, 3 February

Called upon Denis G. and had tea there with him & Harold Lang who was also his guest. This last-named most amusing. Told cruelly funny stories about *all* his friends and the room ached with laughter. Denis insisted on both electric and oil fires and a kettle was singing on the latter; the room was full of tobacco smoke, and steam, the window panes running with condensation and everything terribly samovar and Russian. Harold Lang said my vocal inflections reminded him of Josephine Tweedy. It was probably a calculated insult because I'd already mentioned I'd seen his performance in *Folly To be Wise*[6] and that I thought he was bad. This was a tactical error. There are very few actors who you can talk to like that, and Harold Lang is not one of them. His chief defect is his lisp. A very bad lisp. A lisp is a bad thing.

Saturday, 7 February

'If I were a blackbird/I'd be baked in a pie . . .'[7] John Hussey.

---

5 Astley Harvey, as Black Pirate.

6 1952 film directed by Frank Launder, with Alastair Sim etc.

7 'If I were a Blackbird' had been a hit for the singer and whistler Ronnie Ronalde.

Thursday, 12 February. Wimbledon Park Road, Southsea, on tour
Met a cinema cleaner who told us that in his ashcan last night he found thirty-one fly buttons. This apparently signifies an exciting film, but we forgot to ask its title.

Tuesday, 17 February. Copper Kettle, Norwich
Russell [Thorndike] said tonight that he had found a wonderful book on the stalls here. It is called *Stray Thoughts for Girls* and is rather rude. Terribly funny.

Wednesday, 18 February
Russell Thorndike has invented an outrageous woman called Mrs Cumber. We all keep laughing about her supposed doings. A sort of obscene Mrs Dale,[8] but really entertaining instead of just *dull* like her.

Friday, 20 February
Norwich is a pleasant town, delightfully built on many different levels. It is architecturally interesting despite a monstrous modern tasteless Civic Centre-cum-Police Station, and abounds in derelict churches. Sic transit Christian worship.

Saturday, 21 February
Everyone at the Copper Kettle stayed up late and talked. The awfully boring & hearty commercial traveller became suddenly confidential. He took me aside in the kitchen, in a burst of confession, and explained that he was homosexual. I had to act deliberately nonchalant to cover my dumbfoundedness, confusion and embarrassment. I practically fell over myself in the effort to be casual and burnt my fingers on the gas ring. Life holds so many surprises for us.

Sunday, 22 February
Tour: King's Theatre, Glasgow. Left Norwich at 8 o'c. Arrived Glasgow at 11 o'c!! Met by Stanley and Moira at the station.

Saturday, 28 February
Got 6 rather lovely gin glasses for Stanley and Moira, because I gave them nothing when they were married.

Tuesday, 3 March. Edinburgh
Brought my address book up to date today and was surprised to notice the date I began it – 26 July 1951! Cardiff! That was during the

[8] 'Mrs Dale's Diary', the daytime radio soap-opera. It ran from January 1948 to April 1969, changing its name in February 1962 to 'The Dales'.

Pageant of Wales – that tiny room I used to have at Mrs Mac's! The sunlight and heat of that period. How delightful it all was. I remember that wonderful trip on the boat from Cardiff docks to Minehead or somewhere, anyway it was all very warm, luxurious and pleasant.

Wednesday, 4 March

Got a copy of T.S. Eliot's poems, and bought all the newspapers to read the notices, to find myself consistently ignored by all the reviewers. Furious making.

Tuesday, 10 March. Hanley

The papers here refer to me as 'a magnificent Slightly'. I feel this is a sop for last week's indifference and I refuse to be comforted. Besides, the praise is too lavish and, frankly, uncalled-for.

Tuesday, 17 March. Manchester

I was only thinking in the bath last night, that so many artists are *thin* that it must be significant. Aesthetic people usually seem to be thin. This must have something to do with nervous energy.

Thursday, 19 March

Letter from Peter, saying the Embassy (Laurence Payne) have offered me Feste in *12th Night*, and Osric in *Hamlet*. He (Eade) obviously wants me to take it. I've replied, declining. I loathe that awful play *12th Night*, and Osric is not my cup. Not at all.

Sunday, 22 March

Tour: Theatre Royal, Newcastle. The digs are foul. The letter stated that the distance from the theatre could be walked in ten minutes. In reality, it was half an hour. I felt disgusted and cheated; the landlady complained bitterly of her sciatica, for which I recommended Algipan, but because of her dishonesty I could not feel any real sympathy.

Thursday, 2 April. Bradford

James Donald left the show after smashing the windows of the theatre in protest against lack of fresh air. Understudy took over.

Sunday, 5 April

Tour ends: Bristol. Horrified on arriving here today at 4pm to find that I am sharing the digs with Blowhard (Musical Director) and William Luff – the ancient pirate Cecco. It's all too utterly ghastly. Went to the films to see *Stars In My Crown* which was disgustingly bad. On getting back, there was an awful row, and the landlady made a terrible scene. She told the ancient pair that they can get out as soon as they like etc. etc. O it was awful. Never again. Her name is Flook – Mrs Flook. O! dear o dear!

Wednesday, 15 April
Very few entries from here to May, because I've been up to my eyes in work, with Mother in bed. All very depressing.

Thursday, 7 May
Went to Poll to vote Labour in the Boro' elections. The conservative candidate sent car for us, Mother because of sciatica.

Tuesday, 12 May
The man came to fix my radiogram. He was Burmese and had seen me in *High & Low* at Rangoon!! Fantastic.

Wednesday, 13 May
Went to Equity at Harley St to get digs book because I've heard nothing from B'ham Rep. and I've got to fix accomm. by Saturday!

Friday, 22 May. Birmingham
I am so utterly sick of everything that I cannot come to any proper conclusion about the situation here. Feeling so nervous and apprehensive about joining a new company, I am naturally aggressive and full of adverse comment on things and people. There's nothing really awful about the surroundings: it's me, of course. But knowledge is peculiar. It often enlightens without helping in the least.

Tuesday, 2 June
Coronation of Queen Elizabeth II. Free day, because of the Coronation, and the rain pouring steadily all the time. In the afternoon I met Eric Jones and we talked considerably. Home to bed early.

Monday, 8 June
Dressing with that awful John Arnatt. Ghastly creature.

Wednesday, 10 June
John Arnatt is really quite tolerable in the dressing room. Much nicer than I imagined. The world is full of delicious surprises.

Monday, 13 July
Old Vic, opening night *Henry VI Part One.* Supper with Richard [Burton] and Sybil after the show, at their house in Hampstead. Also Robert Hardy and Rachel Roberts was there. It was delightful to see them all once again.

Wednesday, 22 July
Talked with Benthall[9] today, and left the Vic company. Felt it was a waste of time to be tied for a year to such small parts and unrewarding work. He was charming about it, and enabled me to exit gracefully. I felt that he was secretly delighted.

Wednesday, 9 September
I must obviously get some kind of job soon – or die in the attempt.

Tuesday, 29 September
Peter Eade rang to say I'd got the film part!!! Wishart!! in *The Seekers*, this thing at Pinewood. The leads are Jack Hawkins and Glynis Johns. It seems fantastic. But I know that it is part of the pattern. I am destined to be a good actor.

Saturday, 10 October
I've had the same bottle of ink for about three years now. Shows how much I use the typewriter for all the correspondence. There used to be an idea that typed letters to friends were *rude*. Absolutely fatuous nonsense of course.

Sunday, 11 October
The depression of *waiting* to do a job is ghastly. Almost as bad as unemployment with no sign of work! The conviction now starts to grow in my mind that I shall not be able to act the part anyway. They will have to 'dub' my voice and it will be cut to ribbons etc. and I shall be finished with films for everything – juveniles, character – the lot. How awful life is for actors. Wish I were something ordinary. I wonder lately what *words* really mean. Corruption has become so rife. A word like propaganda for instance that means something quite different now.

Wednesday, 14 October
On a certain plane of analytical reasoning, an argument or discussion can lead directly into a complete vacuum. Psychoanalysis inevitably destroys values. It's a most destructive tendency in modern talking. The fashion of 'debunking' and exposure etc. is a by-product of this kind of thing. Highly dangerous.

Thursday, 15 October
Humour based on satire – irony etc., is part of what I wrote of yesterday. This, too, *can* be a most destructive element. If a person

---

[9] Michael Benthall (1919–74), Director of the Old Vic 1953–61.

does anything incorrect there is only one possible proper moral course (if their incorrectness is at all bad for them). It is to correct them in the appropriate gentle manner.

Friday, 16 October
All actors are playwrights that cannot write plays: all playwrights are actors that cannot act. And I've a sheaf of manuscripts to prove it!

Monday, 19 October
Went down to Pinewood for my first work on this film *The Seekers* – night shots with 'rain' from firemen's hoses pouring down. I was in a trench waist high in cold water. It was awful. I bet I get flu. Back to town by car, and arrived home at sevenish.

Thursday, 22 October
No one has introduced me to Jack Hawkins (who I feel dislikes me with Annakin[10]) and while he could easily speak to me, he avoids doing so, and I cannot very well go up and introduce myself. I'm so frightened of him, but I know I shouldn't be. Obviously I'll have to pluck up courage and go to him and speak up. Say the truth and hope he'll understand.

Friday, 23 October
It appears in the papers that Sir John Gielgud has been arrested on a charge of homosexual importuning. He described himself on the charge sheet as 'a clerk of Cowley Street with an income of £1000 a year'. Why tell these kind of lies? Of course, this is clearly a case of persecution. Poor fellow.

Saturday, 24 October
Found out today from Denis Goacher who'd got it from gossip sources that Ken Annakin did not want me for this film, but that he was over-ruled by the producer (George Brown) who insisted on employing me! One must be *truthful* about everything. I *know* it's HARD, but this seems a fundamental and cardinal truth which is imperative if you're to have proper dealings & confidence with people.

Sunday, 25 October
Spent an abortive day walking about doing nothing but worry over this film job. I hate and deplore these kind of situations. I can't work well if I feel I'm not liked. My confidence pours itself down the drain, and I lean backwards in an effort to appear casual & disinterested. I

---

[10] Ken Annakin (b.1914), the director.

would like to leave the theatre as a profession, but feel that I have no *real* reason. I know that the people who hate me in the profession are people who are bogus anyway. But I am so *weary* of all the queer and anti-queer business. The ironic truth being that I am neither! But I *know* I'm labelled as queer by all the hearties. My face apparently looks effeminate, and people *say* that I speak sibilantly. Well, I don't know . . .

Tuesday, 27 October

Heard this piece of conversation in the bus today, from two tatty women in the front seat:

1) ''Course I don't say nothing to him mind you, but he's getting better . . .'

2) 'I wouldn't put up with any nonsense from mine. I let him get his own supper when I'm on nights.'

1) 'Well I have the cut loaf now, and he puts the butter on his self so I don't hardly do anything, I have to laugh though – last night he sat about fidgeting till about eight, then he says he's going out for some cigarettes! And did I want any? 'Course I knew where he was going all right! Sure enough, back he came just after closing time . . .'

Thursday, 29 October

The telephone was full of regrets. I suspect I'm unpopular. If so, it is hardly surprising. From being a brittle superficial fellow, given to jesting rather well, at the expense of weak or/and absent people (and popular into the bargain) I have become thoughtful, laborious and solemn, given to pondering problems far outside my own particular experience and altogether too serious & pessimistic. At least, that's how I fear it must look. In reality, I am if anything, becoming more *optimistic*, because I'm a bit nearer to understanding the ways of the world, and discovering a few moral values for myself. Today I learned the difference between deprecate and depreciate. I think now about the character in a novel by John Horne Burns, who after searching all round an empty bed murmurs 'Gosh darn it. Not even a teeny weeny lover . . .'[11]

Sunday, 1 November

I think that the converse of 'Do unto others as you would have done unto you' is a truth which we would do well to reflect upon – 'Do unto yourself what you would have done to others.'

---

[11] 'Guy Hudson's hand came back empty after questing all over his narrow bed: – O damn. Not one teeny goddam lover . . .' *Lucifer With a Book*, by John Horne Burns, 1949 (p.48).

Tuesday, 3 November

More and more I am confident that life is relatively unimportant: death is obviously the beginning of something infinitely better. All the crapola that's talked about something being 'just around the corner' really *eats* into one's mind: I found myself really *believing* it once. Disillusion. Then – nothing ever alters – cause & effect go on proving their systole and diastole relationship and nothing alters under the poor old, bored to tears, sky.

Monday, 9 November

Sometimes I feel so unutterably superior to the people surrounding me that I marvel at my ability to live among them. Nothing is more exasperating to me than having to witness the pursuit of evil through ignorance on the part of the pursuer. It makes everything so futile: and human existence is shamed. I reflected today on the qualities necessary in a Director of Acting. He must be introvert enough to understand the extraordinary sensitivity of the good actor: he must be extravert enough to throw the spell of his personality over an entire cast, and have something of the showman. He must *obviously* inspire trust. After all these things, he should know something about the fundamentals of dramatic literature & its presentation on the boards. After this he should know something about the mechanics of electric lighting: carpentry, & all the techniques of stage direction or management. And in this latter, he should always be able to give the impression that he knows far more about it than the manipulator. After this, he should be something of a Gentleman. In the most profound sense of the word (Shavian sense if you will – 'I ask the best from you and in return I will do everything in my power to give you the best of myself') and have reasonably catholic tastes.*

*I have yet to meet such a personality.

Wednesday, 11 November

In the evening to meeting at Town Hall re this by-election caused by death of Labour member, Dr Jeger. His wife[12] is standing for the constituency. Principal speaker was Nye Bevan[13] who was superb.

Tuesday, 17 November

Pinewood. To studio for shots of fight twixt me and Rangiruru. Tony[14]

---

[12] Lena Jeger (later Baroness Jeger of St Pancras), MP for Holborn and St Pancras South 1953–59, 1964–79.

[13] Aneurin Bevan (1897–1960), Minister of Health 1945–51, Minister of Labour and National Service 1951.

[14] TonyErstich.

(who plays Rangiruru) is big and hell to fight with. I am bruised all over and feel awful.

Thursday, 26 November
Feeling very tired and utterly depressed. I am nauseated by my own company. I'm sick of the sight of my white pale face, my bad pitted skin, and measly body. Growing my hair long for this film makes it all worse too. Sitting eating chocolates in front of the fire. This kind of behaviour is a bad sign.

Wednesday, 9 December
In the evening to see Harald & Sue, and was buttonholed about lending them money. It was really unpleasant. I *don't* see why I should provide money for them when Harald doesn't cope with their financial affairs in any way! I gave them a pound.

Wednesday, 30 December
I have only played in 3 productions this year. Yet, I've probably made more money than any other year. Yet, I've been out of work for at least half of it. As to artistic progress? – I think I've lost all calculation method! I don't know now whether I'm getting a better or a worse actor. Certainly I felt awful as I watched the rushes of this last epic. I am sure that this film will not do me any good whatsoever.

1954

Saturday, 2 January
I am obviously not going to get that part in the Christopher Fry play.[1] They asked Peter to wait for one week before they gave an answer, but they rehearse on Monday so it's obvious I am out. Curious really, for I was right for it: and whoever has got it, in my place, should be, at least, a genius. It's a dreadful insult and I have decided to swallow it. So much for Mr Peter Brook, and his laxative fortune.

Friday, 22 January
Took Peter Nichols to lunch. Cost £2. Fantastic. Horrified when I saw the bill. 'What ho! when they lifted the lid'

Wednesday, 27 January
Spent a particularly abortive evening with O[liver] F[ord]. Strange now, to think that he once inspired such incredible emotions. Everything about him seems nebulous. Still the desire to brag and preen himself over his abilities and salary etc. He has no values, poor thing, save the negative material ones, and reminds me of the dispossessed.

Friday, 29 January
Man went to see a psychiatrist – Man: O! I'm in a frightful state doctor! I feel that I am suffering from an inferiority complex. Dr: Perhaps you're inferior. Peter Nichols told me this story – it's the perfect answer to all the psychological bunkum that goes on.

Thursday, 4 February
Masturbation is a physical manifestation of self-love – or perhaps self-satisfaction is the better expression. Anyway, it is gratifying oneself, as far as I am concerned. Sometimes I indulge in it once or twice a week, sometimes not at all. When I do indulge in it, it is because of erotic images which become paramount in my mind, and blot out all other thoughts. These images are all different, but the fundamental

---

[1] Presumably *The Dark is Light Enough*, at the Aldwych.

conception is constant. It is that of *physical power*, the large body, overcoming the weak: the sex is unimportant – relatively – whether male or female – the element of primitive, animal cruelty is always present in the image. The image is my particular devil; for in my general, conscious state, such things are ordinarily barbaric & repulsive to me.

Friday, 5 February

Sexually, I am getting to feel much more settled. I used to think that the reason for my virginity was moral & physical cowardice: part of some psychological fear of responsibility. More & more, however, I am now coming to believe in the *rightness* of abstinence for me. I am convinced that celibacy is an essential quality in my own character. I must never allow myself to be *vulnerable* in the sexual sense. That kind of humiliation would be detrimental in every way.

Saturday, 6 February

The essential thing, for my kind of acting – drama in the professional sense – is *remoteness*. To keep myself at arm's length from physical contact of any kind is to create that 'sense of distance' so essential to *objective* characterising. For me, the actor must *never* be portraying his own emotions, felt in the past, present or future. Not, that is, in the *conscious* sense of portraying. He must always be pretending.

Sunday, 7 February

I have felt curiously cheerful today. Full of daft ideas. Though my language is becoming atrocious. I'll have to watch it. But all my moods are different and when I'm feeling pure then I act horribly pure. I suppose I am a terrible sham really. Yes.

Monday, 8 February

Astonishingly enough, my mood of cheerfulness continues, though the underlying feeling is one of the 'lull before the storm'; doubtless this is all bound up with the subconscious, but I am convinced intuitively that this year is the decisive one for me. It is either *establishment* in my profession, or some other method of earning a living from that motivation only.

Tuesday, 9 February

There are two kinds of people who interest me – 1) The people who want their lives to benefit mankind 2) The people who want their lives to benefit themselves. Of course there are people who don't know what they want to do with their lives, or indeed anybody else's, but one cannot take these kind of folk seriously. The people who are in Category 2, and who, after making lots of money etc. do good, by giving employment, money to charity, endowing hospitals etc. etc. are *not* good people, in the true moral sense: because the methods employed to pile about oneself a mass of material wealth are, of necessity, immoral methods. What most men call 'good business methods' is generally an efficient way of cheating somebody else. The law of leasehold is an excellent example.

Friday, 12 February

Peter Eade rang. I am to meet the casting director of ABC, Jerry Walker, re the film *Dam Busters*, in which all the actors must resemble the RAF men who did this thing!! Of course it is the kind of stupidity which *only* a film company *could* indulge in. Ridiculous to send *me*. I *don't look like anybody*. Except me.

Saturday, 13 February

On my way to Hugh Manning for tea, I passed two decorated young men, and heard this conversation – 'We had a marvellous time last night!' 'Did you? What happened?' 'We had Poetry Readings, à la Margaret Rawlings.'[2] 'Oo! how delicious!' 'Yes! I gave everyone a different author!' 'But heavenly! Hm. What did *you* read?' '*Lady of Shallot*, o'course. I always do.'

Sunday, 28 February

Stanley's visit has made me restless and irritable. He always arouses these emotions. He is suspicious and ungenerous and being with him is like sitting on an oven.

Friday, 12 March

Visit from Philip C. who was violently upset re a jilting session of gaiety. Poor boy. We saw Ed Murrow[3] on TV sending McCarthy sky high! Excellent.

Saturday, 20 March

Denis came for coffee and we talked about Milton and his terrible influence on English Lit. He read aloud from 2 of my Milton volumes and was demonstrably scathing about it. Very proper. I think Milton is terrible. Not a fresh visual image anywhere. Just a sonorous mass

---

[2] Actress, b.1906. 'It has been for her broadcast readings of poetry that she has become best known in recent years' (*Radio Times*, 22 July 1955).

[3] American current-affairs broadcaster (1908–65) famous for wartime reports from London, whose television show 'See it Now' attacked the right-wing demagogue and smear campaigner against 'un-American activities', Senator Joseph McCarthy (1908–57).

of iambic pentameter which goes on and on like a sermon. We went to the Saville, to see Martha Graham and her company dance. I didn't get much enjoyment from this, but Denis was enraptured.

Monday, 22 March

In the evening to see Richard [West] & meet Karin – this Princess of Georgia whom he has married. Great shock.

Saturday, 3 April

Hugh Manning rang me in the middle of my painting walls and I said 'What is it?' and he said 'Don't talk to me like that!' and I was so sick of it all that I rang off. Hugh called on me, and we made a rapprochement. We went to the Curzon to see *Monsieur Hulot's Holiday* which was not very good.

Monday, 5 April

Went to Eade about work and said that I felt I should go to S[outh] A[frica] if I got the right salary and he seemed reasonable about it. I think it's the *only* answer. Without the prospect of S.A. in view, I should be seriously considering the gas oven. I think I should get on with the business of ending the entire wretched futile venture. Another audition *or* interview and I shall *take off*.

Tuesday, 6 April

I now understand why suicides never ask for help before killing themselves. It is an utter rejection of human understanding. I realised last night, whilst walking about the streets crying, that there was *no one* in London I could call on and seek refuge. Even Harald was out. O! Harald has let me down terribly. He could have given me work instead of Barrington. God knows I need something.

Sunday, 11 April

With Harald to Hyde Park where we saw a meeting and heard Pritt[4] speak about the Hydrogen Bomb. And about the Indo-Chinese war in which Mr Dulles[5] wants to engulf us all.

Friday, 23 April

Met McNeile of the Durban Rep. He would not go above £15 a week and I don't think that is enough. Shall put it in the hands of Eade and have him ask for 20 and negotiate with them. Less, I don't accept and shall not go to S.A.

---

[4] D.N. Pritt (1887–1972), pro-Russian Marxist lawyer, campaigner, briefly an MP.

[5] John Foster Dulles (1888–1959), US Secretary of State under Eisenhower.

Monday, 26 April
Saw Eade and he agreed that I should go down to Bridgwater and do some weekly rep. for about 4 productions: decided that Africa could only be done on a bigger salary and directed McNeile to contact Eade – if he doesn't, well, to hell with it.

Saturday, 1 May
Entrained for Bridgwater at Paddington. £4 week F.B. at 59 Victoria Road. This is a strange coincidence, for my last rep. lodgings were at 26, Victoria Road, Salisbury. And this atmosphere isn't so very different. Wilts and Somerset. See.

Monday, 10 May
The opening night of *Traveller's Joy.*[6] Very tatty really. This is the first time I've acted on the stage since *Birmingham* – which is a year ago! I felt like an amateur & probably looked like one!

Wednesday, 12 May
This company is rather frightening. The women come into the men's dressing room. I have put a stop to that kind of thing.

Monday, 24 May
Dress reh. & opening of *Painted Sparrows.*[7] The dialogue is such filth that I feel like vomiting continually. Ashby-Bailey is utterly useless and has *no idea* what he is doing. The whole thing is deplorable. There were only a few people out front – 30 or so – and the evening was very much a flop.

Thursday, 27 May
To the Lunatic Asylum to play to the inmates. Most odd. They started singing at one juncture. And several walked out on the Anthem. Anti-Royalists I suppose.

Thursday, 3 June
There is an appalling atmosphere in this company. The women continually causing trouble and the men like Beck[8] continually *helping* it.

---

6 By Arthur Macrae.
7 By Guy Paxton and Edward V. Hoile.
8 James Beck, d.1973. Achieved fame as Private Walker in 'Dad's Army'.

Thursday, 10 June

Went to tea with [James] Roose[-Evans],[9] talked needlessly, suddenly! it was 7 o'c.! Curtain up 7.30 and we were half an hour away from theatre! Held up a car – lift into town, young man with a blind alsatian – dungarees etc. right to stage door.

Saturday, 12 June

It seems almost incredible to me now, that I have come through 6 weeks of this kind of purgatory. I am genuinely perplexed as to how I have lived through it. How right everyone was in London! What a fool I was to venture near such crap!

Tuesday, 22 June

To Odeon Cinema with Peter Eade to see press show of *The Seekers*. I thought I was quite reasonable and am not half as worried as I imagined I was going to be. No sign of sibilance & all that stuff – the voice was extraordinarily deep – but I accept that.

Monday, 28 June

Saw arrival of King Gustav of Sweden at Westminster Pier, at 12.45. I saw everything very well. The Queen looked exquisite, and rode in an open landau with Gustav. In the second carriage rode Duke of Edinburgh and his Aunt, the Queen of Sweden. They were escorted by units of the Household Cavalry who looked splendid on fine black horses.

Monday, 12 July

1st day rehearsing TV *Misalliance*.[10] Stoll Theatre. I play Bentley Summerhays. Read this play at first rehearsal at the Stoll. It reads very drearily, and I suspect it won't act much better.

Tuesday, 27 July

Rehearsed all day. Transmission of TV production *Misalliance* in the evening.

Wednesday, 28 July

Generally good reports about last night's play. [John] Fernald has offered me the Dauphin in *St Joan* with Siobhan McKenna and I have accepted.

---

[9] Later producer-director; at that time an actor billed simply as 'Roose Evans'.
[10] 1910 comedy by George Bernard Shaw.

Thursday, 29 July
Girl dancing with uniformed fellow asks his designation and is told he is a Gurkha officer, she says she thought they were black, and he says 'No, only our privates are black' and she replies 'My dear, how fantastic.' Johnny Schlesinger told me this story and I think it is very funny.

Thursday, 5 August
There is a standard brand of English acting, wherein 'sincerity' and emotional performances are typified by a pair of swelling nostrils, taut lips and jawline and a constipated voice production. This is often achieved by actors on stages, who in their own moments of suffering look nothing like this.

Tuesday, 10 August
With Michael Harald to Collins' Music Hall where we saw a woman dance with a 14' python wound about her body. Harald said he suspected the python was under the influence of a drug but I don't subscribe to this theory myself – one realises it could be, but I fancy that the reptile was tamed from infancy. There were nudes posing in the show,[11] and during their part in the performance, an unsavoury looking fellow passed up and down the aisles, looking for signs of excitement etc., along each row of seats. However, the 90% male audience remained curiously unaffected throughout.

Monday, 16 August
Went with Michael Harald & Rachel Roberts to the Collins Music Hall at Islington, where we saw another incredible tat show,[12] which seemed even worse than last week. An awful woman who kept singing 'Me and my sha-sha-shadow' (sitting in the row behind) in a relentless monotone made Rachel & Harald hysterical!! The comedian was appalling and had apparently put the show on himself, with £50,000 he won on the football pools. Hm. Very unwise I should have thought.

Friday, 27 August
1st rehearsal of *Joan* at the Arts. The cast seems a very competent, if somewhat frugal one. Fernald I am still undecided about. Ostensibly kind and earnest, but . . . ?

---

[11] *Eve in the Nude.*
[12] Entitled *Eve Goes Gay*. Its successor, the following week, was called *How Naughty can you Get?*

Wednesday, 1 September
Divinity, I believe, is obvious. To deny it is as futile as to deny oxygen. It is something fundamentally *right* and proper to the condition of men. But the *forms* in which this Divinity is observed should never become important in themselves; they should always be subordinate to the original concept; and be dispensable according to the condition of humanity.

Friday, 3 September
Human Love, in any manifestation, never ceases to humble me. These earthly signs of Divinity are noble signposts on the road to God.

Wednesday, 8 September
To Michael Ellis for costume. He insisted on giving me five gins at his club, and I returned to Marchmont Street feeling quite inebriated and slightly boss-eyed.

Sunday, 12 September
In the face of pilotless direction, the actor has the following courses of action: a) to rely on the guidance of some other kind of direction – often a fellow actor who will advise etc. b) produce himself in what will inevitably be a subjective & intuitive fashion c) just say the lines and get through it with the maximum degree of competence. The b) method is the way I generally choose.

Monday, 13 September
He (John Fernald) now tells me the characterisation lacks 'depth' and 'profundity' and 'humanity'. The madness of these words in relation to Dauphin! Who is, as the script says, egocentric, disloyal, guilty, full of physical inferiority, *and* shrewdly cunning.

Monday, 20 September. Cambridge
Dress rehearsed and opened the show. It was all rather mechanical. But audience reaction seemed excellent to me. Perhaps Cambridge is just a 'kind' date?

Wednesday, 29 September
Opening *St Joan* in London. Arts Theatre. Very exciting opening. A success. Lots of congratulations. Went back with Peter Eade and drinks. Chatted till 3 o'c morning.

Thursday, 30 September
Notices are Rotten! Only mentioned in Mail and Chronicle well. The

Telegraph says I was 'satisfactory'. Outrageous. Joan has been rapturously received. Really it isn't proportionate or proper.

Sunday, 3 October

Kenneth Tynan gives me a fine notice in the Observer today. Also Hobson in The Sunday Times. This is very gratifying.

Saturday, 9 October

There is a very amusing cartoon[13] of me in Punch as The Dauphin and I am greatly taken with it.

Sunday, 10 October

I feel perfectly frightful this morning. To make matters worse, Harold Hobson has been curiously insulting about actors to play the Dauphin in the old Sunday Times rag. He says it needs someone at least as good as Guinness!! This from the man that calls Shaw 'class-conscious snobbery . . .' Ugh. He must be a filthy specimen with a sewer of a mind.

Tuesday, 19 October

Interview BBC re variety show with Tony Hancock. I am to play some old Lord in a minute spot. Producer Dennis Main Wilson.

Wednesday, 27 October

How are the future generations to cope with the world? How are they to understand the evil that they are to inherit? How to uncover even one or two fundamental truths from the tissue of lies with which everything has been covered? Man has distorted truth and murdered faith by his own foolish greed and pride. It is not enough for the poets to pity. But where are the poets that can *speak* to the children that are to come?

Saturday, 30 October

BBC 10 a.m. Camden Theatre. Recording of 'Hancock Half Hour' went very well really, and I got through OK. Freddie Treves came and we chatted afterwards.

Sunday, 31 October

Last 2 performances of *St Joan* at the Arts. Party after in snack bar.

---

[13] By Ronald Searle.

Tuesday, 2 November
Tea with Peter Nichols. Electric fire & frugality. Cold day. The Chelsea Embankment bleak and the feeling of fog & pollution in air.

Saturday, 6 November
Recorded the Hancock show in morning. Camden Theatre. I played a Policeman and a Judge. Both badly.

Monday, 8 November
Louie broke a record of Marlene singing 'Black Market'. I felt so angry I just couldn't speak. Got over it OK though, without being filthy rude or anything.

Wednesday, 17 November
Met Eric C. accidentally and he told me of his decision to become a nurse in a Mental Hospital because, he said, homosexuals were 'unwanted' in the ordinary world. I found all his arguments rather specious, and was rather sickened by his insistence regarding Jesus *not* being the Son of God. I tried to point out that it didn't really matter – that it was the whole *idea* of Christianity that was important but he continually blocked one into side arguments & tangents. I fear we were deaf to each other.

Saturday, 11 December
Recorded the Hancock show. I was really very bad indeed. It was a lousy script too.

Saturday, 18 December
Two Hancock broadcasts and the apparatus broke down and we had to fill in for 20 minutes, so I sang old cockney songs and went down very well. They were all very pleased with me.

Wednesday, 22 December
To see Hancock in *Talk of the Town* at the Adelphi. He was v. good but the rest was rather tatty.

Tuesday, 28 December
Any account of the activities of this Christmas period would make wretched miserable reading. The family festivities, the party at Haralds' at Battersea, the pantomime at the Metropolitan, Edgware Road (*Dick Whittington*) played to an empty house. All of it so bare, scant and frugal and abysmally depressing. 1954 has been utterly ghastly as far as I'm concerned. Professionally and socially.

1955

Monday, 3 January
Recorded Hancock Show, at Paris Cinema, as an experiment, at 11.30 in the evening. Pro audience, really. It went down very well. Earlier I sat in Tony's dressing room at the Adelphi and talked. He said I was wasting my time in legit and should go into variety. Like Baxter says. But of course it's the entrée that one needs.

Friday, 7 January
To see Michael Harald, Peter Nichols came too. I was fearfully rude. My behaviour becomes worse, it seems. I apologised to Nichols. Really! I am becoming so utterly futile.

Monday, 17 January
Henry Sherek is to present *Saint Joan* at the St Martin's. It is probably due to rehearse next week. I have been offered the Dauphin, but they're only offering £15, and we're haggling. I think it should carry more.

Tuesday, 8 February
Opening of *Joan* at St Martin's, very enthusiastic reception for Siobhan.

Thursday, 10 February
The show was even worse tonight. Flat, uninspired and utterly dull. Without Siobhan, it would die on its feet. Flat feet. And, ironically, not one critic has attacked, or indeed faulted the production in any way. I am appalled at the lack of standard, discrimination and taste which exists in our theatre today. All these mediocrities should be ruthlessly stamped out.

Friday, 11 February
As I was walking in Marchmont Street this afternoon, a woman cried out 'Fanatical illiterates!' at all and sundry. She seemed very bitter and, I imagine, she was anxious to make an impression of some kind.

It was all rather innocuous, however, for she did not illustrate the object of her invective. We never knew *who* the fanatical illiterates *were*. I passed on my way – bemused.

Wednesday, 16 February

People who talk about the necessity for discipline in the theatre are people who are not of the theatre. Real *actors* are people who feel a sense of responsibility about themselves and their work. The discipline which they exercise (& indirectly inspire, or make for in others) is automatic and unconscious. And this is the only discipline worth having. This is axiomatic.

Thursday, 17 February

Orwell's essay on the work of Henry Miller[1] first interested me in the subject. And now I am lucky enough to acquire a copy of Henry Miller's essays. They are wonderfully refreshing to me and clarify things that were only half-formed in my own mind. He has crystallised for me what I have often *felt* – that the conviction is useless unless it is carried into the flesh. The thought is not enough. And when the thought & the action are one, there is the truth. The only reality that matters. All the rest is bogus: & pernicious. Only in the *being* is there health.

Friday, 18 February

The reason I don't want to act in Shakespeare at the moment is that I want to be associated with voicing the contemporary problems of my own age. I see the greatness of his (S.) poetic vision and its glory. But theatrically it is no longer meaningful for me. The idea of a crowd of people speaking Shakespearean verse on a greensward is somehow incongruous. I'm practically laughing. *Anyway* it won't be done properly because it *can't* be done properly. There aren't the Actors any more. The big heroics etc. can't be encompassed, and the audience has lost touch. This isn't a heroic age. There isn't *room* for heroics. It's *all* heroics now. So the real hero has passed away.

Wednesday, 23 February

To see Dreyer's *Passion of Joan of Arc* at the National Film Theatre. It was superb. Falconetti (Joan) so fabulous I wept.

Friday, 25 February

To Peter Eade re contract signing. Hancock. Last show. Chatted and gossiped. I hear that Donald Pleasence is to play the Dauphin in *Joan*

---

[1] 'Inside the Whale' (1940).

for Tennent's. Well that won't set the Thames on fire. So now then. To supper after with Desmond. Indian restaurant. Met an extraordinary fellow with a trombone. No money. I paid for his meal.

Wednesday, 2 March

On my arrival at the theatre I met Pat (Olivier's personal dresser during the *Beggars' Opera*) and she was dreadfully upset because he sacked her after ten years of loyal service. 'It was my whole life,' she told me, with the suspicion of tear-filled eyes, 'I told him he couldn't do this to me, but he shut the car door and drove off.' I must say, it all sounded mean and despicable, but one doesn't know Larry's side of it. Not that it could matter a ha'penny to me, the whole shoot of knighted actors are extraneous matter. But it's interesting psychologically. Mr Attlee[2] and Hugh Beaumont and John Perry[3] out front tonight.

Tuesday, 15 March

It is incredible how transparent an 'actor' generally is. And it is ironically humorous; for the actor is supposed to be possessed of a talent for disguise, for fraudulent behaviour in an accepted convention, for dissembling. Yet, in fact, the actor makes himself more *obvious* than anyone. I am continually amazed at their naïveté, and their adolescent mawkishness. *Not* their childishness for so often the childlike behaviour has *charm* & redeems itself by its obviousness, its need for affection and security.

Wednesday, 16 March

Reading an article by V.S. Pritchett I came upon sentiments to the effect that genius is only tolerable to the average man when it is dead. I think this is very illuminating. Why is it, I wonder, that brilliance & talent, in any field, is so often resented & decried. It is always a tendency to damn with faint praise, or detract in some way from proper valuation. How often one hears 'Awfully clever, yes – but O! my dear, so difficult I hear . . .' in the theatre.

Thursday, 17 March

The business of actually sustaining a performance night after night is peculiarly difficult for me: my temperament seems so against it. I am

---

[2] (Earl Attlee) 1883–1967. Prime Minister 1945–51.

[3] Hugh 'Binkie' Beaumont, 1908–73. Managing Director of the H.M. Tennent theatrical company. John Perry (b.1906), friend of Beaumont and a director of Tennent's.

by nature erratic – given to enthusiasms which wane after a time; quick to grasp the bones of a subject, slow to develop them.

Saturday, 19 March
More trouble with Siobhan McKenna. Her voice has gone again, and she always becomes bad-tempered with everything about her on such occasions. Everyone in the company is becoming heartily sick of her, & the orgiastic self-pity of these 'scenes' she stages continually.

Sunday, 20 March
Michael Hitchman to lunch. We went to see the Graham Greene film *The End of the Affair*. As with so much else in Greene's writing, the dilemma (sex-religious theme) is ended (and apparently resolved) only in the death. Everybody is inevitably tarnished, sinful & ignoble. His world is a world of dead ideas & dead figures. Everybody in his writing is something seedy & second rate, unable to *live* healthily & properly.

Wednesday, 23 March
Siobhan McKenna told me that John Fernald had written to her saying that her performance was a travesty, and that he had been greatly hurt by hearing that she had adversely criticised his production. Fernald must be psychopathic I think, to write such things to anyone that has to appear on boards. She kept saying that I must not tell a *soul* about the letter, and I said that I wouldn't. Of course I shall.

Saturday, 26 March
The majority, in fact 99% of the people who have talked seriously about this production of *Saint Joan*, inform me that Siobhan McKenna is superb. It is very significant that so many of them have continual recourse to the sentence 'She *is* Joan'. One actor who had seen her performance remarked to me 'There isn't an ounce of technique in her at all', with enormous admiration. And this kind of sentiment, regarding Miss McKenna, seems to me to point the fundamental *error* in her work. The only honest & important criteria [*sic*] upon which we (I) can judge her performance is – *how completely has she conveyed what Shaw wrote?*

Sunday, 27 March
It is apparent in her portrayal of Shaw's Joan that she has never begun to understand or appreciate Shavian dialectic. The joyous quality he had of giving justification to two arguments, the genius for juxtaposing pathos and humour – the sense of *fairness* in his excellent prose – all

this is lost, or never glimpsed in Miss McKenna. She sings monotonously through the part with enormous *conviction* and does all the wrong things with such earnestness & certainty that the undiscriminating audience believes that she is *right*. *Anything* done with the necessary air of absolute conviction will pass for truth, in the absence of proper standards. Standards can be maintained of course only by those who are aware of quality in Art. Those who know the real thing as distinct from the bogus. There is an awful lot of hard slogging in Miss McKenna's work, but none of it has any relationship to Art. One of the most moving things about the part of Joan is the tragedy of *trust* misplaced; Miss McKenna makes it plain from the beginning that she doesn't trust anybody.

Monday, 28 March

Her final lines at the end of the Epilogue are ultimate proof of her inability to act Shaw's Joan. They are delivered with an appalling sense of self-pity & complacency which makes the judicious wince. They cease to represent the question of one of the finer inquiring minds of our age, and become simply an opportunity for Siobhan McKenna to indulge herself again, deliciously, in the last words. There is *no ring* – no inner core of hard truth in these last, wonderful, questioning lines – there is only *whispered complacency* and smug smiling, and the sense of rude intimacy with the Deity, that is vulgar, and almost obscene.

Wednesday, 30 March

Reading Eric Bentley's new book *In Search of Theatre*. It makes me *long* to have a building in which to present plays. A place which would not be an end in itself, but which would supply the *ideas* which feed the minds of men: and a place in which I could evolve a style of acting that suffers neither from inhibition nor the ostentatious *wholesomeness* that marks so much of the American group acting. A style of acting whereby *all* the methods & all the forms could be synthesised & distilled into an *ideal* of human cooperation where each will be taught to understand the paramount importance of cooperation through affection, which will result in the best.

Friday, 1 April

My head is bursting with mental frustration: the knowledge that in this country, it's practically impossible to have truly co-operative acting under inspired dramatic leadership. I fancy I shall go *mad*. Wrote to Erich about *St Joan*.

Monday, 4 April
Siobhan in the shop today, having hair cut.

Tuesday, 5 April
David March, as Stogumber, used to deliver his final lines in the Epilogue on stage, now he walks in silence to the door, and says them off stage. At the matinée, I was so angry that I didn't wait for his final words, I just *cut* in on his lines and went on with the play, for his pausing had become interminable. He came rushing up to me at the end of the show, and made an awful scene, his shoulders twitching and convulsing: it was revolting. I behaved in such a disinterested fashion that he became violently furious and rushed in to see the Stage Director to complain about my behaviour.

Wednesday, 6 April
I resolved to apologise to David March, bethinking that despite all argument, my behaviour was reprehensible, and should be atoned for. In the last analysis, there is no excuse for bad manners. I went to him, and said I was sorry, promising that I would not offend him again in this fashion. He accepted with excellent grace, and was very kind.

Thursday, 7 April
I am glad that this unpleasantness with D. March is concluded, and I *must* learn from this mistake, for the entire chain of unpleasant events occurring twixt myself & others is resultant from the same cause. I must learn to bridle my tongue, I must learn humility, and I must stop making professional judgments. It is really only my business in any company to do my job well. It is, of course, sad that one *cannot* do one's own job well without cooperation, but I simply have to accept that, salvage what I can, and *learn* from this odd, but oft-recurring situation. Even the smallest amount of human endeavour seems to be frustrated in some way.

Sunday, 10 April
With Annette Kerr to see *South* at the Arts, by Julian Green. It's about a young homosexual in love with a normal young man; of course he commits suicide. Really, this is the kind of thing that seems inevitable in all the homosexual writing. They're always killing themselves. Totally misleading & distorted picture of life, for there are a great number of happy homosexuals – at least as happy as heterosexuals. I'm sick of this 'persecuted queer' stuff.

Friday, 15 April

To Aeolian Hall, re the new Hancock series. Apparently Hancock himself is missing & they're hoping he will turn up on time,[4] but in case he doesn't, they're preparing a recording with Harry Secombe instead. We do this from the Camden Theatre on Sunday at 4 o'c.

Sunday, 17 April

I went up to the Camden, where the old crowd were – except Tony Hancock & Moira Lister. The latter is in the Gielgud *Lear* (European tour) and Tony is unwell – apparently it's nervous exhaustion. So his place was taken by Harry Secombe. Harry is a comic in the true 'lunatic grotesque' tradition. His antics are fantastic and very funny. He takes the lifelike ingredient of a character and then proceeds to blow it up to enormously fantastic proportions, the slightest nuance is blown up to embarrassingly revealing proportions and the act is a riot. He played Tony's lines without any attempt to impersonate, just taking them as he came to them, like a thoroughbred horse taking jumps – confidently & with great style. He kept the pace of the show bubbling with laughs and the success of the evening was largely due to him.

Sunday, 1 May

Did the Hancock Show with Harry Secombe. I fluffed & we had to do it again. Bad. I am working too hard lately. That's the trouble.

Saturday, 7 May

Did the reading for Orson Welles, and cued myself. He said afterwards 'I could certainly use someone of your versatility in the company . . .' and we have to meet next week to discuss it further . . . I was rather pleased with myself I must say.

Sunday, 8 May

Hancock show went very well, with Tony once again back in the team. I had about six voices, and one of the script boys suggested using another character man because he said I was doing too much. This is really absurd.

Sunday, 15 May

Rehearsed the Hancock Show at the Camden. It's a bit ribby this week, primarily because I have very little to do.

---

4 Depressed, he had flown to Rome and taken up residence in a *pensione* in Positano.

Sunday, 22 May
I shall take the Orson Welles offer of *Moby Dick*[5] because there has been no definite offer from Sherek for America.[6]

Monday, 23 May
Did the Hancock show from the Playhouse and ran on to the St Martin's in time for *St Joan*. Too hectic. My life is too hectic. The washing machine I ordered from Hoover for Louie arrived today. She is delighted with it.

Saturday, 28 May
Rehearsed morning *Moby Dick*. Last 2 shows of *Saint Joan* and glad to see the end of it all.

Monday, 30 May
Rehearsed *Moby Dick* in morning. Did Hancock show from 2 o'c. to 7.30. Rehearsed *Moby Dick* from 8.30 to midnight.

Wednesday, 1 June
Peter Whitbread, playing juv. lead, is replaced by Gordon Jackson.

Thursday, 2 June
Wrote letter to Siobhan wishing her bon voyage & good luck for America.

Wednesday, 8 June
I wish to God I had never *seen* this rotten play, and Orson Welles and the whole filthy tribe of sycophantic bastards connected with this bogus rubbish. More *theatre* is achieved in weekly Rep. than in London. Ever.

Friday, 10 June
The latest madness from the Welles-Chappell-Edwards[7] trio is *rocking* the cast. We have to play all the scenes staggering at regular intervals! to suggest the motion of a ship. The result is an effective impression of intoxication! Hours and hours are wasted on this kind of nonsense. Everyone is embarrassed by such stupidity.

---

[5] Welles's own adaptation of the Herman Melville novel. KW as 'A Very Serious Actor (afterwards Elijah, Ship's Carpenter, Old Bedford Sailor and others)'.
[6] To tour with *Saint Joan*. The tour did later take place.
[7] William Chappell was Associate Producer: Hylton Edwards not credited.

Saturday, 11 June
Orson Welles may be a brilliant 'personality' but he knows nothing about producing a play. His *lack* of ability is bitterly apparent. The only difference between him & the other bogus English directors is this swank personality, and New Yorker wisecracks.

Thursday, 16 June
Rehearsed from 11 o'c. this morning until 2 o'c. Then back after a lunch break, and on until 6.30. Break. Then we opened for the first night. Peter Eade sent me a bottle of champagne and I drank it all during the performance. I know that I have no objective criticism to offer regarding this production. There is too much about it that I dislike & disapprove of, for me to be at all unbiased. All I know is that the thing is messy, badly rehearsed, acted, & lit. And the sooner it is over, the better.[8]

Saturday, 18 June
An admirer of Welles was discussing him with Rita Hayworth in America and she remarked 'Oh! Orson – yeah, he's clever all right . . .' and added thoughtfully: 'The morning after we were married, I woke up, and I could tell by the expression on his face, he was just waiting for the applause . . .'[9]

Wednesday, 22 June
Audition at St Martin's Theatre for the part of Montgomery in the musical play *The Buccaneer* by Sandy Wilson. I sang very badly. I don't think Tennent's were very impressed. I felt so utterly low & dreary I went to sit in St Giles churchyard among the tombs & beggars. Lunch with Gordon Jackson who played the *Buccaneer* music for me.

Tuesday, 28 June
Orson called me into his room and asked me to do 2 films with him, and said 'Don't do the musical play . . .' I said I'd think about it. I have no desire to work with *him* any more.

Saturday, 2 July
Did the last of the Hancock shows today, at the Camden Theatre. They took away the announcing from me. I was frankly annoyed and

---

[8] On the whole, it was well received, if only as a symptom of Welles's challenging megalomania. KW's distaste may have proceeded from the fact that Welles, as Ahab, indulged in much ad-libbing at the expense of the cast, who, he later said, had been 'young and solemn'.
[9] Welles had married Paola Mori a few weeks earlier in London.

rather hurt. No explanation was forthcoming. 2 shows of *Moby Dick*, drear.

Sunday, 3 July
I accidentally heard a bit of of a radio play tonight by someone called Besant adapted by Howard Agg or Hag or something. It was so atrocious that I kept it on. It was almost funny. That bogus old crapmound Norman Shelley was in it. Terribly funny really.[10]

Saturday, 9 July
Last 2 shows of this ghastly play. Party after, on stage. Awful drear.

Wednesday, 13 July. Shanklin, Isle of Wight
No holiday is really enjoyable when one is alone. I was very lonely really.

Friday, 15 July
Filming *Moby Dick Rehearsed*[11] at Hackney Empire from 8.30 to 6.10.

Thursday, 21 July
Filming from 7 a.m. to 10 p.m. Every day I become more convinced of my desire to leave this profession & get some sort of a guest house. That is what I have always wanted.

Monday, 25 July
First rehearsal of *Buccaneer* was purely a read through. It all went very pleasantly and we finished about 3.30. Orson asked me to play Octavius in his production of *Antony & Cleopatra*. Told me to get out of the Tennent contract. I hummed and hawed.

Thursday, 28 July
Rehearse Globe morning. Filming from 5.30pm to 10pm.

Wednesday, 17 August
Rehearsed from 10am to 9pm. Fed up with the entire poofy set-up.

Tuesday, 23 August. Brighton
I am favourably mentioned in the local paper. Which is nice.

---

[10] *The Golden Butterfly* by Walter Besant and James Rice. Dramatised as a serial in ten parts by Howard Agg. Norman Shelley (1903–80, perennially a favourite actor and narrator on radio) as Joseph Jagenal.
[11] An attempt to make a television film out of the staged play. It was not completed.

Tuesday, 30 August. Southsea
I am favourably mentioned in the local paper. Very gratifying.

Wednesday, 7 September
Dress rehearsal today at 5 o'c. Lyric Hammersmith. I met Adrianne Allen & her son Daniel Massey afterwards. They were enchanting people.

Thursday, 8 September
Opening was an anti-climax. They all expected far too much, & the result was none of the artists came up to it. The patchy & spasmodic direction was shown up in its shoddiest light, and Billy Chappell's[12] face fell steadily throughout the evening.

Friday, 9 September
I am favourably received in all the newspapers. One even goes so far as to call me a 'star'!! Well of course it's all the most blithering rubbish I've *ever* had to appear in, so it's some compensation to be mentioned by the press.

Sunday, 11 September
Walked down to the river & thought a bit. It had been raining and the roads were wet . . . I thought of the last few months, so much material accomplishment but still the spiritual nihilism. Still the deadness of lack of sharing – the *not entering into* life.

Thursday, 6 October
Saw Dr Skolar and he recommends an operation on the mucous membrane of the nose. Says it would mean 6–8 days in hospital. I'm to go to him about it when this play ends.

Tuesday, 25 October
I am too good for the tat, and not good enough for the truly art-purposeful theatre. I am an interesting example of the half-developed competent performer. The actor that is always meaning to work at 'something' and never does.

Wednesday, 26 October
When one has no satisfaction in private life (I mean the satisfaction born of a sense of progression & achievement) then the profession becomes more important than ever. It becomes a fulcrum of existence, and therefore it is appallingly frustrating to be associated with the

---

[12] Director of *The Buccaneer*. KW as Montgomery.

shoddy and inefficient sort of thing that *The Buccaneer* represents.

Thursday, 3 November
2 shows today. Lunched with Desmond Jordan. It was all very pleasant until he said (apropos my work) 'You must have the money rolling in . . .' I do dislike people making remarks about my income. I think it is so impolite to reduce all artistic output to sheer material results.

Sunday, 6 November
November here already and me with no sense of a year going. The first year I have worked practically consistently in London. I suppose this can be regarded as progress but it has certainly not been artistic progress.

Sunday, 4 December
Hancock broadcast from Fortune. It tailed off rather towards the end.

Monday, 5 December
Rehearse *13th Tree*[13] by André Gide (BBC 3rd prog.) at Portland Place 10.30. Only people in the cast I know are Max Adrian and James Thomason.

Wednesday, 14 December
Went early to afternoon showing of *Richard III*, the Olivier film, which opened yesterday. It was certainly a most salutary piece of work. Unfortunately, I felt a complete lack of reality about Larry – it was indeed a theatrical Richard, with funny walk, crookback, unformed hands, and a plasticine nose. This, surrounded by so many realistic performances, looked somewhat bogus.

Thursday, 22 December
2 shows today. This year has certainly been my most profitable year in the theatre, financially. And the most impoverished one, artistically. Economics has largely dictated my career, and I am driven pell-mell about my fear of being poor. I need money for a house. I must have a roof over my head, or under my feet as it were. Useless now to rely upon the idea of L. He has proved a thoroughly emotional fellow and his latest letters, so full of unhealthy talk of repression & so forth that I tore them up straightway. I dislike the vaguest suggestion of sex in my relationship with *anyone*.

---

[13] Billed as 'A Joke by André Gide'. Translated by George D. Painter. Max Adrian as Dr Styx, James Thomason as Priest, KW as Lavignette.

1956

Sunday, 1 January
Did the Hancock show from the Fortune Theatre. Not a very good script, my part was negligible. They're cutting down on the snide character. Too popular. Quite so. Reely. I don't mind. Drinks after with Tony. He is in the London Clinic. Dieting.

Monday, 2 January
The Buccaneer, I hear, may be transferring to a West End theatre when it leaves the Lyric to make way for *Misalliance*. I don't know that I have any positive feelings about it either way.

Tuesday, 3 January
To the London Clinic to see Tony Hancock. We discussed beliefs. Went on & on, till Cicely arrived at 1.30'ish.

Wednesday, 4 January
Only at this juncture of my professional life can I state my worth as an Artist. Only now. Because now I see that in Art is man's striving for the truth – for the order – for the sense, which has evaded him in the stupidity of existence. Only in the recognition of this Truth in Art can my respect be commanded. Here is where my duty as an Actor lies. I must be the perceptive eye. With what fundamental truths I possess, I must judge & work from there. There is not one dramatic organisation in this country which is worthy of my talents. My ability to translate the written thought – mentally and physically – into dramatic action, is *intrinsic*. Thus I can *smell* the bogus miles away, and the London theatre only earns my despite.

Saturday, 7 January
To London Clinic in morning to see Tony. Long chat about anarchy.

Friday, 13 January
O! this day has been so oppressive for me. Suddenly the emptiness of my existence confronted me – hypothetically – I found myself

summing up all the previous year. 1955 was complete dissipation artistically. There is no room in the theatre for me. I don't really *need* it enough. The time is out of joint. It's always out for me. Reading Nietzsche's *Zarathustra* which is incredibly illuminating – a truly brilliant, flashing, poetic mind.

Saturday, 14 January

Read the Peter Wildeblood book about Homosexual Prosecution (Montagu case).[1] It is extremely illuminating in many ways, and should do good for the general enlightenment of thinkers on this subject. Obviously the sex life of consenting adults of same or opposite sex has nothing to do with the State. The present law is so primitively barbaric that it gives rise to more trouble than would ever be, without it.

Monday, 16 January

The leaf that blossoms, dies and falls from the tree is, in the falling, tragic: but I am the leaf that has not blossomed. I am the blighted leaf. My tragedy lies in the knowledge of my failure to blossom. The blossoming of the leaf is the recognition of truth and the *living* of it, the realisation of it. I fail in this realisation. I come always *near* – but never *into* truth. I wait for the sign to show my way. And deep down inside myself I *know* I should be *writing* my own sign. Or I think I know. But all my mind is clouded with a doubt. And still I hope the sign will be given as a gift – a redemption. There is always that *hope*, and with the real *faith*, hope is not an evil thing.

Thursday, 19 January

2 shows and all the drear of Hammersmith redeemed by Richard and Sybil & Rachel who saw the evening performance. It was wonderful to see them. Richard full of fabulously interesting stories about the actors in Hollywood. Marlon Brando dull – etc. It sounded so far off. To supper with them at the Leicester Grill, then back with Richard & Sybil to Hampstead. We talked till 4 o'c in morning. Sybil is a miraculous person.

Friday, 20 January

Went to see James Dean in *Rebel Without a Cause* and was very dis-

---

[1] *Against the Law* (1955), described on the front cover of the 1957 Penguin edition as 'A first-hand account of what it means to be a homosexual'. Wildeblood was sentenced to eighteen months' imprisonment in March 1954 for homosexual offences. ('The case in which I was involved has become known as the "Montagu Case"; because one of the accused men was a peer [Lord Montagu], it received a great deal of publicity.')

appointed. I had greatly looked forward to seeing this brilliant actor once again, since I first saw him in the film *East of Eden*, and which had some splendid things in it for me. But this time it was all wrong somehow. Everything was too slick, the arguments all so bogus, and the acting all so obvious. If American youths *are* like the ones in this movie, then it must be the most frightening community that ever existed! But one simply doesn't believe it. I lost trust in the picture so early on that the entire business was horribly vacuistic. Dean was still very fascinating to watch nonetheless – but exactly the same as *Eden* film – his technique (for I don't believe he is a 'type') is the perfection of transmitting that pathetic uncertainty of the unsure. Almost every gauche movement, every yearning glance is geared to this supreme portrayal. Of its kind, it's undoubtedly the best I've seen.

Sunday, 22 January
I notice in myself a tendency to imitate the handwriting of those I admire. I've done this with Stanley and with Erich.

Monday, 23 January
I walked about in the City area – down Fleet St – reminding myself of boyhood days when my career was to be so different. A lot of new building is going on in the City – Staple Inn has been commendably restored and a fountain plays quietly in the middle. From Fleet St I took an 11 bus to Hammersmith and thought over the business of my own place. The only point in taking a flat would be if the proposition were attractive & the rental small, otherwise it is obviously better to take a property on mortgage and spend money paying for something which is to be mine. For this sort of thing I should need at least a thousand – I am convinced of that.

Tuesday, 31 January
Basil Hodges[2] came to the show last night. Drinks after. He was incredibly changed – I was amazed that a childhood idol of mine could be so different from what I'd imagined! And the voice – so common & the character so transparently inferior.

Friday, 3 February
I now have a thousand pounds deposited, and a current a/c of over one hundred. More money than I've ever had in my life. Still, 400 of the D/A will be used for tax, so I've only about 600 real savings – so things aren't as madly rosy as they may appear.

---

[2] Schoolmaster who taught KW English at Manchester Street School.

Sunday, 5 February

I am becoming more and more desperate about leaving 57. The place has ceased to offer any comfort to me, as a home, and my personality is increasingly stifled. Next week I must do something concrete about taking a flat even if the key money is a large sum. To go on as I am at present is to go completely insane.

Monday, 6 February

I was right not to look forward to the Hancock programme. The script was appalling. I have never felt so acutely embarrassed as I did last night: I had one of those terrible old men to do. The whole thing was just unfunny and incredibly verbose. Eventually we cut it to ribbons. Thank God Tony agreed. Went with him & some others to a flat after, and got rather tight. The entire Sunday was disgusting. A terrible day. I am amazed I've lived through it.

Wednesday, 15 February

Viewed another flat – 817, Endsleigh Court – owned by a Mr & Mrs Russer. A likely story! It's a bachelor apartment, very suitable, but the furnishing is appalling and the decor etc. not good. They're asking £800, and I suspect I shall have to pay it.[3] I simply must get into something of my own, this year.

Sunday, 19 February

Snowing heavily, and icy roads make everything very dangerous. Walked to the Aeolian Hall for rehearsal of 'H[ancock's] H[alf] H[our]'. Vic Oliver was there, rehearsing Variety and the orchestra walked out at 6 o'c.! The musicians are striking for higher pay. It is really atrocious.

Monday, 20 February

I think I must have reached a definite culmination point in my life. My nerves are almost at breaking point – footsteps behind me in the streets get me so I am screaming inside – I'm watching for people to stare and hating them – I want to talk aloud with myself, but there's always people there, and today, for the first time in my life, I went to a cinema (or cinemas) three times from 2 o'c. onwards. I have never *needed* privacy *more* and I have none. I'm weeping a lot too – tears for the plight – the utterly futile predicament of it all.

---

[3] 'Key money'. He did pay it, and was left with £94 in the bank.

Tuesday, 21 February
Rehearse. Apollo, 3.30. I predict a damp squid [*sic*] for the opening night.[4]

Wednesday, 22 February
I am 30 years old today. A sobering thought. Rehearsed with orchestra in morning. Waste of time. Opening was lukewarm. Sandy gave party after at Leicester Grill. I got drunk and became rude.

Friday, 2 March
Met Peter Glenville who is producing a farce with Alec Guinness.[5] He offers me the part of a boy called Maxime in it.

Saturday, 3 March
Signed the vendor agreement about the flat at 817 Endsleigh Court – I wish this transaction would move more quickly.

Monday, 5 March
I could no more share a flat with anyone than I could fly. The very *idea* is absurd. It has been difficult enough sharing a house, but an even smaller area would drive one to distraction.

Tuesday, 6 March
Princess Margaret in to see the show tonight. Looking radiant in Row D, and stealing all the limelight. Really splendid.

Thursday, 8 March
I believe I am coming to understand the nature of faith: and the purpose of eternal continuity, and function: the nature of patient acceptance, and the virtue thereof. Most of my artistic experience in the drama has been bad & frustrating & I railed against it. Now I understand – this is how it is, and always will be, *until* it is given purpose, and nobility. When it ceases to be a commodity, and becomes part of a human consciousness & a nation's culture. When the artist takes it back again from the mammon-worshippers, and recalls its high purpose. As an actor, I know my own value. I'm a reasonable craftsman: I can make a few bricks and sometimes without any straw. My intuitive gift – that of self-advertisement & display without inhibition – is largely wasted through a lack of self-discipline. My own domestic establishment may help me to that end.

---

4 Transfer of *The Buccaneer* to the West End.
5 *Hotel Paradiso*, by Georges Feydeau.

Saturday, 17 March
No rehearsal today, thank goodness. Goodness only knows what I am going to do with this part of Maxime. It contains no really funny lines and so it depends almost entirely on character humour. It is ridiculous to talk seriously about reality in characterisation – everything is personality in a play like this, and that's all that one should concentrate on. Lines, business and cracks – corn – the lot – false noses if necessary – just get your laughs any way you can and devil take the hindmost.

Sunday, 18 March
So now it's over.[6] The long travail is finished: and I am left with a long playing gramophone record to remind me of my first (and doubtless *only*) venture into musical comedy. Well I can't say that I am sorry. It's been a painful & arduous business, accompanied by more ill health than I have ever experienced in any show before.

Saturday, 24 March
Went to Endsleigh Court. Flat 8–17 is now mine.[7] I shall have to do an awful lot to make it right for me, but anyway – it's a start.

Wednesday, 11 April. Birmingham
Matinée and evening show.[8] Peter Eade in evening, we had meal afterwards. He says not to worry about it. Small part but I acquit myself well. That's consoling. I was beginning to feel a complete fraud.

Monday, 16 April. Glasgow
Walked around a bit reviving old memories of Glasgow. This is my third visit.

Thursday, 26 April. Newcastle
Frank Pettingell[9] said goodbye. It was sad for me. I do like him so.

Tuesday, 1 May. London
Frank Pettingell is back in the cast! This is wonderful. Binkie asked him to return. Quite right.

---

6 i.e. *The Buccaneer.*
7 A list of KW's addresses is given in Appendix A, p. 802.
8 Of *Hotel Paradiso*, translated and directed by Peter Glenville.
9 1891–1966. Endearingly bulbous character actor with lop-sided face.

Wednesday, 2 May

Went to Harlequin Films, 1, Soho Square. Interview with Joseph Losey who is directing a film of the play *Someone Waiting.*[10] One of the usual desultory interviews. I get hard, brittle and uncommunicative. The opening was fabulous.[11] Terrifique reception. Alec sent me champagne.

Tuesday, 15 May

Finished all the paintwork in the living room at last! It seemed to be going on for ever. Am having the decorators do the kitchen because I simply can't face that, *and* the hall painting as well!

Friday, 25 May

Alec Guinness took us to dinner at the White Tower. It was all very sycophantic indeed.

Saturday, 23 June

Lance Hamilton rang me & asked me to appear in a sketch with Jimmy Edwards & Zsa Zsa Gabor, at the Palladium, for the Night of the Hundred Stars. So I said yes eventually, which was *mad* because this morning's rehearsal was chaos.

Tuesday, 26 June

Phone call from Lance Hamilton to say the thing at the Palladium is *on* again. A new sketch with Ronnie Shiner and Zsa Zsa Gabor and me as a sort of daft reporter.

Wednesday, 27 June

Rehearsed again at the Palladium and fixed the sketch finally. Zsa Zsa Gabor has no idea about comedy whatsoever. She may succeed in buggering us all up completely. Charming. During the performance tonight Alec Guinness suddenly hissed at me 'Zsa Zsa Gabor to you too!' and I laughed of course.

Thursday, 28 June

The double act with Zsa Zsa Gabor went v. well indeed. Got all our laughs. Nicely.[12]

Thursday, 5 July

Met an American midshipman after show, and brought him back for

---

[10] By Emlyn Williams. The film was entitled *Time Without Pity* (1957).

[11] Of *Paradiso*, at the Winter Garden.

[12] The performance was recorded (sound only) and issued commercially.

coffee, he was called Bruce something. He was a bit aggressive and crude, but it was interesting to talk with him.

Sunday, 29 July
To June Dawes party at 9, Kent Terrace. Why do I go, again and again, to these ridiculous theatrical parties? They're always unpleasant for me – my inferiority rises to the surface, & I start being vicious and acidly funny, and always succeed in entertaining the group I'm not interested in anyway. I can't think why I torture myself in this fashion.

Monday, 30 July
Rose feeling exhausted after last night's party, and dreared through the day like a distraught ghost at the point of bursting [into] tears. The need to cry, like a child, for all the stupid wasting of the thousand chances life has offered me. O! for the real courage to speak out bravely, to do *one* decisive, unselfish and creative deed. Instead of watching the sand run through the glass and let the time trickle through one's hands . . .

Tuesday, 7 August
10.30 Osteopath. I went for treatment but my back still hurts. I hope tomorrow will solve something.

Wednesday, 8 August
1.45 National Orthopaedic Hospital. I was X-rayed and blood tested – both showed nothing wrong. So I'm to be given heat treatment and exercises for the back. What a lot of balls. They simply don't know what is wrong with me, at all.

Sunday, 26 August
Laurie S. called. It was a fantastic let-down. I found it hard to understand how I could ever have cared in the past – how anyone like him could have interested me in any way. He was dull, and quite unattractive.

Friday, 31 August
With Treves and his wife Jean to Battersea Fun Fair. All very gay and high-spirited.

Thursday, 20 September
2 shows. Alec looking quite exhausted.

Thursday, 4 October
2 shows today. The newspapers announce that the play is to come off first week in November. I won't be sorry at all.

Sunday, 7 October
Did the Hancock Show which was death! Went back after with Tony and Cicely. Stayed till 4!

Sunday, 14 October
Hancock show – the 50th one!

Sunday, 21 October
The Hancock script was terrible. Back with Tony to his flat and we talked through the night and I left Monday morning at 9.

Friday, 2 November
This bombing of Egypt by the RAF & the French air force is disgraceful. Eden[13] stated it was not war!! – but 'armed conflict'!! Of course it's fantastic for anyone to be so crass & stupid.

Saturday, 3 November
End of *Paradiso* run. More bombing. The rumour is that British & French troops will land at Egypt on Monday.

Monday, 5 November
Spent day with Tony. We talked of Suez – the action of Eden in Egypt – we deplored it.

Friday, 30 November
Michael Hitchman, 2 o'c. We went to the films and talked of futility and etc.

Sunday, 2 December
Rehearsed & recorded the Hancock show. It went very well. Petrol rationing subject. Got the laughs. I ran off afterwards, very quick to avoid the drears out front waiting to see me. Got home for a quiet sit, washed out me scarves, & went to bed.

Saturday, 8 December
Started taking newspapers today. Manchester Guardian daily & Observer on Sundays.

---

[13] Anthony Eden (Earl of Avon), 1897–1977. Prime Minister 1955–57.

Wednesday, 19 December
Rehearsed *Man Who Could Work Miracles*[14] with cast, including Tony Hancock, at the Piccadilly Studio.

Thursday, 20 December
Tony didn't do as well as I had anticipated. He failed to come up at the end, and I know it was because he didn't believe in what he was saying. If he is philosophically opposed to a script-idea, he doesn't seem to be able to perform it. He has got sincerity for life and sincerity for work hopelessly intermingled and merged.

Saturday, 22 December
Sandy Wilson party at 9'ish. Liz Welch was there. She is superb.

Monday, 31 December
Well it's been the most promising year really. The money has been good, and the work has come along, though in the theatre it's been pretty dull. It's been the year of living in my own place for the first time, and it's taught me the value of privacy – also the melancholy of living alone. To Hattie Jacques party for New Year In.

---

[14] By H.G. Wells. Adapted from the author's screenplay and produced for radio by Dennis Main Wilson. KW as Rev. Silas Maydig. Tony Hancock as George McWhirter Fotheringay. Cast including Dennis Price, Miriam Karlin, Hattie Jacques, Warren Mitchell, Alfie Bass.

1957

Tuesday, 1 January
Saw New Year in at Hattie Jacques party which was a splendid affair – with lots of room and some lovely people. I slipt away at 3 today and slept till 11'ish.

Saturday, 5 January
In afternoon saw Nora [Stapleton] and we called on the Faassens at Spencer Park. Then we went to Islington to Manzi's for pies & mash. Then to Collins Music Hall to see Peaches Page's Nude Show. It was crap. Hal Blue was the comic. Outrageous. The theatre is practically in ruins: the audience moronic. Alack a day.

Sunday, 20 January
Did the Hancock Show, about going back to nature and naked in the woods etc. Quite amusing. Tony has given me a book called *The Suez War*[1] – very good of him.

Tuesday, 29 January
Rose late, tired and dispirited. Made my will.

Monday, 4 February
Sherek telephoned asking me to take over Cliff Gordon's part in [*Under*] *Milk Wood.*[2] I refused on the excuse of lacking an authentic Welsh for the part. The Arts Theatre director Peter Wood rang asking me to play Kite the valet – very funny – in *The Wit To Woo*, which they are doing. But I have to think about *Venus Observed* which conflicts with Kite, and which I've already agreed to do.

Tuesday, 19 February
My first rehearsal for *The Wit To Woo*,[3] directed by Peter Wood, at the

---

[1] By Paul Johnson. Foreword by Aneurin Bevan.
[2] At the New Theatre. Cliff Gordon's main part had been Willy Nilly.
[3] By Mervyn Peake, KW as Kite.

Arts. I like him enormously. The cast includes Wensley Pithey, old friend from *Moby Dick*, and Colin Gordon whom I admire greatly, and George Howe!! and everybody. It's all v. nice. I feel wonderfully wonderful but distrust this elation and feel it will be short-lived. Think I have a cold coming.

Thursday, 21 February
Rushed from rehearsing to BBC for Hancock show, and found I'd hardly any part at all. James Robertson Justice in as Guest Artist! Couldn't bloody care less.

Monday, 25 February
Still this weight of misery dragging me down – it's in the guts of me – and the feeling of deadness permeates the body like a slow sweat and I am always near to tears. I'm more and more conscious of the total lack of reality for me, in this way of life; I imagined this would be dispelled as soon as I became involved in actual work again, but work is no longer able to ward it off. I am *aware all* the time now. My chattering becomes more and more strident, persistent and vacuous in a nervous attempt to cover up, and keep some sort of rhythm going. Systole and diastole.

Tuesday, 26 February
Rehearsals misery because of a boil coming up on my face. O! it's all a bit much. My back, my bum, my feet, my head. And now this! Surely death would be beautiful?

Tuesday, 12 March
The opening of *The Wit To Woo* at the Arts Theatre. I was so nervous.

Wednesday, 13 March
Got some very good notices for my performance last night.

Tuesday, 19 March
To Berman's at 2 o'c for costume for the Hancock TV series. Tyrolean. Should look rather good on me. I've the legs for it, let's face it.

Thursday, 28 March
To see the film *Giant*, with James Dean and Rock Hudson. It was so boring it was bathetic. Dean was rather bad. Rock was the same as ever, looking very concrete mixer, and Liz Taylor aged unconvincingly.

Saturday, 30 March
Rehearsed at TV Centre which is v. modern & pleasant. Then back to town for 2 shows at Arts.

Monday, 1 April
The television went off all right really. Though Tony seemed peculiarly nervous.

Tuesday, 2 April
Gordon [Jackson] came to tea. Burned my curtains with a cigarette! Outrageous. He is very charming though and laughed it off with aristocratic indifference.

Wednesday, 3 April
I can remember nothing really, about today. O! yes – I went up to Gording and did some digging in the garden. Agony, but enjoyed myself greatly.

Wednesday, 10 April
Rehearsed all day. To Dr Newman in evening about my bum. It appears there are 2 growths in the anal passage. He is going to treat them later, I have to contact him after 2 May.

Thursday, 11 April
Again that lowness, that depression. That longing for the end.

Sunday, 14 April
Wrote to Michael Harald to thank him for the wonderful letter he sent me, on my opening at the Arts. His faith in me, and his extraordinary perceptiveness about me personally has always been a source of great encouragement and comfort to me.

Monday, 15 April
Rehearsed all day at Riverside for the TV, and it went out at 8 o'c. Indifferent well. I was not good. Drinks after and supper with Tony & Cicely. [John] Vere got rather pissed as usual & became stupidly maudlin.

Wednesday, 17 April
In the evening to John Vere's for drinks with Tony & Cicely, and we were supposed to be at the Balfours'[4] by 9 o'c, and they kept drinking & sitting, so I got up and left for the Balfours alone. They eventually

---

[4] The actor Michael Balfour and his wife Minty.

arrived at the Balfours' at 11.15. I think that kind of behaviour is appalling. I stayed as long as politeness necessitated, and left with Gordon J. at 1 o'c.

Thursday, 9 May

Dinner with Elaine Tynan, Cyril Connolly, Elizabeth Wharton, Peter Wildeblood and Jill Bennett. A disastrous evening. The Agony continues

Monday, 13 May

Rehearsed all day. Transmission at night. Not bad. *The Waxworks Story.* I was the Polizei. Policeman. Ja. Drinks after. When I got back Gording rang up. He said I was good as the Polizei and v. TBH. Ja.

Tuesday, 14 May

To Dr Newman in evening. He says there is nothing more to worry about apropos the anal passage. He has prescribed some medicine and suggested panacea – trade. Interesting & not without foundation.

Monday, 10 June

Rehearsed all day, and transmitted at 7.30. I played an old dodderer of 80, with an ear trumpet. It was all rather bad. I have been poorly treated throughout these six episodes and had a chat with Tony. I don't think he wants me in the set-up in future. He thinks that 'set' characters make a rut in story routine – the only one he wants back in October is Sidney James. He is mad about him, and nowadays they go everywhere together. Obviously I won't be asked for the October series, so that's that: so much for the obligations of loyalty. Tonight's show was rather dull, I thought. I didn't have a drink with them after – just got the bus and came home, feeling rather sad about it all.

Tuesday, 11 June

With a bank balance down to ten pounds and nothing on the horizon that's definite (apart from the Waller play, and the Codron[5] revue) I am feeling vaguely apprehensive about the future.

Thursday, 13 June

To Cambridge Theatre to meet Eleanor Fazan who is to direct the revue thing. Told her how apprehensive I was, and she wasn't much help either. However, I've agreed to do the show now, so I'm stuck with it.

---

[5] Michael Codron, b.1930, theatrical producer.

Monday, 17 June
Broke lavatory basin in a mad zealous clean-up! Have tried to mend it with some glue. Do hope it works!

Tuesday, 18 June
Walked to the park where there was a fabulous gylrig[6] but not available I fancy. This lavatory repair hasn't worked at all. I must order a new one. O! the expense. Re-reading Thomas Mann – such a stream of understanding.

Thursday, 20 June
Popped into the news theatre in Piccadilly! – phew! the gylrig going on!

Monday, 24 June
Arrived Glasgow at 9.30. Went out to lunch with Baxter and an American. It was all right. In the evening took Moira to the cinema where she fell asleep.

Friday, 28 June
Couldn't stand another minute of this ill-fated visit, so left them in bed and rushed to the station where I bribed a porter to get me on the Royal Scot. Got into Euston 5.30. Wired them – 'Thanks everything, forgive sudden urge return Kenneth'. If they take offence at this, and don't wish to see me any more, it will probably be just as well. Phoned Dennis Price and spent amusing evening with him and went on to the Rouge et Noir.

Wednesday, 3 July
In the evening I saw a traditional piece in the opposite window. Went to the party with John Turner, David, and Herbert Siddens. When I got back I saw the traditional window piece more closely. Charming. James. Gylrig overtures. Religious discussion. Goodnight. Came back about one. To bed, took 4 pills and slept.

Thursday, 4 July
The James rang. It's all too bloody neurotic, can't even enter the block! impolitic etc. I gave up. He says we'll arrange something for tonight. I thought 'We won't y'know' but said all right. All the way

---

[6] Polari term used by KW to denote both a desirable person (this entry) and sexual activity (following entry). Elsewhere virtually synonymous with 'traditional' (3 July entry). The word evidently has its origin in backslang, being 'girl' or even 'girly' in reverse.

to Shepperton for an abortive interview with Henry Cornelius – whole thing ruined by Kenneth More who said I was too young! Fantasy. This actor's work has always struck me as being intrinsically vulgar. Anyway I loathe that entire film world.

Friday, 5 July
James Traditional rang. I fancy a bit piqued about my not being in last night, said he was off, and that he'd contact me when he was in London again. I said OK but I'm not madly keen. Really.

Sunday, 7 July
With David and Michael Hitchman to Southend by steamer. It was the bitter bloody end. Never again. Southend was ghastly. Returned by coach. Altogether an expensive day and ill spent. David came back with me to the flat and had something to eat. No tradition here tonight – I was furious. Reely.

Monday, 8 July
Gordon & Rona,[7] 7.30. – which was as delightful as ever. A sweeter [*sic*] most delectable pair whom I enjoy enormously. But forced myself to leave early because Gordon is filming. Gordon told me about the man swallowing a glass eye & the Doctor saying 'Reely! don't you trust me?'

Tuesday, 9 July
Bamber Gascoigne came to see me about the script for the revue. He talked gaily of this and that, but we accomplished nothing really.

Wednesday, 10 July
Met Bill I. at the cinema, and we spent the evening together. Abortive traditional and said goodnight at 12.30. He is an emotional type with too little altruism to compensate.

Saturday, 13 July
Rehearsed at the Lyric, Hammersmith for the revue.[8] I know nobody except Margaret Smith[9] whom I like v. much. There are others including Philip Gilbert who looks the full sheesh. Eleanor Fazan smiles engagingly, and makes one feel confidently jittery. Bamber Gascoigne is as charming as ever and quite the most delicious humour. I have

---

[7] Gordon Jackson and his actress wife Rona Anderson.
[8] *Share My Lettuce*, mostly written by Bamber Gascoigne.
[9] The future Dame Maggie Smith.

nothing v. much to do in the revue though, so all this talk about it being built round me is so much cock.

Tuesday, 6 August. Brighton
This Brighton period was not entered into the diary at the time it occurred. I was too ill or preoccupied to do it. Everything was ghastly. The evening audiences, small and unenthusiastic, the ridiculous and unending rehearsals which accomplished *nothing*.

Wednesday, 7 August
At rehearsals Fazan had hysterics and left stage. Codron burst on and shouted at us that we weren't cooperative, then Disley Jones (designer) charged Bamber Gascoigne with subversion and ordered him out of the theatre. What an incredible lot of amateurs I am among! What a crock of shit.

Monday, 12 August
From the window of this wretched hotel I saw a dog in the garden – it could only move with difficulty because of obvious dropsy, but wagged its tail incessantly, smelling about the plants etc. I was reminded of the show.

Wednesday, 21 August
V. good opening night, considering all this – they were a very lucky management, because it was only due to individual talent really. The curtains were fantastic. I walked off the stage, and the S/D shouted at me! for disobeying orders. I apologised in my fashion but said I would not take curtain calls to an audience that was leaving the theatre.

Thursday, 22 August
The notices are mixed. Some says I'm good, some that I'm affected!! Terribly funny really.

Saturday, 24 August
This entire *Share Lettuce* period remains appallingly unreal to me; I don't know why – I'm not clever enough to be able to analyse it, but I suppose it's because it has no intrinsic worth that I feel unreal. Like reading muck or comics for days and days, and days.

Sunday, 25 August
To see Margaret Vines and heard all about the break-up of her marriage with Denis [Goacher]. I felt ghastly and on the brink of tears so many times.

Friday, 30 August

I hear now that we move to the Comedy Theatre on the 24th September for about 3 months I bet. This transfer will not work.

Friday, 6 September

Show OK. Terence Rattigan came round to see me and said I was the funniest man in England!

Wednesday, 25 September

Opened at the Comedy to a v. mild house and it was a terrible show – electrics went wrong & the cast were all put off and lacking in confidence. It was terrible, & of course everyone there! Peter Brook – Binkie – J. Perry & all. O! how ghastly it all was.

Friday, 27 September

John Gielgud out front tonight. He said I was 'very droll'. Nice.

Wednesday, 2 October

Did the Kenneth Horne radio show[10] in morning and fluffed a line!! The script was by Eric Merriman and Barry Took. V. good.

Friday, 4 October

Codron & Disley came b/stage to say it was a lousy show and they're coming again tomorrow. In many respects they're right – just because I ad lib a bit, some of the idiots in this cast think they can do likewise.

Tuesday, 8 October

First day of film *Dick & The Duchess*[11] with Sheldon Reynolds out at MGM studios. It was fabulous – first time I've ever really enjoyed this medium since *Trent's Last Case* at Shepperton in '50!!

Wednesday, 23 October

Reh. in morning. Forgot the 5.30 show, went to sleep. Got there at 6 and they'd cancelled it! Went on at night as usual. Everyone very kind to me. Press came & everything.

Thursday, 24 October

The news is front page of Guardian & the Express – 2nd page of Mail, Herald & Sketch, Telegraph & Times! fabulous publicity. Went on television (BBC) at 6.25 tonight to describe it all. Did the show as

---

[10] 'Beyond Our Ken'.

[11] Filmed half-hour comedy series with Patrick O'Neal and Hazel Court.

usual and in the middle, in front of a full house, they gave me an alarm clock.

Tuesday, 29 October
I realise what a stinking deal I've had out of this show. The salary never amounts to more than 30 – and by the time commission comes off, that brings it to 27 and even with Hancock this represents a definite decline in earnings.

Saturday, 23 November
Maggie Smith coming to flat, & Peter Nichols. Then we're all invited to lunch with the Avery lads.[12] They are painters.

2 shows and I was extremely unpleasant to Philip G. This cruel streak must be controlled – it's something venomous that comes pouring out, even when I know it should stop. I think it's all bound up with sexual frustration.

Thursday, 28 November
Up at 6, and Corrigan drove me to Walton, where I play Tizio in *Sword of Freedom*[13] with Edmund Purdom for TV films. All very pleasant and convivial.

Monday, 2 December
I went to buy a television set – a McMichael portable for Louie and Charles, for Xmas.

Wednesday, 4 December
I hear we will transfer to the Duke of York's in January. I don't think this transfer will work. The show's finished by moving it around continually.

Sunday, 15 December
Television excerpt of *Share My Pisspot*, 7.30. Rehearse Shep. Bush Empire at 2 o'c. What a bloody futile business it all is.

As I predicted – it was a ghastly TV excerpt & we died a death. I did not tarry but flew from the studio with all speed back to the flat. Ugh!

Tuesday, 24 December
How hateful all this Xmas period is. How evil and fraudulent: how I

---

[12] Sam and Wilfred Avery.
[13] Adventure serial set in fifteenth-century Italy.

wish I did not have to see my family all the time; this is when I long to live in another country. This is the year in which I have become a 'name' in the profession. Leading in a West End show. Full page in Spotlight etc. Now one will see.

Wednesday, 25 December

It is Christmas morning. A clear bright one, but with the hint of cloud, & forecast of fog to come later. My bookcase for top of bureau has arrived and I suppose I will get used to it, in time. The noises from the next flat are as irritating as usual. Goodwill and consideration to all men. My flat is stuffed with Xmas cards. I am lunching at home, and going to Michael Harald's flat for the evening. I can't stay late, as I have 2 shows tomorrow. It is always this time of the year that I yearn for the thing which life has never given me – physical love: I suppose I'll get over it.

MEMORANDA

It's been a funny sort of year with Hancock, *Wit To Woo*, and *Lettuce* – certainly it's put me on the theatrical map – I got some rave notices and increased my prestige and earned less money than before!! It has taught me that the only way to keep one's position of authority in a cast is to be remote – I made the fatal mistake in *Lettuce* of being one of the 'team' but then I didn't know it was going to make me a celebrity. I haven't matured in any way – sexually I'm as juvenile as ever and unresolved – given a sign I would act on it but no signs come. Perhaps they will in '58.

1958

Thursday, 9 January
Michael Codron says he thinks I've got something on my mind! I didn't discuss it. I can't talk business to someone I know as a friend. All that's on my mind is the fact that I've held this show together on the same money as passengers in the company. Not an offer of an increase, or anything. I think it's shameful.

Friday, 10 January
The Codron Company have offered more money on condition I sign for the run of play & tour! This is dreadful.

Sunday, 12 January
Coffee in morning with Frank Jackson, John Turner and John H[ussey], all very pleasant. In the park afternoon with John Vere who has got over Asian flu, and he came back with me, for tea. In the evening to Freddie Carpenter and Ronnie Waters for dinner – their other guests were Stanley Hall and a grey-haired piece called Noel and Isabel Jeans.[1] The first two I knew, having met them before at George Rose's, but this Jeans woman was a new one on me. Completely Edwardian and clinging to all those dead values, a conception of theatre as ladies & gents stuff and galanterie and the 'old days' – and nobody rings me up now stuff all very pathetic, and all rather dull. She said of Nora Swinburne on TV, in *The Three Sisters*, or *The Cherry Orchard*, or something, 'Of course it would have been much too small in the theatre, but on that little screen, she was really charming – quite charming . . .' and it was this kind of faint praise that she indulged in all the evening. Then they all said Graham Payn[2] would be better off as an agent and I became angry and said what right had they to make such judgments and they all got rather tetchy. The grey-haired piece tried it on, in the car, coming home! Cheek.

---

[1] Senior leading lady, 1891–1985.
[2] b.1918. Noël Coward's lifelong friend, and a frequent performer of his work; later in charge of the Coward estate.

Saturday, 18 January

The cold is still raging, I have the sneezing & eyes watering all the time. After the two shows, I felt better but the voice almost vanished. To the Ken Tynan party at 120 Mount St It was quite fabulous: Gore Vidal, George Nader, Peter Brook, O! loads of fabulous people. I got too drunk and left about 2 o'c.

Wednesday, 29 January

Did the television, BBC, on 'Tonight' with Dilys Laye – 'Peter Patter' – and then rushed to the Garrick for the opening night of the transfer. It went very well considering, but I don't think it will last very long now. I fancy all this movement has rather killed it stone dead.

Sunday, 9 February

To John Vere for a meal and on to the BBC to Viewing Room to see Tony, in *Inspector General*,[3] in which he was superb.

Monday, 10 February

Doing the Hancock show, from the Paris Cinema today, at 10 o'c. Arrived at the Paris to find that the Snide character was *in* the script. When Tony arrived he said he was angry about it, and that it should go. He really believes that it is 'cartoon' and etc. etc. He has certainly gone down in my estimation. Every time he asks me if I mind, I have to say *no* because after all this fuss I'd feel *awful* doing the damned voice! And every single time, he says, in front of everyone, *and me*! – 'It's no good – it's a gimmick voice, and untrue to life . . .' It's a bad argument. O well – I suppose it's a compliment, in a way.

Tuesday, 11 February

9.30. I.B.C. studios. Did the commercials for Murray fruits. Over by eleven.

Wednesday, 12 February

Show went well in the evening. Meal with Ken M. and he came back after for a drink and traditional. Left about 2 o'c. I shall be tired tomorrow.

Friday, 14 February

Charles Laughton came to see the show, and visited me afterwards in the dressing room. He looked tired. We talked of this and that and he said 'I love California. My home is there – my man has been with me for 14 years, and the cook for eleven' and then 'I must bring Elsa

---

[3] By Nikolai Gogol, adapted by Barry Thomas. Hancock as Hlestakov.

(Lanchester)[4] to see this show – she would love it . . .' I said 'Will you really?' and he said 'Yes – it is a promise . . .'

Thursday, 20 February

Collected my cheque for the week, which, with Hancock and the TV *Lettuce*, is 108 pounds. Went to bank and placed it. Then to Halifax where I deposited 200, leaving 32 in current account. This means that I have now £1043 with Halifax: now I must save for the Income Tax in April and the Insurance, about 250 altogether. So now, for the first time, I really am worth a thousand – bit more actually, if I count the M & G shares, but only a hundred or so.

Sunday, 2 March

To Paul Mead party. Traditional Paul F. Charming. Succey de bede [*sic*].

Monday, 3 March

Paul F. stayed overnight and went off this morning about 8.30. He is a sweet fellow of whom I'm inordinately fond.

Monday, 17 March

R.T. brought Edward Seago,[5] the painter, round. We all had dinner afterwards – the drinks in S. flat. Traditional worries. O dear!

Wednesday, 2 April

Out to Pinewood to do practice drilling with a CSM of the Queen's for the film *Carry On Sergeant*.[6]

Monday, 7 April

[P.] F. came round after, to say it was all over – we parted. Probably just as well.

Wednesday, 9 April

Filming at Pinewood. Lot better than last time! Funny how things change completely. It is much more pleasant. *The Seekers* was hateful! How awful everything and everyone was then! Bob Monkhouse is sensitive and kind, Ken Connor is v. amusing, and Norman Rossington a good fellow. The director is Gerry Thomas. V. charming.

---

[4] His wife.

[5] 1910–74. Specialist in East Anglian and seashore subjects.

[6] First of the series: script by Norman Hudis, based on the play *The Bull Boys* by R.F. Delderfield.

Friday, 18 April
Filming all day. 2 shows at the Garrick.

Sunday, 4 May
Did the Hancock show. It went very badly. The scripts seem to get worse & worse. There was a time when Tony would have complained. He seems quite happy with them. They are terrible. This one was a load of inconsequential rubbish about rubbish. Hardly a joke anywhere.

Thursday, 8 May
Went to see Orson Welles in *Touch of Evil* – Joseph Cotten played a Police Doctor in a minute role. Heavily disguised with crepe hair. But I was on to him straightway.

Friday, 9 May
The show was terrible last night, and then Roy Rich came round!! – charming. Said he wanted me for a television thing at Southampton, Aug. 24. So I said I was interested, and he will contact Peter Eade. This is the man who wrote that outrageous letter to Eade, saying he didn't think I could act.

Saturday, 17 May
Last performance of *Share My Lettuce*. A wonderful last night house – not mad & hysterical but properly enjoying themselves. I made a wee speech at the end, and felt very serious and sentimental and sad.

Sunday, 25 May
It seems hardly credible now, that I was ever in *Share My Lettuce* – to have wasted all that time – O! it's fantastic – the entire period, unconnected and unreal. This last year has been nightmarish & confusing. Now, here I am, contemplating a holiday in Jersey! – for the first time in my life! I can't believe I am really going! This week will be fraught for me. The murder of anticipation.

Monday, 16 June
Philips studio, Stanhope Pl. A Murraymint adv. – me as a clerk – Aylmer. And Ken Connor – we had lunch after. The judge was played by Bernard Bresslaw who is a sort of huge Juda Moron on 'The Army Game'.[7] Seems nice enough.

---

[7] TV sitcom in uniform, 1957–62. Bresslaw had the catchphrase 'I only arsked.'

Monday, 7 July
Went to Bermondsey for traditional interest and it was quite fabulous.

Friday, 11 July
Dining with P.S. P.F. was there. It begins again. I am so beyond coping that I'm just letting things go. He came back to the flat. Same old argument, friendships not traditional, no succey de bede.

Monday, 14 July
Stan Walker & Terry, coming for a drink. Also P. – how this is going where it's going etc. – I simply don't know.
It finished tonight.

Sunday, 20 July
Lunch Stanley Walker, 12.30, at the lunch I met Malcolm. O! God. Same thing all over again. All bloody hopeless. Why the agony? Why me? this mortal coil is torture. Bloody torture

Monday, 21 July
Rehearsal Palladium at 2 o'c. Met Jeremy Brett and Dan Massey. They're in the number. All v. pleasant.

Tuesday, 22 July
Malcolm rang, and came round to see me; it was very pleasant, and we discussed poetry, and read some of 'J. Alfred Prufrock'[8] together. He is a delightful person in every way – a sense of honour – rare today – humour, and diligence. We're going out to dinner tomorrow.

Thursday, 24 July
'[The Night of a] Hundred Stars', Palladium tonight. Went off wonderfully for me. A terrific reception when I went on, in 'Bubble Man'[9] with the green suit.

Sunday, 27 July
Malcolm came over – we all went into the country and M. read some poetry & excerpts from Fry beautifully. He is an incredible boy. We talked for a long time after – he doesn't reciprocate fully. I suppose to expect it would be miraculous. The problem at the moment is the modus vivendi – he must be working with a purpose – at the moment he feels anchorless, and futile. Perhaps property is the answer.

---

[8] 'The Love Song of J. Alfred Prufrock' (1917), by T.S. Eliot.
[9] The first-half closer from *Share My Lettuce*.

Tuesday, 29 July
MORNING 'Beyond Our Ken'. AFTERNOON 'Time Out For Peggy'.[10] Malcolm called and we talked. The more I see him, the better it is. We talked of property and he seems to like the idea – it is constructive and would make for a purpose.

Saturday, 9 August
Malcolm called. We rowed over the traditional business, and it was all ghastly. C'est finis. C'est finis . . .

Sunday, 10 August
Peter E. gave me a lift. I told him the biz was over. He was q. understanding.

Tuesday, 19 August
To see the TV film of 'Time Out For Peggy' – it was very good. I did an appearance with Graham Stark.

Tuesday, 2 September
Read thru in the afternoon of *The Noble Spaniard**[11] – I can see it's a crock of shit.

*Margaret Rutherford, Maxine Audley. Directed by Adrian Brown. [*KW annotation*]

Sunday, 14 September
Malcolm called & it all started!! I got away with a few minutes, with his threat of phoning again!

Sunday, 21 September
D. rehearse & transmit *Noble Spaniard*. Never more glad that anything was finished before in my life. Utterly sickening. Dinner after with Maxine which was charming.

Wednesday, 24 September
Broadcast of 'Beyond Our Ken' went very well & I sang some 20's numbers, as a send-up of Bobby Beamish.

Thursday, 25 September
Read the script of *Carry On Nurse* and it's OK. Took it back to Eade. John Vere coming to tea, then we see the Presley picture *King Creole*.

---

[10] Granada TV series starring Billie Whitelaw.
[11] By Somerset Maugham. For BBC TV. KW played Captain Chalford.

Thursday, 9 October
Peter Eade evening. A very pissy affair. Dinner at Belle Etoile & I got rather tight. On the traditional trail evening. Utterly neg.

Sunday, 12 October
These October days – despite afternoon rain, and drear, are sunny and beautiful. I can't remember the month being as lovely as this. Sometimes it's exactly like spring. John H. and I to the Clarendon and Ham'smith for lunch. Very good. To the British Museum in afternoon. The Roman sculpting section – splendid – that wonderful head of Hadrian in purple stone.

Monday, 13 October
Went to see film *Man Upstairs*, very good really. The police were shown as the rotten & corrupt lot they really are. There was a send-up of an Army officer though that was absurd. Adrian Brown in the evening. Pleasant evening & drinks after in a club where I met ein grenade. Traditional. Worked. First time.

Friday, 17 October
Chas & Louie went to look at those flats I found in Rousden St. They found they liked one on the 1st floor. I've sent off the chq. for £225 being ten per cent of the total cost for 99 [year] lease. It will cost me all my capital but it will ensure them of a place to live at low annual cost.

Wednesday, 29 October
The radio script wasn't as good as last week – some lame tags, but it went very well. Feel in a strangely reflective and autumnal mood this afternoon – Dvorak on the radio, the October fog coming down – at 5 o'c. it is too dark to see without electricity – and I am thinking wonderful possibilities – I could write a play, I could be a mad success – (the kind that *I* believed in myself) – but apart from all that, I am grateful for Louie & Charles and some fine friends. Dear J. – and Hitchmanya – and Johnny V. and Nora . . . there have been some wonderful experiences, a lot of warmth – affection – and loyalty . . .

Tuesday, 4 November
Dinner at Wallas's with several people. Noel T. was there. Like a general omnibus. Like a page of Chaucer. I wonder. O I don't want to go thro' the same abortive routine. Why fall?

Wednesday, 5 November
Filming *Carry On Nurse* afternoon – lots of old pals – Terry Longdon,

Ken Connor, Leslie Phillips, Cyril Chamberlain. It was all delightful.

Monday, 10 November

Card from Noel, written on way to Airport. It made my day.

Filming all day at Pinewood. Postcard from Noel made my evening too. Re-reading it.

Friday, 14 November

Saw rushes of the love scene today. They are very good I think. Both Rogers & Gerry T. congratulated me.

Sunday, 23 November

Did the Hancock show from the Piccadilly. It was a general disaster. Really terrible. This team is so dreary to me now! – how different to the jolly warmth of 'B[eyond] O[ur] K[en]' – this crowd, esp. James & Hancock, are so listless and disinterested and their conversation is real pleb stuff. I don't care for any of them at all.

Wednesday, 26 November

Saw Noel in evening and we went to Etoile for dinner. Very pleasant. He gave me a pencil which is lovely. I feel so inarticulate.

Wednesday, 3 December

Up at 6.30 for Pinewood call. Out there all day and never in one shot. Outrageous.

Thursday, 4 December

Rehearsing at 10.30.[12] Wig Creations. The hats are murder, must stop them someway.

Sunday, 7 December

Worked on the Xmas cards. I realise I've ordered too many. 150 would have been enough.

Thursday, 18 December

Reh. in morning for cuts. Opening Night – fair. Louie & Charles, Kaufmanns, Mabel & Gran came round & we all had drinks. Pouring rain but we got a taxi.

Monday, 22 December

With Louie to see about a flat. It will be OK once it's done up. It is at Queen Alexandra Mansions.

---

[12] For *Cinderella*, KW and Ted Durante as the Ugly Sisters.

Monday, 29 December
Noël Coward came to my dressing room after the matinée. He said 'You were wonderful – such a dreadfully vulgar walk.' I said I'd been cut *dreadfully* and he replied 'My dear, put it all back – *gradually*. If I know you – you will . . .'

NOTES
It is funny to look back on 1957 writing and see what I wrote then about myself. All is much the same now, as it was then. Sexually, still unresolved, professionally in the middle and not quite defined, and spiritually – mercurial. Of course there is some progress indicated. I am out of the *Lettuce* revue rut of private jokes and no money. I have done 2 films this year, *Carry On Sergeant* and *Carry On Nurse*. Quite a bit of television, and this *Cinderella* production at the Coliseum – for the first time in my profession I am earning over 100 pounds a week & I feel I'm working for it! I learned last year that in order to obtain respect in a cast you must achieve a certain degree of remoteness. In this company, I have not practised that – so I'm still making exactly the same mistakes. Here I am, in the West End, working with Tommy Steele – a teenage rock'n'roll idol who is very kind and good – Jimmy Edwards who is a sensitive, charming man, and Bruce Trent who is a kind but dull man, Yana, a singer who is considerate and pretty – produced by Fred Carpenter who is loyal & hard-working – not really much to complain about . . .

1959

Thursday, 1 January
Spent New Year's Eve with the Jacksons at Hampstead. Rushed up there by taxi and it was obviously not my night. Just wanted a quiet drink and to wish them a happy N. Year. Instead, they played games. I ordered a taxi for 1 o'c. When it arrived Rona paid the driver to leave. I was rather irritated by it all, and walked away down Heath Drive without speaking to Gordon. I had to walk for a long way before I got a taxi. Got home at five to two. I shall not write to them. Not an auspicious beginning!

Saturday, 3 January
On taking a bath, discovered infection! So of course I was up half the night cleansing it all! This sort of thing makes me feel sick inside. Frank J. gave me some stuff that is for disinfecting called emulsion of Benzyl Benzoate.

Thursday, 8 January
Dinner after the show with Edward Seago. He is *so* selfish really. Kept me up till 1.30. I felt so tired & irritated.

Friday, 9 January
Edward Seago had left in my dressing room some pills for sleeping, and a recording of Schumann's *Fantasiestücke* – I've got it already, but this is infinitely superior to my own. Wrote a letter of thanks to him.

Saturday, 10 January
Letter from Basil Hodges, recalling *The Rose and the Ring,*[1] my first role – in drag – and the present role in Cinderella – in drag. I suppose I can say now that the wheel has turned its full cycle. Properly, now I should leave the stage: I am thinking more and more of getting out of this wretched country with its awful climate – there must be somewhere else that's pleasant to live in . . .

---

[1] By W.M. Thackeray. KW played Princess Angelica at Manchester Street School.

Friday, 6 February
Lunch with Louie. To theatre for 2 performances. One more week and the 2 a day is finis.

Sunday, 22 February
Came back to the flat, and played *Carnaval* – O! what is the mystery of Schumann? – these exquisite sounds that seem to convey a message – for me – such an ecstasy of spiritual feeling – such tentative tenderness that brings tears to my eyes . . . what a gracious soul . . . I am so grateful for Schumann and to the novel that introduced me to *Fantasiestücke* and to Rudi for telling me of *Carnaval*,[2] and to Gordon for giving me the concerto . . .

Tuesday, 24 February
Lunched at Shearns, then to Odeon Leic. Sq. where it was great tradition with fantastic outcome. Cup of tea after & home.

Wednesday, 4 March
'Beyond Our Ken' – every Wednesday, Paris [Studio, formerly Cinema, Lower Regent Street]. 9–12 rehearse. 12–1.15 transmit. Till May 20th.

Did the broadcast from the Paris OK. It was indifferent well. Ron Moody is dropped! and replaced by Bill Pertwee. Negative. Pity to break up a team in this way.

Monday, 9 March
Started filming *Carry On Teacher* at Pinewood. Funny feeling. I expected more warmth on the set. Everyone seemed a bit withdrawn – nice enough, but withdrawn – perhaps it's just the first day.

Saturday, 11 April
Gave last two performances. The usual sentimental rubbish – I got out of the theatre as quickly as possible. Got taxi home with all the stuff. Tommy S. gave me a beautiful miniature German camera.

Tuesday, 14 April
Pinewood 5, for party, end of film. Got rather drunk and behaved stupidly with some electrics and said to meet here on Sat. Of course I shall have to be out.

Wednesday, 15 April
To Harrow for dinner with Gerry Thomas & Peter Rogers. All went

---

2 'Fantasiestücke', Op.12. 'Carnaval', Op.9.

off splendidly. I spoke to Gerry T. about the revue. If I want to, I can do it. We all went to Ken Connor house after. Really delightful.

Saturday, 18 April

When I arrived at the block the electrics (14.4.59) was waiting, in a car with 2 others. I took him aside and paid him off – ostensibly for petrol – for 3 pounds and left. He was good enough to say he would forget the stupidity of Tuesday's conversation in front of the chauffeur.

Wednesday, 22 April

Did B'cast in morning. Flew to Hamburg afternoon, via Düsseldorf. Arrived Continental Hotel. Q. good. Meal & bed.

Thursday, 23 April

Explored town, very beautiful with Venetian-like canals all thro' it. After lunch to Lübeck with the magnificent Cathedral – now practically restored.

Friday, 24 April

Terry arrived in Hamburg. We toured all over town & went round the harbour etc. In the evening to the bar – Stadtcasino where it is all gylrig & fun. Traditional evening for me.

Friday, 1 May. London

I feel so much better now – that cloud over me before I went to Germany was ghastly lowering. The change of environment was v. good for me. Went out on the bike & crashed it into a car. Took it to Freeman who mended puncture etc. My ankle is bashed though, so bandaged it.

Thursday, 7 May

A glorious warm sunny day. To the Coop. Perm. to deposit. I've now got to the limit of £5000. Of course this may look dazzling but it contains next year's Income Tax! – which will be at least half, I'm sure. Went to vote at Malet St.

Friday, 8 May

The result of the vote is that the Tories have got in! They now control St Pancras! So that's got rid of all those Red Flag merchants who have queened it so arrogantly & for so long.

Saturday, 9 May

To see John Vere at Weybridge. It was not very pleasant. He has developed a stutter, and trembles violently at times & the old quality of gaiety has gone. Instead he is now old-maidish and waspish in turn, suddenly lunging into real viciousness which is horrible: it's largely turned on for the vulnerable. I felt like giving him a good kick up the arse I was so angry. But of course we had to smile and laugh it off. The so-called mentally sick get away with murder.

Monday, 11 May
Purchased telephone-bed table from Catesby's. Ordered 500 'with compliments' slips for sending photographs to fans.

Thursday, 21 May
Hitchman & I, to see *Some Like It Hot* – which was really hilariously funny, with the most brilliant tag I've heard in any film. It is a man proposing to a man in drag.

Thursday, 28 May
Philip G. called for me about 1 o'c. and we left for the West Country in his Sunbeam Rapier.

Friday, 29 May
Left Sidmouth for Cornwall. Lunching at Plymouth at Goodbody's – v. good. Then on to Mousehole in Cornwall. A gorgeous little old harbour with a wall originally built by the Phœnicians. We stayed at the Ship Inn. I was known and it was all v. embarrassing. In the evening we met 2 local lads in the bar – Colin & Dudley and after went to their houses for tea & drinks etc.

Saturday, 30 May
Left Mousehole around 10.00 and headed for Land's End which looked wonderful in the brilliant sunlight, also Porthcurno Bay. Really beautiful – then up the northern coast of Cornwall all the way to Newquay where we stay at the Atlantic. Dinner at the Fort restaurant. Funny to be back here, it has changed greatly.

Sunday, 31 May
On to Tintagel which was *fabulous*. Here one can really understand the Arthurian legend.

Monday, 1 June
Left Dulverton, Somerset, at about 10, arrived at Porlock Bay around 11.30 having climbed Dunkery Beacon on the way – my ears singing with pain from wind and height. Sunbathed for about 1 hour. On to Minehead for lunch, and then on to Glastonbury where we saw the ruins of the Abbey, sad in the afternoon sun. Then to London, via

Marlborough & Basingstoke. Arrived flat about 9.30. It was an excellent holiday, but Philip is really a bit of a drag after a while. It's all high flown and etc. but I had to do everything – except drive – which he did handsomely.

Sunday, 7 June

The Hancock series. This started again today after all the talk from Tony about never returning to sound. The script is now geared for Bill & Sid as stalwarts of Tony – good character stuff, and no one else. Hattie Jacques is dropped completely. I was given an innocuous part in one, and a 'spot' in the other, but neither of them worth anything artistically. I think that I am quite superfluous now, & I will telephone Peter tomorrow to get me out of the rest of the series. There is no point in my working in this set-up any more. Also the atmosphere of Kerr, Sid James etc. is utterly stultifying for me – there is simply no point of contact – their world is totally alien to mine, and they & me are better apart.

Friday, 12 June

Letter from John Vere, asking for £100 – I sent it off by return post.

Saturday, 13 June

To Michael Codron at 1 o'c. Lunched with him. He has found some v. good material from a boy called Peter Cook from Cambridge. It sounds excellent. To a party at Neil someone's flat, I got v. drunk.

Sunday, 14 June

Traditional Australian night so woke heavy & full of misgiving.

Sunday, 28 June

In the evening – an abortive dinner party at Hugh Paddick's. There was a Canadian there. Every time you ask them why they like this country they say things like 'So cultural over here . . . so tolerant and cosmopolitan – not bigoted . . .' etc., all *so* untrue. This is a country where Art has never been taken seriously, where bigotry flourishes, and where 'tolerance' is a device to cover a multitude of sins – most of which are based on laziness & stupidity. What these people really mean is that they find more sympathetic queens in London than they did in provincial Canadian cities. What the hell has this to do with culture?

Monday, 13 July

To Bournemouth by car, with Goachers, and spent day with John V.

It was all very successful. Met a trade friend and reconnoitred. V. interesting.

Friday, 24 July

To Aldwych 4 o'c. met Paddy Stone and Peter Cook and Tony Walton. Director, Writer & Designer of the revue. Seems OK. I suggested they call it *Up Your Sleeve.*[3] To Richmond to see the [Robert] Bolts. V. interesting evening.

Monday, 27 July

Daisy[4] died at 4.15 today – comatose – Edith with her – Louie went to telephone and when she returned to the ward, she had gone. It is the first time Death has been brought home to me. The things about me here in the flat, that Daisy made for me – the ornaments – and Clifford – terrible loneliness. I feel very empty and wept to learn of it. I kept thinking of the time Daisy & I went to Romford Market together – she was making me some curtains – she was so sunny & gay that day.

Friday, 31 July

To Daisy's funeral at Hornchurch Crematorium. The cortege passed thro' all the lanes where we used to walk with her when she was so alive – so happy – and that made me cry. There is no real answer to the life of suffering, or unreasonable death . . . it just remains a mysterious, illogical fact . . .

Sunday, 2 August

Met Barry, Corporal – RASC at Woolwich – delightful fellow and traditional conversationalist, we talked all night.

Tuesday, 4 August

First rehearsal of revue. King George Hall, 2.30. A depressing start, in keeping with tradition. Paddy Stone – excellent director – force, energy and imagination, and obv. capable of authority. Fenella [Fielding] & I did lines, & she keeps on apologising for not having characterised fast enough. She'll be OK.

Monday, 10 August

I gave Peter Cook idea for a foreign food sketch which he has written brilliantly.

---

[3] They called it *Pieces of Eight*.

[4] KW's aunt.

Tuesday, 11 August
They've given me another Pinter sketch – a bomb man & a recruit, being kitted out. Quite funny but murder to learn. Rehearsed all day. Learned at night – the humidity and heat appal me.

Monday, 17 August
Rehearsal 10 o'c. Only worked spasmodically. Largely on 'Mardi Gras' which is a sort of fuckabout with balloons. It is quite awful.

Wednesday, 19 August
Gordon & Rona, Sam, and that Canadian Boy to dinner @ 7'ish. Everything went well at dinner party, La Belle Etoile. Afterwards the Canadian Kenneth M. came back & did everything before announcing at the eleventh hour that he wasn't traditionalist. A dreary & sodden conclusion to an otherwise delightful evening.

Saturday, 22 August
M. Codron gave all company a drink in the Horseshoe. Fenella burst into tears on Paddy's shoulder because she thinks nothing has been written for her in the show. She's really furious about Myra De Groot having about 8 numbers to sing! I don't really blame her either. There isn't a man in the show who has *one* number. It's v. wrong.

Sunday, 23 August
Slept afternoon, with fearful dreams: dreams about the opening, and buns being covered with thick cream – all horribly & screamy.

Monday, 31 August. Oxford
Curtain up at 7.25. I hang above flies while cast do the opening & then descend on a wire. It was unadulterated agony. The audience was wonderful. They behaved charmingly throughout. There were quite a few vultures from London but I didn't care reely. Drink afterwards from the management. I received about 50 telegrams.

Sunday, 6 September
Entrained Oxford 11.55. Arrived Liverpool at 5.45'ish. Staying Adelphi – a dreary mausoleum – British Railways.

Monday, 7 September
A disastrous opening with everything going wrong. Went to the Press Club afterwards and got v. tight with all the critics.

Tuesday, 8 September
The press this morning is marvellous.

Wednesday, 9 September
Abortive rehearsals continue. I loathe everything about this rotten stinking show.

Monday, 14 September. Brighton
Travelled to B'ton on the Belle. Performance in evening frightful. House full of sycophantic queens.

Sunday, 20 September
I continually worry about how London will take this revue. I pretend that I am prepared for a flop – but secretly I'm frightened of one – and at the same time equally frightened of a mediocre success! And this first night gaggle of hangers on that flood the dressing room – ugh! and the dread of sycophantic laughter which generally only succeeds in antagonising the rest of the house. I pray for Thurs. when it will all be over.

Monday, 21 September
Fabulous to see my name in lights over the theatre in Shaftesbury Ave.![5] It is v. thrilling for me.

Wednesday, 23 September
Opening night – v. tricky, funny sort of house. Crowd backstage after. I felt empty inside and knew I hadn't been very good.

Thursday, 24 September
The notices are mixed – just the same as *Lettuce* – the same old hints at queerness & affectation – but the Standard is excellent – John Mortimer – calls me a genius! The Mail is good too. Bernard Levin in the Express gives it an absolute stinker! O dear o dear. I'm so depressed – this pile trouble is back again & goodness knows what I shall do. I wish I was dead: I am so sick of everything.

Did a television interview for ITV news, with Fenella. Lark about! Home to Louie for tea. Then to theatre – audience was wonderful. Home to bed about 12.30 after supper with Minnie (Coliseum show) and slept till 8.30! feel better.

Wednesday, 30 September
I turned down the Wilcox film which was 100 a day! I am too tired to cope with that.

---

[5] At the Apollo Theatre.

Friday, 2 October
Decided to move into John H.'s flat. Have set the wheels in motion to sell Endsleigh Court: the sooner I get out of this block, the better. If it doesn't work at John's I will have to find somewhere else. Anyway, *now* I must make the move, or dither in this frightful dump for ever.

Wednesday, 7 October
Moved into 66 Alex., feel much better now I'm out of Endsleigh.

Thursday, 8 October
Went to University College with John H. to vote. Tory. Show went OK. Election results coming in thick & fast. All v. exciting. Tory gains all the time. Labour is going to be crushingly defeated – perhaps that will teach them that the people don't want that outmoded form of socialism.

Tuesday, 20 October
Painted the fireplace in lounge. Very nice. The flat is beginning to look better now. Sir Malcolm Sargent[6] came round to see me after the show, with several friends. All very grand.

Monday, 26 October
The bum is murder again. I really can't stand much more of this you know.

Saturday, 31 October
Went all the way to Lime Grove to see a film sequence for the Julie Andrews show: it turned out to be the wrong print. This script was promised me for Tues. Then Thurs. Then today. I still haven't got it.

Sunday, 1 November
I wrote a stinking letter to Eade and to Michael Codron. I wrote to Eade apropos my not being shoved into the Julie Andrews Show, and to Codron about Fielding. Her pauses are becoming a joke and never hold anyway. I've written asking him to help. If nothing good comes of it, I shall go into hospital after the film and have this operation.

---

[6] 1895–1967, Chief Conductor of the BBC Symphony Orchestra 1950–57, Conductor-in-Chief of the Promenade Concerts 1957–67.

Monday, 9 November
First day filming.[7] The location is a dreary house in Ealing. Water dripping everywhere. Rain pouring down. Charming. And me bum not v. pleasant. Show in evening, drear.

Thursday, 12 November
Filming all day. Fog so bad in evening that my car didn't get to Apollo till 8 o'c.!!! You couldn't see an inch ahead! Packed house & lovely audience.

Friday, 13 November
Filming till 6 o'c. so the understudy did the 1st house.

Saturday, 14 November
Rehearsal notice for the company on the board. I told Jack Hanson that it was in my contract that no reh. were to be called without my permission. He said he didn't know about that! I am not going to rehearse this show any more.

Thursday, 26 November
Filming all day, Pinewood. Show in evening average. The Queen have done a splendid article on me and sent me a copy. Excellent photo by Armstrong-Jones.[8]

Saturday, 5 December
'B.O.K.' 9 o'c. Paris. 2 shows OK.

Friday, 18 December
Finished film & post synch. 1st show at Apollo. Missed the 1st house. 2nd v. rowdy. Party after, on stage. OK. Home 1.30. V. drink [*sic*]

Thursday, 24 December
Got all the presents for the company. Got two lovely silver dishes for Michael Codron – engraved etc. – and lovely cup & saucer for every member of the coy. The show in evening was mediocre.

Saturday, 26 December
Walked thro' the city – it was quiet and raining, really lovely.

Monday, 28 December
Wandered about South London with John H. Show in evening was

---

[7] *Carry On Constable.*
[8] Antony Armstrong-Jones, later the Earl of Snowdon.

quite fabulous. It went like a bomb and was packed out. Codron is to give the coy. a 10% bonus every time they take 2,800 in the week. Worth nothing to me, but it's a charming gesture I think.

Thursday, 31 December

The best thing I did for someone else in '59 was to buy Louie her fur coat – a Siberian Squirrel. And she looks lovely in it.

1960

Friday, 1 January
Well, last year was v. prosperous I suppose, and if we do as well in '60, we'll be all right. The days are becoming more and more unreal. I really don't know what I'm doing. I am by nature an organiser, but I've nothing to organise. I just flit from one bit of rubbish to another, overacting myself silly: but I've made some money – and given away a good proportion of it – a half – the rest set by for tax. My only big possessions – gramophone and desk. The best thing I did for myself in '59 was leaving Endsleigh Court.

Monday, 4 January
Quite a panic in the theatre, because Myra De Groot has vanished. Of course I knew she would go to Berchtesgaden to follow her lover. The understudies coped all right and everything went OK.

Tuesday, 5 January
Lunch at 135 with Louie, and we had quite a chat after. She is to go and have a tooth extracted at 3 o'c. today, so I must ring from theatre and find out how it went – poor Louie! She's like me – can't stand pain.

Monday, 11 January
Went after a flat in St James St. Unfortunately no bathroom or lav. otherwise perfect. But at 350 ex. a year, I think one should have a lavatory. John H. and Cedric Messina to supper after show. It all went very well – duck, champagne and giant prawns to begin. C.M. went on and on about Venice – 'You get out of the train, smell the water, and you start to cry . . .' We all agreed, & nodded in a state of drunken euphoria.

Friday, 15 January
The last capital repayment on *Pieces of Eight* was sent me today – so now the total investment in the show has been repaid. I'm very glad about this. Faith in me as a revue lead has been justified and investors

have been rewarded, and they will make a bit, if the weather doesn't ruin everything.

Monday, 18 January
When I came down on the wire tonight, I dried!! It was quite fantastic.

Tuesday, 19 January
I was supposed to take R. West to dinner, but cancelled it all, because he wanted to bring a dog with him.

Wednesday, 20 January
Lunch with Philipe G. We went to see *West Side Story*, all very modern and 'free' – but the same old formulae. The impressive thing is the new 'form' it's been given. But O dear there's not one really big personality in the whole set-up. It's all wistful littleness. The aggression is not conveyed except in a stagey way, and the pathos, therefore, doesn't quite work either. Consequently all the good 'ensemble' work comes as a successful & welcome relief. Production sound, sets v. real, and music – all too derivative & lacking real melody. No voices to put it over, either.

Thursday, 21 January
Lunch Michael Codron, and the American Mr Cohen,[1] who wants me to do this show in New York. This man wanted me to star with Diana Dors in New York! I said a very firm no thank you. Really! – outrageous these Americans.

Wednesday, 27 January
The show in evening went well, till Madam decided to ad lib one line before the tag in 'Spies'. Of course it threw me completely. This is the last straw. I've reported it to the S/D – and the office and from now on I just behave with politeness – for the rest – she's had it.

Thursday, 28 January
I didn't speak to her at all. Just did my job. In the middle of the spy sketch she broke down and had hysterics, tears etc. Codron came b/ stage with David S[utton].[2] We talked about it & the long & s. of it is, I have to make a rapprochement. You can't win.

Friday, 29 January
To meet Robin T. for lunch. I told him everything & was politely &

---

[1] Probably Alexander H. Cohen (b. 1920). American producer.
[2] Later General Manager of Michael Codron Ltd.

firmly rebuffed. I think I always knew in my heart that this would happen. Made up with Fenella.

Wednesday, 3 February
Visited Park West & viewed a flat, no. 76. Which I like. I saw *Ben Hur* with Terry Theobald and it was all very lush – utterly bad of course, but they got away with it all. The Crucifixion scene was very embarrassing for me. I can't believe in this sort of thing as entertainment.

Thursday, 4 February
The BBC have come thro' with the April offer of 'B.O.K.' – I'm not really very keen on doing it. Must make sure that it doesn't conflict with filming.

Saturday, 6 February
Lunch Michael Codron. 1 o'c. He suggested a television excerpt from the show. I said I wanted to leave it. He seemed rather shocked, but one never quite knows how much M. has really bargained for anyway. I feel at the moment that I would like very much to get out of this in March.

Wednesday, 17 February
Met Terry Theobald and we went to Hackney to see film *Scarface Mob*. The cinema was freezing & an usherette came up to me and said 'Are you Kenneth Williams' so I said 'No, of course not'. Lot of send-ups from Teds who shouted 'Carry On Nurse'.

Thursday, 18 February
Trade show *Carry On Constable*, Studio One. 10.30. With Peter E. It was mediocre & tired. I think everyone knew it. On to the Mirabelle for drinks and chatted with Kenneth Connor. He is without doubt the loveliest character of all. Must write him a note, to take it easy. He looked so tired and strained. Supper at the Caprice. Sherek said 'There's that clever actor Kenneth Williams: at least he says so' and I said 'I do, too' and walked on. The silly old barstard.

Friday, 19 February
The new Prince was born today. Now 2 male heirs to the throne. 2 shows. Cicely Courtneidge in the box laughing like a mad hyena & giving a better performance than anything on the stage.

Saturday, 20 February
Phil Berger of Park West came to the show & after we all went to the Ivy. He paid. It was a great crashing bore of an evening and some

terrible girl with him kept crying out with a Lancashire accent 'Ooh! your expressions on the stage!! I've never seen such expressions . . . !'

Sunday, 21 February

To the Easthams at County Oak. Quite lovely day – Margaret Leighton was quite delightful & we walked down country lanes with some terrible local children who were very funny & we went on swings and Margaret said it was unbelievable that I was 34! All v. lovely.

Monday, 22 February

Give notice to leave company in March.[3]

Staying on for another 3 months. Went to Park West. All the electric stuff is delivered. That's OK. The carpet is down & will be completed by Tuesday.

Wednesday, 24 February

Moved today. Freeborn's were excellent. Everything went well. Louie was wonderful. Thank goodness that's over.

Sunday, 6 March

Bolts. Tea. 4 o'c. Bob Bolt tells me he has an idea for a play for me. It sounds marvellous.

Tuesday, 8 March

Lunch. J. was there. Never was she more futile and boring. 'I just don't want to mix or be friends with coloured people . . .' O dear! She's certainly not depriving them of anything!

Thursday, 17 March

To see *400 Blows* at Curzon. Story of an unwanted child who is sent to remand home. Quite searing & beautifully done. No one allowed to indulge in humanity – the director firmly on the side of the child. Brilliant picture.

Tuesday, 29 March

When I met Stanley he said he'd heard thro' Fenella Fielding that I had loathed the play etc. etc. So that was what really set the whole thing in motion. Of course I just had to crawl out of the impasse on my hands and knees. He came back to the flat after, and we chatted of this and that: but this is really no good at all. Our relationship is continually marred by these incidents and a very shaky ship gets buffeted all over the shop. I'm very fond of the boy in a hundred

---

[3] KW's memo.

ways, but there are a hundred others where I've found him enigmatic & I just don't get thro'. It is surely best to leave the thing alone.

Thursday, 31 March
Performance all to hell – she started on again, La Fielding, about 'I don't know what you're doing in that sketch . . .' so I went back to original script and she is furious. Crying and screaming. I am no longer able to feel any interest – I watch it like some twitching thing – I know it has life but I can't think *what* informs it.

Saturday, 2 April
Fielding seems to be behaving professionally – the work on the stage is OK, but I cannot speak to her offstage. I hope this situation continues, and she accepts it.

Wednesday, 13 April
Did the first 'B.O.K.' in the 3rd series – at the Paris. It went very well, & several friends told me I was splendid. Peter Reeves said it was my show. He is nice.

Good Friday, 15 April
Since I've lived at Park West I've become more and more conscious of nothingness in my life. Work that is done for pure economics – a private life that is monklike, a social life that is barren.

Saturday, 16 April
Walked home, heavy with depression. Much of it is due to the long run of this boring dreary revue, and some due to the futility of my lonely existence – desperately keeping my little life clean & ready for inspection. But there's no inspector.

Sunday, 17 April
When shampooing my hair, about 1 o'c., I felt a stinging in eye, left, and it got steadily worse. At 11 o'c. at Freddie's party I left & Gording took me to Eye Hospital – they didn't do any good – Night Nurse, dying to be rid of me.

Thursday, 21 April
Richard & Sybil Burton to show. It went indifferent well. They came round after, with Tony Richardson* & Doris Lessing and Rachel and Alan. We all went back to the Savoy after. There till 1.30.

*He was being *pro*-Bomb. Said we needed a deterrent.

Wednesday, 22 June
Radio show, Paris. It went off OK. These radio shows leave me feeling quite dead. I feel as though I'm moving in a soporific dream. There is a curious feeling of apathy about all radio entertainment. A negative feeling. The result I suppose of the bifurcated medium – not theatre & not complete sound.

Sunday, 28 August
To Bournemouth with Henry D[avies], met John Vere & spent delightful day with him.

Tuesday, 30 August
Sir Laurence O. out front. He came round afterwards to see me and it was all rather superb. He was magically gracious & I babbled tripe.

Tuesday, 20 September
Terrible row after show with Fenella Fielding. She said 'You have used some of the lowest & meanest tricks I have ever seen in the theatre – haven't you done enough to me? You have deliberately ruined laughs of mine, again and again . . . etc. etc.' What's more she's obviously sincere and believes what she says. 'I know you despise me . . .' she added. It's all such a mess.

Wednesday, 28 September
Show evening – packed. We're doing fab. business still!

Friday, 30 September
Meet with Peter Cook, Michael Codron. I am not happy about the way this material is shaping.[4] It's not right that I should continually have to salvage mediocre material. We must make a stand about this.

Saturday, 1 October
Telephoned Mulvany. He is going to arrange a hospital etc., and I am going to have this operation after the 29th October.

Wednesday, 5 October
To *The Visit* at Royalty to see George Rose. It was the most appalling muck I've seen for some time. The Lunts[5] – an incredible couple of frauds doing a sort of amateur party piece with no semblance to truth

---

[4] For the next revue.
[5] Alfred Lunt (1892–1977) and his wife Lynn Fontanne (1887–1983), America's most famous stage partners: commemorated in the Lunt–Fontanne Theater, New York.

& a cast like a terrible opera chorus & a production of obvious tricks by Brook and a play of cynical dirty nastiness by someone whose name I can't recall[6] & don't want to.

Friday, 7 October

To Grill & C[heese] with John Hussey. He is v. low with no money. Well I can't do any more. I simply can't. I've paid out over a 1000 pounds & it's had no effect whatsoever.

Thursday, 13 October

Met Gording we had lunch at Grill & C. then went to see *Billy Liar*[7] with Albert Finney being v. good: but not as good as he should be. It is really only a medium talent at the moment and all the opportunities are taken at medium strength. It never rises to a moment of acting strength – magnetic etc., it is always cleverly feinted. But clever enough to have misled all the critics into violent praise!

Thursday, 20 October

Tarquin Cole has delivered all my lovely ashtrays specially inscribed with

PIECES OF EIGHT
1959–1960
APOLLO THEATRE

and I have packed them all separately for presentation on the last night.

Saturday, 29 October

All awful. Michael Hitchman died. The police phoned me at 1 o'c. this morning. I really loved M. I know I was better for knowing him.

Sunday, 30 October

Hospital at 5.[8] Had an enema – rush to lav. awful. Everyone v. nice except one Night Sister who cares more for rules than people.

Monday, 31 October

Gording J. came to see me with cigarettes. Lovely. He is off to Tahiti soon for *Mutiny on the Bounty* with Marlon Branding. Reading Erich

---

6 Friedrich Dürrenmatt, 1921–90.

7 By Keith Waterhouse and Willis Hall.

8 For a rectal operation.

Heller on Goethe and it is really fabulous. Asked Gording to look up Ontology for me.[9]

Tuesday, 1 November
At about 12 they injected me and in a state of lovely euphoria I was wheeled to the operating theatre – I took everything in – the surgeon, anaesthetist & conversation of others but could not speak for lethargy & then I came to, about 4 hours later. I was convinced nothing had happened. But in fact – it was all over. Louie came up to see me which was lovely.

Friday, 4 November
Still reading Erich Heller. If any writing should prove the need for the religion of Christ, this does.

Wednesday, 9 November
John Kennedy has been voted President of the USA. This is very exciting to me. To think that, in this kind of world, a man of conscience, integrity, originality & quality *can* win through, against the mud of mediocrity & the fearful political corruption is inspiring in itself. Reading Lewis Mumford on philosophy & the fallacy of systems – dogmas etc. Very interesting. He makes the point about the horror of 'specialisation' in a way so like I've expressed it myself that it's uncanny.

Sunday, 13 November
Corrigan took me back to flat – it was nice to see it all again. Lunched with Louie and Henri D. Then for a walk around park & Henri & I saw Elvis Presley film. Quite good.

Wednesday, 16 November
With Terry & Sam to see *The Alamo*. It was superb. A really magnificent, generous, warm hearted, heroic picture in the classic tradition. Afraid of nothing.

Monday, 28 November
Started [filming] 8.30.[10] Day went well. Same team except Hattie who is replaced by a Liz Fraser.

---

[9] Gordon Jackson responded with a card giving the dictionary definitions of ontogenesis, ontology and sacristy, which KW had presumably also asked for. Finally, Jackson added the definition: 'BUM. N. (Shak.) the buttocks (cf. bump, in sense of swelling)'.

[10] *Carry On Regardless.*

Tuesday, 6 December
Location in Windsor with Yoki the chimp. We only did a few shots before rain came – back to Pinewood for lunch & then home.

Saturday, 17 December
Shopping Xmas presents in morning just for family. Lunch with folks. Then to rehearse TV show produced by James Gilbert. Kathryn Grayson throwing temperaments in sapphire mink. Ostentation gone mad.

Sunday, 18 December
Do the TV show. It was disaster. The sketch which was surefire ('Buy British') in the theatre & on tour, died like some awful damp squib. Everyone saying 'Never mind – the whole show was terrible anyway . . .'

Saturday, 24 December
Wendy Toye, 5.30 on, party. Got to her house & saw 3 queens getting out of a taxi, obviously guests, suddenly lost heart and walked on – got a taxi back to flat, and telephoned an excuse. Went home instead and had drinks with folks on Charles's birthday. Gran was there, in great form.

Friday, 30 December
Pinewood. Got wet again in the House sequence. Suggested gag about the outhouse, greenhouse, washhouse and etc. shithouse, and they put it in! Hope it works. No cold as yet.

MEMORANDA
Time to take stock of the year. It saw my longest run in the theatre – an almost unbearable engagement: my first adult operation – on me bum (which didn't do much good) and my first real flat (apart from one room in Endsleigh). It's a year in which I have earned more money than any other, and in which I have had my name on top, in neon, as a draw outside a theatre. A year in which, I hope, I've learned a little more, & come a little nearer to the spiritual truth which I so desperately need. A year in which my private life has remained as vacuous as ever. All private images and masturbation, more & more dwelling on the sadistic in the mind, more & more conscious of how I'm attracted to this sort of thing: not acting on this knowledge because of the danger it represents to my puritanical way of life, and because it's not an easy world to enter anyway.

1961

Sunday, 1 January
To the Bolts in evening and they gave me the Mozart LP – it's the wonderful Clarinet Quintet – quite superb and a wonderful introduction for me to this music, for in the past M. had always been a blind spot for me. Lovely evening. I argued with Bob about the question of Faith and it was v. challenging. He talked magically about History – especially about the development of the Parliament in England.

Monday, 2 January
1st rehearsal of revue[1] at YMCA. Lance Percival is v. good.

Tuesday, 3 January
Filming at Pinewood. Last day. How I wish all the work could be like this – Peter and Gerald are the loveliest of all bosses & gorgeous to work for. What a fantastic paradise to imagine working in nothing but 'Carry Ons'! On location a child asked Ken Connor for autograph & he said 'Hang on a minute – I'm being directed, son.' And the child said 'O! are you lost then?' This might be the proper verdict on all English directors.

Wednesday, 11 January
John Vere died – overdose of sleeping tablets – in Bournemouth. I felt a premonition of this at the time I said goodbye to him. He was a lovely lovely character.

Thursday, 12 January
I'm very depressed with it all. Sheila Hancock brought me home on the back of her vesper.[2] It was rather exciting. She is a lovely girl, but doesn't quite go over the top like Maggie S. I suppose Maggie *can* because of a fundamental hysteria – S.H. hasn't got this. Maggie has. We share a quiet desperation: which isn't always quiet!

---

[1] *One Over the Eight.*
[2] The Vespa (Italian for wasp) was the fashionable motor-scooter of the day.

Friday, 13 January
Up v. early – 5.30. Sleep v. unsatisfactory so got up & looked at lines etc. & thought of all kinds of things to threaten the buggers with – perhaps if I offered to commit suicide they might listen to my ideas! Why employ comedy actors if you don't think they know about what is funny? It's all too ridiculous & every time I do comedy I find this! You have to work & be funny in *spite* of the management.

Monday, 16 January
Signed lease of flat at Brunswick Gdns.[3] and paid rest of the 5000. Paid 195 pounds solicitor's fees. Sheila Hancock witnessed signature.

Wednesday, 18 January
Broadcast in morning. They did the *Kenneth Williams Story*. It was very funny.

Monday, 6 February. Brighton
Dress rehearsal B'ton. I got v. tight. The Albion, where I'm staying here, is v. tat.

Tuesday, 7 February
Got new script 'Critics' Choice' at 3 o'c., learned it & performed it at opening performance. Evening v. patchy but on the whole it went OK.

Wednesday, 8 February
They gave me a terrible busker number to work – song – with no finish etc. Egg all over my face – and after one abortive rehearsal, I walked off the stage. First temperament I have had on this production. Had a great set to with Michael C. about not having one decent actor in the company. It is disgraceful.

Sunday, 12 February
'B.O.K.' Did broadcast. Vogue came to Paris to photograph me. To White Horse lunch time with folks for a drink. Then on to Decca Studios for Michael Barclay, to record the sketches etc. Finished about 12 o'c. Morale could not be lower in this company.

Monday, 13 February
Returned Brighton on the 3 o'c. Belle. Cook produced sketch for Sheila & me to do. Rehearse at 11 o'c. Read through it, and learned

---

[3] In Kensington. Louie and Charlie's rent had been doubled, so KW bought them this leasehold apartment.

it in dressing room. Show went OK apart from a heckler in a box. Idiot I suppose.

Thursday, 16 February

Michael C. came down for evening show. I said I hated it, and he said 'D'you mean you want me to withdraw it before London?'. I said 'Is that possible?' and he started off about jeopardising the whole cast etc. etc. Which is one way to make me go through what I hate. Dinner after at Albion, where because I brought up my relevant complaints he got v. touchy and called me jew baiter – O dear.

Tuesday, 21 February. Liverpool

Opened here tonight and it was the same old story – & the poor sods bought it. I wish they'd protest or something, but they're so apathetic.

Tuesday, 28 February. London

Put my foot down about the drag sketch, and we stood about, doing nothing. No new material has been forthcoming.

Monday, 6 March

Streatham Hill Theatre. Opening here, despite all mechanical mishaps, was very reasonable & got nice reception.

Saturday, 11 March

I have no enthusiasm left. The artists in this show have been treated like a lot of illiterate infantrymen with an incompetent commander, and an uncertain & dithering H.Q. Both Sheila & I are flogged. My voice almost gone in 2nd house. It went all right, but it was no great triumph. Rona had another baby boy in Queen Charlotte's yesterday. Lovely. Louie went to visit her there.

Sunday, 12 March

Rona looking lovely in hospital and the baby is fine. With Henry D. to see *Flaming Star* with Elvis Presley being superb as usual.

Tuesday, 14 March

I have now given way and agreed to do nine months with the show. I know I'm a fool, but it's the last gesture I am making in the way of compromise. It isn't really noble to keep whittling down the original principles & I'm sick of 'extenuating circumstances'; they are never extenuating for me!

Friday, 17 March
Saw *Carry On Regardless* which was quite quite terrible. An unmitigated disaster.

Monday, 27 March. Blackpool
Blackpool is the *end of the line*. It is the English Siberia. It is pure TORTURE. Hateful, tasteless, witless, bleak, boring, dirty, tat – IT HAS NOTHING. I loathe every disgusting minute of it.

Thursday, 30 March
Tradition dies hard. Up till 4 o'c with Alan at the Imperial here.

Wednesday, 5 April. London
We got away with the opening night of this mediocre little show. The dressing room was bedlam afterwards. What happened tonight at the Duke of York's Theatre? A revue of pathetic trivia, which was the result of utter lack of cooperation. 1) a writer whose ideas were not understood by the director, or cast, and whose ideas, consequently, were never dramatically interpreted 2) a director with *no* idea of what sort of show he was to create on the stage 3) a management that began with talk of being 'utterly different from last time' and ended up aiming at a copy of the previous show 4) a cast that suffered like an army staggering on to the battlefield with no commander, just desperately engaging in personal salvage tactics.

Thursday, 6 April
The press is universally filthy. They say we're all 'camp' etc. etc. O! the attractiveness of obscure rudeness!

Friday, 7 April
Very good house to play to. Rachel Roberts out front & being quite fabulous. When she came round after she was aggressively complimentary* & the obscene epithets were flowing!

*It is extraordinary how feelings of guilt, past loyalties, and a sheer 'fellow feeling of sympathy' can combine to make for an extravagant sort of praise from actors, for fellow actors . . . It is one of the really lovely things about our profession. The way it inspires an inexplicable devotion.

Monday, 10 April
Pinewood 8.20. Leave 7.20. All went well.[4]

Thursday, 13 April
Saw rushes of me playing the Revolutionary Study of Chopin. It all

---

[4] The film was *Raising the Wind*, in effect a musical Carry On.

looked very authentic! Quite unbelievable! I was very pleased and everyone laughed.

Saturday, 15 April
Lunch with Louie. She is moving to Brunswick Gdns. on Tuesday. I shall be glad once she has settled in there.

Monday, 1 May
Noël Coward out front & he came round after – he was superb. I mentioned the bad reviews & he said – 'Of course my dear, that's why you're doing good business . . .' He said also 'Everything you do is completely authentic . . . I can't imagine it being done by anybody else . . . it's quite perfect . . .' But I couldn't really find an adequate reply. What can one say to such a man? Only that I've admired, respected & looked up to him for years and years and years.

Tuesday, 2 May
Did 'Desert Island Discs'[5] with Roy Plomley at B[roadcasting] H[ouse].

Tuesday, 9 May
Filming. Getting very tired. Show evening OK.

Tuesday, 16 May
Sheila Hancock *furious* over the rave reviews for *Beyond The Fringe*, the 3rd London revue, now at the Fortune. She is absolutely speechless with rage at these lovely notices for Cook, when this was the man that practically brought our show to disaster. I said it was best to be indifferent to the whole business.

Thursday, 18 May
To Peter E. to talk about career. I don't really want to go on with 'B.O.K.', but if I have to, then I want a lot of money. Ask for 100 and settle for 50.

Friday, 19 May
Evening show outrageous because of Tex Compton, who brought along Jorge Bolet[6] the famous pianist and their laughter caused a sensation in the theatre. It was so outrageous, half the cast went up with it.

---

[5] Castaway number 545, between Pietro Annigoni and Kingsley Amis. KW did not enjoy the experience (see entry for 30 March 1987, p. 760). He requested, as his one permitted luxury, Michelangelo's 'David'.
[6] 1914–90, Argentinian-born.

Sunday, 21 May
With Lance Percival out in his car. We drove to Maidenhead and lunched at Skindle's. It was very good. Then we sat by the river for a bit, and then it got cloudy so we returned to London, for tea in a little old world café in Gloucester Road, where it was so genteel it practically strangled itself & all the vowel sounds were flattened. Then Lance dropped me back at the flat about 5.30. His Basset hound is called General and was a big success wherever we went. A boy from Eton came shyly to our table for an autograph and called me 'Sir' & I suddenly felt very old.

Monday, 22 May
Lunched with folks and sat in their garden. Heard me on radio doing 'Desert Island Discs'. Not bad, really. Voice came over a bit common and pouffy.

Thursday, 25 May
Eileen (wardrobe) in a state over money. Gave her a cheque for £100 and told her to stop worrying about it.

Thursday, 1 June
It appears that S. has not been able to make the business pay, or get out of debt. The £1200 which I've given has been completely wasted.

Thursday, 15 June
I saw Fenella Fielding today in Connaught Sq. It was a hot day and she was in furs! She looked quite fantastic & oddly fragmented.

Sunday, 18 June
Nice day, v. sunny in the park, with John Hussey. It was all miraculous in Kensington Gdns., the children playing, adults lazing on the grass, the band playing – all suddenly *incredibly* English, and I wanted to weep for love of it all.

Monday, 19 June
The minicabs (1/- per mile) started today, so hired one to take me to the flat after the show. They are excellent. I shall certainly patronise them in future.

Tuesday, 20 June
The show evening went very well and Jorge Bolet & Tex Compton were out front again, and they took Sheila and me to the Ivy. They gave us copies of Jorge Bolet's recordings of Liszt. It was extremely

kind of them and I must return the compliment. I must get them *Pieces of 8* disc and take it down to the Cavendish in Jermyn Street myself.

Monday, 26 June
Did me laundry. Postcard from folks – they are now leaving Cattolica, Charles says they're all very brown etc. They're en route for Menton now. I must say I've missed them both this year, more than any other. The darlings. I hope they're adoring every minute of it.

Saturday, 1 July
Today was the hottest day since 1947, according to the Air Ministry and I can see no reason to doubt them. It was absolutely boiling everywhere. No relief from heat in this city. Absolutely horrible and exhausting. Over 90°. All the nellies in the Parks.

Tuesday, 4 July
Peter Eade came about 3.50 and we went up to see Hal Roach,[7] an American film director who looked like the American cliché and actually succeeded in sounding like one. Pot bellied and conceited and rude. 'I am going to make [you] a comedian, like a Kaye, or a Lewis, or a Chaplin . . .' These are 3 horrible things to be, for me.

Saturday, 15 July
The Bolts came, with Masud[8] (a Pakistani Analyst) and Zoe someone, and that idiot sculptor called Mike. A funny evening, with the Sud boy complaining of the method by which an Earl tried to seduce him. Under cover of his wife. Dinner at the Ivy. Yes – all very odd. Jo Bolt confided after that they didn't really like Sud at all. O dear! – why bring him?

Friday, 21 July
Swimming with Phil Gilbert at P. West. Afterwards we strolled down to Baker St & had tea. Then to a chemist's where a brilliant girl put some drops of Lancôme Cuir – or leather – into a cheap cologne and only charged me 3/3d. Fantastic bargain.

---

[7] 1892–1992, Hollywood comedy pioneer, associated with Harold Lloyd, Laurel and Hardy etc.
[8] M. Masud R. Khan (1924–89), a controversial figure. His obituary, by Mark Paterson, in the journal *Free Associations* (no. 21), begins: 'Masud Khan, prince of princes as he described himself, art collector, womanizer, anti-Semite, snob, charmer, cancer victim.' He trained under Anna Freud and Donald Winnicott.

Sunday, 30 July
This feeling of sexual compulsion with me again. It seems to come with most force in the summer. I remember the last year at Endsleigh, window leaning in the heat. Oh it's appalling.

Wednesday, 9 August
Lunched with Robert Young Drake, he is a very good fellow. And sound on faith. He certainly encouraged me in mine, and as he left me, he said 'Don't forget now – you're doing the Lord's work . . .' and I felt very touched.

Thursday, 17 August
Show went v. well and it was a good house. I made a gag with Sheila Hancock and she said 'O shut up . . .' so I pissed off & didn't speak again during the evening. It was deflation all right. I'm v. easily crushed.

Friday, 18 August
3 o'c. TV commercial for Benson's. This was a film for the trade about Gillette. I used the posh voice, snide, and a high Richardson.

Saturday, 2 September
To see Dirk Bogarde play the homosexual barrister fighting a blackmail ring in the film *Victim* – it was all v. slick, same team as *Sapphire* (Relphs) and like that, superficial and never knocking the real issues. Never touching on what Kenneth Walker[9] once described as 'playing out the tragedy of the heart, alone, with no one knowing of their troubles . . .'

Thursday, 7 September
To Brunswick for tea. Charlie put on the radio to hear news & I retuned it, 'cos it was wrongly set, and he blew up & so did I, and I walked out. Telephoned afterwards to apologise coward's way. My nerves are edgy & screaming inside. I'm amazed I've got through this show as I have. I *know* it's only the result of prayer. Now I must pray for the strength & will to continue for the next few months.

Friday, 8 September
Terrible day. Went to the folks. Charlie digging up all the stuff I planted in the corner of the garden. I could have screamed with anger. And the hospital has told him that he must rest! All the pent-up hatred of the years came up in my throat. And stayed there, thank goodness.

---

[9] 1882–1966. Author of *Sex and a Changing Civilisation*, *Sex Difficulties in the Male*, etc.

All I did was sit silent through the lunch & get away quickly afterwards back to the flat where I went to bed. I imagined that the new flat would help them, but the old malignancies are still there & every time I visit there is the endless bickering. My own life is as vacuous as ever. And to crown it all this terrible show looms like a shadow over me. I suppose the years are showing their vengeance. I feel somehow that if I get through this, I shall be better.

Sunday, 10 September
To the Baxters for the day. Saw Bob Hope on TV. Ghastly joke about President Kennedy – 'I like a man who's got religion. I like to see a man pray – you can see where his hands are . . .' He also said he was not a sick comedian. If this is the comic *well*, that is the joke *rotten*. Comedy is facing an appalling crisis in the west. Partly, or mainly, due to the complete collapse of morality.

Tuesday, 12 September
Out with Henry Davies when I saw that Robert Bolt was in prison. I telephoned Jo – or rather telegrammed and went on to the show, v. dispirited. The usage of the 14th century law (Breaking the peace) originally invoked against pillors [pillagers] and robbers; against civilised people, seeking to change law, is utterly detestable.

Thursday, 14 September
I am feeling terribly uneasy about the situation today. When a country sends a man like Robert Bolt to prison for one month, for a token civil disobedience act done on a Sunday & incurring no harm it seems the kind of savagery one connects with fascist regimes. The issue here is whether one can, in all conscience, be a party to the manufacture & acquiescence in usage of something as horrible as H-bombs. For any honest person the answer can only be *no*. And if, in reply, they say 'Well if you don't use them, the enemy will . . .', the only possible reply for me is 'All right – that's a risk I have to take . . .'

Friday, 15 September
The conviction is in me, that I have to join the demonstration on Sunday, and run the risk of being arrested. But I'm frightened inside about possible reaction for the show. I mustn't prejudice the performance.

Saturday, 16 September
The Editorial of the New Statesman is superb. Condemns the secret police, and overt police action ordered by Butler, and says it will confirm the demonstration on Sunday. And they are exactly right.

The spectacle of a country committing Bertrand Russell, philosopher, O.M. etc., aged 89, to a prison, is disgusting. Butler is the sort of charlatan that the Macmillan sort of mediocrity produces. They are dangerous men in times of crisis, but now they have struck at the intelligentsia of the nation, and we shall see who has the guts to get up and follow, or defend.

Sunday, 17 September

It rained all day, till about 3 o'c. Met John Hussey, and we went to Trafalgar Square – or as near as we could get, which was St Martin's in the Fields. The Police had blocked all entrances to the sq. where the beleaguered committee was sitting it out. The Police used filthy methods of removing limp, passive people – a man dragged by one arm with his head on the ground . . . a woman thrown bodily against a wall . . . a police insp. saying 'If our lads have any more leave stopped, they'll be getting tougher . . .' One saw the fascist, and the savagery in them start to emerge. The entire crowd that I was in was anti-Police – I did not hear, for 2 hours, *one* dissident voice. One thing became abundantly clear. They hated the bomb, and they hated the corrupt government that didn't ban it, and they hated the uniformed bullies that enforce an unjust law. Leaders arrested were John Osborne, Shelagh Delaney, and Vanessa Redgrave. All I seem to be able to do is send me miserable donation and pray for them all. Number of arrests today were 800 odd.

Monday, 18 September

Today I cancelled Telegraph and Sunday Telegraph. They've both sneered at the C.N.D., and neither of those papers has earned the right to sneer. Changed to the Times, which prints admirable & sane letters from Lord Woolton and Chris. Mayhew. Wrote to Vanessa Redgrave and John Osborne, because their behaviour has won my admiration and respect.

Tuesday, 19 September

Supper with Annette [Kerr]. I suggested we get married but she didn't think it would work.

Saturday, 23 September

I was v. proud and moved to receive today two lovely acknowledgments of my thanks, from John Osborne and Vanessa Redgrave, which I shall cherish.[10]

---

[10] Their notes are preserved in the diary.

Sunday, 24 September
Lunched with Annette and we walked all round the city. In the evening, to Jorge Bolet's concert for the Liszt Concerto. He began ragged but seemed to get better. Malcolm Sargent preening like mad – v. ancient and smiling like a corseted clay model.

Monday, 25 September
I dreamed last night that I brought to my mother's home a baby goat – a kid – soft as a woolly poodle, with its head damaged, and me thinking it would mend all right with the years. It came toward me so naturally and muzzled its head in my palm. This afternoon I dreamed I went to a French hospital for treatment – I think it was with Nora [Stapleton] or someone – and the Frenchman came and did something to me – I was naked – and put bulbs, lighted, in my mouth like Musgrove and then squeezed my genitals – all quite cursorily like a routine test, and I leaned forward to kiss him, but he smiled & moved away. Afterwards I was screaming around outside the hospital in the rain & asked directions from two men with an ice-cream barrow, but they just said 'I'm Italian' loudly and I went away.

Thursday, 28 September
Nora for supper. I mentioned marriage again, and she's going to think about it.

Friday, 29 September
Went to see *Taste of Honey* and it began so brilliantly, it was breathtaking. Dora Bryan was fantastic. A superb performance. Never a foot wrong.

Saturday, 30 September
Well, here it is, still running at the theatre, after disastrous notices, and head-shaking and gloomy predictions from everyone. Still running and still getting laughs. More laughs than before. The reason? No.4 on entry for the 5 April in this diary. It's all due to that. I would say, to nothing else. Success despite – the director, the management, the critics, the weather, the competition, the material, the costumes, the lighting, the appalling staff.

Sunday, 1 October
Lunched with folks, and then to Richmond. At the Bolts' were Vanessa Redgrave, Lindsay Anderson, Eileen, Herbert, Diane Cilento, Sean Kenny, and eventually Brewster Mason, who started on his own volition a violent diatribe against C.N.D. and the Committee, because he said, to stop nuclear tests is to 'stand in the way of human progress'

and we didn't need to bother about any country letting them off because 'there is such a thing as human love, and I believe in it, and no one would ever do such a disgraceful – 'etc. etc., an appalling mis mas [*sic*] of 'reasoning' which was really laughable, but unfortunately he is much too neurotic about it all to endure laughter. Also he exhibited a singular lack of grace in launching that kind of diatribe in the house of Robert, who has just come out of prison for his beliefs on the subject.

Friday, 6 October

Tennent's rang Eade & offered me Backbite in *School For Scandal*. I said no thanks immediately. Rotten part, rotten play, and rotten cast (they've got Ralph Richardson and Maggy Rutherford etc. with Gielgud producing, so it's jobs for the boys week!) so they can stick it. Also, someone rang Peter E. offering me a rehash of *Lord Arthur Savile's* Crime![11] Really it is too absurd. Not v. complimentary – the shit I get offered.

Sunday, 8 October

Ever since the business of Robert B. going to prison, I have been terribly unsettled and perturbed. I know that the Christianity of Jesus of Nazareth is the true way of life – not the priestly and theological mess the organised churches have made of it – but the paradox is – they teach it. But how to translate this into action? I try to be honest with myself and with others, except when it will hurt them unnecessarily, I think sex without love is wrong and don't indulge in it – I think killing is wrong – state or individual, and I don't covet other people's goods – and I acknowledge my one true god. But I don't think that's enough. But the facts are, that I move closer to him every day. I perceive the meaning more clearly every day. A man must lose his life before he can find it . . .

Tuesday, 10 October

Fearful row with Sheila H. She said I was ruining other people's perf. by my talking in the wings & that I was inaudible on the stage. I didn't reply. I felt she wanted to row with someone and had chosen me. I shan't speak to her again.

Wednesday, 11 October

This rowing with Hancock does me no good. I find it so difficult to forgive myself. It's unthinkable that I should apologise to her – and she hasn't earned the right to criticise me. But what is worse, I don't

---

[11] Rehashed from Oscar Wilde's short story of 1891.

care. About her. Or the show. I can happily run on, till the end, with meself in a state of siege. I could take Fielding for eighteen months so I'm sure I can take her. Nonetheless I have to face it – I never get on with actresses (or any actors I work with at v. close quarters) for v. long. Sooner or later – there is always a fight. But I hardly ever criticised her work – in fact *never* . . . and she's no paragon . . .

Thursday, 12 October

I read the script of the new Peter Rogers film – *Round the Daisies*[12] – a film version of *Ring for Catty*.[13] They want me for Halfpenny, it's quite good. Eade is asking £5000 but I think he will not get it. More likely 4 or even less.

Friday, 13 October

Collective responsibility for wrong acts is rubbish. The German nation wasn't *all part* of the crime of Nazism. Dwight Macdonald[14] – 'The common people of the world have less and less control over the policies of their governments, while at the same time they are more & more closely identified with those governments . . . as the common man's moral responsibility diminishes, his practical responsibility increases . . .'

Saturday, 14 October

A lot of things in my life lately seem to have happened *deliberately* though at the time I wasn't being deliberate. My choice of books – my being brought up against the idea of *Christian Morality* again and again, in different forms, and then to crown it all – Robert Bolt going to prison as a *moral protest* against the evils of the H-Bomb. Where the morality collapses is the most evil. How ironic that in so many houses they say 'Now let's leave religion out of it . . .' Let's leave the oxygen out of breathing. That's what they've all done.

Sunday, 15 October

Long talk with the Bolts. Robert refused to address a rally in Trafalgar Square. He doesn't want to be made into a public image – he doesn't want to become a Front Man. Ironically enough *he could do it* – and *honestly & well* – but it's the fear he has of being enveloped. The way movements so often corrupt & distort one. R. is a playwright – it is *there* he must make his stand. It is for the singer to sing. We also

---

[12] This became (or already was) *Twice Round the Daffodils*.

[13] By Patrick Cargill and Jack Beale.

[14] 1906–82. American journalist and cultural commentator. The quotation is from *The Responsibility of Peoples* (1957), p.44.

talked on Catholicism and curiously enough, all my objections to it – corruption, princes, hierarchy, dogma – sounded awfully lame to me. I shouted 'Why hasn't the Pope condemned the H-Bomb utterly?' and Eileen (a Catholic) quietly answered 'He has.' This makes me feel unworthy. I could have found that out for myself.

Wednesday, 25 October

'B.O.K.' No. 5. In the 5th series. Went quite well, with a packed house. Took Louie after to see *Fanny* – nice – but no songs! Horst Buchholz was really superb. Most exciting juvenile I've ever seen. Lyrical actor.

Thursday, 26 October

Met Nora & Robert B. for supper in the Grill & C. For some time, I've been feeling a cooling off towards Robert. There *is* an element of patronage – i.e. schoolteacher attitude in his conversation with one – one finds oneself resenting the needless explanations and then there is this extraordinary habit of telling the same story again. And this continual harping on the human inability to live with Truth. The comparison of truth with a blinding light, and people having to close their eyes etc. Of course he is a good man. I don't mean that he isn't. I mean that I'm more and more feeling that he isn't what I thought he was. This isn't his fault. It's mine.

Friday, 3 November

Wonderful to realise that in eight weeks I shall be at the end of this mortification. This has been the worst ordeal of my theatrical experience. But it will soon be over. I still can't believe that Ken Connor is taking over. In my heart I feel this is a fatal mistake, but I want him to have success. Not failure.

Sunday, 5 November

The evening with the Bolts was awful. As usual, too many people there. Some drunken comedian from Australia (sick jokes) who was really the end – with hair all over the place.[15]

Wednesday, 15 November

'B.O.K.' Went OK. As I was leaving building to go [to] Pinewood I was stopped by Bob Monkhouse who was sneeringly rude about me performance. I replied politely 'Thanks ever so much, Bob' and left. I was staggered at the time, but I suppose he is v. unhappy.

---

[15] Unmistakably Barry Humphries (b.1934), who had arrived in London in 1959.

Saturday, 18 November
Lunch with Louie. Maples fixed the door for her, and Charlie started this old nuisance of wanting the old door kept in the cellar & wanting the bill sent to the landlords etc. Of course there was a row. He still insists on this heavy-handed 'cock of the walk' stuff and when I pointed out that I was paying for it he replied 'I'll start looking for other accommodation . . .' which of course is hot air, and sickening. His kind of egocentricism has always disgusted me; but with his illness and old age it becomes increasingly despicable.

Wednesday, 6 December
'B.O.K.' morning. Pinewood afternoon. Now it is a month before the end of this nightmare of a run, and monotonous humiliation. I have been taught the severest lesson of the theatre, and taught it pitilessly. That is – that when what you are offering is inferior, it should be stopped. It's as clear as that. Tennent's sent me a Shaffer one act play. Good part for me. But only one act. Must think about this.

Saturday, 9 December
Paddy Frost, the understudy, really did very well and improved every night. I think we were v. wise not to change horses in mid stream. But it all served to show that Sheila Hancocks don't grow on trees. She has been invaluable to this show.

Friday, 15 December
A day of heartsearching which resolved in my deciding to do the Shaffer play. Eade has gone to meet Tennent's about the terms of my contract.

Saturday, 16 December
I do want my own dog. There's no doubt about that.

Sunday, 17 December
Reh. 2 o'c. C.N.D. show. It was a fiasco. Awful mixture of well meaning charity turns and obligatory clapping. I followed a dreary folk song of homeland! It was ghastly.

Monday, 18 December
The show went off very well. Sheila Hancock's voice is much better. She is giving presents to everyone in the show. I am not. Not giving anything to anyone. They all ought to pay me for keeping them in work for a year.

Wednesday, 20 December
Louie birthday. Take her to lunch. Pat came too, & we had a nice lunch at Biagi. Afterwards I got Louie some calf gloves at Simpson's, then we got some china for Peter E. & Laurena & George B. (cup & saucer) and umbrella for Pat. Came back to flat, and read script of *Carry On Cruising*, the usual crap.

Friday, 29 December
Wrote letter to Mary H.[16] saying it was best to terminate this acquaintanceship. I shall not write any more. You cannot choose to love a person in the human sense. Only in the spiritual sense. In a human relationship, when there is no real affection on both sides, there is a lack of truth which inevitably leads to misunderstanding and trouble. I predict that she will either come to London and forcibly try to see me, or do something desperate and mad.

NOTES
The year has been catastrophe in the way of work. Everything has been rotten. On the money side, ironically, it's been the best ever. The show has been pure murder. Never before in my life have I been called upon to enact such vacuous shit night after night. It has eaten like a worm into me, and I feel like rotting timber. I shall not feel that '61 is over till I'm out of the Duke of York's.

[16] Apparently the victim of an infatuation: an epistolary relationship only. No more is heard of it.

1962

Monday, 1 January
To Berman's for fitting uniforms for film *Carry On Cruising*. The script is a load of old rubbish as usual. After that, I staggered about in the snow and slush with my feet getting colder and damper. Eventually went to Selfridges where they sold me an excellent pair of overshoes for 17/6d and I walked about dry shod. The show tonight was half empty – understandably – people obviously staying at home and not risking transport vagaries.

Saturday, 6 January
A moody overcast day. The day of my freedom. 1st house – shocking. 2nd house – fair to good. Home by car – by 12.

Sunday, 7 January
Woke to realise I'm really free of it. Gone for ever is that cloud that hung over me, like a mushroom. That terrible feeling of shame too, that humiliation of going through the shit every single foul night. No more of that squalid basement dressing room with those awful girls overhead making my nerves scream. Goodbye to all that, and my thankful prayer to God for delivering me.

Monday, 15 January
Pinewood at 10.30. Did one shot after lunch and that was all. Ronnie Stevens whom I abhor is on this picture, as the Drunk. Not such a bad fellow. Rather colourless & suburban but harmless, my abhorrence not warranted. I felt v. sorry for him as I watched him do a scene today. He orders a drink and the waiter says 'Sherry, sir. Yes. Dry, sweet?' Reply: 'Of course I'm dry. And not so much familiarity . . .' and it failed completely. Not an ounce of humour left in it. Very sad indeed.

Thursday, 18 January
Did the commentary for the film of Richard Williams'[1] modern fairy story. He is a young Canadian. I really quite enjoyed it.

Tuesday, 23 January
Pinewood by 8 o'c. Did quite a lot of work – scenes mainly with Sid James in the Captain's Cabin. I wasn't very good. He was.

Wednesday, 31 January
I did a rock & roll number in 'B.O.K.' – 'Running Backwards to Misery'[2] . . . it went v. well.

Friday, 2 February
Pinewood 8.00, worked till 10. Stayed for rushes and lunch, returned by three o'clock and purchased a Baume wrist watch. I must have a really good time keeper.

Every single act of creation is a kind of vulnerability, conscious or otherwise. So much in the theatre is demonstrable proof of this. The more vulnerable an actor is, the better, generally, his work is. The more determined he is that he shan't be vulnerable the worse he becomes. But in both cases, self revelation is involved. Both performances tell one so much.

Monday, 5 February
Pinewood all day. Did nothing. This entire period is mentally a 'fill in' till my holiday which is now assuming gigantic proportions in my mind. I have no interest in the film. It is the usual load of crap, and the company is death. There is nobody now, except Kenneth Connor, that I can talk to. They've all gone. Only the rubbish is left. I can't wait for it to finish and get out of the country.

Saturday, 17 February
Met Hugh Paddick[3] at Air Terminal. Flew to Gibraltar arrived about 6. Car to Spain. Torremolinos. Beautiful coast, sea was filthy. Beaches foul with oil and dirt. Stayed one night in a motel called the RAF. It was dreary. A whole English school staying there. Disgusting & foul beginning to holiday.

---

[1] b.1933, Toronto. Oscar-winning animator; director of animation for *Who Framed Roger Rabbit?* etc.
[2] 'Walkin' Back to Happiness' (Schroeder, Hawker) had been a late-1961 hit for Helen Shapiro.
[3] Colleague and partner-in-camp from the Kenneth Horne shows.

Sunday, 18 February
By car to Malaga. All the hotels full, no one could offer us anything. Back to Torremolinos – this time to Casa Paris, Chez Lucien motel. Damp & terrible with giggling Spanish girls who come & light fires etc. Dinner there was in a small self-conscious candle-lit room with indifferent food served with great pretension.

Wednesday, 21 February
Arrived Gibraltar in lovely sunshine, booked in at the Queen's. Delightful rooms etc. all v. lovely. The rock and everything. But mobbed by people and autograph hunters till it became embarrassing.

Saturday, 24 February
Left Nice airport 5.10, arrived London airport 7.40 and v. glad to be back.

Monday, 26 February
L. at 3 o'c. Together we saw film *Roman Spring of Mrs Stone*, a highly polished 'stylish' production which was v. decadent. And obviously about an old poof and not a woman at all. With L to flat where there was drama over B.'s inability to choose between suitors. Curious how far away I feel from all this sex twaddle. People wanting to possess people. Ridiculous. I felt very glad to return to my clinical little flat. At least there is a *bit* of order in my life – but there, all was disorder and muck.

Thursday, 8 March
Purchased lovely accurate watch 'Ocean Star' – touch of poetry at the Goldsmiths' Assoc., in Regent Street. At last I've got something I can rely on. It was about twenty-five pounds.

Monday, 12 March
To see *Twice Round The Daffodils* press show. With Andrew Ray.[4] It was a good picture on the whole – held together very well. No great highlights but no low drags. Consistently good, but fighting shy of anything original.

Tuesday, 13 March
Down to Pinewood by car and did my dubbing re-pronouncing the word 'impasse' – censor trouble. Ridiculous.

---

[4] b. 1939, actor son of the comedian Ted Ray.

Wednesday, 14 March

Every now and again, I take up the script and try to get this dialogue into my head. But I can't concentrate for more than a few minutes. I use any excuse to do something else. The loneliness of learning lines! It's so marooning – I get frightened & say to myself 'Don't be mad! – you've learned bigger stuff than this!' which of course I have. But every baby is just as hard as the last. Everything gets more difficult.

Friday, 16 March

With Henri Davies to Hammersmith where we got Herbal Cigarettes. I will go on to these for a bit, but I will never go back to tobacco. This I do know. I'm finished with Nicotine. S. & Terry came and we had supper at the Grill and Cheese: S. hinted at being a chauffeur for me at the studios etc., but I didn't bite. After losing 1,600 (minimum) on his restaurant scheme, I certainly don't feel like doing anything more with him.

Monday, 19 March

1st rehearsal of Shaffer play.[5] All very nervous at first, and P[eter] Wood, in luxurious flat, thawed us all out with coffee & talks. First reading and I felt awful. I read it, feeling just reppy, conventional and empty. Maggie [Smith] sounded spontaneous and authentic. Richard Pearson vulnerable and striking marvellous notes of posh bewilderment. I realised during reading how very little I had to do. P. Wood gave us all notes after*, and said roughly that we were all being v. conventional & it couldn't be played like that at all. So that is the beginning of 'cutting the ground from under your feet' stuff, but curiously, I am not worried. I feel this play is fundamentally an old-fashioned drawing room comedy and I think that eventually that is how it will play, whether one likes it or not.

*He actually said of our reading: 'Well that was all very hieratic'[6]

Wednesday, 21 March

Some grim moments with Wood today culminating in his suggestion that I play the part with a cigarette holder! Really. At this juncture. To listen to some of his fatuous suggestions is to feel like screaming. I got out of it with difficulty. A style of playing can only come out of complete ease and mastery of the 'object' in any art. Here the object

---

5 *The Private Ear* and *The Public Eye* was a complementary double-bill, KW appearing (as Julian) in the latter play only.

6 See entry for 28 January 1965, p. 250. KW may be conflating the two occasions, as his footnote here was added later – perhaps after 1965.

is dialogue. He stops the very process at the source. It is really the final treachery in the rehearsal period.

Thursday, 22 March

Evening took Stanley & Moira to Poor Millionaire in Bishopsgate. It was excellent. Afterwards we met three lads who were fans – and we came back to Park West for tea and natter. One of them said ''Course we got a chip on our shoulders, after all, we're children of the war . . .' It was like the cliché in the delinquent film, come true.

Saturday, 24 March

P. Wood said Shaffer said 'Kenneth plays the 1st part in a self-conscious comedy style and then goes into a completely different style with Maggie . . .' What muck. I've never been self-conscious on a stage in my life . . .

Thursday, 29 March

At rehearsal today, I performed differently in view of what P. Wood said, and after he told us 'Never before in my career as a director have I seen my notes so well acted upon . . .' I handled Cristoforou much more timorous & little boyish. It's all right of course, but it can't do much in the way of bravura for the opening. Received nasty letter from a Mrs P. Cook of Bishop's Stortford saying that she thought 'my show' was disgraceful etc. I wasn't in it of course. I wrote back v. reprovingly telling her not to be malignant in the future.

Sunday, 1 April

I suppose when an actor isn't actually acting he is at his lowest really. I keep wondering if I will be able to act this part at all. Desperately working on the 'authenticity' of the speeches.

Monday, 9 April. 1st week of tour, Cambridge

The show went well I would say. And the reception at the end was v. nice. Everyone seems pleased but the general consensus is that the first play needs tightening & pruning. First opening night I've ever done without make-up. I had one or two fluffs & just about managed to get out of them, by the skin of me teeth. Phew! at one point I felt that words were just flying round my head like a flock of starlings . . . I didn't know which one to take.

Thursday, 12 April

Had a small row with Peter Wood about these curtain calls. We're doing 'picture' ones which I think is v. phoney. I prefer straight line-up. Properly.

Saturday, 14 April

Lunched with Mr Blackwood[7] – the Manager of the Arts – who talked of a new method of approach to the 'Life Force' & at one point looked embarrassingly like a medium at a seance. All v. weary.

Monday, 23 April. Oxford

Pierre Shaffer at 12.30. We lunched at Biagi and motored to Oxford via Watlingford & Stadhampton – it was a glorious day. Met Mags at theatre & we all had tea at Randolph. M. is staying with her parents here. Evening performance OK.

Thursday, 26 April

A rather exciting day. Sat in the sun in the morning at the Park, with a thriller, reading. Returned to the hotel and had lunch. After I went to bed for a rest. Then traditional activity and I banged my forehead & it bled. It was all v. significant. Then I went to the theatre & met Shirley (prod. asst.) and we were strolling along, when a striking looking boy passed us, holding a syphon of soda. He smiled & I said 'Hallo' – and I said to Shirley 'I'm convinced I know that boy & his brother who is younger.' Then the performance which went well, tho' Mags fell over, after her scream off!! Back to the hotel where I sat talking to a Mr & Mrs Neves & their son Howard. Then!! *into* the room came the boy of the soda syphon! and we talked, then I joined him and his parents. He is called Richard & the brother is William.

Sunday, 29 April

Richard goes through my head like the bubbles in a glass of champagne,[8] and this way lies madness . . .

Friday, 4 May

Evening performance went a bit to pieces after I'd fluffed. Funny – this feeling of failure I have, once the slip is made – it is almost impossible to carry on. Like making a mistake in a letter & wanting to tear up the whole thing.

Saturday, 5 May

My continual desire nowadays is to have a place of my own where I can hear the rain falling on to wet leaves & see some trees . . . I know that May 10 is going to be v. important. It's a minor blow I'm trying to strike in this performance, but if it succeeds, it will be a major turning point . . .

---

[7] Commander Andrew Blackwood.

[8] A slightly adapted quotation from the song 'You Go to My Head' (Gillespie, Coots).

Thursday, 10 May
Opening night.[9] If I can pull it off tonight, it will be a victory indeed.
It went off all right. I had one fluff which was hardly noticeable and we played to a good house who received us superbly.

Friday, 11 May
The press is excellent. With the exception of Muller in the Mail[10] and that effete creature Worsley in Financial Times (which nobody reads anyway!) All the rest are marvellously good. There's a rave in several.

Tuesday, 15 May
Supper with Sheila Hancock who is finishing *Over the 8* at Streatham Hill. Golders next week is end of it. She is fed up with it, poor dear.

Tuesday, 22 May
I wrote to Wendy Toye and said that I don't want to do the mime film with heraldic drawings by Ronald Searle. I don't like mime, or Ronald Searle.[11]

Thursday, 24 May
Gording at 10.30. It was all v. nice and we lunched at Biagi. He told me many amusing things & I told him about washing me bum and Coward coming in and me saying about me papilli and him saying 'It sounds like an island in the South Seas . . .' Feeling dreadful. Awful boil on my face– skin all painful, and something in my eye which lasted all through performance at the Globe (£568)[12] and made me feel miserable as hell. I walked all the way home and cried in the streets.

Sunday, 27 May
I got a v. nice letter from Wendy Toye about me not doing the film and she was charming about the whole thing. Obviously, in private, she's saying 'I knew he felt like that all the time . . .' etc. But I'm not brave enough to be honest about people to their faces, unless it can be praiseful. I simply can't do it. I know that if I don't get the expected reply from someone who is an acquaintance I get very vexed.

---

[9] At the Globe Theatre.
[10] Robert Muller wrote spontaneously to KW to apologise for the fact that his review had been cut, explaining that 'Unfortunately the paragraph they eliminated was the one in which your performance was (very favourably) discussed.'
[11] But see entry for 9 October 1954 (p. 105). The film was *The King's Breakfast*.
[12] KW often kept a tally of box-office takings – one index of a play's health.

Thursday, 31 May

Photography in dressing room by Helen Craig. She took them for a display in Hampstead designed to raise funds for Roose-Evans's theatre up there. She was sweet – a granddaughter of Gordon Craig. The famous Craig.[13] She was absolutely charming. Wore no make-up which is lovely, I think, and was delightful to get on with. We had a drink in the White Horse afterwards.

Tuesday, 5 June

Took Louie to lunch at Biagi, and after she'd finished an ice cream, she suddenly fell forward on to the table and fainted. It was a ghastly experience. When I got hold of her and sat her upright again, the face was askew on the shoulders – grotesque – the mouth open and the breath gasped noisily like a frightening drunken snore . . . Pierre got her a brandy: and it was eventually all over, and she came round. But she was comatose or unconscious for at least 8 or 10 minutes. During perf. tonight a man shouted 'speak up' & I continued without any kind of pause, entirely ignoring it. There is *no* excuse for this kind of behaviour, even when the complaint is justified (a note can be given to an usherette & conveyed backstage) and in this case my reaction was coming from all parts of the auditorium – so if they could hear, I don't believe in his complaint. But psychologically it was upsetting and made the house uneasy.

Wednesday, 6 June

First house was all right – half deserted, but with the heat outside it was amazing we got anybody! Louie brought Grandma Williams and afterwards we all had tea in Maggie's dressing room. Gran told Mags a rambling story about a neighbour who asked her to buy her a new pair of knickers. Gran said – 'Of course she'd been doing her number two's in 'em and I told her she was a dirty bitch & ought to have her face smacked, and she said "O! it's all right – sit down, and I'll play the piano for you . . ." But it was full of green boots,' she added. Gran kept saying this woman was 'a very well-educated lady . . . definitely . . .'[14]

---

[13] Edward Gordon Craig (1872–1966), designer and philosopher of the stage.

[14] This is not the clearest version KW ever gave of one of his favourite anecdotes, which became known as 'The Green Boots Story'. In his autobiography, he identifies the insanitary neighbour as a Mrs Houth, who kept her shoes in the piano, where they became green with mildew. Despite this encumbrance, Mrs Houth is said to have extracted 'Moonlight and Roses' from the instrument, a feat which KW may have added to the tale.

Sunday, 10 June
I went down to Anne Eastham's 21 birthday party and did a bit of mingling to keep everything going but it was v. hard work. Awful middle class couples doing the twist, it was pathetic. I had too much to drink I'm afraid & became aggressive & loquacious & bawdy.

Monday, 11 June
Paul F. came, not as he said, at 11 o'c. but at 12. Then announced that he had to leave in 20 minutes to go to the country 'with some boys from the ballet . . .' I felt disappointed and hurt that he could behave like this, after not seeing him for a year . . . all those letters – his saying 'You are one of my two best friends' . . . and it really came down to this, his first visit to London in ages: he arrived on Thurs., leaves tomorrow, and I got 20 minutes . . . I suppose one shouldn't expect so much I suppose – oh hell – people are just bloody awful. Sometimes.

Thursday, 14 June
Went to park. Full of girls who sit up, bending over their male companions who are lying down, receiving their kissings & caressings. It is disgusting to watch. No wonder Billy Graham[15] thought our parks so foul. But I'm sure Hyde is the worst. There is so much riff-raff living near.

Tuesday, 19 June
Met P. Shaffer at 2 o'c. and we saw the Bunuel film *Viridiana* at Curzon. It was all v. dreary. Rape and obscenity going on and colossal jibes at organised religion. Bunuel has got a preoccupation with the lame & twisted. All v. distressing but curiously alien. One wasn't touched by any of it.

Wednesday, 20 June
Shaffer has written some v. good things into this play. I suppose all writers must have a certain degree of ignorance or childishness or something, which makes them *try* where many good minds would give up in the knowledge that it's all been done before. I don't refer to the Huge Talents. The geniuses. But the more workaday talents.

I've been thinking more about Bunuel & have read an article on him which has enlightened me considerably. I see his point now. The complete 'decay' idea in the title. Everything going sick unless it fulfils its natural development process, unless all is reduced to decadence. It is true. His film is true.

---

[15] b.1918, American evangelist.

Friday, 22 June
Hancock out front. Who went b/stage to Maggie. After, I was spoken to. V. charming. He went on about the 'power of evil' in the world. He seemed rather drunk to me. That Freddie Ross[16] with him. After all he's said about her in the past! He also said 'We must work together again – not all that old *trick* stuff we were doing . . . but something good . . .' For the truth of that one substitutes 'you' for 'we'. This is the dead end for me and him. There were not any tricks in it for me. All the tricks were by him. This is what he will never see. This is the tragedy of the actor manqué every single time.

Monday, 25 June
My life seems lately to be taking on an atmosphere of trance-like madness, and inner hysteria. What is reality? One thing that stays real for me with the years is the desire to be constructively engaged in loving one particular person. Hermione [Hannen] said to me years ago in Cardiff Castle 'Some of us are not meant to give or receive love in the physical sense . . . but only in the spiritual sense.' I don't seem to be constructively engaged in either . . .

Saturday, 30 June
Sort of climax today to a week of simmering & then boiling frustration. And at the end of every week I'm conscious of some new illness of some kind – since the show, it's been skin, bum, cold, bronchitis, skin again, boils, ulcers in the mouth, and what now? But always this frustration, this screaming desire to have a real relationship to *trust* completely, to *share*. I see I wrote of this on Monday! I'm going the way of Barri Chatt. It's becoming an obsession.

Tuesday, 3 July
Set to, and cleaned the flat, which left me feeling virtuous. Went to the butcher for steak for my lunch. He said to me 'I think you're a bit of prime meself, there you are – four & sixpence my angel . . .' I giggled & felt like a high school girl. It was nice.

Saturday, 7 July
Awful day in the theatre. Friction with Schmidt. She has some awful man whom I dislike in her dressing room a lot. I said so. And she, rightly, defended him as a friend of hers. Sometimes one wonders about one's whole scale of values. And I didn't care. Suddenly I thought 'If it's a question of him or me, she should reject him – I would in her place' and she doesn't. And that's where the whole pack

---

16 Hancock's agent and, from 2 December 1965, his wife.

of cards comes down. I always come to think less of people – I do so admire the passionate devotion, the lifelong loyalty. The hell with *fair* – give me 'I'm on your side, right or wrong . . . all the way . . .'

Sunday, 8 July

After lunch went over to see Phil Gilbert in Fitzroy Square with J.H., then we went to Speakers' Corner – nowadays it's practically all negro. This is a facet of English life they've seized on with affection! They proceed to run down the 'colonialists', 'imperialists' etc., but seem to forget that few other countries would afford them the privilege of freedom to abuse so fearlessly.

Monday, 9 July

On the bus today, the conductor said 'Shaftesbury Avenue' and a man said 'Did you say *let's be having you*?' Conductor: 'I didn't. But do you want to make something of it?' Man: 'Not before I've had me strawberries.' Then he got off the bus.

Friday, 13 July

Ghastly performance. Rebecca West[17] came round after & was v. nice. Said it was like watching the French theatre! After, Mags & I went to Peter Wood for dinner and it was an awful fiasco. We were both terribly rude and the atmosphere was nasty and O, I should never mix with actors at all. Except perhaps one at a time. Home at 3!

Saturday, 14 July

All this week it has been foul weather, wet sticky heat hanging like a blanket of doom over the city. The theatre has been like performing to a dishrag. Today it was so heavy & still that it was putrid, & felt like a plague-ridden town. I'm amazed to see that people aren't covered in spots & sores: but they look incredibly healthy on the whole. I had lunch with Louie & Pat at Brunswick. Then we all went to Brompton Hosp. Charlie looked v. ill, and insisted on showing me his swollen testicles which were larger than a cricket ball. I suddenly felt quite awful. He had a stupid argument with Louie over an idea he'd had to convert a matchcase into a lighter case. It was all so awful & sad. It has certainly been a terrible week. A disaster feels imminent. It seems as if my whole way of life is cracking up like a jerry-built house.

Sunday, 15 July

As I read all the papers today, I had this ever-increasing sense of *madness*. This feeling of living in an atmosphere of such wilful stupidity

---

[17] Dame Rebecca West (Cicily Fairfield), 1892–1983. Feminist, writer, critic.

& wickedness that I was going *screaming* mad. The blatant *untruths* uttered every day by apparently responsible people. It can't be continually shrugged off, with cynical acceptance.

Monday, 16 July

Took Nora out for supper after show. She mentioned this marriage idea & I told her we ought to go through with it.

Thursday, 2 August

John W. for supper after show. Chatted of this and that. I was rebuffed about the traditional issue. Well, I suppose I don't really want to know anyway. Interview dressing room, David Bruxner for profile in Topic. I talked and talked a load of rubbish. Hope he will sort something out. He seemed very reciprocal and almost a perfect audience: just one or two moments of blankness. 'Calling someone epicene is [a] nice way of saying a pouf,' I cried at him.

Friday, 3 August

S. Doorman told me after the show that Charlie was waiting for me in the White Horse. I met him. He went right off about a scheme for making money with a movable height bed and scaffolding and stuff. I could hardly make head or tail of it. Sounded a load of rubbish. A group of gay pieces kept interrupting & asking if I'd have a drink with them. Eventually Charles left & I chatted to them. They were a disgrace. One asked me to meet it there Wed. lunch time, but I shall not be there. I think Charlie might be growing mentally ill. There is something lunatic about the way he talks of making millions etc. etc.

Saturday, 4 August

Lunch with folks. Louie tells me Charles has been telling her that in 3 months she will be so rich she can live where she likes and etc. He has written to his brother Stanley telling him to come to London & become rich. It's all part of the same dream that's always haunted him – a sudden fortune – either from dogs, horses, or movable beds. It is terribly depressing. I come away from that flat with my stomach going over!

Sunday, 5 August

Spent the day alone. Read thro' the Sunday papers, v. interesting article by Cyril Connolly about the Grand Tour of Europe – such an ugly man – such a delightful pen. I remember when I went to dinner with him at the Etoile in Charlotte St with Peter Wildeblood and Ken & Elaine Tynan, and the latter threw ice cubes at the table – a curious evening. We sat next to Edmundo Ros[18] who viewed us all with amusement.

I played some of my Fauré songs – I'm eternally grateful to George Rose for guiding me to them. How much I owe my friends! John Vere for so much in the realm of comedy and painting: Gordon for so many composers & wonderful hospitality and fun: Stanley for opening my eyes in the theatre: Erich for ordering so many of my wandering thoughts & teaching me the ontological mystery, showing me the value of irony. Val Orford for beginning it all – for canalising all that frustration. O! the list is endless – but they're all there held fast in the tissue of my existence – loved forever – I suddenly recall Hitchman with a pang of guilt. He taught me what romanticism meant; I remember him with real affection – and Goacher, teaching me so much about poetry – the greatest blessing.

Monday, 6 August

Charlie turned up in dressing room again. The same dialogue of megalomania and masochism.

Tuesday, 7 August

Louie phoned & Peter Eade. Charlie made him go round there! Told him about making millions etc. It's all so pathetic. The day hangs heavily. Marilyn Monroe killed herself yesterday & today an English actress in sympathy did the same.[19] The pointlessness of our way of life – the awful cheap regard of human life. Show went OK but small house. Rain pouring all the time.

Friday, 17 August

Charlie asked me to do some drawing of this barmy bed idea. I refused. He left the flat in a temper. I really shouldn't visit him at all – I shouldn't go there. All this heaving in my stomach. Why? I scream inside myself. Why? should I be persecuted in this fashion. All my life he gave me nothing, always he either embarrassed or bored me – in the twilight of his, I spent all my savings on providing a home that is better than anything he's ever had and yet *still* this trouble, trouble, trouble – upsetting Louie, being thrown out of I.C.T. – alienating everyone – the hospital refusing to accommodate him because of his outrageous behaviour – *will it ever end*? Will it drag on till Louie has a breakdown? I feel at the end of my tether.

---

[18] b.1910 in Venezuela, bandleader and singer specialising in Latin rhythms.

[19] The reference is to Pat Marlowe, aged twenty-eight, described by the *Daily Mail* as a 'friend of the stars'.

Saturday, 18 August
Supper with Paul F. at G. & C. and then back to flat. What an incredible disappointment. My own fault of course. I'd been flirting with the idea of sharing with him – kidding myself etc. Suddenly faced with it, I knew I didn't want it. Nothing has changed for P. Still the same old moan about regret that he hasn't worked hard enough. Still the guilt about his naturally hedonistic nature, lovable weak creature, to whom I can be a sort of acquaintance, but nothing more.

Tuesday, 21 August
Tony Walton[20] brought some Americans round, and Beatrice Lillie told some stories – you would have thought it was her dressing room, not mine. If these people don't want to be (or cannot) articulate in praise of yr. performance, why do they come round at all? I certainly don't want to meet them.

Sunday, 2 September
I hardly read anything nowadays apart from thrillers and rubbish and the papers. I find myself going in & out of bookshops empty handed. That reoccurring 'What's the point . . .' I know it's daft, but it's a terrific apathy settled on me lately. I know that my real gift lies in getting laughs & curiously that was the very thing which the *tat* revue enabled me to do. Really I'm an impostor in the Shaffer plays: and they have imprisoned me in the very rut I was trying to avoid. Life is full of these kind of ironies. Lot of insomnia lately.

Sunday, 9 September
I wonder when it was that I first started getting the papers? It was the Sundays first – I used to order one at 57 – only on Sundays. I don't remember reading a daily paper until I left home and went to live at Endsleigh. Then it was the News Chronicle. I changed from that to the Telegraph. Last year I went to the Times, but it got [so] ridiculously low on sheer news that I gave it up and went back to the Telegraph. It's a lousy paper policy wise but the coverage is wider than any paper in England. No! I remember now, before the Chronicle I used to take the Guardian. Found it dull after a bit, so changed to the Chronicle. Yes. That is the right sequence. Wonder why I never took a paper at home!

Thursday, 20 September
Reading a novel called *Wingers Landfall*[21] which is incredibly good. V.

---

[20] Production designer.
[21] *Winger's Land-fall*, by Stuart Lauder (1962).

well observed, and fills me with yearning. It's the first time I've fallen for the 'hero' – it's the kind of ordinariness that I so adore – a romantic dream of course – all romantic heroes look ordinary & are capable of great tenderness – strength etc. etc. It's a dream world. Thank God I only enter it in fiction.

Friday, 21 September

Up at seven o'clock. Looking bleary & dreary. And thinking of the Hero. What sort of idiot am I? '. . . and you can be as big a fool at sixty as you were at sixteen . . .' Perhaps nothing in us fundamental, ever really changes – only the form of it. Basically I'm still that silly small child – coquettish – adoring & longing for the big brother who never appears: or if he did I'd run a mile from the B.O. or something.

Saturday, 22 September

You can tell yourself all kinds of lies I suppose and, if you enjoy the illusions, you can keep it going for quite a time. I've been telling myself for years that I enjoy living alone with my books and my records but it's a load of rubbish really. I like people, especially unsophisticated people – in a pub, or the Army barrack room, or on a ship with ratings, I've always gone down well. That's what I enjoy really – being popular with my social kin. I'm really a sort of barrack room 'card'.

Sunday, 23 September

I went over to S. When I saw him again the memory of my writing him sermons on my refusal to lend money suddenly made me blush with embarrassment & I made an excuse to go to the bathroom. The reason is – S. is a v. honest person and how throws [*sic*] one's bogusness up to embarrassing proportions.[22] And it was bogus of me to write telling him to behave etc. One has no right to preach to others and no right to take away their dignity.

Wednesday, 26 September

Evening show v. good really. Then with Mags & Bev[23] to the Establishment to see Frankie Howerd. He was v. good but his performance was marred by an awful woman who kept shouting and interrupting him. I must say, he bore it all with great good humour. She was quite

---

22 To 'show something up to embarrassing proportions' was an odd phrase KW did use elsewhere.

23 Beverley Cross, b.1931, playwright and director, later (1975) husband of Maggie Smith.

impossible & the sort of things she shouted were intended to sound v. smart & clever. In fact, they were banal.

Thursday, 4 October
Never felt so awful in my life as I did during performance. Like my inside was trembling and acceleration going on while outside all was calm. Got through it somehow.

Friday, 5 October
Out with Mags & Bev and Peter O'Toole and his wife Siân Phillips. It was the end. He talks, talks, talks the whole time. Desperately trying to kid himself he's different. Loads of stories about him making other people pipe down – 'I told him' etc. I was quite exhausted by it all. He told several camp stories. I heard them all years ago.

Saturday, 6 October
I think I've been more conscious of loneliness this year than at any other period in my life before. Yet I do the same things that I always did. I suppose it's 'cos all my friends are away – Gordon – George Rose – Stanley – Hussey on tour – etc. etc.

Sunday, 7 October
Annette Kerr arrived at 4 o'clock and we had some tea. 'You do make a lovely cup of tea,' she said, so I replied, 'Well, why don't you share a flat with me?' But she said it would never work out – her smalls in the bathroom, she said, were inevitable . . .

Monday, 8 October
I went to Landau about a suit. Light grey. When I saw meself in their mirror I nearly died. My eyes have great puffs under them. Really awful. Went to the theatre and found a letter from John F.!! asking for seats for tomorrow. It does seem extraordinary to remember that all that happened all that time ago. (1948)

Saturday, 13 October
Lunched Louie. Charlie was there, but left shortly after I arrived. He talked about the ease with which he swindled the railway by not showing tickets at barrier or some such nonsense. Louie in a state because her Post Office Bank book is missing.

Sunday, 14 October
With Henry to lunch at G. & C. – then we walked thro' the city. On my return to the flat there was a message from Louie to say she was at the St Mary Abbot's Hospital where Charles was ill. I went there.

She had gone. They said they were working on Charles & I wouldn't be able to see him for a long time. I went to the flat and found Louie with Pat. Pat had a cold so I didn't stay long. Louie explained that Charles had taken some stuff from a bottle labelled 'Gee's Linctus' which caused him terrible pain. She rang 999 and got a doctor & the police. Apparently they think the bottle contained some sort of cleaning fluid, though how it ever got into the Gee's Linctus bottle is v. mysterious. Anyway they (police) asked all sorts of questions including what was my profession! The upshot of it all, is that Charles is v. ill, and the hospital will call her if there is an emergency. She seems to think it's the end and that he is dying, but I don't think that is true. Surely if it were, the hospital would ask you to stay – oh – I don't know. I'll have to take sleeping pills tonight I suppose.

Monday, 15 October

Telephoned Louie. Charles is all right. The hospital say he is better. I knew this is how it would turn out. Eventually the hospital will send him home, and then it will start all over again. When he went into hospital, Louie found her Post Office Book in his pocket. He had stolen it, forged her signature, and drawn about eight pounds in two days. And on Sat. when I was there, he denied all knowledge of it & said 'What Post Office Book? I don't know what you're talking about . . .'

Met Gordon J. Lunch Scott's. Saw film *Dr No.*

Louie rang 7. Charles died at St Mary Abbot's Hospital at 3 o'c. today. So it's all over. The doctor told Louie his brain was damaged, that the heart was v. impaired, and kidneys in bad condition. That it was, in reality, a good thing, because he would have become much worse.

Show went OK. Audience good. Supper with Mags and Bev. We talked about what Charles could have taken & B. said it sounded like a corrosive poison. He kept saying (Charles did) 'Take these knives out of my stomach . . .'

Tuesday, 16 October

I telephoned Louie. She has to attend the hosp. at 10.30 with Pat to ascertain about the Post Mortem – the doctor requested her permission to hold one, and she assented. I suppose this is to decide why he died – i.e. cause – apropos the Death Certificate. I shall be glad when it's over. She (Louie) is in a state of near hysteria & crying all the time – with Pat aiding the drama. I can't be with them because P. has a raging cold. Louie visited me about three. She told me that there is to be an inquest at Hammersmith Coroner's Court on Friday at 9.30. I think it's best if I do not attend because I would give it undue publicity which could only be harmful to Louie. Peter E[ade]. telephoned & said he would attend with Louie. He is good.

Friday, 19 October
Inquest 9.30. Hammersmith Coroner's Court. Pat rang me at about 10.45 to say they were home. I went over there. Peter E. was with them, having gone to the Court too. Apparently it went all right & Louie behaved superbly. They returned a verdict of Death by Misadventure* or accidental death. I took Louie & Pat shopping. At John Lewis Pat got a lovely coat in black, & Louie got a black dress from D.H. Evans.

*due to corrosive poisoning by carbon tetrachloride.

Saturday, 20 October
Met Louie and Pat. They came to flat, they obtained death certificate from Cheniston Gdns. States death was due to 'Bronchial Pneumonia and Carbon Tetrachloride Poisoning self administered, by accident.' A v. roundabout way of going on.

Tuesday, 23 October
Funeral of Charles, Golders Green Crematorium at 12 o'c. They all came from his family and Cliff, Edith & Siegfried & Alice & Bill from Louie's side.

Wednesday, 24 October
Went to bank at Notting Hill Gate & settled Charlie's overdraft with them. Gave them a cheque for the amount.

Thursday, 25 October
Show went all right. On the way home I saw a terrible fight in the court on way to Brewer St so I flew up Berwick Mkt. and got a policeman, he came back with me to scene of fight. It was quite horrible. Everyone standing watching & doing nothing, tho' it was obvious that the smaller one couldn't defend himself.

Saturday, 27 October
Gave Henry D. lunch in flat, and then we went to see film *The Wild and the Willing*, which was a real old hotchpotch. But there was one actor, *John Hurt*, who was just superb. One of those faces that acts – an actor who lets you see thoughts and hear dialogue about something else. That rare thing – an authentic actor. I think he will become a star. The voice quality had a rare timbre – O! it was a joy to see such acting.

Friday, 16 November
We went to the bank to start Louie getting used to cheque writing, and then went to Biagi for lunch, very nice. Then I walked with Louie all the way back to Kensington through the park. There was no more snow, just a very cold day – the trees almost bare, and a lowering sky. It's the dying time of the year – sad – and full of broken promises & unkept resolutions.

Tuesday, 20 November
Louie came with me to Essex Road where I saw Mr Hazel in Jay's, to choose a cup of silver. Richard P. & I are going to give it to Mags on the last night of her stay. Inscribed 'The Pearson-Williams Award to Maggie Smith, commemorating her superb performances in *The Private Ear and the Public Eye* on over 200 occasions at the Globe Theatre, London.'

Wednesday, 21 November
Thinking about what I wrote on [2 February 1962] regarding acting – I realise now that it is this vulnerability that I don't want to indulge in any more. I don't *want* to show myself to audiences. I have changed over the years – once, this was the very thing I did want. A really superb actor takes pleasure in showing himself. I don't want to. This is why I'm not v. good in the scene with Mags. Yet when I began my career this is the scene I would have played well, and all the other stuff I'd have been lousy or competent at.

Thursday, 29 November
To Binkie's party at Lord North St. It was quite frightening. Nobody but nobody with any grace. Redgrave, obviously high, John Clements forgivably fraught (it was his opening night – *Tulip Tree*[24] at the Haymarket), Celia Johnson looking awful and doing nasal impressions of me to my face. Everyone sitting eating, but Mags & Bev & me had to stand. Rude. That awful Joyce Carey was sitting on a great stool & didn't offer to move over. They were like a lot of elderly, wealthy pigs.

Monday, 3 December
Mags told me that Wanamaker told her the dialogue was so fast he couldn't hear her. So she said 'Not to worry, it's published now, so you can read it . . .'

---

24 By Norman Hunter.

Wednesday, 19 December
Received a letter from Robert Bolt about being in his play about Jack o' the Green. It sounds like a v. difficult role & he has asked about my availability, am I going to America with this play etc. Of course I said no.

Saturday, 22 December
1st house: A Stinker. 2nd house: all right. Lift home after with Mags. As her leaving approaches, it arouses something akin to panic in me. Her scene with Richard is a lesson in Comedy technique & boy – this play really needs it.

Friday, 28 December
Went to Harrod's and got Louie a splendid little Jack Russell – 3 months – well actually 11 weeks old today. Brought him home to my flat where he urinated 5 times on carpet & linotiles, then to Pat's flat where he evacuated copiously. Pat will get in touch with Louie & say he is a present from us both.

Saturday, 29 December
The weather cold and dreary and mediocre audiences made M.'s departure drab & unexciting. I didn't say goodbye or anything, 'cos I'd have cried. But that girl has a magic, and a deftness of touch in comedy that makes you really grateful, and she's capable of a generosity of spirit that is beautiful. She's one of those rare people who make things & places suddenly *marvellous* by just being there. She's adorable.

Sunday, 30 December
A terrific snow blizzard started about 1 o'c. this morning & it was still raging when I started out to Louie's today at 9 o'c. Even with drifts of over a foot on roads, the buses were *running*. The London buses are just *incredible*: wonderful crews, all of them.

NOTES
What a year! My release from that awful revue into the 'sanctuary' of straight theatre. But still they follow me with their rotten barbs – 'outrageous revue actor,' etc. This they call me. Me, who feels so often that I'm almost on the threshold of contact in the theatre – but O so rarely! There is absolutely nothing outrageous either in my approach to my art or the accomplishment. I couldn't be more conventional. It is they who are outrageous – in that they completely fail to respond to proper acting – i.e. vulnerable acting. They shrink from it, they are shocked by it – so a label must be found and it can be conveniently dismissed. Still, it was a good year really. Charlie's death released

Louie from that rat trap of a marriage, and now she's happy with Jack R. who's like a baby to her – I was released from revue – and I proved that I could bring them in apropos box office. One thing I must do next time – have a proper holiday, even if it means paying someone to come with me.

1963

Tuesday, 1 January
Judith Stott[1] was 100% improved last night, after I had a chat with her about the playing. I told her after that no one had responded so quickly to advice. It was excellent. No one there though. She gave me a lift home.

Wednesday, 2 January
Did 'B.O.K.' from the Paris. I was ragging Betty M[arsden] a lot, and felt v. guilty after, because she was v. ill & husband came (Dr) with medicine. I apologised. She was v. nice. We got through the show OK. It was a rehash of an old script. Certainly went over OK.

Thursday, 3 January
Judith S. asked me down to dressing room to meet Carol Reiss[2] some awful film bloke. He talked a lot of rubbish about pace! Said the dialogue was so fast he felt he was 'missing some pearls'. In Shaffer's dialogue this certainly isn't true, but even if it were they'd have been cast before swine with this twot present.

Friday, 4 January
Went to the film *Sodom and Gomorrah* but only the latter bothered to turn up I'm afraid! Still, it was quite fun. I got an invitation to the Savoy for the Evening Standard Drama Awards. I wouldn't attend this kind of shit if they paid me.

Sunday, 6 January
Pleasant time with Andrew [Ray] & Sue[3] but I was afflicted by wind & the odour not v. pleasant. They charmingly ignored it.

---

[1] Who had taken over from Maggie Smith.
[2] Karel Reisz, b.1926. Film director.
[3] His wife (Susan).

Wednesday, 9 January

Letter from Robert Bolt saying that the play was growing, that he'd had lunch with Edith Evans (that old ham) and that 'my part' was becoming larger. It's all v. well doing this sort of thing but I fear Bob doesn't realise that the next stage play I do has got to be v. good for me. I'm sick of helping other people to become names. Precious little thanks one gets for it too.

Thursday, 10 January

Noël Coward waved to us in the auditorium – he was laughing during serious bits of the perf.

Friday, 11 January

This is the coldest winter I can remember – they keep comparing it with 1947, but I don't recall it v. well – tho' I remember how all the pipes used to burst at 57 and Charlie was always out on the roof doing things.

Monday, 14 January

The Evening Standard team who decide the Drama Awards have agreed on Scofield as the Actor of the Year. This is for that chronic Lear at the Aldwych. The whole thing is a farce. (Maggie Smith won it for the best actress.) It should have been me. O! it's a disgrace. They invited me to the Savoy for the presentations. I tore up the invitation. They can stick their awards up their arseholes.

Friday, 18 January

The papers are full of this Vassall enquiry. The reporters giving evidence all talk about homosexual intrigue & hint at dark secrets in high places. All the muck raking is going on. To no advantage. Homosexuality in itself is no vice, a law which makes it one is evil. Had the government acted on the findings of the Wolfenden report, this whole nasty episode would have never occurred.

Monday, 21 January

Read a marvellous book about comparative amateurs who raised & salvaged a huge tanker off the coast of Atlantic City. It sounded really wonderful. That sense of adventure & team spirit, and Achievement. This is what modern life has taken away from the individual. Give a crowd of teenagers a bomb site in London & one would see something happen. But no. We're ringed in by planners, developers, architects, surveyors, solicitors, builders, unions, and it all straggles on.

Tuesday, 22 January
Stott has bashed her face up, tobogganing. She is a great fool.

Wednesday, 23 January
'B.O.K.' The radio show went very well. Eric M[erriman] said I was 'outrageous' – I think I will never know what people mean by this. One spends a deal of energy, time & vulnerability, trying to raise a laugh and one is accused of being outrageous. The critics are exactly the same. They simply don't understand the very thing they're supposed to be watching. They should read Shakespeare's Clowns & see the desperation there. So great that they speak what no one else dares to speak. And they call me 'outrageous'. They don't even begin to see the desperation of my own perilous position.

Saturday, 26 January
Supper with Judith S., who is converging on me more & more. It would be terribly easy to get involved here. I must tread v. warily. In the plays she has made such leaps & bounds it is marvellous. I think we're v. lucky to have got her.

Monday, 28 January
300th Performance at Globe. At the theatre tonight we had the Queen, Prince Philip, The Kents, The Gloucesters and everything. It was all v. distinguished.

Thursday, 31 January
Show in evening. It's now a corpse as far as I'm concerned. Like *St Joan* (in which I was praised) I feel I'm missing out on lots of major points. Nothing I can do about it any more.

Friday, 1 February
Read script of the Peter Rogers film *Call me a Cab*[4] and hated it. Wrote and said I didn't want to do it.

Monday, 4 February
Met Andrew [Ray] for lunch. We went to Olmi's and then bus to St Paul's and walk thro' to the Old Bailey. We heard a case of manslaughter & the defendant – driver of a car which had killed an old lady – suspected of running away after the accident. Prosecution was v. good – so was the Defence. The Judge was terrible. Didn't get a single laugh.

---

[4] Alias *Carry On Cabby*. KW did not appear in the film.

Tuesday, 5 February
Snow and cold. Show evening all right. Took about 6 whiskies, Seconal & Noludar. Opened bedroom window. Slept from about midnight to seven thirty.

Wednesday, 6 February
The matingay was freetening. I giggled a lot. I've definitely had it.

Saturday, 9 February
Went to see early showing of *This Sporting Life* with Rachel Roberts. She is marvellous. Richard Harris is superb in it too. He is unquestionably a *star*. I haven't seen it in him before. You really *care*. I didn't stay to the end tho' 'cos the direction of the film was so awful. Expect it will get rave notices from the posh critics in the Sundays.

Friday, 15 February
Eade telephoned that Ed Murrow wanted me for his television show. I said no thank you. And moreover I'm not going to do another Carry On either. In fact I've got to get this entire work situation in proper perspective. I never want to earn much over ten thousand & I never want to do all that 3 jobs at once stuff again. It's really not worth it.

Tuesday, 19 February
A really terrible day. A depression settled over me & nothing could lift it. I suddenly felt quite trapped by everything. Codron last night with his play, Shaffer on at me about working with him, Robert B. with his play, and the Richard Williams film, and the turning down of the P. Rogers script. I suddenly felt as if I were *really* a pawn. Some clay for a potter to throw.

Wednesday, 20 February
I phoned Robert Bolt. He said that it was a good part which would merit starring. But said obviously I would have to go under Edie Evans. But how far under? I don't know. After all, it will be me that is being a 'draw', not her. Why should I have to prop up these sort of ruins?

Friday, 22 February
Met Baxter & we saw film. When we came out, his car was blocked & he couldn't back out. He didn't mention me getting to the theatre *once*. Only went off about how annoying it was to him. I left him there cursing & got a bus to the theatre. If the roles had been reversed, I would have said 'Never mind about this – you get off to the theatre

– I'll sort it out on my own.' I know now that he is really selfish. I know why the friendship is waning.*

*How stupidly I write when in a hurry! Of course he was irritated & angry about the car & even if it was selfish – so what? – and why should my standards apply to him? It is this idea of 'judgment' that continually *mars* my relationships with others.

Tuesday, 26 February
O! these days of desperation. I feel my stomach going out like a great swelling bumhole. I grow physically & mentally lazy: & increasingly malicious. These days of hunger. I'm always hungry.

Friday, 8 March
I have been doing the remedial exercises every day since Monday. And I've kept on the diet. I feel much better really & don't wake with that awful dizzy drag. I find the Noludar works OK. I'm taking 600mg at night. Will try to reduce this.

Saturday, 9 March
I'm just about sick of this diet business. My eye twitch has returned, my hair has become grey, and my nails have longitudinal ridges – 2 have split. I'm going back to milk tomorrow I can tell you. All this worry about my figure came from the idea of playing this part in R. Bolt's play – this god in garlands. I'll just have to admit I can't wear that kind of costume.

Wednesday, 13 March
350th performance. Frank Stevens, the S/Director, told us that Richard Pasco is to take over the role from me in June. This is a v. pedestrian choice from the management. They'll be short on laughs. But everyone will probably say the usual crap about 'a more truthful performance . . .' etc. etc.

Thursday, 14 March
Met Richard & Pat Pearson & we all lunched at the G. & C. Then we all went to see Schmidt at the Queen's. On the way we met Alastair Sim who said 'Ah! she's the real thing – tell her from me, she's got a secret lover!' Well, she was *marvellous* in the play. A fabulously inventive performance: the others are all quite good: but there's no question she is the best comedienne in this country.

Friday, 15 March
Stanley B. rang me. I was delighted & I shot up there to see him on the 30 bus. He drove out to Bucks & we talked & talked. There are

times (when he is prepared to be vulnerable) when he is just superb. Disarming, honest, charming, and hilariously funny *all* at once. When he's like this one could die for him. It was so good for me to see him.

Wednesday, 20 March

I think Louie looks better now that the dog is gone. He was definitely too much for her, and she hasn't got that worry any more. I met Bev for tea & he showed me the particulars of the cruise to the Greek Islands. We are going to his travel people tomorrow to find out if we can get on it or not. It should be excellent as a set-up, for Bev is very lively & full of style and it is essential to holiday with someone you like.

Thursday, 21 March

Bev's show *Half A Sixpence* with Tommy Steele opened at Cambridge. Quite good notices. I predict a long run.[5] It's a long time since a musical really appealed.

Wednesday, 27 March

Dinner after show with Mags. We had a long chat. I am so delighted to be with her. I always feel so proud of her – she looks so marvellous – her hands are the loveliest I've ever seen. And her humour is always so superb & dry. She talked about Liz Taylor and how frail & vulnerable she looked (she's in this film *VIPs* with Burton & Taylor) and said it's obvious on the set that Taylor is in love with Burton. What a dreadful mess it all sounds. She said Richard is v. grave and calls her 'Elizabeth' – which I must say sounds very charming to me.

Thursday, 28 March

The house was good humoured. Supper after with Mags and Sheila Hancock & we all moaned about the people one has to work with. Home about 12.30. But I bet it's the first time there's been three stage stars at one table in Lyons' Corner House.

Sunday, 31 March

Pat moved in with Louie at Brunswick. I think it will work out all right.

Tuesday, 2 April

It's fantastic what's going on in the City – they're cleaning St Paul's! and all behind there now are new buildings going up. The changes in a few weeks are amazing.

---

[5] It ran for 678 performances.

RIGHT: 'Taken on the roof of my Junior School in Manchester Street – now called the Argyle Street Junior School. It shows me in the school production of the play *The Rose and The Ring*, which Basil Hodges directed: first time I was ever in drag. The second time was '58 at the Coliseum in *Cinderella*.' 11 January 1968.
'Kenneth Williams, with his mincing step and comical demeanour, as Princess Angelica, was a firm favourite with the audience, to whom his snobbishness and pert vivacity made great appeal.' *St Pancras Gazette*, c.1935.

BELOW: 'Jimmy Viccars and I, in *Seven Keys to Baldpate*, Victoria Theatre, Singapore, 1946.' KW's dramatic debut, as Jigs Kennedy; Viccars as Lou Max.

LEFT: KW in CSE's musical revue *High and Low*, Victoria Theatre, Singapore. ('The Brigadier went down lousy!' 3 February 1947.)

BELOW: 'The Three Caballeros', from *High and Low*. With Frank Bale as Bamba, Maurice Weintroub as Samba, and KW as Caramba. ('Dances arranged by Barri Chatt.')

RIGHT: 'Marie [Earley] and I, in Leicester Sq. yesterday – looking quite dreadful! But it *was* a lousy day!' 16 February 1948. (Taken by a street photographer.)

BELOW: Newquay Repertory players in *The Poltergeist*. KW (left) as Vincent Ebury. 'The words are bad in this – people haven't learned their lines properly and it's coming over as a tat production.' 3 August 1948.

ABOVE: New to the profession: studio portrait, c.1948.

RIGHT: Charlie and Louisa Williams on holiday in Devon, 20 June 1948.

RIGHT: Character portrait, from *The Shop at Sly Corner*, Bromley, March 1949. 'Playing the part of blackmailer at the New Theatre this week is Kenneth Williams, a young man with, I'll warrant, a bright future. His is an odious part, played with a sneer that seems to come from the heart – as neat a piece of acting as the company has given us.' HBH in the *Bromley and Kentish Times*.

BELOW: With Annette Kerr in *No Time for Comedy*. 'I love Annette Kerr. She's quite the sweetest person I ever knew.' 10 July 1949.

LEFT: 'Rehearsed *Fools Rush In*. Barbara Murray arrived. She appears quite charming. V. attractive.' Barbara Murray as Pam Dickson, KW as Joe: Margate, April 1950.

BELOW: Very austerity: the 'Still-Life' section of Noël Coward's *Tonight at Eight-Thirty* (the prototype of *Brief Encounter*), with KW as Stanley, carrying the tray, Guildford Theatre. 'This is undoubtedly tat of the most menacing order.' 30 April 1951.

RIGHT: 'Fitting at Wig Creations, where I looked exactly like a tarty lesbian.' KW as the Angel, Barry Jones as the Vicar, in *The Wonderful Visit*, for BBC Television, January 1952.

BELOW: Ronald Searle's caricature of Siobhan McKenna and KW in *St Joan*, *Punch*, 6 October 1954. 'I am greatly taken with it': KW, 9 October. (*Punch*)

LEFT: KW in *St Joan*, September–October 1954: 'a brilliantly fussy Dauphin, ageing without effort into a skinny and abandoned lapdog' (Kenneth Tynan, *Observer*).

LEFT: 'This photograph of me and Sally Bazely was taken in the dressing room at the Lyric, Hammersmith, by Billie Love. I am made up for "Montgomery" in *The Buccaneer*.' 4 February 1956.

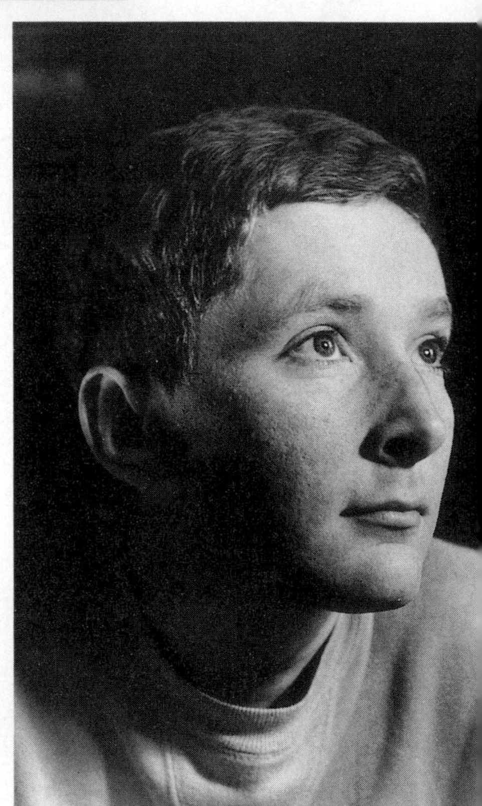

RIGHT: KW with the remains of his *Buccaneer* haircut. Inserted in the diary (as a negative) at 2 May 1956.

Thursday, 4 April

Evening perf. went well. Louie & P. came to see it. After, we all went to the G. & C. with Bev and Mags. Very pleasant evening. Mags told us that Dickie Wattis slapped Jack Palance on the face, & after a pause J.P. said 'You do that again and I'll hit your head so hard it'll match up with your arse . . .' Dickie beat a v. hasty retreat.

Friday, 5 April

Announced in the newspapers that Stanley Baxter is having a nervous breakdown, and left the cast of the play he was doing at the Arts, with Fenella Fielding. I rang Moira but she said he was on the special pills & doctor's orders & seeing no one at the moment.

Monday, 8 April

Patrick Garland came round and we had dinner at a place called Woolf's which was very good. He is an interesting person and talks good sense and is v. lively. I must say I like him enormously. He is convinced that we are all ripe for the H-Bomb & total annihilation for the sick mess we've got ourselves into. I don't. I think that is too neat. I think we'll go on torturing each other & making Hell endlessly, endlessly. I think this Hell is part of the human condition – like pain, anguish and cruelty as well as all the loveliness for which I'm deeply grateful.

Wednesday, 10 April

Went in to town. It was raining, so I walked all the way with my new umbrella. I was in high spirits & sang to myself or muttered dialogue. Forced to use public lav. at Oxf. Circus 'cos I was dying for a pee, flew out again & sang louder to allay fear. Purchased plums from a barrow in Rupert St and a not unattractive cockney said 'I know you like the big ones . . .' with a great leer. I remained quite composed: 'Just so,' I replied airily. Mags popped in to see us at the Globe after & we all read the reports in the paper about Richard Burton's separation from Sybil. Apparently she won't allow a divorce.

Saturday, 13 April

11 to 1 o'c. Rehearse Lime Grove. The running order buggered up by Huw Wheldon[6] with all this 'Of course it's none of my business but I think . . .' to Patrick Garland: so it's all to be changed. Silly really. All due to the whim of this V.I.P.

---

[6] Sir Huw Wheldon (1916–86), Head of Music and Documentary Programmes, BBC, from 1963; later Controller of Programmes (1965–68), Managing Director (1968–75) etc.

Sunday, 14 April

To TV Centre for the Poetry Reading on 'Monitor'. It was appalling. I looked awful. Sounded awful. Lighting was atrociously Arty. Came home fearfully depressed. This is always my reaction to TV. It's simply not my medium.

Wednesday, 17 April

Evening show marred by appalling alliteration in one of my speeches – I heard fire engine bells & in order to distract audience attention from them, began to speak louder and more rapidly & suddenly lost all sense of the speech. Of course I never recovered.

Thursday, 18 April

Lunch Baxters. I think he used the nervous breakdown theory in order to get out of a nasty mess. I don't blame him in the least.

Friday, 19 April

Now I'm 9st. 12, so in about 6 weeks I have lost nine pounds. I think that is considerable.

Saturday, 20 April

Supper with Stott who kept hinting that she'd discovered me to be untrustworthy. I told her that was no discovery. O! these people who want sincerity & trust! How perfectly dreary they all are. And how untalented.

Tuesday, 23 April

Lot of fuss in the papers & crowds in town for this wedding of Princess Alexandra. What a load of old hogwash.

Friday, 26 April

The most appalling reverberating noise above my head all night. I got the porter up at 1.45 in morning, but he couldn't do anything. I pray that something may be done about it, for my life is purgatory with all this kind of noise. Tonight was the 400th Performance in London. Today was really a bit of a write-off for me, because it began so badly and it made me a mess of nerves.

Tuesday, 30 April

I've thought and thought about this Bolt play issue. And the more I do, the more convinced I am that I don't want to be in it. And one of the things I resent most of all about B. is his patronage of me. The last thing that he said was 'One thing I'm certain of is that the part doesn't need you any more – it's strong enough on its own now . . .'

No part is ever strong on its own. As Mr Shaffer is going to find out soon, on June 3rd.

Wednesday, 1 May

M. says she is going to join the National Company in '64 & has been offered v.g. parts. I recoil in horror from the repertoire theatre. Story current at the moment of the Queen chatting to a man at the Buck House gdn. party.

Q: What is your profession?
M: I'm a photographer, Ma'am.
Q: What a coincidence! My brother-in-law is a photographer!
M: Even more of a coincidence, Ma'am, my brother-in-law is a queen!

Friday, 3 May

Went to Le Cheminant in Wigmore St and ordered a lovely gold Omega for 50 pounds, for Richard P[earson]. I'm having engraved on the back '1962/Richard from Kenneth/1963' as a memento of our association in the play. And because he has been a true friend to me, & one whom I want to keep.

Sunday, 12 May

Phone rang twice but I hadn't the courage to answer. 'O to find a voice to meet the voice that you must meet . . .'[7]

Monday, 13 May

That couple of dreary bores Thorndike & Casson got rotten notices for their nasty little recital at the Haymarket. Terrible business box office. Nobody wants to know. What monstrous ego induces these sort of people to recite alone on a stage for 2 hours! (What venom I show in the above sentence! and how unnecessary it is . . . their star is already in the descendant, the embers are about to become ashes, there is no need for me to help this process. I should be quiet. I should be dignified. I should not be vulgar.)

Tuesday, 14 May

At 11.30 this morning I've got Dick Williams coming to discuss the Gogol script for his film *Diary of a Madman*. He came. I read the pieces. V. good I think, and he brought 2 LPs' with music by Shade (Peter)

---

[7] cf. Eliot: 'There will be time, there will be time/To prepare a face to meet the faces that you meet.' ('The Love Song of J. Alfred Prufrock')

for the film. It is *superb*. His music for *Love Me* was marvellous enough but this is a *dream*. This sort of music makes me want to give thanks to God, it shows Him in people, it shows the beauty and the redemption. It gave me buoyancy for the rest of the day. I practically sailed to the theatre. Gave a v.g. performance.

Thursday, 16 May

I keep thinking about property because I will have to find something by end of '64 and I cannot risk any more this endless trouble of rudeness & noise in blocks of flats. Ideally I want a bachelor place that is quiet. I must find quiet. At least quiet from people. I don't really mind impersonal noise, but not people.

Thursday, 23 May

Recording *Diary of a Madman* for Richard Williams. We were at it solidly from 10.30 to 5. It was diabolical. I think it is almost impossible to do this well. Every time it is a compromise between art and technical requirement. Every speech having to be exactly timed within seconds. All the really mad sequences requiring speed and clarity.

Wednesday, 29 May

In between houses, R. & I had tea at Act One & were joined by J[ohn] P[erry] who thanked me for playing for over a year. I suppose it's been the happiest engagement of my life really, and certainly the best acting performance I've ever given.

Saturday, 1 June

Funny sort of day thinking all the while about going off tomorrow. 1st house empty practically. 2nd not much better. Did all my packing & got the hire car at 5 to eleven to take me back to flat.

Sunday, 2 June

Car arrived at 8, picked up Bev at 8.10, plane London Airport 9.50. Arrived Venice at 12. Lunched Danieli. Got the *Romantica* at 6.30. Sailed about 8. It all seems very nice, people on the stodge side but that's inevitable. Wrote to Robert Bolt from Venice saying I didn't want to do his play.

Monday, 3 June

At 6.45 we had the cocktail party with the Captain. Handshakes & bonhomie. Me blowing off v. liberally. But the people. All freetening. The Americans worst. The Germans a close second. Revolting. Pigs. We go ashore tomorrow at Corfu.

Thursday, 6 June
Athens. Arrive 8 o'c. Bev and I went our own way up to the Acropolis. All just as fantastic as one expected, breathtaking spectacle. The capital itself is second rate as a city, but the ancient stuff marvellous. There is a fabulous head of Alexander in the Acropolis Museum.

Sunday, 9 June
Istanbul. All day. Arrived over an hour late due to fog. After 8.30 it cleared & sun came out over the skyline of Istanbul, showing the mosques & towers. Lovely.

Wednesday, 12 June
We arrived in Mykonos which was delightful. Had dinner ashore there. Bev liked it 'cos Lawrence Durrell[8] was dining there too – so he went over and spoke to him & his wife.

Thursday, 13 June
Went to Delphi by coach. We went all over the Temple and the Roman Stadium and the Greek Theatre all fascinating and marvellous. The situation on the top of the mountain there is so dramatic the legend of Apollo is almost believable.

Friday, 14 June
Cruising all day. So boring. I think this cruise is ending not a moment too soon. Eventually a small boat like this is v. restricting & the same old dreary faces around one begin to pall & suddenly you want to be home again.

Saturday, 15 June
Dubrovnik. It was awful. Just unbelievably awful. Architecturally superb, owing to the Austro-Hungarians and the Venetians, but the rest – awful. The shops drab and pitiful. What a terrible place.

Monday, 17 June. Venice
Sitting outside Florian's saw Clifford Evans who went right off. Said the square was 'the drawing room of Europe . . .'[9]

Tuesday, 18 June
Saw Eve Arden in the square, also Dirk Bogarde. They're all here. It's a disgrace.

---

[8] 1912–90. Writer.
[9] A description first applied by Napoleon Bonaparte.

Wednesday, 19 June
Arrived London Airport 3.30. Mags was there with the car. Lovely.

Thursday, 20 June
A flood of mail to be answered. Script of *Carry On Sailor*[10] from Peter Rogers. To be read. Letter from R. Bolt saying he was 'sharply disappointed' about me not doing his play. It's v. tricky. Moral: don't make friends with a playwright.

Saturday, 22 June
Went to the Garrick to see Sheila in *Rattle of a Simple Man*.[11] She was absolutely marvellous. Went round & said so.

Monday, 24 June
In the evening H[enry Davies] and I met Sheila Hancock at Biagi for supper. V. lively. We talked of the moral indignation aroused by the Profumo debate & agreed it was all humbug.

Friday, 28 June
Met Bev at 7 and we went to the Savoy to see *The Masters*[12] with John Clements. One got the impression of watching the second eleven. Acting technique seems to be a dying thing. English artists just muddle thro' with a sort of bellow on the beginning of the line and then a dying fall.

Tuesday, 2 July
We did the wills – Louie leaving equally divided shares to P. & me. I leaving all the stuff to Louie & in the event of her death, to P. Thus, all stays in the fambly.

Saturday, 6 July
Andrew played an LP of Johnny Mathis called *Warm*. It is really the first time I've ever heard this man sing. He is superb technically. Knows exactly how to put over a ballad. Vocally he's obviously the best there is today. Andrew says he's never in the Top Ten or whatever it is.

Tuesday, 9 July
My condition is worsening every day. Inside, I'm like a cauldron of despair. When I hear polite banalities being exchanged, I could scream

---

[10] Subsequently renamed *Carry On Jack*.
[11] By Charles Dyer.
[12] By Ronald Millar.

with anger. I feel that I want to escape from the world that I know, into some primitive ordinariness where there is time & atmosphere for *people* to be important: not *things*. And yet I know that I can't escape anywhere. Wherever you run you take your problem with you.

Saturday, 13 July
Did the 'Juke Box Jury'[13] thing. I think I was awful. I really shouldn't take part in these ad lib things. I'm just not v. good at this kind of thing. Long telegram from Bolt asking would I consider playing 'Jack' for a limited time of say 3 months: I have to go down to Hampshire where he's moved to discuss this with him and Noel Willman who is staying there as a guest.

Sunday, 14 July
By car to the Bolts. Upshot was that I agreed to work with them for limited period, starting from 2nd October.

Monday, 15 July
I must say I liked Noel Willman enormously. I really warmed to him. I should think he would be v.g. as a director, he is a feeling and sensitive person. They told me (he and Bob) that I had a kind of magic that would be right for the role. That only I could do it. I bet when I start to do it, they'll all be saying no, that's not it at all.

Friday, 19 July
11 o'c. at Benson's in Kingsway to do a television commercial in snide voice. A very nasty young man there who was withering, obviously a poof. There is something v. objectionable about these young men in Hardy Amies suits who always have boxes of 50 fags and generate poshery. I'd like to have kicked him up the arse but controlled my temper & said 'Well how do you want it?'

Thursday, 25 July
Went to Eyeline & met Dick Williams. He played me the track of the Gogol script. I thought it was marvellous. It really did suggest the mind gradually disintegrating. I was v. impressed by my own work.[14]

---

[13] Television show, revived in 1990, in which well-known guests gave verdicts on newly released pop records.

[14] So were the critics when the soundtrack, reconstituted by BBC studio manager John Whitehall after KW's death, was broadcast on Radio 4 (3 February 1991). 'Williams gives perhaps the most affecting performance of his career playing, of all things, a Russian who thinks he's the King of Spain' (*Independent*).

Saturday, 3 August
The day was lowering – heavy clouds, dark, and rain pouring. On my way to Louie's I was stopped by a boy who said he was Johnny Savage[15] & could I help him to find Pete Murray who was to help him get a job as a pop singer. I came back to the flat for some money and gave him the fare back to Cardiff & told him to go home.

Monday, 5 August
I suppose I shall go through this phase of crisis in my head again and again. I seem to feel everything again & again: it's as though I'm an echo chamber for everything to bang about in and reverberate. Outside I'm perfectly calm. No one would know. It's truly ironic that I should do the sound track for the *Diary of a Madman*. Perhaps madness is the last refuge for the over-sensitive: perhaps it's the cover of kindness that the world draws over you when you can fight no more.

Wednesday, 7 August
I don't think I could ever go mad. I see myself too clearly. I know even at the moment of no return that it is that moment. I generally know about tomorrow too. I know that nothing is new. I know that nothing remains. I know that all the things we do are largely inventions to pass the time. Sleep is a relief. No wonder some take pills. I know that feeling. I've been taking them since '56.

Saturday, 17 August
Noel W. Dinner 7.30. The same mistakes made. I just went on & on, and talked too much *and* then talked about *that*. O! I wanted to be dead. I drank a bottle of wine. It is my undoing.

Thursday, 22 August
Saw a terrible film & returned to the flat at 4 o'c. The madness screaming up inside me. So many awful thoughts. This terrible sense of doom hanging over me. I wonder if anyone will ever know about the emptiness of my life. I wonder if anyone will ever stand in a room that I have lived in, and touch the things that were once a part of my life, and wonder about me, and ask themselves what manner of man I was. How to ever tell them? How to ever explain? How to say that I never found Love – how to say that it was all my own fault – that when presented with it, I was afraid & so I spurned it, or laughed at it, or was cruel, and killed it: and knew that in the process I was killing myself. Who can say where it all goes wrong? Now I'm thinking all the while of death in some shape or another. Every day is some-

---

[15] No pop singer seems to have recorded under this name.

thing to be got through. All the recipes of the past are no longer valid. I've spent all my life in the mind. I have existed. I know everything vicariously. I have entered into nothing. I've given some sympathy but never empathy.

Monday, 26 August

Saw Barlow in morning & we went over to 62 Farley Court & he measured up and we worked out all the decor in white, and he will fix a wardrobe in the bedroom. I really do like the look of this flat. I feel so buoyant now. Curiously elated. I could fly. I'm so grateful about everything. Just want to get into my new flat so quickly! I know I'm going to feel so superb – the ninth & top floor.

Tuesday, 3 September

Location at Frensham Ponds.[16] Sunny intervals. Bernard Cribbins charming. Charlie Hawtrey unchanging. Juliet Mills delightful. Home by seven v. tired.

Tuesday, 10 September

Pinewood, arrive 7.45. Tank sequence. All day in the bloody rowing boat, till I was aching all over. Charles Hawtrey was pissed. Breath smelled appallingly. It's a disgrace. Still, one must be charitable.

Friday, 13 September

I did a couple of shots at about midnight and we finished around 2.15 in the morning. In the interim periods, we sat about singing rude songs & telling smutty jokes. The reason for most of the smut in the world is boredom. People like to attribute it to reasons more profound. This is part of the general misreading of human affairs: it's the *conceit* that seeks profundity in reasons for behaviour.

Tuesday, 24 September

Peter E. tells me that Edith Evans objects to anyone over the title with her, on the grounds that she is an old lady & may die & this is her last play etc. So I have to decide which sort of line to take.

Thursday, 26 September

The Denning report on the Profumo–Ward case is out. Apparently it says that well known actors were at these filthy parties. It is a disgrace that such people should bring our profession into disrepute in this vile way. Thank the powers that my own private fantasies have been

---

[16] For *Carry On Jack*.

left to wrestle with my own conscience and not in physical acts with others.

Wednesday, 2 October
Up at 6. Car at 7. Out on boat all day. Walk the plank sequence. How dreary they all seem, these people. Nora rang evening. Said that R. Bolt read my part at the reading. Hm. Thank goodness I wasn't there. I *hate* readings. They accomplish nothing.

Friday, 4 October
Woke about 5 o'c. feeling terrible. No wonder people in the film world go bonkers. When you get up in the small hours there is a sort of mad lucidity & life seems awfully petty & worthless. Just looking at the paper this morning – the awful news – I felt sick with depression.

Wednesday, 9 October
Rehearsed with the company today.[17] They look quite interesting & everyone appears to be better than I am. Curiously the Dame is rather dull. Not at all the grand presence. The impression is one of querulousness. But she is charming to me. They started talking about my interpretation today. 'Don't make him evil,' they keep saying. I know they want him to be all animal grace & innocence – the man who is not immoral, but amoral. But so much of the part belies it.

Saturday, 12 October
Moving date. So tired, but so happy. I feel good in this flat.[18] It's the first time I cannot hear the other tenants! All I can hear is traffic. It may be all too good to be true. We will see. O! I hope it's going to be all right!

Monday, 14 October
When I arrived at the Haymarket Tony Chardet told me that Nicholas Meredith with whom I joked & larked on Sat. morning was dead. Heart attack. It is v. shocking.

My bedroom looks out over Regent's Park. The trees are turning now and the sight is beautiful. I can see all the traffic twinkling down the Marylebone Rd. and the gold ladies on the top of the church. It's all so marvellous, I could cry.

Tuesday, 15 October
Donald Mayerson sent me cuttings from New York papers about the

---

[17] In Robert Bolt's *Gentle Jack*, KW as Jack.
[18] 62 Farley Court, Allsop Place, between Baker Street station and the Planetarium.

Shaffer plays. They're a huge success. It's too absurd. What can they be like without me?

Thursday, 17 October

When I arrived at the theatre I said 'O! I've forgotten my script' and Michael B[ryant] said 'I thought you wrote your own material' with a grin. But I did not even smile, or acknowledge it in any way.

Tuesday, 22 October

Today I said 'But you can't say this line "reasonably".' And R. Bolt said 'Say it truthfully.' I could have screamed. The plain truth is that I can't find the *form* to express the part.

Thursday, 24 October

There is a story going around that Dame E.E. goes to Binkie and says 'Why on earth have you cast Kenneth Williams – he's got such a peculiar voice!' Of course it's only funny when the impersonation of her is good: but this was overheard by William Dexter,[19] in the Buxton, & it was said by people who didn't know he was in the company.

Tuesday, 29 October

It's so odd that this play has turned out so like the other one, in that I thought both were too small as parts: but now that I'm actually in the rehearsals I know I'll be good in the part. I know I was right to do this play. It is a good play, and good plays are a rarity in London.

Monday, 4 November

Royal Crescent. Brighton. Booked from now to 23 Nov. inc.

Tuesday, 5 November

Dress rehearsal. White-wet all arms, legs & face, with Max Factor Egyptian. Wore costume for the first time. No one commented from out front. Not a bloody word.

Thursday, 7 November

Evening perf. was slow & dull. Reception dreary.

Monday, 11 November

Show OK. Supper D. E[dith].

Woman at the Dentist's: 'No! not the drill – I can't bear the drill.' 'But it won't hurt, Madam, I assure you –' 'No, not the drill, I'd rather

---

[19] Playing Bilbo in *Gentle Jack*.

have a baby.' 'Well make up yr. mind, Madam, it means changing the position of the chair . . .'

Thursday, 14 November

Tea at Fuller's with Michael Bryant & Tim West. I told them about the Green Boots & Gran. People in the café asked us what the play meant!

Tuesday, 19 November

I have waited a long time for this – and now God has given me the opportunity to use the theatre in its moral sense. The right sense. Bob left a beautiful letter in my room. I shall write back, because I couldn't *talk* about it. It's too private. Again and again in these last weeks I have felt so *grateful*. I feel so *much* to be thankful for. Work – people – and the spirit of *giving*. You can't have it both ways. This play has taught me that, but you can have it *one* way, and that way, when it's right for you, can give you the crystal spirit.[20]

Friday, 22 November

After the show (v. good house) it was suddenly announced that Noel Willman was out front! This! after saying we were to be left alone till London. Supper at Crescent alone. Night porter waiting for a handout. He didn't get it.

The news was announced of the assassination of President Kennedy. I am stunned by it.

Wednesday, 27 November. London

Did the 'B.O.K.' show. It went fair. Lousy crowd. To theatre at seven. Popped into Globe to give Mags the Saint-Simon Journal. Sweet adorable Mags, who copes every day with her problem of perfection. An artist in the real sense. Supper after with R.B. He said that he felt an artist was 'a liar in search of the truth' – and I think it is a very good definition.

Thursday, 28 November

Opening night, Queen's. If ever I have wanted a performance to work I want it tonight. Even if it means a perversion of all the rules, I want it to be a success because R.B. deserves it.

The dressing room is full of wires & presents. O! the letters I'll have to write! The performance was laboured and nervous. The audience was bemused and irritated. The dressing room after, full of unspoken thoughts. I gave no drinks or anything.

---

[20] Phrase from a George Orwell poem; see entry for 9 November 1973 (p. 461, n.).

Friday, 29 November
The notices are appalling, apart from the Mail and the Times. The rest are spiteful and rude. Second House at tonight's performance was mediocre. We haven't had an *easy* night in London *yet*. Nothing to compare with a good night at Brighton. After, I saw Peter Wyngarde & Alan Bates. They were both charming, & wise & understanding about it all & made the evening a great delight. They came back to the flat for a drink and a chat, leaving about 12.45. It was a delight.

Monday, 2 December
R. Bolt rang to chat. He says he thinks the audience will like the play. You can't tell him they won't. They may be fascinated or repelled but they'll never *like* it. It's too sombre and unhappy for them.

Monday, 9 December
Lunch with P.R[ogers] & Gerry Thomas at the Mirabelle. Eating there, one realises why things like the French Revolution occurred. The film they want me for, *Carry On Spying*, is to start about end of January.

Wednesday, 11 December
I telephoned Eade today and Laurena told me that the contract for this play is 12 and a half weeks from the London opening. Which means that I could be free and out of it, by February 22. After which time I will have done over a hundred performances. I think that I shall want to leave then, because the plain fact is that I don't enjoy doing this play.

Tuesday, 17 December
Noel Willman took me to lunch at Bianchi, then we went to see *The Leopard* by Visconti. This is a really superb film. At last, one is able to see the *real thing*. A film of such grandeur, such theatricality, such adult dialogue, such *intent*. I thought everyone in it, from Burt Lancaster down, was marvellous. It is such a delight to be able to say *lovely* – *lovely* to be able to salute a maestro. The first good film for years!

Friday, 20 December
Mags told me over dinner that Larry Olivier said to her, about me 'I think he's got sex appeal.' Of course I don't think it's true, but what a charming thing to have said about one.

Monday, 23 December
How lovely it is to be coming to the end of this diary. I am never sorry to find a year has gone. They're most of them lousy anyway.

The loveliness comes fleetingly, here and there: of course that is as it should be.

Tuesday, 24 December
Went to Jolly's for some of their excellent beef sausages & then returned home – my ears singing with pain from the cold. Louie telephoned that she was busy preparing for tomorrow & I mentioned my holiday in March idea. She said she would come with me. So, whether this show lasts or not, that is what I will do.

Wednesday, 25 December
In the evening to Mags. Same as last time. They gave me v. expensive presents & we had the film show & I left about 11.30. I had to walk all the way home from Kensington to Baker St. All my *loathing* of Christmas and Public Holidays poured over me during the walk home. All those groups of 'merry people', windows open & awful noise of singing, and daft decorations everywhere & drunks and bad driving and just beneath the surface – the extreme rude bestiality. I suppose my worst fault is the instinctive desire to run away from a mess. Instead of trying to do something about it. Run. Get away. No hope of reform I cry. Away from responsibility for work or people, away from commitment, away from affection, away from trouble – away from the community . . . And all the time these *stinking* performances looming ahead of me.

Thursday, 26 December
What is the basis of my insomnia? I think it is because all the subconscious rebels at night, refuses to be dormant as it is most of the day, and gets wildly active. It is proof against drugs, drink and real body fatigue. Nothing defeats it. So all my acquired balance & control of the day is cancelled out by another battle at night. Most nights it's a battle I lose. And, irony of ironies! I'm saying in the play – 'Go on, back to your avoided days, yr. abstract hours, yr. millions of disembodied minutes, and yr. heavy dreams that are destroying you . . . did you know that?'

Monday, 30 December
When I look at what I wrote in the entry 29 Oct. '63, I realise that I just shouldn't be allowed out. You know. I mean it's ridiculous.

Tuesday, 31 December
This year's end is rather like the end of '61. I was in that awful revue & hating it, now I'm in this awful play & hating it. So what is there left to say in conclusion? Well, I've had me first West End flop. I

mean in terms of how many turn up, and taken a bitter blow with the play. I've done quite well financially without busting a gut, and at last I have a decent place to live. No new friendships formed. Certainly the years make me more conservative. Next year I must 1) finish off this lousy play 2) have a holiday 3) do something good.

1964

Wednesday, 1 January
First day of the New Year starting beautifully – as I write this at 9 o'c. before going off to do 'B.O.K.', it is a mild morning and the sun is shining brightly. I begin this with a prayer that we will not suffer another winter like the last, that I get thro' *Gentle Jack* with dignity, and that I give Louie a memorable holiday. Did the 'B.O.K.' recording at the Paris. Went big.

Thursday, 2 January
Peter E. in between shows, about a script – tiny part – they want me to do, in Hollywood for Universal International, but I don't think I want to go all that way for a couple of pages. Still. Went to Eade & read the script. Rubbish. Not interested. Supper after with John H., Bev and Mags at Biagi. Mags said James Donald in *Wings of the Dove* at Lyric has a line 'I walked to St Mark's Square – you know they call it the drawing room of Europe . . .' and she started to laugh! (Cliff Evans quoted it when we were there!)

Friday, 3 January
I am so lucky. It's taken me years to realise it. What Bolt said – 'a liar in search of the truth'. O yes. And I am glad. Glad with all my heart, for living. And I am fundamentally at peace. I know now that my troubles are only scratches on the great periphery of cosmology.

Friday, 10 January
George Rose.[1] Dinner. George started on about America again. How marvellous the Puerto Ricans are. Strange how the puritans are always attracted to the Latin American (Catholic) type. It all comes back to the Storey novel,[2] and Robert Bolt again. Both of them are fascinated by the Animal Innocence, but both see it as a destructive thing – in terms of our civilisation. There is a sickness in the thought of both.

---

1 1920–88, British character actor.
2 Probably *Radcliffe* by David Storey (1963).

The animal thing they invest with a sort of magic. It has none. The animal thing is Animal. Nothing else. There are things in it which we may admire but that doesn't mean we should embrace it. We don't belong to that world.

Sunday, 12 January

Feeling very pale and distraught. Bitterly unhappy in the deep sense. This same old 'unfulfilled' sense. I suddenly thought of trying to love a foreign girl – someone direct & childlike & totally unaffected by the muck of an oversophisticated life. But like all my ideas, it bubbled forth & then collapsed.

Wednesday, 15 January

This morning I suddenly took stock of myself. From here on, I thought, start making some sort of gesture to God. Like in Lent. Give up things. Things you really like. Start with fags, then drink. On every page hereafter, I will record this progress. I had to rush off to Berman's for the fitting at 3 o'c. for *Carry On Spying*. Came out of that at 4 o'c. and walked thro' to Regent St to get the 59 bus home but a revolting pouff sat next to me so I got off at Portman Sq. and walked home.

Thursday, 16 January

My second day not smoking & I'm none the worse for wear.

Saturday, 18 January

In the evening it was really awful. There was simply no audience – about 60 in the stalls, and all evening the noise of drunks singing 'Bread of Heaven' outside the theatre. I have never heard such a rabble.[3]

Sunday, 19 January

My 5th day of no smoking. In future I shall write this as NS. After having a bath today, I looked in the mirror & thought 'How lovely I am . . . how very lovely . . .'

Monday, 20 January

I am reading *Buddenbrooks*[4] at the theatre. This way I am forced to ration myself with reading and it is the most satisfying experience I've ever had with a novel in my whole life. It is just the most fantastic

---

[3] There had been a rugby international between England and Wales that afternoon at Twickenham. The match was drawn 6-all. 'Gone was the tense, Ibsen-like atmosphere which we have come to associate with these particular contests' (*The Times*).

[4] By Thomas Mann (1901).

canvas & so beautifully observed and so startlingly accurate. The astonishing clarity of this man's vision – the diagnosis applies to *us* now. A marvellous book.

Monday, 27 January
13 NS. Went up to see Gordon & Roning. They gave me lunch and I stayed till about 5. I had a lovely time. The boys were marvellous. They're a lovely family. I didn't notice a clock in their room. So I'll get them one. I'd like to get them something. When I got in to theatre [there] was one of those terrible letters about 'Why do you appear in such a lousy play . . .' It takes all the heart out of you.

Thursday, 30 January
I had 4. So bang goes my word about not smoking. I have to accept this weakness I suppose: and ask the forgiveness for being such an abject creature.

Saturday, 1 February
The two performances today seemed fantastically protracted. But at the end all went reasonably well. I arranged car to collect me & all the junk & Pat came & took the awful Lion Binkie gave me, and eventually I was home and dry & finished with that unpleasant experience for ever. Perhaps one day I will be able to think of it all as a rather fine affair. At the moment, I remember only the embarrassment of that stuff to the audience – 'I am a God – a very great God . . .' o dear! I used to feel so awful.

Monday, 3 February
Pinewood 9. A great pleasure to be doing a picture again.[5] Nice to be with Bernard too. Gerald as charming as ever. We did the night shots by the wharf. This is the first picture I've done the 'snide' voice in. I just hope it works.

Thursday, 6 February
I must say I like this Barbara Windsor. She is a charming little girl.

Wednesday, 12 February
The appalling dichotomy of modern living is nowhere more obvious than in the world of the Actor. You meet on the film set, or the stage, plenty of actors with keen & interesting minds, who are all engaged on a role which is otiose. Playing in things which lack any kind of vision. Performing the work of inefficient hacks. The script of this film

---

[5] *Carry On Spying.*

is utterly banal & vacuously so. But all entertainment today echoes the dilemma of our society. Where the permanent values are neglected, where the materialistic grasp has strangled the spirit. What irony, that our progressiveness & expertise and specialisation has resulted in a popular entertainment form that is cruder than anything equivalent to it in, say – Tudor England.

Saturday, 15 February

Read the Lit. Sup. It's always interesting. It occurred to me after reading it that I'm always mostly influenced by Art. Especially writing & music. I can go from the rude style of Henry Miller to the careful beauty of a Motley[6] & still be attentive: from the tentative, sad romantic Schumann to the conviction & superb confidence of Bach and enjoy myself. And now that I've grown to love Mozart I've overcome another silly blind spot. It's after reading poetry – Eliot or Tennyson – that I feel I know something. I hardly ever feel this in *life*. I get all my knowledge from Art: of course it isn't all true. I suppose life does teach me a lot, but what it teaches seems rather the *demonstration* of what I read.

Wednesday, 19 February

I know the question of future work is going to be very very tricky. But I needn't do rubbish in the theatre. I can do that in the cinema. There it's [en]durable – only a few weeks – but in the theatre it's just Agony.

Thursday, 20 February

The script of *Carry On Spying* is so bad that I'm really beginning to wonder. I've changed one or two things but the witless vacuity of it all remains.

Saturday, 22 February

It's fantastic how much this diary shows the transition from enjoyment to disliking this film. At first it's all marvellous and then it just gets boring & shitty. All films are like this, and in a microcosm they are the run of a play. The same turning on each other of the cast, the same disgust with the material etc. It happens more quickly than the theatre because one is with it *all* day, as opposed to just a couple of hours in the evening.

---

[6] John Lothrop Motley (1814–77), best known as the author of *The Rise of the Dutch Republic* (1855).

Sunday, 23 February
It suddenly hit me today that myself and Louie are the givers, the ones who put themselves out and risk being vulnerable. I inherit my talent from Louie.

Tuesday, 25 February
With Nora to supper at Biagi. She again raised this issue of living together. It would never work out. I don't know why we keep on. At least though I'm honest. I've told her that my make-up is far too heterodox. At least I've not covered up in this sense.

Thursday, 27 February
That idiot Cribbins rushed from behind and punched me in the shoulder. Now that is continually painful. It's all in the guise of high spirits & horseplay. He never stops impersonating me. In the beginning, he is fine – it's as the picture progresses that he becomes intolerable.

Friday, 28 February
We went to see *Carry On Jack* at the New Victoria. It was half empty. It was a lousy, badly made film. Really badly made. The editing was all wrong for comedy. I was astonished at the excellence of Charlie Hawtrey. He was superb. So was Cribbins – the best droll I've seen in years. But really good. The rest awful. Including me. My voice sounded so far back and so phoney. So badly recorded. There is something wrong here. The balance on sound radio is not as bad as that.

Saturday, 7 March
With Pat at Victoria to see Louie off to Gatwick, on the start of her holiday to Tenerife. There was snow falling and it was bitterly cold.

Saturday, 14 March
In the evening Stanley Baxter and me went to the Golden Palace and had a Chinese meal. V. nice really. Then we both went to John Schles. party. Everyone was there. Fantasy. I haven't been to one of these theatrical parties for years: and I shall never go again. I must be mad. It is disgraceful to have to mix with people who are artistically so unequal to oneself. It's all so familiar making and democratic and ghastly.

Sunday, 15 March
Snow blizzard whirling outside the windows all day. I hoovered the carpet in the lounge dressing only in bathing trunks. It was v. daring and the atmosphere was charged with sex. If anyone had walked in,

they would have been irresistibly attracted. Read all the papers. Load of rubbish.

Monday, 16 March

Awful day messing about at Pinewood. Doubles never used. V. tricky shot being shoved along the tunnel & I cut both my ankles and stormed off the set saying that I would not do any more. I apologised after to Gerry T. but the damage had been done to myself. I've never done anything like that before in front of a director. To party after in the green room. Met Barbara's husband Ronnie[7] who was charming.

Thursday, 19 March

I was surprised on looking at the '56 journal to find that this was the year I found my first flat: the first time I started to live alone. So it has only been eight years. Hardly that really. But Endsleigh Court seems a long way off now! – and the glamour of the first furnishings! and the materials and the choosings and the painting of the walls! How delightful it all seems! and how bloody miserable it all was! And is.

Saturday, 28 March

Car collecting me at Farley Court at 10.30, then pick up L. and P. Well of course we all arrived at London Airport much too early. Met Barbara [Windsor] & Ronald – got talking & v. nearly missed the plane! Left Lisbon at 5.30. Then a nightmare of a journey began. First a lighter took us out to this ship, and then we started on the voyage to Funchal. It took about 3½ hours. On arriving at the Savoy Hotel, it was just unbelievable. The rooms were all appalling. Bare and nasty. Hard beds. No bathroom. I took loads of pills and went heavy hearted to bed, bitterly recalling Barbara's words 'I'll bet we end up in the khazi.'

Sunday, 29 March

Got us all moved to better rooms. V.g. lunch at 1.30 and things started to look much better.

Monday, 30 March

Lousy day. Rain. In the evening we sat in the bar drinking till about 11.30. Bed. What an awful place this is. I feel like someone who is punch drunk. This is something I had never foreseen. The idea that Madeira could be as awful as this had never occurred to me, and of

---

[7] Ronnie Knight. They later parted and he took refuge from British law in Spain.

course with bad weather, there is simply nothing to do. Everyone is defeated.

Tuesday, 31 March

It developed into a drink session and Louie got v. tight and embarrassed a Portuguese waiter by asking him to dance and generally behaving v. badly. I left them and met a Portuguese boy who took me to the Flamingo which was awful. When I came back to the hotel L. & P. were shouting and bawling at each other. I told them to be quiet and go to sleep.

Thursday, 2 April

Morning cold and raining. In the evening Mike, Ronnie and me played Gin Rummy. The girls came back from Bingo & said it was dreary. Then Barbara got v. shirty and turned on Louie, carrying some sort of moral flag over my behaviour to some old boy who was watching us play cards. I am too old, too tired and too talented to care. No one can imagine the misery of tat holidays. It has to be experienced. I could have done *everything* I've done here on Brighton front. And that's a fact. You can shiver there in extra woollies.

Friday, 3 April

In the evening we went down to the Golden Gate. We all came back to the hotel in good spirits only to make the mistake of having 'one for the road' in the hotel bar; eventually the dreary decor, arum lilies & general funeral parlour atmosphere completely destroyed all we had created. For first time in years, I went to bed without pills.

Sunday, 5 April

Slept till about seven o'c. Not bad. Looked out of the window – black cloud all over the mountain! One falls back on the bed filled with despair.

Saturday, 11 April. Lisbon

Barbara made a dreadful scene in the restaurant 'cos she said the Steak Diane was ill-made. Crying & all. It was the natural climax to an appalling holiday and I really couldn't blame her.

Sunday, 12 April

A mass of letters & my lovely flat. So I am home again, after what must be the most expensive disaster I have ever been associated with. A complete waste of time, which cost me about four hundred pounds.

Thursday, 16 April

At the moment, curiously, I am not unduly worried about not working. When I came back from Greece I wanted v. much to be in a show. Now, back from Portugal, I don't feel that. I'm really not v. keen to go back to the theatre at all. Not unless it is a play which I am mad about.

Tuesday, 21 April

They needn't talk to me about loneliness. I've walked too many miles of pavement. I've scanned so many faces – I've looked with so much furtive hope, but it's never right. Only in my imagination. There, I have marvellous conversations with someone attractive, slow, charmingly phlegmatic & naturally reticent, and with me, he becomes articulate. But in fact, I take a sleeping pill & tell myself to shut up.

Friday, 24 April

I left for Pinewood to go and do some post-synch. and dubbing, and a close-up in the end sequence which we left out of the original. Peter R[ogers] looks overtired and there is a twitching started in the eye. I told him not to overdo things & he said 'Has anyone ever told you what a bore you are' which shut me up straightaway.

Thursday, 30 April

To Peter Eade to collect two Feydeau plays. Both farces. Both quite funny too. I will have to think about them seriously.

Friday, 1 May

Michael Codron rang to say he'd found a marvellous new farce & is sending it here tonight. It is by Philip King & Falkland Cary, called *Big Bad Mouse*, and is a dreary little piece about someone who becomes attractive to everyone because they think he is a sex maniac. It is quite well constructed with good curtains etc. but it belongs to a theatre to which I don't. It's one of those intuitive things one just knows. It's no more 'me' than fly in the air.

Monday, 4 May

Chatted with Wendy [Toye] & Ronald Millar. They're doing this musical of the Barretts of Wimpole St & want a title! Someone suggested 'Under Par' but of course it's too rude. Really. We laughed tho'.[8]

Wednesday, 6 May

Recording session at De Lane Lea Studios at 11 o'c. I went there, and

---

[8] The show became *Robert and Elizabeth*.

that awful young posh poof was in charge again. Too awful. But I held me breath & counted to three & every time he was offensive I pushed my lips forward, looked profound & agreed. I did the whole session conscientiously and well, and it was all a bit dull in the end – largely 'cos of her dictating the inflections. Silly queen.

Thursday, 7 May

I went out at 7.30 to vote in the GLC elections for the council. Tory of course.

Tuesday, 12 May

I got the script of *Carry On Cleo* today and I must say I think it is very funny. I rang Peter R. to tell him so & we are to meet for lunch at the Mirabelle tomorrow.

Thursday, 14 May

Dick Williams came over at about 7. We went to Franco's for dinner. I talked about sexual frustration and he said I should go off and do it somewhere. He said that is what aeroplanes are for. He said it as if jets had been deliberately designed to rush people off to sexual adventures. Of course it's just a lovely idea. I don't know though.

Saturday, 16 May

Michael C. picked me up about 3.15 and we motored down to Brighton. All clientele dreadful but the hotel is good. In the evening we went to a wrestling match. It was obviously rigged. I've got a feeling that this holiday is doomed to disaster. Already I am counting the hours and wondering how we're going to fill in the time.

Whit Sunday, 17 May

Brighton is packed with Rockers and Mods. There were several fights & over 50 arrests. Lovely. I saw a great mass of Mods by the Palace Pier, one boy of about 14 or 15 had a gash & blood pouring all over his face. I was abed by 12 o'c.

Monday, 18 May

It's been a complete waste of time and money. All the things I've done here, I could have done better at home.

Friday, 22 May

Gerry Thomas phoned again. Said that they wouldn't pay any more for the film *Carry On Cleo* – we were asking six – they're offering five. So I rang Eade & said accept their figure. I don't care either way.

Sunday, 24 May
To Louie for lunch. She told me about the Old Lady's funeral which was last Friday. It seems to mark the passing of another age to me. I only knew her slightly compared with Louie, who went to see her every week – I saw her less because she wouldn't come to Brunswick after Charles died. But I'll remember her stories – the woman next door & the bloomers and the piano 'full of green boots . . .'

Sunday, 31 May
I read some poetry and listened to Auden talking about the Sonnets on the 3rd. He sounded so awful. The man has no vocal gift and the hybrid accent, half American and half English, was unpleasant to listen to. He said absolutely nothing original or arresting in twenty minutes, so I turned it off. Amazing that such a drear sounding man could write such lovely poetry.

Friday, 5 June
Rehearse Wandsworth at 10.30.[9] We did a run thro & found we were 78 minutes which is three more than the time prescribed. Bobby H[elpmann] told me it was true that he put his cock on a plate of 'buffet froid' for Vivien Leigh at an Embassy reception. He said she 'very nearly stuck a fork in it . . .'

Saturday, 13 June
It is announced in the Honours List that Robert Helpmann is a Commander of the British Empire.[10] Good for him. Rehearsed at TV Centre from 12 o'c. onwards. Started the Ampex at 7.30. No.3 camera broke down after twenty minutes & we started all over again. It was a sort of nightmare. At one point I gave a bum cue to Robert & he fluffed thro' his reply which rather spoiled his flow. I could have kicked myself & I apologised after. He was charming about it. Afterwards there was an extraordinary party given by David Benedictus in his bed sit. I thanked D.B. when I said goodbye and added 'Thank you for thinking of me for the part'. He said 'Well, if you're stuck for an actor it's always best to get a comedian' and an American said 'Yeah, but they tend to go over the top, y'know?' I said 'You mean a comic. We're talking about comedians,' and the idiot said 'What's the difference?' so I fled.

---

[9] TV play *Catch as Catch Can*, a translation of Anouilh's *La Foire d'Empoigne*, KW as Napoleon, Helpmann as Fouché. Directed by David Benedictus, b.1938, writer and producer, latterly Readings Editor, BBC Radio.
[10] Helpmann (1909–86) was knighted in 1968.

Saturday, 20 June

Walked to the Old Vic to see Mags in *Othello*. It was an astonishing evening. Maggie always surprises me. It's always streets ahead of what one expects. I've had to tear this page out of the diary and start again. She must be the best Desdemona ever. A performance of superb grace and vocally beautiful. Larry [Olivier] was incredibly negroid & v. handsome. He performs with great courage and vulnerability. And this is his triumph – tho' to some it is not acceptable. I find that when he does go out on a limb, I respond. He soars in the role from simple dignity & calm to a wild and terrible anger and wraps the whole part up.

Tuesday, 23 June

The Telegraph states that on Saturday last, 8 productions came off in London. The only theatres soon will be musicals and subsidised ones.

Sunday, 28 June

There was an American actor called Tab Hunter[11] at Johnny Fraser's. A frantic bore who called everyone 'great' or 'fun' & said on the way home 'Gee, it's been a real fun day.' Quite unbelievable.

Friday, 3 July

In the evening, met the Hensons and the Hendersons and we all went to Drury Lane to see Fonteyn & Nureyev dance *Marguérite & Armand*.[12] It was magic – superb theatrical magic. We chatted to Judy Garland who looks fantastic and marvellous. She said 'How is your asp?' which took me aback rather.[13]

Monday, 6 July

With Henry to the Sussex for a snack and then to see *Entertaining Mr Sloane* at Wyndham's. Lousy production and mediocre acting, but a fascinating play I thought. Totally erroneously reported in the newspapers.

Tuesday, 7 July

Up to the Baxters' at 1 o'c. Before I left Stanley I suggested he might like to go off somewhere for a week with me. He seemed quite interested.

---

[11] (A.A. Kelm) b.1931.

[12] Choreography by Frederick Ashton, music by Liszt: the first ballet created for Nureyev (1938–93) after his defection to the West.

[13] A reference to a Peter Cook sketch in *Pieces of Eight* in which the KW character claimed to be carrying a viper ('Not an asp') in his cardboard box.

Saturday, 11 July
Stanley collected me at Farley Court at 8.45 and we went to the airport etc. All went briskly, and we arrived in Amsterdam at 11.30. We met a fellow called Terry Noble who showed us around the place – in the pouring rain.

Sunday, 12 July
To the dreadful clubs again. After one drink I left and went back to the 'hotel' to bed. Lying there, I thought – what am I doing in this sink of iniquity? Walking round unlovely streets in the pouring rain, sitting in clubs with a load of poofs, living at a filthy little lodging house, sitting in lousy council flats and being *bored*! at such expense!!

Monday, 13 July
I told Stanley I'd had it all, so he cancelled the room he'd reserved for me & it was decided I would go home & he would stay. This entire episode is the story of my life I suppose. The run up and the run away. Perhaps death is the only thing that will make me stop running.

Tuesday, 14 July
Met Andrew for lunch G & C. Then we went to a dreadful film with that awful pop singing creature Clifford Richardson[14] or something. It was unbelievably boring.

Wednesday, 15 July
As I left the building to go to the chiropodist, that dreary porter – Grant – said 'Your new hairstyle doesn't suit you at all' and I could have screamed with vexation. I am appalled myself about the hair. It looks barbaric. After the chirop. I came back to the flat and went to bed. I'm in an appalling dilemma all my life. I 'feel' a sexual nature which I am thoroughly ashamed and disgusted by, and it colours all my life. All that I look at is coloured by it. Everything. The madness of imagining I could be different in another environment! Amsterdam or Greece or Constantinople – it's all exactly the same. With Peter E. to see the Royal Tournament. It was splendid to see so many men doing so many remarkable physical feats, possessed of so little brain. It all moved me tremendously and I loved them all.

Friday, 17 July
I realise that Andrew [Ray] has been very important in my life during the past few years. He is always good company even when he's low,

---

14 Where pop singers were concerned, KW tended to affect the same outlook as the High Court judge who famously asked 'Who are the Beatles?'

and he is without any kind of self-pity: he also has that marvellous capacity to enter into the spirit of things, wholly. The thing the Germans call *'entgegenkommen'*.

Sunday, 19 July

Bobby H. told me that Larry O. said to him 'I'm sorry to say this in front of you, Cocky, but I don't think there is any place in the theatre for queers . . .' B. was indignant of course, but in a strange way I know what L. is getting at. Tho' his company at the Vic contradicts it entirely.

Tuesday, 21 July

I would like very much to have been born very handsome. Not for its own sake, but for the sake of being attractive to others. The reason I am so conservative in my tiny circle of friends, and the reason I stay in the house so much, is because I think my face & body unprepossessing. I've no doubt that this is only a superficial excuse for a more profound complaint within me. This is of course the paradox of my own nature. The thing that I am, being the thing which I despise. But I think my despite is justified.

Wednesday, 22 July

Carry On Cleopatra. The Roman costume is murder to get on & off. Did a scene with Kenny Connor. It's all like an incredibly tired echo of the beginning of the series. Surely the wheel can't turn much further?

Saturday, 25 July

Did the interview thing at Riverside for BBC 2.[15] It went off very well. I got loads of laughs. Mugging like mad I'm afraid. Must've looked awful.

Thursday, 30 July

I suddenly realised today that most times when someone is nasty to me my immediate reaction is 'When and how can I be revenged?' It's incredibly primitive. I'm not saying I always act upon this, but it *is* an initial reaction.

Tuesday, 4 August

This Roman tunic I'm wearing in the film is really quite attractive. In white and gold. I continually lift it up and expose my cock & everything at the Unit. They're all rather disgusted and laugh it off, but

---

[15] Probably 'Open House', introduced by Gay Byrne, Peter Haigh etc.

quite a number of them have remarked 'O! Kenny! Not again! – put it away . . .' etc. etc.

And all our trousers shall be taken down and used in evidence against us.

Thursday, 6 August

I wonder how much of this present feeling of despair I can actually take? I suppose one of the effects is to so wear you down that you graduate into utter mediocrity and apathy and eventually – atrophy. And you actually don't notice the rotting process. I can see the land still – though I'm now really adrift – I can still see its outlines, still recognise the reefs and the odd icebergs of danger but for how much longer will I be able to see them? Of necessity, the mind must eventually refuse to see the uncomfortable, accusing things. I know that the utter failure of my life has been caused by the knowledge that has killed the will. I'm almost disgusted by enthusiasm – certainly irritated by it.

Saturday, 8 August

Dreamed I was playing a 'Gentleman' at Stratford – wearing laurels under a helmet – knew none of the lines, the make-up and spirit gum hurting skin like mad and panic on all sides – all my hair falling out of my head – all connected with that inner sense of 'giving up'. Woke full of dread.

Sunday, 9 August

Sat about reading the papers, including a column or two in the Observer called 'In Praise of Carrying On' with a picture of me in the middle. This is v. odd, the way that 'Carry Ons' are just starting to get mentioned: why are they suddenly fashionable? They're even trying to justify the bad scripts now! and talk about the classlessness of them. What hogwash! You can only call a mess a mess.

Monday, 10 August

Dinner at Michael C. with David and Joe Orton,[16] the author of *Entertaining Mr Sloane*. I thought he was really a delightful personality. Obviously wanting to shock though. The friend called Ken comes in on cue & most of the time, before cue. It is v. annoying. One of the most irritating things in the world is when people correct each other.

---

[16] John Kingsley Orton (1933–67), playwright, and his partner (and to some extent editor) Kenneth Halliwell.

Monday, 17 August
I thought I looked very good on the rushes today. Lovely costume too. And the face is actually better than it was a few years ago. In *Nurse* and in *Daffodils* particularly, I looked all lines and v. puffy. Either that, or Alan [Hume] is getting much cleverer at lighting me.

Tuesday, 18 August
Laurena rang at 6 to say that Orson had cabled from Madrid asking if I was free in Oct. Told her to say yes & ask for details.

Wednesday, 19 August
Sun never appeared, but they shot the scene. Me addressing the crowd of extras. They were told not to aim the tomatoes etc. at me, but of course they did. A lot hit the back of my cloak – but I turned v. cleverly and they didn't succeed in getting my face. What a bunch of cretins these extras are.

Thursday, 3 September
Down to Pinewood for the end of picture party. Apart from Jim Dale, I was the only actor there – O! no – Sid James attended – but perhaps the first half of the sentence is still correct.

Friday, 11 September
It's rather marvellous (when I think of the influence Coward has had on my acting) that I should be now recording two of his most famous songs for HMV.

Tuesday, 15 September
Andrew came back to the flat & we started talking about father relationships & parents and where it all seems to go wrong. I talked of Charlie & my inability to 'meet' him, even half way. I suppose I feel guilty about this, still. The feeling that towards the end of his life he must have been terribly lonely – and in need of affection. I was unable or unwilling to give it. I can only redeem this by doing my best for L & P. This is my sole function now – to keep our family together in the only way I know how. That is economically and sentimentally. That's why I'm so glad they're on the Greek cruise.

Friday, 18 September
Walked to EMI studios at 3 Abbey Road, to record the two Coward numbers with Cyril Ornadel & his orchestra. A boy there playing trombone was Johnny Edwards!! He was in C.S.E. in Singapore. Fantastically aged old married man.

Tuesday, 29 September
Hugh Paddick came at 7. We went to Biagi for dinner. He said that Merriman had incurred the wrath of the BBC, and that consequently the series ('B.O.K.') was off. So that is that. That's the end of that little annual source of income, and prestige and everything.

Wednesday, 30 September
The BBC told P.E. that the play I did was to be transmitted at 9.45.[17] Gording agreed to watch with me. It was v. odd to see it, all that time after. I realised as I watched it how utterly wrong I *looked* for a soldier. And a continual error in my performance was the shift of vocal technique again & again which was jarring & looked patently insincere.

Thursday, 1 October
Got a copy of the Times and read a v.g. notice for me, for the TV play last night.

Friday, 2 October
Went to Smith's and changed my paper as from Mon. I'm going to have the Times.

Monday, 5 October
Michael C. phoned me in the evening. Said he would try to push Joe Orton into completing this play where there is a part for me.

Friday, 9 October
Went out to the post, and saw Judith S[tott] driving in Baker St! She stopped & we went and had coffee together nearby. She's now married Dave Allen, the comedian, and they're living in Hampstead again.

Monday, 12 October
I see now that the obvious answer is to vote Liberal. The other two are obviously the 'choix d'embarras' & there is something innocent and honest about the Libs.

Tuesday, 13 October
Note from Michael Codron to say that the Joe Orton play is finished & he will shortly be reading it & will let me know whether we can

---

[17] *Catch as Catch Can* replaced Clive Exton's *The Bone Yard*, postponed indefinitely owing to 'some supposed similarity with the Challoner [police corruption] case' (*Listener*). John Russell Taylor, the *Listener*'s critic, noted that the casting of KW as Napoleon was 'an odd idea which worked rather well in the context'.

do something with it. I'm setting a great store by this & hoping against hope that it will result in our good fortune.

Thursday, 15 October
Went to the school at Lisson Grove, and voted Tory. It's the only practical thing to do. In the evening I went up to Gordon & Rona to watch the election results coming in on television. There were recounts all over the place, but it was obvious by one o'clock that the Tories had lost. Certainly they deserved it. Alice Douglas-Home lost it for them.[18]

Friday, 16 October
I read the new Joe Orton play *Funeral Games*[19] and I think that it is very good – though my part is not vehicular.

Saturday, 17 October
Is my inability to love based on fear of vulnerability & lack of spiritual generosity; or is it the profound belief in the utter hopelessness of human love? I think it is the latter, but it *may be* the former. I've never *tested* the former. I've never once *tried*. It's almost as if I know it's foredoomed; and yet of course I don't know. One thing is certainly true about me at the present moment: I have no desire for *life*. Even as I write this, the awful feeling of guilt about such an admission makes me want to erase it. Why on earth commit such a thing to paper? I suppose all diarists are lonely and uncreative people.

Friday, 23 October
In the evening Joe Orton, Stan W. & Sid. The irony was that Stan & Sid dressed and behaved impeccably, and Joe Orton (who is supposed to be cultivated) did neither. It was the usual polo sweater and army boots, and he talked about himself at every conceivable opportunity. He has gone down considerably in my estimation, and he didn't *listen* to Stan or Sid. Disgrace.

Thursday, 29 October
Went to Eade at 3 o'c. for interview with young man who is writing about me in a university magazine called Isis. I always try to tell the truth when they ask the questions. It's like being psychoanalysed: 'How do you see yourself . . . ?' etc. etc.

---

[18] Having lost the election narrowly (Labour's overall majority was four), Sir Alec Douglas-Home resigned the Tory leadership the following year. His place was taken by Edward Heath.

[19] Early title for what became, at Kenneth Halliwell's suggestion, *Loot*. The title *Funeral Games* was used for a later television play.

Friday, 30 October
Down to Pinewood by 10.00 to do some dubbing on a scene in *Carry On Cleo* – I had to substitute 'bashful' for 'backward' because the censor said it had a homosexual connotation. It was rubbish of course, but it earned me some more money.

Monday, 9 November
Called on Peter Eade to return the script of 'The Avengers',[20] the TV serial I was offered a part in. I said it wasn't worth it – it was a lousy little part which could have been played by anybody.

Wednesday, 11 November
Phone call from Joe Orton asking me over there on Sunday. He says they will serve sandwiches. This will be death. So I'd better be sure to eat something at home first and have nothing there.

When I got home, I discovered a small thing crawling on my sheets! – it was panic stations. I put it into DDT. Watched it die. Then sprayed the entire room, the bed, the mattress, the frame, the linen, everything with DDT. God knows what the thing was. I can't really believe it was vermin, but the horror hit me nonetheless. With all the work, I didn't get to bed till after midnight. The smell of DDT was everywhere.

Thursday, 12 November
To Selfridge's to get a new DDT spray. Came back & cleaned the flat, and then sprayed the bedroom with DDT all over again. Bed frame, mattress, everything, and I put powder DDT in the pillows. Henry D. phoned. I said I was too depressed to see anyone.

Sunday, 15 November
I got the 73 up to Angel, and called on Joe Orton & Ken Halliwell at 25 Noel Road. It was frugal to say the least. The room contained only two easy chairs & Joe had to have a stool all the time. The food was one ham sandwich & the dialogue revolved around it – 'This ham is rather good, don't you think?' Of course if it was, you'd never know anyway, wedged between two slices of that muck we called Bread. O dear. Conversation was endlessly about the play. Every generalisation brought them unerringly back to it. Self-indulgence gone mad. J. told me that Rattigan had asked him to go with him to Hong Kong, with the proviso that J. gives up K.H. It's really fantastic. J. tells it deprecatingly, but he is secretly flattered by the attentions of an old queen.

---

[20] Comedy–thriller series several times revamped, finally as 'The New Avengers' in the seventies.

Wednesday, 18 November
It is agreed that P[eter W[ood] will direct the play *Loot* and he can begin around Feb. 1st. They're agreed on Ian McShane for the boy.

Sunday, 22 November
I've got to the stage now, where I really don't know what I am doing. Apart from keeping up appearances and doing the crossword puzzles. And so I think more and more of death & the possible ways of ending it all. I think I would have to be very tight first, for I'm such a terrible coward, but if it is meant, I shall doubtless find the means.

Monday, 23 November
To the Aeolian to attend this conference with Roy Rich who is now in charge of Entertainment on the Light Programme. The upshot of it all is that we're to have a new series entitled 'It's Ken Again'[21] around Mar–April of '65. They're approaching Barry Took about the actual writing.

Friday, 27 November
Morning began with irate & bitter telephone call from Eric Merriman saying I was disloyal to take part in a radio show which was written by other people after seven yrs. etc. etc. but that he should have expected it because 'I know you're only in the business for what you can get out of it . . .' I said that's right & eventually he rang off with the threat of court action against the new show.

Monday, 30 November
Laurena Dewar phoned. Michael Harald had written there (not knowing my address) asking for money. His wife is to divorce him, and he'd been found dressed in her clothes in Elgin Avenue with no consciousness of the incident. I went round the streets and found his new abode, but no answer to the doorbell. So I put a note and £5 through the letter box. Michael Harald once gave me £10 in the Marchmont St days, so in terms of honour, I owe him a lot more.

Friday, 4 December
Posted another £5 to Michael Harald – no, it was £10 which makes 15 so far. He wrote today asking for more & acknowledging the last lot.

Monday, 7 December
Met Stanley and Andrew, and we all went to the Warner to see

[21] Eventually titled 'Round the Horne'.

Carry On Cleo. It was technically v. good indeed. Well made and well photographed, but the content was diabolical. There wasn't one really funny moment which really caught one.[22]

Friday, 11 December
To meet Andrew. Together we went to the City & had a pie etc. in a little café & then got into the queue for the Old Bailey. We got into No. 4 Court. A lousy one, unless you're in the front row. We saw the trial of a party of youths accused of robbery. The leader is called McVicar and is conducting his own defence v. well.[23]

Saturday, 12 December
We did the 'Juke Box Jury' at 6.15, recording for next week. I spluttered and shouted a bit but generally got through it without too much pausing. Sheila Hancock was v.g. and she's had the nose fixed and she looks marvellous.

Sunday, 13 December
After lunch I went up to see Gordon and Rona. Gordon said that someone reported to him that when asked if I knew Gordon, I had replied 'Know him? I nearly married him.' Now I laughed etc. and agreed. But I have never said anything remotely like that, but I'm not going to deny authorship of such a v.g. line.

Monday, 14 December
Andrew phoned to tell me about his first day on the dustcarts. He said it went all right and the lads were all nice to him, but obviously he didn't really enjoy it.

Tuesday, 15 December
Did the crossword, then Gording telephoned asking me to go ice-skating. I protested that I'd never done it, but he prevailed on me, and I went. He picked me up in the car with Graham, and we all went off to the rink in Queensway. I actually skated, and despite some teetering I did not fall on the ice at all. I found it an interesting experience.

---

22 Posterity tends to disagree, citing KW's own line (as the fleeing Caesar) 'Infamy! Infamy! They've all got it in for me!'

23 John McVicar was charged with robbing a jeweller of £1000, and of possessing offensive weapons. The jury could not agree on a verdict. At a retrial the following February, McVicar was sentenced to eight years' imprisonment. He escaped from Parkhurst, and later from Durham maximum security wing, eventually reformed and told his own story in *McVicar by Himself* (introduction by Goronwy Rees), 1979.

Friday, 25 December

Went over to Brunswick in morning. We had a splendid turkey at lunch & pudding etc. I gave handbags to L. & P. and they gave me ties and a book (architectural). In the evening we watched the Great War series about Verdun and then fell to talking about murderers & Christie[24] at the Old Bailey. The atmosphere between L. & P. does not improve.

Sunday, 27 December

Had a decent night & woke up full of the L.P. problem. I simply must do something about it. But what? If Louie is alone in a flat, will she be happy? And if she isn't, will that be any worse than the present situation? I wonder if the answer is to ask her to come to Farley & share with me.

Thursday, 31 December

Well this is the last time I shall write an entry in this book. Never have I been more glad to see the end of a year. I went to the Dentist, but he only did x-ray of the gold filling and I have to go again tomorrow. At 12 o'clock to De Lane Lea Studios to do a voice for a Wall's Ice Cream advertisement. They all kept saying they knew I must be very busy etc. etc. If they only knew! Rang Gordon and Rona, am going to see them tonight.

I stayed till about 2.30 when G. drove me home. What a friend he has been, over all these years, and how lovely to see a New Year in with such valuable people.

---

[24] John Reginald Halliday Christie, hanged on 15 July 1953 for the murder of his wife, one of several women he had killed at 10 Rillington Place, Notting Hill.

1965

Monday, 4 January
Phone call from P. Wood about the play. Apparently the Chamberlain has made inroads into it, but not irreparably. We are to meet on Wednesday, about amendments etc. He said he had been in hospital with a psychosomatic skin rash all over the body. I suppose he's been overdoing it.

Tuesday, 5 January
Today at 10.30 for the Third Programme, I start rehearsing my first job this year, and my first job for about three months. Last time I played Bentley in *Misalliance* was in July '54 for television. It was a role that was [a] harbinger of good for me then. Olga Lindo was playing the Mother then & she is again now.

Wednesday, 6 January[1]
Peter Wood, 7 o'c. at his home. We discussed *Loot*. He said he wanted to add another character – assistant to the Detective – alter several scenes and *try* to find a new 3rd Act ending. So we're back at the old trial & error game with three weeks to rehearse and no definite script. This play has been around since October of last year, perhaps earlier, and now this sort of activity. I spoke against change *unless* it was something which actually altered the structure of the play, and which was concrete & written. I objected to a new character too.

Thursday, 7 January
I saw Archie Campbell in the BBC canteen and I said 'You never offer

---

[1] John Lahr's excellent biography of Joe Orton, *Prick Up Your Ears*, dramatises the rehearsal period for *Loot* by quoting passages from KW's diaries, starting from this date. These entries were recast by KW for transmission to Lahr, however, and several dates were altered or reassigned. The truth did not always survive the changes (e.g. it is with Peter Wood, not Orton, that KW discusses *Loot* on 6 January, above; and David Battley played Dennis, not Meadows). Among the entries given in these pages are the original versions, on the true dates, of all passages corresponding to those quoted by Lahr.

me a job' v. spitefully & he said 'I must think of something – something where you can sit on a piano' which made me look & feel deservedly foolish, I suppose. Met Robert Bolt at Etoile and we had an excellent meal. Then we were joined by Siân [Phillips] & Peter O'Toole and we all went off to a place called Tiberio where the drink was flowing like mad. I was terribly tight at about 3 o'c. I must be out of my mind behaving like that. Siân & Peter brought me home in their huge Rolls-Royce car & I must say it is fabulously luxurious.

Friday, 8 January

Eventually did the recording from four o'clock to about 7. Charles Lefeaux said there would be about 60 to 70 pieces of editing. The performance standard was not good. Loads of fluffs. Characterisations all poor. If I'd been producing I'd have thought the cast was turning out shoddy work. I felt Charles L. was disappointed. And rightly so. Came back to the flat, feeling dirty, tired & useless. Had bath & changed. Stanley called on me at 8. Dear, delightful Stanley. It's more and more of a pleasure now, every time I meet him.

Monday, 11 January

Chiropody at 9.30, then to rehearsal at D. of Y. for *Loot*. We had a reading of Act One only. Spent rather a panicky lunch with Peter Wood and we bemoaned the lack of standard.

Tuesday, 12 January

I wasn't used till 4 o'c. & then only for one page of dialogue. Took P. Wood aside and said the rehearsals were miles too slow and no work getting done. At one point I was so angry I left the theatre, but then I reconsidered & returned. I had lunch at Lyons with Joe Orton and moaned at him.

Friday, 15 January

I shall be so grateful if this play succeeds. Even a moderate success would be so encouraging. I desperately *need* to wipe out the remembrance of that disaster at the Queen's. Certainly, if this Orton play does work, I shall ask Michael to let me direct something. It is ridiculous that I should so continuously shirk this job. It is something that I would do very well.

Sunday, 17 January

In the evening, Duncan [Macrae] & I went up to the Jacksons' for the evening. He was curiously slow and some of his stories were endless, at one point he said: 'I've never actually looked for drink: I've spent most of my life fighting it off.' And later, about logic, he said 'Say that I tell you I can see Pink Elephants at night: it follows, therefore, that I should provide stables for them.'

Monday, 18 January

Left Wyndham's at 5.45 & hurried to a meeting of the radio team at Aeolian Hall. Barry Took & Marty Feldman now writing the series.[2] We read a sample script & I think it will provide a good sound show. I'm written in very thinly, but doubtless the weight will shift from week to week.

Wednesday, 20 January

I attended the rehearsal of Act I at the YMCA. They're all giving interesting readings and suddenly it's me that is no good. I feel that it will be as much as I can do to get the lines out – I *can't* cope with props. This bloody pipe will have to go. I won't be able to cope with it this week, that's for sure.

Friday, 22 January

Peter Wood picks at things which have no real import in the production at all. My relations with him are getting v. strained and today when he asked me to alter dialogue already learned, he refused. I mean, I refused. I dislike doing this, as I'm well aware that defiance of authority is a bad example to set the cast but there are occasions on which he forces one into rebellion simply because what he's doing is wasteful and futile. Again & again he makes a point about logic or reasonableness, whereas the level on which the play will succeed is *not* this at all. The cast still don't know the lines well enough to use them. We are still mainly occupied with business, geography etc. And there is a curious tiredness creeping in now – despite the fact that there is no real hard work. Loads of talk from P.W. on abstract theory which bemuses the cast & achieves nothing.

Sunday, 24 January

That old fool Harold Hobson carrying on about the Antrobus play at Hampstead saying 'Two of my friends are concerned in this production. No matter. It deserves no mercy.' It is in sentences of this kind that the awful arrogance of the man is revealed. The implication being that *he* should dispense it, by right. It's all would-be 'ex cathedra'. What a pompous and stupid old bore he is. I wandered about the flat feeling strangely relaxed and melancholy. How strange it is that *knowing* can utterly destroy *chance*. I know how much I long for strong arms & the warmth of unquestioning love; and I know

---

[2] 'Round the Horne', replacing 'Beyond Our Ken'.

how quickly I would destroy it: so the chance – even the chance of it – is cancelled out immediately.

Tuesday, 26 January

A very lousy day at the theatre. One never seems to get a real improvement on scenes, nor is the dialogue really flowing with anyone. It is breaks and dries all the way through. I left eventually at six o'clock feeling utterly dispirited and depressed. Moreover, I'm now worried about the play. It seems such a collection of 'bits' at the moment with no sense of wholeness at all.

Wednesday, 27 January

Ian McShane came back to Farley with me, and we worked on the vocal pattern of the two scenes together. He is v. willing and greatly talented. I like him. This morning I corrected him on a wrong reading of a line and said 'If you'd read the script properly you wouldn't make such a mistake . . .' and he said he'd been hurt by my shouting that at him in rehearsal. I apologised. One continually forgets how sensitive people are.

Thursday, 28 January

At the theatre P. Wood made the ridiculous suggestion that a metronome be used throughout the performance to keep the sense of rhythm for the actors!! Really, this man can be so deterring. We had a run-through & I thought it went v. well. P. Wood said at the end that it was all 'much too hieratic', whatever that may mean.

Friday, 29 January

Letter came from Myra De Groot – now she is married and called Mrs Rosenthal. She has a baby boy called Kevin, and seems v. happy.

Saturday, 30 January

Louie has had stye in the eye. She looked washed out to me. We watched the massive funeral procession & service at St Paul's for Winston Churchill. Thank goodness this dreary saga will soon be finished.

Spent the rest of the day drearing about with growing apprehension about the opening of the play. I can't feel any sense of construction in this piece at the moment – perhaps it's the lack of any audience reaction: but this is the worst period of all, waiting to see if the thing will be able to fly.

Monday, 1 February. Cambridge

Evening performance was mediocre. Styles all over the place – my characterisation wrong – too sinister and the audience were mystified. There will be inquests & God knows what will happen. The feeling is hysterical & uncertain.

Wednesday, 3 February
Rehearsed morning and evening, putting the play into two parts, finishing with entrance of McLeavy after the accident. It was a bit rocky, but the management want it tried. My two weak spots are starting to play up. The bum and the throat.

Thursday, 4 February
Matinée – about a hundred there. Quite a lot of people walk out during the show. Joe Orton v. funny about the comments he overhears during the intervals. Supper after show with Mags & Bev who motored down to see it. They were both v. constructive and said it wants more naturalism of playing and re-writing of Truscott and elongating the discovery of money by Detective.

Friday, 5 February
I suddenly realise that all I've been doing for the past few years has been making a living, but as to enjoying anything, I might as well be living in Cheltenham.

Saturday, 6 February
Only Duncan seems to be carrying on superbly and nightly remarks 'I think it is coming on very well' having dried half a dozen times. The thought of being massacred in Brighton next week is hysterical making.

Tuesday, 9 February. Brighton
M. Codron & P. Wood arrived. They brought with them re-writes. I thought that they were lousy and said so. I said, at least see the show, and say if you want such changes afterwards. They did so, and said the re-writes were essential. So now we start all over again. I think there is going to be an endless task ahead of putting patches on a leaking hulk that will never be right because of a basic flaw. The play begins about Fay, and her story is never developed beyond Act I. Had drinks with M.C. & P.W. at Albion & Wood said I always start making people feel insecure and that I was ruining his confidence. Perhaps this is so. After the show, supper with them and went off to see Noel Willman and Peggy. He said he thought I was at my best when I

appeared to be emotionally involved. This is a good clue to what I've been missing.[3]

Wednesday, 10 February
Rehearsed on the rewrites all day. In the evening the result was an unconfident performance and a gain of one laugh for the loss of another. And it had the effect of taking away the character of Truscott. Before, with two interrogations, I had the chance to establish a character; now, with both of them split, I have completely lost it. After the show I felt so suicidally depressed I just didn't know what to do. The utter shambles of this production is totally unbelievable. The cast is demoralised and the script practically in rags and some of it complete nonsense. I wish I had never set foot near the rotten mess of it all.

Thursday, 11 February
Got nowhere with Wood when I pointed out what damage the rewriting is doing to me, as an actor and as a person. He gave a talk to the cast about the evil of negative thinking which was a *lot* of help! I realise now that learning something different to what I'm playing at night is disaster for the performance. I've written to Michael Codron saying that I think we're drifting towards disaster. Sir Laurence came round and said 'You haven't got a play here – that's your trouble' and grinned a lot and kissed me goodnight.

Saturday, 13 February
Tomorrow and Monday are to be marathon tests, because this new stuff has got to go in by Mon. night. It is really frightening to contemplate.

Monday, 15 February. Oxford
We rehearsed all day to put new stuff in, Duncan being a great impediment. Cast is utterly exhausted. We did the performance – just about – and it just about died in the same way as opening night in Cambridge. So we are back in square one.[4]

Tuesday, 16 February
I said in front of the company & Wood that the rewrites were all a

---

[3] Entry ends here: the concluding sentences of the Lahr version, in which KW draws attention to 'The Challenor bit – "I'll have you, you young bugger, etc. . . ."' and notes, 'Every time you get that kind of involvement in the performance – the whole play works,' do not occur in the original entry.

[4] KW's preferred form of the phrase, and possibly the more authentic one. Football commentaries on BBC radio in the thirties were 'mapped' on a grid of squares, the better to enable listeners to visualise the play: hence 'back *in* square one'.

mistake and that our only chance was to go back. P.W. said no. So on we go, to utter failure. Morale so low that people are getting either apathetic or hysterical. I rang Codron and asked him to come as quick as possible – tonight – he refused, saying P.W. had asked him not to come, and a load of crap about 'I must obey my director'. Utterly specious of course. He thinks I'm exaggerating and that all is all right. The performance was dreadful. The hysteria started mounting and by the end of the play, I was barely controlling myself. The laughter that comes from desperation & ludicrousness. It was disgraceful. Geraldine [McEwan] came off stage shouting 'I can't go on with this stuff any more' and crying. I can't come into London with material like this.

Thursday, 18 February
Did the recording of the new radio show 'Round The Horne' and it had some lame moments, but quite a few laughs. Curiously enough I don't feel so dejected. I feel really quite buoyant considering all things.

Friday, 19 February
Show went like a suet pudding. Playing this stuff is like trying to catch bath water. It keeps slipping thro' yr. fingers. Geraldine shaky & ill and tonight in the hotel David Battley started crying uncontrollably & ran out of the room. What an effect this show is having!

Monday, 22 February
We died in the 2nd half at Golders.[5] Never got 'em back again. An inquest after in the restaurant opposite with M.C., David, Peter W. and Joe Orton. Poor Joe looked just beaten into the ground, but Wood keeps on at him to write more. It's obvious the boy's got nothing left to write. My cold seems to be worse. Eyes full of tears.

Wednesday, 24 February
Evening show was terrible, with hesitant unsure performances from all, because of the re-writes. It throws everyone for six. Codron & Albery came round and I started shouting and crying and said I was sick of all this trial and error stuff and I lost all dignity and had to apologise.

On to Baxters'. Stanley had been watching himself on TV and it had been a great success & his phone kept ringing with congratulations. I wished I was Dead dead dead.

---

[5] The Golders Green Hippodrome.

Thursday, 25 February
Wendy Toye and Rona came. They seemed to like it, with reservations. W. hated Macrae. A lot of people do.

Friday, 26 February
Golders Green evening performance went extremely well. A v. gratifying reception afterwards. Michael C. talked to the cast in the dressing room after. Said it would be B'mouth, Manchester and Wimbledon next. So it's nice to know one can live at home for the last week.

Saturday, 27 February
Second House was fantastic. Colossal reception and an absolutely packed house.

Sunday, 28 February
M.C. v. elated about our fabulous reception last night at Golders. We walked in Regent's Park after and saw a Golden Eagle which had escaped from the zoo. It was being harried by gulls and crows.[6]

Monday, 1 March. Bournemouth
Performance went much as one had expected it. They sat shocked and stunned, gasping their 'ohs' and 'ahs' and we got a lukewarm reception.

Wednesday, 3 March
It was madness to send us here. We would have done better in Reykjavik. None of the re-writes that matter have yet arrived, so it's time-wasting and pointless. A great gale blowing and snow.

Monday, 8 March
'Round The Horne' went drearily. No house. I suppose they're all waiting for a regular routine. The material is not v. good, I'm afraid. Rushed out of the Paris and caught the 1.30 Euston to Crewe. Changed and got the 4.30 to Manchester, got in at 5.15. The show at the Opera House went its usual mediocre way with a provincial house. Came out into the street to thick fog.

Wednesday, 10 March
They made us take out 'stopcock' and the rhumba gag 'cos the Watch Committee have objected to it here! Fantastic.

---

[6] The famous 'Goldie' was recaptured on 10 March, only to escape again in December.

Thursday, 11 March
Evening performance drear. Took Joe Orton to supper after at Midland. The poor boy is punch drunk with rewrites.

Saturday, 13 March
Matinée at 5 o'clock. It was awful. After it, Clifford Evans walked in the dressing room and said it was boring, trite, banal and awful. That cheered me up no end. He said 'Whatever you do – get out of it before London.'

Monday, 15 March
The bus crawled (77A) along to Wimbledon & I arrived at 7.15 instead of 7. Cues are not taken up, lines are fluffed, moves are ill-timed & all is disaster. The curtain was so late that we had to ad lib dialogue. After, Codron told cast that there was no theatre, we were in the last week, and that the Phoenix would rather be dark than take us!

Thursday, 18 March
Michael C. talked to the company. Said there was still a chance of the Garrick but nothing definite. I spoke against the show going in. Had Richard Pearson, Doug Livingstone and George Borwick round. R.P. said that it should be seen in town. He also said 'Every time you laugh, you feel ashamed afterwards.'

Friday, 19 March
Geraldine confided to me in the dressing room that she will not come into town with it. So that makes two of us.

Saturday, 20 March
Matinée was ghastly. P. Wood turned up! After ignoring us for a week. Coming to a matinée!! He said he couldn't attend the end perf.! Second house was good. Harry Packers. It went off fairly well. Good reception. Meeting with M.C. and the cast. He said if the company were keen, he could put it in the Lyric, Hammersmith. They said no. So it died tonight after 56 performances of about 3 different editions.

Monday, 22 March
I predicted, when the play was on, that when it came off, we would hear from many sources how good it was, and what a shame etc. M.C. told me that it has started already.

Tuesday, 23 March
Horrible dream about having my hand cut off & they assured me that

it could all be put back on again. In the end, it wouldn't grow back, despite stitches etc. I woke feeling v. frightened. I think the meaning is clear. All the assurances from people that don't really know are utterly worthless.

Wednesday, 7 April
To see Peter E. We talked about the play situation. He gave me a Charles Dyer play to read. It was about two old queens.[7] Really not good enough. Left v. dispirited.

Thursday, 8 April
Found a telegram from John Osborne asking me to telephone his home about the *Meals On Wheels* play by [Charles] Wood. That means he wants to persuade me to do it. Every time I'm persuaded it is disastrous. I wrote a note and said I'd rather not discuss it. But polite, mind you, because I do admire J.O. v. much, and indeed would like to work for him in something I suited.

Monday, 12 April
Met Andrew at Swan & Edgar. He was late, and unshaven; and limping. Thinks he's pulled a muscle. We lunched at G & C and he said that he felt he had lost what little hold he had on life. None of us realise how low we can get, I suppose. We went up the Old Bailey, No. 4 Court.

Saturday, 17 April
Stanley B. rang at 4 o'c. to say that he'd read in the evening papers that Andrew has been admitted to the Middlesex Hospital, unconscious. I have written to him and Susan, saying they're to call me, if there is anything one can do.

Sunday, 18 April
Visited Andrew in the Middlesex. When Stanley said 'After treatment you'll be different' he replied 'I don't want to be different.' There's no doubt he is in a state of manic apathy.

Thursday, 22 April
Lunched with Peter E. and talked about the hopelessness of my poor old tattered career. He said 'You see, they all connect you with high camp.' I said I did see. Funny how, over the years, you actually become the label they put on you. All at once, as I sat eating, I felt all my

---

7 Evidently Dyer's *Staircase*, produced 1966.

accomplishments dripping away from me: I felt naked and awful. But I kept the chat going. Never let on.

Monday, 26 April
Visited Andrew at 5.30. He's in a private room. He is being given psychiatric treatment. He said they came round the ward today offering everyone a trip to Watney's Brewery. I must say, I thought that was a waste of everybody's time. He said he turned it down. I mean declined. Quite right.

Tuesday, 27 April
I have to earn at least two thousand a year in order to live, and in this profession I average ten thousand a year. Where else could I do that, with no qualifications? Nowhere.

Tuesday, 4 May
Had passport photograph taken at the same place as I originally went to in 1950! And it came out as I wanted it. The camera operator said 'You must smile!' But I ignored the stupid fool. I must look as I usually look, & that is *not* smiling. Laurena Dewar[8] rang me at the dubbing session [for Pearl & Dean] to ask me fly to *Paris* to do dubbing for Orson Welles. I said no. She (Laurena) was *furious* and made a great thing about 'turning down seventy-five guineas.'

Thursday, 6 May
Peter Glenville wants to meet me tomorrow. He is to make a film of *Paradiso* and wants to see me about playing my old part in it (Maxime). It's a lousy part really & it would conflict with the 'Carry On', but I really wouldn't mind doing it, and it would be nice to say no to the Rogers crowd, and let them get some other fool.

Friday, 7 May
Brompton Square at 2.15. Eventually I was shown up. Would I do a test on Monday? Certainly, I smiled. Go to Berman's straightway – here is a script etc. etc. At Berman's I learned 3 other actors were being tested for the same part! I said 'Don't bother about a suit for me' and left. Told Laurena Dewar (Peter in San Francisco) and she said I should never have agreed to test in the first place. It was all a bit of a cheek.

Monday, 10 May
Laurena Dewar rang to say she had told MGM I can't do the Glenville

---

[8] Of the Peter Eade office.

crap because of the Carry On crap. She behaved as if it were world-shattering. Ridiculous.

Wednesday, 12 May
In the park about 3.30. Saw Ken Halliwell with Joe Orton and we all sat in deck chairs and had the chats. They're off to Tangier on the 24 May – so that is an idea for a week. Have to be injected tho'! I mean vaccinated. I think.

Friday, 14 May
Met Andrew R. about 12 o'c. And we had a boat out in Regent's Park & then sat in a deckchair. Then we met Joe O. and Kenneth H. That rather spoiled the afternoon. They kept on and on about their play-writing etc. We went to that café in the park for tea and intruded on a woman who sat alone. We kept on and on shouting and bawling at each other till eventually she left. Got the Carry On script. It's the part of the Judge in a Western town. Not v. good or right for me, but I might be able to make something of it.

Sunday, 16 May
Tom & Clive arrived about 1.30 and Stanley B. about 2 o'c. We sat and talked till 4 when the weather cleared, then we all went down to Maidenhead. Back to town and dinner at Biagi where we fell into a religious discussion and all became v. serious. Stanley stayed on a bit and we talked about how we had both become so jaded, disinterested, and disillusioned. I said that with no private life, there was only the profession to make up for it & that had fallen apart. The dream of a theatre group & plays reflecting the moral problem of our own time was just a dream.

Tuesday, 18 May
I've started to grow sideburns again. I shall need them for the film anyway – might have to try a moustache as well. One of those stragglers.

Saturday, 22 May
Rang Mags to ask if Bev was going on holiday this year, and she asked me down to the country. We drove down together to their country place at Beaumont. I told Bev I could be free after the 10th June till 3 July and by good fortune, he can fit in to this period. It is extremely lucky for me, because Bev is a superb companion for a holiday.

Wednesday, 26 May
Stanley B. rang. I was delighted. He asked me to see *High Wind in*

Jamaica. It was absolutely terrible. S. drove me home about eleven after we'd watched that absurd fight with Cassius Clay 'knocking out' Sonny Liston after one minute, no count, no punch, no fight. Everyone shouting 'FIXED'.

Friday, 28 May

I sometimes think that there is no longer any point in social intercourse for me. Invariably they are not half so entertaining as I am, and consequently I do most of the work: this was all right when I was young and enjoyed showing off, but now I no longer enjoy it.

Sunday, 30 May

In the evening Rona, G. & I all went up to the Baxters'. That awful Eamonn Andrews came on [TV] with his terrible guests. When he asked Clement Freud what his crest should be, Freud said 'A broiler chicken being goosed with a ball point pen, and the inscription "Don't Let The Good Life Stop".'

Monday, 31 May

Met D. at Vega. Terrible fat ear wigger at next table. I said loudly to D. 'Had any trade lately?' and he grew fearfully discomforted 'cos he said the fat party leaned forward approvingly nodding!

Thursday, 10 June

We flew from London Airport at 7.15 for Frankfurt. Left by Ethiopian Airlines at 10.00. Arriving Athens at 00.15. We had drinks in the Square (Constitution) at 2 o'c in the morning and the air was balmy.

Saturday, 12 June

We boarded the Turkish Maritime vessel M.V. *Marmara* for Istanbul via Izmir. Holiday is going beautifully so far.

Monday, 14 June

This ship's orchestra played 'Ramona' in the Sea of Marmara. I thought it was fantastic. I mean. Turkish Maritime. No one met us at Istanbul docks. It was like a beargarden. Our hearts sank when we saw this awful Hiltonish hotel. We went for a swim but the krauts had grabbed all the best places on the plage.

Tuesday, 15 June. Istanbul

This is the embarrassment des riches. Eastern fantasy. A lovely day in this fantastic city.

Tuesday, 22 June. Crete

Visited Heraklion Museum which had some interesting frescoes of Knossos, and then we got a taxi out to Florida Beach. Bev went in for a swim, but I sat in the shade of a taverna. There was a v. handsome Greek Airman & before he left he gave me a note '22–53–Stelios'. The whole incident made me feel excited & erotic. Read the Times in Liberty Square & had a coffee. Kept thinking of Stelios. Madness. Met Bev on the terrace for drinks at 7 o'c. We went up Dirty Alley for dinner – donner kebab and sailors were all round us. When we left I got the winks and kisses blown. What it is to be a pouf. In any language. My self-despite starts to rise. I went off on me own in the evening and got in with some Greeks in a bar, v. sleazy, and I was pissed at 12 o'c. & eating apricots with crème de menthe. Disgusting. Don't remember much about the rest of the evening.

Monday, 28 June

Endless drive from Sitea to this filthy monastery at Toplou. This awful old monk with lice crawling on him. Really disgraceful.

Tuesday, 29 June

I discovered today that two traveller's cheques had been stolen from the drawer in my room. I know the numbers etc., but don't feel like calling the police etc. because I just think it's awful and unclean. Theft is something that really disgusts me. It makes me feel hateful towards this whole wretched island. Anyway I've had this place. I've never come upon so many cadgers in my life. I shall be glad to get back to my own country. To be able to have a cup of tea – one's own way – ah! the delight of being able to be cool. How many times must I do it, before I learn that travel is illusion. (In this case, it was good for me because it started the rhythms going. They'd practically stopped.)

Saturday, 3 July. Naples

It's a question now of living through the days. We found a little restaurant & had a v.g. meal. I drank a lot and talked about suicide.

Sunday, 4 July

Arrived London at 6.50. The relief to breathe clear air! The temperature here is about twenty degrees lower, but it's all worth it.

Tuesday, 13 July

Left at 7 for Pinewood. I'm playing the Judge with greyed hair and moustache and a 50'ish voice.[9] I only hope that it works. Quite a bit of trouble with the sound man over my voice. Oh! dear.

Thursday, 15 July
Gerald T. told me today that they were pleased with me in the rushes, so I hope that my Hal Roach characterisation is going to work. It is quite a challenge for me, 'cos I've never played character in a film before.

Friday, 16 July
P.E. gave me a play to read called *The Platinum Cat* by someone called Longrigg,[10] from David Conville (v. young management) and I think it is v. engaging. One will have to find an enchanting young girl. Every line you read in the part says Maggie S.

Sunday, 18 July
I told Bev I was interested in *Platinum Cat* and he says he will direct it.

Friday, 23 July
Saw the rushes today. The make-up etc. was all right but the voice took a bit of getting used to. I see what the trouble is. It's really too old & wheezy for the face. It's a shame really but of course I'm stuck with it now.

Wednesday, 28 July
Pinewood at 8. Met John Le Mesurier who was looking well. Had a chat with him and he said Hancock was drinking away his career. Dreadful business in Hollywood where his work was a fiasco.[11]

Tuesday, 3 August
Played the Fauré Requiem tonight. Some of it makes me want to weep, and always I feel purged after hearing it. I inwardly beg to be forgiven. Beg to be pardoned for all the errors, the unworthy thoughts, and especially the malicious things my tongue finds to say.

Monday, 16 August
Pinewood 8 o'c. Saloon scenes. Rather tedious and of course I found I'd left the watch on the wrist! Dread the thought of rushes.

---

[9] In *Carry On Cowboy*.
[10] Roger Longrigg, b.1929, novelist, first-time playwright, and latterly an author specialising in country pursuits and the turf. His *Who's Who* entry does not mention *The Platinum Cat*. Also wrote novels under the name Rosalind Erskine.
[11] He had begun *The Adventures of Bullwhip Griffin* for Disney, but was replaced.

Wednesday, 25 August
Saloon stuff with the cow hides – accusing Rumpo of rustling etc. Pleasant day really. Me being v. cheeky. I said to Gerry T. 'A lot of people think we should take a cut in these films instead of a salary' and he said 'You'd have to wait two years for your money'. Which I think indicates that he doesn't approve of such a thing. But it might be an idea to pursue it with Peter Rogers. I certainly don't want to earn a lot of money in this financial year. I feel quite buoyant lately. Must be heading for a fall.

Thursday, 26 August
To Rushes at 1.25. I wasn't any good. In fact, whether it's the writing or not, I don't know, but I haven't been at all funny in my eyes since it started. It's a character that is essentially a reaction one. It bounces off others. Sydney Bromley would have been excellent in my part. And really funny. His character is marvellous. Perhaps I've come to the end of my inventiveness; actually, I wonder if it ever existed.

Tuesday, 31 August
Shot in the Doc's room. My last sequence. I was playing up a bit and being outrageous. Feeling everyone's bum and miming pissing behind the flats. As I drove away from Pinewood I felt v. much as if it was my last day. More sad than I've ever felt before. I wonder why? I've never noticed a last day so emphatically.

Wednesday, 1 September
Met Joe Orton at Goodge St at 5.45 and we went to the Middlesex to visit Kenneth Halliwell who's had the appendix operation. He looked quite well. The episode reminded me of when I was in the Middlesex before – to see Andrew Ray. It is a depressing experience. Returned to flat for coffee and George Borwick came over. We chatted about Tangier till about 10 o'c. when they both went off.

Friday, 3 September
Pinewood for end of picture party. It was v. nice. Peter Rogers said that they always wanted me in their pictures and that 'we've even had you in them when it wasn't really necessary.' This man talks in riddles the whole time.

Monday, 6 September
Went to see a revival of the Leslie Howard picture *Pimpernel Smith*. The charm and radiance of L.H. still triumphs over technical & artistic badness. His was the most mysterious quality. One of the few actors I've ever seen who could convey gentleness, charm, humour, attrac-

tiveness, strength, intellect, humility, compassion, all instantaneously. He was a sort of genius.

Tuesday, 7 September
It is ironic that in so many ways I resemble my father so much. We are alike in so many things, both of us shared a sense of inferiority, both of us disliked the governing class & its accent; we disliked any kind of ceremony even in dress; preferred the company of men to women, smoked far too much, was troubled by insomnia, dreamed of travel & another way of life (as I do), and when I'm most unguarded, my handwriting is just like his was.

Thursday, 9 September
Found some marvellous lines of Cicero – 'To be wholly idle is not idle, and wholly alone, is not alone . . .'[12]

Saturday, 11 September
Went up to Highgate after lunch to call on Moira. We walked in the woods, and several squirrels came right up to us! When I put out my hand to one, he bit the finger – quite gently – as tho' to test if it were food: close to, they are v. like rats.

Tuesday, 14 September
Bev came over about 6 o'c. We went along to Biagi for dinner. After the meal we went to the White Horse for a drink & then the Salisbury which was v. theatrical. Met John Hurt in there and asked him why he'd left his wife & he looked shocked & said 'It's not a question I can answer, standing in the Salisbury' and proceeded to answer it, saying 'I just didn't *know* myself then . . .' I got v. high and was giving bogus phone numbers to everyone. O dear.

Tuesday, 21 September
Rehearsed Kingsway 10.30. Got the No. 1 bus home. I sat behind the driver and saw that he was young, handsome and incredibly blonde: I particularly noticed it: then at Warren Street I realised he wasn't using the indicator for the turn left, so I banged on the glass & signalled the direction. He turned round, acknowledged it with a nod, and did as I bid. After, the conductress said 'That was good of you, love, to keep your eye on him – I was upstairs getting the fares you see & he doesn't know this route at all – he's been switched from Catford, you

---

12 *'Numquam se minus otiosum esse quam cum otiosus, nec minus solum quam cum solus esset.'* Cicero, *De Officiis*. If KW saw this quotation in its Latin form, it may well have confirmed his marked liking for the adjective 'otiose'.

know – only country buses – and he's not used to the West End at all – all this traffic makes him nervous.'

Friday, 24 September

Got a v. nice letter from the editor of Film thanking me for the article I did on Richard Williams. I wrote it straight on to the typewriter and 'just as I speak' – it read quite well. Like everything in my life, it proves that whatever is *easy* is entertaining. Whenever it's hard work, it's boring. Went to Wembley Studios. In the end, we recorded it about 7 o'c. and the audience was lousy and I felt stale, and the whole thing rather fizzled out. These half hour things should never rehearse more than two days and studio for one.

Monday, 27 September

It's the first rehearsal today at Queen's Theatre rehearsal room. I am full of various apprehensions. Will this Caroline Mortimer be able to play comedy?

Wednesday, 29 September

Several times I mentioned preponderance of pauses & need for picking up cues, but Bev didn't support me. It is extraordinary that in every production I do, oneself is not regarded as any kind of authority on delivery. They seem to think one achieves one's position by accident or something.

Tuesday, 5 October

Worked Act III afternoon. Then tea with Bev and Tony Valentine & the girl Susan Tebbs at Act 1 Scene 1. I told 'em about the operation on me bum and Bev said 'After that, I need a good stiff drink.'

Saturday, 9 October

Rang Bev at 9 o'c. and asked to see him this morning. I apologised for my stupidity in talking & advising actors in the play, contrarily to his direction. I felt considerably better afterwards.

Saturday, 16 October

V. dangerous spending too much time on a comedy. We need an audience now. I feel so grateful for everything. First God – then my job – then all the rest of the blessings. I suppose this is one of the best periods of my life.

Tuesday, 19 October

To Cecil Gee for fitting. The blue corduroy trousers are still not right. So I went to the basement & got a pair of ready made ones. All the exercises have paid off! These are a 28 waist trouser which I could never have worn before! I've been 30 for ages.

Monday, 25 October. Brighton

Opening night. It went off reasonably. I had one fluff, apparently C. M[ortimer] went tearing along much too fast & the audience couldn't really take it in – but I don't care about complaints about speed. Bev suddenly announced his marriage to a v. attractive girl at the table called Gayden. He is marrying her on Friday! There's no one I wish more well.

Friday, 29 October

Up at 7 with Bev to London on the 8.36. To Kensington, walked to the Registry Office. There was John Wood & Sylvia Glory & Peter (Earl of Faversham), Michael Abrahams, Bev and Gayden Collins. They were married by a charming Registrar & we were all back at Eldon Rd. having champagne by 1 o'c. It was really a waste of time my going all that way, 'cos Bev didn't use me as a witness. He had Abrahams. I must own to being v. disappointed & hurt. I'd imagined this honour would have gone to me. When I got back to Brighton I was seized with melancholy and shot into the pictures to see a film called *Shenandoah* – as I turned up the carpeted stairs of the cinema there was a woman on the landing with her knickers off – urinating! It was pouring down the stairs. I called the usher & manager. It was disgraceful. They said 'Oh! we know her – she used to work here.' Evening perf. went v. well.

Saturday, 30 October

Dougie Byng came round. He said 'You've got a new quality in yr. work – it is *charm*.'

Sunday, 31 October

Read the new Carry On, 'Screaming', & wrote to Peter Rogers that I didn't want to play another 'old' character. If he offers to make the age younger, I'll do it, not otherwise. I'd rather play my own age.

Wednesday, 3 November. Oxford

Gerald Thomas came to see show in evening. Said he thought it was a thin little piece, but that it was mildly amusing. He said they're making my character in the film younger, and he will be the brother instead of the father of Virula. They've offered Virula to Fenella Fielding.

Saturday, 6 November

Met Bev and Gayden and we went to Lincoln College and took sherry with Brian Simpson[13] in the Wesley Room. Then we were joined by Vivian Green[14] (College Chaplain) and we had lunch in the Williams Room. It was sumptuous with a raspberry sweet worthy of the Mirabelle. Conversation was mediocre. Certainly not of the level one might expect from such academic minds. V.G. said he liked the Beatles and I told him that he ought to know better.

Monday, 8 November. Birmingham

The performance was mediocre. Suddenly it is *all quite clear: I've done it again.* Landed myself in another load of mediocrity & no talent or technique around me to help me disguise it.

Sunday, 14 November

My stomach is out again. The corduroy trousers are too tight for me to get on. Threw them in dustbin. Never liked 'em in the first place.

Tuesday, 16 November

Opening Night, Wyndham's. Suddenly it was all inhibited and tight. Voice was like a croak with nerves, and all the ease and by-play went for nothing. Anyway, I knew, standing in the wings, that we were plummeting to a flop. I know the notices will be disastrous.

Wednesday, 17 November

They are. There isn't any gleam of consolation. Gordon J. rang and with superb consideration asked me to lunch with him at the house. He and Rona were splendid.

Friday, 19 November

Once this six months' term has been served (if it has to be served) one must disappear from the theatre and leave it to rot into limbo.

Sunday, 21 November

All the Sunday papers are nice to me! Fantastic.

Tuesday, 30 November

Evening performance good. Afterwards Maggie S. came round. She looked marvellous. Said that the show was no good and added 'You're

---

[13] Then Fellow and Tutor; latterly Professor of Law, University of Michigan.

[14] Rev. Vivian Green, b.1915, historian and memoirist. Bills himself in *Debrett's Distinguished People of Today* as 'the man on whom John Le Carré partly modelled the character of George Smiley'. Honorary Fellow, Lincoln College, from 1987.

acting for all five of them! It must be exhausting darling!' We had supper after in Biagi and were joined there by Robert Stephens. This is Maggie's new love. V. good mind.[15]

Monday, 6 December
Feeling terrible. To show in the evening & just about got through it. Almost fainted at one point & bashed me face, and cut it just below eye. Had to play all last scene with it bleeding.

Tuesday, 7 December
Rang Patrick and told him I was worse. The body hot & aching everywhere. Complete lassitude. He said he would write to the management. I can't go on. Took to the bed. Suicidally depressed. If only there was a way out.

Thursday, 9 December
Patrick rang to say that the company were sending an Insurance Doctor. Obviously to check on whether I'm really ill. It is disgusting the way people treat one. Laid in bed thinking of suicide and all the letters I would have to write to those people who have been good to me. I don't want to appear on a stage ever again. Whatever it is in one that makes for an entertainer – live sense – is dead in me, at the moment.

Friday, 10 December
The Insurance Doctor said 'Frankly, I'm amazed you stuck it as long as you did.' At 6 o'c. John Gale telephoned. He told me that he had withdrawn the show as from Sat. and that I wasn't to worry about anything except getting better, and that we would do something together in the future. John Hussey went out to Flanagan's for some fish for us to eat. Turbot v. nice, and chips. Ate the lot we did.

Sunday, 12 December
At 10.20 tonight, I was suddenly gripped by a terrible fear that I was going to die. Suddenly. And I realised how little I'd done. And I realised that I was afraid. And *needing* God. Needing as I have never ever known in my existence. Had to get out of bed & have a drink.

Monday, 13 December
Moira came over at 12.30 and she told me that Stanley is going to Beirut (Lebanon) for a few days, so if I went there, we could meet up together. It is an idea. And it would be sunny.

---

[15] They were married in 1967 (marriage dissolved 1975), and had two sons.

Thursday, 16 December
10.00 Moira just rang. She said that Stanley is trying to get to Beirut before the 30th!! I don't deserve it I know, but if *anyone* can help me at this dreadful period, it is *him*. No one else. It was him I turned to, in my head, at Wyndham's on that dreadful night and it's been him I've been thinking of, ever since. Just to be with. Just to talk to – a faithful hand that takes all the chaff & grain together, keeps what's worth keeping, and with a breath of kindness, blows the rest away.[16]

Friday, 17 December
London Airport. Via Frankfurt and Belgrade and Istanbul arriving Beirut at 18.30. After getting in and unpacking, I had a walk round the streets. It's all v. Levant & just like Greece and Turkey at night. I was accosted by a youth who offered me delights in the Turkish Bath with Massage and 'you know Sir – all that you like . . .' But I said I was a man of God and that rather stumped him.

Saturday, 18 December
Cable from Stanley. He arrives Beirut Xmas morning at 9.35. I must meet the plane. He is wonderful.

Friday, 24 December
Letters from Louie, Annette and Gordon & cable from the Pearsons. Wrote letters to all & had a rest in the afternoon.

Saturday, 25 December
Met Stanley. Dear, understanding Stanley. It did my heart good to see him & that's a fact.

Monday, 27 December
We're both rather dispirited in this place & S. said today 'I don't feel any kind of sympathy in this city.' I agree. The people think of you only in terms of money, and of taking advantage of yr. ignorance to overcharge the whole time. Now I know how Americans feel in Europe.

Thursday, 30 December
Direct flight to London. They invited me & S. into the cockpit or Flight Deck and we sat with pilots and watched it all. Got into flat & floor was littered with letters. Three were bills.

---

16 For the original context of these phrases, see entry for 10 November 1980 (p. 621, n.).

Friday, 31 December
In evening I went up to Gordon & Rona. Lovely evening. So that is the end of it. The worst year ever, I suppose. The third flop, giving me the feeling that I don't want to do anything in the theatre again. Just at the moment, I don't know what the answer is. All I know is that if you're going to live at all you've got to fight. At the present there isn't much fight left in me. I'll have to take stock, go carefully and regain my buoyancy and start all over again.

1966

Sunday, 2 January
Went out and got the papers. The usual load of rubbish, apart from an interesting piece by Philip Toynbee[1] on the boring pointlessness of the writing of Beckett and Burroughs. He should have cast his net wider, to include Osborne.[2] He made the point that this kind of writing treats of despair despairingly. He rightly says that this is a fundamental misconception of Art.

Monday, 3 January
At 7.30 Hayley and Juliet Mills came, with Russell.[3] They took me to dinner at La Terrace, off Mount Street. Returned to Juliet's flat for a brandy. Hayley played her record of the Red Army Ensemble which I said was awful and she said 'Oh! you are a swine!' which was amusing. I thought several times during the evening what a lovely person Juliet is. Practical and good, and patient and loving. Why don't I ever meet a girl like that, who cares for me?

Thursday, 6 January
Still thinking about this accommodation for Louie. We had lunch together at Hook Line & S. and agreed to look at a flat which Peachey have got at Osnaburgh St., quite near to me. I don't think we'd get anything much better in a central area.

Friday, 7 January
In the evening went to see Joe Orton & Ken Halliwell. Watched some television, 'The Avengers', which was puerile, and Joe O. gave me a copy of his play *Mr Sloane* which is a v. handsome present.

---

[1] 1916–81. Author and *Observer* book reviewer.
[2] Who had suddenly declined in KW's estimation (see entry for 8 April 1965, p. 256).
[3] Russell Alquist, then the husband of Juliet Mills.

Monday, 10 January
I telephoned Freeborn's and arranged the removal of Louie on the 21st.

Tuesday, 11 January
Ordered the car in the evening to take me to Judith Stott & Dave Allen at Hampstead. Dave asked me if I'd do an interview thing on his pilot show for the BBC and I said yes. I like him and moreover, I like his work.

Wednesday, 12 January
It is with rueful acceptance that I acknowledge Stanley Baxter's ignoring of me since the return from Beirut. I have telephoned etc. but nothing. Now that I look back on it, I can see that there was no intellectual justification for thinking S. was the *one friend* who could help me in that last crisis. It was an emotional idea. Linked with him in similar circumstances.

Thursday, 13 January
I went out and got the Noel Coward LP record on which I've done 'Mad Dogs' and 'Mrs Worthington' for HMV. I listened to the whole thing & I honestly think I'm the best thing on it, I really do. None of them have the quality that is right for Coward – that self send-up sophistication. It's the most indifferent disc I've ever heard.

Friday, 14 January
Pinewood about 9.45.[4] Clothes are vaguely Victorian, frock coat, cravat etc. and make-up dead pale to look 'from the dead', as it were. Everyone on the set was nice to me. Alan Hume, lighting, took me aside and said 'No joking, Kenny, it really is good to have you back on the set' – I could hardly reply, I was so touched and pleased. Technicians & stage hands – loads of people came up to me and said lovely things. It was the most beautiful day of the year. It's a wonderful thing to be liked.

Monday, 17 January
Jim Dale said 'We all take the acting pace from you, Ken' – I must admit, it's all v. gratifying.

Wednesday, 19 January
Did stuff with the Oddbods – all that revolting mummy make-up, and teeth. Made me feel sick. One of them told me about his experiences

---

[4] For *Carry On Screaming*.

at a sex orgy. I realised how utterly disgusted I am by this kind of thing.

Phoned Louie. I know now that I'm in a ridiculous state about this whole move. I'm landed with an annual outlay of more than a thousand pounds, and the loss of about six thousand in terms of an asset. It's not that I am mean, it's the knowledge that such obligations force me into an economic trap which becomes increasingly difficult to escape from.

Thursday, 20 January

Saw Charles Chaplin in the restaurant today. Looking grey, yellow, and bent. Pathetic. He's doing a picture with Marlon Brando.[5] Haven't seen him yet.

Friday, 21 January

Did one shot entering the Hall with Fenella. Thinking all the time of Louie moving[6] & hoping all was going according to plan. Got Charles, the driver, to take some flowers to the new flat at midday.

Tuesday, 25 January

Doing these Carry On films is as though nothing has changed since '57, when I started the first one. Since then, as a style or burlesque they've established themselves as part of the British entertainment scene and they have made a way of life possible for me. I have never missed being in one.[7] When I started I was doing *Lettuce* at night & had an upstairs room at Pinewood. Now I'm downstairs in the star dressing room and do nothing at night.

Tuesday, 1 February

Location shots at South Gate of Studios and after, at Windsor. I had to sit in this coach with Fenella Fielding who said 'Why is your bum so hard? Do you leave it out at night?' which made me laugh I must say. She is such an enigmatic creature! I went into her dressing room afterwards and told her truthfully 'I haven't laughed so much for years.'

Monday, 7 February

The shot was me, backing away from the reincarnated Pharaoh and falling into a great trough of dough, struggling out again and then falling into the vat with the monster. It wasn't pleasant. The dough

---

[5] Chaplin, in his seventy-seventh year, was directing *A Countess from Hong Kong*.

[6] To Marlborough House, Osnaburgh Street, NW1.

[7] Not so: he had turned down *Carry On Cabby* (1963).

stuck into hair *everywhere* and it was the devil's own job to remove it. Still, luckily, with these kind of scenes, the clothes are so ruined that they can't go again. Trouble is, they had a Mitchell camera as well, so with all that noise I shall have to post-synch everything. Returned to Farley early and had a rest before venturing out to the TV Centre to do a spot [on] the Dave Allen Show. It is a lousy little studio; but they were better by the time I got on and we got some laughs out of them.

Tuesday, 8 February
Pinewood at 12 o'c. Warren Beatty said 'Hallo Kenny, how's it going?' which was v. forward of him but secretly pleased me enormously.

Wednesday, 9 February
To Studio One, to see the Trade show of *Carry On Cowboy*: it was marvellous. It's the first good British comedy in years, the first time a British Western has ever been done, and the first 'Carry On' to be a success on every level. It's got laughs, and pathos, some lovely people and ugly people. Mind you, it's an alarming thought that they'll never top this one.

Friday, 11 February
The result of the debate on Homosexuality in the Commons is a victory for the supporters of the private member's bill advocating freedom for consenting male adults. It certainly surprised me. I would never have dreamed it would get by in a country like this. Certainly it will be enormously encouraging to the people who have worked so hard on the Albany Trust.[8]

Tuesday, 22 February
Birthday. Pinewood at 8.30. At lunchtime Gerald sent me a bottle of champagne. Peter Butterworth gave me champagne too. In the afternoon, they wheeled a huge birthday cake on to the set & I was photographed cutting it! Home by 6.30. At 7 o'c. Stanley B. and Tom & Clive came and we all went to Biagi's restaurant for supper. I suppose it was my best birthday ever. Well, I've been waiting a long time to be forty. I'm certainly starting to look it, I think.

Monday, 28 February
General Election announced for March 31. I rang Stanley and he let

[8] 'The only movement to which I ever attached myself was the Albany Trust, because its espoused aim was to change the law concerning cohabitation between consenting male adults.' KW to Monday Club meeting of the Campaign for Homosexual Equity, 27 June 1977 (from pencil notes for speech).

me go up there to see Harold Wilson on television. It was v. good. I think he will win & predict a majority of about fifty. Of course I shall vote Tory, but I know that they will lose in the country.

Thursday, 3 March
To Rona in the evening. We had a very nice meal and afterwards we saw television. A 'blue comedian' was interviewed, and as he tried desperately to justify the awful work he was engaged in, I suddenly understood why I was so sympathetic to him: my dilemma is exactly the same. I do a dirty Carry On film because I can't afford to be *moral* about my work. This is the economic trap.

Wednesday, 9 March
'Round The Horne', Paris [Theatre]. We had a v. good house to start off with & it all went extremely well. Lots of laughs. George enjoyed it v. much. He is off on Friday to Marrakesh. Lovely.

Saturday, 12 March
Alistair Cooke who reads 'Letter From America' on radio is regarded with great respect as a journalist & commentator. People speak of him as though he was something special. In actual fact, he is a v. bad reader. He sounds as if he smokes a pipe. And probably does.[9] Bores the arse off me.

Tuesday, 15 March
Walked over to Louie's flat in evening to see the Liberal Party B'cast on television. Done with great sensibility by Ludovic Kennedy. And after, a dramatisation of the assassination of President Kennedy.[10] An actor called Tony Bill* played Lee Harvey Oswald (the alleged Assassin) and it was interesting to see the stuff that was never *verified & established* now being treated as factual & true. There will never be a *true* picture for us about what happened in Dallas on that fateful & dreadful day, *because* Oswald was never given a chance to defend himself & is now dead, *because* the truth about the appalling corruption of the Dallas Police will never be told, and *because* the Warren Report is the official & efficient hindrance to a proper inquiry.

*a staggeringly good performance in a mass of mediocrity – a personal triumph.

---

[9] Alastair Cooke says (28 January 1993) that he smoked a pipe for six months at Cambridge, but gave it up when he realised it didn't look as masculine as he had hoped.

[10] *Lee Oswald – Assassin*, by Rudolph Cartier and Reed de Rouen, from a documentary play by Felix Lützkendorf. Kenneth Allsop, narrator.

Friday, 25 March

Up to see Stanley in the evening and we did some recording of dialogue for this Irish accent he wanted. In the evening we watched some television, which confirmed my opinion that this is essentially the medium for nonentities.

Sunday, 27 March

At 5 o'c. to TV Centre to do 'Call My Bluff' panel game. Our side was Joan Sims & me, under Frank Muir, and their side was John Neville and Diana Sands under Roberta Morley. We won of course. After, we had a few drinks and a chat, and a man called Barry Lupino (bearded) asked me if I'd be interested in doing an hour spot on TV in a show of my own devising. I said I would be, on condition the script was right.

Wednesday, 30 March

Listened to the show 'Round The Horne' on the wireless. I thought a lot of it was inaudible. But the sound of all the enjoyment & laughter was v. infectious I must say. Still, the fact that I listen at all is a sure sign of boredom!

Thursday, 31 March

Went to vote at Lisson Grove at 9 o'c. I voted for a Mr Capel who is the Liberal candidate. Not a hope in hell I don't suppose. That awful Hogg[11] will stay in, I expect – judging by all the prosperous looking idiots at the polling station. Nora Stapleton came over and saw me about 2.30. She was attacked by a gang at Drury Lane. They tied her up & made away with two thousand pounds. She was still v. upset by it all, and began to cry when telling me. I'm afraid I sat there and laughed.

Friday, 1 April

Labour have a majority of about ninety-five.[12] My own prediction was 50. Liberals are back with 10 seats bless 'em.

Sunday, 3 April

There are no words to express the deep unhappiness that possesses me. The economic trap that I'm in – with money obligations to Louie – and to P. both force me to maintain this kind of life: I have no privacy in the streets, always there is the moron's nudge or cretin's

---

[11] Quintin Hogg, Baron Hailsham of St Marylebone, b.1907. Lord High Chancellor 1970–74, 1979–87.

[12] Actuallyninety-six.

wink to make me hasten away: always there is the emptiness of existence to which I return. I think now, that I am approaching a crisis. I don't think it is possible to go on like this. There must be *another* way. There must be. This is a living death.

Monday, 4 April

To Victoria to see Morecambe & Wise in film *That Riviera Touch*. These two have always been my unfavourite comedians, but there were some v. funny & original things in this film, which was v. well done. These two came out of it v. well indeed – v. much innocents abroad and at times a real note of pathos established.

Tuesday, 5 April

Joe Orton & Kenneth Halliwell arrived at about 6 o'c. They talked about the play *The Erpingham Camp* which Joe has done for television. Said it was marvellous. Joe told me he'd been to see his play done in Berlin (*Loot*) and that it was also being done by the Manchester Theatre with someone called Chagrin in my part. Singularly appropriate name. I reproved Joe Orton for not having written anything for me. 'I tear around for 7 weeks on a terrible tour for you,' I said, 'and I get no reward. It's the same with Bolt. Appear in a flop in the West End for him and when it comes to his screenplays – *nothing* is offered me . . .' Oh yes, I became very bitter and scornful. Then Joe told me about the woman downstairs[13] who spilled a cup of hot tea between her legs and had to be taken to hospital. Kenneth H. said 'It came up the size of an apple – a terrible blister' and the old lady said of her treatment in hospital 'I had *every* attention, including Top Class penicillin . . .'

Wednesday, 6 April

'R[ound] T[he] H[orne]'. At the rehearsal John Simmonds the producer said there'd been criticism of the fact that the visual performance has been outweighing the vocal: he said this is particularly irritating to people listening to the radio because they're hearing gales of unexplained laughter. I said 'It's me you're really getting at, isn't it?' and he said yes. In so many words he did. It all went very well & we had a packed house.

Thursday, 7 April

To Broadcasting House to record a talk on 'Woman's Hour' on what I felt like & ate at breakfast. I said it was generally coffee & a cigarette and that it was a *doom* laden affair. Which it is.

---

[13] Identified in *The Orton Diaries* as Hilda Corden (1915–81).

Sunday, 10 April

Michael C. told me this story about Lady Dorothy Macmillan saying to Mme. De Gaulle at a banquet at the Elysée Palace 'Now that yr. husband has achieved so much, is there any particular wish, any desire you have for the future?' and Madame replied 'Yes – a penis.' Whereupon Gen. De Gaulle leaned over and said 'No, my dear, in English it is pronounced Happiness.'

Monday, 11 April

Gordon rang me at 2 o'c. and asked me over. When we were talking about people being either instinctive or intellectual, G. said 'Without your intellectual capacity I should think *you* would go mad.' I more or less agreed with him, and he said 'Of course, underneath you are colossally emotional' and I asked how he *knew* this. He said 'Oh! I just *know* it – I can often see you in my mind's eye, sitting in your flat alone – and just crying. I don't mean out of self-pity either. It's the *bigness* of it that is so admirable . . .' It's amazing how much he knows about me.

Tuesday, 12 April

I know now that the reason I cannot indulge in promiscuous sex is because I've come – no, because I've *always* equated it with *sin*. I think that the natural goodness and dignity of man is bound up with regard for these qualities, and that if you use someone else physically, with no other motive than sexual stimulus etc., then you degrade them, you take away from their natural goodness & their dignity (and of course your own.) I think that this is forgivable in the auto-erotic function, because one is only concerning oneself with oneself, and though its mental consequences can be bad, nevertheless it is infinitely preferable to the former. I think that the reason I've never had intercourse with someone is because I've never *trusted* them with the *knowledge of me*. It seems to me to be *so much* to offer of oneself – such an act of vulnerability – that it would require a v. special person to entrust it to. I don't think I've ever met such a person.

Thursday, 14 April

Gordon J. mentioned that he was taking the family to Foxhole in Pwllheli, N. Wales in a week or so, and I said I might pop up & visit them. I asked if there was a hotel near where they were staying and he said he didn't think so, but why didn't I stay *with them* 'cos they had a spare bedroom. I said I would think about it. Then later on, Rona said 'Well you're welcome for 3 days, but I honestly couldn't allow any longer . . .' I was really appalled. This kind of rejection is so *lowering* to me and I can't pretend indifference to it. I wanted to shout out 'Don't bother yourself dear – I shan't come *near* you for 3 bloody minutes, let alone three days – I don't want to even see your rotten cottage in the country – stick it up your arse' etc. etc. But I just said 'Well, it's the weather actually, that would decide it for me . . . I will wait and see what that is like.'

Sunday, 17 April

In desperation I phoned Terry. I took him to lunch and filled him with fantasies about sexual licence in Morocco. By the time I'd finished he was v. anxious to go there, but I was rather punctured at the end, when he asked when I'd been there & I had to confess that I never had been there. After that we wandered disconsolately round Speakers' Corner and watched a speaker being heckled by a man who shouted 'You're supposed to love your fellow man.' 'What do you think I am – a homosexual?' Great laugh from the crowd. Then to see Jean-Paul Belmondo in the film *Pierrot Le Fou*, and in a sequence about lack of identity, the girl asks 'Who are you?' and he replies 'I am a homosexual' (joking of course). Great laugh from the audience. When we came out the depression was all over me like a *pall*. I said a hurried goodbye and walked home in the cold. Found myself crying.

Saturday, 23 April

I leave this morning from Paddington for Pwllheli. I am really dreading it, and I think I must have been mad to agree in the first place. Gordon & the boys met me at Pwllheli, where, mercifully, some local lads asked me for autographs. Obviously not so Siberian as the territory appears from the train window. We drove to the cottage at Llanbedrog – right on the beach.

We talked about the 'Moors Case'. This is the business of a man called Brady and a girl called Hindley who are accused of murdering children and burying them on the moors. It has touches of Gilles De Rais & the Marquis de Sade and sounds quite revolting. One feels in cases like this that such people *should* be painlessly put away. All one's carefully proposed arguments about capital punishment being wrong drain away on reading about this sort of filth.

Sunday, 24 April

In the evening Rona gave us boiled eggs. I thought the meal was a sort of tea, and that dinner would follow. But nothing else was forthcoming. Charming. One really can't say that the culinary effort has ever been essayed! There was considerable argument about me staying on tomorrow & Gordon offered to drive me to Bangor to catch the 7.30pm arriving Paddington at 2 o'c.!! in the morning. But in the end I prevailed.

Monday, 25 April
I left Pwllheli at 8.20. All my original misgivings were justified. It was a great mistake and a very expensive one.

Thursday, 5 May
I wrote a letter to Gordon & Rona when I left Pwllheli. I had no acknowledgment. I am wondering why there's been such a silence ever since. Somehow, I can't get it out of my head that the visit was symbolic of something.

Wednesday, 18 May
Peter E. rang. Said that Sir Laurence O. had been on the phone about me joining the National. Seemed quite interested according to P.E. I will wait & see what they come up with.

Saturday, 21 May
At 10 o'c. to party at Pembroke Square. It was the same crowd. Dickie Wattis sitting moodily in a corner commenting on an American friend 'He only wants to cuddle – doesn't really know *what* he is . . .' Don dancing with a bearded Swiss-German of twenty-three called Martin, who on being asked his reaction to a kiss said 'Why don't you just *do* it? All this questioning is so analytical & clinical – it *kills* romance . . .' A very tall and dishy boy on the stairs is touched up by someone who says he looks very fit, and the rejoinder is 'I'm not complaining.' I hung around making desultory passes at people and then running away.

Thursday, 26 May
Met George Borwick for lunch at G & C at 12.30. He said he'd booked us on a flight to Tangier via Paris on Sat. 11 June. He said that he thought I was a good and loyal friend. He was sincere.

Monday, 30 May
Wandered round to the Hedleys' at 3 o'c. Rona was there, and before long, she had begun a reproof for my behaviour in Wales. She said they'd been v. hurt that my letter merely said I'd got home all right and didn't say thank you for the stay with them. She said 'We went to no end of trouble, taking the electric blanket off Graham's bed and giving it to you – and when we drove you all the way to Portmeirion all you did was to say you'd rather be in the sun than cooped up in a car.' I replied 'Oh! yes, you put yourself out all right – so much so that my dinner on Sunday night was two boiled eggs:' and she said 'Lucky to get them!' But one realises after this, that it's the result of taking people for granted – you imagine, because you're such old

friends, that you don't have to bother with the conventional courtesies. But in actual fact – you do. Nonetheless, looking back on the whole thing, esp. Rona's attitude over the invitation in the first place, I feel without guilt. I should, however, have stuck to my guns about the *initial* reaction, and not gone at all.

Thursday, 2 June

When I fall out with friends, it is because I feel something unfair has happened. Of course there is the counsel that says 'Don't be childish about it – be big enough & generous enough to forget it: people *are* unfair. You probably do similar things yourself. Don't ruminate & brood over it.' But the fact is, I *am* childish. If I'm not indulged & loved by people, then I actually *want* – physically – *to run away* and never see them again. One thing I have learned, over the years, is that I am truly independent of friendship. When it is good & honourable, I value it, but when it's not there, I can do without it. I don't say that it's joyous, but I can do without it.

Saturday, 4 June

All my friendships are under a strain at the moment – Andrew, Hussey, Gordon and Baxter. And I'm seeing less of Henry D., strain there too. This year saw the eclipse of the Beverley Cross relationship as well. The only friendship that is consistently functioning is George Borwick, who has proved incredibly loyal over the last six years.

Monday, 6 June

Mike Smith, to discuss making a record of some kind. He came up with no ideas or scripts of any kind. I found myself suggesting recording some of the Rambling Syd Rumpo songs & he agreed.

Saturday, 11 June

Arrived in Tangier at 1.30. Driven to the flat, which is all v. baroque, and reached by a cul de sac, quite charming. We went round loads of bars & met loads of people. Everyone knew everyone else. It's practically a parish here.

Sunday, 12 June

George B. had a bath & used all the hot water. I washed up & prepared for the evening party. We had Hubert, Malcolm, Hans & Peter (from the Pergola), Joe Orton and Ken Halliwell. Went v. well.

Monday, 13 June

We had the appalling misfortune to meet a dreadful drunk called Kinnaird. We got dragged back to his awful flat for dinner & there was an Irishman serving Irish stew, with no tie & a general air of truculence. This Kinnaird creature was so far gone, she was saying 'Price Vesident' instead of Vice President and 'a lovely Wren City in the church'. I have never been treated to such an embarrassing load of codswallop.

Thursday, 16 June
Tea at the Pergola where I chatted with Warren Beatty. We're to meet tomorrow at 3 o'c.

Friday, 17 June
Went down to the Windmill. Chatted to Ian & Terry & met Mohammed & Hassan. The latter had 2 front teeth missing. Joe Orton and Ken H. came & were deeply offended because a woman appeared on the sun terrace. 'It's a bloody disgrace,' said Joe and went off for a swim. We had lunch there and then made our way to the Pergola for the 3 o'c. appt. with Warren Beatty. He turned up there at 2.45 sitting down to lunch with Kraut royalty, so we got the bum's rush. I flew back to the Windmill and saw Mohammed and invited him back to tea instead. He has a face like a Byzantine portrait. The sort of head you see on the icons in Constantinople. Met Tony & Nobby after for drinks in Stefan's bar. An incredible young man called Paul who lives at Blackheath talked to us & kept using expressions like 'It's no life for a white lady, darling.' I said he should go home to his wife.

Saturday, 18 June
Coffee at the parade where Joe made me laugh a lot about advertisements like 'Since I started using whatsit, my life has become blissful' etc.

Sunday, 19 June
Went down to the beach for the last time. The blazing sun, the golden sands, the holiday makers, the rent, the pimps, the drunks, the whole fantastic set-up. Took off about 2.20. Arrived London at 6.20. For all the money I spend on fares etc. I would do better to invest in a decent holiday cottage or flat in England, where I would be sure of peace & quiet and decent furnishings.

Thursday, 23 June
Gordon & I went to La Ronde café 'cos it poured with rain. We were sitting on stools at the counter having coffee, and a woman asked me to move. I think she was the manageress. She said I was impeding the service. I just smiled and said no. She insisted, so I said 'I've no

intention of moving so I suggest you call the police . . .' and then she moved off in high dudgeon.

Friday, 24 June

Peter E. rang me back about the Eamonn Andrews engagement and said he'd fixed the fee. 'That's the quickest £250 you've ever made,' he said. I was v. taken aback. It's certainly a ridiculous figure. I'd expected something like 30 or 40. They must have money to burn, these people.

Sunday, 26 June

I have to do the Eamonn Andrews TV show tonight & the trepidation grows as the hour approaches. O dear. The thousand natural shocks that flesh is heir to . . .

Monday, 27 June

Phone rang a lot. People to say they thought I was good last night. Back to the flat, and Tom Sloan rang for BBC TV, offering me M.C. on a TV show called 'International Cabaret' to start next Tues.[14] I said I would like to do it. I think it's high time I had a shot at this kind of thing. Other idiots have been getting away with it for years. Peter E. said they'd mentioned a fee of £400 for a show. I think this is excessive myself.

Tuesday, 28 June

I went into an office with John Law[15] and we bashed out some outrageous material, mostly purloined & did about 4 mins.' dialogue. Certainly feel delighted to be working at something. Feel quite buoyant. It's interesting to reflect that if I *had not* returned to England last Sunday, I wouldn't have appeared on TV and my career would not have taken the turn that it has done.

Tuesday, 5 July

Worked with John Law till about lunchtime, then to the theatre. We had a run thro' at 6 o'c. My spirits started dropping and by the time the show started they were in my boots. I've never felt so apprehensive and so inadequate. When I eventually made my entrance it was appalling. The reaction was virtually non-existent. It's left me with a very nasty feeling and that's not conducive to confidence or ability

---

[14] Tom Sloan (d.1970), BBC TV Head of Light Entertainment. Has a major TV series ever been offered and accepted at shorter notice?

[15] Scriptwriter who had contributed lyrics to *One Over the Eight*.

to think up any funny ideas for the future. It's as though one has been shat on from a great height.

Wednesday, 6 July
The full horror of last night, and 'dying' in front of an audience etc. really hit me today. At 7 o'c. I went to Gordon and Rona. What a haven they are to me. The gratitude will never be expressed.

Friday, 8 July
At last today, Stewart Morris took me & John Law along to Lime Grove to watch a playback on video tape of the show we did on Tuesday. It was perfectly all right. If I had seen all this before, I wouldn't have gone through all this agony.

Tuesday, 12 July
We went on the air, live, at 7.30. There was no doubt about it, it went really well. It is not easy to do, because, in compering, you have to keep re-establishing yrself and re-creating atmosphere.

Wednesday, 13 July
Met George B. for lunch at the G & C. A waiter there showed me a filthy notice for last night's TV show in the Daily Mirror, which said I was pathetic and added that he 'was letting me off lightly' – the fantastic arrogance of these people! So back I go to the death wish and the desire to leave the whole rotten, corrupt bloody broiling. Went to bed. Peter Eade phoned and said he thought I was repetitive on the show last night, and so did Laurena, and she said my shirt looked wrong! I wish I was dead.

Saturday, 16 July
After dinner Stanley and I shot over to see Joe Orton & Kenneth H. at Noel Road. Stanley read aloud some of Joe's 'Edna'[16] correspondence and made it sound v. funny indeed.

Tuesday, 19 July
The show went well. Peter E. said he thought I was better tonight. Big F. deal. Tom Sloan buttonholed me and said I was to go on with a whole series of these until Christmas! I said yes because otherwise we'd have been arguing all night over it.

---

[16] It was a hobby of Orton's to write letters of painfully suburban remonstrance to newspaper editors, critics, public servants and manufacturers of perishable goods under the name of 'Edna Welthorpe'.

Thursday, 21 July
It is amazing how elated I felt today. Writing these scripts has been quite an eye-opener to me. It proves that one can do *anything* if the need is urgent and there is a deadline – one minute there isn't an idea in yr. head & the next day the stuff seems to flow from one.

Tuesday, 26 July
John Law & I to the theatre for a run-thro'. I said to Johnny Mathis 'Do you want any special kind of announcement?' He said 'Oh! yeah – give it all that bit about unique vocal talent and stuff and then say 'our STAR OF THE EVENING' – then give it a pause while the harp does a gliss, and then stretch yr. arm wide and say 'MR JOHNNY MATHIS . . .' and he patted me on the cheek. He's a disgrace. I've been announced on a few programmes myself but I've certainly never patronised anyone in *that* fashion.

Tuesday, 2 August
We went on the air live at 8 o'c. and got off to a terrible start when the girls bearing the props smashed all the plates which the See Hee Brothers from Formosa were supposed to juggle with! They refused to go on, then relented after persuasion and did *one* trick & walked off. They asked Juliette Greco if she would do an extra number & she said 'Tell them they are out of their minds!' and refused. I tried to make my bits go further but all to no avail. Heartbreaking.

Saturday, 6 August
Stanley complimented me on the Cabaret show. He was particularly amused by me saying in the opening spot 'Handel was a dab hand at the old philately' and said it made him laugh. It is, of course, a code reference to fellatio.

Tuesday, 9 August
One thing I must record about these TV shows: with hardly any study, I know the lines. I certainly knew it all last night and this is without any rehearsal of any kind.

Friday, 12 August.
To the Centre. Bill Cotton[17] came in. He said it was lunatic to leave a series when it's just starting to jell. I said I agreed. I know what is basically urging me forward in this job – I *like* creating this work and I like turning up at the Centre and working on material. It's not the

---

[17] b.1928. Then Assistant Head of Light Entertainment. Later Controller BBC1 (1977–81), Managing Director, Television, BBC (1984–88).

money angle – I am going to tell Tom Sloan to lower the figure if I continue because (a) we'll need money for extra material and (b) I am overpaid at £500 a show anyway. It's a ludicrously high figure.

Monday, 15 August
Meeting with Bill Cotton and John Law. It was agreed that we will need to have six scripts in hand by the 31st Aug. or by the latest Sept. 10th – it can't be any later, 'cos by the time the film begins on the 12th, all I can worry about thereafter will be learning.

Tuesday, 16 August
I had a private word with Bill Cotton about my salary on TV and told him I thought it was excessive and he promised to speak to Peter Eade. Peter rang me and said he'd compromised on 400 guineas, so I agreed to that.

Sunday, 21 August
I had a walk round to get the papers. They were drilling in the road, and one particularly attractive youth who wore no shirt – just his jeans – looked over to me and smiled as I was passing & gave me the thumbs-up sign & said he approved of my acting. It was a delightful moment. I smiled in return but felt too embarrassed to look back as he started telling his mates who I was. O! the joy of these sort of men! their *directness* & their clumsy charm – it's disarming and heartwarming. Of course my reaction is basically homosexual etc. & probably *they* don't share that at all, but it's still lovely all the same.

Wednesday, 24 August
Centre at 10 o'c. We got out most of [script] No. 16, and that means there's only three to go. It's incredible what we've accomplished – in fact, if we stop here, we've still got enough ahead to tackle the other three in November.

Tuesday, 30 August
The show tonight died the death of all time. Worse than anything we've ever done. The Russians – Ygrouchky Trio – went like a bomb and Nana Mouskouri brought the place down – but they didn't want to know me. Audience must have been all Greek & Russian I think.

Thursday, 1 September
John called (Violet's son). He is a v. self-opinionated* lad & extraordinarily self-possessed.

*I think this is very similar to the sort of phase I went thro' from about fourteen to at least eighteen. Outwardly it takes the form of cockiness, snobbishness & rudeness – inwardly it is a colossal desire to be loved.

Thursday, 8 September

Curious dream about meeting a marvellous Arab sheik and saying I loved him, in which he replied 'Come round tomorrow afternoon and we can watch some television' in an American accent. Woke up feeling so awful that I thought of asking Patrick to send me to a hospital & getting me a psychiatrist.

Sunday, 11 September

I said to Nora 'D'you know what a half-caste is?' and she said 'No'. I said 'It's someone who's been *promised* the part.' She laughed.

Tuesday, 13 September

Filming *Don't Lose Your Head*[18] at Pinewood. Finished at 5.20. TV Theatre at 6 o'c. for 'Int. Cabaret'. The star is Gilbert Bécaud. At the run-thro' I said at one point 'How do I go off?' and Stewart Morris bawled out on the P.A. 'Very easily, ducky!' and everyone laughed. Charming.

Wednesday, 14 September

Pinewood. Did the boudoir stuff with Joan Sims & Peter B[utterworth]. Got awfully stymied with the props. I can't handle dialogue *and* props. I'm no good at it.

Sunday, 18 September

Read some of the Harold Nicolson[19] diary in the Sunday paper. Interesting to read that he felt ashamed of journalism etc. & threw in his lot with Tom (Oswald) Mosley and lost, and then felt he had ruined his reputation. What a different story it would have been if Tom had won! But he couldn't. Because his was a policy 'in extremis' and that can never succeed in England – not in the England after the Victorians. The history of this Island after that is one of utter mediocrity politically, and with the success of the Labour Party the creeping rottenness of socialism has succeeded in crippling the one thing that made this country great – from Drake downwards – the spirit of private enterprise & profit motive. We've exchanged all that for the dead cushion of the Welfare State with all its attendant bureaucratic muddling –

---

[18] Sometimes billed as *Carry On – Don't Lose Your Head.*

[19] (1886–1968), diplomat, MP and author, husband of Vita Sackville-West.

the 'sit on your arse for 50 years & hang your hat on a pension' idea, which Louis MacNeice expressed so bitterly & eloquently.[20]

Monday, 19 September

Repeated phone calls from *Tony Hancock* asking me to appear in his show on Thursday. He has taken the Festival Hall! I didn't go to the phone because I was on the lot. Instructed Peter Eade to say no. T.H. phoned three times. The sheer impertinence of this man is phenomenal! First he makes my position in the radio show embarrassing & cuts down the parts to nothing – actual *one-liners* – & ends up by insulting me in front of everyone about the 'snide' characterisation so I leave the show. Then he comes to the Shaffer plays, years later, and goes to Maggie's room – not mine. No attempt to see me. When I *did* meet him, accidentally, he said he was doing [the] *Punch & Judy Man* film (which he'd written himself and it was the flop of all time) and said 'I'm really excited about this – I'm doing the sort of comedy I've always wanted to do – I'd like you to do something with me – not those funny voice "cardboard" characters of yours – but comedy based on truth . . .' One stood there being patronised & denigrated and one smiled and said thank you. Now, he wants me to work with him again! He must be either very stupid, or *mad*. I'd rather leave the business than work with such a philistine nit. When I told Sid James he said 'You're joking?' I said 'No' and he said 'You'd be mad to work with him again – the man is a megalomaniac.'

Tuesday, 20 September

Pinewood. Car at 7.45. To TV Centre at 6 o'c. I ate too quickly. Drank too much. Sick all thro' the show. Vomiting in the wings – and sick in dressing room. *Don't know how* I actually did the show – everything was going round and I saw everything twice.

Wednesday, 21 September

Rang Peter Eade & told him the whole ghastly saga. He said he'd get on to the BBC & see whether the work was good or bad or what. Gerry Thomas came up and said 'I know you were pissed on TV last night.' Charming.

Saturday, 24 September

Gerald Thomas, 7.30, Burnham. Barbara (G.'s wife) had a streaming cold & I was furious. It seems barmy of G. to ask me to spend an evening in a room full of germs, when I'm working with him! I got thro' the evening somehow – letting slip the odd 'fuck' and 'shit' and

---

20 In his poem 'Bagpipe Music'.

'pisspot' and 'bumhole' and 'fart' – sometimes they got a laugh, but mostly, an embarrassed silence. I should not be allowed out.

Monday, 26 September
It was one of those days when all humour departed from me & I behaved like a pig to everyone. At heart I am so *low* I could weep. This is the sort of time in my life when I long for strong arms to comfort me – I am desperate for this kind of affection. There's never been any strength in my life apart from my own. No one on whom I could lean – just for a little time – not even a teeny weeny lover. There's no doubt I am a complete mess. I'm getting worse with the years, not better.

Friday, 30 September
Really dreadful day. At lunchtime, I was launching into a dirty song at the restaurant and Joan Sims said 'Give it a rest ducky – we've all had enough for one day' and I was furious. I said 'You stupid cow – why don't you go to another table if you don't like the conversation?' and I spent the rest of the day ignoring her.

Sunday, 2 October
I notice all these awful diaries of Sir Harold Nicolson have got marvellous reviews. *And* all the reviews for Joe Orton's *Loot* at the Jeannetta Cochrane theatre are marvellous too.

Friday, 7 October
Pinewood. Peter Butterworth asked me to meet a friend of his who is a monk. He was v. disturbing. He said 'Listening to you on the radio, I get the feeling that you're going on *too* much – that you're so full of despair that you're using the work almost in desperation . . .' And a lot more in that vein. I agreed with everything – but really the studio is no place for these kind of profundities.

It is ironic to reflect that I have made so much money this year, and have been involved in so little work! March, April, May & June consisted of about an hour's work ('R.T.H.') one day a week!

Monday, 10 October
When I think of the shameless way I behave in the studios – anything for a cheap laugh, the dirty mimes, the dirty songs, the obscene dialogue – and the person that I really am, at home with myself, it is almost a Jekyll & Hyde existence: and the first half gives me guilt and remorse. The obvious remedy is to stop the lewd behaviour, but then I'm loth to relinquish the laughs, and the crowd that gathers about me. I need them like other (healthy) people need the affection of a

partner. I don't believe I've ever been vain or conceited. I have certainly been arrogant and rude, but mostly I've used such qualities as a form of defence. Half the time I'm unaware of the damage they cause *because* I don't believe I'm that important. It always comes as something of a shock to find that people are influenced in *any* way by my behaviour; and when I do learn that I've succeeded in wounding anyone, I do *try* to put it right as soon as I can.

Tuesday, 11 October
J.D. asked me to dinner. Eventually arrived at a flat where there were seven people to dinner. A dreadful man with a Great Dane informed us that it had had intercourse with a woman. I had difficulty in concealing my disgust. This sort of thing represents a sort of ultimate filth which leaves me so revolted that I'm stunned.

Sunday, 23 October
To Gordon and Rona at 5.30. At 7 Simone Signoret arrived. I didn't like her at all. I mentioned Dany Robin[21] and she was v. scathing – 'She is not rich – she was an ingénue, a dancer for the chorus . . .' and more in this vein. Then when I gave my reasons for disliking Gaskill (who directed the disastrous *Macbeth* she's been slated in) she said 'I think that just sounds like gossip' and I didn't say that she'd just been doing the same thing. Afterwards I told G. I didn't like her & he was shouting in her defence in the car. He was v. heated. I realised that he felt particularly involved, so I took a different line in conversation. We parted amicably, but there was the feeling of an atmosphere.

Monday, 31 October
Pinewood. Didn't work till about 12 o'c. They gave a party at 5.20 for end of picture. It wasn't much like a party. Lots of moaning from everyone about their meanness. One of the waitresses told me that Charlie Hawtrey asked her for a carrier bag full of the left-over snacks from the buffet, to take home with him. The sadness of it all.

Sunday, 6 November
My seclusion seems to be getting worse over the years. Stayed in all day with occasional attempts to learn lines – how I hate that! – and reading and listening to Schumann and Brahms. On the visits to the lavatory I note the reflection of my white, strained face in the bathroom mirror – ruefully contemplating the many grey hairs, the pock-

---

21 French actress, b.1927, then shooting *Don't Lose Your Head* with KW.

marked skin and the recession. Outside the windows, there is the murky fog again.

Monday, 14 November

Peter Eade telephoned and said Binkie had been on the phone about me doing a new Feydeau farce to be directed over here by a French bloke. There is a suggestion that I go to Paris to talk about it! I discounted this but told P.E. to let it be known I was v. keen on the idea – John Mortimer is to do the translation.

Thursday, 17 November

Arrived at the Royal Court just on 7.30. The play, *Macbeth*, had some v. interesting things in it – Alec Guinness giving a performance of great vulnerability, but Gordon J. being the shiningly best thing in it – a performance of radiant integrity & charm – the 'Martlet' speech was really beautiful. Simone Signoret simply can't speak the verse & that's that. Went round after & told her she was marvellous.

Sunday, 20 November

Tried to learn some lines but my heart's not really in it. The utter limbo of my Sundays! Even masturbation denied me today, 'cos I caught my cock in the zip fastener and it's quite painful. O! the irony of it. Played the Brahms 4 Serious Songs and then the Fauré Requiem. Here is where all my gratitude lies. This is, to me, the most beautiful and moving thing in all of life – the giving of comfort. Wherever I have felt or seen or heard of this, it has never ceased to touch my heart and leave me better. I find it most in literature and music, and occasionally with people – but this latter v. rarely – and I am always so grateful. Like tonight when I wept with reciprocation. And there is always a moment in the exaltation when I ask for the sign – to tell me that there is some purpose for my life – an emperorship somewhere – where I shall exert the sway of sensible & polite power, which will be read about in later years by admiring scholars who learn amazedly about this worthless actor who became a mighty ruler.

Monday, 21 November

My dick still sore from the zip fastener mishap. At 7 o'c. to Louie, to see the Cabaret on television. Just as my stuff *starts* to create an atmosphere, you are back in the banality of these terrible acts.

Tuesday, 22 November

TV show. Star was called Jacqueline François & I forgot her name! Had to try it 3 times before I got it right. All my comedy went v. well indeed. Cheating in a lot of camp. After, Bill Cotton asked if I would be willing to go on with the show until March, if the Channel approved. I indicated that I would.

Wednesday, 23 November
P.E. rang and asked if I would like to do Eamonn Andrews' Show again. Apparently Joe Orton is to be on it, and they thought I would like to be with him. They're wrong.

Monday, 28 November
'Round The Horne'. For the first time, we did it without Kenneth Horne and it really made no difference. The laughs were all there as usual and the entire show went like a bomb.[22]

Thursday, 1 December
December here again! Last year I was in that filthy disaster which caused me so much pain and anguish. What a recovery this year has been for me! Set me right up again. I've got a more mature kind of confidence back, and I've done solo, stand-up comedy for the first time in my life in England, an incredible challenge: and I feel I have scored a victory in the face of tremendous odds. I'm very grateful.

Friday, 2 December
To Centre at 10.15. Worked with John Law, and completed [script] 22. If anyone had told me, when I signed for 6 episodes in the first place, that I should end up doing thirty, I'd have thought they were raving mad.

Saturday, 3 December
Announced on the 6 o'c. news tonight that Giles Cooper had been found dead on the railway line near Surbiton. He was 49. It sounds v. odd to me. They said 'Apparently he had fallen from the train.'[23] I acted with him at Newquay quite a lot. Always remember him as the Archangel Gabriel or Raphael in *Tobias and the Angel*. He told Henry D. that it was me who made him leave acting and become a playwright.

Thursday, 15 December
To Myles Rudge at 4.30. Barry Worth – the arranger – was there already – he is a delightful fellow and always rather excites me. I want to please him, want him to laugh at my jokes & sallies. He does,

---

[22] A show for Christmas Day. 'Kenneth Horne himself was not able to take part in today's Christmas programme but the others go round without him, wishing him well as they go' (note in *Radio Times*).

[23] The jury returned, without retiring, a verdict of Death by Misadventure. Travelling home from a 'dramatists' dinner', Cooper had a high blood-alcohol level.

moderately, but when we're alone, it's curiously silent. Ted Dicks came about 10 minutes later – dear Ted – and we all chatted merrily. Then we rehearsed the four numbers for tomorrow, and talked about a title. Myles & Ted thought of 'Kenneth Williams On Pleasure Bent' and I think it is brilliant.

Friday, 16 December

Recording session at AdVision. It was bloody murder. One is shoved into a booth and expected to have all the genius of a professional singer when you can't even recognise a beat and there's no conductor giving you one. Everything was abortive and eventually I left at 1 o'c. without saying goodbye to anyone. Just walked out into the street with my stomach in a turmoil and wanting to weep with anger and frustration. It has flung me into the pit again. It's worse than a nasty review.

Sunday, 18 December

To the Centre to do this game, 'Call My Bluff'. Frank Muir was suddenly ill, and they got Alan Bennett & I had to be chairman for both teams! We lost the first and won the second. Alan B. was superb at it.

Tuesday, 20 December

Talking with John Law I said that I was waiting for death, rather dramatically. He said 'Well there's a couple of things you could do while you're waiting.' I said 'What' and he said 'Well you could buy a settee and throw a party for a start . . .' It was so funny I was transfixed. This is his humour par excellence – the ability to be funny and constructive at the same time. I suddenly realised how v. fond I am of him.

Monday, 26 December

I told Gordon about J[ohn] L[aw] giving me the entire Beethoven sonatas and he asked if he could borrow them for a tape recording and I said 'I never lend things' and he looked v. crestfallen and Rona said 'Now – he's hurt because it costs him a lot to ask such a thing' and I felt perfectly dreadful.

Tuesday, 27 December

Life is really incredibly monotonous. The endless, unchanging pattern of nature is in itself monotonous. No wonder some men try desperate measures – no wonder our mental hospitals have so much to cope with. The creeping boredom carries paralysis in its wake – compared with this the old fashioned vices are childlike. I suppose there must come a time for all intellectuals, when it seems that there is simply 'no more to do . . .', 'no more to be done' – 'no point in doing anything . . .'

Thursday, 29 December
I do think it's good, the way my career has gone this year. I never thought I could be funny solo, and I've made records of myself singing & I never thought of myself as a singer and now I hear professional musicians saying what a good ear I've got & it's *all* lovely. I know of course I'm being a jack of all and master of none – but in my case that is right *not* because I'm incapable of the mastership but because all the 'masters' in acting are such pretentious bores! I suppose that's what horrifies me most – the thought that I might start taking myself (and talent) seriously! What a pretentious nit I'd become!

Friday, 30 December
Did all the remaining work on the LP. I did the 'Boiled Egg' of Michael Hitchman. I felt a particular delight in this, because it's my small way of [paying] a tribute to him, and a way of perpetuating his poem.

Saturday, 31 December
Me last entry in this diary – given to me by Gordon – still my best friend he is – it has been a year of recovery for me. My first year *entirely* out of the theatre and I haven't even missed it. I've done the sound radio, two films, and the television series, and made an awful lot of money. The most significant change in home life has been moving Louie into her own flat.

Went up to Gordon and Rona. Saw myself in the 'Cabaret' with Dickie Valentine. Lots of laughs, and certainly better than anything else on any other channel. We all had the toast in champagne and I couldn't have spent the eve with better people in the whole wide world.

1967

Sunday, 1 January
A brilliant day to start the New Year – a shining morning of dazzling sunshine and sky of Mediterranean blue – it's balmy – one might be in Beirut! Though thank goodness I'm not. The papers are full of the N. Year Honours. One knight is a football team manager called Alf Ramsey! Dorothy Tutenkarman[1] gets OBE and Rutherford becomes a Dame!! It is really the cheap day returns.

Tuesday, 3 January
Worked with John Law on another script for 'Int. Cabaret', and finished it. Then we worked out a script for the spot I'm doing on the Rolf Harris show on the 21st. Stars of the show tonight are the Swingle Singers who hum Bach. They're terrible. P.E. gave me a lift home & lectured me about being mean & not tipping people – esp. the stage door.

Wednesday, 4 January
Myles Rudge came at 7 o'c. and we went to Biagi for dinner. M. said 'Well of course I think it was outrageous rudeness when you said the orchestrations were a load of shit and Barry (the orchestrator) was actually sitting in the same room and obviously heard *all* you were saying . . .' So at last, albeit in dribs & drabs, the truth starts to emerge.

Thursday, 5 January
Tom & Clive came about five, and after a cup of tea, we all went into town to see the film *The Family Way*. It wasn't terribly well done – at times I was reminded of a Carry On, but Naughton's[2] script took the strain with consummate ease & soared out of the screen: the result is a marvellous picture.

---

[1] Dorothy Tutin, b.1931. Actress. The Tutenkhamun joke was a standard item of wordplay between KW and Gordon Jackson, though not appreciated by the victim (see entry for 7 February 1982, p. 647).
[2] Bill Naughton (d.1992).

Saturday, 7 January

I read Ecclesiastes. It is v. moving and sad . . . 'when desire fails . . .' and made me realise yet again that I must get a decent King James bible – this copy I've got is modern and the prose simply hasn't got the beauty.[3] I wept as I read some of it, and fell to thinking about tears and the general significance of them – especially since I cried so much on Thursday night about the Naughton film script – it's love that moves me – always. It never ceases to affect my heart – generosity of spirit – compassion, gentleness – the strong *giving* – these things make me weep.

Wednesday, 11 January

On the bus, I got talking to the conductor who said he'd given up being a page at the Berkeley because the Head Porter was keeping all the tips – he asked me if I was anti coloured people & luckily I said no, 'cos he then showed me a photograph of his Indian wife. It is really marvellous how this boy of nineteen gets married to a foreigner, has a lovely child, works on the buses & has an ambition to drive one, when he is twenty-one. It was charming.

Sunday, 15 January

To the Centre at 5 o'c. and did 2 'Call My Bluff' sessions. Lost them. My teams were Leslie Sands ('Z Cars') and Lisa Daniely and after, Richard Wattis and Dilys Laye. She was brilliant and v. good at it. Came away after feeling bitter & depressed. This was largely due to an encounter with an ugly & stupid old woman who was somebody's guest in the hospitality room – she said something to me about 'Nobody likes losing' and I said 'Rubbish – I'm a v. gracious and good loser' (which is true of my performance on the box) and she said 'There is no such thing as a good loser' and I said 'Just think for a minute about what you're saying: think for instance of Smuts'[4] and she said 'He won' & I said 'The Boers won?' and she said 'Yes' and it was then that I decided to go home. I don't like women anyway, but these sort of ignorant bores make me puke & they always seem to imagine that their femininity protects them – gives them privileges or something.

---

[3] In the King James version: 'Also when they shall be afraid of that which is high, and fears shall be in the way, and the almond tree shall flourish, and the grasshopper shall be a burden, and desire shall fail: because man goeth to his long home, and the mourners go about the streets.' Ecclesiastes 12:5.

[4] Field Marshal Jan Christiaan Smuts (1870–1950), South African commander and Prime Minister, an enemy in the Boer War and an ally in World War II.

Monday, 16 January
'Round The Horne' – it was as if one had been doing it for years and no respite. The script was singularly uninspired I think – no innovations or bright ideas for the beginning of a new series, just the same old warming of hands at the camp fire. For the first time I am beginning to feel that this show is rather dated and tired.

Thursday, 19 January
M[ichael Codron] announced that he'd booked a table at the Post Office Tower!! so we went! It was certainly the most exciting experience and strangely moving, because London looks so beautiful from up there – and the restaurant revolves all the time so that your view changes. The food was v. good and we had champagne cocktails at 18/- each! Pure fantasy.

Friday, 20 January
Went off to hairdresser, and met Joe Orton on the way who has agreed to be on my team for the 12 Feb.[5]

Saturday, 21 January
It seemed like an endless day, rehearsing. Eventually we started at 8.10 and my opening spot with Rolf went very well. Then towards the end of the show I did my solo. The first half, the wine tasting, went fine up to 'I'm on the fish, Muriel, and you're on the game so I think it leans towards a claret . . .' but after that, when I moved on to the census form stuff, it went down in tempo.

Monday, 23 January
'Round The Horne'. The show went v. well, but I think the fact that Roy Rich showed up signifies that it's 'being watched' as a show. There have been one or two moves to clean up the script this series which haven't evinced themselves before. Sounds like a wee purgeette is on, to me. I couldn't care less myself. I think this show is quite dead artistically & the format has completely atrophied itself – it is moribund now. I think I will have to withdraw after this series.

Thursday, 26 January
The porter delivered a parcel – it was a beautiful King James Bible from Tom. I was astonished, touched and delighted. A really beautiful present.

---

[5] For the panel game 'Call My Bluff'. This and subsequent meetings between Orton and KW can be seen from the other man's point of view in *The Orton Diaries*, ed. John Lahr (1986).

Monday, 6 February
Called on Joe Orton & Kenneth H. and Joe gave me a copy of *Loot* – I must say it is v. funny, but it's ironic that I am not the originator!*

*Of course I am the originator – what this means is, it's ironic that I'm not mentioned in this script because Joe has not mentioned the first production.[6]

Sunday, 12 February
Gordon came at 3 o'c. & drove me to the Centre. My teams were Joe Orton and Maxine Audley, and Gordon and Wendy Hall. With the first I lost, and with G – and my last game – I won! It was a deep joy indeed. Joe was v. good at the game.

Tuesday, 14 February
Went down to Shepherd's Bush at about 5 o'c. Star is Gene Pitney. I was doing very well till the last spot, where I had an appalling dry & had to be handed the script. They'll have to edit that out. I continued after with great success and ended v. well. I was left with that awful feeling of unprofessionalness, and a job badly done. Pat W[illiams] came round with some awful people who made me take a tape recording of their work etc. I was so angry I was practically dumb.

Wednesday, 15 February
I wrote a v. stiff note to P. saying that if it *ever* happened again, I would cut her out of my life utterly, finally, completely. And I certainly mean it.

Wednesday, 22 February
Lunched with Andrew. Walked to the junction of Hanover Sq. & Bond St where a dreadful man swung his umbrella & hit me. I rounded on him – 'Watch where you swing your umbrella!'

'I'm sorry' (v. shortly)

'I don't want your filthy muck on me –'

'Sorry.'

'You great old poof.'

As I walked away I saw that Andrew was scarlet. I asked him why

---

[6] It is customary to preface the published texts of plays with a cast-list crediting the participants in the original production (whom KW calls 'the originators'). In the Methuen edition of *Loot*, however, Orton gave the cast-list of the original *London* production, performed at the Jeannetta Cochrane Theatre by the London Traverse Theatre Company, with Michael Bates as Truscott. In this way, Orton avoided raising embarrassing memories of the touring Ur-*Loot*, whose text, he will have claimed, was different anyway.

& he said 'Well I thought you were going on about it – the bloke had apologised . . .'

Friday, 24 February

To the Centre to see John Law. We met Stewart Morris & he said that the high-ups were v. pleased with the Cabaret & that the figures are encouraging. He says they want to bring it back in October for 26 episodes, colour, etc.[7] & probably do two a week: he said we would have to talk about it. I'll say we will. The writing is going to be murder.

Saturday, 4 March

Woke early, feeling absolutely deathly. So low and depressed and weak. Suicidal. Just couldn't make any kind of effort. Did not shave or dress. Just went back to bed. With these bloody colds I go thro' the same old routines, waiting for the congestion to ease – the drops, the capsules, the faintness, the awful look round the eyes, the vague sweats – the wanting to die. Dreared around the flat in the dressing gown and the utter loneliness of it all was overwhelming. There is really no point in my existence at all. I suddenly think 'What am I doing here?' The day looks bright and sunny, but windy. All the *nits* crowding round outside the waxworks. How I loathe them *and* Madame Tussaud. To retire to the side furthest from Picra & watch the doom of the whole broiling![8]

Thursday, 9 March

I just hope that Tangé is going to be sunny and pleasant. If it's as good as Malaga in Feb. ('60) it will be all right – what one can't cope with is rain.

Saturday, 11 March

Walked up to see Joe & Kenneth at Islington. They told me about their stay in Libya and how disastrous it is. Tripoli sounds like a nightmare – foul place and foul English-Americans. All the hotels were full and they were forced to spend the night on a terrible cruise ship owned by Chandris, in a tiny cabin, for which they paid £10

---

[7] BBC2 began regular broadcasting in colour on 1 July 1967.

[8] The original from which KW makes this adaptation runs:

> The ruling class will think I am on their side
> And make friendly overtures, but I shall retire
> To the side further from Picra and write some poems
> About the doom of the whole broiling.

From 'Translation', by Roy Fuller.

sterling – shocking. They got the same plane back & when they said how ghastly it was, the stewardess said 'Oh! didn't you know?' – 'cos apparently everyone else does. They gave me a lovely bit of haddock for supper. Really tasty. It was a v. nice evening. They are both kind and hospitable.

Monday, 13 March
L came over at 7 o'c., dear L – we have been friends now since '49, and it's always worked on some level or other, completely successfully. The humour is shared. That's the great thing. We sat & talked about the holiday in Tangé. I gave him the snack-ette and he left about eleven.

Tuesday, 14 March
Incredible how changed one becomes by illness. It colours everything. I have to face the fact that I can't take suffering of any kind, with any real 'grace'.

Thursday, 16 March [Press cutting enclosed]
Both these letters are in this month's Plays & Players and are both from the pen of Joe Orton himself. He showed me the originals. It's a v. funny spoof I must say! I love Edna W[elthorpe].[9]

Friday, 17 March
Ended up at Dunhill's getting a gold lighter for £95. I am having *John Law* engraved on the cap. It is a great expense, but I think it's the sort of thing he would like.

Sunday, 19 March
Got up feeling terrible – skin trouble on the face & looking like death. Suddenly Robert Bolt turned up at the flat & drove me down to the Mill House for lunch. It transformed my day completely. Suddenly one is *wanted* – there is this extraordinary quality he has of making you feel important & special – gives you renewed confidence, a new lease of life – my God he is a *dear*, good man. Noel Willman came

---

[9] Edna had written: '. . . no one should seriously nominate as the play of the year a piece of indecent tomfoolery like *Loot*. Drama should be uplifting. The plays of Joe Orton have a most unpleasant effect on me. I was plunged into the dumps for weeks after seeing his *Entertaining Mr Sloane*. I saw *Loot* with my young niece; we both fled from the theatre in horror and amazement well before the end. I could see no humour in it. Yet it is widely advertised as a rib-tickler. Surely this is wrong? These plays do nothing but harm to our image abroad, presenting us as the slaves of sensation and unnatural practice.' The other letter appeared over the signature of 'Donald H. Hartley'.

too and that just made the whole thing magical and I could have wept at the sheer good fortune of it all. I could weep even now. Perhaps I go over the top, perhaps it's all ridiculous. But it's truly how I feel today – so moved and happy and so grateful for these dear friends who have enriched my life & to whom I'm so eternally indebted.

Monday, 20 March
My goodness, but yesterday was a marvellous day. Quite a turn-over for me. An exception[al] day indeed. 'Round The Horne' went v. well. Script was v. good indeed and the audience splendid – a great deal of affection there, one felt.

Friday, 24 March
We arrived London Airport at 12 & all went smoothly. George B. waiting for us. He brought us to the flat at 5, Rue Dante & showed us everything. After to Denis, then to Bryon's, then to El Piano, and a typical Tangé arrivé[e]. Pissed. The evening is warm & one doesn't need overcoat, but one must have the woollen on.

Saturday, 25 March
Sat in the sun having coffee & then G. took us both on the tour of Tangé – Medina, Kasbah, Sultan's Palace, York Castle & we finished up in the Socco Chico having coffee with Terry (ex-Apollo Club). There were two dreadful queens with slap on, & one smoking a yellow pipe. I've got news for her.

Tuesday, 28 March
We walked right into Dennis 'My dear I know Danny La Rue terribly well . . . & introduced Tennessee Williams to loads of trade' etc. etc. & so we got landed with the round of drinks and the polari. Got away eventually & had a v. good dinner. Naf polone asked for autograph. Then to have a drink at Bryon's. I started on Pernod but Bryon changed me to Ricard half way. It was fatal. Back at the flat I was sick. Terrible terrible night. I shouldn't be allowed out.

Wednesday, 29 March
L. & I walked to Magoga – on the Malabata road. We walked by way of the beach – paddling across little streams. The beach was endless & nobody about: and when we reached Magoga we wandered up the hillside for a bit and found eucalyptus trees – heavenly smell – and wild thyme and miniature irises & loads of wonderful wild flowers. We got the bus back to Tangé for 30 cents. Saw Helge who confessed

to taking 3 Supponeryls[10] last night. I said he must have been mad! He could hardly keep his balance, or his eyes open. I said to L I don't know how he got them up there & he said 'His difficulty, my dear, will be keeping them there . . .'

Saturday, 1 April
Went to Magoga & were joined on the beach by Mochta. Several Moroccans shouted out 'You fuck Moroccan boy tonight' and other disgusting slogans. Got the bus back to G. Hardy for lunch and there was Lionel B[art][11] and loads of friends. We were all introduced & Lionel asked me & L to dinner tomorrow night.

Thursday, 6 April
Dinner at El Djenina rather bad. 2 naf queens anglais Marconi[12] ad nauseam. Really this was a completely wasted evening because it was the last chance for trade alliances, and it's funny but, after dawdling about on the platform for hours one suddenly wants to jump on the train simply *because* it's about to go. Not 'cos one wants to travel! So that's it really. My second visit to Morocco & much better than the first.

Thursday, 13 April
Went along to the Polling Station at Lisson Grove to vote Tory in the GLC election: there is a strong hope that we will win County Hall this time! I hope so – it would be a nice smack in the eye for the socialists. Went to the butcher's for some chops & Joyce thanked me for the card from Morocco. Received a disgraceful letter from Joe O. accusing me of throwing french letters into pillar boxes. To Joe O. and Ken H. at 5.45 at Noel Road. We had the haddock, and chatted away merrily. I told him of the adventures in Tangé & about the Barri Chatt business & he laughed & wrote some of it down 'cos he said he could use it in a sequence he is going to do later on. They are both going to Morocco for May–June & have taken the flat that I used in '66. On my way down Pentonville Hill I passed four youths, and they cried out 'Can't you find us a spot in your films Kenny – we're v. good!' & expressed *no* surprise at meeting me. I simply laughed & passed on. 'Just like Morocco,' I thought.

---

[10] The suppository version of the sleeping pill Soneryl.

[11] b.1930. Composer, lyricist and playwright.

[12] Eavesdropping. The mental picture is of headphones clamped tightly to the ears.

Monday, 17 April
Berman's at 3 for costume fitting.[13] That Philip pulled off the breeches and a pin scratched all my leg and it wouldn't stop bleeding. V. inconvenient. Met Peter Butterworth there. He told me that Sid James is out! and they're having Phil Silvers[14] in the lead!! He is just terrible, so it's a worthy successor. Then we sat in St James's Park and after went to see Paul Newman in *Hombre* – v. good but the hero gets *killed* again! I'm sick of these immoral endings. I told Peter B. how angry I felt when the hero in a fiction piece is killed & how utterly immoral it seemed to me & he said 'I'd no idea you were such a romantic – I love you for it – if this place weren't so public, I'd give you a hug.'

Wednesday, 19 April
Met Peter E. and he took me to the Centre where we chatted with Bill Cotton about the projected series for Sept.–October. They want to do it from Talk of the Town and they talked me into it. Rang B.C. after I'd got back, and said *don't* put up the money. It is ludicrous that I should have to ask my employers *not* to give me money. It is quite ridiculous.

Tuesday, 25 April
Clive came at 6 o'c. to do the plug for me. Joe O., and Ken H. and Tom came about 6.30–7. Took them all to Biagi for dinner. Desultory conversation. They came back for coffee & left about 11 o'c.

Wednesday, 26 April
Listened to a bit of 'R.T.H.' on the radio. Fantastic difference to what it used to be like. Just before, I had been playing some Hancock excerpts on disc and they now seem so *slow* and pretentious. Sid James & Bill Kerr & Hattie Jacques were just awful. Reading lines like they had scripts in their hands. Recitative. Hancock doing his pompous bit in too slow a tempo. I think this was the great defect with H.: the absence of real professional expertise & technical cleverness. The sort of rough ability he *did* have was sufficient for a duo of the Morecambe & Wise type of act, but not for the more advanced kind of comedy which he really admired (Benny, Tati etc.) It's really the difference between a comic and a comedian. H. never properly decided on either.

Thursday, 27 April
Peter E. drove me down to Windsor in 40 minutes (motorway) and

---

[13] For *(Carry On) Follow that Camel.*
[14] 1912–85. American vaudevillian, best known for his TV characterisation of Sergeant Bilko.

we saw *Don't Lose Your Head* at the local ABC. It wasn't bad, but I realise there is no need to do all this character make-up. It just doesn't work for comedy. The thing is to look as pleasant as possible. I really should stop making all these faces too! They're quite absurd and unfunny. The fight sequence went on too long & Sid James really does look terribly battered and old. V. unattractive when he's making love to the girls in it – all rather disgusting.

Saturday, 29 April

Andrew told me that Harry Fowler said of me 'I don't mind Ken swearing in front of Kay because with him, it comes from the heart . . .'!! as if sincerity absolves one from good manners. H.F. is obviously more conventional than I'd ever imagined!

Sunday, 30 April

Meet Joe O. & Ken H. Regent's Park. It was quite pleasant & sunny at first but all cloud by lunch time. We had a stroll round to Biagi & then, after the lunch, the Hyde P.*

*Joe talked about p[ick]/u[p] with a fellow who told him 'I often get picked up by these queers & some of them have very nice apartments . . . they're obviously on quite good money . . . I've had as much as thirty shillings from some of them . . . they're not all effeminate either, some of them are really manly & you'd never dream that they were queer, not from the look of 'em. But I can always tell 'cos they've all got L.P.'s of Judy Garland . . . that's the first sign of a queer: that's the big give-away.' I said 'You've an extraordinary ability to remember dialogue as well as accents! You really capture the flavour of the personality you're describing . . . that's worth recording.' He agreed. 'Yes, I think I'll start writing a diary.'[15] I said Pepys's ref. were in code so no one would know. Joe said 'I don't care who knows.'

Tuesday, 2 May. On location, Rye, Sussex

Went up to the Fort they've erected on Camber Sands. I've got the monocle which I fancy is going to give me trouble. Eventually we're all in the dining room with Gerry, and P[hil Silvers] started to sing *Ole Man River* & tell us about a routine he did as Paul Robeson & I'm laughing so much but daren't show it & Jim D. is desperately keeping

---

[15] He had been writing one since 20 December the previous year. A long account of this Hyde Park visit appears in the published Orton diaries, but there is no mention of an exchange about diaries. A possible explanation is that this second paragraph of KW's (certainly written later than the first, in a much hastier script) is a reminiscence added after Orton's death, and referring to a much earlier meeting in the same setting, e.g. 12 May 1965. But Orton was cagey about his diary-writing: he told his agent Peggy Ramsay about it only on 30 May ('I'm keeping a journal, to be published long after my death'– *The Orton Diaries*, ed. Lahr, p.13). To complicate the matter further, this passage by KW is also quoted by Lahr (p.11) but in a version slightly expanded and rewritten for Lahr's benefit by KW; and in this version, KW quotes Orton as saying, 'Yes, I've started a diary.'

a serious face and Gerald is kicking me under the table, till eventually the hysteria was at boiling point. Feel as though I've been here for years.

Wednesday, 3 May
First thing on the location, P. said 'It was great last night – having congenial company. 'Cos the thing I can't stand is a *bore*.' We said we couldn't stand them either, then he said 'A Bore is a *thief*, you know that? He's a thief because he steals your time' and I said that was very true. Jim scarcely repressing laughter. In the marquee P. starts again and asks me to get him a 'Coke' so I say 'Get fucked' and he says that reminds him of a story about Rita Hayworth. Big deal. But this fellow really *wants* waiting on *and listening to*.

Thursday, 4 May
There seems to be no respite from this kind of man. Refuses to relax and shut up. You mention the county of Kent and he says 'O! you Kent do that!' and you're supposed to fall about. The awful truth is that he is not v. funny. I get more laughs on the set than he does. He said to me 'There are two Indians, see? One of 'em is a Big Indian and the other is a little Indian, and the little Indian is the other one's son but the Big Indian isn't his father – what is the relationship?' So I said 'His mother' and after a pause he said 'Yeah! – well most people don't get it . . . they say aunt . . .'

Saturday, 6 May
P[eter Rogers] told me that he would like to do a *Carry On Doctor* as the last, and then 'say goodbye to the Carry Ons . . .' rather sad really.

Monday, 8 May
Dinner ruined by P.S. This time we had *all* the Sinatra stories again *plus* an account of the audience with the Pope. No point is *ever* reached. One screams out for a tag line. Nothing. The horizon vacant for miles. Gerald kicking me under the table. Hysteria & despair battle inside one.

Wednesday, 10 May
P. Rogers came on the set and started touching up P.S. – when he got to the dick P[hil] said 'If you find anything there, let me know' which certainly made me laugh. If he stuck to the contemporaneous & extemporaneous he'd be wonderful. The involuntary crack. This he does superbly.

Friday, 12 May

Had an extraordinary dream. Andrew R. telephoned me to say that I was to be investigated. When I asked *why?* he said he couldn't say over the phone. Eventually I got asked to go to the Police. He was there – Andrew. Suddenly I realised intuitively that they were searching my room in my absence. I got away somehow & went to the house where I lodged. I could see thro' the windows all these people searching thro' my things. I started to smash all the windows. Then the police came and said I was completely vindicated! I asked what of? and they said 'Racialism' and I looked round at the roomful of people and said, after great hesitation, 'I thought it was homosexuality.' Then I was sitting on a beach and saw 3 policemen save a woman's pram from the sea. When she asked them to take off their trousers to have them dried, they all refused, smiled & went away, soaking wet.

Sunday, 21 May

I had one of those emissions last night – a colossal remembrance of the dream that caused it – me copping it in the north[16] with a fortyish tough guy.

Tuesday, 23 May

In the evening, Moira B[axter] came over. She talked about her Crochet Class at the Hornsey Institute & about her cat getting cancer & her trying to cure it with purple leaves got from a herbalist, which have left stains all over the house. She said 'Who would've thought the cat would get cancer?' and I said 'Well let's face it darling, he *was* a very heavy smoker' and that made her laugh.

Tuesday, 30 May

Pinewood at 8. Helped Phil Silvers with the lines but all to no avail. He blew on so many takes that he got humiliated and burst into tears on the set. Put my arm around him and talked & talked him out of it. He is v. depressed and low. He continually says that he is 'only half a person' and hints at greater powers & talents which have been taken from him when his wife & 5 daughters elected to leave him. I should think they were all bored out of their minds.

Thursday, 1 June

It's atrocious trying to work with P.S. Doesn't know a bloody line of the script: and the breath smells dreadfully. Today they chalked all the dialogue on a blackboard for her & she fluffed *that*!! Of course it threw me eventually till I started to go too!

---

16 Rhyming slang: north and south (mouth).

Wednesday, 7 June
Pinewood. I really hate that incompetent fool P.S. now & it's barely disguised. When he came out with a line today, I said 'Oh! you know it? – it's fantastic, how do you do it? – go to bed with a record under your pillow or something?' Some people said it was rude of me. Angela [Douglas] said 'Oh! you go too far . . .' etc., but I'm too exhausted to care.

Thursday, 8 June
Latest news is of fighting on the East of the Suez Canal. Israel is winning. One thing this has proved – these Levantines are all superb at the mob hysteria stuff and good at setting fire to Embassies etc., but utterly useless at soldiering.

Monday, 12 June
'R.T.H.' at the Paris, went like a bomb as usual, and K.H. gave us all a luncheon in the loggia room at the Hyde Park Hotel. I had a conversation with John Simmonds which was v. disquieting. He said he envisaged dropping everyone from the show, except K.H. and myself, in order 'to give the writers some new impetus . . .' This sounds v. reckless to me.

Monday, 19 June
Off to 'R.T.H.' for the last of the recordings. *It went fantastically*. The longest & warmest round of applause was for the Rambling Syd bit. It was to the tune of 'The Girl I Left Behind Me' – I broke down twice through laughing. It was a disgrace. I have written to Marty & Barry thanking them for such a marvellous series of scripts.

Monday, 26 June
It was v. pleasant working at the Centre again with dear John Law. I am v. fond of him I must say & we do laugh a lot.

Monday, 3 July
I went along to the Aeolian Hall to rehearse with Eddie Braden and Terry (guitar) for the LP of 'Rambling Syd' which we are doing tonight at EMI. To EMI studios at Abbey Road at 7 o'c. Then we did it, with about two hundred people at about 9 o'c. It went like a bomb. The organisation at EMI was utterly appalling. This man Tony Palmer has absolutely no idea! At the end of the session everyone was allowed up into the Control box!! It was pandemonium! I left with Peter Eade & went to Biagi where we had supper. I said that this Palmer creature was a silly fat slob.

Wednesday, 5 July

Louie came at 6.30 'cos she'd got a demand for excess rates from Park West – so I dealt with it – Joe Orton & Ken Halliwell were there & we all chatted of this & that. Joe O. was full of the Tangier holiday from which they've just returned & said that it was all a great success in the flat. They're going again in October & probably November. Joe O. said that he liked Louie very much and said 'You come out with everything in front of her, don't you? – she likes a joke obviously – v. different from my mother. I could never talk like that with her.' He also said he'd started a diary[17] which would contain details of all the sexual encounters in his life. Stan W. said after, of Joe and Ken, 'Aren't they both boring? They're always talking about themselves.'

Thursday, 13 July

The Lords have passed Leo Abse's[18] bill, legalising homosexuality in England: it's all right between consenting adults in private except the services! and in Scotland. So it won't do any good for the queens of Dundee & the like.

Friday, 14 July

Stanley [Baxter] suddenly said he fancied going to an East End pub. I said the only one I knew was the Bridge Tavern at Canning Town so we drove there. Once in the bar, we got besieged by young lads asking for the autograph etc., and met a very nice lad called Alan who was a boxer, and a friend called Paul who said 'I'm the wife' – all v. Brian Rix – there was a dreadful youth boasting that he'd been in *Oliver* who kept shouting 'I'll fuck you' & I said 'Charming!' rather weakly & kept laughing it off. Another boy started taking off his trousers but the landlady said 'That's enough' & I said to the landlord 'It's too much' v. grandly. I must admit I enjoyed it v. much myself. A great pleasure to be surrounded by thoroughly unpretentious men.

Saturday, 15 July

Went to the film *Man For All Seasons* which was undeniably superb. It's a marvellous fabric which Bolt has woven with consummate skill, care and affection. Suddenly realised how brilliant this man really is. This work has had an extraordinary effect on me – the play had too: but I disliked Scofield so much, but in this he is very good indeed & the stageyness has gone. What a pity I couldn't have been in a success for Robert – it would have been so good to have done *him* a service.

---

[17] See entry for 30 April 1967, p. 303, n.

[18] b.1917. Labour MP for Pontypool 1958–83, for Torfaen 1983–87.

Saturday, 22 July
Met Noel W. at Biagi. I confessed all the sexual upheaval to him & told him how it was plaguing me. He was v. rational about it, but made it clear how dangerous a game it could become. He said that one could only live properly, if it was *for* a person or for God: and that if one had neither one could only relate to people promiscuously. This is where the *danger* lies. We also talked about the labyrinth of romantic pursuit. The one where you disappear up your own arsehole.

Sunday, 23 July
Went up to see Joe Orton & Kenneth. They were v. kind. We chatted about homosexuality and the effect the new clause would have. We agreed it would accomplish little. Joe walked with me to King's X. We also talked about his inability to love, his horror of involvement, & his *need* to be utterly free, and Ken H. disagreed with this, saying that love is involvement, and you can't live without love.

I must be approaching some sort of crisis – this incessant noise, the skin disease, the preponderant sexual problem. One day I think it's overcome, & then the sight of a navvy working in the street, stripped to the waist, and gold tanned flesh and muscles & I am back in square one. Full of guilt and shame. Even if I *did* it, I know I couldn't *live* with sex. I must be going slightly mad. The heart bangs dreadfully. Don't talk to me about psychosomatic symptoms. No good telling me not to think about things – they're there larger than life & twice as natural.

Monday, 24 July
Wrote to Joe Orton thanking him for being so kind yesterday. He listened so patiently to all my problems – so did Kenneth Halliwell. They were both so kind to me. It is v. nice to have them as neighbours I must say, it's good to be able to walk up there and see them.

Monday, 31 July
We completed Script No. 23. Bill Cotton took us down to viewing to see the Sammy Davis show which had been a sensation at Talk of the Town last night. When I hear that things are fabulous I just don't want to know. I didn't stay long. I have no generosity for that kind of thing. The man is too clever by half – no wonder there are racial troubles in America.

Tuesday, 8 August
Tried 3 times to phone F., eventually got thro' and he said 'I'm sorry but I've been on the phone for 45 minutes, talking to Joe Orton – he's having trouble with his dick & wants a good doctor.' When he

came to the flat he talked about Joe again, & I said that all this promiscuity was dangerous and wrong: but I said 'I think Joe's heart's in the right place . . .'

Wednesday, 9 August
John Hussey telephoned me at 4.45, he'd read in the paper that Joe Orton and Kenneth Halliwell are dead. Apparently it is a murder and a suicide. The BBC wanted me to go on TV and talk about Joe, but the Police will not name Joe Orton as being dead: so the programme has been cancelled. I rang Gordon and told him. I said no to the BBC anyway. I couldn't talk about Joe in public – not at the moment.

To Peter Butterworth & Janet [Brown] at Montpelier Sq. And then we went to see *El Dorado* with John Wayne and Robert Mitchum being superb. Suddenly realised when I left them that the Joe Orton business had gone out of my mind for a few hours! It soon came back again. There is something so dark and horrible about the circumstances. Joe Orton – in pyjamas with head injuries, a hammer nearby – and on the floor the body of Ken Halliwell, dead from suicide. Did he have a hallucination or something? Did he fear J. might drop him? It's all so odd. When I think of the generosity of Joe – his warmth and affection – his kindness to me when I was so depressed – I just want to cry.

Thursday, 10 August
Lots of phoning – people on about Joe Orton's death. Everyone says the same thing, *why*? I think the motive was Halliwell loved Joe. Halliwell felt that something v. big & important threatened that love. He couldn't kill that, so he killed J.O. This is the only thing that makes any sense – if there is any sense in murder.

They delivered the script of *Carry On Doctor* today and I read it. It's really a v. good vehicle for Frankie Howerd but all the other parts are lousy. I think that is it. This is the straw that breaks the camel's back. I wrote a nice letter to Peter Rogers saying I didn't want to play the part.

Friday, 11 August
Off to Morocco again. Eventually arrived at the Rembrandt Hotel. Went up to El Piano at about 1.45 and had the drinkettes. Found that the plane that Tom & Clive came on, to Gibraltar, got diverted to Tangé – so they're here!

Saturday, 12 August
The weather is absolutely fabulous. Tangé looks really wonderful, I'm so glad I came. We all went to LP [El Piano] and then all bundled

into your taxi and went to Stefan's. I lost the way so a marve boy called Absalom took us there. There was definite partiality. I got v. high and all the usual rubbish, waltzing over rubbish dumps and drinking in local hostelries. Finished up shouting 'You're no gentleman – this wouldn't happen at the G & C and I am your actual quality' outside the Rembrandt.

Tuesday, 15 August
Telegram from Peter Rogers saying Frankie Howerd out, and offering me the part!! Of course it's impossible, so I'll have to wire or phone London or something! Stomach going over with worry about it all.

Tuesday, 22 August
Suddenly realised I've been here quite long enough so I went to Bland's and altered my ticket to Sunday 27th direct flight to London. I bought a bottle of champagne 'cos it's Tom & Clive's 3rd Anniversary.

Thursday, 24 August
Some days ago, I read in the Times that the Orton inquest had been deferred until a friend of his returned from abroad, whose evidence might help the judgment. Now, I had the feeling when I read it, that this friend is me. I think I shall have to get on to Derek Bluston about it: it might well be that my giving any kind of testimony is neither in Joe's posthumous interest or in my living one.

Sunday, 27 August
When I came thro' the customs today, the officer said 'Hallo Mr Williams – your 3rd visit to Morocco isn't it?' & I said yes, & he said 'What's the attraction?' & I said 'Well, it's very sunny . . .' rather lamely.

Wednesday, 30 August
Out to Ryman's to get some tape to repair the binding of this volume, which inexplicably got cut during the flight to Maroc from London. I am wondering if it was searched. To my horror, I realised in Tangé that both cases were unlocked.

Saturday, 2 September
Noel Willman rang & said Peggy Ramsay was offering me my letters to Joe. I think that is simply splendid of her. It was not me wanted for the inquest, but a doctor who was treating Halliwell.

Monday, 4 September [press cutting enclosed]
Cut this out of the paper.[19] It represents all that can be known about the last hours of Joe. Curiously I have no anger for Halliwell – only sorrow – though the more one considers it, the more horrible it all seems. Now, that is the end. No doubt someone will write a book about it all – and time will eventually heal the terrible pain of those who cared for them.

Sunday, 10 September
To Talk of the Town for the show. The tops was Tony Martin[20] & Cyd Charisse and they were absolutely terrible. Lost the house halfway. Marty Feldman came round with Loretta and was very sweet about it all. He actually said 'The show was going fine till Burke and Hare came on . . .' which is really true.[21]

Thursday, 14 September
First day of film, *Carry On Doctor*. I was home by 5 o'c. Went to see *Bonnie & Clyde* at the Warner. The film is certainly v. daring. A scene showing an unsuccessful attempt at intercourse with Warren B[eatty] rolling off the girl & lying there crestfallen, and then she tries to go down on him for the old fellatio and he looks appalled and stops her. The entire cinema welcomed this episode – in the W/End! – and there were cries of approval from the auditorium. It was disgraceful, but I had to laugh; not at the episode, but at the audience reaction – that kind of nervous 'Oh! Hallo! what's going on *now*!' laughter.

Saturday, 16 September
Charles Hawtrey phoned with some rambling story about refusing to give my telephone number to a journalist. Said he'd been playing Portsmouth and that every morning he woke to find his flat full of pipkins and sailors' cigarette packets.

---

[19] An account from that day's *Evening Standard* of the inquest into the deaths of Joe Orton and Kenneth Halliwell, under the headline: 'Orton Murder – "hammer attack frenzy". Flat-mate's "enormous" overdose of drugs'. The article begins: 'Joe Orton, the 34-year-old award-winning playwright, was battered to death with a hammer in "a deliberate form of frenzy". The murderer: his 41-year-old flat-mate, Kenneth Halliwell, who committed suicide with "an enormous overdose" of drugs. The St Pancras deputy coroner, Dr John Burton, recording this verdict at the inquest today, said: "It is quite clear Mr Halliwell struck Mr Orton while he was asleep. There is no question of a suicide pact – nothing to suggest that Orton was a party to this. The evidence is overwhelming that Orton was killed by Halliwell. In a note he said he had done it intentionally. By inference there was trouble between them for some time. It appears it came to a head."'

[20] b. 1912. Original name variously given as Alfred Norris, Alvin Morris etc. Singing star of stage, screen and radio; husband of Cyd Charisse.

[21] This (recorded) edition of the programme was not broadcast.

Thursday, 28 September
Pinewood at 8 o'c. Lunched with Frankie Howerd. He is undoubtedly a very boring man. Loves talking, but there is no really cultivated mind. He continually says 'eksetra' which is irritating.

Sunday, 1 October
The tops on the show was Vince Hill of whom I've never heard.[22]

Friday, 6 October
At 9 o'c. the bell rang. It was a nun asking for money. I refused smilingly and closed the door. It's the impertinence that I object to. Telephoned the Head Porter and made my views known on canvassing. During dinner, Tom said he'd told Clive that if he ever left him, he (Tom) would come to live with me. Actually I think I would welcome it – the idea I mean – but I also know that we should need a much larger establishment.

Monday, 9 October
Finished the operating theatre sequence & started the scene in the room with Matron, Hattie. Hurt my back & moving the head forward is now painful. Always these films are painful for me. Should have stuck to my original decision not to do this one. 7.30, listened to Isaiah Berlin on the Romantic movement in Europe, on the Third Programme. Superb, lucid, and brilliantly explained.[23]

Sunday, 15 October
Jane Morgan[24] was v. nice to me & said she'd seen all my films in America. Her husband, Gerry, said that my stuff on the show tonight would *all* be cut in America – he said they would never allow the camp, & he added 'but you could make a fortune in cabaret over there . . .' All these Americans seem to regard New York as a theatrical Mecca. It is ludicrous. I haven't the slightest desire to see any part of their country, but I should love to play Australia.

Tuesday, 31 October
Listened to the 5th lecture by Isaiah Berlin, in which he talked about the Romantic concept of all Structure as Death – all that which has been *done* is useless & must be rejected. A constitution that has been written is necessarily a dead one, etc. etc. The more I hear him talk

---

[22] Singer, b.1932, who had almost topped the charts in February with 'Edelweiss'.
[23] 'Some Sources of Romanticism', six lectures by Sir Isaiah Berlin, b.1909, philosopher.
[24] Singer (b. Jane Currier), best known for 'The Day the Rains Came' (1958).

about Romanticism the more I come to think I am not sharing in this ideal at all. I'm continually stunned by the incredible *speed* of the man, the mind is so fast, and the diction sometimes tumbles over itself and it's so *refreshing* and invigorating.

Saturday, 4 November

I listened to 'R.T.H.' on the radio. It was really very funny – me doing a send-up of a Southern American jazz trumpeter[25] – it was a v. good voice I used: the whole programme was full of wit and invention and infectious humour.

Thursday, 16 November

One of those dark, rainy mornings that I love. I watch it pouring down on these builders on the Nash site & they're all wet & miserable & I am delighted. I've reported Tussaud's smoking chimney to the Westminster Council & a man is coming to view it all.

Tuesday, 21 November

There is a lot in the paper about devaluation. Wilson has said in the Commons that it does not affect money in savings etc. in England*, and the Chancellor has said that it means a lowering in the standard of living etc.

*quote: 'It will not affect the pound in your pocket'!!

Thursday, 23 November

Dinner at Biagi with Tom, Clive & Billy McNeile. It was awful. I never want to go thro' anything like it again. Tom told me that he'd lunched with Stanley and told him *everything* I had said. Of course this has caused endless trouble now.

Saturday, 25 November

All my reactions to this Tom business are the same. I really want to finish with him and Clive. I really want not to see them again. They have been an appalling disappointment to me. Everything that was good in the relationship has been completely soured. To Lime Grove for the Simon Dee Show.[26] I babbled on talking rubbish and came away feeling suicidal.

[*Enclosure*] Simon gave me this print of the television transmission. It's the bit where he held my hand & said 'Honestly I just like looking at you.' He has the most fantastic self-possession.

---

25 'Bix Spiderthrust'.

26 'Dee Time'. Host, Simon Dee (b. Carl Henty-Dodd, 1934).

Sunday, 26 November

I had a talk with Tom & Clive & I think there is no doubt about their acknowledging the seriousness of what has happened. There is no animosity on my part now, I just want to make it clear, so that it doesn't happen again.

Monday, 27 November

Went out to Barking, and as I tried to board a bus, a man shouted 'Hallo my friend!! – would you care to ride with me? – Mister Cabaray Poof Sir?' I stood like a frozen idiot while people stared at my embarrassment, then I turned on my heel and walked, as fast as was decently possible, away; I felt the blood rushing to my heart & my head, and had the awful desire to cry. Not so much at the *words*, but at the *desire* of a perfect stranger to want to humiliate & hurt me. He certainly succeeded. Lit a fag & pulled meself together & then got another bus home.

Thursday, 30 November

Maggie S. came at 6.30 & drove me to the Old Vic where we saw *Rosencrantz & Guildenstern are Dead.*[27] I have never sat through such tedious boredom, I felt the anger rising within me. By the interval I was furious. Maggie asked me if I was enjoying it & I said I was bored to tears. She said 'Well it's a free country, you can leave right now if you want to . . .' which I thought was awful.

Friday, 1 December

The BBC recorded a message from me, for colour TV. Then Stewart B. arrived; we went to these friends for drinks. I got far too drunk & eventually arrived at Wyndham's feeling awful.[28] When I got to Alec G.'s dressing room he said why wasn't I doing something in the theatre & I said I couldn't face 8 performances a week and A.G. said 'Well I do it' and I said 'Yes but you get these early release clauses . . .' and Redgrave pointedly said 'Goodnight Alec and thank you again'. When they'd gone, I rushed to the mirror and said 'My hair is a terrible mess' and Alec stroked his bald dome and said 'O! I so agree – I can't do a thing with mine either' but at the time I just couldn't reciprocate because I was so drunk and I just went on and on talking too much.

Saturday, 2 December

I rang Gordon about last night & said how dreadful I felt and he said 'Well I would have been happier if you'd been sober' and that is the

---

[27] By Tom Stoppard.

[28] To see *Wise Child* by Simon Gray.

nearest to a rebuke one will ever get from Gordon. So that is the proof. I *was* dreadful and the evening was ruined by me.

Sunday, 3 December

Rose jaded & disenchanted, still full of guilt about the recent events & vaguely resentful of all the people who have contributed to those events. The lesson is always the same. *Trust your initial reactions* – and act on them. If I had done that with Maggie I would never have gone to the Old Vic at all. *Every time I go there I hate it.* It has always spelled disaster for me. Now that's a resolution I will *act on*. Never, ever, go to the Old Vic again, no matter who is on the stage, or who invites me.

Monday, 11 December

To Louie's & watched the 'Int. Cabaret' show – Eckstine one. I had been cut by Lupino in both spots. The last 4 minute one was gone completely. I was furious & incensed at this sort of philistinism. I rang Tom Sloan at his home & went on about it.

Tuesday, 12 December

On getting up, I decided that this issue would have to be forced. I rang the BBC & said I would *not* work with Lupino any longer. That's it. Final. Result is that Stewart is doing Sunday's show, and thereafter John Street. So I have won.

Wednesday, 13 December

I had a phone call from Tom Sloan asking me to go back to square one & work with Barry Lupino on the show! I said all the same things again & he said all right, they'd get Stewart Morris to do this Sunday. He said a lot of things about the man's livelihood etc.: but that's totally irrelevant really.

Tuesday, 19 December

To BEA and booked seats for Alyn Ainsworth & me, to go to Maroc on the 31st and return on the 5th January. Taxi to Tom & Clive where we had a lovely evening & talked about decadent art.

Wednesday, 20 December

Alyn Ainsworth came over & I gave him something to eat and we talked about our trip etc.: and I realised suddenly what a terrible bore he is.

Saturday, 23 December

To Maggie and Robert at Eldon Road. There was her dresser, and

Coral Browne and Jeremy Brett. A very curious mixture indeed. Coral is one of those dramatic and stunning looking women with a marvellous face and head & she is v. funny in that New Yorkerish way. Jeremy is v. good looking & charming, and this dresser was a rather plump cockney queen from Edgware Road. I kissed everyone goodnight and was about to shake hands with him when he pulled me to him and kissed me twice. I was staggered by the temerity of it all & exited bemusedly into my taxi.

Tuesday, 26 December

The phone has rung a lot – someone who knows the code. Three rings & start again, but I still didn't answer. There is an awful lot of this 'social chat' stuff over the Christmas period, and I can't be doing with it.

Wednesday, 27 December

I've had Louie every day & it's happening again tomorrow when we go to the pantomime! Once a week is all right but every day simply won't do. The wavelengths are not at all similar.

Thursday, 28 December

George Rose rang me and I gave him lunch at Biagi. We met Harry Andrews and Basil in there, and joined them for coffee. H.A. said that 'Roseybum' play at the National was very good so he must be quite senile now, tho' he looks quite good. To Golders Green to see what must have been the most disgraceful evening in the theatre that I've ever witnessed. Not a jot of talent anywhere and private jokes with the cast falling about at themselves. We had to lie like *mad* after, because someone had bought us the seats! He made us go down to Danny La Rue's D/room where we were plied with champagne. It was ghastly.

Sunday, 31 December

Got to Tangé at 12.10. It's funny being here at New Year, I'm reminded a lot of Beirut. Which I never would have visited that time if I had known about this place. I've been here in July, March and August, Sept. and now December and it has never let me down yet! Always blue skies, always the incredible atmosphere and always these unchanging & delightful people.

1968

Wednesday, 3 January
At 7 o'c. to Dickie Bird's apartment for drinks. V. heterosexual and crowded with crashing bores. Mark Gilbey was there & as he was invited to the Eliots for dinner, he drove us there in his great Mercedes with the liveried adonis chauffeur.

Thursday, 4 January
We got the 6 o'c. plane out of Gib., it was a Comet. Norman Wisdom on board, so we had the chat. He is a good person. Home by nine o'clock. Realised when I was lying in bed that the drumming noise from the fans has started all over again, so I had to take the Supponeryl to get to sleep.

Sunday, 7 January
This drumming noise continues to dominate my life – I think in circles and come back to it every time: every place I've lived in, I've had to leave because of noise – Endsleigh Court, Park West and now this place, which I thought was a haven. I just don't know what to do any more – it is hard to know what my life is *about* – work that gives me no real joy, or sense of artistic achievement: a way of life that is repugnant – where I can't walk about in public without the moron's nudge and the cretin's wink – where there is absolutely no physical relationship and let's face it, friends are all very well & indeed valuable, but they have their own lives to lead. Talk of the Town at 5.35. Tops is Georgie Fame. Lovely voice.

Monday, 15 January
Mayfair Heating called in their expert, Mr Kemp, and he has fixed the fan! There is no longer any thumping overhead! I'm enormously grateful to him.

Friday, 19 January
The lovely Ken B. rang & I've agreed to meet him next Monday. I am probably mad, but I'll have to do this – then I can work it so that

it develops platonically – the irony is that he quite fancies me! – at least he *appears* to. But our ends never know our beginnings and it is a tortured web that we weave etc. etc. I purchased this Brian Howard book today[1] – about this young homosexual who 'failed' in the materialistic sense, all his life. Sounds delightful to me. Of course I realise how *lucky* I am to have got a talent which reaps such rewards. It enables me to live a life of great *ease* and comfort without really doing anything.

Monday, 22 January
Ken B. came to see me. He said during the evening that I always looked as though I had make-up on my face! I was quite taken aback, because apart from the fact that it's untrue, I am conscious of the fact that I've a bad skin & that there are obvious blemishes and when I look at photographs I am always bemoaning this crater-like surface. It was all on a plate etc. but I suddenly realised I didn't want to know. I think now that I haven't wanted to know *all my life* – I don't have a *need* for love: not even companionship: but of course I *like* companionship. With this sort of young man I feel like some awful old queen tarting around and because of the disparity in age & lack of any real common ground, the conversation was difficult and often banal.

Tuesday, 23 January
I played the Grieg sonatas and fell to musing on my condition. I can't have sex 'cos I just can't cope on that level, and so I'm only really left with work – and that pays me too much money (due to the Tax situation) so I can't afford to do very much of that. It's all very difficult really. I have never gone through such a period of *hating* the government, such as I am going through now.

Tuesday, 30 January
Lunch G & C with the adorable Gording. His play finished at Wyndham's on Saturday so he's free again. He said that Alec Guinness (in drag for the part in *Wise Child*) checked all the props in the handbag and said 'You know, Gordon, it may seem rather silly and sentimental to you, but I'm going to miss this old bag . . .' and then walked on to the stage . . . He also told me that some nights Guinness is saying,

---

[1] Brian Howard (1905–58). Aesthete, occasional writer, suicide. *Brian Howard: Portrait of a Failure*, ed. M.J. Lancaster. In a famous 1929 hoax when some bright young things invented and exhibited a fictitious German painter called Bruno Hat, the faked paintings were supplied by Howard. Evelyn Waugh once wrote (*A Little Learning*) that 'The characters in my novels often wrongly identified with Harold Acton were to a great extent drawn from him.'

very roguishly – 'Oh! I can't play it tonight my dear, I've got the curse . . .'

Wednesday, 31 January

Reading Camus. More & more with this writer you realise how utterly naive most thinkers are. He makes a fascinating case for Art being rebellion. Rebellion, in this case, *against* disorder and chaos in the natural world, and by its vision imposing an order & a poetry of its own, into the mess. Of course this is romantic – in so far as it is putting a *false frame* on infinity. He makes the marvellous point that there is no such thing as realism in Art. To be real, the description of a character in a novel would be *endless*. Just as the painter catching an arrested movement is *false* insofar as, in reality, this was only *part* of another movement & reality would show us all, not a fragment which contains all the bias of the selector.

Monday, 5 February

'R.T.H.' at the Paris Cinema. Now there are 4 writers on it! It is unbelievable really. Four. For half an hour of crap with not a memorable line anywhere: well – perhaps the odd one. Well of course one goes on and flogs it gutless and gets the rubbish by.

Tuesday, 6 February

Peter Eade telephoned:

'Can you keep a secret?'

'Yes, of course. For a certain time.'

'I've just had a call from Delfont. You're to be voted – no – have been voted the Radio Personality of the Year, by the Variety Artists' Club. This is a great honour – the theatre one goes to Edith Evans & film to Scofield.'

'Well ring Delfont & politely decline.'

'Are you serious?'

'Of course. I despise the entire Delfont world, the Variety Artist crap, and Scofield & Edith Evans [&] the whole bag full of hob jobbery and snobbery that they comprise.'

I must say it gives me considerable satisfaction to turn down one of these spurious 'awards'. I guide my own career in theatre – well almost – oh! hell.

Monday, 12 February

Did 'Round The Horne' at the Paris. It went very well. The writing is really good I must say. I only hope they keep up the standard. Got the script of *Up The Khyber* Carry On film. They're offering me the part of Khasi. Which is Hindustani for lavatory.[2] I imagine they think it's appropriate. It's not a v. long part. Went up to see Gordon & Rona. We watched the cabaret on the television. I thought I came over like a stupid poof and that's a fact.

Wednesday, 14 February

I went and got the Nat King Cole recording of 'I Wish You Love'[3] which I heard at Tom's flat. For some reason it makes me cry. Spirits were reasonably high today 'cos the bum was quiet and I walked about the streets being v. jovial & jocular and made faces at people: many of them looked startled and hurried on. Some laughed & turned away & then did a double take.

Thursday, 15 February

I see that the actress Virginia Maskell has taken her own life.[4] I think I have seen her work – a v. sensitive face – she was the mother of two children & they lived in the country – she took these sleeping pills and laid down in a wood near their home. She was found dead & suffering from exposure. A letter was left which signified 'no hope – just despair'. It is terrible that a girl like that should have been so desperately unhappy.

Saturday, 17 February

To bed in the afternoon. Up at 4. Copious evacuation. It is all v. odd, the bum seems to be living a life of its own. I shall be glad when this weekend & Monday's work is over. I shall be glad when next week is over. I shall be glad when everything is over. Gordon came at 7.30. He told me that Donald Wolfit had died. It's all happening.

Monday, 19 February

To the St John & Elizabeth [Hospital]. By six o'clock I'd had the enema & the evacuation. Sister Xavier popped in but our conversation was terminated by me rushing to the commode. Mr Mulvany visited me at 7.45. We had a long talk about the problem of materialism in modern society. He said he would inject the piles tomorrow and look at the inside of the rectum etc.

---

[2] Most dictionaries of slang, including Eric Partridge's famous work, advise against a search for any Eastern derivation of 'karsi' and its variants; they are nothing more than the simple Italian 'casa' in disguise.

[3] Originally 'Que reste-t-il de nos amours?', by Charles Trenet.

[4] Aged thirty-two. KW had certainly seen her in *The Wild and the Willing* in October 1962.

Tuesday, 20 February
I recall being wheeled on a stretcher and someone saying 'Give me your arm' and then nothing more until I woke again about 2 o'c. At about 9 I saw Sister Xavier & she told me there had been a great fissure & the entire area inflamed. So – now one knows why there had been so much pain and discomfort.

Wednesday, 21 February
Barium enema. I hated every minute of it. Mr Mulvany came in at 12 o'c. and said I could go, if I wanted to.

Thursday, 22 February
Got lots of birthday greetings & threw them all in the dustbin. Only realised at about 5 o'c. that I am forty-two today. Forty-two! – it's an adult age, that is. You can't be childish at forty-two and get away with it but nonetheless, I shall try.

Saturday, 24 February
Well, I have got through the day without pain from the bum, and I am grateful. I would like very much to enter softly into the room of the sufferers, and read something beautiful to them, so that for a little while at least, their mind was transported and comforted. A voice is all I've got. It's all that I've ever had. I read a lot of poetry tonight – the Patmore one about chiding his son and then regretting it, made me cry.[5] Always the inhumanity in the world makes one weep. We've all of us been weeping all our lives. The weeping will never be done.

Monday, 26 February
To the Paris to do 'R.T.H.' The bum became *murder* from about 10 o'c. onwards. My spirits plummeting to zero. The bum has gone from just irritation to irritation and pain. I feel hopelessly, irretrievably lost. This endless movement in the anus like some awful worm till you could scream & all the nerves are frayed & stretched to breaking point. Took 8 tablets & had a glass of sherry feeling quite *mad* at 1 o'c. in the morning. Took a Mandrax tablet & went to bed feeling utterly lunatic.

Wednesday, 28 February
John Gale[6] telephoned. 'I am putting on a revue starring Hermione Gingold and I wondered if you would like to be her leading man . . .'

---

[5] 'The Toys' by Coventry Patmore (1823–96).
[6] Theatrical producer, b.1929.

Me: 'Have you any Sal Volatile?' Gale: 'What?' Me: 'I think I shall need about a dozen bottles.'

Thursday, 29 February

Tom came, & Clive. I took them all to Biagi. After, we drove to the Spartan, where I was disgraceful. There's no question about my being v. frustrated. Once I get into these homosexual clubs and have a few drinks I start behaving in a way that I would ordinarily deplore. It's the full 'common as muck' queen, dying for the touch-up. Pathetic. If I didn't have to worry about economics and Louie, I really would change my way of life and perhaps get out of England or change the job or something. I have no real interest in acting *per se*.

Monday, 4 March

To Louie. We watched the TV show. I was very good indeed I must say. A fragmented beauty with a great dignity.

Saturday, 9 March

I question everything in my life: I suppose I always have. I find myself asking if I deserve *anything* – at the moment I am questioning whether I deserve to be taking this holiday on the 18th. I suppose it's the puritan legacy. What a stinker that is, to inherit. Here I am now, at the end of the day with the bum quiet & feeling content, with just the desk light on, looking down on the ribbon of light in the Marylebone Road – they've almost rebuilt the York Terrace main house – the entire Nash Terraces on the left are still being done, and on the other side, where the old Marylebone Workhouse stood, the new Regent St Polytechnic Annexe is going up. I went out this morning but the staring & the nudging drove me quickly back indoors.

Sunday, 10 March

Washed me hair & shaved and went out for the papers. When I came back I went into the bathroom to comb me hair & thought 'You don't look half bad for forty-two'. There's no doubt about it, on a good day, I look quite lovely in your actual gamin fashion.

Tuesday, 12 March

2.30 B[roadcasting] H[ouse]. I did the interview for the Woman's magazine programme (Rosemary Hart). 3.30 Second interview, for 'World At One' with Susan MacGregor.[7] This girl was awfully nice, but the talk didn't go quite as well as the first. Not enough humour.

---

[7] Sue MacGregor, b.1941. Broadcaster. Arrived in England from South Africa 1967.

Wednesday, 13 March
This has been a remarkable day. The first time for ages that I have walked comfortably. It continued to behave like a proper bum all the time: at one point I almost forgot it! I am enormously grateful.

Sunday, 17 March
The show went well but I was v. nervous. Peter E. sent champagne. Lovely. John Law and I had the glass in the dressing room before. Star was Vikki Carr.[8] She cried through all her numbers. Disgraceful really.

Monday, 18 March. Gibraltar
'R.T.H.' at 9.30. At Gatwick I signed photographs. The Captain asked me on to the flight deck but I was too tired & I went to sleep. Eventually we all met up for the drink-ette in the bar here & then trolled into town. We all went to Sugar's bar where we joined a load of lads from HMS *Reclaim*. It was drinks and dirty songs till 12 o'c. Sugar did the dance with the castanets and kissed me and was v. bold. So was Maggie the barmaid.

Tuesday, 19 March
9.30 plane to Tangé. To Claridge for dinner. Excellent. Then to Stefan's Bar where I met Hammet and he came back to Rue Dante. In the middle, I had to get up to let in Terry and friend. Got off to sleep about 3 o'c. eventually.

Wednesday, 20 March
Woke to find the lip was damaged thro' the violent amour. It's a disgrace. To the chemist for hydrocortisone etc.

Sunday, 24 March
I had the bowel motion and went to tip my fag ash down the loo and burned me cock. There's always something.

Tuesday, 26 March
I really am beginning to wonder if I should come to Morocco again. The nearness to England – the inexpensive nature of the trip and the prospect of the sun: these are the obvious attractions, but certainly the society isn't. It does become a frightful bore having to listen to these endless sagas from the queens about their dreary affairs and

---

[8] b. El Paso, Texas, as Florencia Bisenta de Castillas Martinez Cardona. Her hit of the day was 'It Must be Him'.

their money troubles or their bum troubles. Perhaps I should start scouting around for something different next time?

Saturday, 30 March
The last stroll down to the beach. Plane left at 6.10. Eventually, bed at 2 o'c.

Tuesday, 2 April
Met Noel Willman at Biagi's at about 7.30. Our careers (ironically) have both suffered appallingly since *Gentle Jack* – which I never wanted to do in the first place – so Robert Bolt should put us both on a pension: instead of handing out money to all these dreary charities. This year I have given about seven hundred to friends that need it – that is certainly better than cheques to all these daft organisations.

Wednesday, 3 April
BBC studios in Maida Vale for the talk with Peter Haigh on 'Movicgo-round'. He asked me for a definition of 'camp'. I said 'To some it means that which is fundamentally frivolous, to others the baroque as opposed to the puritanical (classical), and to others – a load of poofs.'

Friday, 5 April
Went to Dr Black at the Rank Org. and had the medical. Got away with Peter Butterworth and we lunched at the G & C where he told me the saga of Hawtrey moving into the one room at his house. It was unbelievably sordid & terribly funny.

Monday, 8 April
'R.T.H.' Barry Took was in a v. funny mood and suddenly got quite snappy about the show becoming filthy. 'We might as well write a series called Get Your Cock Out,' he kept crying. I think he's a bit demented.

Sunday, 14 April
The bum is playing up badly – now it has become so erratic that there's no knowing what is going to happen from one hour to another! The irritation, the soreness, the continual washing; and the farting becomes vicious & rasping. All sentiment apart: to die would be a release for me, from a life that has been physically and mentally a continually painful business: there's really no sense in it anywhere.

Tuesday, 16 April
First day's work on *Up The Khyber*. It was a lousy little scene between

me and Sid James but he blows a raspberry in the middle which will get a big laugh. Roy [Castle] is v. good in the rushes & photographs v. handsomely: he is incredibly naive & ingenuous.

Wednesday, 17 April

As I came in to the studio, Peter Rogers stopped me and said he wanted a word with me – he said 'Come into the caravan, I don't want to say it before the rest of the cast – you've been working with us for about ten years now and it's time some home truths were told, the fact is, that you stink' and thereupon handed me a huge bottle of La Plus Belle Lavande!!! I was practically speechless! It's this sort of gesture – thoughtful and kind, that Peter is so often making, and it's one of the most endearing things about him. What sort of life would I have had without Peter and Gerald? – oh! dear! the mind boggles.

Sunday, 28 April

Tom & Clive came with this blonde bombshell from Bath: a very pleasant young man but of course lacking any real fluency or style. All rather stolid & loutish and after the loveliness has worn off you start getting awfully bored. I advised him to join the Metropolitan Police: he said he was interested and that he would apply.

Monday, 29 April

Listened to the radio show 'R.T.H.' tonight. It was quite funny in parts, and totally decadent. This period of our history must surely be very comparable to the Platonic period in Greece when the Gods are fallen into disrepute and morality is practically eroded away. All the humour in this show was anarchic or homosexual and it was *all* applauded. It is like playing to a load of hopeless drunks – show them another drunk and they *fall about*. If I cared about this world of ours I'd be really frightened – indeed I used to be – but now I don't care. The society of a civilised & gracious people is almost always a minority that flourishes rarely.

Friday, 3 May

At one point while rehearsing with Joan, I farted very loudly & she got up crying out 'Pooh! it's disgusting, I can't sit here with this going on – the dirty sod.' I said aggressively 'Rudolf Valentino used to blow off' and Gerald T. said 'Yes, but they were *silent* films' and everybody laughed.[9]

---

[9] KW's favourite chat-show anecdote, rivalled only by the 'Green Boots'.

Tuesday, 7 May
I feel the need to sleep more and more these days. I am getting old. I am in the twilight of my life. I see in the papers that my friend Oliver Ford got fined 700 pounds 'cos of what they call 'gross indecency' with a guardsman. Well it's not my cup of tea. No sex is. But I think it's high time all these daft charges were dropped. Some men will always pay to have a woman and some to have a man. It's a perfectly reasonable idea and there isn't a law in any land that will ever change it.

Friday, 10 May
I saw Robert Stephens in Mags' caravan & we had the chat. They're doing *Miss Jean Brodie* there, on the adjoining set.

Saturday, 11 May
Tom & Clive came and drove me to the Garden. Eventually B. arrived with David – a guardsman I'd never met. Brian & Tony turned up with a guardsman called Peter. There is an extraordinary ambiguity about guardsmen – indeed, about all homosexual rent. On the one hand, they like certain aspects of the camp and often indulge in it themselves, but they resent bitterly any slur upon their heterosexual capabilities and this makes for an uneasy dichotomy in their behaviour. I heard after from Clive that one woman, leaving with the husband & daughter, looked distastefully at our table of eight males and said 'There isn't a single lady at that table – they're all men' which apart from its irrelevance was a totally untrue statement. Got home with that awful feeling of waste and disappointment at 12.30. It cost me about £28.10.0 altogether and it wasn't worth a penny of it. Not a penny. I felt cheap and degraded and nasty.

Sunday, 12 May
Clive collected me and drove me to Highgate. They are fabe hosts and no mistake. Tom described having it away and I got half a colin, Clive said 'Well get it out then – come on, show us' but I laughed it off.

Monday, 13 May
At the studios today, to brighten things up, I hid my cock between my legs and impersonated a vagina for Angela Douglas. She sunk her head in her hands and moaned 'Oh! God – how horrible' and didn't find it amusing at all. This is where she lacks graciousness.

Thursday, 16 May
That nasty old man who's 74 and is supposed to do wardrobe came up to me and said 'You don't like me, do you?' and I said 'No, I don't' and he went to Peter Rogers and started crying his eyes out. P.R. came

to me and remonstrated. So I went to this old man and put my arms round the horrid, self-pitying spectacle and said 'You mustn't take any notice of me! I say lots of things in a temper which I don't really mean – now come along & don't upset yourself my dear . . .' etc. etc. The full fawning load of crap. Did the love scene on the bed with Joanie Sims. She had seen all the business with the old boy & she said 'You are really *wicked* aren't you? – demonic little bastard . . .'

Monday, 20 May

'R.T.H.' went very well, including 'Hawkin' Me Greens' which got a great clap. I caught the 3.5 to Bangor. Car at station drove us to the Royal Goat Hotel, Beddgelert, Snowdonia. Film locations always begin as an adventure, and invariably become purgatory.

Wednesday, 22 May

The barman says Charlie Hawtrey consumed 2 and a half bottles of port, a whisky & a pot of tea last night! Last night I heard him shouting and bawling on the stairs, well past midnight, so I'm prepared to believe it. It's not the eccentricity, or the grotesquerie, or the homosexuality that puts one off Charles: it is the excruciating boredom.

Monday, 27 May

'R.T.H.' at the Paris. Last one of the series – there was a buffet party & drinks, but I had to leave for Pinewood. The script was all right I suppose, & got loads of laughs, but the playing discipline is practically non-existent.

Wednesday, 5 June

The whole day made unreal and horrible by the shooting of Robert Kennedy. This senseless mad awful act has resulted in him being operated on, for removal of a bullet from the brain. Everyone seems utterly stunned by it.[10] Phoned a cable to Tangier saying about the arrival time.

Friday, 7 June. Tangier

One always forgets the essentials of Tangé. The poverty, the friendliness, the curiously childish mercenary thing – the instinct to 'beg for alms' that goes on, on so many levels.

Wednesday, 12 June

Johnny said he hadn't come the night before 'because I am frightened

[10] Senator Robert F. Kennedy (b.1925), fatally shot at the Ambassadors Hotel, Los Angeles.

you look at me and you say go away' so again it was arranged. We all went off to the Piano and sure enough he did come. We sat drinking and then walked home to the hotel together and I paid for his taxi back. He kept saying 'No good tonight – you pissed' which was completely untrue – it's the old ploy of accusing the other person of what you're suffering from yourself.

Friday, 14 June

I walked down to the Windmill and on the promenade a group of British drears approached and said 'Ee! it's Kenny! Hallo Kenny!' but I continued walking and they cried out 'What's the matter with him, then?' – impossible to explain that one comes to this continent purposely to avoid all that they represent. Went at 9.30 to the Villa Augusta. Their two guests Dieter and Wolfgang were there and I asked Dieter to show me the gardens, he took me to the roof and kissed me passionately – the tongue exploring the mouth – and said 'When I come to London I shall come to see only you – no one else . . .' He is certainly the most handsome German I've ever met, but I quickly came down from the roof and re-entered the drawing room saying 'What a lovely garden' and I returned to the Rembrandt at about 2 o'c. in the morning.

Saturday, 15 June

Gradually they all come pestering – the Moroccans with 'Allo Kennet are you all right?' and the dreary English queens with 'May I say how much I enjoy your performances?' One feels like retorting 'You should see me wanking dear' but I am too weary and gutless for that.

Sunday, 16 June

To tea with Mrs Wilton. She is an old lady of ninety who looks as if she's stuck together with stamp paper and her aggressiveness is totally tiresome because it precludes anyone joining in the conversation. She said that she wanted written on her tombstone 'Thank God she's gone . . .' which was reasonable in the circumstances. I originally wanted to stay out here for at least a month, until all the painting was finished but now I shall take the first direct flight I think.

Sunday, 23 June

The last day & the usual feeling of relief and regret. I've been here too often and I know too many faces. The number of handsome Moroccans has certainly decreased since I first came & the number of English bores has increased alarmingly. I was home by 9 o'c. and I got into my *redecorated flat*. It is completely transformed and it looks lovely. All the walls are bare – all the pictures down – and I'm going to keep it that way.

Tuesday, 25 June

It says in the Times that Tony Hancock has been found dead, in a suburb of Sydney. It doesn't mention the circumstances. He was 44. It seems a futile end, but the man was incredibly destructive all his life – never did anyone *waste* people & opportunities, as he did. I went up to see Gordon in the evening. We watched the television news and it said that Hancock had taken an overdose of barbiturates. Sid James said 'I was deeply shocked' which was kind of novel, and Tom Sloan went on television after the news and talked about Hancock as a 'Colossus of Comedy' and a crapulous eulogy about 'original clown – wit and invention' etc. etc. No one saying the real truth – an indifferent performer saved by two of the most brilliant scriptwriters of the decade, Galton and Simpson, whom he rejected. Thereafter, it was all downhill.

Wednesday, 26 June

Again Laurena Dewar phoned about doing a job. Station announcer gimmick for the opening night of Tyne-Tees Television. I said no again. She was furious. If this goes on much more, I shall have a dreadful row & leave the entire set-up.

Friday, 28 June

Andrew F. telephoned to say that John Windeatt[11] had committed suicide: he said 'My dear, it's so inconsiderate! we were supposed to be going to Sicily together on Monday . . .'

Tuesday, 2 July

Next time I get a desk diary I must try for a black one, then everything on the desk will match. Cleaned and polished my Carry On mug and displayed it on top of the bookcase. Let's face it, it's the only reward I've ever got so I might as well show it, pathetic though it undoubtedly is.

Saturday, 13 July

Tom & Clive came at 6 o'c. I gave them the steaks and did a tomato salad, and black cherries for sweet. Afterwards I read them a lot of Hitchmania – how that good man lives *on* in my life – and quite a bit of the '65 Diary, and they left about 11.30.

---

[11] Friend and (chiefly) correspondent of KW.

Tuesday, 16 July
I thought, when I left De Lane Lea Studios today 'Well that's a quick way to make money – 15 minutes at 300 pounds.' But people passing me in the street were unimpressed by the tat raincoat, and tieless creature wobbling along.

Tuesday, 30 July
We talked of the holiday in Tangier and it's all taken for granted that I'm to share the flat with the boys but I think from the bum point of view I'll need the bath en suite so I think I shall make them see the wisdom of my going to the Rembrandt.

Monday, 5 August
Had David Hatch[12] on the phone asking me to do six programmes in his radio series 'Just A Minute' – unfortunately it means working with that Parsons fellow, but I said yes, 'cos it will be a nice fill-in.

Monday, 12 August
I heard the tribute to Hancock programme on the radio tonight. It was terrible. The excerpts were all slow, tedious & unfunny. Hattie Jacques was doing her 'pompous' bit, and Sid James, the inevitable shyster, and me with character voices so heavy that the diction was sometimes totally obscured. There was a painful speech in the middle from Dennis Main Wilson. He finished by saying 'and this I really believe, in fact I'm prepared to swear – that Hancock's genius was so great, that it was beyond his ken . . .' Now, to have chosen, as his last 3 words, the title of a radio show which paralleled & eventually superseded 'Hancock's Half Hour' was not only tasteless & inept, but stupid as well.

Wednesday, 21 August
To the G & C for lunch with Joan Sims & Angela Douglas, we were a dreadful trio of gigglers. When I asked for the bill to be split three ways, Joanie said to the waitress 'He's the last of the big spenders' and then we all went to Piccadilly where I got a taxi and I went with Angela to do some shopping.

Friday, 23 August. Gibraltar
The boys came & Louie made the tea etc. and then we all took the car at 5.20 to London Airport. Of course the sun and heat of London makes you wonder why you are leaving at all! I went into their room at the Queen's & they gave me the Alka S. and Clive undressed & all

---

[12] b.1939. Latterly Special Advisor to the Director General of the BBC.

so I thought it was time to go. Then I went to bed early only to wake about 3 o'c. because of the nocturnal emission. I was furious. Staggering about cleaning everything up and absolutely bug-eyed with tiredness.

Saturday, 24 August. Tangier

Clive already has a better colour than the rest of us. G. refused to go to Piano with me so I hurled abuse at him and flew off narrowly missing being run over and went on me own. I got absolutely stinking and Dennis got me a taxi. Returned Rembrandt and was sick in the loo. Always the same here – I never learn.

Sunday, 25 August

Barry tells me that all those Americans have got crabs. It does seem v. unhygienic. G. launched into a great account of a queen who got them in the moustache because of the plate of ham.[13] Conversation was high flown indeed.

Wednesday, 28 August

I met that Harry who said Tom picked up a boy in the Piano and Harry said 'It's got a huge cock so Tom is silly, with that pile and all . . .' so I thought hallo! it certainly gets around in Tangier. How I *loathe* this place. It is definitely the *swan song*. Whatever happens, I must remember the Heat (wet), the Tedium, the Flies everywhere, the smells, the bores, the *noise* (shouting, barking, singing, crowing, transistors etc.) and either find somewhere else, or cut out the holidays, that's all – I've *had it*.

Sunday, 1 September

There are undercurrents with T & C. I don't know, all the time, what they're due to, but I do know they're there: perhaps our entire trio relationship is an unhealthy one – I don't know. Certainly it is a neurotic business. The excessive badinage is proof of that – half the time our laughter is a thin cover for appalling hysteria.

Tuesday, 3 September

When we walked with that boy yesterday in the party to Magoga, he said 'I met a homo once – actually I thought he was having me on . . .' and Tom said afterwards 'He was walking with eight queers at the time' which made me laugh at the sheer idiotic irony of it all.

---

[13] Rhyming slang = gam = oral sex.

Wednesday, 4 September
What a dreadful round they all are. W. with his eternal fixation on serviceman sex and conventional behaviour, G. with his penchant for fellatio and being bashed by the lover manqué, and queens with cigarette burns all up the arms – it is practically a mad house. One would do well to steer clear of the whole rotten broiling, because there will be a dreadful retribution one day.

Sunday, 8 September
We got into London at 7.30. Got to the Customs. T[om] in front & the Insp. said 'Have you anything to declare?' and T. said 'Only this leather pouffe' & I said 'He don't mean me, it's just my tan . . .' The customs men roared with laughter. I said goodbye to the boys & said that I would phone etc. but I've dropped it to Tom that it will all have to be rested. I shall need time to get over it all. I commented on the flat being kept so immaculately & the new linen put out etc. & I said to Louie 'What on earth would I do without you?' – and she smiled & reciprocated, but how can you really list it all? – the endless tissue, the walks, the houses, the furniture, the giggles – the whole sharing bit we've had with each other – the only one I've ever really trusted & the only one in my life who's ever shown in every bit of her life, her devotion to me, in complete altruition. Clive told me yesterday that when he and Tom were feeling so depressed, Tom clasped him in his arms and said 'Never mind, whatever happens – at least we have each other . . .' Clive said 'After he said that, I really didn't care . . .' and I thought to myself 'Neither do I . . . about either of you'. Such sentimental twaddle made me irritable.

Wednesday, 11 September
To the Grafton for this radio production. John Simmonds directing. It is called 'A Bannister Called Freda' and again Myles [Rudge] has written a brilliant script and Ted Dicks two marvellous songs. Joan Sims & me playing all the parts & John Moffatt doing the Narrator – superbly. Of course this is a pilot show & we've yet to see if the powers approve it.

Friday, 13 September
The script of *Carry On Camping* arrived & I read it. That's OK. Went along to the Playhouse & had a bit of rehearsing with the team of 'Just A Minute' – chairman: Nicholas Parsons, rest – Clement Freud and Geraldine Jones. It was death & I couldn't get on to it at all. But when we came to the performance I just about managed and scraped through. But Nicholas was a great help and so was Clement Freud. David Hatch (who produces the show) was very nice to me before

(when I was v. nervous) and afterwards. I like him v. much – always have actually.

Played the Brahms violin sonatas and then the *Vier Ernste Gesänge* sung by Hermann Prey[14] and then the Mendelssohn Piano Trios. When the Prey songs were being sung, I found myself clasping my hands in complete ecstasy. It is this personal affirmation of faith by man which transports, moves and makes me better: always I come back with repentance and rue to the 'divinity which shapes our ends' – I'll never be able to enter into organised religion & churches seem to me an anachronism but when Faith is manifest in Art, or in the superb individual, that is when I come to God.

Monday, 16 September

Got a Penguin of Longer Poems, including Auden's Letter to Lord Byron. It is fascinating writing, and one is suddenly aware of the 'professional' having to do the odd stanza rather badly etc. – it is the *whole* in art that always matters. It's like the odd line in Shakespeare like – 'I go my Lord and doubt not so to do.' Which you *know* isn't very good, but it is *sayable* and it gets you off the stage, if done with a flourish.

Wednesday, 18 September

The lovely GPO have changed me number. I am WEL[beck] 8803 from now on and precious few people are going to know that. I told Louie, George [Borwick], Peter E., Rona, Nora, Stanley B. That's all, at the moment.

Sunday, 22 September

Went to Wembley for the Frost Show. I was landed with Laurence Harvey! He moved, behaved and looked like a raddled old queen. He camped it up, he told bad taste jokes and endless anecdotes with no point at all . . . He brought a great retinue to the studios with him – a young queer boy, and John Ireland and some bird to make it look good, but it didn't kid me brother! I mean Sister.

Monday, 23 September

In Crawford St a motor car stopped and a man called Justin introduced himself & asked me to go and have tea with Twiggy[15] at Holland Park on Wednesday. I agreed.

---

14 Op.121 by Brahms. Recorded by Prey in 1958 with Martin Mälzer (piano).
15 Lesley Hornby, b.1949. Model and actress.

Wednesday, 25 September
At 4 o'c. Frank (the chauffeur) picked me up and drove me to Holland Park where I had tea with Twiggy and Justin de Villeneuve ('my real name was Nigel Davis'). They have a flat right at the top of one of those rambling Victorian monstrosities, full of gimmicks & toys and photographs of the 20's. Twiggy is delightfully unaffected and Justin v. charming indeed. They were really v. kind, childlike & direct. She models & designs dresses & talks like a cockney factory hand, & he is rather Italian-looking with long Florentine hair, and he twitches the eyes & nostrils a lot nervously, is a photographer, and promotes her ideas & manufactures clothing under her name. They have an enormous Rolls-Royce, talk in terms of thousands of pounds, & live in circumstances & surroundings one would associate with the average young actor, all a bit 'home made' – very curious. The conversation was themselves, newspapers, television, & pop stars & pop music. Very lowering indeed.

Sunday, 29 September
To the Playhouse to do 2 'Just A Minute' shows. I chaired the first one and was on the panel in the next. These two were both v. good, and we were all on form & the audience was absolutely splendid.

Tuesday, 1 October
Today I got Melvyn Bragg's[16] novel *The Second Inheritance* and I haven't been so impressed by good writing for years and years. It is a marvellous story and one with great humour, authenticity and feeling. What a lovely mind this Bragg must have. The Ackerley book[17] showed me the futility of waiting for ideal love – life is not about that, and now this marvellous Bragg novel shows the real warmth and satisfaction and love in domestic life – again and again in the cycle of nature, the purpose is shown to one. *Why* oh! *why* did I keep on and on *postponing* experiences until it was too late to have them? I'm like someone who *wanted* – indeed *ached* to swim, but never dared put my foot in the water. Just sat and watched others doing it, till eventually the very idea of the water is alien and frightening. I am the living proof of the futility of *thought* without *action*.

Monday, 7 October
First day of *Carry On Camping* at Pinewood. Most of the action is outside & they have turned the orchard into a Camping site. My

---

[16] b.1939. Writer, TV presenter, head of Arts, London Weekend Television etc.
[17] *My Father and Myself*, autobiography by J.R. Ackerley, 1968.

stand-in is Micky Clark who I really like. He is great, and calls the Bingo Sessions on the Granada circuit and comes from Feltham. Married with kids and everything, but v. boyish and lots of intelligence & charm.

Tuesday, 8 October
Gerald said to me today 'I notice your jaw is receding and it is probably due to tooth decay & gum recession – yes – you'll soon have to wear a pad or something there 'cos it's very age-making on the screen . . .' This is part of Gerald's tack. He told me in *Sergeant* that I'd go bald in a couple of years!

Saturday, 12 October
I read the Melvyn Bragg novel *For Want of a Nail*. This was marred for me by the interior monologue which runs thro' at the same time as the story narration & at times it's difficult to know whether you're reading about a happening or something which is imaginary. V. annoying: but it is the great humanity of the man that is so marvellous – one adores him, and his bigness of spirit.

Sunday, 13 October
Listened on the 3rd Programme to F.R. Leavis, talking on the poetry of T.S. Eliot.[18] It was fascinating and profound. His diction wasn't v. good and the accent was quite extraordinary: ugly at times, but the shining & beautifully illuminating burden of his talk redeemed the whole. It *can't* be an accident that I listened in tonight. That I fasted today. That all I know about value judgments teaches me to reject what modern society offers me.

Monday, 21 October
I hate not waking naturally, but having to get up when the alarm clock rings. How I long for the day when it all stops, and when the whole idea of having to work for a living has ended for me. Ironically, I expect that by the time it happens, I shall be dead anyway.

Tuesday, 22 October
Pinewood, still out in the orchard. I particularly noticed one of the property men today, and I said to Andy (i/c props) 'Who is that tall boy in the jeans & white shirt, with the fair hair?' and he told me he was called Alf. Andy obviously mentioned my interest, because in a few minutes, Alf came over & said to me 'I think you're going to be

[18] F.R. Leavis (1895–1978), Cambridge critic and lecturer. 'T.S. Eliot and the Life of English Literature' was a public lecture given at Cheltenham.

a fan of mine.' I was amazed by such outspokenness & said 'You've got quite a few on the unit already – Charlie Hawtrey buys you bars of chocolate . . . he'll make a pass at you, before long . . .' He smiled and said 'It wouldn't worry me.' I was sitting next to Barbara Windsor who said after 'I might have been a blade of bleeding grass for all the notice he took of me . . .' He went on to tell me he was unmarried, and he was 27, and lived with his parents & brothers & sisters, in Cowley – local. All the time he was talking to me I felt a physical excitement that really made my heart pound.

Thursday, 24 October

Gerald took me aside and said we'd been friends long enough for him to talk frankly about my work, and that I had been bad in the scene because I had been mugging & pulling faces and lost the 'character' of the Headmaster & that the scene had lacked credibility because of this. Peter Rogers said 'It was like watching Kenneth Williams doing himself on television, instead of playing a character . . .' Of course by this time the ego was on the ground and covered in mud. I said things like 'Well of course I see your point & an actor can't be objective about his own work' etc. etc., but inside I was dying. The essence of being funny is confidence & buoyancy, and the pair of them certainly destroyed both qualities in me, for the day. The fact is, the role as written is totally without credibility and so of course one falls back on personality playing & all one's old tricks.

Wednesday, 30 October

At one point I said to Gerald 'You can leave me out of the next film you make' and he said 'In the next one you are playing a coloured witch doctor' and I replied 'Don't bother to ask me' and Barbara cried out 'I'll do it Gerald' which was quite funny.

Tuesday, 5 November

It was freezing cold in the orchard & the mud is thicker than ever! I forgot I was wearing a throat mike & said dreadful things to Barbara Windsor – 'Get out of it you dirty little whore' etc. and she said 'Oh! it's dreadful, we've been treated like shit here this morning . . .' and they got it all on tape and Gerald heard everything! Barbara was terribly embarrassed! Gerald said to me after this incident 'Barbara really meant what she said on that sound track you know, and that is where she is different from you. You often say you've been treated like a load of rubbish, but it's always in fun and gets a laugh on the set, but she really meant it . . .' It is interesting that this is all taken with that degree of seriousness.

Thursday, 7 November
Regarding that Alf Props, I have certainly gone off him! It seems extraordinary now that I should ever have been bothered by him. He is an ignorant lout and that's all there is to it. I told him I no longer admire him, I said 'I used to think you were a great dish & get an erection when I was near you, but now it has all died completely.' He looked surprised & embarrassed, poor sod. Good job it was only a mental affair.

Saturday, 9 November
[Enclosure: cutting of a photograph from The Times *of same date, captioned 'The Prince of Wales dressed for the part of a padre in Joe Orton's play ''Erpingham Camp'', which will have its final performance tomorrow by the Dryden Society of Trinity College, Cambridge.']*

Had to cut this out and keep it – it really is the most ironic thing I've ever seen in a newspaper. A prince of the realm playing the part of a priest in a play by Joe! If only he were alive to appreciate the mad joke of it all. Joe never stopped attacking the formal virtue which is the very thing for which the monarchy stands! Quite apart from the fact that he sends up religion cruelly, and the Prince couldn't be there without religion and the organised church.

Saturday, 16 November
To the Lime Grove studios at 4. Eventually we went on (Barbara & I) at 6.30 with [Simon] Dee saying 'Welcome to Kenneth Windsor & Barbara Williams . . .' and other daft, lame cracks. He is a fool of an interviewer and again he left a gigantic pause! which I commented on. I mouthed vacuous 'nothings' and the whole thing died the death. At the end, Rita Webb ('Oh! I wish I had nice legs, because mine are fucking awful') appeared, coming out of a huge birthday cake because it was the 100th Simon Dee Show.

Sunday, 17 November
Rang B. and he asked me over. He also had a guest called Leslie someone. He later revealed that he'd a cancer condition of the anus & that he was being treated by a German surgeon in Munich. One suddenly realised how *little* one really *cared* about suffering & distress: and in a way, that is *healthy* and proper. There is no point in caring if you're incapable of help, and I am, in this context. He also said he liked people to be sincere & added 'A lot of actors are insincere . . .' & I really went for him there: the actor's need of facade etc. & how sincerity was no virtue anyway. Hitler was probably sincere. I said a concern for the truth was infinitely preferable to sincerity.

Saturday, 23 November
The boys took me to B's party at 8 o'c. It was *death*. All old queens and mothers and Sally G. – this must be the ogre of all time. She said to Clive 'I want a man.' 'I'm sorry I can't help you.' 'Well give me threepence ha'penny – that's the price of a fag.'

Monday, 2 December
At 11.30 to the photographer David Bailey at Gloucester Ave. He just chatted to me and took photographs and I was away by 12 o'c. He's a young fellow – only about 25 and v. mod and with it. He made me laugh when he said 'You can't be a royal photographer if you've been divorced' & I said 'Have you?' and he said 'Oh! yes – three or four times . . .' At 3 o'c. to the photographer Godfrey Argent at Queen's Gate and I liked him v. much – he's ex-Corporal of the Horse in the Lifeguards.

Tuesday, 3 December
To the Centre. Worked with dear old John L. on the script of the 'Kenneth Williams Spectacular' – it's just 15 minutes of me. Nothing else. 1 camera. Finish. Terribly funny. At lunch we were joined by Stanley B. and the lovely Terry Hughes. We all chatted merrily & at one point I turned to John & said 'But I don't want to bore you with my homosexual reminiscences' and he said 'Why make an exception of today?' Everyone laughed.

Sunday, 8 December
During my visit to T & C they played the LP of the revue *One Over The Eight*: it was incredible to hear those dreadful sketches all over again, and the absorption I had with daft baby voices and silly pronunciation. O! dear. And not a tag line anywhere in sight. Poor Sheila and I, struggling with material which just didn't exist. Toni Eden's songs all sounded marvellous. That girl could certainly sing! and ironically, she hasn't been heard of since.

Wednesday, 11 December
I have been asked again and again (by people in the street even!) why I'm not doing 'International Cabaret' again! And there's even been stuff in the papers about it. When the new edition came out, The Stage said how much it missed 'our Kenny'. What a joke it all is, when you consider the filthy notices that greeted me when it started!

Monday, 16 December
Riverside at 10 o'c. – it was pure agony. Reading these children's

stories[19] and trying to characterise loads of characters is like running a marathon: and cards keep appearing saying 'Go faster' etc. I'm dressed in a kaftan of blue silk and gold embroidery – all very lovely, I suppose. The great happening is Jonathan Cohen. He does the music, is over 6 feet, darkly handsome, & 23. With gifted & lovely people like him around, the whole rotten Riverside bit is redeemed.

Thursday, 19 December
My letter to Erich [Heller] has produced results! I had a Christmas card and message from him at the Northwestern University, Evanston, Illinois. I replied today.

Thursday, 26 December
In Portman Square a negro chap came up and asked me for a match because he was anxious to light a boiler. I hadn't a match so I gave him my old Ronson lighter – I've had it for years, since '63 in fact. So I can get a new one with good excuse.

NOTES
This diary began in Tangier, and I visited the place *four* times, during its writing. On all the occasions, I fled to Morocco because of some inner despair. There wasn't one really successful visit, in the sense of spiritual replenishment, but they all worked after a fashion, because new rhythms were created, and this is the essential purpose of life – to keep the rhythm going. The pendulum must swing. It's when the pendulum is motionless or barely moving at all – that is the time of suicidal despair. Above all, I have learned that in my work *I know best* and it's my taste that is truly informing and that it is my personal vision that is worthwhile.

---

[19] *The Land of Green Ginger* by Noel Langley, for the BBC's 'Jackanory'.

1969

Wednesday, 1 January
Bill and Barry came and I gave them dinner at Spot III. We talked about Joe Orton and the Mrs Cawdon vagina saga[1] and the fag packet thrown out of the window at Bury St Edmunds. A thin, elderly spinster handed back a used cigarette packet to a blowsy vulgar woman who'd just thrown it out of the car window, at the traffic lights. Spinster: 'I believe this belongs to you!' Woman: 'I just threw it away – I don't want it.' Spinster: 'And neither does Bury St Edmunds.'

Thursday, 2 January
The morning was brightened by the letter from the marvellous Jonathan Cohen. Even writing his name gives me pleasure. I replied asking what evening he is free and we can have dinner together.

Sunday, 5 January
I reflected how I would like to become a monk. The materialism & alienation in modern society are not for me.

Wednesday, 8 January
I feel curiously content these days – in fact I think I'm very nearly happy. A voice within me cries out warningly 'Watch it! it's going . . .' Read and read the Holroyd book on Strachey.[2] It is full of riches and wonderfully rewarding, sometimes I go back several times over a particularly trenchant passage. O! to have this objective brilliance, yet keep the warmth & humorous irony of it all, as he does. I reflected today that I'm only able to lead this leisured life of reading and writing and listening to my gramophone because of the Carry On films: the banal vulgarity of these pictures provides the wherewithal for me to sit reading my books of poetry and biography & reflecting upon the

---

[1] See entry for 5 April 1966 (p. 276).

[2] Lytton Strachey (1880–1932), biographer and essayist. The biography by Michael Holroyd (b.1935) is a two-part work: *The Unknown Years* (1967) and *The Years of Achievement* (1968).

utterly civilised values. It's irony all right. I wander into the kitchen for a cigarette & drink innumerable cups of coffee, stare out of the window at the Post Office Tower, and like being alone: it's all v. pleasant. I also read *A Woman Of No Importance*,[3] and I think it's very good.

Friday, 10 January

Jonathan Cohen came & I took him to supper at the Garden. It was all very pleasant because he is a charming and talented boy, a delight to be with.

Saturday, 11 January

All this reading has taken me back through the years. It wasn't for nothing that I spent so many years in Bloomsbury. I know all the pavements that Lytton trod, and in Russell Square I always think of T.S.E[liot] and Prufrock. It reminds me too of that period when I was a regular visitor to the Goachers' flat in Museum Street and how Denis used to talk about 'that old queen Angus Wilson[4] mincing in and out of the British Museum' which impressed me enormously, and Harold Lang (whom I met with him) whom I thought so bogus.

Monday, 13 January

Dr C. gave me the ordinary 'flu injection. He said I should find a 'suitable companion' to share my life with, he said 'You don't have to go too far – a little mutual masturbation – that kind of thing, preferably someone older than yourself, someone who can share with you – not someone who's after your money – you will get a lot of pleasure out of it – of course, a little pain too, but it's worth it I can tell you . . .' I walked down Churton St after thinking of likely lovers, but not a *type* entered my head.

It was just gone 7 o'c. this evening when I finished the Holroyd biography of Strachey. I was weeping at the end. I was not crying about the death – not so much – tho' it moved me deeply – as for the inconsolable grief it gave to those around him – the wonderful *steadfastness* of all those friends who just came, and were *near* to someone who was greatly loved by them all. This strange, gentle, unhappy and wonderfully civilised man who was so unable to find complete & shared love, and who was, at the end, surrounded by love. I think there are things in this book which have affected me deeply & I think that Holroyd himself has clarified (what were for me) some strange

---

[3] By Oscar Wilde.

[4] Sir Angus Wilson (1913–91), novelist, biographer and short-story writer.

inconsistencies & worries in my own life. I think this book will go on affecting me, and will reverberate for the rest of my life.

Thursday, 16 January

I had a look at the money situation today. A rough valuation of the investments now totals about twenty thousand pounds, leaving out the question of my 99-year lease of this flat, and Nat. Sav. Certificates and the 2 life policies which mature at about 3,000. I am mindful of my position as head of the family, since Charles's death. I am completely responsible for Louie – at the moment (and for the last 5 years) I maintain her at £20 per week, but I may have to reconsider this sum v. shortly, and I have part responsibility for Pat. I consider therefore that I am properly discharging my duties in the family.

Friday, 17 January

We did the two shows[5] and I behaved disgracefully, shouting and bawling and taking my shoes off and lifting up my trousers to show my legs etc. Nothing to do with sound radio. At one point my hypocrisy rose to gargantuan levels & I cried out to Nicholas Parsons 'Oh! you are a *lovely* chairman!' and the entire house clapped. Rushed out of the side entrance after and into the car, refusing to sign autographs for girls all standing in the rain.

Saturday, 18 January

Before I retired, I read the '64 diary and was surprised at the amount of depression and despair in it. I don't think I'm like that any more. Found myself asking 'Why?' – perhaps it's because I now steer clear of friendship with the depressives. There's no question – they do lower me. But in the last analysis, it always comes back to thanking God.

Sunday, 19 January

Between the two shows, I cracked the joke about the dentist – 'not the drill, anything but the drill!' – and it got a colossal laugh! and a clap. So that was no audience for the sort of fantasy script we wrote! They both ran 20 mins. (both written for 15 mins.) and Bill C[otton] wants it kept down to 15, he said 'I think that 20 minutes is really pushing your luck . . . people sitting looking at one set and one face for *all that time* . . .' He talked as if it were a party political broadcast. His parting words were 'Well if it doesn't get on the air, it won't be because of me . . .'[6]

---

[5] 'Just a Minute'.

[6] 'The Kenneth Williams Spectacular'. The eventual fate of these solo pilot shows was implicit in Cotton's words. He suggested a series of six revue-format shows instead.

Tuesday, 21 January
It is extraordinary, the effect of *time* on the mind: yesterday I was really concerned apropos the acceptance or rejection of the pilot shows. Today, I couldn't care less: I'm glad now that I've arranged to go on holiday with Louie. I can forget the whole broiling for a bit. Walked in the park till 1.30. Had the elated feeling and rapture of being near to God and the creative centre of things: said the Lord's prayer to myself & felt it *meant* something.

Tuesday, 28 January
Arrived Liverpool at 2.10. A coach took us to the *Monte Anaga*. There's no question but the passengers on this ship are a dreadful lot. They look like a crowd of mental defectives being given a holiday and the white coated stewards could all double as male nurses. I'm becoming increasingly aware of the confined nature of this boat – she is a cargo carrier of 10,000 tons, and I imagine the arse will be dropping off with boredom by the time we reach Las Palmas.

Thursday, 30 January
We were up to the sweet at lunch when the ship shuddered with an impact and the captain rushed from his table in the dining room and shot up to the bridge. A lot of passengers went running up to the deck, and practically emptied the room. I stayed for the coffee. Later it transpired that we'd hit a fishing boat amidships, cutting it in half & sinking it. We lowered a lifeboat and circled for survivors, and picked up four. There was one dead, and a further four missing. Another fishing boat hove to, and the crew shouted obscenities at our ship. Now, with the survivors on board, we have turned round and are making for Corunna, which is where the fishermen hail from. Obviously this will wreak havoc with our holiday plans. This fellow Bill on board organised a fund for the survivors of the disaster with the help of a priest and between 65 passengers we raised a measly 23 pounds which was quite shame making. The radio officer said that you couldn't see the bows of the ship because we were sailing into the sun & it was blinding.

Friday, 31 January
Joined Marjorie and Dick for Scrabble. It was one of those lousy games that never really got off the ground and I argued with Dick about rules. He said if one player goes out, the game is finished, but I pointed out Rule 9 which states that play continues until all *possible plays* have been carried out. He was very shirty about it all and made pitiful remarks to his wife like 'Well that's the way we've always played it

before, though of course we've never played it with great Shakespearean minds . . .'

Tuesday, 4 February. Hotel Metropole, Las Palmas
We were writing postcards in the lounge when a dreadful woman smelling of drink & accompanied by a huge cretin suddenly barged in on us with all that 'Am I boring you?' stuff. After about 10 minutes of her rudeness – 'Anyone could do your job ducky – Danny La Rue is better than you' & her shouting to waiters 'He's a film star he is!' I got up & politely but firmly said goodbye.

Thursday, 6 February
So far it's turning out all right really. I'm better with families than all these queens.

Sunday, 9 February
We sailed into the dining room at 8.45 and our table had been taken. Louie was furious and had a great scene with the Head Waiter so he ordered a bottle of champagne for the table. Though well meant, the gesture couldn't have been worse. The food was all lousy, so the drink was even more potent and we'd already been drinking a white wine and then we started giggling and behaving appallingly in the dining room, going from table to table and Louie crying out 'Bugger this hotel – it's a disgrace!'

Thursday, 13 February. Aboard the Monte Umbe
This ship is still rolling a lot, and the wind is howling through the rigging and the waves are crashing high and huge spray rising on the crests. Sat on the promenade deck with the Crossleys during the morning, till 11.30 when Fred gave us all champagne in the Robles Lounge, then went down to lunch. Roast lamb – v. good and returned to cabin to pen this. The roll of the ship getting steadily worse, and the whole structure shuddering as her propeller comes out of the water with the rise of the stern on each pitch & toss: loads of them are confined to the cabins with mal de mer. After lunch, sat on the promenade deck in a deck chair, with my overcoat, cap, gloves and sunglasses on, and went to sleep for an hour. They are showing *Carry On Doctor* in the ship's cinema today at 5 o'c. They had it coming out as well! I'm staying in the cabin. See enough of my face in the mirror every day.

Saturday, 15 February
Somebody said they'd picked up the BBC on radio & that Kenneth Horne had died. I felt quite stunned when the news hit me. I loved

that man. His unselfish nature, his kindness, tolerance and gentleness were an example to everyone. God knows what will happen to the series now.[7]

Monday, 17 February. London

Forces Network, recorded a brief tribute to Kenneth Horne for the troops in Germany which will go out from Cologne tomorrow. I steered clear of the hushed & eulogistic tones. Producer was Bryan Bass: he was v. tactful & kind to me, but I was trembling – not 'cos of nerves – but 'cos suddenly the grief of it hit me.

Thursday, 20 February

I had a dream last night that I was in bed making love to this Lothario – a foreman like 40ish working class – even in the dream I was rejected. I wonder how much significance dreams have?

Monday, 24 February

Meeting with Took, Cooke & Mortimer and Paddick, Sims & me to discuss the new show. The format will be revue, roughly same as before, and the tentative title is to be 'It's Bold' which sounds all right to me.[8] To the TV Centre for 2 editions of 'Call My Bluff'. That Wendy Craig was on the opp. team. At one point I said 'I don't believe your definition dear, because you were far too actressy . . .' & she said 'Well you should know honey!' and the audience fell about & I was left with egg on me face all right.

Wednesday, 26 February

Nicholas arrived! at 10 o'c. We went to the Steak Ho. in Baker Street for supper and a talk. He came back to Farley after and left at about 12.45. All follows the usual pattern of my life and we shall develop into friends. 'I shall sit here serving tea to . . .'[9] We lay on the bed, fully clothed. There was intermittent kissing, but mostly talking. I'm afraid it doesn't work. It has become much colder and I put an extra blanket on the bed tonight.

Thursday, 27 February

I must learn from this. I must stop all this Mister Right crap and involving other people in my fantasies. It isn't fair to them & only

---

[7] A letter from Kenneth Horne was awaiting KW on his return. He kept it in the diary.

[8] What emerged instead was 'Stop Messing About', written not by Brian Cooke and Johnnie Mortimer (d.1992) but by Myles Rudge.

[9] 'I shall sit here, serving tea to friends . . .' From 'Portrait of a Lady', poem by T.S. Eliot.

succeeds in vexation ultimately. The parties are to be avoided. And the drinks.

Friday, 28 February
To the film *Prime of Miss Jean Brodie* – Maggie was *astounding* – at one point I actually almost got up out of my seat! What a performance! One could go on and on about it & never find adequate words for it.

Saturday, 1 March
Letter from Nicholas about meeting tonight. I telephoned him & said it's best that we don't meet again. He sounded rather bewildered but accepted it all, dazedly.

Wednesday, 5 March
Sent wire to Stanley at the Queen's Theatre for his opening night in *What The Butler Saw* and said 'Big success for you tonight is fervent wish of Fred Bummel & all the boys at the Fleet Club Wanchai, Edna Welthorpe fun with a Frankfurter and No Need for Filth Kenneth Williams'.

Thursday, 6 March
The only personal mention for S. is in the Telegraph which praises his farce timing – but the play gets knocked by everyone. Apparently the Gallery started *booing*! Oh! I just felt 'Thank goodness I'm *out* of it all!'

Monday, 17 March
The hair looked terrible, so I had to wash it this morning, for the radio show which starts today at the Paris. It's called 'Stop Messing About' – I do hope it goes well, 'cos we've got a lot to outlive. Later: it didn't. It was mediocre and played to a half empty house. I suppose a lot could be due to the start of a new series – it takes some time for the timing to get run-in, and for the audience to be cultivated, but nonetheless it was a great disappointment. I think everyone felt this. Joan [Sims] said 'Let's face it dear, our careers are in the ash can . . .'

Wednesday, 19 March
Pinewood at 8. Sometimes on this picture,[10] just before a 'take', I've suddenly had the feeling 'What on earth am I doing?' and it's almost unnerving. I realise that you get nerves from *realising the importance* of what you're doing. I'm all right when I have the jokes – then just go on and *do* it – without self-consciousness.

---

[10] *Carry On Again Doctor.*

Sunday, 23 March
To Gordon & Rona at 7 o'c. I made a stupid lot of remarks to Gordon about how bad the *Hamlet* production at the Roundhouse[11] is (he is Horatio in it) – all without having seen it and said I'd 'heard' about it. It was disgraceful & I regretted it, because it obviously nettled him. Gordon is not enjoying any of it. He said that Nicol Williamson (Hamlet) stopped the performance the other night and said 'I can't go on – I am simply exhausted, and I'm not giving you my best. In fact I'm fucked . . .' and then walked off the stage. Well I don't think that's got much to do with acting. He also said that there's 15 actors to a dressing room and they all sing folk songs with guitars – while the play is on! It sounds more like a madhouse than a roundhouse.

Thursday, 27 March
Lunched alone and that awful Michael Redgrave came over to my table & started talking. He said 'It is ridiculous us sitting facing each other for three days without speaking' and then asked about my picture. I said it was the same story with different costumes and asked him how he was enjoying working with Bette Davis in *Connecting Rooms* and he said 'She is wonderful' which she very obviously isn't. Bette herself avoids lunching with him and was at another table, with the Vicar – that daft blond bloke who is 'Chaplain to the Rank Organisation', and obviously she wasn't enjoying herself, poor bitch.

Friday, 28 March
Picked up Louie and we went to the St George for dinner. I said to Louie 'You know, after a few drinks I feel quite sexy' & she replied 'It was the other way round with your father – after a few drinks with Charlie you knew you were in for a safe night . . .' I said the waiters at the St George were not as good as the Metropole & she said 'No, there they were very grand – you remember that dark one with wavy hair who always showed us to the table?' I said 'Yes – you fancied him a bit, didn't you?' 'Hm. Well he was nice.' 'Yes – everyone is really after a bit – they all want to get stuck-in.' 'Never mind getting it in, it's getting it out that worries me . . .'

Wednesday, 2 April
All the shots were corridor & stairs & reaction scenes. Dreary. Some awful scoutmaster was put through to the set and asked me to meet his scouts and become an honorary member of the group! Of course I refused.

---

[11] Directed by Tony Richardson.

Sunday, 6 April

The boys arrived and we drove to B.'s luncheon party. It was rather splendid. After the lunch – caviare, cold turkey & champagne – B. started putting blankets all over the windows. I enquired the purpose and she cried 'My dear, we're all going to watch a dirty film!' I flew out of the house and got the 30 bus home: not thro' prudishness etc. but because one knows that pornography is basically futile and despairing, and my morale would not take that kind of buffeting.

Saturday, 12 April

I suppose that the Camus definition of moderation being rebellion is really epitomised by me. I realise that the forces of destruction are in oneself & that the task is to control & use them. I think I've learned to exercise control so well that I've almost annihilated the *will to act* : this latter only seems to manifest itself now in drink – when alcohol uninhibits this corseted personality I've created.

Monday, 14 April

To Paris Cinema for 'S[top] M[essing] A[bout]' (4). It went like a *bomb*. I was very pleased with the marvellous reception because at last it is a vindication of all my arguments etc. and it's a *triumph* in the face of the terrible adversity of K[enneth] H[orne]'s death. Standing in that corridor today having coffee – I suddenly felt he was walking in again – I felt him behind me – smiling and genial with that carnation in his lapel . . . but when I turned round, it wasn't him. It was someone quite unlike.[12] I miss him dreadfully. I could weep for all that *goodness* gone from our atmosphere at the show. But I must *keep going* and not let it have the real impact on me.

Tuesday, 15 April. Pinewood

At lunch I had the great shouting match with Joan Sims. Her patronage & assumption at times that she should tell me what to do is intolerable. Hattie intervened & told me to stop it. The Budget News is out. Watched Peter Jay discuss it on television. He is fabulous. Exactly the sort of bloke I adore.[13]

---

[12] According to Horne's biographer Norman Hackforth (in *Solo for Horne*), it was Douglas Smith, the announcer.

[13] The Hon. Peter Jay (b.1937), then Economics Editor of *The Times*. Later British Ambassador to the United States (1977–79), Chief of Staff to Robert Maxwell, and latterly Editor, Economics, Business, News and Current Affairs, BBC TV.

Sunday, 20 April
When I went out to get the papers a lady called Miss Weisz (her brother was 'Vicky' the cartoonist[14]) talked to me about the noise from the fans.

Monday, 21 April
Did 'S.M.A.' at the Paris. Joan S. was v. buoyant and performed quite brilliantly in the show – her characterisations & singing are quite superb. There's no doubt, she's an asset all right. I wasn't v. good – I'm too full of congestion. John Musgrove gave me a prescription for Benylin Expectorant and an antibiotic called Ilosone – both 3 times daily. The girl in front of me collecting a prescription was called Tuesday Weld[15] – can you imagine? What a daft name.

Thursday, 24 April
Peter Rogers started on at me about this Television Carry On series which I don't want to do. He said he would do it anyway, with other people, adding 'Don't worry duckie, I can live without you . . .' which of course is quite true. Peter Rogers said 'We've got to go into television sooner or later, because in a few years, there won't be any more feature films being made for the cinema – it's all steadily dying.' I think he's probably right, but it will take a lot longer than that to die entirely. I think film production will have to adapt itself to a less profitable market, and turn more to television methods. Came away from Pinewood today feeling the chill wind of the 'end of an era' blowing.

Wednesday, 7 May
Lunch with Peter Eade. What do I want to do with myself – what work, apart from Carry Ons? I say I want to do *nothing* but end up agreeing to read some play he's been sent. I can't even write properly. Everything is becoming disintegrated. Only one arm moves when I walk. Returned to the flat at 2 o'c. Went to bed. Woke about 4. Talked to myself. Played ridiculous scenes about frustration to myself. P.E. rang – would I take part in a TV series where you do the thing that nobody sees you in usually? Like a comic who plays Hamlet etc. etc. Highly fucking original. I said to *stick it*.

Monday, 12 May
'S.M.A.' John Simmonds said 'Our audience is changing – there are more youngsters than before – I'm afraid it's developing into a

---

[14] Victor Weisz (1913–67), and Elisabeth Weisz, b.1910.
[15] Susan Ker Weld (b.1943), film actress. Married Dudley Moore in 1975.

Kenneth Williams Cult Show and that isn't what I wanted . . .' It's incredible that people can stand and insult you, to your face, with no kind of embarrassment or guilt. What the hell does John Simmonds *expect* of a radio show that puts my name at the top of the bill & bears a title which is a catchphrase I've used ever since Galton & Simpson wrote it for me twelve years ago?

Tuesday, 13 May
Steak House with T & C and John H. and afterwards we all came back to Farley. We all ended up talking about the political situation. Clive recommending a Fascist takeover to pull the country out of the mire, and me raving hysterically about the futility of a mixed economy. They all left & I did the clearing up etc. and had the wank & got off to sleep about 1 o'c.

Saturday, 17 May
I see that old idiot Adrian Boult[16] had the double hernia operation, and that ghastly old man Lewis Casson is dead: let's hope his wife takes the hint too – dreadful pair of charlatans! It is certainly proving a good year for deaths. They're dropping like flies in insecticide.

Monday, 19 May
Peter E. rang. He had Eric Portman ill at his flat and it's quite a lot to cope with. I told him I wasn't going away over Whitsun for lack of a travelling companion. But I told him I'd fixed to go July 3rd–17th with T & C. I am really rather apprehensive of going on this 'package' holiday. I think I was a little bit *mad* when I made the arrangements.

Wednesday, 21 May
To Cinecenta to see *The Sergeant* – a tale of an Army sergeant who falls in love with a soldier, gets rebuffed and shoots himself. It had the effect of sending my spirits to zero. One was back in the world of 20 years ago – all *The City and the Pillar* stuff. All black and white. Normals shown hand-in-hand walking through forests, and sunlight thro' the leaves, or having cosy family dinners with laughing happy children, and the queer sergeant lonely, pot bellied and drinking himself into a stupor. Another load of muck to sit through.

Thursday, 22 May
There was a letter today from Bill Cotton about me doing 'something in the nature of a sketch show' in the autumn. I replied saying I was too piqued about the pilot shows which *they turned down*.

---

16 Sir Adrian Boult (1889–1983), orchestral conductor.

Friday, 30 May

Gordon rang and asked me up there this evening, so I went to Clare's shop and got chocolates for Rona. The woman in the shop told me that Vicky – the cartoonist – brother of Elisabeth Weisz who lives in my block here, actually committed suicide.[17] I didn't know that.

Monday, 2 June

Bill Cotton, John Law. We talked about the format for the 'Kenneth Williams Show' and agreed on a lay-out. I shall have to safeguard myself in this series by saying, from the beginning, that I must have a large say in acting direction & the artists must agree beforehand or I'm not working with them. I told Peter E. that I would not do the next Carry On if the script did not appeal to me.

Wednesday, 4 June

Peter E. rang to say they want me on the Simon Dee show. I said no. I can't stand the idiot.

Tuesday, 10 June

Dinner at Spot III. I got quite high. I should have gone home *then* if I'd had any sense, but no! I suggested going on to the Spartan for a drink and H. said 'Let's go instead to Tattersall's, and if that's dreary, we can go *on* to the Spartan.' So to Knightsbridge we went and there we were joined by two boys from the Horseguards and one thing led to another and these two – Mick and Jeffrey, came back to Farley! Me trying the philately with M. & no go – 'I've had too much to drink' etc. etc. and then we talk & talk till 3 in the morning when that old Irish night porter found them a taxi. I dreared about the flat after, clearing up the mess and feeling unclean. I gave Jeffrey the radio because he said he liked it and didn't possess one. I don't think I shall replace it. I went to bed at 4 o'c. with the room growing lighter.

Wednesday, 11 June

Woke about 6 o'c. with guilt heavy upon me. I think I should see a psychiatrist. Letter with appalling news! They made a mistake with the figures for year ending April '68!! and I've got to find about £500 *back tax*!! Woke with those dreadful palpitations banging in my ears. Noticed during shaving that the skin is peeling. Overhead the *fans* are *thumping again* – and I wish I was dead. I would like to walk out of this existence for *ever*. All I could think of in the bathroom was the line 'to cease upon the midnight with no pain . . .' I walked all thro' Hyde Park, with the same line running through my head – 'to cease

---

[17] Found dead 23 February 1967.

upon the midnight with no pain . . .'[18] The suicidal feeling mounted and mounted all the way: at Hyde Park Corner I got the bus back and just went to bed and gave up. Peter Eade telephoned. We had a row about the Comedy Playhouse fee. They're offering 600 & I think it is too much.

Thursday, 12 June
I went to Electrical Services in Marylebone Rd. and got a VHF radio for £19.11.9. It is much better reception.

Saturday, 14 June
David Frost's house for a talk about what we're to do on the show with Frankie Howerd. Talked with Neil Shand[19] & Frankie Howerd and the producer suddenly said everyone should go into the street to see the Concorde fly overhead so they all trooped out and watched this earth-shattering event. I sat alone, smoking & drinking Krug champagne on a v. empty stomach. Eventually Frost returned & he and Frank decided they should talk alone, so I went out of the room and talked to Neil. Eventually I went home terribly pissed. On the doorstep David Frost looking at me and Frankie H. said 'Many people would say – there stands English Comedy.' I thought to myself 'Then many people would be lacking in perception' but shouted drunken goodbyes and reeled down the street into a taxi. Joined Frank and David in front of the cameras at about 7.30, mouthed a lot of innocuous rubbish and then went with Peter E. to the Garden for dinner.

Sunday, 15 June
That Beatle who is married to an Asiatic lady was on the Frost Programme. The man is long haired & unprepossessing, with tin spectacles and this curious nasal Liverpudlian delivery: the appearance is either grotesque or quaint & the overall impression is one of great foolishness. He and his wife are often 'interviewed' from inside *bags* in order to achieve 'objectivity' and they have 'lie-ins' whereby they stay in bed for long periods & allow a certain number of people into the room. I think this man's name is Ringo Star or something [No – it's John Lennon][20] but he began as a 'singer' and instrumentalist with this group called The Beatles and one searches in vain for any valid reason for his being interviewed *at all*. What this ex-pop-singer is

---

[18] 'Now more than ever seems it rich to die,/To cease upon the midnight with no pain': Keats, 'Ode to a Nightingale'.
[19] Scriptwriter.
[20] KW's annotation.

doing pontificating about the state of humanity, I cannot imagine. It's mind-bending to listen to.

Wednesday, 18 June

Tom and Clive came at 5.50 and we went to see *Ring of Bright Water* which was about as bad as you can get in movies. Even the otter was amateur. On our way to the cinema we met a soldier on leave from Farnborough who said 'I'm looking for a bird' & I cautioned him against venereal disease & said 'You'd be better off having the wank . . .' He reacted nervously and fled in the direction of Tottenham Ct. Road.

Sunday, 22 June

Clive came at 12 o'c. and took me to Dale Lodge – drinks & chat & then lunch. After, we sat till 3.30 talking about Singapore and all the ridiculous camp of those days. Then we all went to Epping Forest and joined hands round a rotted stump and chanted 'Fairy, Fairy of the Glade, Send us all a bit of trade . . .' till some bypassers came along & we were silenced. Then we all lay on the ground on a travelling rug which C. got from the car. I recited bits from songs of yesteryear – 'It happened up Monte Rey, a long time ago . . .' etc.[21] Clive has given me the two Greek busts I wanted of Hermes: they're really *lovely*.

Monday, 23 June

Another lousy night – nothing helped by the news this morning of the death of Judy Garland, that talented and brilliant shooting star who was so full of anguish and despair underneath all the showbiz glam. facade.

Wednesday, 25 June

Went to the Charantelle restaurant. There was a dreadful scene at a nearby table made by a v. common queen who shouted at her companion 'You dirty liar – don't try to be funny with me – I made you what you are & I can *beat* you at it!' When the other one left, she screamed after him 'You take the dog with you . . . do you hear?' and then she said to me 'You look worse *off* than you do *on* – thank you for a great disappointment . . .' She was really quite hilarious.

Thursday, 26 June

I seem to be full of negative resolutions these days! A letter to Gerald

---

[21] Monte Rey: stage name of James Montgomery Fyfe (1900–82), dance-band era singer. 'It Happened in Monterey', 1930 pop song (Wayne, Rose).

Thomas saying I'm not keen on being in the next film, and another to Michael Mills saying I don't want to do his television production.

Tuesday, 1 July

Got reply from Gerald Thomas. No concession whatsoever and sentiments maintaining I am no different to any other main member of the cast. If I am no different than he certainly won't miss me not being in the next one.

Monday, 7 July

Gerald came to the flat at 12.15 and we had a talk. He said he was sorry if I felt I'd been treated badly on *Camping* and that he would try to see that it did not happen again. That is good enough for me. I have found myself very rhapsodic today – singing hymns and intoning great romantic themes and crying out passionately to myself and thinking it isn't dead yet. There is *still a chance*, a chance to show some really spiritual and selfless love – the love that lies thigh to thigh and toe to toe with the leper – I must find the courage.

My heart is too full tonight. Too full for containment and I fear I shall spill over well past my bed time. I am full of the feeling of nearness to God. That means I have to define what I mean by God. For me God means Truth and Goodness and Beauty. This is manifested by man, to man. I have learned these things from man. So I know the truth about the need to communicate and that in certain essential senses we are indeed bound up & involved with each other, but that there are certain areas where we must have solitude in order to have His company in our hearts. And that is the God I worship. It's not a mythical deity, it's Truth & Goodness & Beauty in Men. I do find it in them. Every time I find it I am transformed, uplifted & ennobled by the discovery. It has, for me, no element of the dark or the deathly – it's all to do with light and airiness – lyrical & laudable. The whole mess that is existence and mundane things is shot through and transformed by human love & understanding. This is what Jesus meant about redemption. It is the *only* way . . . one real act of *love* . . . please let me be capable of it. Just one chance and don't let me be a moral coward or a physical one and tonight I am *full* of joy. This hasn't to do with emotional silliness & flights of fancy. It is the result of mental discipline. On any civilised level, there will always be the task of weeding, cleaning, irrigating etc. As Eliot says – we must be for ever rebuilding the temple. I think what I've really learned tonight is that one must be seen to be rebuilding it. That's something I've been successfully avoiding for *years* – 7th July/midnight.

Thursday, 10 July
Wrote a long air letter to the boys 'cos I had to say thank you for their two marvellous missives that I've just received. Those two letters mean a great deal to me at this particular moment. I sympathised with their holiday condition – 'cos they make Pesaro sound perfectly awful.

Wednesday, 16 July
To Centre at 10.15. Worked with J.L. on the script – we did about 2 pages. Every now & again (it's becoming more & more frequent lately) John Law decides to dig in his heels, and become aggressively dictatorial. When I said 'But surely you can't make probability a criteria [*sic*] in this kind of comedy – you don't think *that*, do you?' and he shouts 'I don't *think* – I *know*!!' He likes to imply that we occupy separate worlds. His, the realm of the professional writer, with its own inalienable laws – Mine, the world of the actor, a world of chance in technique etc. I'm a temporary dilettante on his territory with no *real qualifications* etc. etc. Whereas in fact Law's literary ability is nil. He has no originality – he's got the journalist's *hack* ability and a lot of TV knowledge. He's never had a solo comedy-writing success ever: either in the aesthetic or the commercial sense. Poor sod. I feel v. sorry for him. He's past it now.

Thursday, 17 July
I sometimes wonder where I learned all the rubbishy 'beliefs' I used to hold. This stuff about 'I don't *like* people.' It's not true. I actually get enormous pleasure out of them, obviously from communication but also from just observing. And the other one, 'I'm not a star – I'm essentially a member of the team', that's a load of rubbish. It's been a way of avoiding responsibility of leadership in my work for *years*. Again and again you see that the only way to execute & convey *your* vision, you have to sit down and *do it yourself*. There is no other way.

Friday, 18 July
I'm utterly sick of the moon. The papers never stop giving it headlines, but nobody mentions it in conversation: on the rare occasions it has come up, people pronounce their indifference. Bertrand Russell said last week that the attempt to put a man on the moon was an act of 'impiety'.

Saturday, 19 July
As the bum has been so curious – all this tingling etc., and unlike past symptoms, I tried something new this morning & put that Johnson's Foot Powder up there. I'll just see how that affects it.

Monday, 21 July

The papers are carrying headlines about the moon landing. They've succeeded in getting the men on to it. One of the astronauts said it's 'a leap for all mankind.'[22] Whatever that may mean. Tom came at 5.30 and we had the casserole and fresh gooseberries.

Tuesday, 22 July

I noticed J.L. was shaking a lot – the hands are quite unsteady. I wonder what is wrong with him?

Sunday, 10 August

We drove thro' lovely by-roads to Danehill & found P. Butterworth sitting in the garden and he gave us all a lovely welcome and cups of tea. We all sat in the afternoon sunlight and Tyler & Emma came and chatted. Driving back thro' the country side with the air full of the smell of new mown hay and the sun like a great red ball of fire going down thro' the trees and winking thro' the hedgerows – goodness but I owe such a lot to these two! On the way back we stopped at Streatham and Tom got us all Wimpys & we had them in the car, scoffing and sneering at some appalling furniture in a nearby shop window & saying 'Oh! what a lovely wardrobe there! – fancy having that in your actual abode.'

Tuesday, 12 August

I would never go to see a play called *Who's Afraid of Virginia Woolf*[23] – the title itself smells of the meretricious, and neither would I go to see *Boys in the Band*,[24] which simply mirrors a bogus world of homosexual 'parties', it is the same as 'drag' which has always been distasteful to me: I think people who enjoy all these things are really unhealthy, and curiously dirty, in a way.

Saturday, 16 August

There is something so sad in the spectacle of someone trying to give pleasure to others and not succeeding. Ironically, there are those who by deliberately choosing to please themselves, give a lot of pleasure to others.

Monday, 18 August

In the Post Office at 10.45 a woman said 'I have seen you on television

---

[22] Neil Armstrong, Commander of Apollo 11, evidently intended to say: 'That's one small step for a man, one giant leap for mankind,' though the utterance came out slightly garbled in the excitement of the moment.

[23] By Edward Albee (1962).

[24] By Mart Crowley.

& I didn't think you were so good'. I replied 'When I ask you about your profession you can talk to me about mine, until then, be quiet' and walked out.

Tuesday, 19 August
To BEA & I got on the BE 066 flight to Tangier (via Gib.) tomorrow.

Wednesday, 20 August
Driven to the Rembrandt & ensconced in Room 405 by 6.30 local time. Hamadi greeted me warmly and all the pages and my lovely chamber maid – she is a sweet woman.

Thursday, 21 August
Dinner with Chris & George at Claridge's where the waiter squeezed my cock as he laid the tablecloth and said it was lovely to see me again.

Saturday, 23 August
With J.M. at 8 o'c. to the Nautilus where we had dinner – then to the Lizba where I met a flame of '68 who was a philatelist. Michael B. came over & I mentioned the problem of the accommodation for philately and he said to wait while he fixed something up and he went off. After a time I became utterly sick of the noise & the boys and I walked out and went home to bed, resolving to apologise at a later date. I got off to sleep, woke up, and found myself peeing all over the writing table in the hotel room! Luckily there were newspapers on it, so it was them that became wet.

Sunday, 24 August
When Elizabeth came in, I saw her looking at the writing table & when I got up, I noticed that some of the pee was underneath the glass of the table top! so I had to quickly clean that up. I threw the urine-stained newspaper down the lav. Dickie B. told a marvellous story about Michael D. turning up at a grand house, in drag as Queen Mother, and the butler saying 'Oh no sir – you can't come in – she's here already.' Which is about one of the best stories I've ever heard – certainly the best in Tangier.

Wednesday, 27 August
Traditional night of self regard and got off about 1.15 – awoke about 8.30. A bloke in the Socco asked me 'You want some stuff?' meaning drugs. The impertinence! and me there to buy china! Dined at the Alhambra. Coffee at the Café de Paris. Went to the Piano but left at about 11 o'c. Chris & me went to the Lizba, then to Blow Thro'. Then

I returned to the Lizba and met Jafa & eventually he took me to a sleazy apartment house in the Medina where a Spanish queen with an ill-fitting toupée showed us into a wretched chamber for 15D. & I gave Jafa 20D. He did a bit with the belt but the noise was deafening in the quiet – it was 1.30 by then! so had to desist. There was a considerable amount of amour and he played with his cock in a totally unselfconscious way, but I would permit no ejaculations. He suspected the wig of watching so hung a towel over the door handle. Eventually we left there about 1.45 and returned to the Lizba where he said he'd like my Ronson and I said tomorrow, but I shan't give it. I returned to the Rembrandt at 2.30 & thought 'I'll have another bit of that tomorrow.'

Thursday, 28 August
This time he took me to the Marie and that lame porter showed us into a v. elegant chamber and he lay there smoking & giggling & then produced a packet of marijuana but I declined politely and then without much more ado apart from the hand flag, dressed and left! He asked for the lighter but I had decided he was a greedy bastard and so I never brought it with me. He was furious. A youth in the street said 'Your eyes are narrow – you drink too much' and I said to mind his own business and went off to bed reflecting on the frailty of human nature, and the palpable impudence of Moroccans.

Sunday, 31 August
I came home at 11 o'c. I was lying in bed & felt the irritation in the pubes & thought it was one of those ants. Went to the bathroom & looked and found crabs. Rang F. in panic. He was utterly practical. Meet me in 7 mins. outside the Café de France. I did. He took me to a pharmacy at 11.30 and got me the Benzyl stuff. I could have cried with gratitude. I felt like a pariah. Got home and did it all & felt v. relieved. I actually saw two of the bloody things. Black. Ugh. Made me feel sick. Well I know who's responsible. Jafa is the only thing I've been naked with. There is no other explanation, the dirty little swine.

Monday, 1 September
On washing, I found only one relic. It was dead.

Thursday, 4 September. London
The script came for *Carry On Jungle Boy*. My part has now gone to Frankie Howerd and I'm offered a bit which starts on page 74 (of a 90-page script) and looks like it might have been written for Hawtrey. Right now, I want nothing to do with that set-up *ever* again.

Saturday, 6 September
I was slightly disquieted to find – after going to the loo – that there was a slight spermatozoa discharge! But I quickly washed etc. & it didn't re-occur. Nonetheless it led me to wondering: also, it suddenly hit me! If Jafa was the one with the parasites it is utterly sickening to think I did a bit of the old philately! phew! What disgusting webs we mortals weave.

Tuesday, 30 September
George B. gave me this cutting on Monday,[25] which he cut from a newspaper which is called the International Times and is some sort of weekly broadsheet which is fashionable in the hippie circles. Why my name appears I do not know, since I'm not a contributor to any journal or paper, but I seem to be in very elevated & talented company! And the illustration is very pleasant I suppose. G. says the inference is that all the names on the list are homosexuals. 'Good gracious,' I cried, 'one learns something every day!' and affected indifference, but secretly I thought to myself 'I rather *like* the billing . . .'

Thursday, 2 October
To Peter Eade. Quite a scene there. He said 'You are getting very bitter and people are saying to me "What's wrong with Kenneth?" – you have become a very unhappy person – nothing seems to interest you at all, you don't want to work, you have this phobia about the theatre' – and a lot more in this vein. At 5.40 Tom arrived and we got the taxi up to Dale Lodge. They gave us drinks & canapés and then roast lamb and blackberry pie. Stanley (who arrived at 7.45) said the meat was delicious. At one point when I said to S. 'I sometimes feel I am so useless I just want to die . . .' He said 'Oh well, if you did I should just follow you. I don't think I could go on then . . . I really don't . . .' I was utterly overwhelmed. I could've hugged him.

Monday, 6 October
A woman asked for my autograph in Langham Place; when I shook my head she shouted after me 'You dirty snob.' At Peter's office I recorded nine minutes of talk about Noël Coward and his lyrics and the philosophical implications of his writing. He informed me that the Dublin TV chat show is fixed for the 18th.

---

[25] The unexplained list of well-known people (ranging from Plato to J. Edgar Hoover) appears under a photograph in which two young men, one black, one white, exchange a kiss.

Wednesday, 8 October

Wendy Toye phoned at 4 o'c. to say that John Law has been put into the Intensive Care Section of the Brompton Hospital. She says that his heart actually stopped beating, but responded to massage, and is going again. Wendy said no one is to know this, & she will keep me informed. To Louie in the evening to watch the Sarstedt show (as Bill Cotton requested).[26] I sat on my own 'cos Louie went to her dance club. It was quite eerie sitting there in that flat without her – like a sort of presentiment of her death and me wandering about her empty abode. Everything so clean and neat – it made me want to weep. The Sarstedt show was so appalling I only stayed a minute.

Friday, 10 October

To the Paris Cinema. We had that woman Moira Lister: she decided she was going to be very funny, and when she started losing she began silly challenges on the 'If I can't do it, then neither shall you' basis. When she did it to me, I was furious and showed it and proceeded to use every trick & *won* the game, shouting & bawling and preening myself for all the world as if I *cared* desperately. It was an appalling exhibition. I left the theatre with the heart pounding and a feeling of utter self-loathing & shame. I shouldn't do these games at all.

Saturday, 11 October

I feel like Lytton Strachey today. There is some satisfaction to be got from actually setting things down on paper. (I think what I would really like to do is *write* and live in a cottage in some lonely place.)

Thursday, 16 October

Got the Spectator on the way home and was staggered to find they'd published my letter! Suddenly seeing one's name & address in print is a shock! I got another copy & took out of it the appropriate page, & posted it with a note to Erich, in the Northwestern University at Evanston, Illinois:[27] I think it will interest him to see the way he still influences my thought.

Saturday, 18 October. Dublin

Jeremy [Swan] met me at the airport and we drove to Dublin. To Shelah Richards' house. We sat in an elegant & untidy room and

---

[26] 'Peter Sarstedt: On Cool. The Thoughts and Attitudes of a Contemporary Songwriter' (BBC2).

[27] Where he was now Professor of German. In his letter to the *Spectator*, KW quoted a passage from Heller's *The Disinherited Mind*.

talked and were joined by Siobhan McKenna!! which was lovely. She looked staggeringly well – quite blossoming & lovely and a girl from the press and a photographer (Irish Press) and then I went with Jeremy to the studios. I opened the show with Gay Byrne interviewing me. It didn't go well. The audience was dull and very provincial. I got the laughs but they weren't easy.

Sunday, 19 October
Thought a lot about the trip to Dublin. The atmosphere of *seediness* and decay about the city, and the feeling of utter provinciality combined to make me feel depressed. There is something terribly doomed about the Irish. They've got the poetry – you can hear it in their speech and feel it in their art: but they need the organising genius to prosper. They need the *English*. They need a nation of shopkeepers, mercenary philistines, to counterbalance them: and ironically they reject them (quite reasonably of course judging from the past) but one sees that Wales would go irrevocably to the same kind of arable-ism if she severed her ties with England.

Tuesday, 21 October
Austin Steele on the telephone today. John Law has been unconscious for the last eight days. His position is very precarious. Austin said he would contact me in a couple of weeks and that we could try to knock out the other 2 shows then. I would like to have a go at this because I like him.

Wednesday, 22 October
These last two days (and probably tomorrow will be!) are curiously disjointed. I have not been keeping to my traditional chores & the diary has suffered. It's all been over this daft desire to write letters to the papers and see my name in print & have people think 'There's clever!' I know I'm not lovely, so I'm desperate to be thought clever.

Saturday, 25 October
I had the great self-fulfilment session. The image alternated between J.M. (I was going down to him in a taxi) and a large handsome sailor: then everyone became ambidextrous. None of your passive or active hard and fast lines. Well nothing fast. It was all v. enjoyable on the loo: but after, the insistent ever-returning thought 'You'd never want to see them afterwards – not in real life . . .'

Sunday, 2 November
We all rushed out to see *Daddy's Gone A-Hunting*. I was enormously impressed by a new actor in films called Scott Hylands. He looks like

the David Apollo head and acts with the kind of precision and authority that seems to come from a *powerhouse* of talent. I was spellbound every time he appeared. I've not seen *one* good notice of this film.

Friday, 7 November

Gordon telephoned, said he'd been to see my lovely Scott Hylands in the film and left before the end: he didn't care for it at all. He said 'I can see why you adore him – he looks like you would have looked at that age . . . and he is called Kenneth in the picture . . . subconsciously you were identifying with him throughout . . .' Now this is an interesting idea, but it's not true. It's the Apolline look, esp. of the neck, that is most enchanting about Scott, and certainly I was *never* fortunate enough to have those kind of good looks when I was 25. I must try to get a photograph. T & C gave me dinner. We rushed thro' and they whirled me up to Muswell Hill where we saw *Daddy's Gone A Hunting* for the second time: again I was struck by the superb economy of the direction and again by the utterly captivating quality of Scott Hylands. It is not a sexual reaction, he looks like a statue a lot of the time, it is the utter alchemy of the actor for *me*. I am committed. I can't help myself.

Wednesday, 26 November

A letter from George Rose in New York to whom I wrote desperate for information on Scott Hylands. He actually *knows* him! And was just as impressed by Scott as I was! Says he's very very normal and gave me a Los Angeles address. Wrote straightway.[28]

Thursday, 27 November. Gibraltar

Tried to book on the Tangier plane and we were told that the morning one was fully booked. We ended up with a group of officers from HMS *Blake*. All the time in the bar with the sailors I was shouting 'Of course I'm queer – what d'you think I'm in here for?' and these officers were obviously embarrassed.

Friday, 28 November

Phoned at 9 o'c. by the porter. No plane! Fully booked until Sunday but we could be wait-listed! Instructed him to get us on the first available London plane, rang Tom and told him the worst. Plane took off at 12.10 and we reached London at 3.30 in the morning.

---

[28] Nothing seems to have come of this.

Saturday, 29 November
Complete waste of about seventy-five pounds. Snow blizzard whirling outside.

Thursday, 4 December
Bright spot provided by the Durham University Magazine who have printed my article! It is very gratifying to see it in print.

Sunday, 7 December
Clive drove me to Dale Lodge. In the evening we watched an interview: Noël Coward talked with Patrick Garland. Noël at 70 was immaculate. The old boy had to keep everything going himself. It was disgraceful: but there was one delightful moment when Coward said that in his youth he read a lot: 'I was a regular visitor to the Battersea Public Lavatory – I mean – Library . . . Oh dear! Quite a Freudian slip there, I'm afraid . . .' and a little laugh and then a quick pull on the cigarette which was ever in the right up-poised hand.

Monday, 8 December
I visited Louie at Marlborough Ho. She showed me the Morgan family Bible, in which her father, Henry Morgan, inscribed all the names of his children. It was fascinating: and she showed me her birth certificate issued (in lieu of original) as Work Permit (Factories Act) in 1915! And we looked at the cameo portrait of her mother which she keeps in a brooch. I always call her Louise or Louie, but my mother's name is really Louisa Alexandra![29] Her mother's name was Louisa. Curious they should have chosen the German form instead of the French. Today, two leading actors died – both of whom had been kind to me. Eric Portman, and Hugh Williams.

Wednesday, 10 December
To the Metropole to see *Carry On Again Doctor*. It was very good indeed, and should have got excellent reviews from the press. It moves along at a spanking pace, the cutting is excellent and the situations all hold. My performance as Carver, the surgeon, is remarkably authoritative and the incredibly banal lines which I have to say are made quite acceptable by the sort of style and panache I bring to the role. I was surprised and pleased, save for the fact that the greying hair was quite noticeable at times. Alas! my youth has left me. This should be the last film I do.

---

[29] In his Army paybook, KW gives the name as Alexandrina.

Monday, 15 December
Suicidally depressed with these damned fans. Intermittent thumping again and again. I'm really getting to my wits' end about it. I know I should try to sell & get out, but with the noise of the builders & the mess opposite, I don't think I would stand a chance.

Thursday, 18 December
Fans were turned on again at 6.30 and, of course, woke my slumbers. How utterly loathsome it all is.

Friday, 19 December
Decided this morning that I can stand it no longer. Telephoned Noel [Willman] and asked him if I could come to his house & he said yes, that we could try it for a week or so. So I am going to pack the bags and go over there tonight, after I've seen the engineers who are coming to the flat with Mr Williamson, the architect.

Saturday, 20 December
Noel showed me his basement – the conversion is half finished. I said it would be a marvellous place for me to move into & begged him to let me have it. I met him later at the cinema and suddenly my spirits started to *sink* again. While I was watching the film I started to have misgivings about the 'move idea' and about living in a basement and in Chelsea and with a friend and an emotional tie and I started to wish I was actually dead. I thought of going to buy hundreds of aspirins and getting drunk & taking them *all*. I thought of all the comments that people might make about my death and the conclusions they might draw. My mind became like a kaleidoscope and then there was a scene in the film which was very moving and my attention was engaged and I started to cry. When we came out I thought I'd never be able to control myself and as we talked my voice cracked and I found myself crying again. Noel ignored it and just kept talking, very sensibly, & I returned to Farley. I feel that my mind is going & that I should be in a nursing home.

Sunday, 21 December
I know all about the mind being damaged and impaired. I know how it happens. I know because it's happened to me. It seems when something becomes *obsessive* – so much so, that it pervades *everything* and distorts the whole of existence. What began as an irritating noise in this flat has become such a *continual* worry that I had actually started to let it engulf me. I had started to view it all as a *persecution* and the property owners as evil etc.

Monday, 22 December
Went to Shepherd's Bush at 11.30 and rehearsed all day. Eventually we did the show at 8 o'c. The audience was awful. Ended up with Tom driving me home. Rang the porter at 1 o'c. to turn off the fans and he did. Then it was quiet. Hardly slept all night. Up at 4 o'c. and took a pill. Desperation.

Tuesday, 23 December
No wonder the responsibility of starring in a series sends some people off their rockers! It's the importance it assumes in the mind – one is no longer able to do the job and *go away*.

Wednesday, 24 December
It is extraordinary the way these fans no longer perturb me. If a buyer came along and did take the flat, goodness knows what I should do! I got a charming letter from Peter Rogers saying he wants me to be in the next film: that is around April usually, and I would certainly like to be with them again at Pinewood.

Thursday, 25 December
Went over to Louie. Watched one of those dreadful pantomimes and was amazed to see Ian Paterson (*Share My Lettuce*) playing the Prince Charming & looking about 28. This is ridiculous 'cos I knew him in 1957 and he looked about thirty then! It's extraordinary. I remember I fell v. much in love with him & asked A. to intercede but nothing came of it. Ah! the wrecks that are strewn about the beach of my unrequited love.

Friday, 26 December
Dear Tom arrived, said his father had driven him to the station saying 'My prayer every night is to see you with a girl on your arm and you having a son that will bear my name.'

Wednesday, 31 December
So that's the end of this rotten year. It contained more deaths than I can remember, and was full of trouble for me in one way or another: the biggest disappointment being my one man show idea which the BBC would only offer £400 for. I *know* it was worth more than that. So I'm landed with this dreary old revue format and the awful title 'The Kenneth Williams Show'!! By the time I come along in Feb., camp will be on the way out and they will *pan* them all. Heigh ho. One good thing about the year – it made me resolve to leave this flat. If I can get a buyer I will go.

1970

Thursday, 1 January

In the papers it says Noël Coward is now a Knight! (the fool should have refused it! how silly to be vain at his age!) and Maggie Smith gets the C.B.E. (I always said she wanted to be a Dame – so she's gone the way of the others! what a pity!)

Friday, 2 January

Got up feeling curiously elated. The newspapers have announced that the travel restriction of 50 pounds a year is to stop. We are all going to be allowed 300 a journey! Well that is nice. Government obviously trying to win the next election.

Monday, 5 January

Again & again I keep asking myself '*How* are you living thro' this period? How are you remaining sane?' It's as though the top of my head was *open* with every nerve & brain cell exposed.

Tuesday, 6 January

Roger Ordish in the viewing room played us the No. 2 show. Very pleased with it I must say. Went up to have the congratulatory drink when David Climie & Austin Steele[1] came over and the former said 'You heard about John Law? He's dead' and I was really shocked. So, at last, after about 5 months in a coma, John is dead. He was actually only 40 years old. I have no time for grief – only time to work on his writing of this series, and make it funny, as he would have wanted it.

Thursday, 8 January

Met Bev & Gay and we departed for Biagi. All I can think of is moving. I am utterly *obsessed* by it. I started to get drunk quite deliberately. I drank 2 enormous Negronis and then had a lot of wine and then had Strega. I was shouting and bawling and people were looking. I think

---

[1] Scriptwriters and editors.

I am slowly splintering as a personality. Feel as tho' I'm stuck together with stamp paper. Used a Suppon. but only had sleep till 3.30. Rest of the time I lay awake. The mind screaming. I feel utterly defeated and broken in spirit.

Thursday, 22 January

Laurena Dewar rang, saying that Helen Fry wanted me to read poetry & talk about it, to a live audience, for Radio 4 – and I have to compile it all, and talk about it! *Ludicrous* – at their money. They will offer you twenty quid for this. I told Laurena that I wasn't interested.

Monday, 2 February

The phone rang at 9.30!! It was George B. 'I wanted to say thank you for lunch on Saturday.' I said 'Really? I thought it was terrible.' He said 'Oh! I just put it down to your being in low spirits' but I was v. cursory. Then at 10 o'c. Dennis telephoned 'I wondered how you were feeling?' They're obviously all set for a suicide. I haven't the guts I'm afraid.

Wednesday, 4 February

Interview with Mr Last for The Sun[2] – as usual, I talked too much – all the poof stuff came out and the 'waiting for death' bit. I am obviously becoming slightly unhinged. At one point he said 'You seem to be facing a dilemma similar to Tony Hancock's.'

Monday, 9 February

Helen Fry at the BBC. Walked to B.H. through the windy blustering streets. She had got the script typed out[3] & I was quite pleased with the look of it. Read thro' some of it for timing and decided to finish on my own 'unemployed' poem. It's a bit of a cheek, but she was all for it.

Tuesday, 10 February

I realised my TV series started last night![4] That janitor fellow who is often at the paper stall accosted me there this morning with 'Your show last night was a load of shit, why don't you get another script writer?' but I was too wearied by it to reply, and simply walked away. Why do people want to wound so senselessly? Went over to Scanlon's to get some smoked haddock and that John (bacon counter) said he

---

[2] Richard Last, b.1927. Later chief television critic of the *Daily Telegraph*.

[3] For 'With Great Pleasure'.

[4] 'The Kenneth Williams Show'.

thought it was a 'rotten show' so obviously one has to accept that it's not liked by the public.

Saturday, 14 February
It is odd – here I am with a solo radio show to do – reading the work of many different kinds of poets and prose writers, and I'm not doing any real work on it, in advance: just relying on ability to sight-read all of it. At 7 o'c. Eric Whitby, Controller of Radio 4, introduced me and I went on and skated nervously at first, then got into my stride. Stanley B.'s lyric 'Berlin in the Twenties' went terribly well – lots of laughs – so did the Louis MacNeice, also the Death of Dryden and Shallot – for the serious bits they were attentive & kind.

Tuesday, 17 February. Tangier
Did the packing, had an early lunch and wrote two soulful notes to George and Stanley and phoned goodbye to Louie. I was ensconced in the Rembrandt by 9 o'c. It is hard to explain the fascination of this place. Above all there is the feeling of *ease* – the feeling that you don't have to bother about what people think, and, out of season like this, there aren't those ghastly package tourists about, and no one recognises you and starts the nudging as you approach, and then there is the *tat*. The incredible air of tat that hangs over everything – nothing is really quite *right* – always there is something *off* – often in a way that's intangible – an entirely instinctive knowledge tells it to you, and one likes them *for* it. The people are marvellous. They make the place.

Thursday, 19 February
It seems odd here, not to have Isabel my old chambermaid. Hamadi told me that she died. I should have come at Christmas & I would have seen her. She always understood me – always remember her getting the blind fixed for me in the front room. Think I'll try these new suedes today for the odd strollette. At about 10.45 we all went to the Lizba. That Omar appeared behind me when I was in the loo! and advanced slowly undoing his flies – it was all very theatrical. I gave him 10D. and said not to bother because it wasn't the right ambience & he really needed a shave. Afterwards we went to the Blow Up. Several advances were made by the renters and it was all happening. At one point both the owner & me were queueing for the loo. Sid drove me home at 2.30 and I cut me toe struggling to undress myself. O! the folly.

Saturday, 21 February
I walked back to the Rembrandt at 2.30 because I wanted to wash

me hair & have the barclays. Michael York and his wife Pat came for a drink with me at the bar of the Rembrandt and it was quite delightful. He is really quite small with a curious gangling graceless walk and this marvellous face and blonde hair which he continually brushes back from the eyes and a charming shyness which is adorable. I kept looking at him so much I began to feel guilty. He told me his real name is Johnson and he is spending a tax year out of Britain. Seeing them both created a marvellous atmosphere for me.

Sunday, 22 February

Everyone gave me drinks on my birthday and Dennis rang me at the bar and sang 'Happy Birthday' and I got cables and cards etc. That Jafa made overtures but I just had me shoes cleaned. I fixed to go with Omar who took me to the flat in the Casbah for the tradeola, 20D. all in. Back to Blow Up for drinks. Then I had to have more – this time Omar & Mohammed & me à trois back to the same flat. All very pleasant and they got me back to the hotel at 4 o'c. in the morning. I've certainly never had a birthday like it before – in my life!

Monday, 23 February

On undressing, I discovered the infestation *again*! so I had to get dressed and procure the taxi and he knew where I wanted to go, and he waited for me! The all-night chemist in the Rue de Fez gave me the Benzyl Benzoate & I returned to the hotel. Put it all on and lay in bed with my balls on fire. Really it can't be an accident! This happened last time I was here! All these boys must be dirty. The only one who I've known with no mishap is Mohammed Halimi and he seems to have left Tangier. One thing is certain – it puts one off for years as far as I'm concerned! All the attraction flies out of the window and one just feels total revulsion.

Tuesday, 24 February

The place is alive with American sailors – all of them that pasty white colour and all of 'em on the Ugly Pills.

Thursday, 26 February

That Tom gushed over Omar Infest this morning! So I expect she's got them too, by now. Sid said 'If her pubics are like the riah,[5] the crabs are going to have a v. thin time' – & I laughed, 'cos he is nearly bald.

---

[5] Backslang for hair.

Friday, 27 February

I said to Robert 'I told Ian Horrabin you'd said he was a rotten bridge player.' He was furious. At 8.30 a Mrs Lebus collected me for the Herbert dinner. When I entered the house, David said 'Isn't it wonderful? Rex is here!' and I was introduced to Rex Harrison, who appeared baggy-eyed and slightly bemused with this girl Elizabeth from Bridgend. He seems to have a propensity for girls from South Wales. Everyone there said he'd left Rachel 'cos she was always drunk, but as the evening progressed he became increasingly incoherent himself, with vodka and wine. David excitedly announced that we were all invited aboard Rex's yacht tomorrow for lunch, but I said I had to check the engagement book. Mrs Lebus said that the young were different thinkers compared with the middle-aged and Rex said 'Bollocks' and people tittered embarrassedly but Mrs L. was furious and said in the car on the return that she wasn't going to the luncheon and that she thought he was a dreadful man. Someone called Peggy (married to a Dutchman called Dan) told of the first night of marriage sleeping between him and his friend Louis who kept saying he was homosexual and she said 'I quite understand my dear! all these tits and everything – it's too much.' Rex said that Larry O. was a 'stupid bastard obsessed with folie de grandeur'.

Sunday, 1 March

Went to bed in despair. Woke up about 6. Talked to myself till 7.30 about a French officer who decides to read the Songs of Solomon to an almost inarticulate French Legionnaire (who is pilloried by his unit & accused of a dreadful crime), and in so doing loses his ennui and becomes involved in *life*.

Tuesday, 3 March

It was announced that London Airport would be closed from 6 o'c. tonight! & I got in at 5.20!! so I *just* made it! I found a note from Louie saying she had fallen on the stairs at Bickenhall and fractured her leg! When I went round to see her, the leg was in plaster and she *hates* it.

Saturday, 7 March

The script has arrived of *Carry On Loving*. I am offered the part of Snooper (which looks interchangeable with Charlie Hawtrey) which is certainly a small part – well no – a support I suppose, but really thankless. The end is a big party shambles where everyone throws custard pies and seems to be the bottom of the barrel, but for Talbot Rothwell[6] bottoms are capable of infinite variety.

Monday, 9 March

Peter E. lunch. He told me that he'd met Ordish who confided that Bill Cotton thought the series was 'disastrous' and that this seems to be the general consensus of opinion. Tom told me research confirmed no enthusiasm except in the southern area and of course Scotland turned it down anyway. Obviously it's thank goodness for Peter & Gerald! It was lovely irony that on last night's show, I actually said, right into camera, '50% of this country is against this show and the other 50% don't care either way . . . and frankly, neither do I . . .' and all the audience laughed. Returned home feeling really quite tranquil. Indeed I had the barclays.

Sunday, 15 March

I returned to Farley for the barclays which was very pleasant really. I played it all American. There is a lengthy article on Spike Milligan in the Observer. He is in Kenya doing the airline commercials which I turned down before I went to Morocco. There's quite a lot about finding out that Sellers and Secombe got much more money than he did, and one can sense the bitterness that's there: but the anarchy of the Goons inevitably means the collapse or destruction of someone & in this case, it appears to be him.

Monday, 16 March

Letter from Val Orford who *again* writes to say 'No one has a good word to say for your TV series' and goes on to say it is because I 'overact'. I ignored all this in his first letter: and I will have to ignore it again. My theory about the critics is that, like Val, they hate it too, but because of the death of J.L. they've decided silence is best.

Tuesday, 24 March

Mr Godden showed us No. 80 Queen Alexandra Mansions. It is 2 rooms, K & B. A v. good layout. 42 year lease. It is a flat with its own entrance way, and is on the ground floor – no stairs to climb. In so far as one ever knows anything, this is an area I belong in: the flat can be made very comfortable & if it does prove noisy the sound proofing will deaden a lot. Clive phoned but I couldn't give away the secret of the move. Not yet.

---

[6] 1917–81. Screenwriter for most of the Carry Ons.

Saturday, 28 March
Amazed to find an invitation to Downing Street in the post! I am invited to a reception given by the Prime Minister for the Swedish Ambassador! I replied to the private secretary saying 'I have to decline because these grand functions fill me with awe and I become hopelessly inhibited, Sincerely yours, etc.' I think it is best to be honest. Here am I, trying to move into a tenement block in King's Cross, and getting the invite from Whitehall!! It is all malapropos.[7]

Wednesday, 1 April
I was accosted by a man in Piccadilly who said 'I like you because I'm *like* you.' I said 'Eh?' and he said 'I'm a queer too – I'm a sailor – come & have a drink with me Kenny!' but I fled up Vigo Street & taxi home for the barclays.

Friday, 3 April
Our dear old G & C is to close in June. It is really sad. It has been one of my favourite haunts for so many years! Oh dear! 'I grow old, I grow old, I shall wear the bottoms of my trousers rolled . . .'[8] I have been happy today. Happier than I've been for a long time. Wrote a long letter to Maggie S. saying how much I love her. O yes – it's been a lovely day.

Wednesday, 8 April
Seems strange to be starting a 'Carry On' after so long an absence. We are the only film being made down there! I've never known it so desolate: but of course it means we have the lovely dressing rooms and the best stages instead of being shoved into I-block like the old days. Oh! it was all just marvellous, I can't express the joy of it. I telephoned Freeborn's and they're going to move me on Saturday morning to 80 Q.A.M.[9]

Saturday, 11 April
At 11.30 the men came on the phone & said they were leaving Farley and Mr Booth's stuff was all coming in! They arrived here at about 12 o'c. and had unloaded everything into 80 by about 1.30. The leader of the crew said of Farley 'There was a definite humming noise there – there is something wrong somewhere . . .'

---

[7] He kept the invitation in his diary, though.
[8] From 'The Love Song of J. Alfred Prufrock', by T.S. Eliot.
[9] In Hastings Street, WC1.

Thursday, 16 April
I went down to No. 80 to have a look round.[10] Brian has done the basic work on the very large kitchen cupboard and stacked a lot of my stuff on the shelves. Overhead there was the sort of bashing and thumping which sounds as if someone was mending shoes: there is the roar every so often of the underground trains running underneath! Oh! there's no doubt but that I certainly pick them!

Sunday, 19 April
Listened to my Poetry Programme. I thought the delivery was all a bit too fast. Stanley B. telephoned after. He said he thought the reading of 'Shallot' was the best he'd ever heard in his life! Well this is praise indeed, 'cos he never flannels me. I was so pleased! He said he'd been listening with Evelyn Laye and that she'd been agreeably surprised by the whole programme.

Thursday, 23 April
Replied to the fan letters apropos the poetry reading. They're all raves! I was still at it at 5 o'c.! The most wonderful letter is from Sir Francis Meynell whose mother was Alice Meynell.[11] He says he was proud to be in my company!

Wednesday, 29 April
From about 1.30 onwards, I had the most awful stomach pains. I couldn't find any position to relieve it at all. The exchange put me on to an emergency service and by 6 o'c. a Doctor came. I telephoned Tom and he came over at 5.45. He was marvellous and went to the chemist for me. I woke at 10 o'c. to find the pain had gone! I was so relieved. I had a cup of coffee & a piece of cheese, took 1 more of the Doctor's tablets (as prescribed) and one mogadon, with 3 spoonfuls of some liquid he'd also prescribed. Within five minutes I was in *agony* again. It was a repeat performance exactly and the feeling of an iron bar clamping in your stomach, the nerves start screaming with the tension and it's like a *nightmare*.

Thursday, 30 April
Pinewood, arriving at 10.40. I had a glass of milk on the set. Lovely. I lunched with Bernard Bresslaw. Lovely man. Saw the beautiful Barry Andrews[12] in the restaurant – phew – he is so beautiful it's breath-

---

[10] While work was being done on his new flat, KW was staying in a friend's apartment in the same block (No. 92).
[11] Sir Francis Meynell (1891–1975), publisher, book designer, poet. Alice Meynell (1847–1922), poet.
[12] Actor, b.1944.

taking. I have given thanks to God for delivering me from that *filthy* pain. I can't remember anything as bad for sheer lasting continuity, in my life.

Monday, 4 May
To the Paris at 10 o'c. and we did 'S.M.A.' No. 6, & it went like a bomb. Really the reactions are certainly as good as in the best days of a successful series.

Tuesday, 5 May
More letters to answer about the poetry programme. All of them talk about 'How nice to hear this *other* side of your personality . . .' It is not really saying that they're pleased to find a cultivated mind where they'd expected banality or superficiality, it is saying 'How nice to find you're one of us . . .' in the snob sense.

Sunday, 10 May
T & C arrived at 9.15 & we left for Deal. We called at Middle Street & Charlie [Hawtrey] came to the door in his undervest, unshaven. On entering, we saw his lunch steaming on the table, so we went off for more drinks till he was ready. He was still unshaven but showed us all over the house which is rambling and incredibly tat – like a lodging house which all the boarders have suddenly deserted and that revolting smell of rising damp & cat's fish everywhere. She produced male physique magazines with a great flourish and meaningful remarks, but they were all quite innocuous. I was horrified to learn then that Charles was travelling back with us! 'cos Tom had foolishly offered him a lift to London and Miss Cadge jumped at it. So we had her all the way! A nightmare journey of 3 hours and she *had* to lose her cigarette holder and search the car at Victoria (where we dumped her) to find the wretched thing. She pressed us all to come again & 'please regard it as your second home.' Before I do that, I'll need the Rest Home.

Saturday, 23 May
Noel came at 7.15 and we went to Conway St for dinner with Hester Chapman.[13] The house is dingy and dirty and orange-box tat of appalling gloom and decay with the smell of rising damp. She was swathed in a vast evening dress of a bronze metallic material & matching stole. She told some marvellous anecdotes. She *knew* the Stracheys! 'I used to have to read detective stories aloud to Lady Strachey and would bawl out – 'cos she was deaf – 'I WON'T BOTHER WITH THE CHAPTER HEAD-

---

[13] 1899–1976. Historian, novelist.

INGS, Lady Strachey!' who mournfully replied 'They're the only bits I *like*!' and when Marjorie was leaving the house to see *Back To Methuselah* and Lady Strachey said 'Where are you going?', Marjorie said 'As far as thought can reach, Mother . . .' She said that when she stayed with Lytton he was moaning about the huge car which Carrington could never start and he piped 'It won't *go* – it won't *go* – we'll have to turn it into a summer house . . .' Hester said the wonderful thing about the Stracheys was the totally equal way that they approached one. She said 'They made you feel as clever and as grand as they were . . . which was rather nice . . .' Noel and I struggled with her dreadful food – crab soup, cold & nasty lumps – and shepherd's pie! with cauliflower that tasted of *soap*. But *she* was superb. Sometimes as she drew the stole around her and smiled she looked like a girl and incredibly radiant. Really lovely.

Wednesday, 27 May

A letter from Peter Porter[14] to whom I complained 'cos he called my anthology 'sanctimonious & camp' – he says that he didn't intend to hurt and apologised for a 'thoughtless criticism' – that is good of him, so I wrote a letter of thanks. I met Ivy Hammond!! and her husband!! We had a long chat. She said 'Oh! I remember you when you was little and you'd just been circumcised & I said to Louie "Don't *pull it off*, Lou! It might bleed" . . .' Listened to some marvellous playing on the 3rd programme. What a beautiful thing radio can be – and what a boon to the person who likes to enjoy such things, alone. Had the barclays and went to bed about 10.45.

Monday, 8 June

Went to Bush House for interview on World Service with Jeremy Verity. It went all right & I got terribly worked up and left the building all excited and preened about & pranced into Kingsway and smirked at a lorry driver on the zebra, who smiled & waved and I jumped on the 77 bus very buoyantly indeed.

Thursday, 11 June

I keep getting very apprehensive about the flat – either it's all too good to be true and I don't deserve it, or it will all be got ready and I will die, or someone will go in and steal everything.

Saturday, 13 June

Started reading *The Mill on the Floss*. It's the first novel of George Eliot that I've ever read. I kept thinking of Melvyn Bragg for some reason.

---

[14] Australian poet, b.1929. Then radio critic of the *New Statesman*.

Much of the moral philosophising is very sound indeed and the observation is sometimes incredibly acute. Her characters are well drawn in the small parts, but the two central characters make no sense. This Tom Tulliver can only be explained if you believe in a man who is totally obsessed by the ideal of *justice*. Nowhere in the book does he seek human affection and indeed, nowhere does he really get it, except from Maggie his sister. She sacrifices two lovers for him and eventually drowns with him in the river Floss. But it remains compulsive reading. Perhaps there are indeed people who are only sustained in life by their *ideas* of justice and have little or no interest in sexual matters or anything else. I didn't finish it till 12.30! Then went to bed.

Thursday, 18 June

We started watching the election results coming in, and contrary to *all* the opinion polls, the swing to Tories was marvellous!! Tom stayed graphing it all, and Clive drove me home, and we reflected on the astounding and marvellous victory! Long ago, in Flanagan's, Tom gave a toast 'Here's to 1970 – to Ken getting his own flat & getting out of Farley into something *right* for him, and to our having a lovely *cruise*, and to returning to find a Tory victory and Labour *out* –' So far, two of those desires have been realised!

Saturday, 20 June

GREAT DAY. MOVED TO 80 Q.A.M. Henry Gess rang to say he was on his way. I'd just about finished scrubbing when he came, with the lads and the carpet. I could hardly conceal my excitement. It is the most beautiful off-white-oatmeal colour I've ever seen. By about 9 o'c. I had a coffee and a fag and apart from making the bed, everything was shipshape. I have never moved into a flat and felt such happiness before, in my life. At last I am back at my dear little desk which I've not sat at since 11 April. Horrified to find, when I was sitting in the kitchen about 12 o'c. in the dressing gown, that the fridge makes a noise! It is utterly infuriating because my last one (same model) never did.

Sunday, 21 June

T & C came at 12 o'c. and were amazed that I'd moved in! I showed them all round and they approved everything. They were my *first guests* and *rightly* so.

Monday, 22 June

Spent the entire evening cleaning things and arranging etc., playing my Schumann and with the orange lamps on in the living room it's enchanting – the prettiest flat I've ever had in my life. What will happen to *mar* this loveliness? Please God to keep me in such contentment: and never a move again! My heart is full of gratitude.

Wednesday, 8 July
Got up at 9.40. Found a dead spider. I was furious. These are the very creatures I do *not* want killed. They do a wonderful job. I think this is the first day I've started to relax in my new home. I can see the oatmeal carpet getting filthy in the hall & I think 'It doesn't matter' – I always expected the hall to get dirty anyway.

Wednesday, 15 July
Walked to Egton House[15] to see Michael Bell regarding this music programme. We prepared 18 items of music & tonight I must write the links. Came back on foot to 80 and I was appalled to see a woman moving in to the flat below and she's got a *piano*! I heard her playing it. Terrible row. I *knew* my conditions here were too good to be true. I've soundproofed till I'm blue in the face, but the noise of a piano you cannot guard against. It's as though it was playing in the same room! And it seems to be coming from the bedroom! But whatever happens, I can't move. Not again. She's got no carpets down and the noise of them walking in and out is dreadful. They move something in and then she plays another trill on the piano. It's almost triumphant. At 10.30 I heard the piano being bashed and she sang that she 'loved those dear hearts and gentle people that live and love in my home town' – I just wished she would revisit them immediately! When it started on again, I played Malcazinsky[16] doing the Chopin Ballades *v. loudly indeed* – just to remind her that this block is not soundproof and at 11 o'clock I switched off.

Thursday, 16 July
At 10.30 she started playing the piano! She played 'I'll Walk Beside You', 'Parlez-Moi d'Amour', and 'Climb Every Mountain' and 'All The King's Horses' and 'Please Release Me' and 'Souvenirs' and 'Auf Wiederseh'n' and goodness knows what else, singing all the while in a wobbly soprano – occasionally forgetting the lyrics and faltering a bit, then picking up again. I stole outside the block and looked in her window. No curtains. There she was, sitting at the piano – a woman of about 40 with the moustache look and spectacles and dark hair and a reddish nose – no make-up – bolt upright banging the keys and singing away like there was no tomorrow.

---

[15] A BBC building adjacent to Broadcasting House.
[16] Witold Malcuzynski (1914–77).

Friday, 17 July

Now the piano below is bashing out 'Café Mozart' and the 'Harry Lime Theme'. Brian agreed we'd have to start all over again and try insulating the floor. I walked into Hastings Street & the idiot was lying on the settee with sheets & blankets and in a night dress with the lights full on – no curtains – eating sweets and reading the Daily Sketch. The sagging tits v. much in evidence. I was amazed. One wonders whether she's being deliberately provocative to passers-by or whether she is completely unselfconscious.

Wednesday, 22 July

To Noel and Limerston Street where I met Rosamond Lehmann,[17] she's another Hester Chapman! All flowing gowns and expansive hairdos and make-up etc. used to give an appearance of youthfulness. We had a great argument about 'a man can be deplorable in many ways & still be a great man and a good man' and R.L. quoted Tolstoy. Then we got into the theatre and I quoted the rehearsal of Richard II with Guinness in the lead and Ken Connor playing the servant, and Ralph Richardson who was directing the play stomping round Kenneth all the time crying out 'Ham! Ham! Ham!' ad infinitum ad nauseam. I said it was appalling behaviour; they replied 'Yes, but what a marvellous *actor* he is!' and I know he isn't. He's hidden for so long behind the mask of eccentricity that he's actually become eccentric. His work is fundamentally *ludicrous*. Significantly they both said Falstaff was his finest performance. I left about 11.15 after confessing to Rosamond that I wore my best suit because I was to meet her.

Sunday, 26 July

After the washing-up I did the troll. King's X seems to be a sort of melting pot for the odds & sods and one delectable vanished up the York Way which had seemed a possibility but I returned to 80 at 1 o'c. and fell into troubled sleep on my virginal couch. In Hyde Park tonight where we walked after the cinema I started singing 'In My Own Little Corner'[18] and dancing and doing *mad* voices with absurd gestures and tried to make T & C laugh but they were a bit embarrassed at such cavortings in public: I don't know what else to do. It's either this act or I'm going to voice the despair and manic depression that's really inside of me, and they've had a belly full of that. I can't talk to Louie 'cos she won't sleep for worry over me, so it's that screaming inside my head. Noises in my head. Skin disease and crying.

---

[17] 1901–90, novelist.

[18] A memory of *Cinderella*. Song by Rodgers & Hammerstein, as sung by Yana in the show.

Monday, 27 July

I am beginning to feel more and more unreal. Living in this flat and in this block is like serving a *prison sentence* and I feel the bedroom is a *cell*. I feel I must get out – but I have spent all this money, I have tried everything to make it soundproof – it hasn't worked and I am back to where I started. I keep weeping at the utter desolation inside me. This continual recognition and people asking for my autograph when I want to scream *fuck off* – leave me *alone* you bloody cannibals . . . they don't *like* their actors, they want to eat them, they want to eat them alive. We are *them* trotted out for a bolder show,[19] the stocks, the pillory etc. I am actually saying 'Well there you are' in a resigned & daft way, because I don't know what to say that isn't despairing.

Tuesday, 28 July

Met Mr Fox[20] (Sunday Times magazine) and talked about Joe Orton – especially with reference to Edna Welthorpe. Then he took me to lunch and I got more and more uninhibited, till of course I suggested he come back to the flat and out came the letters and the photographs and I actually gave him one of the prints!! for reproduction in his newspaper! Afterwards I sat feeling awful. Felt that I had told things which should be kept private, but comforted by the fact that no one has been mentioned who could be hurt. I'm the only one apart from K.H. who really knew Joe, and if the public are to read anything about him in the Sunday Times, it should be stuff which is authentic and not the rubbishy ravings of silly queens who were only on the fringe of his acquaintance. Saw the film *Kes* which was too amateur to really engage me. Returned to the flat at 11.30 and tried to get the muck out of this *spot* on the cheek. Standing, looking in the mirror at the blood all over my face and the drops of it flicked all over the glass from my frantic stabbing with the needle, and seeing the rash on the chin, and the dandruff in the hair and I can only think of suicide. How *can* one go on and on like this? It's as though you are walking but the same piece of ground is under you all the time. I have asked, begged and prayed to God to give me peace. Just one room where there is quiet. I don't get it. So I am back to walking the streets and crying. I seem to be crying all the time. I'm just continuing on a sort of behavioural pattern evolved from Acting. I don't know what to do any more. I actually don't know what to do.

---

[19] cf. 'Tulips turned inside out for a bolder show': from 'Funeral Wreaths' by Ruth Pitter. See entry for 20 February 1977, p. 535.

[20] James Fox, b.1945. Later author of *White Mischief*.

Wednesday, 29 July
I had awful dreams about insects in my hair and washing it, only to find complete baldness and rowing with George B. over his having a cold! And saying to a military sentry 'You've never *ever* given me a kiss' and he said 'You've never come up to the guardroom where I sleep' and then he brushed my lips with his and went off. It's all v. disturbing. Probably the gradual approach of insanity. The idiot still away so there is quiet.

Monday, 3 August
Hans Schmidt[21] came, and we went to Biagi for dinner. He is here for a few weeks and is eventually to return and teach here for 2 years. When, at one point, he said apropos Protestantism & Luther 'So often I think, the Dogmatist is the Heretic,' I mentioned the Calogero argument on this subject, i.e. the cornerstone of liberalism in philosophy must be 'It is my duty to admit Doubt', and the trap: one has written one's first line of dogma . . . We went on to speak of these endless paradoxical truths in life and he said that Hegel had come nearest to trying to solve it, in the form of synthesis.

Tuesday, 4 August
Nora drove me in the new red Opel car to Byfleet, and Robert Bolt. He gave us a drink and the phone *never* stopped ringing & he had to go and answer it. We had lunch on the lawn, served by his Spanish girl. Her husband's name is Jesus and he said that on last week's shopping list the latter had wanted some materials for carpentry, and the Catholic maid they've got had been shocked to read 'Long nails for Jesus' and Robert laughed at this. I noticed that he looked at me closely. He knew, I'm sure, that such tastelessness shocks and appals me. I silently prayed 'Forgive, forgive . . .' as tho' it were a magic formula. When I said 'After I've gone, they'll say "He seemed quite normal to me, I never thought he would kill himself",' he replied 'Rubbish. There was never anything *normal* about you . . .'

Wednesday, 5 August
Corrections to the Television Who's Who entry.[22] They had got down: 'Single, supports Mother & Sister . . .' so I wrote 'Omit this. Sounds like a sob story . . .'

Friday, 7 August
Went to the Playhouse for the 'J.A.M.' sessions. It is Clement alone

---

21 KW's German pen-friend.
22 *Who's Who on Television* ('A *TV Times* Extra'), 1970.

who I'm really sympathetic towards. The shows went all right I suppose.

Wednesday, 12 August
The postman said 'Sorry to get you up, but I couldn't get this packet through the door . . .' and it was a book from Peggy Ramsay! Written by John Lahr (about his father)[23] and there was a letter saying he wanted to write a book about Joe Orton. I replied saying it was all right if Peggy approved. S. & J. came round at 12 o'c.! J. said 'The world is so unreal that one clings to sex as a *reality* – I mean, when you're sucking someone's cock, it is *real* – there is something to hold on to . . .' I agreed that it would seem to be so.

Thursday, 13 August
I sat reading and from below, she started singing 'When you want someone who won't want you, perhaps you'll think of me . . .' I thought 'Poor old cow . . .' I feel sadness and despite for her at the same time.

Friday, 14 August
T & C came along about 6.15 and Tom told a hair raising story of picking up a skinhead and etc. in the bushes on Hampstead Heath and as he pulled the head down for sixtynine, the wig came off in his hand! He said 'I was off like a shot – and left her lying there . . .' What with having the dick bitten by a docker and now picking up a bald queen, the sex life seems turbulent indeed.

Saturday, 15 August
Letter from Laurence Harbottle[24] returning all my Joe Orton letters! They make rather embarrassing reading. One suddenly realises the difference between what is written for publication & what is written for amusement of friends! I had *never* seen it so nakedly before.

Monday, 17 August
Sitting at the desk. The eyes full of tears. I am so *lonely*. I am so unhappy. I always have been. I move from places but it makes no difference, there is never any peace – always the noise, always the savagery, the nightmares, and horrible dreams.

---

[23] *Notes on a Cowardly Lion*, on the comedian Bert Lahr (1895–1968), who played the part of the Cowardly Lion in the film *The Wizard of Oz* (1939).
[24] b.1924. Senior partner, Harbottle & Lewis, solicitors.

Friday, 21 August
Called on Peter Eade. I told him & Laurena about the carbuncle, and offered them my trousered leg. I said 'You feel how big it is' and both of them said 'No thank you' with that kind of distaste that makes you feel like a pariah, so I just turned on my heel and walked out. I *loathe* the pair of them: smug, bigoted fools. Got the 73 bus home. Girl ran after me in Tonbridge Street: 'Could I have your autograph please?' I said 'No thank you.' Went to the Spartan. I was bawling and shouting 'Mutual masturbation?' to everyone; most of them said 'No thank you.'

Friday, 28 August
Peter Eade phoned to say that even Gerald 'has heard you've become a drunk . . .' so I telephoned Gerald & he said a hairdresser called Dominic had said he'd seen me in a club 'pissed out of my mind'. I told Gerald that he might well have done so. I am supposed to be going on holiday tomorrow. If I go, I will never have left this country in such low spirits. Where in this whole wide world will my restless spirit and deep dissatisfaction find release? Of course, death seems to be the only answer, and of course one's thinking tells one that it is wrong, but more & more one comes to feel it is the only solution. The over-sensitive mind will always either *have* to use a facade (& be forced into duality & hypocrisy) or *break*. All those I know who've done it (broken) I feel colossal empathy with. Perhaps this is stupid & mistaken, but I feel it impulsively, naturally, & consistently.

Saturday, 29 August
The car is collecting T & C at Dale Lodge at 11.15 and coming on to me afterwards & we depart for Gatwick. Instead of 2.30 take-off, we got delayed messages over the tannoy and the whole thing became nightmarish. We eventually took off at 11 o'c. and arrived in Venice at 1.30 on the 30 Aug. It would be pointless to try to recall all the ghastly tedium of waiting about at Gatwick and of all the autographs and the pestering that went on the whole time.

Sunday, 30 August
Up and about around 10 o'c. and explored the ship – it all looks rather nice & there seems to be a pleasant cross-section of people. Alex (Staff Captain) asked us *all* to dinner! So of course we went. It was delightful. Then Alex said 'Now you come to the night club & see the Ballet . . .' and took us through to a special table, reserved specially and these 6 girls danced marvellously despite the roll of the boat & a Belgian comic did tricks that never worked. After, I congratulated them all & bought them drinks and persuaded them to join Alex and us and we had a

marvellous party! We sang songs & drank long after the bar had closed and Tom played the piano and all the girls danced with us & I stuck me bum out and oh! what larks Pip!

Tuesday, 1 September
We are docked in Piraeus. Pissed off to that taverna on the Plaka and had shish kebab and salad & retsina, and then went to the Parthenon to see the Amphitheatres. Forgot to mention that at Aeolian Hall on Aug. 27 I saw John Simmonds and he told me that they were going to drop 'S.M.A.' from the air. He said that Muggeridge (one Controller)[25] liked it, but that Eric Whitby (another Controller) hated it, and that there'd been complaints about how dirty the script was etc. He said 'You wouldn't *mind*, would you?' and I said 'Not at all' etc. Inwardly, I was furious, but what's the good? It's a sad end to about 12 years of radio comedy. Our appreciation was always about 60%.

Wednesday, 2 September
We got on the buses and were taken up very high in the mountains to Neomoni which is an 11th century monastery with some superb mosaics in the Byzantine fashion but lacking the usual rigidity & formality – they were extraordinarily alive, and some of the groupings were utterly modern. I was astonished to find such beauty. One particularly, Christ washing the feet of the disciples, was lyrically lovely. Drinks with two fellows from Texas, Glyn and Dick (the latter plays Bass in the San Antonio Symphony Orch.) before lunch. The latter told us that a girl sent him a p.c. from Bald Knob (Arkansas) with 'Thinking of you' written on the back, which I thought was v. funny 'cos I thought it meant no pubes around the dick. It didn't.

Wednesday, 9 September
I rowed with Tom and said I would not go for a holiday with him again and that's a fact. In return, he said 'Let's face it, you don't really get on with anybody for long – it's the same with all your friends – you get *bored* with them all eventually. Of course Louie bears the brunt of all your frustration and bad temper . . .' I said 'Oh dear! it's all coming out now, isn't it?' It is Jugoslavia tomorrow and they say that going ashore is made v. difficult by the police and the Customs etc. If it's *that* difficult I shan't bother. It is the Fancy Dress rubbish tonight, so I returned to the cabin and put one up.

Sunday, 13 September. London
At 8 o'c. I could hear a radio going through the floor. So much for

---

[25] Douglas Muggeridge, Controller of Radios 1 and 2.

sound proofing. I read the script of *Carry On Henry* and I think it's abysmal. My part (Cromwell) seems to equate to the thing I did in *Don't Lose Yr. Head*. It is liberally sprinkled with filth.

Thursday, 17 September

Julie, below, started playing the records at 12 o'c.! tonight and the sound just floats up, a bit muted, but the same as before. The piano is as clear as ever. Curiously, it did not make me start that old screaming inside, I suppose because I know her now, and I know that there is no malignance of any kind.

Saturday, 19 September

Julie called. She told me a long rambling account of the 2 marriages, [and] how she'd had 12 children. She continually reiterates that 'no one knows what I've been through' and it certainly appears to have been an adventurous & bizarre life.

Monday, 21 September

Stanley came over and we talked about lots of things. I told him my play idea – the bogus messiah – and he said 'I think it's rotten' which certainly rather deflated me. He said I should go back on television 'in any show where you get a chance to chat . . . that is what you're good at . . .' He said there should be some format devised where I was the eternal guest.

Wednesday, 23 September

To see Julie at 7 o'c. The place is in astonishing confusion and there is a sort of mindlessness about it which would drive me mad. A carpet has been laid in the front room, which is an incredible vivid red pattern and smelled appallingly (I imagine it's been stored in a damp warehouse or something) so I came back to 80, got me spray, & returned and deodorised it! She told me a curious & very funny story about going off to an hotel in Victoria where a man asked her to chase him round the room and tickle him with a feather duster. She said that she 'felt she was a nuisance' because of the piano playing and I said we'd have to learn to live with it: I had her go up to my flat and listen to me play the piano. She admitted 'Yes, you can hear it . . . though it's not as loud as down here of course . . .' She read aloud to me her speech at the Mormon Church at Norwood 'Youth and Heritage' which expressed excellent sentiments: it's amazing that a woman who has experienced such continuous adversity should remain so light of heart – or perhaps it's all a facade to cover an inner despair?

Sunday, 27 September
I must start to realise my true position. So far, the Carry Ons have cushioned me economically, but now, with the radio going, and the probability that the films will go too, there is going to be the need to look around & probably return to the theatre.

Tuesday, 29 September
Taxi to the TV Centre. Bill Cotton is now H.L.E. – Head of Light Entertainment in TV. He said, in the absence of a better plan, we should reintroduce 'International Cabaret' at the Talk of the Town, and he came up with Myles Rudge as writer and I agreed. Predictably, Peter E. rang & said 'O dear! that again?' It is ironic that all complaints of unoriginality come from people who haven't an original thought in their bodies. Like most newspaper critics. I listened on the radio to a programme about whales and the detestable whaling industry which is steadily and ruthlessly wiping out these marvellous creatures. O! it makes one want to cry out and die alongside them. My disgust & despite for this sort of factory fishing is endless. It upset the entire evening for me.

Sunday, 4 October
To Dale Lodge. At one point, Tom said 'I think you deserve more than two rooms in a tenement block . . .' and suddenly my life was encapsulated. I was labelled. I was sprawling on the pin[26] and my spirits started drooping. I know all about my dilemma. I *long* to be unknown. Because I'm not a star and have never earned those astronomical sums I am not rich and cannot afford the seclusion of the country retreat. If I do, I lose all the capital so carefully acquired which is to be a standby in the event of real need – on Louie's behalf or my own. I must stop this writing 'cos I'm on the verge of tears again.

Monday, 5 October
Reading Leavis. When I came to his argument about 'Yes I have heard of the philosophical thought of Wordsworth but I'm only concerned with the poetry of Wordsworth'[27] I started to fume inwardly at this senseless divorce of a poet's natural powers of reason, intellect etc. being suddenly 'suspended' when it comes to his writing poetry. If it were true, then you would have great poetry which contained *no thought* whatsoever, and of course you haven't: it doesn't exist. It all

---

[26] cf. Eliot's 'Prufrock': 'And when I am formulated, sprawling on a pin,/When I am pinned and wriggling on the wall,/Then how should I begin/To spit out all the butt-ends of my days and ways?'
[27] The passage (which takes in Blake and Shelley as well) occurs in 'Criticism and Philosophy', an essay in *The Common Pursuit* (1952).

comes back to this intellectual passion for *labelling* and compartmenting everything. You can either be a literary critic, or you can be a philosopher – you can't be both. Why ever not? It's like the old 'motorist' and 'pedestrian' nonsense: it seems superficially to be two different things, and on examination, it is proved to be neither, it is simply a *man*. One has been reading for ages about the various dramatic changes that are taking place in the world and there is glib talk about the new kind of man – the new generation of 'the Sixties' etc. It is all nonsense. Fundamental man doesn't change at all. The questing creature faced eternally with the postulations '*I am nothing in a world of something*' and '*I am something in a world of nothing*' – and the paradox is endless.

Wednesday, 7 October

To the Dorchester where Peter Rogers held his champagne party for launching of his 21st Carry On. The only actors there were: Charlie Hawtrey & me, and Joan Sims and Barbara Windsor. The reporters all asked me 'What are you doing in these sort of films?' and one man from the Guardian said 'Why are you associated with this chamber-pot kind of comedy?' I said that in our kind of society there was and should be room for all kinds of entertainment *if it worked on its own level* and that the only charge to be taken seriously by us would be the one that the comedy (burlesque in this case) didn't work: that it wasn't funny.

Monday, 12 October

First day of filming *Carry On Henry*. Gerald & Peter were both charming to me and the former remarked 'I like to have you on the set on the first day' which was v. gratifying.

Friday, 16 October

Laurena Dewar showed me a letter from Binkie Beaumont to Peter, suggesting I should play Drinkwater in *Captain Brassbound's Conversion* which he was going to present with Ingrid Bergman in the leading role. I took down my Shaw Works, and read it. It certainly starts v. well, and then rather peters out, but there are opportunities for comedy and in the absence of anything better, it would certainly be worth considering.

Wednesday, 21 October

To Lord North St and I met Binkie, who introduced me to Ingrid Bergman. She was charming and lovely. Joss Ackland was there, who will play Brassbound and was v. nice, and Frith Banbury[28] who was kindness itself. Everyone agreed that they liked each other and Binkie cried 'Are you with us?' and I said 'Yes' and he said 'Then I can ring the Daily Mail?' and I said 'Let's wait & sign contracts.' Ingrid told an incredible story about Lewis Milestone & Joan Crawford, the [former] picking out a v. handsome extra and saying 'Miss Crawford, here is your flatterer. This man will be engaged to tell you how wonderful you are in every scene we shoot . . .'

Wednesday, 28 October

They are doing 'This Is Your Life' (ITV) on Talbot Rothwell at Pinewood this evening, and we were all asked to stay behind and walk on to the set and all 'stand around Talbot', with egg all over our faces doubtless! But I was finished so I pissed off at 3 o'c.

Tuesday, 3 November

It was the banquet scene with Henry throwing the table over! Sid did it all very well. I was being demonic & rushing all over the set telling stories, singing dirty songs and miming in a masturbatory fashion and shouting at Gerald about how the scene should be directed. When he told me off at one point, I shouted 'I have the privilege of old acquaintance' and he said '*Old* is right, looking at your face' which everyone laughed at. But there is no doubt about it, on that set, I do have privileges! and I get more fond of Gerald and Peter every time I see them. It is because, in all the years of working together, they have never lost faith in my ability, tho' goodness knows I've often lost it myself.

Friday, 13 November

It was another 'Here is Sir Roger's Retraction' sequence with Sid James. While rehearsing it with him, I ad-libbed *one line* and he threw his great tantrum '*I am a serious actor*' bit, and shouted 'Can we ever have *one* straight rehearsal?' and there was quite an atmosphere created. Of course the scene was lifeless after that. James does this kind of thing because he is basically a very insecure man when surrounded by real actors. As he can't act himself and is fundamentally aware of his bogus nature, he really resents any kind of talent near him, and this kind of outburst really typifies that resentment.

Sunday, 15 November

Clive suggested going out for tea, I said 'Where?' and he said 'Lyons or somewhere . . .' and I said 'Oh no, better to go back to your place

[28] b.1912. Actor and director.

& have it there' and he said 'Yeah! and *you* won't have to *pay* for it . . .' I muttered something about paying for the pictures – 3 tickets at the Metropole on Friday – and then lapsed into silence because this recriminatory slant on money has been occurring a lot lately. When Tom said 'Madam has gone very silent' I suddenly flared into temper about it all. In reply, Clive shouted that I was a 'nasty little queen'. I said 'Just stop the car and I will get out' and he screamed 'I'll fucking stop and fucking kick you out . . .' and there was a lot more obscenity but no actually pulling in to stop. When it came to the Portman Square turn-off, the lights were red so I said 'This will do' and got out of the car and walked home. I am well aware that this row is caused by me and that it is foolish if viewed objectively, but I am not objective, and what *stays* in the mind is the extraordinary venom of Clive. It was the same in Gibraltar and his malignance then; basically he does not like me. I suppose I've really known this all along. It is the reason I have so often thought the *trio* relationship is a *bad* one.

Sunday, 22 November

In the Sunday Times colour supplement I found the article on Joe Orton,[29] with a huge colour reproduction of the photograph which George Borwick took on the terrace of the Windmill with me in the centre and Joe and Ken on each side of me. I notice that nowhere in the article does the author acknowledge that I *told* him about Edna Welthorpe. No one else knew about her, and I told him about the correspondence hoax for a purpose: that was that he should bring out in his article that joyous & truly funny side of Joe: but no – instead he has chosen the old hackneyed crap about 'note of foreboding' and the 'sense of doom' with the murder of Joe as the natural climax to a bit of reportage in the style of a journalist on crime.

Wednesday, 2 December

To the TV Centre.[30] Well of course the nerves went to me head like alcohol and I got worse and worse: I did 'smite thee with the pisspot', 'lavatory paper', the Malvolio letter scene, common sailor, lay on the floor reciting, Grandma & Mrs Houth doing it in the bloomers, critics being like eunuchs, 'sitting here holding me dick' (Clement [Freud] interrupted and said 'No – you're actually holding *mine*') and the audience laughed but it was a disgrace. Of course afterwards I felt bitterly ashamed and self-disgust took possession completely. Washed out shirts & socks for penance and therapy.

---

[29] By James Fox. See entry for 28 July 1970, p. 379.

[30] For the chat-show '(If it's Saturday it must be) Nimmo'.

Friday, 4 December
I walked to the Playhouse to do 'Just A Minute'. There was an awful moment when Freud said of Beauty & the Beast 'My wife played the part of Beauty in a production of this play . . .' & Nimmo interrupted with 'Deviation – I've seen his wife and she could never play Beauty.' There was a laugh from the house, Freud was smiling but silent, and then Nimmo asked for his words to be retracted & said he was sorry.

Thursday, 10 December
Call from BBC told me not to go to the Playhouse because of Power Cut, so I went to the Concert Hall at Broadcasting House and we did the 'J.A.M.' shows from there. After the b'cast the producer asked the audience to clap those people who had made it possible to keep the show going in spite of the Electric Workers' strike and I cried out about the strikers: 'May they rot and perish' and the entire audience applauded.

Monday, 14 December
At the restaurant tonight, Paul F. said he admired my Mont Blanc pen so I gave it to him. I shall have to get another one anyway 'cos the screw threads hurt my fingers after a while.

Thursday, 17 December
Tom came at 6.30. I said how deeply offended I'd been by his friend & he pretended a different version entirely and said I had offended Clive! by saying 'Let's have tea at your place, it's cheaper in Highgate . . .' which I did *not* say, and he added that 'Clive is tremendously generous to you – driving you up to Highgate every Sunday, as he did . . . practically acting as a chauffeur for you . . .' When it comes down to this kind of banality it's best to forget it – forget the entire relationship I mean.

Saturday, 19 December
While talking to Paul I carefully stole his pen, & substituted the *new* Mont Blanc, and so now I've got my old pen back, and he doesn't know it. I am so glad because this nib is so much better.

Tuesday, 22 December
A letter came by late post from Clive & it says a sweet message of goodwill and an unsaying of any hurt. I should not have occasioned such writing: it puts the boy in an awful position. I telephoned him and said 'You have made a beautiful gesture' and I knew from his voice that it was at Tom's bidding: nevertheless he has *made* it, and that is bigger spirited than I am.

Friday, 25 December
Took down the venetian blinds in the F/room and washed them. They were filthy. I walked all the way to Gordon & Rona, arriving at about 1.30. It is uphill all the way and one of me bags broke at Swiss Cottage! oh! I was furious. We had champagne cocktails! It was all lovely.

Thursday, 31 December
The phone went at 10 o'c. – it was Laurena to say that a man called Wilson had rung to say that Michael Harald (Cotton) had died of cancer and was to be buried today. It was only a few months ago I saw him doing courier work in Gower Street. Pat rang at 10.45 – 'I just wanted to wish you a Happy New Year . . .' I said 'Thank you' and replaced the receiver. Rent demand came in & I sent off the cheque. I washed the camel cardigan. To Geoffrey & John's party. Home at 3 o'c.

1971

Monday, 4 January
There was a dreary read thro' which showed how awful they all were, except for Ingrid, Gibby[1] and the American captain.

Tuesday, 5 January
Cavendish for a press reception. I got hopelessly pissed and was being ridiculously indiscreet and giving the phone number to everybody. Went with all these journalists to a pub where I was telling a Duncan Macrae anecdote when a capped & muffled Irishman interrupted with 'You talk too much – you're a bore – I've seen you on the television – you are always boring . . .' I smiled acquiescence and said 'How true, O King!' & eventually got a taxi to the flat at about 10.30. I had a terrible head and was extraordinarily drunk.

Wednesday, 13 January
I said to Joss 'All your walking up & down & psychological philosophising over the role is self-indulgent and boring – Shaw's dialogue needs to be *said,* not emoted over' and he was furious and Banbury said I was wrong to talk like that and 'Everyone rehearses differently . . .' God! they're all so *boring*.

Friday, 15 January
Could not face another rehearsal with Banbury and so I went over to the Doctor and got a certificate to be off for 2 weeks! This sinus condition will have to be looked at.

Saturday, 16 January
At 9.30 my bell rang. I opened the door an inch to Griffith James – the Stage Director! He started on about 'We are all very worried about you . . .' I expect he'd been sent to check on whether the voice is bad, or whether Ada Bagwash is shamming. I couldn't begin to care.

---

[1] Ingrid Bergman played the role of Lady Cicely Wayneflete; James Gibson played the missionary Rankin.

Monday, 18 January

Woke with those tightening pains round the stomach which make you undo your trousers etc. and then it worsened till it became pure agony. I was crying out to God to help me, and mouthing imprecations, and asking to die. I kept thinking about crushing all the aspirins I could find and taking them but there weren't *any* in the house. I feel it is a punishment for my own arrogance – leaving rehearsals on Friday and behaving selfishly – it's as tho' God said 'We'll give him something to be *ill* about . . .'

Tuesday, 19 January

I got to the theatre at 10 o'c. – the Palace – and we rehearsed Act II. Frith admitted he was 'a little worried' about Ingrid going to so many theatres at night (she went to see *Lulu*[2] at the Apollo last night) and not learning her lines.

Wednesday, 20 January

I played it exactly the same as Monday and this time he said at the end: 'You are all on one kind of note . . . it sounds very monotonous . . .' No criticism of Gibson in the same scene who *still* doesn't know it! and who 'ums' and 'ahs' all over the shop. Then because I move up to the window as Banbury instructed me, he said 'You walk upstage & seem to be doing a *number* on your own!' That finished me. I shouted 'You want to get the bloody cues picked up instead of picking me to bits . . .'

HIM: 'That will come, we've got another ten days yet . . .'
ME: 'Yes! It's been "coming" for the last fortnight, it will still be "coming" in Brighton.'
HIM: 'Don't start shouting like that! We can all raise our voices you know . . .'
ME: 'I'm very glad you can! Mine is practically gone thro' trying to rehearse this properly . . .'
HIM: 'Now come along & stop being selfish.'
ME: 'Selfish? I have learned my lines and rehearsed as well as I know how, if that's what you call selfish then I've been wasting a lot of time in this profession . . .'

Then after a bit of rehearsal, I walked out of the theatre and he came after me & I told him this continual criticism was undermining my confidence & I told him I couldn't take any more of it. He actually said 'All right . . . in future I'll give you your notes privately . . .' Of course, he's *mad*.

---

[2] By Frank Wedekind, adapted by Peter Barnes.

Friday, 22 January
Run-through of the play. Ingrid stumbled through it. She hasn't taken hold of a scene *once*. Not on one single occasion has she made a sentence *exciting*. It's a lady with a foreign accent who doesn't know the script very well. Got home about 7 o'c. & spent the evening talking to myself and reading house columns in the paper. I still dream of the little house I might have some day.

Thursday, 28 January
I tackled Banbury personally. It was awful. One suddenly realised he didn't know what to do about Bergman! He said apropos her not knowing the lines 'If I start being severe with her, she may lose her confidence and then where should we be?' Then he went to her room, but the dresser told him 'Miss Bergman has gone home . . .'

Saturday, 30 January
Frith said one or two general things and announced his departure. I said 'But you have called a word rehearsal for this afternoon – aren't you going to attend it?' and he muttered something about 'Mister Beaumont ordered the word rehearsal' and left. We returned for the word run. I suggested we do moves as well, and as it progressed, Ingrid (starting to assert herself at last) gradually introduced various moves and changes which helped the scene, and when it came to the Trial I suggested she really move about and dominate it as a Prosecuting Counsel really *would*, and she jumped at it! All the actors on stage said how much better it was.

Monday, 1 February. Brighton
I got a small round of applause on the entrance which embarrassed me 'cos it ruins the delivery of lines. In the 2nd act they took up the curtain without checking on me, so I was off for the entrance!! Walter Brown went on in my stead and filled in. I think he enjoyed the emergency more than anybody else. The concluding duologue with Ingrid & Joss got rather bogged down 'cos she lost the lines, but the applause at the end was very good indeed. Frith Banbury said of the opening '*What an escape*!' thus echoing Shaw's last line of the play and indulging in the only bit of humorous irony I've ever heard from him.

Tuesday, 2 February
At lunchtime today I bumped into Dame Flora Robson who played Lady Cicely in 1950.[3] She said that afterwards, in Marrakesh, when

---

[3] 1948, at the Lyric, Hammersmith.

a native Berber offered his hand for money, she took it and said 'How d'you do' just as in the play! and added 'I suddenly became Lady Cicely in real life.' It was a charming anecdote.

Monday, 15 February. London
The D/rehearsal at the Cambridge was farcical. There were loads of photographers in the stalls and it was impossible to work seriously under such conditions so I got the giggles and larked about the whole time, winking at Ingrid & Joss and sending up Gibby who was appalling on the lines. Peter E. said he'd noticed me larking about and said 'You behaved disgracefully.' I said 'Yes – I always do when I'm faced with boredom.'

Thursday, 18 February
Binkie on the telephone. Would I please attend rehearsal today to keep Ingrid in the theatre! She's been sick all night – it is probably nerves, they all think. Got to the theatre to find the room full of presents and – most prized of all, a note from Ingrid: 'Be my next director – feed out of your hand, I would . . .' The show went through competently and at the end there were nine curtains and Ingrid had to take 3 solo calls. The house obviously adored her, and rightly so.

Friday, 19 February
Rang Peter E. and he advised not to buy the papers, 'cos they are all rotten for me *and* the play. I hope it doesn't hurt Ingrid.

Sunday, 21 February
Clive drove me up to Highgate and we had the lovely lunch – sirloin of beef and champagne.

Monday, 22 February
Birthday cards delivered from Tom & Clive, and B & G, by hand, and great present from Fred!! Bottles of drink! The postal strike continues. I did the accounts on the new Decimal forms.[4]

Wednesday, 24 February
Ingrid is still doing some lines well and some lines badly . . . it is because the lack of stage technique makes her unable to *sustain* moments, or comedy effects . . . Nevertheless I *adore* this woman and will forgive everything from someone who has her sweetness, radiance and generosity of spirit *and* who *packs* the theatre as she does. It is really marvellous to play to such houses.

---

[4] Decimal currency had been introduced on 15 February.

Friday, 26 February
Walked to the Paris to do the spot – about 15 minutes' chat. It was a lousy house and they certainly needed a kick up the arse so I told the blowing-off story about the Carry On – *yet* again. Walked to the theatre at 6.30. Went up to Joss's room for the chat and he showed me some appalling notices in the weeklies! They are really dreadful.

Monday, 1 March
Went to the Centre, where Stewart Morris, looking much thinner and younger, told us about the format of the show, and provided an office for Myles Rudge & me. Most of it fell to me, so I plodded on so that one got about two pages of usable stuff.

Friday, 5 March
Saw Bill Cotton and told him about all the writing problems. He agrees with me. He actually suggested to Myles that he write a script on his own and submit it to the BBC. Left the Centre and met John Maynard[5] – I asked him if he would write with me and he said 'I'd love to, but for comedy – no – I'm not good enough . . .' It's interesting that everyone is willing to say whether comedy material is good or bad but hardly anyone is willing to sit down and write it.

Sunday, 7 March
There is something strangely paradoxical in that so many people in the frivolous business of entertainment are seriously professional without pretentiousness or mystique, and in the serious business of entertainment pretentiousness and mystique abound. You get more work done (and entertainment as a result) with comedians in the variety side than you ever do with actors. This is why places like the National Theatre do not produce anything funny. The nearest they got was the genius of Maggie Smith but then she was a star before she got there really.

Tuesday, 9 March
Hilary [Minster][6] came and we drove to the Centre. We worked sporadically and did only half a script. In the lift I talked to Huw Wheldon about the difficulties of writing comedy and he said 'Oh bollocks! you just go out, find your situation, and then come back and write it down!' We returned to the Cambridge. There I read the Carry On script which Eade had left at the S/Door. It is terrible for me. I'm required to be *old*, but a lot of the stuff is exterior! And you can't fake

---

[5] Latterly Script Editor of the BBC soap opera 'Eldorado'.
[6] Actor, later prominent as Von Klinkerhoffen in the BBC sitcom ''Allo 'Allo'.

age in the open air, there is loads of location stuff and the dialogue is awful, with that inevitable 'girl seducing me' scene. I rang Peter Eade & said we must get out of it.

Sunday, 14 March

Suddenly couldn't face the evening alone, so I rang Rona and she asked me up there. Gordon told me this story of two young cockneys talking about the film of Marie Antoinette – apropos the scene where she asks the priest why she has to die, and one said 'That bit was good, when she says "How comes this then? I done fuck all and I'm getting topped in the morning!"'

Tuesday, 16 March

Peter E. came round. I told him of my apprehension about all these bloody scripts and of my suspicion that 'International Cabaret' had been dropped by the BBC and 'Meanwhile on BBC2' was really a separate show into which I'd been shoved at the last minute.

Wednesday, 17 March

By 5 o'c. I had finished script No. 5 – it is the first script I've ever done which wasn't written with anyone else in the room with me. It will be interesting to see if it gets any laughs at all!

Monday, 22 March

Eade telephoned. His cowardice is amazing! I told him that it was to be a condition on the next film that they did the car, and *now* he informs me that 'they couldn't possibly agree to that' so we're back in square one! on the same money! and for a longer period! 7 weeks! and he didn't *tell* me till today, so it's too late to change etc. So I have to fix my own transport. There's no doubt, as far as business is concerned, he's a lousy agent. The show was fair, but it's now become a penance as far as I'm concerned. T & C came around & we went to Peter Mario. Two Jewish couples sat right next to us – tho' the place was empty – and talked so loudly that we moved a table away. At one point I said 'They represent the worst kind of Jewry – the Hendon, Golders Green kind . . . totally unintelligent . . .' and they heard. One man said 'They're only a load of pooves . . . I feel sorry for them myself . . . haven't they gone quiet!' as indeed we had! I was staggered by the reaction! I never dreamed they'd overhear my remark. We all beat a hasty retreat.

Friday, 26 March

My mind keeps returning to the idea of moving. I don't really like this place – I don't like the behaviour of the people and I don't like the streets and I don't like the size of these poky little rooms that I've got. I want a bit of spaciousness. I liked having a study and I liked having enough room to put the Hoover round everywhere quickly. I want all that back *and* I want central heating back – I don't like getting up in the morning shivering, and having this measly little bath with not enough hot water to cover me properly.

Friday, 2 April

At Pinewood it was comparatively easy with little work to do.[7] Lunch with Bernie Bresslaw and Kenneth Cope.

It takes only the smallest sort of hurt to destroy me, and in the process, destroy my work as well. The saddest part of it all is that most of the cruelty which causes this sort of destructiveness is born of wrong-headedness – not malice. The stupid notice which Helen Dawson[8] wrote in Plays & Players was shown (by some fool) to Ingrid! – with the result that she cried, and her weeping doesn't result in a better show but a worse one. The 'cruel to be kind' attitude simply doesn't work with actors. It destroys them: whereas you can *change* them and help them and *improve* them, with humour and affection – above all, affection.

Sunday, 4 April

Most of the time nowadays it's tears, tears, tears. Tears welling up inside of me. I feel the bleeding going on inside – every day I die more consciously. The staring, the stopping in the street, the nudging of people when they recognise me – my fear of them – my *hate* of them, my desire to get away from their prying eyes . . . and always this longing for a quiet death. What is the point of *pretending*? All this stuff about 'You've done some good with your life!' that I get from my friends – what good is it, if it's not good for *me*? It's the utter loneliness of the existence.

Monday, 5 April

Hilary Minster came into the D/room but I said 'No – I don't want to talk to anyone' and he left in a huff. But I can't help it. The despair

---

[7] On *Carry On at Your Convenience*.

[8] Critic and author, who married (1978) John Osborne, as his fifth wife. Her review (*Plays and Players*, April 1971), concentrates on Ingrid Bergman: 'I can see that she is blessed with a pleasing, perfect profile, but for me, the face is almost antiseptically free of cut, thrust, and, at least from a seat a few rows back in the stalls, any evidence of the interesting trials of life . . . Miss Bergman has no voice for projection and she reacts wildly when she's not being spoken to and hardly at all when she is. Also she has a tendency to cut in on other people's lines while dispensing with quite a few of her own.' Ensuring KW's disapproval, she goes on to characterise his contribution as 'not so much a performance as a turn, and also largely inaudible'.

is too *large* in me at the moment & I could spill over any minute.

Tuesday, 6 April

I was grieved to hear of the suicide of James Mossman.[9] He was a good fellow – apparently the death of both his mother and his friend had made life unbearable for him. He suffered deep depression – the dear man – may he be comforted.

Wednesday, 7 April

Pinewood. Finished by 10.30, washed the hair etc. then foolishly went into the bar, and talked with Peter Rogers who insisted on my having a drink – I ended up having two so of course I was pissed by lunchtime! Kenneth Cope sat next to me at lunch and I've always thought him most exciting so of course I was coming out with all the stupid stuff like 'What does it feel like to be so desirable?' & generally embarrassing him dreadfully.

Thursday, 8 April

I had smoked 3 cigarettes today by 2 o'c. and then I decided to kick it. Did not smoke for the rest of the day. By the end of the evening my breathing was better. I will give up drink as well for certainly I've never really enjoyed it.

Sunday, 11 April

To Shepherd's Bush. I went in to the theatre and suddenly I was *plunged* back into that other atmosphere of illusion, lights, razzmatazz and rubbish. It was marvellous. The Young Generation was splendid. Howard Keel sang 'Oh What A Beautiful Morning' etc. All my stuff went all right. Stewart Morris said 'It went like a bomb! Better than any of your other shows . . .'

Friday, 16 April

Griffith James came up and said 'I saw you stick your tongue out when you were facing upstage at James Kennedy . . . when you thought the audience couldn't see you . . .' I replied 'Oh well, if I did, I did, but one can't be *good* every night . . . actors are not automatons' and of course the stomach started churning and my heart started banging so that by the third Act I lost all my confidence and walked thro' the play. At the curtain I said to him 'Next time you criticise my performance, do it at the end of the show – you ruined my third act completely – ruined it.' Went to the D/room so upset I could have wept. Came

---

[9] b.1926. Journalist and television interviewer.

home and smoked 2 cigarettes & drank gin and felt suicidally depressed.

Monday, 19 April

Pinewood – everyone expressing their derision at my smoking again! Gerald said the next one is *Carry On Matron* – it seems the hospital jokes are unending. Felt quite buoyant on the set today. I notice that whenever I'm volatile etc., Sid James gets really irritated!! He doesn't like it when he's alongside someone who is getting the attention in an amusing way: as an entertainer himself he's talentless & resents it in others – but as a man he is kind and generous, albeit a philistine.

Tuesday, 20 April

There is this joke about two men chatting:

FIRST MAN: I can't wait to get home and tear off my wife's knickers . . .
SECOND MAN: Why?
FIRST MAN: They're too *tight* for me.

Of course the tag line has to be delivered with the right degree of restrained wriggling. It was told to me by Hattie Jacques. She did it brilliantly and then burst into peals of laughter about it.

Wednesday, 21 April

The show went in mediocre fashion because Ingrid fluffs appallingly and tonight she was lousy. At the curtain she said 'Oh! let's get this over and then all get drunk.' I don't think she is very happy inside herself in spite of the apparent serenity of it all.

Thursday, 29 April

Pinewood. We did the Factory Yard scene – I was doing the wanking mime and Renée Houston shouted 'Don't do that sort of thing in front of me – I don't like it . . .' but Hattie poured oil on troubled waters. Houston is just an old woman who drinks too much and whose career has been on the skids for so long that it's made her a bag of nerves. She couldn't get it right – never knew the lines – and we had to do several takes.

Friday, 30 April

On my entrance with the chair in Act I, I was late – about 5 seconds – and Bergman was furious. When she came off I said 'I apologise for being late . . .' and she was graceless and said 'I don't speak your language so I can't extemporise.' I thought she was quite horrid about it – it's the *only* time it has happened in the run and I am doing several other jobs. If she got censured every time she dried or ruined a line, she'd be in the pillory perpetually. Walked home depressed thro' the cold streets.

Monday, 10 May

Marianne Stone told me at lunch today that Harold Lang was dead! He was only 46 and died in Cairo, about four months ago, of a heart attack.[10] It brought back all those memories of Goacher and that set in Museum Street – oh! I am *glad* I got out of all that – the bitterness, the dishonesty of it all! Ugh!

Tuesday, 11 May

Walked to Le Cheminant with Louie and ordered a silver salver to be inscribed: '*Presented to Miss Ingrid Bergman on the occasion of the 100th performance of* Captain Brassbound's Conversion *at the Cambridge Theatre, London, 17.5.71, with the admiration and affection of the cast.*' They said they think they can have it ready by Friday. I certainly hope so! Otherwise it is all rather pointless.

Thursday, 13 May

I took a great dislike to the travelling clock which I purchased yesterday, so I chucked it in the dustbin. Actually I put it on top, so if the collector wants it he can have it. I'm getting the head banging palpitations and headaches and body aches and I'm walking about like an old man. But ironically – I have been very happy during this period.

Friday, 14 May

Joss frightened me by saying 'Poor Ingrid . . . she isn't *well*, you know' and last night, with his encouragement, she was impersonating me in the wings! Face, voice etc. I said 'Stop doing it! It's a disgrace!' and she said 'I bet you go round impersonating *me*!' Obviously there's a lot of chat goes on in this company which I don't know of, 'cos my room is away from everyone else, and I do so many other jobs I don't see much of them.

Monday, 17 May

Tom & I went to the party and I gave Ingrid the engraved salver, and made a speech and the press took the photographs. Ingrid said 'Nothing like this has happened to me . . . I shall treasure it . . .' but she left the party very early 'cos she said there was no air in the place.

---

[10] Lang died in November 1970.

Tuesday, 18 May
Lots of members of the cast asked me if they could contribute something to the salver but I said not to bother 'cos it's only the gesture which really matters & they all endorsed it and said it was a very good idea and that it made the occasion. I walked home thro' the mild streets reflecting that it *was* a good thing that I did *Brassbound* because it's meant that I returned to the theatre after six years, and returned in a big success. Barclays and bed at about 12 o'c. with 2 mogs.

Thursday, 20 May
Evening show OK and after!!! – I went up to see Sir Noël Coward in Ingrid's room. He was with Coley[11] and Graham Payn. I sat at his feet and told him about Stanley and me passing the Nat. Gallery today & me quoting 'We've seen the National Gallery opened, the Houses of Parliament burn, the introduction of Income Tax which gave us quite a turn . . .'[12] and Stanley saying 'Coward, of course – who else?' He was adorable and said my performance was very good. 'You are one of the few actors I know who can be outrageous and get away with it . . . and we love you for it.' At one point when Ingrid mentioned Eleonora Duse[13] he said 'I saw her . . . she over-acted dreadfully . . . even when playing an eighteen-year-old at sixty she never had a shred of make-up . . . and her hair was snow-white, done up in a sort of terrible bun at the back . . . it was all most discouraging . . .' He looked very good and kissed me on both cheeks with real affection. Impossible to tell him what I *really* owe him but I did say 'My debt to you is infinite & your dialogue *and* your lyrics go on delighting me and reverberating thro' me every year . . . there's not a day when you're not with me . . . esp. when I sing "Now In the Clear Bright Morning"[14] and he replied 'That's my favourite sentimental lyric' and he said I was clever to remember the words. When he'd gone I said to Ingrid 'It's been a beautiful evening and you have made it all possible . . . you don't realise how much warmth, delight and *love* you bring into a room with you . . .' Walked home thanking God for bringing all my dreams to fruition . . . couldn't sleep for excitement.

Friday, 21 May
Griff James told me that Coward overheard him taking a party round the theatre last night & Griff was saying to them 'I will tell you how the lights work, how the curtain is operated and how . . .' and Noël

---

[11] Cole Lesley (Leonard Cole, 1911–80). First valet, then secretary, manager and biographer of Coward.
[12] Lines from 'Oh What a Century it's Been', in *After the Ball*.
[13] 1858–1924, Italian actress who toured the world.
[14] From *After the Ball*.

interjected 'And tell them what an enormous profit Binkie is making . . .'

Sunday, 23 May
On shaving I thought again how lovely my face is . . . perhaps I shall decline into an Indian Summer beauty. Wrote to Edward Heath saying I admire him very much: do hope he gets us into Europe, and to the Spectator saying I thought their cover was distasteful and vulgar.

Tuesday, 25 May
The show went OK – v. big house – but I farted very loudly during the 2nd act and there were muttered cries of 'dirty sod' and 'pooh!' from the cast. Ingrid didn't notice.

Wednesday, 26 May
I walked up to Louie and then we went to various shops looking for a fur coat. At Dickins & Jones we found two marvellous coats. A Queen Christina long coat in mink and leather for £410 and a Jacket at £480. Louie chose the Jacket. It's gorgeous – there's no doubt of that.

Thursday, 27 May
Joss's fly zip broke and all the company fell about giggling and some people left the auditorium. Discipline is at a low ebb, and the supports all know there is little that anyone can do.

Friday, 28 May
To TV Centre to do the interview with Ken Everett (apparently he's a disc jockey) who was very pleasant. Gave me the telephone number and said 'Come down some time when you want a bit of peace in the country . . .' which was very sweet of him.

Friday, 4 June
Off to the Paris for this radio series 'Secret World of KW'. A strange collection of BBC rep. types – none of whom are laugh getters, but my stuff went all right & I think on the whole, it was a success for a start to a new series. Walked to the theatre at 6.45 just saying to myself 'Thank God for being alive.' During the performance, I noticed everyone was being v. good, & then they said 'Alfred Hitchcock[15] is out front!' Ingrid asked me up for drinks with him. He was enchanting, and we all went off to Inigo Jones for dinner. At the restaurant Hitch

---

[15] 1899–1980. He had directed Bergman in *Spellbound* (1945), *Notorious* (1946) and *Under Capricorn* (1949).

'Two photographs of me on the beach at Brighton, 30 June 1957. It was hot and sunny, but a good sea breeze, and altogether very pleasant indeed. M[ichael Hitchman] went into the sea but I didn't.'

Gordon Jackson, 8–9 August 1957, Brighton. 'Gording and Rona came down...This Brighton period was not entered into the diary at the time it occurred. I was too ill or pre-occupied to do it. Everything was ghastly.'

BELOW: Captioned (by Gordon Jackson): 'Mine's as big as my *hat*!!' Brighton, 8–9 August 1957

ABOVE: 'John Vere gave me the photo...he is Fauntleroy in a Hancock TV.' 18 August 1957. From left: Hattie Jacques, Clive Dunn, John Vere, Tony Hancock.

RIGHT: 'A photograph Stanley [Baxter] and I did, in a "Take It Yourself" machine – it's not at all bad. Reely.' Brighton, 5 November 1957.

ABOVE: Bill Kerr and KW argufy, Tony Hancock draws his own conclusions (and keeps control of the script). 'Hancock's Half-Hour', 1958. (*Radio Times*)

LEFT: 'Broadcast of *Beyond Our Ken* went very well & I sang some 20's numbers, as a send-up of Bobby Beamish. Must listen in on Wednesday next (evening) at 8.' 24 September 1958. KW rescued by the original cast: Kenneth Horne, Patricia Lancaster and Betty Marsden, with (behind) Hugh Paddick and Ron Moody. (*Radio Times*)

'Spent day with Michael Hitchman.' 21 June 1960: Hitchman and KW in Trafalgar Square.

'This passport photo looks startled and plump to me. V. nasty.' 29 September 1960.

ABOVE: 'Photograph of me, Sheila Hancock, and Lynda Baron and Toni Eden in a barouche at Blackpool.' 29–30 March 1961.

LEFT: 'Photography in dressing room by Helen Craig. She took them for a display in Hampstead designed to raise funds for Roose-Evans's theatre up there. She was sweet – a grand-daughter of Gordon Craig. Wore no make-up which is lovely, I think, and was delightful to get on with. We had a drink in the White Horse afterwards.' 31 May 1962. (*Helen Craig*)

'I went down to Broxbourne by minicab. Mags and Bev at cottage down there, we sunbathed on the lawn. A really lovely Sunday, my first for ages. The Aga had gone out and Bev had a terrible job relighting it and consequently Mags' casserole was a bit dicey but it tasted v. good to me. I was starving. Beverley took the photograph.' 3 June 1962: KW, Maggie Smith and Tuffet.

KW and Beverley Cross in Venice, 17 June 1963. 'Evening gondola serenata. 2 hours. Fascinating. Back to bed.'

LEFT: 'This photograph was taken when Louie and I were walking on the front at Brighton. We walked to Roedean and then got the bus to Rottingdean where we had lunch. We caught the 5.25 Pullman back, having tea and Welsh rarebit.' 10 May 1964.

BELOW: 'Had passport photograph taken at the same place as I originally went to in 1950! And it came out as I wanted it. The camera operator said "You must smile!" But I ignored the stupid fool. I must look as I usually look, & that is *not* smiling.' 4 May 1965.

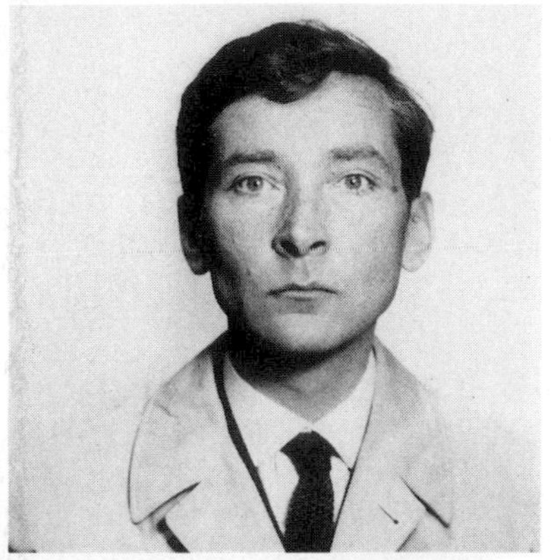

BELOW: 'To Lime Grove for the Simon Dee show. I babbled on talking rubbish and came away feeling suicidal. Simon gave me this print of the television transmission. It's the bit where he held my hand & said "Honestly I just like looking at you." He has the most fantastic self-possession.' 25 November 1967.

said that during *The Birds* he said in one sequence (where all these birds came down the chimney & attacked Jessica Tandy) 'Listen Jessica . . . if one of them gets up your skirt, grab it! Because a bird in the hand . . .' & that was certainly one of the funniest lines I've ever heard about filming!

Sunday, 6 June
TV Theatre at 5 o'c. Spots 1 & 2 died the death, and 3 and 4 went very well. The Stupids – a Swedish gymnastic act – livened things up considerably.

Monday, 7 June
Start of the new 'Just A Minute' series, Nos. 1 & 2. They both went rather well and I was behaving v. badly & shouting & bawling & lying like mad.

Tuesday, 8 June
I bought a lovely table lighter for Louie. This year, so far, has been the busiest of my life! Stage, television, film and two radio shows! It is ludicrous.

Friday, 11 June
Had to go to Ingrid for an autograph for Perihan and she sweetly wrote 'From her uncle's leading lady . . .' I should think Bergman is the *best person* I've ever met who is an International Star. I said to her in the wings 'You are being splendid tonight' & she said 'Yes, I'm in good voice too.' I said 'Yes, but the entrance was superb! So grand, so composed . . . utterly serene' and she replied 'Well you know about actors – you can't just switch it on – some nights it all just goes *right* . . .' It is true.

Tuesday, 15 June
Called on Domenic at the Garden to arrange the dinner tonight for Ingrid & Gordon & Louie & me, at the Grange, in the far room. Gordon was absolutely marvellous because he knew about *all* her films, right from *Intermezzo*. I said to her on the way out 'You are the best person I have worked with *ever* . . .' and she replied 'Oh! my dear, there will be others . . . many others . . .'

Wednesday, 16 June
Got up at 7 o'c. and sat drinking coffee & smoking fags and feeling totally disorientated: I'm like a rudderless boat on the Caspian Sea . . . I am in a thousand tiny pieces. I don't know how I am going to get thro' the day. Great barclays at 8.30 with a vision of navvies on

a building site . . . thought I'd cut my letter out of the Spectator and stick it on this page.[16]

Sunday, 20 June
Washed the hair etc. for the TV tonight, 'cos I noticed in the viewing room on Thursday that the unwashed hair looked rather spikey and tat. Tonight is No. 10 and the *last*! Car to TV Theatre at 4.30. The star was Vera Lynn. All my stuff went down like yesterday's news. Stewart Morris said that he would 'put in a bit more laughter' but I was past caring. I got back to the flat at 11.45. Stood in the bedroom, heard the clock ticking & said to myself 'Over now . . . the dream is over now, maybe it really wasn't so important anyhow . . .', quoting Noël Coward.[17] For 10 weeks I've had ten opening nights on television with the most unrewarding audiences I've ever faced and I never want to do stand-up work again. The loneliness, the vulnerability and the level of banality required eventually succeed in diminishing one to a point of suicidal depressiveness. Took the Suppon. and mog.

Monday, 21 June
To the Garden to meet this Malcolm Williams who is to write this piece on me in the Radio Times. The interview went the 'too serious' way & he kept on about me being 'defensive' and 'not really coming to any conclusions' and I eventually said 'There aren't any to come to . . . except the obvious one; which is unprintable – that I'm a dead thing . . . I ceased to be an actor *years* ago . . .' Left him feeling utterly depressed and suicidal.

Thursday, 24 June
Second performance was dreadful. Gibson said 'Lazy Cicely' instead of Lady Cicely and everyone fell about 'cos I farted very loudly just after.

Monday, 28 June
By the time I'd bathed, washed the hair (Selsun) etc. and done the fingernails etc. and sloshed Monsieur Givenchy all over meself, I looked in the mirror and marvelled – I may be going to pot completely, but no one would know it! – all so lovely, I had the barclays.

---

[16] 'Sir: I agree with the letter (22 May) about the typography and lay-out of your paper. In truth, I used to *like* having the *Spectator* lying on my table but I don't now. I think the cover is particularly vulgar and the drawings distasteful. There used to be an admirable simplicity and dignity about the paper and I miss it now. I go on taking it, I must admit, but I always turn it face downwards.'
[17] 'The Dream is Over': the original version, written in the twenties, does not contain these lines.

Wednesday, 30 June
In the park for an hour and then to do the Children's Programme at B.H. At the interview, one small boy asked 'Was your nose always that funny shape?'

Wednesday, 7 July
Booked on the Direct Flight to Tangier on August 1st with a return for 3 weeks. So, as the play ends, I will go the next morning.

Tuesday, 20 July
To BBC. The discussion on Wilde, Corvo & Solzhenitsyn[18] was chaired by Derek Parker & was with Marie Rambert, Jennie Lee & me.[19] I agreed with J.L. on Wilde, but disagreed with both of them on Solzhenitsyn. I said that I thought *One Day in the Life of Ivan Denisovich* was rotten. I think it is. It may be excellent as a report on conditions in a political prison etc. but as a realistic novel, it is rotten.

Friday, 23 July
Car to the Paris for the last of my series. Today's had a proper adult audience and it worked all right. Party after & I got into one of those fundamental arguments with Keith Williams's wife!! and said things like 'Your kind of argument makes me very angry' which annoyed her. (I said this because, having told me that she was an atheist, she then said she didn't know the difference between Nazarene and Pauline Christianity.) Of course I was drinking too much . . . I dimly saw Peter Eade blinking thro' the haze, but I was stoned by 3 o'c. and returned to the flat to lie down and recover.

Saturday, 24 July
This production [*Brassbound*] was a boat that was never launched gracefully into the sea, but which bumbled and lurched down the slipway, made a few desperate voyages, overballasted and taking in water, and is now visibly sinking.

Tuesday, 27 July
Letter from Joyce saying *James* is in London, married, with a child! Oh! I would like to see James – just a look I mean . . . but could one take up the threads of all those years ago? It was at least as early as 1939 . . . I shall always remember walking down Tonbridge St on the

---

[18] Oscar Wilde (1854–1900), Frederick Rolfe ('Baron Corvo', 1860–1913), Alexander Solzhenitsyn (b.1918).

[19] Dame Marie Rambert (1888–1982): Polish-born dancer; founder and director of Ballet Rambert. Jennie Lee (1904–88): Labour MP at age twenty-four; Minister for the Arts 1964–70; widow of Aneurin Bevan.

way to the Regent (demolished) Cinema, when he said 'With my brawn and your brains we're a marvellous combination' and I hadn't the generosity to reciprocate. So Spender is right: 'and you lacked the courage to choose . . . and you have only yourself to blame . . .'[20] Louie was looking lousy. Bags under the eyes and the hair with that 'just done' look – the full 'Gracie Fields gone off' bit.

Saturday, 31 July
The second house was packed and v. enthusiastic. Ingrid came into the wings and was very affectionate, put her arms around me, and said 'So, at last my dear! To think I stood here and wished you luck half a year ago!' It appeared in the papers tonight that she has broken all records for a limited season in London by taking £250,000 in 6 months. Quite a few members of the company became rather sentimental and there were quite a few moments of underlining in performances! When I came to the line 'Dear me! We comes in with vanity and we departs in darkness, don't we guvnor?' I suddenly realised that when the lights went out tonight on this production, it would vanish for ever: this poor old creaking and rickety affair which was greeted with hostility by the press and grudgingly by a lot of people in our profession has proved a wild success commercially and entertained a lot of people. It must have entertained them or we would never have got the consistent laughs we have had night after night. I did all my packing and shot out to the car at 10.45. I am *free* of it . . . free of the endless bane of it . . . that awful humiliation of a thankless small part . . . ugh!

Sunday, 1 August. Tangier
Got to the Rembrandt by 10 o'c. and saw my beloved Hamadi and embraced him warmly and presented the shoes which pleased him. George took me to the Grenouille where Frank gave me a splendid welcome. Charles joined us and told of the panic during the coup here but all is now back to normal. There is something about this place that finds an answer in my spirit.

Friday, 6 August
Diarrhoea *again*. So all the medicine yesterday and all the medicine today has not cured the condition. This boy took me to the Casbah 'You meet lovely soldier – very strong'. Shown into this little room where a pathetically skinny Moroccan was lying in the actual torn undervest and pants which outdid Ada Bagwash. I embraced him for

[20] Concluding lines of Stephen Spender's poem 'The Double Shame'. Correctly, 'And you lacked the confidence to choose'.

the sheer pathos of it all, gave him 10D and left. Returned Lizba where the procurer said 'You can have me for 25' and I cried out 'Oh! you're too generous! I'll meet you here tomorrow!' with no intention of doing so.

Saturday, 21 August

Never has a holiday become so utterly boring and dreary as this (apart from Madeira). I went down to the Windmill & chatted to the same old crowd. I gave T & C lunch and then we walked to Magoga. Then we got involved with a young flaxen-haired American who had been kicked in the groin by some Moroccan thugs. Then I returned to the Windmill to settle my bill and found myself involved in a drinks 'do' at Anthony's & Francis's flat. Dinner with George in the Grenouille. I left the party at 11 o'c. and sat with a load of sailors from Belfast in the B'vard till about 1 o'c. when I returned to the Rembrandt. It has been a rotten holiday with undertones of unpleasantness and the ever-present hatred of the natives here. It is certainly time to go.

Monday, 23 August. London

When all is said and done, the fact remains that the sheer change of scenery does accomplish something in one's spirits and in that sense, Tangier does the trick. Its great drawback is really the fact that one knows it too well, which is at once the advantage and the disadvantage of the place. What has changed tremendously is the prosperity of the country – the number of cars about now is colossal compared with '66 or '67 and the number of male whores has diminished colossally too because now, there is literally nothing to choose from even if you wanted to, and I certainly don't. The one factor that has remained constant is the appallingly boring & meretricious nature of the expatriate settlers out there. They are the true parasites in that country and have earned real despite from the indigenous people.

Tuesday, 24 August

Up to Highgate. Clive had done a splendid meal and after we saw an interesting documentary on Axel Springer of the German newspaper fame. It was fascinating but there is no doubt that the BBC has a big left wing bias! And some of the 'angles' in the film were impertinent – especially considering they had Axel's cooperation & could never have done it without him. After, there was a lot of claptrap about Negro Black Militants with the ridiculous queen Baldwin[21] being all emotional and volatile and saying very foolish things like 'You English

[21] James Baldwin (1924–87), black American novelist and essayist.

created America with your convict settlement there . . .' I think she was mixing it up with Australia.

Thursday, 26 August
Met John Lahr who is writing the Orton biography. Again it started. All this raking over the old ground. He is to come to the flat to see the Orton letters! He asked if he could see *mine* to Joe!! but I don't think I can do that.

Tuesday, 31 August
He rang the bell promptly and I gave him all the letters and I read relevant bits of the journal, including all the stuff about the production of *Loot*. At one point John Lahr said 'I'd probably have been a bit bored with Joe if he'd been self-indulgent about his work . . . he'd have probably tried to grope me or something . . .' It made me laugh & I couldn't forbear saying 'I don't think so. You wouldn't have been his type . . .'

Thursday, 2 September
I played the Goldberg Variations, listened to Beethoven on the wireless and then heard Bernard Williams (Professor of Moral Philosophy at Cambridge)[22] talk. An interesting point he made was a personal one – that a moral philosopher should not pursue a moral belief which had no validity for himself: that if he did so, he couldn't profit by it in the sense of knowledge. This seems to me an admission of the uselessness of objectivity and to prove that the subjective is invariably man's imperative in any pursuit. The 'objectiveness' can only ever be relative, never absolute. It's a daft illusion to imagine it can be.

Thursday, 9 September
Louie came over. We went to the Nat. Gallery and I showed Louie the Guercino ['The Incredulity of Thomas']. It never fails to give me satisfaction. I think it shows a depth of vision and a sense of physical beauty totally in harmony with its spiritual counterpart. Here is a Jesus who is strong enough to be really compassionate, strong enough to accommodate the weak and the faint hearted and so beautiful that you know he is divine. It is at once tragic *and* triumphant – you *know* he is too good for *us*. You are led through tears to silence: to the peace of the inner sanctuary . . . where 'no bomb that ever burst shatters the crystal spirit.'[23]

I think so often nowadays of London as Byzantine. So much *form*

---

[22] b.1929. Knightbridge Professor of Philosophy, Cambridge, 1967–79, etc.
[23] George Orwell.

remains and so much *content* is vanishing. Again and again you feel in this city that despair is washing the walls and is eating into hearts of people and so the music gets noisier, the dancing more frenetic & fragmented, the conversations more wry and ruefully cynical (again & again you hear 'Oh! it's all a *con*') and the confrontations more & more stalemate – Ulster and terrorism, Trade Unionism and the Establishment problem, all of them talking from only one standpoint & thro' their own lenses [&] out of their own blinkers and the terrible *pride*, self-conceit, arrogance that brings whole nations into jeopardy.

Friday, 17 September

Walked to the Playhouse. Sheila Hancock said 'The reason the shows were rotten yesterday is because you were *sulking* . . .' After, I had a drink with David Hatch, Nick Parsons, Peter Jones etc. in the Sherlock Holmes. Nick Parsons kindly drove me to Highgate after 'cos I was dining with T & C. They were both in good form. I wrote a load of pornographic filth on their toilet roll and left them to discover it . . . I was giggling all through the pee in their bathroom. They drove me home at 12.30. I was up till 2 o'c. with the barclays. A charming laughing boy and jeans and policemen and hussars all flitted through my frenzied imagination and then there was all the clearing up in the bathroom and the benedictory ending from this dream lover saying 'Now you go to sleep . . . now you know what it's like . . . it's humiliating & all the rest of it, but I have to do it to you like that . . . it's for your own good . . . yes of course I love you . . . you fool . . . go to sleep . . .'

Thursday, 23 September

To Gordon & Rona. Gordon told me that Bette Davis was v. funny on the film and after every burst of rudeness she always added 'but thank you kindly all the same . . .' She was livid 'cos he gave her a round jigsaw puzzle – 'What are you trying to do to me? I want *straight* edges!!' and he said that Robert Wagner told him that Clark Gable had advised him (when working with Spencer Tracy) to 'grab the nearest prop and keep going.'

Tuesday, 5 October

I was walking home in Berners Street when I saw that Negro Orator with the mutilated hand & we had a chat. He said 'Things are very bad with me, man – very bad' so I gave him £2 – slipped it into his pocket for him – and he waved his arms and said 'Man! it's a lovely day!'

Monday, 11 October

First day of *Carry On Matron*. It was a murderous scene with medical dictionary talk plus thermometer in my mouth & taking the pulse and remembering every bit of business and I buggered it completely. By the time it got to take number seven I heard Gerald say to the cameraman 'Oh! let's keep that one and print it . . . it won't get any better . . .' and of course he was right.

Wednesday, 13 October

I read – or re-read – Heller's *Hazard of Modern Poetry*[24] and thought again of my great debt to this man. I suppose his singling me out for attention is one of the greatest compliments in my life that I know of. I have never met, before or since, such a man. The mind is wonderfully able to comprehend the complex and paradoxical nature of modern life, and incredibly, to foresee so much that has actually happened since the actual writing took place, in the field of modern literature. He echoes much of Auden's 'We must love one another or die' and eloquently stresses the need, the desperate need, for us to put *back* into our lives the absolute validity of the Human Affections. There is a particularly apt sentence: 'It is the truly pathetic fallacy of empiricism that it offers as safe harbour what is the ocean itself, the storms, the waves and the shipwrecks, namely man's experience of himself and the "objective world". The history of human kind is a repository of scuttled objective truths, and a museum of irrefutable facts – refuted not by empirical discoveries, but by man's mysterious decisions to experience differently from time to time. All relevant objective truths are born and die as absurdities . . .'[25] I wish I could write the entire paragraph because it becomes almost poetic. Starting with the language almost of a barrister it ends by sounding like Shakespeare.

Sunday, 24 October

I tried writing a piece for The Listener – it is about the essential vocal neutrality in a good newsreader – I don't know if it's any good really but I posted it off to the Deputy Editor because they've asked if I have got anything.

Monday, 25 October

I am glad I ate nothing yesterday because the belly was becoming

---

[24] In its original form, a series of BBC Third Programme talks; later added, as a final chapter, to reissues of *The Disinherited Mind*.

[25] This version, from the Penguin edition (1961), differs slightly from KW's transcription.

protuberant: when I looked down, it was obscuring the view of my penis and that would never do.

Tuesday, 26 October
During the filming this morning, I had a sausage in a roll and Gerald said 'Shouldn't eat all that bread . . . it is fattening . . .' I said 'You don't want to worry about me! My belly isn't sticking out' & he said 'No, but your arse is.'

Monday, 1 November
Off to hairdressers at 10.30. Henry told me of the IRA bomb explosion at the Post Office Tower! This is terrible news. It is one of our finest buildings and a telegraph communications centre. I wish they'd get these filthy Irish thugs and shoot them all.

Tuesday, 2 November
In the evening I listened to a man called [Philip] Oakes[26] talking about Tony Hancock and why he killed himself and he described Tony's death as 'an overdose of sleeping tablets washed down with vodka' and in that phrase, which cheapened & degraded the appalling occasion of human despair, this man Oakes revealed himself. When he said later 'I loved Tony Hancock' you realised that you were listening to a journalist finishing his column. Sid James said he'd seen him tottering drunkenly down Piccadilly and hadn't been able to stop his car and talk to him – 'That was the last I saw of him'; and Duncan Wood said he was a perfectionist who could never rehearse enough (after we'd heard how he'd played snooker all day *instead* of rehearsing.) It was only interesting to hear *between* the lines. V. depressing programme & meretricious in the extreme.

Tuesday, 9 November
To the Curzon Cinema because Michael C[odron] recommended the picture there. It is *The Conformist*, and Michael said it was 'absolutely marvellous.' I found it tiresome, cynical, stupid, inexpertly made, and depressing. Walked home afterwards saying to myself 'You are a Prince of the blood royal . . . you are a sensitive aristocrat in the midst of mud & mundanity . . .'[27]

Saturday, 13 November
I am really rather unhappy about my writing for The Listener. It is

---

[26] Author, critic and poet, b.1928. Co-wrote *The Punch and Judy Man* with Hancock in 1962.
[27] A persistent fantasy since childhood.

on my conscience (about the reference to announcers wearing wigs) because it's a disparagement of a human weakness, and as such, it is unworthy and uncharitable to write in this vein.[28]

Thursday, 18 November

The End of Picture Party was held in the Green Room at Pinewood and there was a superb buffet spread and lots of drinks. I talked to Hattie and Sid, Ken Cope, Ken Connor, Bernard Bresslaw, Charlie Hawtrey and two policemen from Langley. Gerald told me that he was 6 and a half days *ahead* of schedule. He said it was a record for him. I should think it's a record for the *industry*!

Monday, 22 November

Listened to my programme 'Secret Life of Kenneth Williams'[29] and thought it was bloody awful. Dirty and dreary and badly produced & badly acted. No *pace*.

Friday, 10 December

Laurena Dewar rang. Would I go on Thames Television and chat to Michael Parkinson? I said certainly not. North Country nit.

Monday, 13 December

Went out to the post at 11 o'c. and was surprised to find it sunny and mild, a really balmy delightful day. It seems incredible that on such a day, someone, somewhere, is being murdered.

I am in my decline now, and accepting it with tremendous panache.

Tuesday, 14 December

Tom arrived at 6 o'c. He came alone because Clive is having Australian trade. We went to the Colosseo and were surrounded by the sort of accents that make one want to *smash* the English moneyed class. Voices that are actually *cultivated* to *sound* like something instead of *conveying* that something. Their complacent loudness is offensive in itself. This is the sort of thing which throws me right into the arms of the working class: I belong there atavistically and sexually. I got into a long argument with Tom over South Africa, insisting that it

---

[28] The published 'Views' column by KW (*Listener*, 23 December 1971) concluded: 'The magazine news programmes on radio, with announcers trading quips and esoteric asides to each other, are invalidating their own comment, and the television spectacle of gentlemen in make-up and colourful clothes performing rather than reading the news debases a coin they'll all want to use later. I want to use it now.' The phrase 'colourful clothes' replaced 'human hair wigs' at KW's request, the page-editor, Mary-Kay Wilmers, complying 'regretfully' with this emendation.

[29] Written by R.D. Wingfield.

was a chauvinistic, nationalistic, repressive and brutal state which exercised a tyranny over liberalism. You can't keep sneering at Liberalism without also sneering at what is best and dearest in English society. Tom kept reiterating this old cliché about the Africans not being ready for civilised government etc. etc. This is always being advanced as a reasonable argument but unfortunately it is not what the struggle is about. Whether or not a man should behave in a certain way in his *own house* is not the point, the point is that to deprive him of the means of ever getting his own house is immoral and wicked. This is why S.A. is guilty of crimes against humanity and it is why she will, one day, be condemned and destroyed by the very inhumanity she is creating.

Wednesday, 22 December

I had a feeling that my article would be out today and went to the station bookstall, and there, sure enough, was my name on the front of The Listener!! They've invalidated my writing, by putting on the same page a great drawing which lampoons me, and by placing on the opposite page the entire script of a 'Secret Life of KW' programme. It is utterly stupid.

Why do I always remember being very young – about 10 or 12, and being so happy on top of a bus in Kingsway on a raining afternoon going to Woolworth's in the Strand to buy pens and paper and paper clips . . . Oh! I loved *stationery* and all the accoutrements of *writing*.

Thursday, 23 December

In last year's diary I had an article I wrote for an undergraduate magazine so I suppose this year represents an advance.

Friday, 24 December

A great parcel arrived from Robert Bolt!! It was 3 bottles of gin! This is both generous and kind! He always remembers me. I got wine for T & C and chocolates. I shall take this up to their house tomorrow – 3 bottles of Graves & chocolates and 200 cigarettes, and a bottle of Gordon's gin ('cos they like the odd gin and I don't) and the bonded razor for Clive. T & C came and I gave them dinner. Then we drove to St Paul's for the service. The cathedral was packed. Donald Swann did the warm-up. Carols at the piano. The service was conducted by a bad speaker with an Australian accent and we were surrounded by Swedes & Danes. Tom went to the altar rail & received communion. Clive & me stayed put but sang our hymns as valiantly as we could to the worst organ accompaniment you could ever imagine.

Saturday, 25 December

We saw the television 'Christmas With The Stars' – stars indeed!! what a *joke*. It's all the 'jobs for the boys in the BBC' stuff with inane excerpts from 'Dad's Army' & etc. Television has really succeeded in creating a number of rep companies, with all the same provincial tattiness and the same sort of factious following and internecine rivalries. Utter muck.

Tuesday, 28 December

Back to Dale Lodge to see *The Great Escape* and the Panorama Year Review. This latter was an absolute disgrace. Morality has departed it seems. The incredible feat of man orbiting the moon etc. was shown, and intercut with shots of puppet mice and an idiotic commentary for children sending it all up. A sermon, spoken by a clergyman about 'our God-given country & all our riches' etc. was soundtracked over vision of smoke-filled cities and slag heaps and utter devastation and that was sent up too. Northern Ireland was reported so the Army actually *looked* fascistic and the IRA gangs made to look heroic! The BBC must be absolutely full of socialistic or communistic sympathisers. The organisation is rotten to the core.

Wednesday, 29 December

As this diary draws to a close, I can at least acknowledge some self-improvements. I am becoming more charming with the years and gradually learning that one must expect nothing of anybody with the exception of G[eorge] B[orwick]. He is totally consistent with the years: and totally loyal.

Friday, 31 December

Got a taxi to Gordon & Rona. The house was looking beautiful, with a huge Christmas tree dominating the drawing room, and I suddenly felt so *safe* there. These are the friends to be really cherished, because even the times when we have had disagreements are all informed by a professional awareness of what we are as *actors* – I suppose that is why the only really good permanent relationships that *work* for me are the ones with fellow artists. Gordon played *Valse Ultime* and Rona & he sang it in French & as usual it enchanted me. When I drank a champagne toast with them to 1972 as Big Ben struck, I just adored them both. They've given me a wonderful present – the Oxford Companion to Eng. Lit.!!

1972

Sunday, 2 January
Of all the utter fatuities in the New Year's Honours list, the theatre one is the greatest! They've made that idiot Courtneidge mediocrity a Dame! They've put *that* alongside Edith Evans, Peggy Ashcroft and Flora Robson! Oh dear! these three should send all their insignias straight back!

Monday, 3 January
In the evening I had the extraordinary good fortune to hear a Lieder recital by Ian Partridge[1] accompanied by his sister at the piano. It was some Schubert and the Schumann Liederkreis. I was able to follow everything with my book of Lieder which Gordon gave me. It was a rare treat and I sat down at 11.30 and wrote a letter of appreciation to Ian Partridge – I will have to look out for some of his recordings because he sings most beautifully.

Tuesday, 4 January
I got a recording of Ian Partridge singing 'Wenlock Edge' songs[2] and some songs of Blake. The setting of the Housman poems by Vaughan Williams is almost an *essay* of misunderstanding. Hardly any of the Housman poems even comes off as a song: the first impression is one of dirgelike intoning which is reminiscent of church singing, and the sheer editing or 'placing' of the words, and their musical emphasis, is atrocious. All this is redeemed by the fact that Partridge soars above this indifference with his sheer musical talent and lyrical ability.

Saturday, 8 January
I was astonished to find myself looking so lovely in the mirror: the longer hair flatters the appearance, as it frames such pale beauty. Cut me toe while doing the nail 'cos it was ingrowing but found, in such

---

[1] Concert tenor, b.1938. Frequently performed with his sister Jennifer.
[2] Recorded January 1970 with the Music Group of London. Words from A.E. Housman's *A Shropshire Lad*.

circumstances, it is best to continue the process of separation (nail from skin) under the water tap because that helps.

Monday, 10 January

At 2 o'c. I walked through the city to Shoreditch & returned via Old Street, Goswell Rd. and Mount Pleasant. Some of the areas are utterly sordid and the soulless concrete blocks which are replacing the old slums have an equally depressing effect on the environment. I saw one schoolboy wandering along, lost in a world of his imagination, & I thought 'Romantic dreams have given hope to so many young people who have to grow up in aesthetically revolting surroundings, and I ought to know, because I was one of them.' When you see the filth and the squalor of the East End you *marvel* that the year is 1972! One has come all this way, and supposed there had been civic enlightenment, but here it is as dark as ever. Called at the chemist at King's Cross & the assistant said 'You are looking peaky!' which irritated me & I replied 'I have suffered many things.' She said 'What things?' & I said 'Things that cannot be discussed with you.' I got the Gevral & left.

Tuesday, 11 January

Postman brought me a parcel which turned out to be *Wenlock Edge*!! Ian Partridge has sent me his recital of these songs as a gift! This is a charming gesture.

Sunday, 16 January

Read the papers and the stuff written by Goronwy Rees[3] about the Burgess–Maclean scandal is muck-raking in the most incredible bad taste: one wonders how such a man could *ever* have become the friend & confidant of *anyone*, and out of his own mouth he has condemned himself. I gave lunch to G & B. B produced some homosexual fantasy drawings (of policemen whipping a boy & then having him) which were very exciting indeed but embarrassing to peruse with B. watching one closely the while.

---

[3] 1909–79. Journalist, novelist and academic. A Marxist at Oxford, Rees was a close friend of Guy Burgess, who defected to the Soviet Union in 1951, as did his fellow spy Donald Maclean. Kim Philby, the 'third man', followed them in 1963. It seems likely that KW was reading advance extracts of Rees's autobiographical book *A Chapter of Accidents*, published in February 1972. Rees's view was unlikely to commend itself to KW, since Rees was 'a heterosexual and a theatrical Marxist' who 'observed this queer, perverted personality [Burgess] with affectionate tolerance' (A.P. Ryan, reviewing the book in *The Times*, 10 February). KW interprets what Ryan called 'the Boswellising of Burgess' as a betrayal.

Sunday, 23 January
The day was bleak & cold and there was a march of students shouting slogans & chanting mindlessly, all down Regent Street, accompanied by hundreds of policemen *all* denied their weekend leave. There were barriers at Downing Street and mounted police. It depressed me very much. The bawling long-haired youths shouting '*Thatcher out*!'[4] and carrying coffins expressing sentiments like 'Maggie Dead' etc. was the spectacle of only another form of fascism: and it's the same old mob instinct . . .

Monday, 31 January
There are warnings of power cuts because of these filthy mining strikes. Oh! what a scourge and a blight is the English working man! What a dishonest, lazy bastard! Only exceeded by the Welsh and the skiving Scots.

Friday, 4 February
Read an interesting piece in the TLS on pornography.[5] It maintained that it was *never* good literature and that it was self-denigrating & anti-social but that it was essentially the by-product of a highly literate society. It also mentioned that Anna Freud[6] had described the dilemma of the invert as being the result of 'a dread of emotional surrender' and this seems to be absolutely correct, as a diagnosis, to me.

Saturday, 5 February
Louie asked if I'd heard anything from the dreaded lurgies at Highgate & I said no, & that they were *out*. She said 'I can't get over them saying "We gave you Christmas!" without any thought apparently of what you have given *them* over the years! And they make so much of their little acts of giving you lunch or something!' I said 'Yes, well you are right, but it's over now . . . I don't want them in my life any more.'

Monday, 7 February
Walked to Laurena to tell her about my decision apropos the [Marcel]

---

[4] Mrs Thatcher was then Secretary of State for Education and Science. The previous June she had announced plans to end free school milk, earning her nickname of the time, 'Milk-Snatcher'.

[5] Article by M. Masud R. Khan (see entry for 15 July 1961, note, p. 174), 'The Abuses of Literacy: 4'. 'Anna Freud has diagnosed the essential predicament in perversion-formations as dread of emotional surrender. One could argue that the crucial predicament in pornography resides in the incapacity for sensual surrender.'

[6] 1895–1982. Psychoanalyst and writer, daughter of Sigmund Freud.

Achard[7] play. She said drily 'Well I suppose we will learn about the wisdom of the decision if and when it becomes a great hit!' This refers obliquely to the fact that I have turned down loads of plays which, later on, turned out to be great successes with long profitable runs: I was offered *No Sex [Please] We're British*[8] over 4 years ago & said no. But my decisions have not been based on whether I was turning down something profitable, they've been based on whether I would find the *acting* enjoyable. It is easy to suffer a bad script with rotten actors in radio, TV or films, but to endure it *night after night* is like a sort of Chinese water torture to me.

Tuesday, 8 February

More and more nowadays, I can feel the *mind* going . . . the concentration becomes so *local* that I'm staring at a wall tile and seeing murderously clinical *whiteness* . . . things start to take on new & startling dimensions. To Rona at 7.20. We talked about getting older and Rona said 'I have hated being forty! Have you?' & I replied 'I have hated *all* of it – all the years and all the ages.' It is true. The sooner I leave this vale of tears the better.

Thursday, 10 February

Delighted to find a letter from Gayden [Cross] in Seillans so that decided me. I've written to ask if they can fix some hotel or something & said that I will travel out there on the 21st February. It is sheer providence, given by the Almighty, which brings her message to me when I am so low and in need of a change of surroundings.

Wednesday, 16 February

Letter from Bev saying all that we discussed on the phone. He has written 'All longing to see you,' the kind of phrase that makes my winter heart sing. Did some more writing. A sort of play about the effect of a coup d'état in Maroc on the expatriate English community: up to page 36 – mind, it's all scribble, scribble, but it is incredible the way that characters do start writing themselves after a time.

Friday, 18 February

A telegram boy delivered this wire which I have stuck in the diary.[9] I thought it might be a hoax, till I rang the Dorchester Press Office where they'd confirmed it. I haven't worked with Richard Burton

---

[7] 1899–1974, French playwright.

[8] By Anthony Marriott and Alistair Foot. Ran more than ten years at the Strand, transferred to the Garrick.

[9] This telegram from Elizabeth Taylor, inviting KW to the Intercontinental Hotel, Budapest, 'to help me celebrate my big 40', occupies three whole telegram forms.

since that early time in Swansea when he was married to Sybil. This birthday is for Elizabeth Taylor and Christopher, her son by the Michael Wilding marriage. They're filming in Budapest at the moment. I told the press agent at the Dorchester to say I couldn't make it 'cos I was going to France.

Sunday, 20 February

Suddenly – a dream: I am in a beautiful drawing room, it is evening and the windows are open on to a terrace. It is a still summer evening . . . I am walking from the room to the terrace. There is a man playing the piano for me, and the air is full of the notes spiralling up to the heavens . . . and I know that in this moment I have found happiness and that I am intensely grateful. I hope he knows it, but I haven't the ability to convey my gratitude to the man at the piano who has made it all possible. It is not the first time I've had this picture in my mind.

Monday, 21 February

Took off for Nice. Sat next to a couple from Edinburgh & she said 'Do you not like to be recognised? I'd never have thought you could have looked so solemn!' The steward whispered in my ear 'The first class compartment is empty if you'd prefer to go and sit there' but I declined, not wanting to snub the Edinburgh pair. As soon as we came through Customs I saw Bev & Gay and we waved madly to each other, my heart swelling with affection for them both. The hotel is full of dreadful cyclists who are on some sort of race competition & there are portable massage tables and the smell of embrocation everywhere. They are revolting. At dinner they sang communal songs. The food is very good.

Tuesday, 22 February

Drove thro' the mountains via Muy to St Tropez. It was divine. A little cluster of red brick & tiles round an enchanting little harbour. I am a little uneasy at the way Beverley is paying for everything. He wouldn't let me take the bill today & cried out 'Rubbish! It's your birthday!'

Wednesday, 23 February

Bev started to show me the ramparts of the old town but the wind was so gusty that we turned into the side streets & walked right into Virginia Gallico who said we must have drinks at the house. We went & were shown all over this luxurious abode & met Paul Gallico[10] who

---

[10] 1897–1976. Hungaro-American novelist.

said 'I am delighted to meet Kenneth Williams because he has given me so much pleasure' & I was taken aback & muttered 'You are most kind' and we had champagne and it was very pleasant. Then they introduced two Americans who write musicals (they did the ill-fated *Ambassador* at Her Majesty's recently); one was called Hal and the other was called Larry? Grossmith,[11] and they were both engaging.

Thursday, 24 February

Gayden gave us a cold supper which was v. good and after talk about the generation gap she went to bed. Bev lent me his torch and I did manage to walk back to the hotel on my own but I reflected ruefully that it was hard on my lovely shoes by Bally. They're not for the mountain goat.

Monday, 28 February

Bev came alone and said that Gayden was 'too exhausted to come to the airport.' We drove to Nice in comparative silence. At the airport we both flew to the lavatory and on the way out I saw Richard West with a nose like an electric light bulb sitting in the hairdressers'! He called me inside and got hold of my hand and kept repeating 'You know I love you dearly!' and the assistant with the hairdryer was considerably disquieted. I was stuck throughout the journey and he cadged a lift from Heathrow to Gloucester Road! Got home at 4.30.

Thursday, 2 March

To the Royal Court in the evening to see *Veterans*. It is spiritless and depressing. Endless trivia delighting in bad taste like a man exposing his penis, and two men measuring the lengths of each other's sword knots – i.e. phallic ref. again – and denigration of queers and laughing at queers and the terrible masochistic self-indulgence of Gielgud! oh! one became so sick of the half strangulated elongated vowels and breathlessness, and he is dreadfully unattractive. Gordon gave a v. lively and engaging account of himself, but the others have mistaken Charles Wood's writing for a latter-day Chekhov & treat it as boringly as most English productions are, of that mistreated Russian author. At the interval I told Rona flatly that I couldn't stand any more of it. She was cross and said 'You must see the second half' but I know all about this kind of rubbish within ten minutes of the first act, and as Gordon wasn't going to reappear, I had no intention of allowing myself to be further debilitated.

---

[11] The songs in *Ambassador* (at her Majesty's) were credited to Hal Hackady and Don Gohman.

Friday, 3 March
Curious dream that I was in *Charley's Aunt*[12] for only one matinée weekly, with John Gielgud, and I was hating every minute of it! I was so relieved on waking to realise it was all untrue! It is a dark rainy morning & very me.

Saturday, 11 March
Lovely letter from Fred H. to which I must reply promptly. He says complimentary things about my letter writing which give me a great deal of satisfaction and pleasure. It is wonderful to find such reciprocity in correspondence. Perhaps all one's life should be conducted on this level. I suppose actually that most of mine is. Practically all my existence is lived at one (or sometimes several) removes from reality (and by reality I mean what 'seems' to happen in the lives of average people) and I certainly lack the capacity to physically share a relationship with anyone . . . every time I've got near to it, I've been overwhelmed by pity for the utter pathos of people: and I can't adore where I pity. After every masturbatory episode I think 'Only *love* can redeem our ugliness, only great love can purge our ugly thoughts' and I know that it is true.

Friday, 17 March
Spent the morning bashing out this column for the Radio Times and finished at 1 o'c. I walked to Peter Eade's office to meet the bloke from Radio Times. He chopped my article from 500 to 240 words and altered the tone entirely. Made it much lighter and send-uppish. Then changed and went to Angela [Douglas] & Kenneth More's party. Rachel Roberts burst in and said 'You don't look any different to when you played Hugo and I was Olga in *Crime Passionel.*' I introduced her to everyone in the group, but she ignored them and went on about our affairs, and Swansea: 'I never see the Burtons. Richard is *still* telling the *same* old stories . . . it's so dreary.' (I thought 'You're not telling any new ones yourself!') It was a collection of appalling bores. All crashers.

Saturday, 18 March
Spent the evening listening to the Brahms on radio and the Sayers play and Redhead.[13] This latter is fast losing his touch. Tonight apropos letters which prove useful to a biographer he said 'The writer probably wasn't being truthful at all, but just thinking *this will make them wonder*

---

[12] The venerable farce by Brandon Thomas, first produced 1892.

[13] *'Unnatural Death*: The novel by Dorothy L. Sayers dramatised for radio by David Geary'. Brian Redhead, b.1929, chaired 'A Word in Edgeways'.

and doing it for the *effect* of eventual disclosure to the public.' Even if letter writers do behave like this – which I doubt – to say such things is hardly likely to advance the cause of biography or history: it sets out to demolish the validity of all sources. Ironically Elizabeth Longford[14] took this up, by adding 'Nowadays all people who keep diaries are suspect.' One felt like saying 'Suspected of what?' Diaries are written so that one has a record of events, and because there are certain events one *wants* to remember. There is perhaps also the element of the confessional in them, and that isn't a bad thing in my eyes. It has certainly eased my loneliness. The accusation of falsity comes because they say one isn't really objective, and only puts down 'what one wants to.' Of course one does. One puts down what *one* wants: not what *others* want. That is what is so delightful about the diary, it is what the self wants to say. All the inconsistencies and the bad judgments are glaringly revealed, but then so, in the process, is the self. The diarist is the classicist because he does want to make some order out of the jumble and accident and coincidence of the happenings of his day.

Monday, 20 March

Eade phoned and said 'Would you like to work with David Bell on 6 episodes of a comedy series for London Weekend?' and I said certainly not. Eade was furious and said 'You haven't had a peep out of the BBC . . . they've not come up with anything' and then we started on the same old merry-go-round of 'Where is the material?' at the end of which he admits 'There isn't any.' I must perforce admit, I am getting tired of these conversations with Eade and if it gets any worse I will tell him it's got to stop, or we shall stop. Stop being represented by him.

Thursday, 13 April

Walked to Peter Eade, and we had dinner at Casa Mario & then went to see *Dirty Harry*, the latest Clint Eastwood picture. It was v. good indeed & technically brilliant. Peter was going on about 'those nasty shirts you wear . . . cheap little stiff collars on them, like an awful bus inspector or something . . .' I said 'They're not cheap shirts! This one cost £1.60 pence!' and he smiled derisively and said 'Oh dear! that is *nothing* for a shirt!' He is extraordinarily snobbish about the daftest things. I left him at Shaftesbury Avenue and walked home thro' the back streets, trying hard to dodge out of the way of undesirables. That is an aspect of London that never used to be. One was never afraid, on the streets, in my youth. Today it is all very different

---

14 Elizabeth Pakenham, Countess of Longford, b.1906. Biographer.

and there are gangs of ruffians who lurk about Soho intent on trouble-making at a profit and drug addicts and drop outs and heaven knows what else.

Saturday, 15 April

The morality behind the [Don] Siegel film (*Dirty Harry*) is almost Homeric and epic. One man tries to do his job properly and, when he does it for the *last* time under Promethean provocation, he resigns from the police force. It is the story of an individual conscience & it is beautifully shown. One is very glad that such pictures are being made and I hope they make a lot of money at the box office. I have the instinctive feeling that Michael Codron is not speaking to me. Gordon thinks it's because I walked out of the Royal Court. I am sick and tired of wondering whether people are offended or not. My crimes are nothing compared with those of Genghis Khan.

Sunday, 16 April

Looked at the lines of the film script and marvelled that anyone can seriously consider such otiose material. There is a voice inside that says 'Keep going . . . you must keep going . . .'

'Why? There is really no point . . . it's all pain.'

'Memory will create illusions.'

'All we live for is really illusions . . .'

There is a line about that in Somerset Maugham: 'What do we any of us live for, but our illusions? And what do we ask of others, but that we be allowed to keep them?'[15] The choice is between selfishness and altruism. I chose the self. It was the right choice for me I think, but the journey gets lonelier all the time.

Tuesday, 18 April

Pinewood at 7.40. We are in the new K & J Block. The first day, for me, of *Carry On Abroad*. If you'd told me in '58 that I'd still be coming out to Pinewood to make these films I'd have said you were mad. Though it was the first day, there was an air of staleness over everything. A feeling of 'I have been here before' and I thought the acting standard was rather bad throughout.

Wednesday, 19 April

Joan Sims confided that she'd won the Mabel Temelly award for grace and charm in movement at RADA and added 'I got ten pounds on that day!' and Kenny Connor said 'And that's what she's still getting' which made me laugh, 'cos we all consider the daily rate on the Carry

---

[15] Spoken by Mrs Tabret in the last act of Somerset Maugham's *The Sacred Flame*.

Ons is derisory. David Kernan and [Jimmy] Logan both remarked on my ability to learn a lot of lines. They speak as though it is remarkable: of course it isn't. It is our job. I've got about five scenes to learn tonight. I do hate learning. It's a good job I don't have to do much of it. I only have to look at it a couple of times and then it's in the head all right.

Thursday, 20 April
I sat next to Gale Grainger on the bus coming out. I rather like her. She is a good actress and a sincere person with a willingness & a kind of humility which means you can make a suggestion & she will act on it. There is another girl called Carol [Hawkins] who is sweet and a girl named Sally [Geeson] who is adorable. When you meet girls like these you understand why men fall in love with the opposite sex: they're gentler, kinder, and understanding about vulnerability. I talked to Kenny Connor a lot and he said it was ludicrous that we were working for the same money we got in 1960 and said 'That crowd out there asking for our autographs think that we are rich, and we ain't even got a pen to sign their books with!' and I suppose it's true. Certainly it is daft that my film salary should be roughly 130 pounds a day! I should earn in a film daily rate what I earn in a theatre weekly rate, so I should be on at least 200 a day.

Friday, 21 April
Coach to Slough High Street to continue the exterior stuff. In the coach, Kenny Connor came aboard with his wife (played by June Whitfield) and asked Sid James: 'You wouldn't happen to have some spare bromide would you? – you see, the jogging of the coach excites my wife . . .' and Sid and Joanie started laughing & that set the tone for the day. Kenny is one of the most mirthful people and one of the most authentic ad-lib men that I know. Talked with Bernard Bresslaw who was fascinating on the subject of Judaism and the problem of the progressive v. orthodox in Israel. Bernard is an enchanting and lovable person. I always enjoy his company.

Monday, 24 April
Sat in the coach waiting & later in the caravan with Sid James. He talked at length about Hancock and said that he used to go about the flat naked with excreta & vomit about and that his sexual appetites were depraved & that Matt Monro told him he'd woken up one night to find Hancock going down on him for the fellatio, and that Matt had 'given him a right hander.' This is certainly a new twist. I'd never heard that Hancock was interested in homosexuality. Sid said 'It got so that he'd try *anything* . . .' Of course one wonders how much

of this is factual and how much gossip put together from disjointed accounts.

Monday, 1 May

Didn't work till 2.45. It was bedroom scene, me in pyjamas. I did the 'vagina' business by pushing the cock between my legs & the wardrobe women cried out 'Oh! stop it! It's revolting!' and kept making disapproving noises. They have no sense of humour.

Friday, 5 May

Feel leaden and uninterested in anything. I should give up fags but I like inhaling. I should give up drink but I like the idea of drink. There are no other pleasures for me. O I don't mind about dying – not at all – but I am frightened to death about pain: and there is another aspect of it: I have a secret contempt for all weakness, including my own.

Saturday, 6 May

Walked up Charing X Road to Foyle's. I passed an innocuous looking middle-aged man who was respectably dressed à la Dunn's gents' outfitters who said loudly & without looking directly at me: 'Oh yes. Funny! Very funny little man, but I bet he can't *fight* . . .' and then he shouted at me 'Queen!' as I passed him. The depression is heavy upon me. It can't really be the nasty remarks of the man – one knows that he must be disturbed – though that incident probably sparked it off. Everything is so fraught with unreality . . . the feeling that one is walking in a trance life & that all round one is misery. I suppose that the dropping of the horrors has brought home to me the desert of my existence. Not that I want that relationship back again. Even if it had a germ of goodness it was still right to relinquish something so meretricious. I must welcome the next thing God sends me. He always does send something. The mentors come. Just in time. But nevertheless they come.

Wednesday, 10 May

I was talking to Dave (the painter) and cadging some emulsion paint for the bathroom and he told me that George Bradford – the painter on the last film – was dying. He said that all those black spots on his body & face had turned out to be cancer and that he only had a week to live. I suddenly remembered how George had confided in me, on the set, about his anxieties regarding the black spots. They had removed *one mole* from his body and within weeks, he was covered in these black spots. Car came and we drove to Wexham Park Hospital by 5.45 and Sister Bromley showed me into a private room where George was dozing. She woke him gently and he looked at me and smiled and reached out his poor hand which was covered with all these black marks. I took it and I said 'Everyone was asking where you were on the set and we missed you very much . . . all the gags and the giggles we used to have! And I only heard today from Dave that you were in hospital . . .' He talked coherently and certainly knew me, and said 'Tell Bernard to get his cricket bat out and we'll play a game when I get back . . . and remember me to Gerald Thomas will you? and Barbara Windsor, don't forget' so I realised he doesn't know about the imminence of death. We talked for a bit and I said he must relax and not worry about anything and at 6.10 his eyes were closing with tiredness. I squeezed his hand and tiptoed out. Drove back on the M4 in pouring rain and half way home, the sky cleared, the rain stopped and there was a huge double rainbow. It was beautiful. The whole day was full of meaning.

Thursday, 11 May

The latest sick story is the surgeon saying to the patient: 'Well there is good news and bad news, I'm afraid, so here is the bad news first: we've had to amputate both your legs. Now, here is the good news: a man at the end of the ward is interested in buying your carpet slippers . . .'

Tuesday, 16 May

They told me today that George Bradford died last night, so my visit last Wednesday was just in time. Apparently it's in the papers that the actor Nigel Green has died from an overdose. Everyone on the set today complaining of tiredness and I am full of lassitude myself. Peter told me on the telephone that this was to be the only Carry On film this year!

Sunday, 21 May

Brian drove me to Gordon & Rona. We sat in the garden in the afternoon sun and it was truly deliciosa. Rona gave us a salad supper and I felt like a great glutton at the end of the day. I told the story of the revolting looking woman with a parrot on her shoulder, saying to a man passing by 'If you can guess what I've got on my shoulder, you can have me.' He replies 'Oh. Er . . . a crocodile?' whereupon she cries 'That's near enough' and grabs him in a passionate embrace.

Wednesday, 31 May

I know, even as I'm planning to go away, that it will solve nothing and probably end up proving a great bore and inconvenient to boot. In the restaurant I kept on about death and said to Louie 'You will be all right if I kick the bucket . . . there will be money to provide for you' and she said 'Oh! don't be so morbid . . . anyway, if you go, I will have nothing to live for . . . I wouldn't want to go on.' I know I shouldn't have talked like that with her 'cos it only succeeds in depressing her dreadfully, but the despair was so engulfing it all spilled over I'm afraid. Got home about 11.30, the taxi driver saying 'I reckon your films are very good' which is an opinion I wish I could share.

Thursday, 1 June
Pinewood at 9 o'c. I did 60 loops by 12.30. There was one *stinker* – an ad lib sequence where I went under an umbrella. I couldn't do it at all and I didn't really care either. They said they would try & juggle it technically.

Friday, 2 June
Left for the airport at 9.30. The stewards insisted on me having champagne with them, up forward, and I was very high by the time we arrived at Tangier at 2.35. Everyone in the Rembrandt was charming and the welcome was delightful. And it happened *again*!! that feeling of 'It is wonderful to be back in this place' – the sight, sounds and smells of it all are enchanting to me.

Sunday, 4 June
Went to the Grenouille where there was a great crowd at the bar. After, we returned to [the] Rembrandt and stood chatting there while a couple of soldiers shadowed us for the tradiola. Certainly, a few years ago, this would have greatly intrigued me but now, alas, I know that with this kind of encounter, there is much *less* than meets the eye.

Tuesday, 13 June
Eventually walked to the Grenouille and had dinner. It was crowded at 9 o'c. and several people were waiting for tables. V. was shouting and bawling at the bar and eventually went outside to be violently sick in the gutter. There is something about this resort which brings out the worst in people. Had coffee at the Café de Paris where a procession of male whores shamelessly paraded by the tables in a desperate endeavour to look inviting and make a profit at the same time. I fear most of them were out of luck, yet, like incurable punters, they all [come] back for the next race. At the moment, I really feel like packing it in and just going home, but perhaps things will change in the next couple of days.

Thursday, 15 June
We went to the B. Hotel. In the bar we met Norbert (the owner) and

three boys. I went off to one of the rooms with Mohammed (Bambi) heartened by Norbert's remark 'All my boys are clean & reliable – you know' and we rolled about amorously & it was all very silly and unfulfilled. The setting was all perfect but I couldn't have an ejaculation or anything. I never have been able to, with anyone. Only in masturbation does it work with me. Martin gave us a lift back to the Rembrandt which was most kind and thoughtful of him. He certainly appeared in a far more pleasant light tonight, perhaps because of a shared sense of guilt – we were all there for a purpose which we secretly feel to be wrong. All our morality teaches us that you should never use another human being for base purposes because in the process you degrade both them and yourself. I long to be free of the temptation. My only consolation is that the years seem to diminish the incidents and they do become farther and farther between.

Friday, 16 June

Up at about 9 o'c. and of course, found your actual parasite so had to go to the chemist for DDT powder and start *all that*! Then found the skin of the dick was slightly abrased! I thought I felt the teeth last night! Oh! these adventures always leave me disgusted and impaired.

Saturday, 17 June

I think that God did not intend me to have a sexual relationship of any kind, and that is why all these dire consequences occur whenever I defy his ruling.

Tuesday, 20 June

This time, when I get back to London, I really must do something positive about finding a place to live that is *me*. I really must start being selfish for a change and create the kind of surroundings which I really want, instead of living in conditions which give me no peace or aesthetic satisfaction. I have a feeling that it will have to be well out of the centre, but the travelling will all be worth while if I enjoy the destination.

Thursday, 22 June

Called on David Hatch at Aeolian Hall. He said about the pilot show on Sunday 'I hope you and Ted [Ray] both kick the script about a lot . . . I only want you to use it as a framework not as something to be stuck to . . . It's not Shakespeare . . .' All of which suggests that he is relying more on artists than he is on the script.

Sunday, 25 June

Walked to the Playhouse. The show went all right. Not a smash. Just all right, and a lot of things could have been better. Afterwards I had a drink with David Hatch & he seems to think it stands a chance of success, but told me that the writers are a problem. Someone will have to go. Today I achieved an ambition. I've always wanted to work with Ted and now I've done it.[16]

Tuesday, 27 June

Called on Phil Berger and talked about flats. He said that the flat next to Louie is under offer, at £13,500, but that if the people don't complete by the 30th he would give me first refusal. I went to Marlborough and looked at it and I think I could make it all right – it's not ideal by any means – but it could be all right if I furnished differently. I always say 'It's the last time', and then *start all over again* because I really do need to live in town & an apartment is the only way.

Friday, 30 June

Telephone call from Phil Berger: 'You can have that flat if you want it' and if I take Louie's as well, he is willing to knock the two into one price of £24,500. That means it is worth it.

Monday, 3 July

Tom rang me at 10.30. I said the slanderous stuff he was hearing was untrue. He said he would come down to the flat for coffee. I am acting here on Stanley's advice that it is best not to have a recriminatory atmosphere. I was shocked at his appearance. He had the lines of exhaustion round the eyes and his hair as long as a woman. It was mutually agreed that there was misunderstanding on both sides.

Wednesday, 5 July

Taxi to Peter Eade and told him all the plans re the move. He said that obviously I would have to be less choosy about the work in future – that is horribly true.

Friday, 21 July

I went to Peter E. and got the script of the play which Michael Codron has given him for me to read – *The Fat Dress* by a man called Laurence.[17] I read it as soon as I got home and it is very good indeed with a marvellous part for me. At last it has happened! Michael has found a good script for me! I wrote him a letter and posted it straightway.

---

[16] On radio, KW presumably meant; they had worked together on *Carry On Teacher*.
[17] Later *My Fat Friend*, by Charles Laurence: his first theatre play. He had written the Sheila Hancock sitcom 'Now Take My Wife . . .' for television.

Sunday, 23 July
At 11 o'c. T & C arrived and we drove to Henley where I gave them lunch at the Two Brewers.

Wednesday, 2 August
Now I am sitting in the bedroom on my last night here and writing at this desk which I bought at Catesby's in Tottenham Ct. Rd. (now gone) for my room at 66 Alex. with John Hussey in '59. What are my feelings now? No regrets about leaving certainly, for I've never really *liked* this place. It provided a cheap base from which to work and served to remind me of poverty and privation. I feel I have become old here & a part of my life is finished. Now I shall start on the twilight period.

Thursday, 3 August
MOVE TO MARLBOROUGH.[18] Tom & Clive arrived at 5.30 and Tom brought with him 6 bottles of Chablis & one was already cooled so we opened it & had the first drink in the new flat. At 8.15 we all went to Carrier's for dinner. Coffee with Louie in her flat and I returned to mine at about 12.30.

Friday, 4 August
We went to Imhof's and got a colour TV for Louie for £280. I am gradually getting sorted out and feel much happier than I have been for a *long long* time.

Sunday, 13 August
Interesting things on TV – including a show called *Who Do You Do?* with Freddie Starr who has great talent. Very clever indeed. Can't understand why I've never heard of him! He is brilliant.

Thursday, 17 August
This is the first time I have ever had a west facing flat and the sun floods in during the afternoon. It is one of the things I have always envied in any other house I've visited where it's happened. Endsleigh was east facing and cold, Park West was south & a backyard, Farley was east, cold, and the endless spectacle of Tussaud's dustbins and tourists. This is the nicest (most precise) apartment I've had yet.

Thursday, 24 August
I met Peter Eade who began 'Now, if you do this play you really must take direction because you know how naughty you can be when you

---

[18] 8 Marlborough House, Osnaburgh Street, NW1; the flat adjacent to Louie's.

feel it all needs gingering up a bit and you come outside the framework of the play and do a sort of front cloth act with it . . . you have got to get back to the good things you did in the theatre like *St Joan* and the Shaffer plays . . . that's what people remember . . . you know how outrageous you were in the Bolt play when it wasn't going very well . . . I am the only person who can tell this to you. If Eric Thompson[19] does this play of yours, do give him a chance . . .' etc. etc. I listened with patience to all this mouthing because I know he is well-intentioned. He took me to the Cambridge to see *Journey's End* directed by Eric Thompson. It is reppy, uninspired pedestrian muck. If this is an example of Eric Thompson's lovely direction he can stick it up his arse.

Friday, 25 August

To the Playhouse for the 'J.A.M.' opening. Audience was good. After, I walked to the Osteria Lariana to meet T & C and Stanley. On about the third mouthful of food the stomach pains began. The pain was like iron bands round the guts. I was pouring sweat and longing to vomit. Got a taxi home where I tried everything from 8.30 to midnight. I drank endless cups of hot water till eventually I did vomit into the lavatory pan. The pain still didn't go.

Saturday, 26 August

Thank goodness the pain has diminished. I feel like a rag. Tom came at 10.15 and Clive drove us to London Airport. At Nice it was a joy to see Beverley at the airport and we drove to Seillans. Tom was very enthusiastic about the place and in the afternoon sunlight it all looked very tranquil.

Sunday, 27 August

Here in Seillans thinking about the theatre & whether Eric Thompson is any good or not, you realise that it doesn't matter one iota. The thing to do, in any circumstance, is to appear to know exactly what you are doing and at the same time convey casual doubts about the abilities of everybody else & undermine their confidence.

Thursday, 31 August. London

To the bank to change francs and trav. cheques. The franc coins I put into traffic parking meters. Spoke to Eric Thompson on the phone at

---

[19] 1929–82. Actor, writer and director, best known for his adaptation and narration of the television series 'The Magic Roundabout'. Father of Emma Thompson.

Nottingham and he sounded very pleasant. They're considering Barbara Ferris and a girl called Linden[20] at the moment.

Friday, 8 September

I went to Michael Codron. There I met Bernard Holley (who is to play the lover manqué) and Eric Thompson and Charles Laurence. There was a great discussion about rewriting the play and all sorts of ideas about telescoping bits here & there and I eventually said 'Leave well alone.' I walked with Charles and said 'Don't let them bugger your play about. *They* don't know about the loneliness of creating a piece of literature & in removing all these bricks from here & there, the whole wall can fall down . . .' I have a horror of rewrites and mutilations from my experience with the Woods and the Willmans of this world. At the Playhouse it was an all-male game. Nimmo, Jones, Freud & me. David Hatch said after that it was all right.

Monday, 18 September

In the evening I walked to Harrow Road in the rain to see *Joe Kidd* with Clint Eastwood. It was, as usual with this actor, excellent. On the way home I became conscious of the neck pain which never seems to leave me & started envisaging suicide & letters to friends and coroners. Of course nobody really *cares* about the pain of others – if they did they would have little energy for getting thro' their own affairs. Selfishness is the mainspring of most action and compassion for the plight of others has to be secondary.

Thursday, 21 September

'J.A.M.' recordings. It was Aimi Macdonald. I said 'Shut your row you ignorant nit' at one point & after the show Nick Parsons said 'You shouldn't do things like that to Aimi 'cos she is a very sensitive little girl.'

Friday, 22 September

There is something curiously *wrong* with me. Every now and then, mostly coming home at night, I become assailed by a feeling of *not belonging* – of not having any real place to go to, of not knowing any real place and of not being real myself. I know that it dates from when I moved from Farley Court into 92 Q.A.M. I did something I should never have done. I moved into a temporary abode which is the worst thing I could have done. As all my life is an act and a hollow sham, the concrete things like my belongings & my privacy & my books & things are *necessary* – they're the only reassurance I have. In moving

---

[20] The part went to Jennie Linden, b.1939.

into that flat I cut myself off from all that reassurance. I was forced to fall back on myself and the utter emptiness of my existence was revealed in a way it never should have been. You *should* be able to take *some* things for granted. Now I find I can't. I'm even unsure and alien about the place that I live in. Before, I didn't question that. It has raised the trivial & ordinary to a dimension of ridiculous proportions and threatens to topple over and destroy me underneath its rubble.

Saturday, 23 September
To bed full of visions of an early death and then got out and prayed to God repeating my eternal cry 'Help me, please help me . . .'

Tuesday, 26 September
We drove to Eric. There was Bernard Holley there, and the boy who plays the Scot, but no lady because the actress they've engaged – Miss Linden – is on holiday in Ireland. I was alarmed from the start when Eric began to want cuts on the first page! My first speech to be cut and then the line about 'I want to pee' because, he said, 'It can be acted, it doesn't need saying.' When I ventured the suggestion that this comedy writing had natural rhythm and that the cuts destroyed it & used the 'I say, I say' example to illustrate the argument, Eric replied 'There is no "I say, I say" in this play & there mustn't be. If the audience start thinking of Kenneth Williams and not the character we are sunk . . . that mustn't happen.' I began to wonder why I was cast!

Wednesday, 27 September
Woke full of worry and foreboding. My instincts are: Eric Thompson is no good for this play. It is full of literary niceties & artifice, it is to do with theatrical illusion & exaggerated metaphor – he wants to turn it into a thing of documentary reality and *truth*. He doesn't see that a series of lies and improbabilities convey the truth in this kind of art. He continually analyses the text with questions like 'Would this really happen?' Later on when Charles tried to stop another cut in the play by saying 'Kenneth read it very well,' Eric replied 'Kenneth would be funny reading the telephone book' which is the sort of untrue cliché that frightens me.

Thursday, 5 October
Gave Peter E. dinner at Casa Mario and then we went to Comedy Theatre to see Eric Thompson's production of *Time & Time Again*.[21] It

---

[21] By Alan Ayckbourn.

is very neatly and deftly done and would be a credit to something like York or Birmingham Rep.

Friday, 6 October

I wrote a letter to Eric Thompson to say how beautifully he had directed the play at the Comedy. Rang Michael Codron and said what a wonderful play he'd got at the Comedy and how beautifully Eric had directed it etc. I am practically going round with their boot laces in me mouth. The arse crawling hypocrisy of it all is totally sickening. It is *me* that should be being wooed! I am the one who is going out on a limb with this play! *not them*!

On September 23 when I knelt down to say my prayers in the dark, my knee hit the edge of the bed and the pain made lights in my head. It is a continual mental debate with me: 'Does it matter *how* you pray, as long as you pray?' but fundamentally I know one *should* be on one's knees. Every time I have forgotten to do it, I lie in bed justifying it all by saying 'I think of God just as well in this position.'

Monday, 16 October

To the Paris for the 'Betty Witherspoon Show'. They were a small house and they were not very good. They were good for me but not for the show and not particularly good for Ted. I finished the show with a send-up of Sydney Carton and it played very well with Miriam Margolyes & a lot of pantomime & larking about. At the chat after, I told Simon Brett (producer) to put the *snide* character into the opening spot with Ted. I rushed to the St James Church Hall, Piccadilly for the first rehearsal of *My Fat Friend*. There were press photographers there & all that hoohah. After one speech of mine beginning 'Victoria Hope spinster of this parish . . .' he [Eric Thompson] said 'Now would you go through all that again and this time would you just speak it naturally . . . don't act it . . . just be it . . . just say it all as if you were almost thinking it for the first time . . . to yourself . . .' and I said 'Yes' and did it. Of course the comedy goes out of the window but I thought: 'We must cooperate with this man.'

Tuesday, 17 October

Stanley came at 7 o'c., took off his shoes and socks and said 'The temperature in this flat is just right! I love getting the air to my feet' and proceeded to phone Capability Brown endlessly till he got a table. We got there and he asked what *coley* fish was & the waiter said 'It's like cod but not as pretty' and Stanley said 'Oh! I like it to be pretty. I haven't come all this way to eat ugly fish' and it made me laugh straightway. He was in v. good form and I told him how much I'd enjoyed his TV performance and he launched into a great account of the technical difficulties involved.

Tuesday, 24 October
Rehearse at 10 o'c. Eric Thompson giving more homilies on the underlying seriousness of the scene. He said 'Now this could easily develop into a romp . . . and just be funny . . .' Afterwards, Charles Laurence (who happened to be present for the first time today) said 'That is what it should be . . . that is what I intended.' Every single comedy idea of mine has been rejected at the moment it was tentatively proffered.

Monday, 30 October
Run through in front of the management. It went haltingly along with occasional laughter from Michael and at the end he came round & said it was wonderful & moving & beautiful. It took a lot of persuading to actually get into his office. There, I told him how unhappy I was & Eric said he was amazed & had no idea etc. Eric Thompson said 'You are unhappy 'cos I have taken away all your lovely little tricks and your funny voices . . . I didn't want them . . . I thought your first reading of the role was awful. I never said so 'cos I knew you'd go to Michael & say you didn't want to work with me . . . but if this play is done it is going to be done *my way* otherwise I'll go right now . . . you can get anyone you want to replace me.' Michael said to me 'I am not going to allow you to cheapen my production & turn it into some vulgar funny little piece.' And then I knew! *That* is what he & Eric have been thinking I would do to this play. The meeting was a great eye-opener & a bitter blow. Now I know why Codron's never cast me till this play came up. I'm in the 'vulgar queen' category.

Tuesday, 31 October
Michael rang at 9.10. He said conciliatory things. Eric came up and simply squeezed my arm and said nothing of yesterday's events. It was charming and disarming. The rest of the day was fine. Only one black moment when I said (of Jennie) to Eric 'Couldn't she top me there?' and Jennie said 'Yes I can hear you. My name is Jennie & I am trying to study the part' and when Eric remonstrated she said 'Well I never once refer to him in that way but he is always calling me *she*' and I went over and apologised.

Saturday, 4 November
Charles Laurence telephoned. He told me that he'd been present at one of the run-throughs. He said Michael remarked 'Ken seems a bit down, doesn't he?' and Charles replied 'No, it is the same performance

he gave on Monday . . . that is what Eric wants from him' and Charles added (to me) 'Perhaps this is the first glimmer we've had from Michael that he realises the play-direction is wrong.'

Sunday, 5 November

I do know about comedy, and when I go on to that stage tomorrow with an audience out front for the first time, I am going to do what my intuitive knowledge tells me to do. Not what some pretentious little director manqué tells me. I keep remembering Jennie Linden's words about me rehearsing comedy lines with no reaction for 3 weeks. She said 'It is awful to watch you going through it . . . it is like cruelty to animals . . .'

Monday, 6 November

Went to the Paris to do the 'B.W. Show'. It was absolute death. If I had been producing it I would have said that the whole thing was a complete write-off. T & C drove me to Brighton by 3 o'c. exactly. We did the D/rehearsal at 3.20. Thompson gave notes till 6 o'c. Eventually the curtain went up at 7.50 and in my nervousness I walked on without the props! I was so nervous I couldn't *hold* anything. The newspaper was trembling in my hands. The audience was superb. It was as if one had friends out front. We took a modest 3 curtains.

Thursday, 9 November

I have not had one note from Thompson about my performance. He has not said that I am no longer playing as he directed it. I am gradually cutting out all the awful pauses he put into it and getting the thing moving in the way it always should have moved.

Monday, 13 November. Wilmslow

E.T. drove us to the [Rex] theatre. It is like playing to a long tunnel and I fear that the microphones distort one's voice terribly. The play was very well received.

Tuesday, 14 November

Had a great talk with Eric in Dressing Room. He said 'It is the dark side of this play which I want to bring out but I know you'll never feel happy playing it my way . . .' I went on the stage and I did it his way. I lost ground everywhere. I lost laughs, command, presence and lines. I must stop it. I must return to the method I know. Eric came round and said 'That was marvellous! That is the best you've ever done.'

Wednesday, 15 November
Up at about 9 o'c. washed the hair & had the barclays. Eric drove Jennie & me to a pub where the locals were rather rude & he said 'We don't like being hemmed in! We'll move on!' and we all left. Then we visited Mottram Hall where he pocketed a copper ash tray & Jennie said 'Oh! you're a thief!', then we went to rehearse at 2 o'c. at the theatre. I said quietly 'I think all this analysis of the script is very dangerous . . . we've got to go on at night and perform it' whereupon he said 'All right, that's it. You get on with it . . . do it yourselves . . .' and he walked off the stage and drove off. The company were all rather shaken. Jennie said 'I think there is something wrong with him that we don't know about.' At 6.20 a page brought me a drink from Eric!! & I went to thank him and he put his arms round me & said 'Sorry – very sorry.' Decided to perform from now on according to my own dictates.

Saturday, 18 November
I left at 11.5 with Peter [Eade] in his Mercedes, for London. I asked him what he thought of the show. He said I was playing it too queenly & too slickly. I think now that Eric Thompson was probably right in his idea but wrong in his method.

Monday, 20 November
To the Paris and again the whole thing died the death. Now it's really got to the point at which one wants to discontinue the series. Went with Simon [Brett] to the pub after and got stoned.

Wednesday, 29 November
Michael Codron rang me: 'Is it true that you want *both* the downstairs rooms at the Globe?' I said it was. He said 'I didn't know that they had ever been *both* used by the star of the show . . .' I said 'Oh yes, Maggie had them both' and he said 'Oh! yes . . . well all right . . .' Afterwards I thought about it and remembered that, in fact, the other was occupied by Terence Scully – that's why we had to whisper when we talked about the play! During rehearsals, apropos the cut he made, Eric Thompson said 'You really *must* trust me – please trust me . . .' I felt like saying 'Not after I've seen you stealing the ashtray from Mottram Hall.' Ugh! his morality must be in a shocking state of disarray.

Wednesday, 6 December
Had the lie down till 6 o'c. when the Dressing Room started filling up with presents and telegrams! One from Ingrid, and Maggie and Bev, & George B., and Robert & Sarah! All lovely. The performance

was hard work – not an easy house – they were all right but not lavish in reciprocity, but the script triumphed. After I went with my party to the Osteria Romana. At the end Tom & Clive drove me to Fleet Street where Tom got a proof of the Irving Wardle notice. It is marvellous!

Thursday, 7 December

Peter E. rang and said 'You have got some marvellous notices!' Michael rang and read me a rave from Milton Shulman in the Standard! Rona rang. Wendy rang. It's all going on! So good that I'm sure there's a catch in it! The show went well.

Friday, 8 December

Walked to the theatre for the 1st house. It went all right for a small house & after Ingrid came round! She looked lovely and the company came down to the dressing room to meet her, and she chatted to them about the show, praised them fulsomely and behaved with generosity and charm. She was v. funny about *Brassbound* in America. The 2nd house was good, and T & C were there & Tom coped with everything including opening the champagne and showering me with half the bottle & soaking me shirt! In the middle of all this, in walked Maggie & Robert with Christopher [Downes]. It was *fantastic*! I simply wanted to cry with delight & joy! I hugged & hugged her and we opened more champagne and sat and sat chatting about everything till suddenly it was midnight! Lovely Martin Beckwith found a phone book & I rang Gloria at Peter Mario and she agreed to have us all to dinner – all seven of us! and we walked round there and had a marvellous evening.

Sunday, 10 December

I went in to Louie and we watched *Random Harvest*. In the end, the tears were running down my cheeks! I suppose the critics would say that the plot was thin and improbable, like Cinderella – but why does it make you cry? I returned to my flat and wept again, and the speech from our play 'Few people have the courage to begin again . . .' started going through my head. Now that the strain is easing and the pressures are coming off, I am starting to see how lucky – no – how good God has been to me.

Monday, 11 December

Paris for 'B.W.S.' The script was much better and it went well. Maggie had sent to my dressing room a bottle of champagne and a letter that contains some of the loveliest thoughts that anyone has ever expressed to me. God has been so good to me with my friends – I fear I don't deserve all this joy – the wonderful success of the play, & the radio & this great reunion with the one most marvellous actress I ever really loved. I fear I am too excited even to sleep tonight!

Tuesday, 12 December
I went to give the blood at Margaret Street and they made my next appointment for March 13, 1973. Had the rest till about 5.15 before leaving for the theatre. I walked there, buying cigars on the way for Bernard Holley 'cos he likes them. The evening performance went like a bomb.

Wednesday, 20 December
Jennie Linden was super tonight. She gets better all the time. I told her so & she said 'No . . . it's all due to working with you my angel!' Rushed off to Louie's party at Peter Mario where they did the cake and the singing etc. Went to bed at about 3 o'c. and put a Suppon. up because I really must sleep.

Friday, 22 December
I found a letter and presents from Louie on my desk. She says 'Perhaps next year, I won't go away and we can have dinner together . . .' & of course I started weeping. I replied to her & put it in her letter box. It is absurd that we correspond like this (next door to each other) but to actually *say* heartfelt things would see us both crying. We are both too aware of our precarious vulnerability.

Saturday, 23 December
I had supper with Maggie & Robert & Chris Downes. Maggie said 'Well you were away from the theatre for ages but you've certainly come back with a bang! Those notices were absolutely marvellous!' which I loved hearing. I said 'Oh! I am so glad that I have met you all over again . . . this incredible coincidence of being next door to each other . . . just like it was ten years ago when you did *Mary Mary*[22] . . . and I was in the Shaffer plays at the Globe . . . no . . . it isn't a coincidence! God intends all these things & he intends all the intricacies of special relationships . . .' Maggie drove us home. She said 'The awful thing about success is that it gets *harder* every time, not easier . . . I suppose we were carefree in the early days because we were young and arrogant . . . now we see all the pitfalls.'

Monday, 25 December
T & C came at 12 o'c. We drove to Hattie by about 1 o'c. She served

---

[22] By Jean Kerr.

a splendid lunch and Joan Sims was terribly funny handing out presents like a bountiful fairy. Of course Hattie got the most and as the pile of gifts grew and grew to mountainous proportions on the table in front of her, Joan handed yet another huge parcel to her, saying with a bitter smile 'Here's *another* bleedin' present for you Hattie! and it couldn't happen to a nicer person . . .' by which time everyone was laughing hysterically! My face actually *ached* with the pain of laughter. First Christmas day that I've ever known such hilarity.

Wednesday, 27 December
When I got into the dressing room I found a charming letter from Eric Thompson! What a turn up for the book! For the first time in this entire production he actually praises my work! – well he talks about the show rather than me specifically, but it is certainly a climb down from Delphi as far as he is concerned. I must admit I was pleased to receive it.

Sunday, 31 December
I walked to Gordon & Rona. Eileen Atkins said of our piece at the Globe 'I just think it dies when you go off the stage . . . when you are on, I believe in it and it lives . . .' We sang songs round the piano but most were keys too high for me. It was a lovely evening. I was with dear dear friends at the end of this year.

1973

PERSONAL NOTES

[*From enclosed cutting:*]

'In the second part of his *Journey*, when he is in the Hebrides, Johnson[1] is acutely conscious of foreshortened time, time lost because not recorded in writing:

"Written learning is a fixed luminary, which, after the cloud that had hidden it has past away, is again bright in its proper station. (Oral) Tradition is but a meteor, which, if once it falls, cannot be rekindled."'

I found this in the TLS last year and it supplied Gordon with the burden of his speech at the opening of a new bookshop in Glasgow, 'cos he quoted the lines about 'written learning' and this was a particularly apt occasion for them. So, it is right that this year starts with my beloved Johnson and my dear friend Gordon, so associated.

Wednesday, 3 January

I went to the BBC & met Tony Gould and read from the diary to him for his programme. He let me go on from 11.15 to 1.15 before saying he didn't think it was suitable. He suggested I go away & write another kind of journal 'palatable for the general public' but without losing the 'intimate' touch of 'your own writing for yourself.' I said I would have a go. But I secretly resolved that I would get out of it all. I resented that I'd told so much about myself all to no avail.

Thursday, 4 January

At Gt. Portland Street, three boys were fighting and I said 'You can stop that immediately! How dreadful to attack each other in a world as full of misery as this! How old are you?' and the eldest boy, looking at the ground, said 'Firteen Mister' and I said 'Oh! that makes it

---

[1] Dr Samuel Johnson (1709–84). Essayist, critic and lexicographer. An enduring hero of KW's. The article he quotes appeared in *The Times Literary Supplement* on 20 October 1972.

worse!' and a smaller boy cried out 'We was only playing Mister!' and I said 'Oh! well that's all right then! Here is 50p to share among yourselves and never hit each other again' & I departed grandly, crossing the road, holding up my hand to stop the traffic and beaming at all and sundry. Performance went very well! During Jennie's speech apropos the fur hat – 'Henry's not going to wear it during the film is he . . .' a small boy cried out 'Yes he is!' and the auditorium loved it! It is extraordinary how many children attend this play! There is no question of suitable morality etc. How different from my own youth!

Sunday, 7 January

I am drinking the bitter waters of contrition regarding Eric. All along, he has been right about the quality of performance – where I've disagreed is about form – and as to content he has been correct. It is irony indeed that his truths have come home to roost and that his repeated warnings in rehearsals have now been justified demonstrably.

Monday, 8 January

Paris studio for 'B.W.S.' I thought the script was good. Miriam Margolyes told me that Dick Emery[2] is in St Mary's Hospital! So I sent him a get well telegram. He's always made me laugh.

Tuesday, 9 January

Mags came in at the end and we went to Peter Mario. First time we've been *alone* with each other for years. I said 'Periods in life are sometimes like a long dark tunnel but you come out into the light eventually.' She said 'I think I'm on the Inner Circle.' And of course it's in this kind of remark, funny & sane, that you realise how her extraordinary awareness equips her to face practically anything. I've always adored her but tonight was a sort of Everest in relationships.

Thursday, 18 January

I met Maggie at Wardour St and we went to a private screening of *Love and Pain and the Whole Damn Thing*. Maggie is superb. The boy Timothy Bottoms is good & the direction is lyrically romantic. I cried me eyes out. We went to Mags' dressing room for coffee. Every time I see this girl act I am filled with admiration. I was so proud and privileged today to be sitting next to such an actress. Such incomparable style, such careful delineation, such vulnerable fragility . . .

---

[2] 1917–83. Television comedian. His most famous character was a ripe, busty female whose catchphrase was 'Ooh, you are awful – but I like you!'

Wednesday, 24 January
Next door to see Maggie. I went in to her dressing room and the crowd was horrific. Maggie said 'You know Franco of course' and Zeffirelli[3] came & shook my hand and said 'Of course! We met in Maggie's dressing room when you were acting with her in '62 . . .' which I was sure was a lie and I said so. He then said 'Will you do me the honour of being my guest for this evening?' & I gushed 'Yes! I shall be delighted' and he added 'Just for dinner, I mean' & I thought to meself 'Don't overestimate yourself, Franco!' but I said nothing. When we all arrived at this filthy little restaurant in Beauchamp Place we were kept waiting in a tiny overcrowded dark filthy room & I knew I could take no more of it. I walked out – after asking Mags to do likewise, but she said 'How can I? It's Franco!' I got a taxi home by 11.45.

Thursday, 25 January
As soon as I entered the dressing room I *knew* someone had been in there. Various cupboards had been interfered with and they had stolen my Paper Mate pen which Kenneth Horne gave me with 'R.T.H.' inscribed on it! They stole my stamps as well! But they left table lighter and letter opener etc. and drinks! It is all most peculiar.

Wednesday, 31 January
Maggie came round and we went to Peter Mario. At the meal when I told Maggie how incredibly her talent had matured in *Love, Pain . . .* (film) she said 'I learned all that from you . . . It was you who taught me about the end thought being present from the beginning, that the breath must be taken right and the inflection *rise* at the end for the collocutor . . . not fall . . .' I thought 'How receptive and willing you have been!' She is the most striking example of a serious artist – one with an infinite capacity for taking pains . . . and one totally without pretension.

Tuesday, 6 February
Maggie came round! We had dinner at Peter Mario. Came back to the flat for coffee and talked till 4 o'c.!! It was foolish but this girl draws me like a magnet, and I am inextricably involved with her. It is a knot I will never want, or be able, to untie.

Monday, 12 February
Backstage after, I had Ian Partridge & his wife, Paul Gallico & Virginia,

---

[3] b.1923. Director-producer-designer for stage and screen.

Tom Meyer & Fleur Cowles,[4] Sheila Hancock & her agent, Norman. Fleur Cowles said 'I listen to you in "Just A Minute" and I really *hate* you . . . you know?'

Friday, 16 February
At the curtain, I rushed away because Maggie was waiting in my room to discuss the [Michael] Parkinson [Show]. I showed her the 'Death in Leamington' poem by Betjeman[5] and suggested we might do it together and that since Betjeman himself was on the programme with us, it might be appropriate. She seemed agreeable to the idea.

Saturday, 17 February
To TV studios for the 'Parkinson Show'. I was introduced to Sir John Betjeman and he was a great delight. One of the most lovable and kindly, gentle people I've ever met. On the show itself, it all got very woolly and serious and Maggie went terribly *posh*. She was obviously intensely nervous. When I got on, I wasn't much better and I was foolishly blabbing about train strikes being against the essence of socialism etc. so I will doubtless reap the whirlwind of indiscretion. I read the Betjeman poem with Maggie – holding the book between us – and it worked very well.

Thursday, 22 February
Up at 7 o'c. and put a pound note in an envelope for the postman – they have to get up early in the morning & it must be pleasant to have a surprise occasionally. [Birthday] Supper with Gordon, Rona, Louie, Martin and Maggie at Peter Mario.

Saturday, 24 February
Coming up Villiers St I saw Jimmy Gibson!! that ancient derelict, tottering along! He said 'They've flown me down from Glasgow for a telly . . .' & I thought 'They'll need a bier to get you back again!' but I said 'You look marvellous!' as I gazed on the wrinkled clay-like skin.

Sunday, 25 February
T & C arrived. We went to the Odeon at Edgware Road to see a film but a crowd of hooligans shouted 'Hallo Kenny, you queer!' and more in this vein till I got up and went over to them and asked 'Who is making these remarks? And who has the guts to stand up and say

---

[4] Magazine editor and society hostess. Tom Montague Meyer, her husband from 1955.

[5] 1906–84. Poet and guardian of the architectural heritage. Poet Laureate from 1972.

them to my face?' and there was silence. God! Why don't people leave one alone?

Thursday, 1 March
Walked to Briglin Pottery at Crawford St where Brigitta showed me the ashtrays she's done for me. They are splendid – some lovely blue colours and the inscription 'GLOBE THEATRE, MY FAT FRIEND 1972–1973' on each one. It will be the 100th performance in London on Friday – tomorrow.

Saturday, 3 March
Michael rang. After I'd railed at him he said 'I am just sick to death of all your endless complaints. You complain about the production, you complain about the cast, you complain about the lines & moments in the scene being delivered wrongly, you complain to Martin about there being no 100-performance board outside the theatre . . . all you do is *complain* and I have had it, I'm sorry . . .' I said 'I am sorry if I've upset you. I don't really want to hurt you, ever.'

Sunday, 4 March
Delivered a letter to Michael by hand saying I was sorry to have become such a bane to him & quoted the Housman 'All's wrong I've ever done or said, and nought to help it in this dull head' but dared not complete the verse.[6]

Monday, 5 March
No one will ever explain why I telephoned Maggie this morning. I got an answer. I walked all the way to meet her. All through Hyde Park where I saw spring burgeoning thro' the twigs & branches and the swans flapping furiously on the lake . . . I walked to Coq Au Vin at Harriet St and we had lunch together . . . she looked *marvellous* . . . rested and yet translucent. We talked and talked and time flew, till I walked home at 4 o'c.

Friday, 16 March
Brendan (Stage Door keeper) said he'd told Frankie Howerd I was not to be disturbed!! so I will have to write him a letter of apology. Brendan means well but can't sort out the chaff from the grain.

---

[6] 'Shake hands, we shall never be friends, all's over;/I only vex you the more I try./All's wrong that ever I've done or said,/And nought to help it in this dull head:/Shake hands, here's luck, goodbye.' *More Poems*, xxx, by A.E. Housman.

Thursday, 22 March
Michael phoned me at 10.15 to say Binkie Beaumont had died! He said 'The maid found him in bed – he was still warm . . . but he was dead . . .' I said I was glad he'd gone while still working. At 12 o'c. Richard Pearson came and we had lunch at this pub in Gt. Portland St. It was a joy to see him again. I am deeply fond of Richard – he's going off to Chichester to do *Seagull* and an Anouilh play.

Friday, 23 March
Linden played it as tho' in a trance. I was full of anger. Went to Linden's room and had a blazing row with her. She said she was ill so I said she should go home. She ordered me out of her room. At the end, Eric Thompson turned up & gave a little homily on company relations. She said 'I don't think there's any need to make a trauma out of this . . .'[7]

Saturday, 24 March
2nd performance: Marvellous! The *best* performance *ever* of this play! Linden was way out on top – the breakfast scene was fab! Holley played his last scene with Linden & him being so good that– even in the wings – one listened as if it were *new*! Astonishing evening. The audience reception was ecstatic & as Jennie rightly said 'We could have gone *on* taking curtain calls . . .'

Monday, 26 March
My beloved Noël Coward has died in Jamaica. This is certainly proving to be a vengeful month! Coward was my inspiration and the standard for the style of acting which I used as a criterion – the method of enunciation, breath control, acting technique, timing, everything I based on him. I cried on the way to the theatre. Went in to see Mags at the Queen's – she cried too & said 'I don't know how I'm going to say those lines tonight . . .'[8]

Friday, 30 March
It is the *last matinée on a Friday* – dearly purchased by me by agreeing to stay on till June '74!! – but curiously I don't feel very tired. The bum started playing up dreadfully. At the end of the show, S/door rang down to say 'An American called Jack Klugman[9] is here to see

---

[7] This did not stop KW from keeping a log of changes or deficiencies in the performances; according to a dated carbon, he typed it up on 27 April.
[8] She was playing in Coward's *Private Lives*.
[9] b.1922. American film actor, familiar from the TV series 'The Odd Couple'.

you' & I said 'Get rid of him.' I see anyone who writes or is properly introduced.

Sunday, 1 April
Went in to Louie for lunch & she confided 'Old Johnson's on the drink again! Dirty old sod! It must be awful for his poor wife!' Louie sits making judgments like this, and adds: 'Old men's dicks! Nothing to do with me! No thank *you* very much!' Oh! she does make me laugh.

Sunday, 8 April
Nose running, eyes watering, head full of rheum, body aching everywhere & a feeling of utter lassitude. I don't want to go back to that theatre and act that play ever again. It is as though *waves* of infection keep bashing at me.

Tuesday, 10 April
To the Globe where I stood outside the theatre for one hour with Martin Beckwith selling flags for the blind. We did very well really.

Wednesday, 11 April
Since I wrote to T & C on April 3 suggesting we forget the Sundays for a bit, there has been total silence. No reply. Nothing. Ludicrously childish. The show went like a bomb! I wrote the lines:

'Oh what can you say at the end of the day?
Was the plot so sound? Or the lines profound?
Was there rather less grain than chaff?
Oh what can you say at the end of the day?
You can say that you made them laugh.'

I will send them to Maggie 'cos they're apt.

Thursday, 12 April
Went to the post with Louie, then to Netley St school where we voted Tory for the GLC election. Performance was excellent from cast. Walked home singing songs I made up as I went, titles like 'My Time is Fully Occupied with Me', & revolved a couplet:

'Found his attraction made me tremble at the knees
Got into bed with it & contracted a disease . . .'

Bed at about 12 o'c. 2 mog.

Sunday, 15 April
Stanley came and we drove to the Adelphi for the Emergency Meeting of the Union called by the militants of the left, asking for the removal of the Equity Council. Of course the speakers were Tom Kempinski & Corin Redgrave, both reds. They were superbly refuted by Raymond – no, Trevor Baxter in a withering speech and thank God, the Council was saved.

Wednesday, 18 April
I walked to the hotel where I had lunch with Paul [F.]. He was v. grave and adorable, with his huge spectacles scanning the menu. He met an American on the travels and I asked 'Did you fuck him?' and he said 'Well, I, er, well . . . yes' which made me smile. After lunch we went to his room & he showed me some v. good pornography and kissed me so hard that I've a rash all over the chin. I hastily grabbed the present he gave me and said 'Well I really must go now' and returned to the flat for the barclays & slept for about an hour.

Thursday, 19 April
Bill Cotton rang & suggested I do 'What's My Line?'[10] as a member of the panel, in August, for 5 episodes on a Sunday & I said yes.

Saturday, 28 April
Whatever else I've learned from this play, it is *this*: my heart sinks when I look at the 'actors' around me in this piece . . . and they look at me like drowning sailors shouting 'Keep us afloat' and I do . . . night after night . . . but I'm sick of being a life saver to such an unlovely & rotten bunch as this. Always excepting Holley. His good nature is constant, on and off.

Tuesday, 1 May
I gave supper to Stanley. He said what Maggie said: 'Be *off* the show . . . let them see what it's like without you . . .'

Thursday, 3 May
Did the rectal wash out several times so that it would be clean for Mr Mulvany's examination. He examined me and said that he would treat me in hospital. I am to go in on Sunday. He said the inflammation is now worse than it was before, and that there is an ulcer in the rectum. Michael said 'Could you delay the hospital business for us to at least get a replacement?' I said I was willing to ask Mulvany. He

---

[10] Panel game of American origin, for a time in the fifties the most popular programme on television. Briefly revived for the seventies.

kept asking me to *stay on* with the play & doesn't seem to comprehend that it's the play that's causing the misery.

Friday, 4 May

Went to meet Codron & [Toby] Rowland at 2.30. It was *awful.* It continued with hectoring, bullying, threatening, till 4.30. Returned with Peter to his office. We both agreed we wanted an honourable compromise, so Peter offered to have me ask Mulvany to delay the real hospital lengthy stay till 3 months' time. Dinner with Mags. She said 'What if you were ill like this, but playing with *me* in that theatre?' & I said 'I'd be asking for the run to be extended!'

Saturday, 5 May

Gordon telephoned and said he would pick me up tonight from the theatre and drive me to the hospital after the show. He is surely the best friend in the world. I got to the hospital at 11.20. Michael Codron rang. I told him that I may have to stay on & return here, after the shows.

Wednesday, 9 May

Mr Mulvany examined me & the proctoscope was agony. He said there was an improvement and that I could go today since the work would all get disorganised. Returned to flat at 4 o'c. Went to the theatre. There is no doubt but that I have to supply the energy for the whole show.

Thursday, 10 May

Paris for 'J.A.M.', it was *packed*. We had to turn away 200 people!! It is fantastic how well this show goes! The [evening] performance was ghastly. I flew out the side door with Maggie and we went to Lariana for dinner. Maggie said 'Jonathan Miller thinks you ought to play Peter in *Peter Pan* . . . and that you would be frighteningly good.' I said 'with my *bum*? all that harness & flying?' She agreed it was mad.

Tuesday, 29 May

Telephoned the Codron office – David Sutton spoke to me. Told him that the pain was worsening & that I was to see Mulvany at 4.30. He examined me & said it was, as he predicted, trouble in the colon. I've now got to have a barium x-ray done! Go in to hospital Thursday night. Walked to theatre. The house was awful, and alas, so were we.

Thursday, 31 May

Astonished to read in the paper that Kenneth Allsop[11] (the TV celebrity) had taken an overdose of barbiturates and died holding a copy of Dorothy Parker's phrases about the worthlessness of life. He must have been deeply depressed. Regency picked me up & took me to the St John & Elizabeth. I went to my old room again.

Friday, 1 June

I went to X-ray and had the barium enema. Saw Mr Mulvany and he said that negatives showed that the colon was affected & he said 'Now we have proof if they want their own doctors to see it . . .' I left the hospital at 11.30. Took Louie to lunch at Lariana. Michael C. rang. I said I *had* to leave end August. Performance was like a *nightmare*! Maggie was waiting for me! We went to dinner at Peter Mario. She asked me to give her a coffee and said 'I'll only stay for a moment' but of course we talked till 4 o'c. in the morning.

Monday, 4 June

The show was atrocious. I practically dried twice in the first scene. Don't know what I am *saying* any more. I have reached a point of no return. I will have to go to Mulvany now. I can't face this any more. It is slowly undermining me as a person & as a performer. Couldn't sleep for the abdomen. Took Codis & 3 Doriden.

Tuesday, 5 June

Telephoned Mr Mulvany's secretary and she arranged for me to go into the St John & Elizabeth this evening. I walked to Johnson & he manipulated me. On the way back, I met Mr Mulvany in Harley St. He said it was right that I should go in because 'otherwise you are just deteriorating.' Packed my bags and wrote a note to Louie and then the car came and took me to the hospital. Mr Mulvany came. I told him it was the production that was causing all the trouble. I am not going back to that dreadful play. I don't care what happens. I will go to a psychiatrist if necessary, or leave the business entirely. The plain fact is, as it stands, the piece had a run of 6 months after which every part of the jerry-built structure was starting to give at the seams.

---

[11] b.1920. Journalist, author, sometime Literary Editor of the *Daily Mail*; popular interviewer on the 'Tonight' programme, etc. Allsop had lost a leg many years before, and his long suffering of pain was said to have influenced his state of mind. An inquest at Bridport heard that he had underlined two passages in *The Collected Dorothy Parker*: 'There is nothing good in life that will not be taken away,' and 'She could find no other means that could deal with the pain of living.' Allsop had taken four times the lethal dose of barbiturates, but since there was no evidence as to how he came to do this, an Open verdict was recorded.

Wednesday, 6 June

Bernard Holley telephoned me and when he said 'When are you coming back?' I foolishly said 'Never'. I said 'Don't speak to anyone about your conversation with me.' Louie came to see me. I told her that I could no longer face going into that theatre and she agreed that it was making me neurotic and said 'I knew on Saturday that you were getting into a state . . .' It is true. I was. The hateful nature of that play was colouring everything in my life.

Thursday, 7 June

Read the papers – I see Jimmy Clitheroe[12] is dead! This year seems to be nothing but deaths!

Friday, 8 June

Mr Musgrove came. He said the pain in the ear was due to a boil & prescribed some stuff. He told me he'd got Jack Hawkins as a patient at East Grinstead – 'I don't think he will last much longer than a fortnight' – suffering from cancer. Apparently [the play] is to terminate on June 30. So the cast are going to be forced to go through this charade for another three weeks! Hattie Jacques and Joan Sims rang me & were v. sweet.

Saturday, 9 June

Mr Mulvany said he'd spoken to Codron and that 'he took it very well, but wants me to write him a letter about your condition.' He also said I would need to be here for about 3 weeks and then have about six weeks' further treatment outside hospital.

Monday, 11 June

Letter arrived from Eric Thompson!! It was easily the *best* letter I've had apropos my indisposition. He said 'At least you can console yourself that you won't have to do that play again . . .' and that is exactly the sentiment one wants to see expressed by an understanding observer. Goodness, but Eric is an enigma! Stanley came in! He promptly took his shoes off & socks & tie and went & sat on the balcony throwing me bits of conversation from a distance. Gordon came in at 6.30 and he and Baix chatted about Hillhead or Headhill – their old school.[13] It was quite a day!

---

[12] High-pitched 'perpetual schoolboy' comedian, found dying on the day of his mother's cremation. The Blackpool coroner decided that death was accidental.

[13] Hillhead High School, Glasgow.

Thursday, 14 June
Maggie came and I was able to offer her some tea from my own pot. She said 'All the women go thro' that phase of being attracted by you . . . you're such an enigma to them.' I said 'It is ludicrous! You know all there is to know about me: there is nothing enigmatic about it' and she said 'Yes there is . . . no one quite understands the sex thing – they can't understand your lack of interest in it . . . women are always intrigued by the unattainable.' I thought the conversation was curious because it echoed everything that Hattie said when she was here the other evening.

Friday, 15 June
Mr Mulvany came. Said I could go after another week. He said that it would obviously be better to go away from London on release from hospital – preferably abroad.

Tuesday, 19 June
I was injected and then taken down to the operating theatre for the sigmoidoscope examination. The euphoric sensation of the drugs made me utterly relaxed and tho' I heard what people were saying I had no desire to reply. The entire experience was utterly delightful.

Friday, 22 June
Back in the flat by 10 o'c. The letters were stacked on my desk!! All commiseration from fans! I threw the lot into the dustbin 'cos I just haven't the energy to cope with any of it.

Monday, 25 June. Taunton
Clive drove all the way to Andover by 12.55 and got as far as Sidmouth by 5 o'c. By 6.30 we got to Taunton where we found the Castle Hotel which was civilised.

Tuesday, 26 June
Awful truth is, this has not worked at all. Clive is fearfully boring after a while and the weather and preponderance of tourists is making the whole situation untenable. Don't know how I can keep going.

Wednesday, 27 June
Went on to Wells and the streets were lined with police and small children waving flags, and we were told it was a visit from Princess Anne! It was too much. Motored on to Cheddar. Full of idiots in plastic macs! I was horrified. After the filthy lunch, we went on to Bristol. Death. On to Bath, where the Francis [Hotel] can only put us up for tonight! I laid on the bed in the filthy little cupboard of a room

which smelled dreadfully & listened to the noise of builders outside & suddenly I just gave up . . . I knew I could go on with this charade no longer. When Clive reappeared, I said I wanted to go back and he said 'OK . . . I'll drive you to the station' & he did. I could hardly believe it was all happening to me! He must credit me with strength I don't have. I wanted to weep and cry out 'Drive me home' but knew that I couldn't. The train was late. Everyone stared at me. I just wanted to die. Got home. Thank God for Louie. She was in.

Saturday, 30 June
Thank God it is Saturday and that play will be coming off tonight.

Sunday, 1 July
Checked with Regency about the car for Louie. The chauffeur came with a vast car to take her to Southampton. I returned to my flat feeling utterly desolate without her. She is all I've got. She has got me through these terrible days . . . I could never have done it without her . . . I just sat down and wept.

Tuesday, 17 July
Did some research on the questions for 'J.A.M.' tonight. Walked to the Playhouse and David Hatch was very kind: 'It is good to see you back again' and Clement Freud said 'Thank God you're back again! It's been awful . . .' Clement said he was the Liberal Candidate for the Isle of Ely and seemed greatly optimistic about his chances.

Tuesday, 24 July
Tube to TV Centre. Lunch with Isobel Barnett,[14] William Franklyn, Anna Quayle – the panel for the TV game 'What's My Line?'. It was all v. convivial and we watched a re-run of the old series. I realise now that I really do enjoy the company of pro's. I enjoyed the entire episode.

Friday, 27 July
The good news is that the Liberals have taken *both* seats in the two by-elections! So Clement Freud is now M.P. for the Isle of Ely.[15] I am delighted. His will be one of the few lively, intelligent & witty minds in the House of Commons.

---

[14] Lady Barnett (1918–80). Doctor, magistrate and a star of the heyday of 'What's My Line?'

[15] And remained so until 1983. Represented Cambridgeshire North-East 1983–87. Knighted 1987.

Saturday, 28 July
Went to the Westminster Hospital where I saw this Mr Holborow. I leaned over his desk while he was absent from the room and looked at the letter from Dr Clarke to him. It said (apropos me) 'This famous actor has got a sore tongue . . .' It was unbelievably naïve. Simply not the sort of clinical language a doctor should use. Ridiculous referring to my career. It's got nothing to do with my complaint.

Sunday, 5 August
We went up to Birmingham to do the TV show. The audience was excellent. The celebrity was Michael Crawford – the step was so light when he came on that I (wearing the mask) thought it was a woman & said 'You're an actress? I can smell the perfume' but he said gruffly 'No.' After we'd discovered who he was (Isobel) I wished I hadn't said it.

Monday, 6 August
Barbara Windsor telephoned me. It is her birthday tomorrow, and I am going to see her and Ronnie at 8 o'c. She said that the Carry On show at the Victoria Palace was ill-prepared and that she wasn't looking forward to it, adding 'You know Sid *hates* Kenny Connor . . .' Actually I didn't! Can't understand anyone hating Kenny Connor – he is a very good actor and I've always found him vastly amusing which is a sight more than I can say for Sid James.

Thursday, 9 August
Today there's an invitation from Cliff Richard & Dora Bryan in the post – to meet Billy Graham!! Is the world going mad?

Sunday, 12 August
It was a Mercedes Benz so we had a better journey to Birmingham than that awful Vauxhall last week. After the games & about 3 retakes, we went to hospitality. After about half an hour I said to Bill Franklyn about going and he began all this send-up stuff about 'Oh! she's stamping her foot . . .' I went and waited in the foyer. Eventually he came down shouting 'Oh! he's waiting with his hand on his hip!' and I simply walked to the car and sat in the front seat. He got in the back and went v. quiet. By the time we reached Luton he asked me for a cigarette & said 'I'm unhappy and cold' and we chatted amiably and on arriving home he said 'Goodnight Kenneth and bless you' and I was equally pleasant. I just can't stand send-ups from pro's. That's all.

Monday, 13 August
Went to lunch at Peter Mario with Bernard Holley. He said 'After you left the show people asked for their money back . . .'

Sunday, 19 August
Drove to Birmingham for the TV. One of the celebrities was Hattie!! So of course I travelled back in her car and we had the great chat. It was lovely to see her. Hattie said to me in the car: 'Bill Cotton thinks you are terrific and he really only put this on as a vehicle for you . . .'

Tuesday, 28 August
Went to see Peter Eade. He said 'Between these four walls, you were just determined to get out of that play at the Globe, weren't you?' and I replied truthfully 'Yes . . . when you're in a long run the play lives with you night & day and if the conditions under which you perform it are continually frustrating it ends by driving you to dementia and a nervous breakdown . . .'

Wednesday, 29 August
Eade rang. 'Would you be interested in going to the Isle of Man for that radio show with Pete Murray?' I said yes. Of course it's all an absurd expense for a radio show to go all the way to the Isle of Man but I've never been there and I believe there have been some rather famous Manxmen. I think Fletcher Christian was one.[16]

Saturday, 1 September
Had a long discussion with Stanley. When we left the restaurant we went to a cinema in Brewer St to get fags 'cos he'd run out of them and a boy behind the grille there said, after I'd talked to a lady in the confectionery kiosk, 'I thought you were a queer . . . you know, a *queen* . . .' and when I spluttered something like 'I beg your pardon,' he articulated louder and more clearly 'You know . . . a POOVE . . . I think you are an old poove . . .' I found myself smiling mirthlessly and repeating (as if it were a denial of the accusation) the words 'I am an actor' and then the lady asked me for my autograph and this boy sneered 'Oh! so you are a famous actor, are you? I never heard of you . . .' After, in the car, I confessed to Stanley that the entire incident succeeded in depressing me horribly. It was the calculated desire to make someone *wriggle* on the hook, to needle, and to denigrate.

---

16 'Fletcher Christian was of good Manx–Cumberland stock.' Richard Hough, *Captain Bligh and Mr Christian*, 1972.

Sunday, 2 September

I remember thinking as I lay in bed last night 'I am *falling* . . . I am falling . . . all my life has been a process of falling . . .' I know what Stevie Smith meant! They all think I'm waving but I'm drowning.[17] My acting career has been the waving.

Wednesday, 5 September

Met some American fellow called Burton and an Australian chap and Burton said 'I met you at Richard's party' and I recalled he'd been v. rude. We all went to the Intrepid Fox and of course it started . . . all the jokes and etc. Suddenly there appeared this boy called John from Wales, with short dark hair and a v. attractive sculptured sort of face and Burton simply put him in the taxi with me and said 'Now you go home with him and *be nice*! You understand? Be nice!' and John nodded agreement. He came back to the flat for an hour or so and he was nice all right – eventually I got him a taxi in Euston Rd. and returned drunkenly to the flat and was violently sick.

Thursday, 6 September

Louie came in & said 'Is this your tie lying out here on the landing?' and it was! I must have been in a shocking state last night. Car came and I got to the airport at 12.20. We took off for Douglas I.O.M. There was a conference there with Pete getting to know everyone in the show including a young comedian, Johnny More, who is in cabaret here & is to impersonate *me* on the show! I was aware throughout the day that I looked awful and felt quite shaky.

Friday, 7 September

At the theatre the broadcast had begun. Johnny More never stopped talking to me in the wings and I wanted peace. Eventually I went and found a packed house and within minutes the P.A. system broke down & they were shouting 'Can't hear!' A child wandered up & sat in my lap, a little blonde girl who said she didn't know where she came from. I asked her what she'd say to a policeman & she replied 'I'd say I was lost' which seemed logical if unhelpful. After the show we signed autographs till 12 o'c. We got off the plane at about 4.15. London full of heat and sunshine.

Saturday, 8 September

On returning to my flat I realised that the itching in the crotch was due to parasite infection! Ugh! I found one and covered the body

---

[17] 'I was much too far out all my life/And not waving but drowning.' Stevie Smith (1902–71), 'Not Waving But Drowning'.

with Amphytria before going to bed. Casual trade *always* has this consequence for me!

Sunday, 9 September

Played the Bach Double Violin Concerto and dressed for this party tonight. The first person I met was Richard Wattis, who told me he's forbidden spirits by the Doctor, adding 'My only pleasure used to be getting drunk all the time! And as for sex . . . I long ago realised I'll only get it if I pay for it . . . so my "love life" is a series of rather sordid monetary transactions . . .' Hattie was looking rather drawn and apparently she's been in hospital and they've discovered arthritis but everyone at the party was hinting at worse disorders.

Monday, 10 September

After reading the news – more about terrorist bombs in London – I started on this blasted script again. I realise now that my choice throughout has been biased in the sense of belief – an asseveration apropos the validity of the ontological belief . . . so far I'm simply instancing the poetry which mirrors that belief but sooner or later I must clinch the argument with prose. I will have to *state* the substance of the opposition to belief and deal with the materialists & the determinists & the Marxists and show that the very language we use in our lives contradicts the assumptions which they make. Determinism taken to its proper conclusion makes nonsense of apportioning praise or blame. It certainly invalidates judgment of any kind and in human affairs, all men have to make judgments, whether they like it or not. Marxism, with its dismissal of the spiritual life of man & denial of God puts the categoric imperative on to the State, so men are at the mercy of a ruling clique and totalitarianism triumphs at the expense of the individual: the free thinker has to be punished & humiliated (Solzhenitsyn etc.) and we're in a world little different from the Czarist persecution of Dostoyevsky.

Wednesday, 12 September

Went to see Helen Fry at about 3.30 and got all this guff from the Commissionaire about 'Who are you?' etc. while another attendant, standing beside me was saying 'I think you're very good on the TV.' Talked to Helen about the Poetry & she agreed to the idea of basing it round the Ontological argument, said she wants an *hour*!! phew! I had not expected *that*!

Wednesday, 19 September

Went to post office to send telegram to Ingrid who opens tonight at the Albery. Gordon came at about 6.20 and we drove in his Jaguar to town to see this play *The Constant Wife*.[18] The curtain rose on a set that was idiotic. A grand piano (never used) dominating the scene *painted brown* – something you'd never see in England. The acting was full of this 'I am going to make a speech' recitative variety, and the production unimaginative, wooden, obvious, and sometimes pretty vulgar. Ingrid had been dressed horribly, in clothes that made her look heavy & *big*. You realise how circumvoluted and pompous & stupid Maugham's dialogue is! Half of it sounded like a cross between an attempt at Wilde, and an imitation of Shaw, because of the would-be epigrammatic and the exposition of women's emancipation, but none of it worked. Gielgud pink-faced, overfed and beaming at his awful production. Gordon & I went round after & congratulated Ingrid & John McCallum.

Saturday, 22 September

Louie left the paper for me. She is a darling – wish I could make it up to her – Oh! my whole life is spent trying to make it up to her. Trying to erase all the sadness and the loneliness and only succeeding in making more loneliness 'cos the nights I don't spend with her serve to emphasise the others, or vice versa. Or something. I do love Louie. After my fashion. She's the only person I've ever loved. By love I mean caring so much that it's altruistic, and feeling her presence when she's not physically there, and missing her and knowing how she'll react to things and then being stunned at finding something *different* in her.

Tuesday, 25 September

Walked to the BBC Enterprises party at the Langham and saw the launching of the records *Unique Hancock* etc. and posed for photographs with Ray Galton and Alan Simpson. I shouted at some man 'You keep away from us! I can tell by the redness of your nose you've got cold germs!! Keep away!' and he scuttled off revealing *white clogs* on his feet! I shouted 'And get rid of those ridiculous shoes too!' and someone nearby said 'He's the design expert for BBC Enterprises' and I replied 'Then he should know better.' We went to a pub where I cried out to Jack de Manio[19] 'You never use me on your programme!' and he said 'What are you doing Monday?' and was charming.

Wednesday, 26 September

To the Playhouse for 'J.A.M.' Both the shows were *outrageous*. Derek Nimmo & me just attacked Parsons till he got cowed & spluttery, and

---

[18] By Somerset Maugham, 1926.

[19] 1914–88. Radio presenter with touches of wilfulness and eccentricity.

Aimi Macdonald blethered on with me crying out 'Oh shut your row! You're obviously mad!' and Clement Freud said that William the Conqueror defeated Hereward the Wake instead of Harold at Hastings. I had a drink after with everyone in the pub and David [Hatch] said 'Yes, it was all appalling . . . absolute anarchy . . . it got out of hand, I'm afraid.'

Saturday, 29 September

Home in time to hear on the news – the death of Auden. A gathering of idiots like Adrian Henri & George (Lisp) MacBeth[20] talked about Auden with self-conscious dryness. No affection.

Wednesday, 3 October

Walked to the Playhouse for the champagne party. Clement Freud moved pointedly away from me – this is because, last night during the show, he told me to keep my voice down and I told him to shut up, adding: 'Don't tell me how to perform' whereupon he took to stroking my jacket in a placating fashion but I didn't speak after that.

Friday, 12 October

Motored down to Bristol. Introduced to Mary, the Baroness Stocks, Richard Marsh,[21] and Isobel Lady Barnett, whom I already know – lovely seeing her. We went on the air with 'Any Questions' at 8.30. I let it down in one place, where emotion got the better of me and the fluency dried up – it was in discussing Quintin Hogg's plea for compassion for the engine driver who lost his life in that train robbery . . . I said he was the only one whose voice was raised on behalf of this victim and then I faded away with 'I find that very moving . . . I was very moved . . .' and simpered myself off the bill.

Tuesday, 16 October

It was pouring down as I made my way to B.H. for this programme with Jack de Manio. He seemed a bit pissed – all the reactions were rather slow and there was a sort of smiling unconcern which threw me rather. Shot out of there at 11 o'c. Worked on the script amendments.

---

20 W.H. Auden (b.1907); Henri (b.1932) and MacBeth (1932–92), poets.

21 Mary Stocks (1891–1975), economist, writer, broadcaster. Richard Marsh, later Baron Marsh of Mannington, b.1928. Minister of Transport 1968–69, etc.

Friday, 19 October
In the afternoon through the pouring rain to Eade to collect script for TV Commercial. This one is for a cider-champagne and apparently the idea is to put the voice on a storyboard and etc. If the clients approve, I then make it as a *visual* commercial!! and am paid ten thousand. Actually I hate the idea of doing a visual. I have never done such a thing before and I think it's unethical tat unless the product (or cause) is a good one, and the commercial is witty. This isn't. It's a Carry On dirty postcard formula.

Tuesday, 23 October
I shall be so glad when this rotten year is over. The very number 73 is rotten. I abhor the remembrance of that ghastly play, the *mad* nature of the reunion with Mags and those weird dinners with Robert and her and Chris Downes. How far away it all seems.

Wednesday, 24 October
Watched the fight between Baby Boy Rolle and John Conteh from Nottingham. Baby stood up to some punishment and Conteh (Commonwealth Light-Heavyweight Champion) won on points but there was a lot of booing from the house. Babe kept falling on to John and holding him – avoiding real fighting.

Wednesday, 31 October
I went on to do this chat spot with Russell Harty at 8.40. The interview rambled about and weaved from one thing to another in a most inconsequential fashion. The one certain thing you can always feel with an audience is their *desire* for authority. Once they're assured that you are assured then everything follows smoothly; but if they feel 'Oh dear, he doesn't know what he's doing' etc., then their behaviour becomes anxious (on your behalf) then irritated, and sometimes angry or indifferent. One of the researchers on the programme took me to dinner. On the return I met two boys from Kuwait in the lift and invited myself to their flat and the good looking one – Bader – flung me on the bed and made violent love to me. I was saying 'This is madness, Bader! I am pissed!' and I fell off the bed and cut my elbow.

Thursday, 1 November
On my knees at one point saying to God 'Oh! I am so ashamed!' and begging to be forgiven.

Friday, 9 November

To the Playhouse for a run-through at 5.15.[22] Helen then decided she wanted *more* rewrites and a complete cutting of the [Gray's] Elegy to what I had suggested in the first script – i.e. begin with 'Yet e'en these bones . . .' as indicated by Johnson. Eventually we started at 7.35. I went thro' at a good measured pace I think, stopping & going back on several mistakes. Trouble with a few coughers but there always is. Certainly there wasn't a laugh in the script and they were asked to be attentive to an unusual degree, and they were. The Chesterton 'Wise Men' went rather well, I thought – it seemed to hold. Applause was warm at the end & it had been 55 minutes.

Wednesday, 14 November

Watched the Royal Wedding on the television. The scene in the Abbey was magnificent and Princess Anne & Mark Phillips looked a handsome couple but the most enchanting sight of all was Prince Edward who was a page behind her, with Lady Sarah Linley.[23] Edward is so beautiful, so composed, so aware . . . It was very moving to see Anne proceed down the aisle on the arm of Prince Philip.

The more I hear commercial radio the more repellent I find it. The din created by the half-baked talking to the half-educated is horrible.

Friday, 23 November

Received an interesting letter from Fred White who knew Grandad Williams in Bingfield Street. He mended a fuse for Fred! – Grandad – Henry Williams was the one who did all the lights on the dome of the Coliseum – he was in electrics. Rang Phyllis to find out about all this and she said she remembered him. He lived at 66 Bingfield Street and his father was a licensed moneylender and a Bessie Wells was his second cousin. My grandad John Williams and his wife Elizabeth lived at No. 64 in the house of Mr & Mrs Neal. This latter, Louie Neal, was the sister of Bob Ward (who had a shop on the corner for second hand clothes etc.) and his son Tom Ward married Lili (Elizabeth) Williams (daughter of John & Elizabeth). She also said that Aunt Soph's daughter, Dolly Kiff, still lives at Delhi Street! The Williams family must go something like this:

---

[22] Of his radio programme 'The Crystal Spirit'. The title was taken from a George Orwell poem appended by him to his own 1942 essay 'Looking Back at the Spanish War': 'No bomb that ever burst/Shatters the crystal spirit.' See entry for 9 September 1971, p. 408.

[23] Actually Lady Sarah Armstrong-Jones (daughter of Princess Margaret, and sister of Viscount Linley).

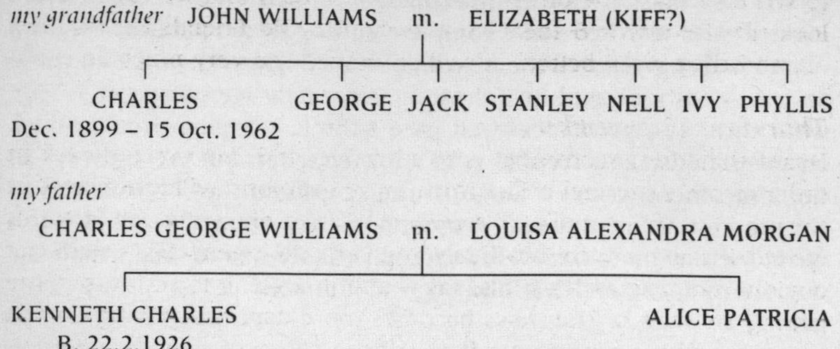

I must fill in more of this when I get the time.

Monday, 26 November
I had a call from Peter E. to say that Hattie is all right. Apparently there is some obstruction in the fallopian tube but it can be put right. I wrote her a letter and went out to get a card 'cos Louie wants to send one.

Sunday, 2 December
Arrived at Fred by 12.30. He had an interesting collection of people. There was Norman, who boldly stated 'I said to this young sailor in bed the other night – you are not the man your father was – and my dears, it was true . . .' Leslie bragged about the length of his penis, Henrik said of someone 'He has a beautiful arse, and very hairy, like a jungle, you know . . .' and everyone nodded as if they did. Fred was full of enthusiasm for his imminent departure for Greece where he said he'd found 'the most divine policeman who wants me to take him one or two things from Cartier's.' I spent the evening with Louie & she wanted to see the Royal Command Performance on TV. It was *dire*. It had no shape, no taste, and no talent.

Wednesday, 5 December
To Basil Jellicoe Hall for the Old Folks' Christmas Party. The Mayor came in and said to me 'You're doing a grand job' while I was in the middle of a particularly dirty story to a lady of eighty.

Monday, 10 December
Lovely letter from Myra De Groot!! She's in New Zealand now! Robert

Bolt called and gave me the Blake biography of Disraeli.[24] I asked him to write in my copy of his *Man For All Seasons* and he did. I didn't look till afterwards & then I saw he'd put 'Old Friends are the best . . . and they grow better . . .' which moved me very much.

Thursday, 13 December

Heard that the government is to introduce a *3 day working week* in order to meet the fuel crisis! Apparently everyone will lose wages in the process! And it applies to *everything*! Banks, offices, shops, factories etc etc. It's all mad 'cos obviously you can't do it generally – with the obvious example of hospitals, say – and it is going to result in some glaring anomalies. The news becomes more depressing every day as we watch democracy simper itself off the bill.

Friday, 14 December

By tube to Lime Grove for the last of the 'Jackanorys'. The electricians' strike was on! So the lighting was reduced to one lamp!

Saturday, 15 December

To Desmond's party. It was all very entertaining. Apart from some wide eyed idiot from Eire who kept calling me Mister Williams and saying 'Can you help me? I'm a *star* really . . .' I talked to a BBC camera boy who was charming and Sandy Wilson and the dreadful Chinese boy from Hong Kong and Wilson said 'I never realised when I met you . . . you're quite a scholar, aren't you?' I went with a fellow called Percy to his home & then to Liverpool Street station with a James R. Home to Alka Seltzer and dreadful headaches. O! Why? Why get pissed all the time . . . the guilt will overwhelm me tomorrow.

Sunday, 16 December

Went in to see Louie in the evening and found there was nothing but rubbish on the television. Old films! – including *Don't Lose Your Head* with me and Jim Dale and Sid James. This latter looked really awful. One forgets if one is away from the face for long enough, but it is so bashed and creviced that it gets in the way of any articulation; and oh dear! he is such a *bad* actor – he reveals his embarrassment at every line. Each utterance is done in the 'I have got to get rid of this' sort of fashion and the embarrassment is passed straight on to the viewer. I was as bad as ever, all posh voice and sneers and convincing no one. It was funny to see Peter Gilmore as Robespierre!! Now of course he is famous as the Captain in the 'Onedin Line',[25] but then

---

[24] Robert Blake (Lord Blake), b.1916. *Disraeli* published 1966.

[25] A saga of nineteenth-century shipping which ran until 1978.

he was moaning about having no future and the wife left him and married Nick Henson.

Wednesday, 19 December
Arrived at Manchester. 1st show was restrained and dull. Marty Feldman was the guest celebrity. In the second show, it was the wonderful Mike Yarwood. He was splendid. Taxi to the hotel with Isobel and Nanette [Newman]. Sat in the Midland having coffee. It was in this hotel that I stayed with Maggie in '62 when she stood outside my room singing 'Noludar' to the tune of 'Joshua' 'cos she wanted a sleeping pill.

Thursday, 20 December
Caught the 7.30 train. I had cornflakes, kippers, toast & marmalade @ 95p. which was very good. Marty gave me a lift home and said 'You have become much more relaxed over the years . . . quite different from the old days . . .'

Monday, 24 December
Now that Louie is gone, I feel utterly alone and miserable. Find myself crying stupidly. Don't think I've ever felt so wretched at Christmas.

Friday, 28 December
Awful dream of Louie returning with 2 suits for me from Hepworths and saying goodbye! 'I've got a big flat by the Strand . . . trouble is, no one wants to know my poor old man . . . they're all digging into my handbag I'm afraid.' When I cried, and said 'What am I going to do with your flat at Osnaburgh Street?' she laughed nervously. It was all horrible.

Sunday, 30 December
Hilton Hotel for the Alan Walker party. Hattie was there, looking fit and better than ever. There was a girl called Eva and I said 'You have a wonderfully pretty face' and she said 'I think that is very rude! Commenting on people's looks!' so I moved away quickly. Dickie Wattis was shouting and bawling a mixture of flattery and insult at me. He always does. At about 11 o'c. I left with Wattis in a cab. He said 'Come in for just one drink' but I refused for I knew I was already drunk.

Monday, 31 December
Hattie rang & asked me over there for New Year's Party but I said I was going elsewhere for fear of offending her, whereas, in fact, I am going nowhere. If I attend *one* more party I shall go stark raving mad.

1974

Tuesday, 1 January

It is the first time in my life that this day has been a national holiday. The only papers were evening ones! It is little short of scandalous.

Wednesday, 2 January

Did 'Open House' with Pete Murray. I wasn't very inspired but I did mention the virtue of prayer. Went in to Louie and saw the TV. This programme 'Softly Softly'[1] is becoming very odd indeed. This week the subject was a young (and seemingly passionate) fascistic constable with a racial prejudice, power complex, and goodness knows what. Even assuming there are a lot of ambitious & power-ridden policemen about, that is no excuse for such a damnable indictment of a noble army of understaffed & underpaid servants of the state. There are enough sinister forces for evil at work in the world without fabricating the same qualities in the British police.

Wednesday, 9 January. Manchester

To the studios with Isobel, Bill & Nanette [Newman]. I must admit the state of the country depresses me dreadfully – it was so difficult to get through the shows . . . I did a bit of chatting to the house & got a few laughs, but my heart was like lead.

Thursday, 10 January

We learned there was nothing in or out of Euston (because of ASLEF not the NUR) and we would be conveyed as far as Watford Junction. David Jacobs found us seats on the suburban train out of Watford which was packed with vexed & irritated passengers. One, from Lancaster, said 'We all seem to be taking these ridiculous measures like a load of sheep . . . nobody is protesting . . . no coal, no transport . . . nothing.' And you feel this in all conversation; the belief that the crisis is really unnecessary . . . that it has gone too far . . . that the 3

---

[1] Popular police series (1966–76).

day week etc. is all rubbish and the miners should be paid. Oh it's ghastly.

Tuesday, 15 January

A very nice driver (Bruce) drove us up to Manchester because there is a train strike. Celebrity was the tennis star Virginia Wade. That was fine. I had said 'Do balls come into it?' and she said 'You'd look pretty silly if they didn't.'

Wednesday, 16 January

We walked around the square and Isobel said 'That's enough exercise for me' and we returned to the hotel for lunch. Went to the studios. First celebrity was Dickie Henderson – I couldn't guess anywhere near him – and the other was Peter Gilmore! I was delighted! I've always been v. fond of Peter. He announced that he was leaving 'The Onedin Line' and the audience all cried out 'Ah no!' which shows his popularity.

Monday, 21 January. Manchester

The first game was fine and the celebrity was Vic Feather,[2] who said (apropos his becoming a Lord) 'I have to see the Garter King of Arms . . . I would rather see the Brassière one myself' and jokes of a similar nature: a genial ill-bred creature. Afterwards, in hospitality, Eve (research) said 'Vic Feather kept pinching my bottom all the time . . . it is a bit much you know' and Isobel said 'Yes, he did it to me on "Any Questions" . . .'

Thursday, 31 January

I walked to Peter Eade and read the script of *Carry On Dick* – said I'd do it if they cut the stocks scene (where I'm pelted with rubbish) and pay the salary after the tax period, i.e. April 6th. The script is utterly banal. It is incredible that human minds can put such muck on to paper.

Tuesday, 5 February

I went to De Lane Lea Studios where I did a voice-over for a tuition film about North Sea Gas (playing the Will o' the Wisp – voice of Natural Gas) with Jack – no – someone Hawkins (Peter Hawkins) with whom I worked at High Wycombe *years* ago. He said 'I do hundreds of

---

[2] 1908–76. General Secretary of the Trades Union Congress 1969–73.

voice-overs . . . it's all so screamingly boring' and he told me of the awful frustration of it.[3]

Friday, 8 February
Stanley came and we went to Lariana. Stanley had very little to say really. I was waspish and nasty and eventually he said he felt feverish and was sure he'd caught a cold and would I mind if he left? I said 'I've very little time for illness' and joined Stan W.'s table instead & he went home.

Sunday, 10 February
A note from the girl below says that she is going to play her filthy clarinet for an hour & a half every night. Lackaday and rue. Saw the news on television and I suddenly realised: it is *more* than depressing! This entire period is like a nightmare. There seems to be walking insanity abroad and various *unreal* dialogues are broadcast which desperately try to disguise the yawning chasm of meaninglessness.

Friday, 15 February
Got the paper. There was certainly nothing worth reading in it, so I turned instead to the shooting script of the Carry On which arrived yesterday. If anything it is worse than the previous version. It is appalling. It lacks verbal wit, it lacks comic situation, it lacks any credible characters. It is a Carry On.

Tuesday, 19 February
Got to Manchester and we did the two shows which were OK 'cos the audience was a merry one and fell about at such descriptions as 'faggot packer' etc. The first celebrity was [Michael] Parkinson (I got him) whom I loathe and after him Jack Warner whom I love. I couldn't face any of them after and on arriving back at the Midland I went straight to my room. The further you go in this profession the more you realise its utter hollowness – what Erich called 'the looking glass world' where the values are simply those of either fashion or the market place and little else matters at all. I shall be glad to leave this town, and the show.

Friday, 22 February
Went to Thames Television and walked through a picket line to do the chat show with a woman called Mavis Nicholson[4] who was quite

---

[3] Peter Hawkins had provided the voices of such television favourites as the Flowerpot Men, the Daleks, and Captain Pugwash, among many others.
[4] b.1930. Journalist and TV interviewer.

nervous. It went thro' all right. Bit bogged down in the middle but otherwise OK. Returned to flat to meet Andrew. We went to see *McQ* at ABC One in Shaftesbury Avenue. Quite a good fascist picture about a corrupt police force.

Tuesday, 26 February

A fabulous surprise from Charles Laurence!! A copy of the play is sent to me! And he's written a marvellous inscription on the fly leaf! This is the best present I've had for years and years. I sent him a telegram of thanks. Interviewed by a girl from the Liverpool Post – 'Why do you *act* on "What's My Line?" when the others are simply themselves . . . ?' Here we go round the Mulberry Bush.

Wednesday, 27 February

To Bristol. I met the producer, Pamela Howe, and Amanda Theunissen who was *enchanting* – the kind of girl I want to touch – and exquisite. She looks about 15 but is married with two children & lives in Bristol with her husband who teaches at the Polytechnic. Arthur Marshall arrived and we had the lunch and then did the broadcast.[5] It was awful. All bits and pieces and fits and starts.

Friday, 1 March

It's the right weather for the election results! Apparently the Tories are defeated. I feel it's a personal affront. It is an unsatisfactory and muddled result of a *stupid election* fought on unsatisfactory & muddled issues.

Monday, 4 March

Curious to reflect that this[6] is the first film I have done from this address. Car at 7.15 and we arrived at Pinewood at about 7.50. The road is greatly altered now & and in parts I had difficulty in recognising the route. Once in the studio, however, there was little change! All the same old hangers-on and overfed potbellied people that cling to this industry like flies to excrement. Of course the dialogue was all filth and innuendo 'Do you know Big Dick?' etc. etc. and one's heart sank . . . but I kept my countenance.[7] The news is that Heath has resigned and Wilson has gone to see the Queen tonight.

---

[5] 'Can't Put it Down' (broadcast 6 March): 'Kenneth Williams, Arthur Marshall and Amanda Theunissen meet their doom in darkest Sussex.' The programme was a discussion of Stella Gibbons' *Cold Comfort Farm*.

[6] *Carry On Dick*.

[7] A phrase for which KW showed an increasing fondness, probably recalling Eliot's 'I keep my countenance/I remain self-possessed', from 'Portrait of a Lady'.

Wednesday, 6 March
Still the Inn sequence of which everyone is heartily sick. Sid James complaining that it's a lousy script 'All talk and no action' and very angry with Kenneth Connor who he said 'makes private jokes on stage at the Victoria Palace and doesn't play it as rehearsed' but of course one *knows why*. Kenny is a comedian and Sid isn't.

Friday, 8 March
My stand-in, Michael Clark, told me that the extras are all 'tough guys' and said that one of them has a three page entry in the book on the Kray Brothers! The film industry attracts some dreadful creatures.

Saturday, 9 March
Went to bed & dreamed that I was attending a political meeting addressed by Harold Wilson: I was talking to him & he was complaining of the sparse attendance, and I saw Heath in the front row smiling and wearing a ridiculous square shouldered ladies' musquash coat. It was absurd. Read a lot of poems aloud from the Larkin Oxford collection. The Flecker one about the Canal is fine.[8] I sat, revolving many memories and weeping.

There was a young lady called Gloria
Who was fucked by Sir Gerald du Maurier
Jack Hylton, Jack Payne, Jack Hylton again,
And the band at the Waldorf Astoria.

Wednesday, 13 March
Everyone is so *weary* on this film! Except Jack Douglas who is endlessly suggesting bits of business to me, discussing Queen Anne furniture to others and giving curry recipes to Joan Sims. I'm horribly afraid that most of his ideas are rather good.

Thursday, 14 March
Lunch with Kenneth Connor and his son Jeremy: he is playing a footpad in this film! I said to him 'I remember when they brought you on the set at Pinewood when you were only three years old, and you had a scene with your dad in the hospital in *Carry On Nurse*.' He is a good-looking and sensitive boy. I was treated like some old hack

---

[8] 'Oxford Canal' by James Elroy Flecker (1884–1915), in *The Oxford Book of Twentieth Century English Verse*, edited by Philip Larkin (1973). The verse about Gloria, pencilled in by KW, does not appear in Larkin's anthology.

you keep around in case of need but don't bother with overmuch: of course, that is exactly how they regard me.

Friday, 15 March

Dreadful notices for the new Charles Laurence play[9] with Maggie Smith!! Awful in the Times, filthy in the Express and rude in the Mail with a reference to his first play being redeemed by *my* presence! Compliment indeed!

Tuesday, 19 March

We did all the 'drag' sequence with Sid James who kept saying 'I hate bloody drag . . . can't *stand* being in wigs and dresses' and obviously meant it. At lunch, it was Ken Connor, Peter Butterworth and Bernard Bresslaw – no girls – and conversation was consequently more interesting. I had far too much to drink and shouted at Gerald who was giving lunch to Ernie Stewart 'The moths will fly out of your wallet' and other rudenesses. On the set after, he said 'That was very rude of you . . . I've often taken you to lunch' & I said 'But you are *moneyed*! I've only got two rooms' & he replied 'Yes and the stove is covered in cellophane . . .' which is quite true.

Wednesday, 20 March

Only one nasty moment when I was in the wrong clothes. Gerald was saying 'Hurry up, or we'll lose the sun!' and when I quoted some poetry from Gray to him, he said 'We're not here to shoot poetry! We're here to shoot a load of shit.' First time I've ever heard him talk in such a blatant fashion. After, he said 'I bet you quote that in some interview!' A lot of people commented on my horse manner & I haven't done any riding since the Kirtlington days![10] But I had Diana – a v. good mare.

Thursday, 21 March

Jack Douglas suggested two script amendments and Gerald suggested a tag for the pigeon sequence –

Me: I have the smell of success.
Jack: I thought it was the pigeon . . .

Which was very apt and rounded the scene off beautifully. Barbara Windsor said of the man with the horses 'I'm mad about him! I've given my Ronnie grounds for divorce four times in five minutes just

---

[9] *Snap.*

[10] During KW's wartime evacuation period at nearby Bicester, chez Mr Chisholm.

looking at him!' She is immensely likeable and vulnerable and funny! Totally adorable. I can think of no actress I'd rather be with.

Friday, 22 March

It was all interior of the church with Sid James in the pulpit – a sight at once sacrilegious and scandalous. The entire sequence – sermon & hymn singing – in this filthy script is abhorrent to me. Day redeemed by presence of Hattie: she is a constant joy, and dear Bernard . . . we all lunched together.

Monday, 25 March

I have learned that I can no longer afford to cut my hair very short. In the old days it always had a youthful effect and I could get away with it, but now the recession on the temple is so extensive that it looks awful, and the side greyness is worse than anywhere else, so I need the fullness of top hair to help this. The face has aged considerably in the last year or so. The other thing I've noticed is the inertia in my personality. In the past I delighted in dominating a conversation and challenging all points of view but now I have little desire to converse with anyone save the real *old* friend or the truly sympathetic acquaintance. All the rest – it's just nods and smiles and often no sound issues from me at all.

Tuesday, 2 April

Driven to Stoke Poges for the 'stocks' sequence. It was hateful and hurt my neck to stand in that fashion with the head & wrists imprisoned. Kenneth Connor pointed out that they were not stocks but pillories & suggested a new end sequence:

Me: Oh! what would my family say?
Jack: You won't have any family!
Me: Why?
Jack: You're on the pill-ory!

which certainly made the unit laugh and was a great improvement on the script, but Gerald shot both versions so I expect it will be Peter who will pronounce judgment.[11] All the muck that was flung at me made me feel filthy and smell too! And Gerald said 'That's your last shot!' which rather surprised me.

Saturday, 13 April

Letter from Russell Harty[12] in the post asking if he can publish my

---

[11] The pill-ory line does not appear in the surviving (video) version of the film.

[12] 1934–88. TV arts journalist and chat-show host. Book: *Russell Harty Plus* ('Based on the television series from London Weekend Television Ltd'). The interviewees

interview with him thro' Hamish Hamilton! I think not. The impromptu dialogue, once set down on paper, is a dangerously permanent record of one's indiscretion. Ingrid telephoned: she asked me to a party on the 26th.

Tuesday, 16 April

Went in to see Louie in the evening and when preparing supper I said 'Oh hurry up you silly cow' and she replied 'You'll be sorry you spoke like that when I'm not here.' 'What do you mean, when you're not here?' 'When I'm gone! Dead of course!' 'But you know I care for you as I care for nobody else in the world! That is the reason I am totally uninhibited when I'm talking to you.' 'Oh, I know you don't mean it . . . I was joking . . .' Of course the irony is that when Louie talks of death she little realises that it has been (and will continue to be) a dreadful apprehension for me. God knows what I should do without her!

Friday, 26 April

I went to David Hatch at 2 o'c. and went thro' scripts. They're all pretty terrible. I found myself lying with aplomb . . . 'Yes, that is quite funny really . . .' and will be landed with performing all this rubbish in the autumn. To Mount St for Ingrid's party. John Gielgud said 'Are you fit now? Can you return to the theatre? I always think it's fair to give them nine months. Noël would only do 12 weeks but of course he wrote it all himself you see.' Emlyn Williams said in mock awe 'Oh! it's the Superstar Sir John Gielgud!' and of me 'That's my very talented nephew!' Ingrid said 'Tonight we can all get drunk and smash the flat up! 'Cos I am leaving it after this . . .'

Thursday, 2 May

Letter from David Hatch saying I hadn't read his letter! I rang him and quoted from it! (I had stupidly returned it among the scripts.)

Saturday, 4 May

A letter from David Hatch raising the entire script issue all over again! People will not accept no for an answer but must worry you like a dog with a bone! I don't want to perform his bloody script: I write and say I'm not up to it: he replies arguing that I *should* do it: and round & round we go.

---

whose words were reprinted ranged from Frankie Howerd and Gary Glitter to Dame Sybil Thorndike and Gore Vidal.

Sunday, 5 May
To Gordon & Rona. I foolishly asked for my poetry programme ('Crystal Spirit') at 10.15 and they listened for a bit. They all said they didn't care for 'that kind of poetry' and turned it off. From what I heard, it sounded *awful* – over-emphasised and monotonous and *bad.*

Friday, 10 May
Peter E. phoned 'Leslie Grade says he will pay you anything you ask to come and be in the pantomime at the Palladium.' I said the prospect would fill me with horror. That theatre in Argyle Street seems to epitomise all that is reprehensible in show business.

Tuesday, 14 May
Load of letters about the poetry sent by Helen Fry's secretary. Laurena phoned & I went to Eade's office to collect another lot of letters! They seem to be unending regarding this poetry programme! I returned and spent about six hours writing the replies. Some you can do in a few lines but others need elaboration of some kind. Superb letter from Arthur Darlington, a farmer in Wales. It is easily the most interesting and most authentic letter I've received apropos broadcasting, ever! I shall have to compose a good reply, for this kind of thoroughness deserves reciprocity.

Tuesday, 21 May
Rushed off at 10 o'c. to meet Beverley at Peter Mario. He said the notices for his play at the Mermaid had been fair but not enthusiastic – it is called *The Great Society*. Maggie joined us at 10.45 and we had a lively supper together. Mags drove us home at 1 o'c. and I ran alongside the car shouting 'Hard right! back away . . . down on the wheel' and Bev said 'Piss off before you get run over!' It was a lovely evening.

Friday, 24 May
With Louie to the Playhouse. Guest was Jean Marsh. We have a new producer, John Lloyd.[13] Very nice boy. Feel I've seen the face somewhere before. The eyes are deep blue and v. beautiful.

Saturday, 1 June
Taxi to TV Theatre for the TV show 'Read All About It' with the guest author Julian Symons.[14] My stomach was going over and over at the

---

13 b.1951. Later associated with a younger generation of broadcast comedy, e.g. 'Spitting Image'.
14 b.1912. Author, critic and historian of detective fiction.

end. Difficult to know what made me so angry but I was. The second half (where each member was supposed to discuss his book choice) was a waste of time – instead of the books being discussed they were all dismissed in a moment or two and the little time that was left fell to a discussion of what limits a biographer should set himself in terms of intimate revelation. I found myself *disliking* Melvyn Bragg. I felt that I wasn't being *used* on the programme – I can talk well on certain subjects and was never given the opportunity. I came away feeling cheated & angry. Antonia Fraser I *loved*. She gave me a lift home. She was the redemption of the day for me.

Tuesday, 4 June
Went to meet Geoffrey Cannon at the Radio Times Building. We walked in the park and he explained the new format & policy of the paper and wants me to write for it. I said: 'Will you have an alternative writer in case my stuff turns out to be useless . . .' He said 'If I agreed to that, the exercise would be foredoomed . . . I know you will do something absolutely splendid.' God! I wish I had such confidence in myself.

Friday, 7 June
George gave me dinner & took me to the Victoria Palace to see *Carry On London*. It was like watching human beings *forced* into a pig sty & desperately trying to make light of their plight. The show is a pathetic rag-bag of end-of-the-pier and would-be Cochran type revue with glamour girls and chorus boys. Perhaps the saddest thing is the audience. At the end Sid James came forward & said 'We're gonna do the whole bloody thing all over again!' and they cried out approvingly. When he had the temerity to ask 'Did you enjoy it?' they shouted 'Yes!' George & I went backstage to see Barbara and she greeted us affectionately and all the team were kind to me.

Sunday, 9 June
I tried writing this stuff for Radio Times all over again. It's no good, I just can't get it going. If anything is ever made out of it, it will be as a result of a brilliant editor cutting & shaping it.

Monday, 10 June
Geoffrey Cannon phoned & said that he'd rearranged the order of paragraphs & read them out to me. He added 'I think you will like it when you see it in print and I think it will give you confidence for next time because I shall be after you to do it again.' Stewart Morris phoned about bringing back 'Int. Cab.' and would I meet a writer he's found on Thursday.

Saturday, 15 June
Saw Ronnie Corbett on television. Jokes about 'The vicar gives me a blessing and I'm late getting home & the wife says *''You've been blessed again, haven't you?''* ' The blatant denigration of religious practice made one sick. I turned it off.

Monday, 17 June
Found that Geoffrey Cannon had sent me a proof copy of Radio Times with my 'Preview' in it: must confess I find it ordinary: written with the competence of a good journalist, no more. I wrote saying I would do a further three: of course I'm mad but his charming letter is a powerfully persuasive instrument. Got the tube to Shepherd's Bush & worked with Peter Robinson on the script for Int. Cab. We roughed out about half a show. He showed me some of my earlier scripts which he'd got from Archive and I was amazed at how well they read. Returned to flat feeling quite good. The effort of going somewhere and doing something does give a sense of accomplishment.

Wednesday, 19 June
There are pickets at the gates of the BBC – the P[ersonal] A[ssistant]s are on strike – and there is a newspaper dispute affecting all publications! So after all that work on the Radio Times article I needn't have bothered 'cos it won't come out anyway!

Friday, 28 June
Relieved to find the bumps behind the ears have subsided, now the uvula pain has returned however, so I'm not alone: if physical ailments are a form of company, I'm one of the world's socialites. Went to the Centre. Worked till 4 o'c. and produced about half a page. It is deeply disappointing. Went in to Louie. We saw 'Ironside' – this has gone off terribly. One sees again and again that all the programmes are straining against the language itself. There is only *so much* you can say . . . beyond that, it's all been done. The Tarbuck show is an example. 'The Two Ronnies' has better material but is curiously charmless – it is apparently slick etc., but you *don't care* . . . the only comedian who rouses affection is Les Dawson – there's a sort of sad & rugged courage there & a lot of rueful fun.

Saturday, 29 June
Went to the fete at Lambeth Palace which was ruined by pestering children & adults, asking for autographs. A woman said 'Would you do the auction stall for us?' and I said no and she said 'Well frankly I only asked you because someone said you were well known but I've never heard of you myself . . .'

Thursday, 4 July
Went to the Playhouse through the drizzling rain of what could have been an October afternoon. The ['Just a Minute'] games were rather dreary but the audience was marvellous. Diana S. (who is blind) was there with her husband and before the game started she gave me an envelope & said 'Read this . . . but don't let it lie around anywhere . . . it is personal.' Home by 7.45. Read the stuff from Diana. It is all about her attempt to write a biography about me and being told by everyone: 'Oh! he's a queer' and says that she ended up not wanting to write it at all.

Tuesday, 9 July
Letters from Val Orford – 'Your TV series was a failure' and Eliza – no, Edith Butler: 'Your radio series (Witherspoon) must have come out of the ark, where did you find all those awful old jokes?' The telephone rings a lot these days. I let it ring. Don't want to know.

Wednesday, 10 July
To see *Carry On Dick* (trade show) at Studio One in a downpour of rain. Met Peter Butterworth & sat with him. It was diabolical. The pace is deadly . . . at one point I thought it looked as if everyone was *ill* or something.

Friday, 12 July
Went to the Playhouse to do the game. At one point I shouted 'Shut your row' to Clement Freud, & Parsons remarked 'He doesn't talk to you like that!' & I said ''Course he doesn't! He's not got my vocabulary' and the audience laughed and applauded! I behaved disgracefully.

Monday, 22 July
Did some letters and then went by tube to TV Centre and dictated Script 7 and Script 8 and so this wretched business of travelling back & forth is over. Peter R. is a charming fellow but he provides *nothing* in the way of comedy. He actually said 'What will you say if they ask us to do some more?' I replied that they'd asked for 8 and I'd done 8.

Thursday, 25 July
A foolish woman called Patterson has sent me religious writings – 'to help you' which are obviously written for halfwits. Consigned that to the WPB.

Lest I be guilty of arrogance, I read the book which Mrs Patterson sent. It is issued by the Jehovah's Witness organisation and is appallingly banal: reconsigned it to the WPB. I shall not reply, or acknowledge it. If there is any further rubbish from her, I shall say a belated thankyou. I must not speak to her in a disparaging fashion about her faith.

Saturday, 27 July
In the evening I saw John Wayne in a submarine film which was v. good.[15] He has the capacity for bigness in acting – bigness in every sense: physical and mental. I think this is inseparable from the man himself & it was confirmed when I saw him in real life conversing with Parkinson: it was gratifying to see his generous and amiable nature steadfastly refusing to be provoked by the needling small-mindedness of the interviewer & remaining utterly polite throughout. He has a natural distrust of pretension & sophistry. He is about as decent a man as we're ever likely to see.

Sunday, 28 July
Walked with George to the café at Peter Robinson in Oxford St & we had coffee & a chat. He said 'The Western world is becoming totally decadent' and pointed out the gimcrack nature of Oxford Street & Coventry Street with the amusement arcades full of pop music noise & long-haired drifters & layabouts . . . the streets are filthy and people are actually lying in doorways and there is this mindless boredom & despair. He said there was soon going to be nowhere you could flee to. I said South Africa would last about 5 to 10 years. I think all dictatorships will be *out* by then.

Friday, 2 August
I took Gordon to Peter Mario. I was longing for something good to eat, in spite of the pain from the bloody tooth. It was all a desperate attempt to cheer up. My mind is preoccupied with suicide. I certainly would love to go.

Saturday, 3 August
Typed out the article for R[adio] T[imes]. It ain't very good 'cos it lacks cohesion and some of the stuff is almost 'contrived' in the literal sense but I'm past caring really and should they object to the quality of the writing I'll have the perfect chance to say 'Yes well I hate doing it anyway, so get someone else.' I'm long past the period when I got a kick out of seeing my name in print.

Tuesday, 6 August
Tooth: agony – esp. on biting or contact etc. Went to the dentist at

---

[15] *Operation Pacific* (1951).

5.30 and at 6.15 he extracted it, and showed me the root (one of three) that had caused all the trouble. It was a murderous extraction. The nurse held my head. He wrenched and pulled for about 4 minutes before he got it out in *two* pieces, separately. There are marks all round my mouth and the lips. In my heart I know it's a *dying* process. I am 48 but I should have been dead a long time ago: it is a useless life . . . one that goes on with a facade but which is a sort of daft vacuum.

Thursday, 8 August
Lovely letter about my Preview from Geoffrey Cannon. This man is so encouraging and charitable.

Saturday, 10 August
The news was full of the aftermath of the Nixon resignation (yesterday) and heralding a new 'honest' era under President Ford who is nothing to do with motor cars but apparently has a good record in baseball. Seems rather like asking Don Revie[16] to become Prime Minister. Might not be such a bad idea at that! He'd certainly make a better impression than Wilson or Heath.

Monday, 12 August
To the hairdresser at 2.45. Henry is away so Mr Sugarman did it with his usual ruthless abandon. When I said I thought Eastbourne (his holiday resort) was a bit posh for me, he said 'Perhaps you could find something near a sewer to suit you' and I cried 'Ah! how apt' whilst thinking 'How rude.'

Thursday, 22 August
I went with Louie to Peter Mario for lunch and she talked to Henry Cooper[17] who was charming to her and she adores him. After, we went to D.H. Evans where Louie got a new fur (Canadian Squirrel) for £450. She paid herself. Her other squirrel was Siberian (130) and she got it in 1959; they told her it's not worth remodelling 'cos of the worn nature of some of the skins.

Monday, 26 August
There was a strange little playlet written by Galton & Simpson about a package holiday, *Holiday With Strings*, in which Les Dawson played the stuff they used to write for Hancock. There was *one* sequence – his sitting next to a queen in the plane – and it was the only one that worked. It is *dialogue* – especially duologue which these boys can

---

[16] Manager of England football team 1974–77.
[17] b.1934. Professional heavyweight boxer 1954–71, subsequently an entertainer.

write, and once they establish a relationship (albeit a stereotype like this) it starts to work. Their women (in this case Patricia Hayes) are all aggressive and rude, and largely unsuccessful. The whole thing was unsatisfactory and pure *radio* in technique.

Sunday, 1 September

I suppose all violence (including that done to the mind as well as the physical kind) is the result of *limited intellect* (or of passion limiting it in the temporary sense). The fine mind and the thinking mind must *stop short* of violence because it attacks the very basis of civilised values – the supreme importance of the Individual: that people are ends in themselves and not the means and that their end (for me) lies in the realisation of their authentic spirit . . . the acknowledging of God within them & therefore in others. The world of the mind or spirit differs vastly from the mundane world and man's faith represents the eternal *tension* (dynamic) between conscience and reality. He walks a tightrope towards his goal (God) with humility on the one hand and appalling arrogance on the other. Some make this journey gracefully, some stumbling & teetering, some falling off and hanging by one arm occasionally, but none ever fall because the infinite mercy of God is there, like a vast hand stretched to save them. 'He misses not one of all.'[18]

Monday, 2 September

Up at 6.45. Heard a bit of my own trailer for the programme 'S[tart] T[he] W[eek]' at about 5 to 7! It sounded slightly mad. Walked the wet streets to B.H., and went on the air at 9.5. I tended towards over-rapidity thro' nerves but I didn't stumble overmuch. Sheridan Morley, Bill Franklyn, Kenneth Robinson and Michael Klinger[19] were all good talkers and I wasn't left with egg on me face at all. Peter E. telephoned & said I've been asked to record *Northanger Abbey** by BBC Transcription department. Quite a nice compliment.

*No, it is *Nightmare Abbey* (Peacock)[20] so it ain't such a compliment.

Tuesday, 3 September

Dreamed that I had hidden from the police under the skirts of a lady who was on the loo & that thereafter experienced trepidation lest I be recognised. Read the Charles Williams preface to the Oxford Milton.

---

[18] cf. the poem 'Nod' by Walter de la Mare: 'his blind old sheepdog, Slumber-soon,/ Misses not one of all.'

[19] 1921–89. Film producer.

[20] Prose satire (1818) by Thomas Love Peacock (1785–1866).

Wednesday, 4 September

The TV was *dismal*. Really pathetic. Ronnie Barker is embarked on a disastrous course – comedy set in a *prison*! It is drab and anachronistic and utterly foolish in conception.[21]

Thursday, 5 September

Read the Pepys Diaries 'cos we may discuss him on the *STW* programme: found them inordinately dull. What a dreary little creature he must have been. Lunch with Ernest Maxin apropos 'Int. Cab.' and the burden of it was: cut the scripts by 3 minutes. Quite a bombshell at this late juncture. It is infuriating 'cos it means that one has slaved away at it for nothing.

Thursday, 12 September. Bristol

Got the to the studio at 10 o'c. and worked till about 6.[22] All through it, you could feel the word 'disappointing' ringing thro' the air. We left the studio at 6 and Pamela [Howe] drove me to the Theunissen house. Amanda said 'You won't come down here again – I can feel that you won't' and she's dead right. Her children are heavenly but I couldn't believe it when she asked me to *read* the Gawain story to them!! – after being stuck in a studio reading stories all day till the voice was a croak! Still I did it & the children liked it – the boy said 'You're better than Mummy' and I replied 'Yes but she is prettier.'

Sunday, 15 September

Went to the Talk of the Town thro' the pouring rain carrying me stuff in the suitcase. My opening spot went well but I was conscious of the left leg trembling v. badly. Second spot was lousy – I got lost in the opening lines! Peter Robinson walked off with my lighter & fags saying 'It went very well indeed! I've marked all the laughs . . .' and he had – in the script.

Monday, 16 September

C. came. He said he'd been to the Escort with Harry & some docker & a Welsh boy – Keith, & this latter had been approached by a Prince Ali who asked 'How much do you earn?' & Keith said '25 pounds a week.' 'I will pay you 50 & give you a flat in Sloane Square – I will visit you & ravage you three days a week' and Keith replied earnestly

---

[21] 'Porridge', by Dick Clement and Ian La Frenais.

[22] On reading a radio adaptation of *Cold Comfort Farm*.

'What do I do on the other four?' C. said 'He's ingenuous but very practical.'

Wednesday, 18 September
Saw Paul Richardson (my neighbour) and he told me there had been 3 attempts at arson at the White House.[23] A pity they all failed.

Saturday, 28 September
Interesting sentence in the TLS about 'the danger that attends upon an ideal of *aesthetic totality* once it enters the stage of man's social or moral existence . . . therein may lie the explanation of one of the most awful & puzzling phenomena of modern Europe, namely, how artistic and intelligent minds can have accepted the sacrifice of the individual as some beautifully necessary tragedy in the fulfilment of the interests of the whole.'

Sunday, 29 September
Walked to the Talk of the Town. The house was v. thin with loads of empty tables. They were good humoured & very *nellie*. My opening was fair, the second spot fair and I dried completely in the 4th!! Peter had to come on and give me the prompt. When I told the audience 'I've forgotten my lines', they all began to applaud loudly! I stopped them, saying 'Never clap incompetence' and then went on.

Saturday, 5 October
Spent the day learning the lines: a task I hate. My appalling dilemma is having to learn stuff which I have no real respect for and which I know is otiose. The very idea of standing up on a stage & talking to a lot of people drinking Veuve Du Vernay and pretending that everything is funny when our world is tottering on the dark & giddy precipice of meaningless existence . . . it's either mindless or mad. I suppose the thinking actor *is* mad.

Monday, 7 October
Still full of guilt about my behaviour with the audience last night. At one point I took the trousers down and said 'Look at the lovely hairy legs' (after the recording of course) and generally played for every cheap laugh in the book. It was disgraceful.

Thursday, 10 October
GENERAL ELECTION. Set out on foot to Gordon & Rona at Hampstead. We saw the election result start on BBC TV with the polls forecasting

---

[23] The hotel across the road.

a Labour landslide of at least 100 majority but by 1 o'c. in the morning, this figure had shrunk to 20!* and we realised that these polls are useless.

*in fact Labour's overall majority in the House is *three*.

Monday, 14 October

Found that the post had arrived and Erich has sent me his new book on Kafka! How sweet of him to think of me. In the afternoon I went to Swan's at Tottenham Ct. Rd. and booked Louie and me on the P & O Christmas cruise on the *Canberra*. It is about 650 each. Came back & told Louie. She said 'Oh! I'll need lots of frocks! They're posh buggers on the *Canberra* . . .'

Tuesday, 22 October

In the afternoon Helen Montagu[24] rang: 'I've had a letter from Charles Laurence about the Feydeau and he thinks the only person for it is *you*! Shall I say that you are interested etc. and perhaps we can arrange a get-together with the three of us to discuss it?' I said yes.

Wednesday, 23 October

Went in to see Louie for supper and we watched *Carry On Jack*. It is amazing how well these early Carry Ons stand up! At one or two moments I was v. good indeed & talk about economy! I get words out quicker than anyone else on the screen! Self-indulgence in acting is totally alien to me.

Sunday, 27 October

By mistake, instead of Sunday Times I got the Observer and suddenly realised that awful claque is *still there*! The Tynans, the Russell Davieses and the A.J.P. Taylors . . . all the old hangers-on still hanging . . . still churning out lines from the dried imagination and the dead pen. Davies was insulting about *Man For All Seasons* so I wrote to the editor. It might get printed.[25]

Tuesday, 29 October

Went in to Louie and saw the State Opening of Parliament on TV. It was terribly *funny*. The Queen in fabulous robes talking about 'my government's need to economise because of balance of payments

---

[24] Of the H.M. Tennent organisation.

[25] It did. 'Your reviewer of films reveals a most pitiful ambition in his spiteful lines about the film *A Man for All Seasons*, and he also reveals his ignorance . . .' (*Observer*, 10 November 1974).

deficits' and wearing a Crown with enough precious stones to raise several millions. When she came to the bit about a Wealth Tax I thought she ought to stop, point to the crown and say 'I hope you're not going to include *this*?' It would have got a big laugh.

Sunday, 3 November
Walked to the Talk of the Town. It was *awful*. Rotten house full of foreigners or elderly drears. Gilbert Bécaud was drinking neat whisky out of a bottle backstage. It was a dreadful end to a series.

Sunday, 10 November
Saw myself in 'International Cabaret'. I look lean and intellectual in the way that Peter Cushing looks . . . the voice tends toward the *posh* and the face is often severe & aesthetic when it should be smiling and jolly. The general impression of my performance is someone superior being forced to pander to the inferior; and that is roughly the truth of the situation.

Friday, 15 November
Walked to the Playhouse for the revue type show called 'Get On With It' with Lance Percival and Miriam Margolyes. I went to a pub with the crowd after and bought them all drinks . . . suddenly it was quite like the old days of radio shows . . . one knew one had really created a bit of fun . . . the audience was very responsive.

Sunday, 1 December
Never seen London so *empty* . . . the streets deserted . . . no one in Embankment Gardens except a drunk on a bench singing disjointedly like Ophelia. Louie was walking listlessly and I said 'You can become infected with the depression of these times . . . the bombs, the strikes, the threats, the shortages and the inflation' and she paused & said 'You are quite right . . . it works through eventually . . . you can't *keep* shrugging it off . . .'

Wednesday, 11 December
Peter [Rogers]'s Party. Peter had the menu written with 'Le Nosh Up' on the cover which suited the dreadful restaurant. Guests: Kenny Connor, Bernard Bresslaw, Barbara W., Sid J., Hattie, Joan S., P. Butterworth and Jack Douglas. Gerald said 'There is a v. good part for you in our next one in March! It is *Carry On Behind* and it's about an archaeological dig and you're this professor in charge . . .' He told me 'South Africa banned *Dick* 'cos of our use of the church . . . playing Sid as a crooked Vicar . . .' Ironic that it takes a government like

that to do something about such appalling sacrilegiousness while *our* government pass it without a qualm.

Saturday, 14 December

Caught the wrong train to Southampton Central instead of the Docks. Boarded the ship at 11 o'c. Lunch in the Pacific Restaurant: all v. Lyons Corner House decor and terrible service. We are sat next to Sid & Edna who teach Ballroom Dancing and are amicable. During the meal a drunken woman staggered up to my table & cried 'You didn't smile at me, so *up* you dear!' and her companion whispered 'She's had quite a few drinks!' as if that was the perfect excuse. I was asked to kiss this intoxicated lady and sing Happy Birthday To You. We saw the Isle of Wight disappearing. Louie said 'It is always sad when you're leaving your own country.' The Up You lady reappeared and was again pissed and shouts 'You didn't come to my party so *up* you dear!'

Monday, 16 December

Lisbon at 6.30. The Tagus bridge looked magnificent and the setting sun like a great orange ball of fire behind it. Drinks in Crow's Nest with Fred, Doreen and Ann. Went ashore with David (a Major in the Green Howards) and Miriam, a Jewish girl with little to say except 'When I wore my mink in the Regent Palace a woman shouted: "What d'you have to do to get *that*?" . . . I felt awful . . .' and we nodded sympathy.

Saturday, 21 December

After dinner I had drinks with the Beasleys & then went to bed, with Ann C. shouting 'You selfish sod . . . you're spoiling your mother's evening . . . always going to bed . . .' She is a great stirrer and should have been avoided.

Sunday, 22 December

Cocktails in the evening. Diana, Fred & Ann in the Card Room with hardly anyone present. Jack C. in Peacock Room, and then to the Huggetts in the Casino Room. At one point I passed Captain Chester saying 'I'm on my way to the third party!' and he said 'I'm doing my fourth!' After, drinks in the Meridian with Ann shouting 'You rotten sod' when I went to bed.

Monday, 23 December

11 o'c. With Beasleys to 2nd head waiter's cabin where we sat cramped and hot, listening to dirty records. Left at 12 o'c. with Ann C. shouting 'You rotten sod' etc. etc.

Wednesday, 25 December
We're on the Equator. It is *hot* and very humid. Horrid atmosphere. Louie's feet are swollen. So are mine. All this *standing* at parties. Agony. 12 o'c. Ken P. party in cabin with orchestra including an electric organ! A waiter spilled Campari all over white dress worn by Ann C. She is furious. Adrianne sang 'The Holy City'. It was hot making. 7.30 Party given by Peter M. Death. 7.50 Derek H. party. Photographed with cripples & dwarf etc. 9 o'c. Louie pissed at dinner. Edna & Sid saying to her 'Go on! Have another!' We got embroiled in a dreadful trio – Chiquita, Dennis & Molly. Bed at 3 o'c.

Friday, 27 December
We arrived at Dakar in Senegal at 6 o'c. No launches leaving *Canberra* 'cos the sea was too rough. 6.30. Lifeboats took us ashore for the Senegal Night Club, and the Native dancing. They served a whole lamb on a spit for each table. Ludicrous waste. Half the world is starving. The dancing was non-existent. Just drums banging and bottoms & tits jerked about. I had a martini with *pepper* in it! Oh! it was a mad evening. In the cabin I got an electric shock from a faulty switch. Rang for electrician who came at 1.30 and defused it.

Saturday, 28 December
7 o'c. Cocktail Party: Nat and Miriam. The latter having started with David now transfers her affections to Nat and is saying 'I suppose I am the most notorious woman on this ship!' (Peacock Room.) 10 o'c. Meridian Room. Ann C. making a dreadful scene – 'You rotten bastard! You unsociable sod' and a lot more in that vein.

Sunday, 29 December
6.15 Masonic Party. Speeches . . . Fred, President & Captain . . . 'honourable brethren . . .' etc. etc. It was *ludicrous*.

Tuesday, 31 December
Santa Cruz, Tenerife. Went ashore with Louie and got linctus and antibiotic throat tablets. We had coffee at the café on the main square and a man cleaned my shoes very well for 25 pesetas. Cocktail parties in the evening. Bore. Bed at 11 o'c.

1975

Wednesday, 1 January
First New Year's Day I've spent on a ship! There is a row between Bert & Joyce. They've stayed in the cabin for two days. Went alone to have drinks with officer who was pissed. I got away as gracefully & quickly as possible, and fled to the Beasleys' Party.

Thursday, 2 January
Arrived at Gibraltar, North Mole, at 9.30. Seems years since I came here! I made Louie buy a rainproof jacket (£2.60) and we saw a v. pretty beaded white dress which she got for £25. Afterwards I sat for a bit talking to Roy (invalid) whose wife had left him to play Bingo, and after conversing he said 'You have verbal diarrhoea' which was my thanks for attempting to divert him. Heigh ho! Wheeled him to the Meridian.

Saturday, 4 January
To the Meridian Room for coffee. All of them slumped in armchairs like some monstrous asylum for geriatrics. Fled to the Crow's Nest where an elderly man fell and collapsed on to a table of drinks and smashed the lot. The ship is rolling considerably.

Sunday, 5 January
London is mild, overcast and quiet. I was unpacked by 3 o'c. and exhausted. It is the first holiday I've ever had that was a continual nightmare of staring endless rudeness. So strange to be lying here after all those days in that cramped little cabin.

Monday, 6 January
At 7 o'c. Tom & Clive arrived and we went to the Cosmo. The relationship fitted together again like a new-found old key turning the same lock.

Friday, 10 January
To Peter Nichols by 8.30. Met his wife Thelma, and children Louise

and Daniel, there was another little girl[1] but she hardly spoke. There was a certain stiffness at first & then we talked easily & I was astonished at Peter's phenomenal memory. He recalls things about Marchmont St and Louie and me which I had completely forgotten. He said he'd love to see Louie again so I suggested a Sunday which he'll have to name.

Thursday, 16 January
Went to see *Blow Out* at the Continentale. I left after about 40 minutes of boring rubbish. Came back and there was a great session of Arthur's Erotica[2] with astonishing success.

Friday, 17 January
Saw Louie in the evening and watched 'Hawaii 5–0'[3] and a v. good series called 'Rising Damp' with Leonard Rossiter being quite brilliant. What a lovely actor! And the speed of delivery was machine-gun like and retained clarity throughout.

Wednesday, 22 January
Read the *Carry On Behind* script. It is the *worst* I've ever read. The part for me, Roland Crump, is small, it is unfunny, and is mostly concerned with heavily contrived slapstick. Don't know why on earth they offer it to me.

Saturday, 1 February
When I went in to see Louie at 11.45 she said 'It's been on the radio that Richard Wattis is dead!' and we had a v. subdued lunch in consequence. The BBC rang and asked me talk about him. I went round to B.H. and recalled his kindness to me, beginning with *Dick & the Duchess* and told the Jack Palance story. Later: listened to the programme and found they'd cut out all the interesting stuff and left in only the innocuous kind of rubbish that could be said by anyone.

Wednesday, 5 February
Peter Eade rang. 'I've had Weidenfeld & Nicolson on to me about you writing a book for them . . . this man there, he said you're such a fascinating and extraordinary character that they would be glad to publish *anything* of yours . . .' I said 'I am not a writer' and he said 'But you *are*! You write very well' and I said 'I don't think so, and even the column for the Radio Times is a chore' and he dropped it

---

[1] Catherine.
[2] Rhyming slang at one remove ('J. Arthur Rank').
[3] American detective series: well over 200 episodes from 1968 on.

after that. Heath has resigned the Tory leadership! It appears now to be a battle between Whitelaw and Thatcher. I quite like Margaret Thatcher but I think Whitelaw is an old Bumble.

Friday, 7 February

William Dexter (or Peacock, as he called himself) has died. Extraordinary. He was quite young. Played that part in *Gentle Jack*. V. suave. Quite liked him.

Tuesday, 11 February

Read more of the Wain biog. of Johnson.[4] It is heartwarming – the way J. clings so devotedly to the old & lasting friendships. Since Rona said 'He was teetotal', I said to her, on the phone, 'I should re-read it, dear! The night with Langton & Beauclerk was spent drinking *punch*' and there is an account of Garrick doing his impersonation of J. (with his Staffordshire accent) crying out 'Who's for poonsch?' The news is that Margaret Thatcher is leader of the Tory party! It is certainly revolutionary!

Friday, 21 February

Arrived at Bristol. Stood with a BBC chauffeur vainly trying to recognise James Michie (poet & publisher at the Bodley Head) who eventually introduced himself: he looked like a University Edition of José Ferrer. At the BBC there, we met Pamela Howe, Amanda Theunissen, Patrick Kavanagh[5] and Sarah (secretary) & had lunch. It was a lively conversation, and a lot better than the broadcast quiz/discussion that followed. Patrick asked questions and we had to say who wrote them etc. Oh dear! our world seems full of these terrible *games*! And whom do they satisfy? Not the learned, and not the unlettered either! Some middling section I suppose, which listens for the sake of a celebrity & little else . . . certainly not from a love of literature.

Saturday, 22 February

Lots of cards which will go straight into the dustbin.

Tuesday, 25 February

There is a school of English acting which *announces itself* instead of allowing us to interpret it. It comes on, saying 'I am an English eccentric & drily amusing' or 'I'm an Englishman of aristocratic connections'

---

[4] *Samuel Johnson* (1974), by John Wain, b.1925.

[5] P.J. Kavanagh, b.1931. Writer. Chairman of 'Read Any Good Books?', on which the others were panellists.

or 'I'm frustrated but lovable' and so on: whereas in fact these qualities are what we should *discover*. In 'Kojak'[6] it is because Telly Savalas looks at people so intently & is patently interested in them and the meticulous details of their lives that his compassionate nature is conveyed to us. He *announces* nothing in those terms. What he announces, in fact, is vanity about his wardrobe & a determination not to take *anything* too seriously except injustice.

Wednesday, 26 February

Gave Beverley dinner. He was wearing a fine jacket of cashmere by Turnbull & Asser. We talked at length about Mags & he admitted: 'I've given more time to this production of *Private Lives*[7] than I've ever given to one of my own plays . . .' He said that he and Mags had loved getting my letters, which pleased me greatly. As we left the restaurant, a man dining alone called out to me 'You're another bloody queer' and I said lamely 'Yes indeed . . . that is true . . . it's all part of life's rich pageant . . .' Beverley said 'D'you want me to bash his face?' and I said 'No, don't bother' and got him a taxi in Shaftesbury Avenue. I walked home reflecting on the hatred I arouse in many people.

Friday, 28 February

I walked to Berman's and in Stanhope Street they were drilling the road and I noticed the blond man handling the pneumatic was v. handsome . . . then his friend alongside saw me & called out 'Hallo Ken! You're looking well!' and they both chorused greetings to me. I loved it & simpered my 'Thank you very much' like a schoolboy receiving unexpected praise. O! I do adore these kind of men. God sent that incident to me, in compensation for the insult in public on Wednesday. We saw on TV news the account of a bad accident at Moorgate . . . the train accelerated & crashed into the wall of the tube tunnel . . . about 30 people dead. One of the firemen spoke to a cameraman and he was so utterly absorbed in doing his job, but finding time to say 'They've got a lot of courage down there . . .' about the victims, that it made me cry.

Wednesday, 5 March

The BBC showed a pathetic thing called 'Last of the Summer Wine' with Michael Bates, Peter Sallis and that Rowbotham or Owen[8] being

---

[6] Adventures of lollipop-sucking New York cop, 1973–77.

[7] Playing in New York.

[8] Series by Roy Clarke, with Bill Owen (né Rowbotham) as 'Compo'. Still running (and originating new episodes) in 1993.

repulsive. It was banal dialogue and had the laughter dubbed on. It was chronic.

Saturday, 8 March

The new passport arrived. The photograph certainly makes me look awful: and *old*. What a going-off was here! It is obvious from the ruinous nature of the face, that the qualities in one *do* affect the *looks* of one. In my younger photographs, the lips are generous & the eyes wide with hope: now the lips are thin & pursed with the ungenerous nature showing thro' them, & the eyes are narrow with distrust & scepticism & the lines round them show the tired ennui with which it's all viewed.

Monday, 10 March

One woman to another: 'What have you done to your hair! It looks like a wig!' 'It is a wig.' 'Oh! is it? . . . you'd *never* know . . .'

Wednesday, 12 March

For the first time at Pinewood[9] I am in the *star* dressing room – well, suite. It has sitting room and waiting room and dressing room and bathroom. All very grand and quite unsuitable for me. Met Ian[10] (the boy from 'Dad's Army') and Adrienne Posta at lunch, with Joan Sims, and dear Bernard Bresslaw. Gerald said 'The man who is most brilliant at coordinating dialogue, movement and props, is Kenneth Connor' and I found myself in total accord.

Thursday, 13 March

Ken Connor told me of a v. funny incident during the shooting of *Trio* . . . after a stupendous take a painter went up to the author's chair & said 'You've got another winner there, Somerset.' And another story about a women's lib. wife who flung away the bra & the husband said 'It makes you look 10 years younger . . . now that they're hanging down like that, it's taken all the wrinkles out of your face.'

Saturday, 15 March

It is impossible to set down the names that have given me lasting pleasure. I suppose I find myself humming Brahms (*Vier Ernste Gesänge*) mostly, or Schumann, or Quilter, but *lines* I owe to a hundred sources: the delicate tenderness of De La Mare, the sheer daring in Brooke, the grandeur and serenity of Tennyson, but then, I love

---

[9] For *Carry On Behind*.
[10] Ian Lavender, b.1946.

Henley too – 'a late lark singing . . .'[11] Oh! that is wonderful to me. The lasting pleasure comes from that intrinsically *eternal* quality in these men's works. The enduring thing, for me, is that they enshrine *eternal* values. I mean, I knew the passage from Corinthians was great writing *before* I heard *Vier Ernste Gesänge, but* the Brahms setting did something else for me: it told me of Brahms' reaction to such magnificence . . . and that added another dimension and significance to it all. Like watching a fine actor and then hearing your own verdict endorsed by a mind you greatly admire – the thing *goes* from the bricks & mortar *into* the cathedral.

Thursday, 20 March
Yet another journalist brought on to the set! (Sunday People) He said 'I want to write about all the fun that goes on *behind* the scenes . . .' and Kenny Connor said 'Mission impossible.' Long discussion with Ken & Bernard with the latter saying 'We have been betrayed by false prophets and the most false was Marx . . . we have taken material growth for granted . . . never stopping to question whether it was good or bad . . . right or wrong . . . we seem powerless against the *weight* of inertia caused by decadence . . .'

Sunday, 30 March
There is a throbbing pain coming from the rectum. I've had it before but it's never lasted as long as this. The pain from the bum makes me think of death and I immediately see myself taking the overdose and imagine what my last acts would be. The irritating thing about most suicides is that they don't leave proper explanations and the newspapers simply say that 'notes were left' for the coroner or somebody, whereas it is the *public* that should be informed. Quite apart from celestial visions I know that I welcome my own passing, because life has always been painful to me: the pleasures have come from the spirit and the vicariously communicated experience of fine people . . . not the actual.

Thursday, 3 April
Taken out to the Paddock or Orchard, where they've erected the Holiday Camp. Started filming in sunny weather, then at 10.40 there was a *blizzard* with snow whirling everywhere and we all sat in the caravan. Joan Sims, Bernard, Sherry, Carol Hawkins, Windsor Davies, Jack Douglas played the Initial Game & the time passed agreeably . . . Windsor revealing a considerable amount of Biblical knowledge.

---

[11] 'My wages taken, and in my heart/Some late lark singing'; from 'Margaritae Sorori', by W.E. Henley (1846–1903).

Thursday, 10 April

Lunch with Bernard (Anti-E.E.C.) and Elke [Sommer] & me who are pro-E.E.C. Quite long discussion. Bernard maintains it is a false union and that it will inevitably lead to trouble 'but I admit that I think the issue (referendum) will be won by the Marketeers . . .'[12]

Friday, 11 April

Saw Richard Briers in a comedy series.[13] It was terrible. Not a laugh line in it. When the wife said that the Matabele tribe ate insects, Briers' reply was 'Silly sods' and there were shots of him holding a gun to the head of a chicken . . . it was all tasteless and unpleasant . . . when a cock bird was indifferent to a hen, Briers' line was 'Perhaps he's a queer . . .' Oh dear.

Tuesday, 22 April

Got Trav. cheques for the Malta trip. Walked to the City Lit. to do this talk. Audience was sparse. I went *on and on* . . . talked too much & left full of self-loathing. Walked home by 9.30. Found that my flat had been burgled. They'd been thro' all the drawers and the cupboards. All I can find missing is the Travellers' Cheques and the money (about 50 to 60 pounds in notes, and 200 in T.C.) and 4 pairs of shoes and the shoe trees! And they'd taken a big Ryman's bag to put all the stuff in. Obviously they'd got some sort of skeleton key 'cos the door had been neatly opened. Obviously I'll have to get a mortice dead lock. It is curious what they did not take . . . the Bulova Accutron watch was left hanging in the bathroom! Heigh ho. I have never been burgled before. Went to bed, full of perturbation, at about 1 o'c.

Saturday, 26 April. Valletta

We drove as far as Olympia before I realised that I'd left the passport in the flat. We met T & C in the departure lounge & then joined one of those daft endless queues to board the plane. The Grand Excelsior is a v. good hotel. There was quite a cluster of waiters for the autographs etc. and all the usual rubbish about 'You are very funny man' etc. etc.

Friday, 2 May

Met Maurice, Louie & Clive and drove to M'dina near Rabat: a magnificent 15th century city with ancient walls and bastions, churches

---

[12] The result of the Common Market referendum of 6 June was: in favour, 67.2 per cent; against, 32.8 per cent.

[13] 'The Good Life' by John Esmonde and Bob Larbey. 'The Goods introduce livestock into Surbiton to the apprehension of their neighbours.'

and idyllic quiet squares of tranquillity and silence. Returned to the Excelsior at 1 o'c. and the staff presented me with a framed photograph of myself with them all, on the terrace (taken by the newspaper) and I made appropriate thanks to each.

Saturday, 3 May
Maurice presented us all with beautiful goblets with 'Malta' inscribed on them! I was v. touched. We were all unanimous about the holiday being a most interesting & successful week.

Sunday, 4 May. London
Sent a cable to Maurice and Georgina. Rested till 6 o'c. After, I set out to see Erich Heller. Erich has put on a bit of weight and seems to blink a lot under heavy lids. He greeted me affectionately and gave me a sherry while he poured himself whisky and added ice. I was surprised to hear him *repeat* himself on several occasions – 'Anthony Thorlby[14] is the Professor of Comparative Literature at Sussex University . . . I found him unbelievably beautiful . . . now he has three children. He is a Catholic . . .' and he told me that *same* story about Isaiah Berlin (in the lift, with the matron saying at the end of his diatribe on Immanuel Kant[15] 'Don't believe a *word* of it') and was surprised at how childish his humour has remained – no not childish – innocent. Again, he said 'I look forward to the day when I see you doing something really splendid on the stage . . .'

Tuesday, 6 May
Peter E. telephoned: the BBC asked me to do a half-hour programme on Bloomsbury & my favourite districts etc. and we signified agreement and asked for a 100 and they came back today and said they hadn't got *that* sort of money. It is unbelievable. Do they really expect to get anyone decent to appear, and write material for TV [@] half-hour for 25?

Wednesday, 7 May
Ian Messiter rang. Would I take part in a broadcast for no payment, apropos the E.E.C.? I said yes of course.

Thursday, 8 May
To Peter E. where Ian Messiter[16] came with a tape recorder and we

---

[14] b.1928. Heller pays tribute to him in the preface to *The Ironic German*.
[15] 1724–1804, German philosopher.
[16] b.1920. Best known as a producer and deviser of panel games, including 'Just a Minute'.

did a few words about the Common Market. I am Pro. In the afternoon I did a bit of cleaning & the vacuum cleaner sucked in one of my ties! It blocked the pipe and I had great difficulty removing it, but eventually succeeded with screwdrivers and the Maggie Smith scissors! These have now done *everything* from paper cutting to extracting birds' nests from air bricks and now clearing a vacuum cleaner!

Monday, 19 May
I walked to Peter Mario to meet Mags & Bev. Mags was looking fine & so was Bev, but he confided that she'd been overtired with the New York run of *Private Lives* & she said 'Holding the whole thing *up* dear' & sounded glad to be out of it.

Wednesday, 21 May
Gerald Thomas gave me lunch. Leslie Linder came over & asked 'Are you the voice on Brobat loo advertising?' & I said 'Yes, but I'm not doing it for money, but in the interests of hygiene.'

Thursday, 22 May
To John Musgrove party at Portland Place. Stanley arrived with Moira and we had the chats. Stanley looked fine and talked about his work with the usual self-absorption.

Saturday, 24 May
Michael W. drove us to Oxford where we mounted the winding stairs to the balcony of St Mary's church tower & obtained a superb view of the city . . . it was magnificent! The old Bodleian and Balliol looking superb, and the bells ringing for evensong . . . the organ was playing some Buxtehude, so everything was perfect. M. drove us then to Woodstock where we had tea & scones before returning to London. On the journey he played some Hubert Parry choir music which was simply beautiful and the Toccata & Fugue in G of Bach, and the sheer *endeavour* of it all was overwhelming & wonderful. No car ride has been so enjoyable since the Mags days (when we were touring with the Shaffers) when she found the right radio programmes every time.

Saturday, 31 May
Went to see Gordon & Rona. Gordon said 'Alec Guinness asked me to play a small joke with him for some American guests who'd seen me as Hudson the butler (in the TV series[17]). Rona & I had to arrive early & I had to hide in the kitchen. Rona was introduced as Mrs Rona Trossach and then he clapped his hands and called out "*Hoyle*!"

---

[17] 'Upstairs Downstairs'.

and I had to enter with the tray and the Americans shrieked "Oh my God, Alec!!"' I said I thought it was a tasteless piece of vulgarity.

Sunday, 1 June
Lunch with Louie and at 1 o'c. we went to the park. We saw two v. beautiful youths who sat near, and smiled charmingly. One held a rose. They ate some food & placed the litter carefully in the bin and waved a farewell to both Louie & me before departing as gracefully as they'd arrived. It was one of those rare moments of polite unspoken reciprocity that stays in the mind for ever.

Sunday, 8 June
Tony Laryea came at 9 o'c. and we drove to the 1st location: British Museum. I did the first take without a fluff & instead of accepting it and getting *on*, Laryea starts 'directing'. Oh dear oh dear. We ended up doing about a dozen takes – none of them any better than the first. Then to Bedford Square and more trouble and then back to Tonbridge St. A horrible wind ruined the sound; traffic noise & people combined to spoil take after take, it was awful. Then Russell Sq. then Marchmont Street. That was the final horror. A gang of yobs started the catcalls, the idiots came out in their hundreds and unselfconscious acting became impossible. I said I couldn't go on with it. The crew said after '*You* made the day for us,' which pleased me enormously. I've never been so frustratedly exhausted in my life.

Monday, 9 June
I am still using the Formula 16 on the hair but it makes it so matted and greasy that the appearance is revolting. There's no doubt about its efficacy! The silvery white bits of hair on the sides of the head have been turned to a shade that is quite blonde.

Tuesday, 10 June
At 1.30 I went to the dentist and we drove to Malden where the new teeth were fitted & coloured. Norman put them all on. The teeth are superb copies of my old ones, and the matching is brilliant.

Saturday, 14 June
Had a rest in the afternoon. Curious dream about Louie & Charles at 57 inviting everyone in to watch television and me pulling a huge curtain behind which I was going to sleep & when Charles protested I said 'It was you who taught me the habit.' There was a moment when I was going down the basement stairs & I looked at the linoleum & with a great pang I thought of the number of times Louie had cleaned that floor. Went in to see the news etc. We talked, and I

fixed labels on the cases for her. There is a terrible sadness about her going.

Tuesday, 17 June

Saw the TV news and had some mince, tomatoes, cheese and biscuits at Louie's. I wonder how she is enjoying her cruise? She must be in Norwegian waters by now. I always tell her to go off and enjoy herself on any holidays which she can manage because she deserves the breaks, and while she has the health I want her to travel, but oh! how I *hate* it when she is away! The empty flat next door makes me want to weep: I start to remember every sort of thing she does & says, and all the affection comes surging over me like a wave: I'm overwhelmed. I will never (and have never) loved anyone as much as I love her.

Wednesday, 18 June

Tom came at 4.45. We had a talk about the holiday & he owned he was more interested in trade than in travel.

Saturday, 21 June

Stanley came and I took him to the St George. At the table, we sat looking over the rooftops of a sleepy London, watching a slow sunset. I said 'One thinks of Wordsworth's "all that mighty heart is lying still" . . .' and Stanley (looking out at the evening) said dreamily 'Oh yes! Wordsworth, really lovely . . . greatly underrated . . . like that other woman . . . what's her name . . . Doris Day!' When we talked about acting he said 'We're both alike . . . there is a streak of madness in us both . . . the desperate clinging to *privacy* . . . the rejection of a potentially hostile world . . .'

Wednesday, 25 June

To the Paris for 'J.A.M.' I got furious with Freud 'cos he ruined a bit of my stuff with only one intention: to get in on the last 3 seconds. It was so obviously shoddy and cheap. I said after: 'You're a stupid cunt' and he wrote on a piece of paper 'You should never be angry with your friend' and I wrote back 'To err is human' and he smiled.

Thursday, 3 July

The tennis was interesting – my beloved Roscoe Tanner lost to Jimmy Connors which saddened me but oh! he was a joy to behold, and I loved him more than ever when he questioned an umpire's ruling on a late call (which he couldn't hear and neither could the BBC commentator) which was patently unfair.

Thursday, 24 July
At 6.15 I heard the revue format show. It was all right but oh dear! the material was thin. At 8.45 I heard myself on the programme 'Homosexuality – The Years of Change'. Lord Arran[18] sounded splendid; Leo Abse sounded muddled & incompetent, I sounded irrelevant! I was going on about queer stereotypes & endeavouring to defend a concept which patently was indefensible. And the producer cut the very bit I wanted *in* . . . the stuff about the individual conscience, and the morality of society.

Tuesday, 29 July
Got a taxi to Buckingham Palace and met Anona Winn in the forecourt, with Terry Wogan and Adrienne Posta and Rod Hull (who did his Emu act). Anona confided that Hermione Gingold was being very difficult & the latter remarked (when she saw the marquee in which we were to perform) 'It's a disgrace to expect artists to work under such conditions' and she (Hermione) told me 'It is utterly daunting to die the death at this sort of function and it is demoralising when you have a show to do in the theatre afterwards . . .' At the opening of the show, Wogan got up to chat at the microphone & it broke down & the lights went off and the main fuse had been blown. A conjuror, El Condor, was v. good & produced a magnificent Eagle Owl! It was lovely. Hermione Gingold decided to leave at this point and refused to have her photograph taken with the rest of the cast. I died the death and heard one small laugh throughout the entire 6 minutes which seemed like an eternity. At the conclusion, Wogan beat a v. hasty retreat.

Wednesday, 6 August
Curious dream. Richard Pearson arriving after a *second* burglary in my flat & me saying 'If they can get through a mortice dead lock it really *is* sinister . . .' But it was all a dream and I woke to find all was normal, and *then*! – I found my letters not on the floor, but placed on the kitchen table! Then Louie came & said 'The electricity man came to read the meter so I let him in . . .'

Saturday, 9 August
Michael W[hittaker] came for me and went for dinner at Giovanni's. Elaine Stritch came and put her arms round me 'I'm so glad to be able to see you . . . you're terrific . . . I love this restaurant . . . it's the sort of place you feel you can just burst into song!' and she did. She suddenly burst into a Streisand number, and did it very well.

---

[18] 8th Earl of Arran (1910–83). Journalist.

Then she said 'I'm with Janet Leigh over there . . . don't run away . . . we can have brandy & coffee together . . .' Then a gentleman in a white beard rose and recited a monologue about a yokel buying a quartern of beer and carrying it home in his trilby hat & everyone applauded. Elaine: 'He's got *guts* . . .' The owner, Giovanni, said 'I met Ingrid Bergman in Rome & she said you were a marvellous person.' I said thank you.

Thursday, 21 August
Stanley came and we drove to dinner. Stanley said he would go to Rhodes alone. I said 'You will find plenty to do.' He said 'Yes . . . sitting in the sun by the pool.' I replied 'There's more to Greece than that . . . don't you look at the ruins?' & he said 'No, I let them look at me' and everyone fell about.

Sunday, 24 August
Certainly this year and next is obviously going to be rotten in terms of work and I may have to return to the theatre: if I do, I shall certainly not make the mistake of working with any bogus director.

Tuesday, 26 August
I must have shown my depression to Louie 'cos she said 'I think you'd be better off if you did some work . . .' She's never said that before, but it's obviously been on her mind.

Tuesday, 2 September
Lunch with George. Harry Secombe came over to the table and was v. kind to me. I told him he was superb in the Vera Lynn Speech at the Savoy and he sent over drinks to both George and myself! He is a delightful person. When he said 'What are you doing?' I said 'Nothing . . . haven't had a murmur . . . Bill Cotton was scathing about "Int. Cab." and said the figures were rotten . . .' Harry said: 'Don't worry . . . I'll have a word with them . . . I *can* you know!' Ah! he is a dear man – I've liked Harry without reservation since I worked with him at the Camden when he took over from Hancock and was so brilliant! Goodness, what a *lift* he gave to that series! And how much better he was than the absentee.

Friday, 5 September
Peter E. rang to tell me that Helen Montagu had sent the Feydeau! (It's been translated by Christopher Hampton.[19]) I went to his office

---

[19] b.1946. Playwright and screenwriter.

and read it. It is quite funny but needs meticulous casting, and I suspect the mother will be v. difficult to fit.

Sunday, 7 September
Lunch with Louie and after, we walked to the Rose garden which was full of horrid people slumped in deckchairs . . . there was a bit of sun but it soon clouded over: then there was the hint of cold, of evenings shortening, of winter and trouble. The summer is just beginning to be wearisome and then, it is dying. For years now, I've been taking Louie to this same park . . . even as a child, in '32 when I borrowed 6d from a parkkeeper for food and my father accompanied me there, the following week, to find & repay him . . . and as this year runs out I feel I am dying too. There *is* a sense in which nothing is ever the same again.

Tuesday, 9 September
By tube to TV Centre for the meeting with Terry Hughes and the writers. Terry said to them 'I want to do this sketch show with Kenneth and I want you all to write specifically for him.' There was an awkward pause and I started talking about ideas I'd had but it all rather died the death. I passed two workmen at Shepherd's Bush who recognised me and shouted 'Kennif Willyams! Load of crap!' and I began to think they weren't far wrong.

Saturday, 13 September
I pulled out the file to do the accounts only to find that I have earned nothing & there is therefore nothing to record. O God! the utter depression of it all.

Tuesday, 16 September
To meet Helen Montagu and Christopher Hampton. Helen said it would be marvellous to get Hattie J. for the part of Mama, & second there was Peggy Mount or there was Elspeth March. She added 'You would be ready about February wouldn't you?' & I said yes . . .

Thursday, 25 September
It is amazing that we are nearly in October and only three months before the end of this diary. Days that have passed, Days that have passed. Days pass so fast, Days when I've wondered if I'd ever last. It has taken this year to make me realise that I am not rich any more, that the days of dining out, giving luncheons and presents etc. are over. When one looks at the actual figures and sees that in this financial year it is already about Eight Thousand it looks good. But in fact it is *bad*. If I were alone in the world, I'd try to sell these flats,

move to the country & get a little abode, and seek a local ordinary job.

Friday, 26 September

Tube to Paddington and leisurely picked a paper from the bookstall before getting the [Bristol] train. A man at my elbow said 'Hallo Ken! Remember me? That show at the Watergate Theatre? Phew! What a play that was! Of course I've left that all now . . . I'm with the IBA' and I interjected various 'ohs' and 'ahs' but since I've never worked at the Watergate or ever met *him* the entire episode was meaningless. Pamela Howe met me & drove me to the studio. Did the recording.[20] It was lousy. I think it was because too much was being squeezed into 14 and a half minutes. The Engineer (lady) lunched with us and said 'D'you know why racing drivers have bent cocks? Because they have to piss round corners . . .'

Monday, 6 October

Spent most of the day reading Spender on Eliot.[21] He points to a mass of inconsistency in the latter's critical writing as if it invalidated the criticism: it doesn't. It is in the nature of human beings to contradict themselves (and others) in the course of their lives. Eliot was continually battling with his conscience: fighting a war between *living* with all its materialism & inevitable compromise & betrayals, and *knowing* the spiritual truths and duties which conflict and trouble us. There *are* passages in his critical writing which seem to be incomprehensible. The stuff about the poet not being a thinker is utter rubbish taken on the level of common sense: but he is making a case for the essential neutrality of the poet, and saying that 'the singer has to sing the song' and not necessarily *compose* it as well. This argument acquits the poet from any charge of political propaganda or philosophical tendentiousness and suits Eliot for that moment. Of course it doesn't suit him later, when he points to the essential need for *faith* if Art is to have real significance and value in society.

Monday, 13 October

I'm frightened about this hand and that's a fact. Walked over to the Hospital at 9.25. I was given a bed in a large ward & then made to bath, dressed in surgical gown etc. and injected at about 12.45. Woke up in the post-operative ward & kept laughing. I was laughing quite loudly. It wasn't about anything funny, I just couldn't help laughing.

---

[20] Of 'Christmas at Cold Comfort Farm', broadcast as the 'Morning Story' on Christmas Eve.

[21] *T.S. Eliot*, 1975. Sir Stephen Spender, poet and critic, b.1909.

Sister O'Keeffe telephoned Louie, who came over at about 5.20 and took me home – my hand in a vast bandage and arm in a sling.

Tuesday, 14 October
Can't write with right hand so am using bandaged hand. It's not to be disturbed till 30 October! I wish the days would go like lightning so I could get the whole thing *off* and be able to use my left hand properly.

Wednesday, 15 October
Got up and did the washing *and* shaving with the right hand! It's incredible what one can manage to do as long as one allows plenty of time.

Friday, 17 October
Telephoned Miss Marley about this bandage and she said 'Come over now . . . Mr Watson is here . . .' so I went at 12 o'c. and saw him. He put on an Elastoplast. He said 'We removed a lump . . . like a piece of boiled rice, from your hand . . . it's been sent to the laboratory for analysis . . . don't let your arm hang down . . . use it like Napoleon . . . it helps the healing process.'

Monday, 27 October
To interview at Eade office with journalist from South Africa. She appeared to be in physical distress and sat with ashen face, clutching the stomach and muttering about a spastic colon. Peter said 'With that trouble, she shouldn't be a journalist' & I said 'There are some who'd say of me: with his arse he shouldn't be an actor' and he smiled & said 'They'd be right!'

Wednesday, 29 October
Up at 9 o'c. Heavyhearted. O! to exchange it all for the Schopenhauer 'never having been.'[22] To TV Centre. Terry Hughes showed me some of the material and I was surprised by the quality of it *and* the literacy.

Friday, 31 October
I thought quite practically last night about *suicide*. It would be a blessed end to all this misery. I can hardly *think* straight what with the pain in the hand (which I never had before that bloody operation) and

---

[22] The tone of the pessimism of the German philosopher Arthur Schopenhauer (1788–1860) is remarkably similar to KW's. e.g.: 'Does it not look as if existence were an error the consequences of which gradually grow more and more manifest?' *Parerga und Paralipomena*, 1851. See also entry for 25 September 1978, p. 565.

now this ghastly agony in the windpipe. Laurena phoned: 'Would you do "Jackanory" on the 4th & 5th Dec.?' I pointed out that I'd got the radio show on the 5th and she said 'Oh dear! I hadn't realised . . .'

Tuesday, 4 November

Find myself thinking more and more about suicide in practical terms; what is the most effective and quick and practical way? Even as I'm shaving I think 'What's the use?'

Thursday, 6 November

Joe Bulaitis drove me to his studio to judge the Children's Photograph Competition. The fellow judges were Anna Scher and Terry Mancini.[23] After making decisions, we all went upstairs for refreshment served by Joe's wife Gloria. Then a lively discussion ensued and Terry was delightful about his work, telling us of the misrepresentation and the bogus people involved in it. He returned yesterday from Istanbul where his team (Arsenal) won by 3 goals. He said 'We had nothing but champagne & orange juice on the plane coming back, so we were all a bit Brahms . . .' but he looked superbly fit and healthy. When he left, he said to me 'I could stay here all night talking to you . . . I'd like to meet you again . . . this could go on for ever as far as I am concerned.' I was so pleased and flattered and touched. More than I've been for years.

Friday, 21 November

Curious dreams about Mags & Bev at the White House & remembrance of that feeling that it would last for ever . . . the hot summer & Mags & Judith collecting blackberries . . . all gone gone gone. The panic and the madness inside me are only *just* being contained. I am keeping my countenance, but inside, there is *screaming*. There is now, ever present, the knowledge of the otiose nature of this existence. The civilised will always be a minority: the barbarians will always destroy. Whether it is strikes, muggings, crime, assassination, bombing, kidnapping . . . whatever.

Monday, 24 November

Phone call from Terry Hughes: 'Will you bring in tomorrow any old scripts you've got with dialogue we could use again? People never remember what they've heard in the past in a stand-up comedy spot . . .' I said I'd have a look thro' some of the stuff.

---

[23] Joe Bulaitis, photographer. Anna Scher, Founder and Principal of the Anna Scher Children's Theatre. Terry Mancini, central defender of Arsenal F.C.

Tuesday, 25 November

Walked to Addison Road to talk to Patrick Garland[24] about the Feydeau, in his studio (v. posh) amid paintings and plants . . . all so piss elegant . . . with the classical music in the background. He suggested some names for the parts which I don't agree with . . . Dandy Nichols for the Mother . . . but I hadn't the guts to say no.

Wednesday, 26 November

Rehearsed at North Acton. It amounted to one run through of each sketch and was useless. In the restaurant I talked to Gordon and to Ronnie Barker and several actors. It was like Old Home Week. The only lovely thing was Julian Smedley who came to rehearse the guitar for Rambling Syd with me. In the lift on the way out, Jack Warner said 'Would you like to see my birthday present?' and showed me a model of a little boy urinating. I said 'Oh! that *is* clever!' and fled.

Friday, 28 November

To the Paris Cinema to rehearse with Lance & Miriam – I have never been so fortunate with a cast before *in my life*. They are both marvellous. The audience was sparse. Simon said 'It went very well considering.' I had supper with Louie and then went to my flat and typed till midnight to get the R.T. article off my back.

Saturday, 29 November

I saw the TV news. 'Dr Who'[25] gets more & more silly. Bruce Forsyth too ill to do his 'Generation Game' so Roy Castle took it over. He is marvellous. Can't understand why he's never become a big *name*, he's got talent, looks & technical brilliance . . . lovely person.

Wednesday, 3 December

Bright day, and a lovely letter with olive branch from Denis Goacher – really superb and very generous! I am worried about tonight. I've had my own TV show before and it's not really worked and this time it's make or break.

The show began with a *packed* house at about 8.10 and it was a nightmare of changes! It was out of one costume and into another all the time and it seemed I never stopped talking. The voice got more and more like gravel & on the last note of the French song[26] it *cracked*. The *house was a dream* – I've always been right to reject all this 'good

---

[24] b.1935. Director-producer, writer.

[25] Science-fiction series for children and addicts, from 1963.

[26] A compendium of familiar French phrases entitled 'Crepe Suzette', sung as a love song.

luck' rubbish from a cast, or anyone else. I *hate* it before a show. It's nothing to do with luck, it's God deciding to *give you something*. He gave it to me tonight. It was nothing to do with material or acting. He gave me an atmosphere of such *love* and affection that I couldn't go wrong. Terry Hughes said 'I've never done a TV show that's gone so well *in every number* . . .' and Peter E. said 'You were superb! You were really inspired tonight . . .' I was glad I'd invited *no one*.

Thursday, 4 December

The sleep was short and the body is still whirling with the excitement of last night! The applause was like a heady drug to me. I gave thanks to God last night when I said my prayers . . . the misery of the last few weeks was lifted away by Him & I was given an astonishing & lovely experience.

Monday, 8 December

Read the book of poems Denis Goacher sent me. One about old friends is moving & beautiful, but too much of the time (like so much modern poetry) he forgets to *tell us the story*. Went to bed with head full of words. It was 1954 when he gave me those poems! And now after twenty-one years I read with my eyes full of tears . . .

Sunday, 14 December

Watched the 'Carry On Laughing' series.[27] It is diabolical. The writing is mean minded, cheap, derivative and degrading, and the actors were all lousy with the exception of Kenneth Connor who was splendid. Sid James looks like something which has been taken out of a pickling jar and that mirthless laugh he uses to cover the embarrassment of a laugh not received is sickening. Altogether, a dreadful experience and one which Peter E. was right to keep me out of.

Friday, 19 December

I started trying to rough out the Preview column after having lunch with Louie. I was in the middle of typing when Robert Bolt rang. It was infuriating! I had just started to write! He said 'Can I come round and deliver yr. Christmas present?' and he came. Pipe tobacco everywhere, the carpet marked so much I had to Hoover and three ashtrays filled after half an hour. He gave me a book of Chronological Tables. I had to leave at 2.30 and go to the Paris for 'Get On With It'.

---

[27] A series of TV comedy half-hours, made by ATV and written by various hands, in which most of the Carry On regulars joined. Familiar historical and fictional characters and milieux were, as ever, pastiched.

Wednesday, 24 December

That ghastly series 'Porridge' about prison life was showing . . . Oh! how that ever became accepted for television is beyond me! The tastelessness, the romanticising of villainy . . . the business of making criminals attractive . . . the winking at corruption within the prison service . . . it is sickening and disgusting. Went to bed thinking of Blunden's 'Some bell-like evening when the May's in bloom . . .' and Owen's 'eternal reciprocity of tears . . .'[28] and reflecting that if I've ever *loved* anything, it is poetry.

Thursday, 25 December

Tom came and we drove to Oak Avenue where Clive greeted us and we exchanged presents (theirs to us were *lavish*) and Keith and David came and the lunch was *superb*! Tennis Elbow[29] was played. There was singing round the piano, discussions of psychic activity, poetry, painting, Homosexual Law Reform, Doctor jokes & situation gags, trials of Florence Maybrick and the Wallace case,[30] and thrillers. At 2.15 in the morning I was waxing enthusiastic about Claude Chabrol.

Wednesday, 31 December

Quite a few letters complimenting me on the choice of poems at Christmas time which went out on Radio 4.[31] I wish I'd got a transcript of that programme. Spent the evening replying. Louie went off with friends to a New Year's Eve affair. I sat in the flat and read. It was mercifully quiet in the block. So, this is the end of the year . . . all the doom forecasters (including Wilson) are saying that next year is going to be dreadful etc. etc. but then, there are always enough natural *and* man-made disasters to justify this prognostication.

---

[28] Last line of 'Almswomen' by Edmund Blunden (1896–1974); phrase from 'Insensibility', (VI), by Wilfrid Owen (1893–1918).

[29] 'The Tennis Elbow Foot Game', one of Ian Messiter's radio parlour games.

[30] Two celebrated murder trials, of 1889 and 1931 respectively, both at Liverpool.

[31] In 'Woman's Hour', 23 December ('Christmas Anthology: Kenneth Williams with his own selection of seasonal music and poetry'). As he wrote, KW was being broadcast on 'Start the Year with Richard Baker', subtitled 'Carry On Surviving'.

1976

Saturday, 3 January
In the evening, Louie went to a dance at Archway. I went in to her flat and saw the Marx Brothers in *Night At The Opera* and marvelled again at the delicious quality they had! All of them. They're the most lovable comedy team I've ever seen in my life. Harpo is glorious (his harp sequence in this was glorious) Groucho marvellously funny and the Italian one is incredibly attractive.

Wednesday, 7 January
There is a letter from John Bratby[1] saying he will paint my portrait! What a compliment! Peter E. rang and said they wanted me for a 'Jackanory' in March and that the Feydeau would rehearse at the end of March.

Sunday, 11 January
Dreared about shaving and packing etc. Michael arrived at 9.40. Drove us to Heathrow by 10.30 and we found that leaking oil in the boot had stained Louie's case. Landed at Tenerife at 4.10. Coach took us to various hotels and we landed up at the Las Vegas at about 6.30.

Tuesday, 13 January
The hotel is the same as the ship for all the pestering and one longs to scream out 'piss off' sometimes, but everyone is surprisingly pleasant here. One is struck by the love and attention bestowed by the Spanish staff on all the children.

Monday, 19 January
Sat with the Scots set & Joan joined us. Laurence said he was feeling better. The awful old man from Miami came up & interrupted the conversation: 'What are you up to, Kenny?' 'Mind your own business.' 'I beg your pardon?' 'Don't beg, you can have it for nothing.'

---

[1] R.A., 1928–92.

And he left in a huff. I don't see by what *right* these idiot bores imagine they can *impose* themselves on others without so much as a by your leave. Eventually went up to bed. On the way I saw Howard and went to speak to Lorraine but she seemed uninterested so I left v. quickly. Made a *great* noise by shouting to myself in the room till the Germans next door banged on the wall. I was delighted. They've annoyed me endlessly.

Thursday, 22 January

Met a lady in the foyer who said 'We saw your show on television last night' & the husband said 'It got quite good.'[2] Thank goodness I'm not in U.K. for any inquests.

Friday, 23 January

By the pool in the afternoon & talked to the tall blond dish who walks like a dream. West Country. 'I'm a copper' – and me thinking it was Swedish! Dinner with Joan, Laurence & Louie and on to the Royal Coach with the Scots as well. I ordered champagne for 8.

Saturday, 24 January

The sea sparkling in the morning sunshine underneath my balcony . . . soon, all of it coming to an end . . . my last full day here . . . I think I've enjoyed this fortnight more than any other holiday 'cos the people have been fun and the children & parents are all marvellous. Sat by the pool with Bob and Paula (the policeman from Budleigh Salterton). Walked to Square for tea with Andy & Gladys. Told the manager that his hotel was splendid. We went to the Irish Bar and we were followed by a group from the hotel including Peter ('My wife left me with my two daughters') and the farmer Tom (from Norfolk) and his chum, and Claire and Mark ('I'm here with my Dad') and Bill ('I've got this chicken farm') and the sing-song ensued.

Sunday, 25 January

The friends all waved us off – Joan & Laurence etc. – and it was all rather moving. We got in at 9.25. Tom & Clive waiting for us and a gladsome sight they were! Tom said my TV show had been very good and that we're to go up to his house to see it on Wednesday. I think I enjoyed the Tenerife holiday more than any holiday I've ever had in my life.

---

[2] This was 'The Kenneth Williams Show', starring KW with Lance Percival, Anna Karen and Claire Nielson. Producer Terry Hughes.

Wednesday, 28 January

Tom came and took Louie & me to Dale Lodge. After dinner, he showed us the 'KW Show' which he'd recorded on his video machine. It wasn't bad but some of the cutting was lousy. I now see why everyone was going on about the French Song . . . it was the last item so of course it's the one that stays in the memory.

Saturday, 31 January

Horrible dream about the play. This is the second one I've had! The cast all singing and larking & me going off to find the management to protest!

Tuesday, 3 February

To Peter E. for interview with Nick Davies for the Sunday Mirror. He was pleasant to me & said Joan Sims had told him about a violent quarrel we once had! And that she'd said 'But he *did* apologise afterwards . . .' I told him it was about me telling dirty stories at the lunch table etc. He asked 'Did you ever learn of any sexual intrigues taking place on a Carry On film . . .' and I said no. Extraordinary stuff to be asked!

Thursday, 5 February

'This Week' featured Margaret Thatcher and several sharp but firmly polite snubs to her interviewer Llew Gardner. She gave the impression of one with a real grasp of her subject and one who was not to be browbeaten by an upstart journalist. It would be good to see her as PM . . . it's something this country needs.

Wednesday, 11 February

Watched the Olympics from Innsbruck and saw, to my delight, John Curry win the gold medal for skating. As the commentator said 'He never put a foot wrong' and the poor Russian champion fell on his bum in the first jump! Interviewed after, Curry said 'No, I wasn't nervous in the least . . . I knew I had nothing to fear in the way of competition . . . now, I'd like to spend a few days with my mother . . .' He's the most self-possessed and stylish champion . . . altogether delightful.

Thursday, 12 February

At 3 o'c. telephone call from Roger Gale 'Would you stand for the

Equity Council[3]?' and I said no. After a few minutes I rang him back and said 'You've made me feel very guilty . . . I will stand.' Went to B.H. and saw him and signed the papers (seconded by Greta Gouriet). Returning home I was nearly run over by a car (I had *started* crossing, but the lights turned as I was a third over) and I shouted at the driver 'You might at least give me a chance . . .' and he said 'If you will let me speak . . .' but I walked away. This was v. rude & I am sorry now.

Friday, 13 February
A letter has come from North Western University, Illinois, asking if I want to be a subscriber to the memorial volume (Festschrift) for Erich's 65th Birthday. I consider it a privilege. I would honour this dear man in any way that is possible.

Wednesday, 18 February
In the evening I walked to James Roose-Evans. The guests included Stephen (composer).[4] A knock from the floor below at 12.30 reminded us that the noise of talk was disturbing others & at 1.20 I left with Stephen. We walked home. He talked about Donne and quoted lines with superb understanding. Gave him my number 'cos I want to see him again.

Thursday, 19 February
Walked to the bookshop called Griff's 'cos they stock this Anglo-Welsh review which I'm interested in: but I saw the owner smoking a cigar, moodily staring at the ashtray, and I fled . . . it all looked somehow hopeless.

Saturday, 21 February
Tom & Clive came. They drove Louie & me to Michael where they'd gathered a great crowd for the birthday drinks: Gordon & Rona, Pat [Williams], Miriam Margolyes & friend, Keith and David, Stephen, Harry, and it was quite a crowd! At 10 to 12 I said we should be going & Louie shouted protests & that endless tirade about the spoiling of her pleasure, while Gordon & Rona (who were giving us a lift home) were patiently waiting by the lift.

Sunday, 22 February
Went to get the papers. When I returned Louie gave me La Plus Belle

---

[3] The general representative body, or parliament, of the actors' union. Members may vote (1992–94) for twenty-nine candidates in the General list, and for others in specialised areas of performance and stagecraft.
[4] Stephen Oliver, 1950–92.

Lavande & wished me Happy 50th birthday. It was so mild and pleasant that we went to the park and walked right round by [the] zoo and the lake: there weren't many people about so it was better than usual.

Friday, 27 February

Found several letters awaiting me including one from a little boy who writes enchantingly. Interesting that I've *never* received an unpleasant letter from a child: all the nasty missives are penned by adults.

Saturday, 6 March

Got to the Centre at 11 o'c. The day seemed endless as far as work was concerned. Both episodes[5] were full of difficult writing. Voices coming on top of one another, thick & fast. The second was endless stops & starts and I was *lousy*. Worse than I have ever been on a 'Jackanory'. I suppose it's because I'm getting old but certainly I never fluffed so much in the old days. The cameraman was enchanting: one of those calm and efficient Englishmen who does his job superbly and has that delightfully humorous twinkle which lightens the dreariest occasion. The dresser (Stephen) was kind & considerate: in fact I was surrounded by delightful folk all the time.

Monday, 8 March

Letter from Richard Pearson. He doesn't want to be in the Feydeau. Everyone I suggest doesn't want to be in it! Hattie, Sims, Connor . . . the list is growing every day . . . Oh yes! *and* Gordon and M[ichael] Aldridge. Telephone call from Vernon Sproxton[6] regarding the religious spot on his television programme: 'Would you like to come and have lunch at Kensington House on Wednesday?' and I said yes. Always it is the small job which entails a *personal* statement that is the most difficult.

Wednesday, 10 March

Walked to Kensington Ho. to meet Vernon Sproxton. I read him the script & he made one amendment, or rather addition, saying 'Put this in your own words . . .' I was on my way out when I met George (transcription) and he told me 'These are my last days here for I retire at the end of the week . . .' so I went in to his office to have a drink with him. Showed him the script for my religious b'cast & he made loads of amendments and corrections. He said 'You're one of the very

---

[5] Of 'Dust-Up at the Royal Disco', by Norman Hunter. 'More extraordinary tales from the Kingdom of Incrediblania.'

[6] Rev. Vernon Sproxton, b.1920. Radio and TV producer, 1957–77, then freelance.

few comedians with a *mind*' and then Bernard Palmer came in & worked with us. Lovely man. After, George recited a large extract from 'Ulysses' & when he got to 'to strive, to seek, to find & not to yield . . .'[7] he wept uncontrollably. Bernard & I were both moved. George said 'Alas, Kenny, I'm not a pro . . . forgive the emotion, but I'm daunted by this retirement thing . . . I shall miss it all terribly . . .' Bernard said 'Come, George! Churchill's career didn't start till he was over sixty' & George snorted 'But *he* wasn't with the BBC . . .'

Tuesday, 16 March

Louie left me a paper & I had a read before starting on the washing of the kitchen ceiling & walls. All of it was filthy. At about 12.30 Laurena telephoned and *told me that Harold Wilson has resigned! What a time to leave the sinking pound!* There was all the usual humbug and obligatory compliments from erstwhile ministers: only Edward Heath spoke truthfully when he said that the Wilson brand of pragmatism often appeared as deceit and hypocrisy & that there was *no* formulative *vision* in the man.

Thursday, 18 March

To Drury Lane at 3 o'c. Sat in the stalls with Patrick [Garland] & Helen [Montagu] and looked at handsome young men: alas, none of them funny. Then Paul Hardwick came out & he was delightful & a little man called [Peter] Glaze – v. honest. The girls were all awful and on came Carol [Hawkins] who read so badly it was a joke, but I know she can act so I told Patrick & Helen to get her. I walked back to Leic. Sq. with Patrick who is *still* insisting on the 'tropic' sets & wants me to look at them on Tuesday with him: it is irritating. He is frightened about 'so many Feydeaus have been around & I do want to get away from the *usual* look of them . . .'

Monday, 22 March

Taxi for Peter Nichols. When I arrived they were trying to find the cause of their smoke-filled rooms, and Peter went next door, returned, and said 'There is a fire in the next house!' and Thelma telephoned the Fire Brigade. Peter gave me a draft of his new play about C.S.E.!! I was very touched when he said 'This is the piece you helped me to write . . .'

---

7 Last line of the 'Ulysses' of Alfred, Lord Tennyson (1809–92). Passage includes the lines: 'Death closes all: but something ere the end/Some work of noble note, may yet be done.'

Tuesday, 23 March

I read Peter Nichols' play *Privates On Parade*. He's done some clever & adroit things with it but the obscenity and the blasphemy are unwarranted: the second half is not as good as the first and a proper dénouement is lacking. The character Terri (based on Barri Chatt I should think) is a gift for somebody. He's got a capacity for creating an evil & corrupt atmosphere of astonishing nastiness, with amazing economy.

Wednesday, 24 March

Patrick G. phoned: 'Carol Hawkins has turned down the part ... apparently she has been offered something better ...' This surprises me! She certainly conveyed nothing of this to me, and goodness knows, she was on the telephone often enough! Peter E. on the phone: 'Tennent's have arranged for you to play Bristol and Nottingham & then Edinburgh & Glasgow ...' I said 'Well, Helen told me Oxford and Eastbourne, so if they're changing their tune I'm changing mine and you can date the contract as 6 months from the opening of the play on tour ...' He demurred but I went on about it. Adamantly.

Thursday, 25 March

Gerald Thomas telephoned: 'We'd like you to play this part in the Carry On we're doing in May ... can I send you a script? It would involve about 5 or 6 days' work.' I said I'd be pleased to be in it, but that I didn't know if the touring dates would allow it. By chance, I saw the Old Time Music Hall and there was Ted Durante being v. funny as the Drunk in the Tart by the Lamppost sketch ... he looked the same delightful clown as he was all those years ago on the *Devonshire* troopship.[8]

Friday, 26 March

By taxi to Patrick Garland. He said he'd found a v. good young man, Alan Lewis, and a girl – Celia Bannerman*, for the juveniles. He took me to Stefan's flat (set designer) and we looked at the designs. It is all as Patrick planned. Martinique-French colonial style. A fait accompli really. Bumble Dawson[9] showed me her designs for the clothes and (apart from servants) they're all very good. *All* of them, Stefan, Bumble and Patrick said they were afraid of the fact that there were so many Feydeau farces about (Phoenix and Stratford Bow) and 'they're all so predictable.' They're all desperate for a *new look* and this isn't what Feydeau is about at all. Returned to the flat, full of disquiet.

*she later withdrew, saying of the salary 'If I earned *that* I'd have to sell my furniture.'

---

[8] He had also been KW's fellow Ugly Sister in *Cinderella* in 1958.

[9] Beatrice Dawson, called 'B' in youth, hence Bumble.

Sunday, 28 March
The religious spot I'm to do today is v. much on my mind. Changed into a blue suit & got a taxi (£1.50) to TV Centre and did the VTR at 3.15. The director relayed the message through the F[loor] M[anager] – 'Look down at your hands, look up on the signal, and start to speak, and, at the end, look down at your hands again . . .' When I asked why, the reply was 'It is a good precedent established by Savonarola.'[10] I thought it was irrelevant & placing an unwonted habit on my own style. Nevertheless, I obeyed: you cannot have everyone on the ship aspiring to captaincy.

Saturday, 3 April
In the evening Louie went to her dance and I stayed in to watch *Carry On Up The Jungle* which was a Carry On which I did not appear in. It was quite funny and at one point I was laughing aloud. I was staggered to see what they got away with!! A snake going up the skirt of Joan Sims! & her look of horror turning to delight!! Kenny Connor was quite marvellous, and Terry Scott was excellent as Tarzan. Sid James doing the same old tired automaton recitation . . . nothing at all to do with acting . . . one asked oneself: 'How on earth did he get away with it?' but of course he did, & the incredible thing about his 'career' is that it spans everything from South African Boxing, the American musical, Revue (*Touch & Go*) and conventional English theatre, and radio, and TV, and v. successful film career. All built on a 'persona' but nothing to do with talent.

Monday, 5 April
Peter Nichols rang: asked me to post his play *Privates On Parade* back to him 'cos he wants to work on it, in France. Supper with Louie and we watched the news announcing the succession of Callaghan as Prime Minister: there is something fishy about the resignation of Wilson and the ushering into power of this mediocre man.

Tuesday, 6 April
Denis Goacher telephoned & we've arranged to meet tomorrow at the B.M. main gate. His voice sounded superb: I had forgotten how beautiful an instrument it was: suddenly realised how few people really *spoke beautifully* but without affectation, as he does.

Wednesday, 7 April
Up at 7.30 to find a letter from Equity telling me that I have been

---

[10] Fra Girolamo Savonarola (1452–98). Austere Dominican monk and religious reformer.

elected a Councillor! I am in the top 6 of the voting numbers! Telephoned Rona and fixed to go with her to the Victoria Palace on Sunday for the Equity Meeting. Agreed to be godfather to Isabel Chidell's grandson Robert, and the ceremony is on Sunday 25 April. I met Denis Goacher and gave him lunch. He talked a lot of good sense about faith and the human situation and said he thought he could earn money teaching English in Greece: it is a ludicrous waste of talent.

Thursday, 8 April
Costume fitting. Bumble was late. She said 'I've been with Larry all day . . . he sent you his love . . .' I was greatly pleased.

Sunday, 11 April
Rona came, looking divine, & we got to the Victoria Palace all right. Sat near Wendy & John Moffatt. One forgets how disgusting and how barbaric these meetings are, till you're actually faced with it all over again. It started *straightway*, challenging standing orders, challenging rule of the Chairman, challenging the right to make speeches . . . *all from the left* and the speakers mainly illiterate & dressed in outlandish garb.

Monday, 12 April
At the YMCA for a read-through of the play.[11] There are some amusing moments. Altogether, nothing to write home about. Dinner with Helen Montagu. I talked endlessly about C.S.E. and the Nichols play & about the family etc. O! I do go *on* so . . . dear Helen is so patient with me. Went in to Louie & saw myself on the TV Religious programme. I looked very aesthetic and posh . . . whole thing rather overcultivated. The look & the sound get in the way of the message. The hymn sung before and after was an intrusion & malapropos. Pity. Great pity.

Tuesday, 13 April
Rehearsals at YMCA. Again & again I want to scream out to actors – 'do it like *this* . . . can't you see?' and I restrain myself. I must not tell anyone how to do anything. They must find their own way. At the Equity meeting this morning Clifford Mollison complimented me on the religious talk last night and I was deeply touched . . . truly kind. O! yes, I sat next to Nigel Davenport at the Council meeting. I like him. He behaved in the most reticent & politic fashion. I was furious about the non-smoking ban but he was complaisant & reproved me for objecting.

---

[11] *Signed and Sealed*, by Georges Feydeau, KW as Barillon.

Wednesday, 14 April
Telephone rang but I could not be bothered to answer it: there is nothing I want to know. I am greatly relieved that T & C haven't bothered me at all & hope they're away for Easter.

Friday, 16 April
Learned from Patrick that Bumble Dawson is dead. I was chatting with her yesterday! She was lively and bright as a button: now she is gone. Patrick said something beautifully: 'She has designed all the costumes for this play: let us play in them well, *for her . . .*'

Sunday, 18 April
Up at 7 o'c. with these filthy birds making their screaming racket! Oh for an airgun to shoot them. Lunch with Louie and then returned to flat to try to learn lines . . . trouble is, I continually want to re-write them.

Tuesday, 20 April
All my suggestions apropos script revision were accepted, except that Patrick would not allow 'tough bananas' & he's right, 'cos it's malapropos. All the amendments were praised by the cast & Peggy [Mount] said 'Thank you for those lovely new bits, Kenneth.'

Wednesday, 21 April
Helen Montagu (no E on the end! I must remember!) came to see us at about 4.5. She's always infectiously happy . . . a lovely sunny personality. We were talking about John Perry & I told them the story about him saying of B.W. (in *The Buccaneer*, about her billing, where she wanted an AND in front of her name) 'If she's not very careful, it will be BUT Betty Warren!' & they all fell about.[12] It's the wittiest remark about billing I've ever heard.

Friday, 23 April
Found this rubbish in the TLS!! written by Russell Davies apropos cabaret & revue. So I'm an emblem of decadence am I? On BBC television? The only cabaret I did for them was compering variety acts in '66 to '69 and I've not done it since! and how can Huw be a 'current ideologue' when he left the BBC some time ago? This is the same

---

[12] Betty Warren played Mrs Barraclough in *The Buccaneer*.

creature who disparaged Robert Bolt. Sounds like a nasty piece of work.[13]

Sunday, 25 April
I had a rest before getting dressed to go to the ceremony of Anthony Chidell's (and Angie Chidell's) child, Robert. I held Robert Anthony Russell Chidell in my arms and there's no question but that he is a beautiful baby . . . magnificent. I held him throughout the ceremony at the font but, just at the last moment, he roared his disapproval & I handed him to Angie . . .

Monday, 26 April
Gerald James told me today that Ronnie Radd is dead. Only 47. Apparently it was a heart attack, and all v. quick! So odd that I'd been talking of him (in the Feydeau *and* Sandy Wilson) to the cast of this play only last week! Saw Louie at 5.45 for a meal. Returned to flat at 9.15. Peter E. phoned – 'I thought you should know . . . Sid James died tonight . . .' Ah me. Poor Sid. He was 61. I never liked his work but oh! it's a terrible thing to die while preparing for a twice nightly summer season of rubbish at Torquay*: no one deserves that.

*in fact, it was Sunderland. Audience of 400.

Saturday, 1 May
Returned to the flat and re-bound the crossword book 'cos it was falling to pieces! It was given to me in '59 by Sheila Hancock & it has been more used than the Erich Heller book!

Sunday, 2 May
Michael Whittaker came at 7 o'c. and trod all over the carpet in spite of my endless injunctions.

Monday, 3 May
George disquieted me by saying 'What a nasty article in the News of the World about you in the Carry Ons! All that stuff about their paying

---

[13] Huw Wheldon did not leave the BBC until 1977, and was still a Special Advisor in 1976. KW misconstrued my point. Arguing in favour of a true satirical-political cabaret on television (and hoping for something less cautiously wholesome than the usual fare), I had remarked: 'Given that the BBC's current ideologue is Sir Huw Wheldon and its emblem of decadence Kenneth Williams, who expects the present regime to revive the idea?' KW had been for some years the BBC's most generously-licensed exponent of non-political camp, but this position was being wrested from him at about this time (see entry for 10 January 1977, p. 533). For the BBC's reaction when KW did engage in political polemic, see entry for 27 October 1982, p. 663.

you nothing while they roll around in the Rolls Royces . . .' and said that the tenor of the writing was horrid.

Wednesday, 5 May

Quite an argument with Patrick about the validity of pauses in a farce. They only work when there's been a *noise*. No one seems to comprehend that. I feel a gulf yawning & a pit of sinking misery inside . . . a sense of futility . . . me doing French farce in a period of appalling crisis . . . the country lurching from one deficit to another . . .

Saturday, 8 May

Went in to Louie's empty flat – she's away on this outing – and felt unutterably lonely. When she is away I feel lousy. I started crying in the kitchen. Returned to my own flat after having the lunch Louie had prepared. I miss her terribly: it's like a great nagging inside of me. Tried to forget it all by getting out the cases and sorting the stuff I shall need for the tour.

Monday, 10 May. Bristol

Up at 8.20 but awake since 6 o'c., noise of ducks on the river is disconcerting. How I hate all bird noises: rather have traffic any day. D/rehearsal was quite spirited till the 3rd Act where it dropped badly. The first night was rather like an amateur company carefully playing something which *had been funny* years ago in the hands of professional comedians. There was some applause but not much. Everyone was in a lather of sweat and exhaustion.

Tuesday, 11 May

Patrick said 'I have to admit the set is distracting.' Oh dear oh dear. I called on Pamela Howe. She admitted she'd seen the show last night! Never came round. She thought it was awful. Helen told Patrick she wanted to see me alone and went to Harvey's. She said she was prepared to have a new set if Stefan didn't re-do the present one.

Wednesday, 12 May

Did the voice-over for Unigate & was back rehearsing by 11.30. I stayed onstage giving my own ideas for reorganising the scenes and giving them movement & life. I re-staged the opening with books, dustsheets etc. & got [Barry] Stanton & [Peter] Glaze to bring it *up* à la double act. Patrick was quite cooperative and said: 'Thank you for helping like this.' The evening performance began well, with the opening going much better and the rest stuttering along dreadfully.

Thursday, 13 May

Lunched with Pamela Howe who said 'Actors, in circumstances like yours, have to be very brave, don't they?' and I found myself in rueful agreement. Had a talk with Bryan P[ringle] whom I like. He said 'We must not get depressed, we must all work to make it as good as possible.' Helen came down from London to see it. She said 'The first Act is enormously improved and Patrick says that it is largely due to you . . . he says he thinks you've been wonderful & unselfish & worked entirely for the sake of the show.' I staged a fall for Peggy today (at rehearsal) and when she did it tonight it worked like a dream. Got a lovely laugh.

Saturday, 15 May

It has been a curious week. The Monday: a horrifying disappointment and then, a gradual improvement & an amazingly good morale in the company. We're v. lucky to have such a good collection of people and *all* have worked as hard as they can to make the play work.

Wednesday, 19 May. Nottingham

The fact remains that the jokes are *not there* . . . again and again it is the stuff *put in* that gets results. I think Helen is right. It wants a gag man to be brought in. If I suggest something, P.G. says 'It's not period.'

Sunday, 23 May

It seems unbelievable that I've got 3 more weeks of the nightmare of this stinking tour! I can hardly believe I'm living thro' the horror & the shame of it all! If it's my punishment for something . . . well then, I'm paying the price all right. I had lunch with Louie. She said 'The management should take it off' and she's so right. I telephoned Helen. She said 'I will come to Glasgow, and we will have to decide something drastic there . . .' We certainly will. It can't go on drifting like this.

Monday, 24 May. Glasgow

Photographed by local paper sitting in the gutter with Peggy Mount. Ludicrous. Cast addressed by Helen Montagu. She gave copious notes & directions to be followed & was v. enlightening about the piece. I am really being asked to be a director of comedy *and* play a leading role.

Wednesday, 26 May

Gerald said 'You must stop helping others, Kenneth, and start helping yourself!' I gave Floella[14] a new line about 'His harpoon gun didn't go off!' and it got a laugh. Plowman gave me 'Let the blood rush to her feet' for Madame Jambert's faint and that worked too. Also gave Flo a song 'When my lover comes' with the broom, to open the 3 Act and it gives it fluidity. There are loads of things I could do with this play if I was on my own 'cos the cast trust me and can see that what I suggest is practical.

Thursday, 27 May
It's amazing how – because of the work on the play – my own morale has gone up. I had lunch with Jane Carr and felt v. tired, so she said 'Go to your hotel and lie down.' I did. Noise from above was dreadful. I complained & they said 'You're under the Royal Suite . . .' Princess Margaret is here. I got changed from 9 to 7 floor. Our new curtain for Act 2 worked. It's not a yok[15] but it is practical.

Friday, 28 May
Performance at night was very good. Returned to Albany for talk with Helen. She said 'I can't thank you enough . . . this proves you can direct a play' & I said 'Yes, I should have done it in the first place.'

Saturday, 29 May
Went to bed exhausted and truly dispirited. The cast got away with it last night because of concentration and energy from *everyone* and tonight (apart from a few) they let it go, thinking the stuff would stand up on its own. It won't. What is so depressing is the knowledge that their stupidity is not malignant but simply appalling ignorance of their own dilemma.

Tuesday, 1 June. Edinburgh
Peter E. telephoned. 'Codron rang me and said his play at Wyndham's was a flop and did we want the theatre?' I can't be bothered about West End theatres at the moment. We need all the out of town experience we can get: and I need to get this cast on my own and do the necessary polishing.

Thursday, 3 June
A man screamed & threw coins at me in the street 'You may need a penny some day!' I need one now! Went to theatre at 6 o'c. Paul & Flo rehearsing like mad, Gerald checking on dialogue, Peggy

---

14 Floella Benjamin. Actress best known for her many appearances on children's television, e.g. 'Play School'.
15 A big laugh.

reminding people of new moves, Jane going over it and everyone anxious to do their best. The performance was high keyed & unrelaxed but purposeful. The audience was rotten. No indulgence here, but comparable to a sticky first night.

Friday, 4 June

Went down to the bar & met a belted & jeaned Adonis called Peter. All going well till a drunk intervened. We got rid of it & I took the boy to lunch & then got the invite to the house – 'My mother won't return till 5 o'c.' – so rushed into a cab for the suburbs. On entry all was lost. Old Mother Riley had taken afternoon *off*! So we all had tea & the chat about bourgeois values!! I brought Flo and Jane back to the Caledonian for drinks and we had a long talk. Flo spoke about the animosity of neighbours throwing ordure on windows & through the letter box & of the struggle of her mother to bring up 6 children, and Jane told of neighbours spitting & hitting her because of the class warfare in her street. Both said the adversity had spurred them on to spiritual victory. Returned to my room at about 12.30 with the head spinning with Adonis and played an entire scene on the strength of remembering. It was unbelievably real. Couldn't get to sleep until about 2 o'c. in the morning. Today was really an extraordinary experience.

Monday, 7 June. Newcastle

Helen & Christopher [Hampton] came round. Helen said 'It's played just like people saying lines . . . there is no argument developed and people aren't *listening* to each other, or to what they're saying themselves . . .' She wanted the show to open in the second week after tour, with *previews*. I said 'Have a dress rehearsal & open.' Forget the rest. She said 'You have shaken me considerably!' By this time we had talked for 4 hours. It was 2 o'c. in the morning.

Saturday, 12 June

Peter E. came backstage. I said 'If nothing else comes of it, I've learned that a cast does respond to me and I can direct . . .' We drove home on the motorway and P.E. dropped me at 3.10 at my door. He is a good friend & a loyal man.

Tuesday, 15 June

Another one of these sweltering days. I wish this terrible heat would stop. To Stefan's awful flat at Holland Park to see the new version of the set. It is simply the old one, painted white.

Friday, 18 June
The sun was hot but there was a breeze. Hardly anyone about . . . Louie said 'They've all gone to Lord's' – in this country, the silly season is rotten TV, Lord's, Wimbledon & Ascot . . . it's all dressing up & larking about, as economic disaster looms nearer and nearer.

Monday, 21 June
Dress rehearsal. It is incredible to be in such a small theatre! It seems years since I was there with *Lettuce* and dear, dear Maggie.

Tuesday, 22 June
On stage for notes from P.G. at 5 o'c. I started mentioning certain points before Judy[16] got hers out & Bryan Pringle shouted 'Shut up' to me. He said it was because I was impolite to Patrick & added after 'I may want a job from him one day.' The Preview went fairly well.

Wednesday, 23 June
To the theatre. Room full of presents. Bob Bolt came in. I didn't know he was coming! Hadn't opened the telegrams! The show went fair 1st Act, dropped like a lead balloon in the Odyssey sequence & came up a bit in the 3rd Act. Applause was fair but the auditorium was a sea of waving programmes & dreadful *humid heat* . . . the sweat pouring off everyone.

Thursday, 24 June
The papers have all got filthy notices for it. The people who are singled out & given special mention are: Paul, Gerald and Peggy. I get all the 'Carry On frenetically' abuse & there is much talk of grimacing. Coffee with Peter E. & a talk. We agreed we're in the shit.

Friday, 25 June
The boiling sun is relentless: the sort of weather which one loves on a holiday & loathes in London. I feel actually *angry* as I look at it & know the damage it's doing to people, to business and to spirits . . . one is sweating before the day begins & I have one sheet over me on the bed & it's still uncomfortable. To the theatre thro' sweltering streets . . . everyone standing *outside* pubs holding beer in their hands . . . in Titchfield Street they shouted 'Don't go in tonight, Kenny! There'll be no bugger there!' and I smiled sickly. In the event, the auditorium had about two hundred in it, and they were very kind and indulgent.

---

[16] Patrick Garland.

Saturday, 26 June

Louie suggested a brilliant idea: 'I'll make some sun blinds for you, out of those old sheets of yours . . .' By 2.30 she had made me some *fabulous* candy stripe curtains which keep the sun out of both rooms excellently! I realise now – *I can take this flop*. I can take it because the derision comes from a despicable source and because I'm not conscience-stricken. In dreadful circumstances I did my best.

Monday, 28 June

I wrote letters cancelling all appointments – Erich Heller, Martin Braun, Peter Nichols . . . etc. Told 'em I'm like a dog with a wound & I want to lick it in solitude . . . I'm lousy company at the moment. Don't really want to meet Baix tomorrow 'cos the relationship is taut at the best of times. Sat in the D/room feeling suicidal . . . all the critics yesterday (and the dailies) panned *me*, not the play, director or cast or set. Just *me*. I have to go on a stage pretending I don't know I'm lousy. In the event, we played to a handful. Company went *mad*. I was appalling. The sight of them sent me tumbling into rubbish myself & by the 3rd Act, I was gone. Giggling etc. Helen Montagu came round. She said 'We'd better have a talk on Wednesday . . .' and looked & sounded pretty grim.

Tuesday, 29 June

Stanley came and drove me to Barbino where it was air conditioned! It was *bliss*. He said 'Don't worry about this show . . . I've got a feeling they will cut their losses and take it off . . .' Walked to the theatre in a daze of hopeless uncertainty. Don't know how I even got words out of my mouth . . . even collecting the key at the S/Door was a nightmare . . . The first Act was simply a question of trying to speak . . . my nerves were so shot to pieces that I had to keep swallowing . . . but [by] the 2nd Act, I'd recovered a little. I suppose the enormity of the failure hadn't hit me till today.

Wednesday, 30 June

Went to the Globe to see Helen. She was *marvellous*. 'I don't want to prolong your agony any further than I have to . . .' She said she was surprised at the vituperative nature of the critics. 'I thought your performance on the opening night was exactly right . . .' She's the best employer I've ever had.

Thursday, 1 July

The bedroom seems to *hold* the heat and one can find no air . . . I keep thinking of Spender's line 'You've got to live through the time when everything hurts . . .'[17] Trouble is it's been hurting me for years. Why live at all? There is nothing here of real value that wouldn't stay with the spirit always . . . O! it would be such a relief . . . In the evening, we played to 143 pounds. One tried and tried but it's no good . . . like a party which no one's attending . . . the atmosphere is death.

Friday, 2 July

More letters to answer. The heart like lead. I know I'm being depressing for Louie . . . we sit thro' meals in silence that is screaming with pain: she's full of anguish when I'm in a flop . . . or unhappy in any way. They said they would know if this show was to run by Friday (today) and if I hear that it will come off and put us all out of our misery it would be miraculous, but the futility of perpetuating this meretricious muck is too appalling to contemplate. I shall finish it all off at the weekend. I wrote my goodbye letters to Peter E. and to Louie. I was crying on to the blotter. Silly fool. I think God's hand will catch me when I fall . . . but shall I have the courage?

Went in to do the show & found there was the usual handful but we all had a go & went on gamely. At the end, Paul Hardwick said 'The electrician asked Martin Beckwith about the get-out next Saturday . . . we're coming off . . .' I was staggered. No one has informed me & yet the FOH manager *knew* before the show tonight! It is unbelievable that I should find out in this fashion. Gave my thanks to God for saving me from this dire situation. It has been a punishment I suppose. The lesson I've been taught is that all institutional work is compromise & when (as in '73) I left a show, I shouldn't have done so.

Thursday, 8 July

I rushed out of the flat to catch a bus (53) and the conductor shouted at me 'Do your flies up!' and turned to the other passengers & said 'Isn't it disgusting? I get 'em all on this bus . . . filthy people . . .' etc. etc. It hardly showed in fact & he must have been looking at my trousers in the 10 seconds it took me to get to my seat, so he must have been an unhealthy & maladjusted creature. The evening performance was *dire*. Berserk with mad vulgarity and funny voices. With this collection of amateurs one is forced to give up.*

*see Jan. 31st entry. It predicts this would happen. It is extraordinary.

---

[17] 'You must live through the time when everything hurts': first line of Spender's 'The Double Shame'.

Saturday, 10 July

Matinée was £149, and Evening was £183. In a theatre which can take a thousand pounds, it is derisory indeed. It has certainly proved that (without good notices and proper weather) I am *no* draw at all, as far as box office is concerned. I thank God I am delivered from this awful fiasco. Helen was displeased with the performance. She was pleasant to me but I think disillusionment has set in.

Wednesday, 14 July

At about 12.30 I left for the Punch luncheon at Tudor Street. Miles Kington greeted me and I met Alan Coren, the editor,[18] Larry Adler, Bill Grundy, Sheridan Morley & quite a few others. That ghastly Alan Brien[19] was there. He said 'Peter Cook told me that you weren't interested in sex . . . you'd rather have a wank and a Mars Bar . . .' & I replied 'It's only half true . . .'* and launched into the story of wanking at Endsleigh Court & breaking the lavatory in the process. Perhaps it's tiredness or stupidity . . . I don't know . . . but certainly I feel disgusted with myself. The jaded nastiness of their conversation and their appalling cynicism was astonishing to me. I mentioned my admiration for General Gordon[20] and they sent him up . . . made jokes about his death . . . they've no decency at all. I couldn't *wait* to get out. I walked up Bouverie Street with the cartoonist Mr Dickens[21] & Larry Adler who went on & on about 'the greats' and said 'When I last played Bridge it was with Ingrid Bergman, Jack Benny and who d'you think made up the fourth? – yes . . . it was Garbo!' and we all looked properly astonished & awed.

*I never eat Mars Bars

Friday, 16 July

Reflected that the emptiness of my life shows the utter waste of a selfish life. Life without real sharing is a pointless affair & my life is pointless. One keeps the despair at bay with various activities but knows *that* is what one is doing. I know I don't want to share because I don't want to be involved in the *mess*: most people are a mess. I may be pointless but I'm not a mess. Not yet.

---

[18] The editor was William Davis, b.1933; Alan Coren, b.1938, became editor in 1978. Larry Adler, harmonica player and writer, b.1914; Bill Grundy (1923–93), television presenter and journalist; Sheridan Morley, drama critic, author and broadcaster, b.1941.

[19] b.1925. Columnist, critic and author.

[20] Charles George Gordon (1833–85), killed at Khartoum.

[21] Frank Dickens, creator of the 'Bristow' cartoon strip.

Sunday, 18 July

Met Paul Richardson (Flat 29) and we sat talking from 10 o'c. till about 4 o'c.!! The time flew by! I rather like him & we chatted about theatre. He told me all about Sadler's Wells & the companies he'd been with.

Monday, 2 August

Got the contract for 'J.A.M.' and thought 'Bless the BBC' before I posted it at 9.30 when I got the papers. Peter E. telephoned & asked: 'Are you getting bored?' & I lied smoothly 'Oh no! there is plenty to do . . .'

Thursday, 12 August

Eade telephoned & said Tatler had rung so I said give my number to them & was contacted by Robert Lightfoot asking me to write for Tatler – 900 words and a practically free rein. I said all right. I think it is all meant: whether I like it or not, more & more I'm propelled in the direction of writing. Quite the barclays before bed. Masturbatory success is the result of imaginative conceit.

Friday, 13 August

Walked to the Rose Garden with the Leishman translations of Rilke[22] and sat in a deck chair reading. It was hot and humid. The paper has a notice about the death of Tom Driberg[23] and mentions his diary (which may be published) and says he was a well-known homosexual. Amazing how papers love saying this sort of thing as soon as people are dead but wouldn't dare do so when they were alive.

Tuesday, 17 August

At 2 o'c. I walked thro' the hot dirty streets to John Wood Studios to do a v/o for McVitie's biscuits – a bottle talking to Alice in Wonderland. I was the bottle. I was away in half an hour. Strolled back & saw headlines on newsstands – WATER PRESSURE CUT IN LONDON, so obviously the capital is at last acknowledging the drought.

Friday, 20 August

A man telephoned saying 'I'm from the International Opera . . . we got your number from Equity . . . it's about our production of *Salome* . . . are you free during next month?' I said 'I beg yr. pardon?' & he replied 'You are the Ken Williams who works at Greenwich, aren't

---

22 Rainer Maria Rilke (1875–1926), German poet. Translations by J.B. Leishman.

23 Baron Bradwell, b.1905. Independent, then Labour MP, journalist and gossip.

you? . . . the black dancer?' When I said no, he said 'Oh! what a curious cross tangle! I'm sorry to have troubled you . . .'

Wednesday, 25 August
Government has appointed that fool Howell[24] (Minister of Sport!!) to be Minister of Water under these emergency drought conditions. I am not bathing. Just washing in a basin & conserving water.

Thursday, 26 August
Oh dear! the heat is relentless. Had to ring R.T. about a mistake in my typing. Came as something of a shock to me when I realised that I'd started writing for them in June '74!! Didn't realise I'd been at it for over two years. Pat collected us with a friend and drove us to I.C.L. at Putney for drinks celebration apropos her 21 years with the firm. The manager presented her with a superb freezer for her new flat. There's little doubt but that Pat is very popular indeed with the people at her firm. The liking is expressed without reserve.

Saturday, 28 August
To Harry for drinks. Harry told me off for pronouncing *toll* as in Moll – 'It should sound like tole, dear! You say *poll booth* as *pole,* don't you?' and I admitted I didn't. Well, we're always learning. I said 'In correcting me in the middle of a sentence, you're committing a solecism.' Back by 12 o'c. Full of traditional preoccupation.

Sunday, 29 August
Michael came and we went to Robert Bolt at the Mill House. He is leaving on Tuesday so this was farewell to the abode. They had a lavish party laid on. Talked to Antonia Fraser (who admitted 'Yes, Melvyn *was* rather curt with you on that Book Programme . . .') and John Hurt who seems to have *taken on* the Quentin Crisp persona!![25] He was behaving very badly and kissing everyone. I saw Finney & Rex Harrison & Eileen Atkins but I'm not interested in the first two.

Friday, 3 September
I am using 3 blankets now! The weather changed completely after August thank goodness.

---

[24] Denis Howell, MP for Birmingham Small Heath from 1961.
[25] Having played the flamboyantly homosexual Crisp on television in Philip Mackie's 'The Naked Civil Servant' (1975).

Monday, 6 September
Went to Pye Studios at 5 o'c. and ran thro' the script of the *Jule & Sand Album* (LP) with Hugh Paddick and Barry Took. The former never seems to alter, he still looks as slim and youthful as he did when 'RTH' was on. The audience was very tolerant: it takes a lot of patience to listen to the polari excerpts for all that time. There were several retakes, and we had to do a version specifically deleting references to *record* & substituting *cassette*.

Saturday, 11 September
Evening with T & C. They put on the 'KW Show' on Video Tape & Fred told me 'L. *wiped* the French Song . . . it's gone completely.' I said it was hurtful. Tom said, 'Oh nonsense, I've wiped your show completely! You can't waste 17 pounds preserving your work dearie . . .' That deflated me. I had always thought he would keep my show, as a record. Why does one expect so much from close friends?

Sunday, 12 September
On the video tape last night, I remarked how old, haggard & tired I looked. I am now looking like the elderly preserved queen I used to meet pityingly at parties & always gave a little attention to, thinking it was gracious & kind to do so. Oh dear.

Tuesday, 14 September
Gordon & Rona came & I gave them dinner at Peter Mario in spite of the pain in my tooth. Gordon said 'Do you really not need glasses to read this?' when we were perusing the menu. He added 'I bet you have a pair at home for reading!' & I told him I didn't have.

Tuesday, 21 September
Equity meeting. Miriam Karlin said 'Fenella Fielding came to see my new house in Wandsworth and she said "It's really splendid, my dear . . . are you going to bring it into town?"' Louis Mahoney asked me to sign a protest against the S. African regime & I did. Miriam said surprisedly 'Well! I didn't know you supported *that*!' and I said 'No one with a conscience could not' and spoke of my abhorrence for the racist state.

Monday, 27 September
A man calling himself James Green (Evening News) rang & asked questions for an article he's writing about me in Wednesday's edition. He said 'How is your Feydeau play going? Are you enjoying it?' & I

told him it finished several months ago: the press are v. contemporary in this country.

Monday, 4 October
I've got to go all the way to Blackheath for this sitting with the painter John Bratby. I got the 53 bus at 9.15 and I was outside his door at 10.10. I sat in a chair & talked, and at 12.15 he said 'Have a look at this . . . how does it strike you?' and I looked at the easel. It is a marvellous portrait of me! He captured the aspiration, the theatricality, the arrogance & the 'boyish' aspect. I was staggered by the cleverness and speed of it! He is a quiet man who has lived in the area for some time & obviously likes it. He says v. little but encourages one to talk a lot. He is immensely likeable. He gave me a book of reproductions of his work. I got the 53 bus home by 1.45. When John Bratby asked me, later: 'Do you really like it?' I said 'Yes enormously, but it does flatter me . . . I look like a boy' & he replied 'You look like one.' I said 'I was born in '26' & he smiled: 'You wear your years very well.' Peter Eade has said that there is to be a Carry On made in Jan./Feb. The money would just about see me thro' an extremely uncomfortable year. Of course, it could be argued that I shouldn't have spent the capital on [an] annuity for Louie, but to go on paying her out of my own salary had two drawbacks: 1) it couldn't be guaranteed 2) it didn't give her independence.

Thursday, 7 October
Letter from Bratby offering me that canvas for 350!! I can't afford it! How embarrassing.

Wednesday, 13 October
Went to Trafalgar Square and held banner protesting about the arrest of actors in South Africa. I stood with Kenneth Haigh, Eileen Atkins, Sheila Hancock, Robert Morley & Albert Finney. The Embassy allowed only *one* person in, to read the letter of protest, and that was Albert . . . he went alone . . . and suddenly looked very courageous.

Tuesday, 19 October
Peter E. rang: 'We can't have you sitting about with the odd "Just A Minute" and writing for the Tatler . . .' When I said 'I'm obviously unfashionable at the moment,' he replied, 'Well it's not happened to you before and you've got a lot to fall back on' which staggered me till I realised he was referring to talent. Walked in the park & there was a pale winter sun . . . all the grass is thick and green again; you would never know we'd had 3 months of drought. I purchased 4 grapefruit for 30p and two pears, and ate them all greedily. Delicious.

Sunday, 24 October

'One who was tortured by the past' should be written on my grave. Everything came to haunt me today: seeing 'Boy From Barnardo's' and writing to Russell Cotes & becoming pen-friends with Jimmy Johnson, the appalling hand-made lamp from Freddie Berry (O! the love that must have gone into it!) Getting the Vachell book & re-reading the rubbish which once made me weep. Our yesterdays often prove to be our tomorrows.

Monday, 25 October

Set out in rain for P. Mario to find Maggie & Beverley. Mags embraced me warmly and Bev & I banged our heads together after I'd hugged him & bent to sit down: we were all nervous. Mags looked *marvellous.* Like a radiant young girl. Bev told me (when she went to the loo) 'Her Cleopatra is superb! Her authority and sheer presence are colossal . . .' Mags said: 'Oh isn't London filthy! Honestly it feels unhealthy just walking thro' Coventry Street . . . everything is so *dirty* and squalid . . . different from the days when we used to go to the Grill & Bumhole . . .' She was v. funny about Coral Browne warning her about Cleopatra: 'It's the breathing you've got to worry about dear! It's bloody *murder* . . . uphill all the way' & Mags added ruefully 'She is dead right.' I went with them to Waterloo & saw them off to Guildford . . . another piece of my life goes away on a platform.

Friday, 29 October

Went to the Paris Studio for 'J.A.M.' It was awful. Patrick Moore[26] successfully challenging my line on Macready: 'One of the great Actor Managers of England' by saying 'England's never been managed' and the idiot Parsons allowing it! Oh my loathing for this rotten game!

Tuesday, 9 November

Equity meeting. Row about John Curry (ice skating champion) having the same name as one of our members! The skater is applying for membership of Equity for his show at the Cambridge. We agreed to special conditions and provisos, and vetoed 3 American skaters he wants to use.

Thursday, 11 November

Peter E. rang: 'The S. Times want you to review a book . . .' I said yes. I can't very well say no. The S. Times delivered it and I read it

---

[26] b.1923. Television presenter and spokesman for astronomy.

in about three hours. Drafted out a sort of review eventually.[27] It's incredible how much correction one's writing needs. I go wrong in delineation as well as with punctuation & it's amazing how often I repeat myself, forgetting I've already used a particular phrase. It was 12.30 by the time I'd done the polishing. That's another thing: there is a point in all work, where you should *commit* and then, leave it alone. Stare long enough and you'll find something wrong with *everthing* [*sic*].

Saturday, 13 November
There is a charming letter from Dr Ball of the Middlesex Hospital saying that there is an impairment in the rear of the brain which causes Louie to experience lack of balance at times, but his diagnosis otherwise is that the outlook is good. Must reply to this considerate letter.

Monday, 15 November
P. Eade telephoned: 'Punch want you to write an article for their Christmas issue . . . what I've always wanted for Christmas . . . about 400 words.' I wonder about this writing business . . . it's as if God was saying 'I will put some writing work in his way' and I've never needed alternative employment *more*!

Wednesday, 17 November
Lunch with Mavis Nicholson. Talked about the Diary programme and ironed out a format. She is vivacious & lively but was depressed by a programme she'd done with Margaret Thatcher; she felt the inhibition hadn't been overcome: she's a perfectionist. She was v. funny about Kingsley Amis:[28] 'He screamed *Commie* at me! I said not commie but *left* . . . he thinks all right thinking is of the Right . . .' I said 'He's right; learning is by nature conservative' & she said 'I thought you might agree with *his* views.' Left at 2.50. The depression is colossal. One knows it's something one has got to live thro'. Thankfully I have the '68 diary to remind me of a similar period and I know from that, that the situation doesn't last.

Monday, 22 November
Ever conscious of the *bum* & wondering 'Will it get better without

---

[27] *Stand Up Virgin Soldiers* by Leslie Thomas, reviewed by KW in the *Sunday Times* colour magazine, 19 December 1976: '. . . he has a good ear for the repetitive banalities of army conversation, the obscene rudeness and derisive comment reserved for the rookies – "Get some in," "Get your knees brown." In their illiterate phraseology he conveys the helplessness of those caught up in events they feel powerless to control.'
[28] Sir Kingsley Amis, b.1922. Author.

surgery?' Peter Eade has sent contract for the Mavis Nicholson show @ £35. This is derisory. I returned the contract.

Tuesday, 23 November

Peter E. said: 'Thames TV say that they will raise the fee to 50 pounds' & I said they could stick it. Laurena rang: 'Thames Television have agreed to pay you £100 for the diary programme.' I said all right but it's a pyrrhic victory.

Saturday, 4 December

Got the 30 bus in the evening to B. It was very shabby. I wrote in the visitors' book 'A dreadful evening . . . not even a sandwich . . . thanks for nothing' and he got quite shirty with me & tried to grab hold of me . . . very nearly tore my overcoat.

Monday, 6 December

I could hardly summon up enough energy to talk to Louie. We sat in her freezing cold kitchen eating this pathetic lunch of cold meat. She is looking white and strained and not at all well. I think she worries about money . . . she does buy the food for both of us, all out of her own money *and* seems to manage (goodness knows how!) And I thought that I was going to provide a pleasant old age for her!

Monday, 20 December

Lunch Louie at 12.30. Wished her a Happy Birthday – it must be the first year I haven't given Louie a present! I'm afraid money is low. Tom collected us at 6.45. At the end of the dinner, they brought in a birthday cake. But you'd never have thought it was *her* birthday with chat about things she's uninterested in. Several times I tried to change this by saying 'Well dear! How does it feel to be 75?' but always somebody diverted conversation back to self.

Saturday, 25 December

Up at about 9 o'c. feeling as low as hell. The depression that comes from fear of physical pain and from the despair of my private life. Can't remember any Christmas as awful . . . except perhaps the '65 period. Tom came at about 10.50. We had champagne before lunch and then went thro' for the superb dinner. Clive did pears to begin, then a marvellous turkey, and then the pièce de résistance, an Eva Pudding. It was delectable. I had two lots and was quite the pig-ette. Those two gave us a splendid day, but then, they always do: their hospitality is lavish & there is always a generous atmosphere.

Tuesday, 28 December

Bum worse than ever. I have never known such pain on walking. It's not so bad if I'm still. God knows what is going to happen to me. I just can't continue like this & yet . . . medically it's not considered serious & the NHS will not give it any priority.

Friday, 31 December

Telephoned the doctor for Louie 'cos I don't want her walking with the bad foot. Telephoned Gordon & Rona and said that with Louie's illness & low spirits I thought I should stay in tonight and he agreed entirely. We had one glass of wine at 12 o'c. and so I saw the New Year in with the best friend I've ever had.

1977

Wednesday, 5 January
Did a rectal washout and went to the Middlesex Hospital where I was seen by a Mr Slack (I believe) who inserted various instruments up the bum and it was all very painful. He said 'There is no internal trouble so that is good news; there is a patch of inflammation near the entrance & I'm going to give you some suppositories for that and an astringent lotion to dry up the area where there is some weeping.' He said that no bowel motions should be strained and that I should have bran every day. Came home & put up the new medicine and kept the lotion (on lint) in the area with sticky tape.

Monday, 10 January
Peter E. telephoned. We talked about why there'd been no offers of work of any kind & he pointed out that the Grayson TV Show is a complete crib of my stuff, and that Inman is doing the same thing on the BBC! It hadn't *hit* me before! *Of course*! they've found other people to do it, and *cheaper* people in every sense. I would love to go right away from England for a year. Of course, it's impossible, Louie, property etc., it's all too complicated, but it would remove the endless humiliation of these years. The television was diabolical. Only good thing was 'Coronation Street' and there was quite a moment when Ray Langton[1] (thinking his wife asleep) confided to another woman in the hospital ward: 'I love her.' It was utterly direct, honest and moving: a lesson to *all* pretentious actors.

Wednesday, 19 January
Laurena phoned: 'Would you like to go to Toronto for a 15-minute chat show? They're willing to fly you out there . . .' I could hardly believe it. All that way for a chat show! Of 15 minutes!! I said I couldn't face the plane journey.

---

[1] Played by Neville Buswell.

Wednesday, 26 January
Went in to see Louie. The heart *sinks* as we look at the wound and find it's back to square *one*. The same old weeping infection look (tho' the hosp. says there is no infection) and no sign of the real healing for which one is waiting.

Sunday, 13 February
We saw the Dennis Potter[2] interview. He was splendid. One knows he is in continual pain and that engages sympathy at once, but thereafter, it is his self-torturing desire to speak truthfully which is so admirable. He actually tries to explain profundities, occasionally giving up: 'Words are really no good for this kind of thing . . .' and 'I feel this' rather than *think* this. There is the frank admittance of doubt, and the acknowledging of 'the need for tension' which is so startlingly engaging & fresh in a television interview. The interviewer said 'I know you don't admire us clerics . . .' and Potter didn't deny it. But he did say 'I want the church to be there . . . someday I might need it' and expressed his dilemma.

Wednesday, 16 February
Walked to Gordon & Rona. After a superb dinner from Rona, Roderick came downstairs & said 'Watch the Party Political B'cast! It's a hoot!' and we did. Every time Margaret Thatcher began the slow & solicitous replies to questions, Rona fell about. We discussed the tat of Variety Club awards etc. When I said 'I'm unfashionable at the moment' Gordon said 'You'll never be unfashionable. You're always being quoted. Thoroughly authentic.' He gave me some Schubert Trios at the end of the evening with a lovely note. What a dear friend he has always been to me.

Thursday, 17 February
Peter said 'You really must think about doing something in the theatre' and said it had got around that I was difficult 'to fit into a company' etc. etc. I told him James Roose-Evans had suggested 'An Evening With' and he thought it was a v. good idea.

Saturday, 19 February
C. came and we drove to his flat. Harry came. He refused wine and held up his glass 'Another vod dear please!' and by the end of the meal he was almost inarticulate: 'You see my dears I love Larry Grayson my dears because he sort of stays within his own character my dears, if

---

2 b.1935. Playwright, author and journalist. 'The Anno Domini Interview', conducted by Colin Morris.

you know what I mean. Oh my dears, I'm putting this very badly but my dears, he doesn't ever do what is *alien* to him! You see my dears . . . he's always rather *cosy* . . . my dears . . . of course I saw him years ago in this drag show at the Stratford Bow Theatre Royal . . . my dears he was a very polished music hall artist. Very polished he was.' Later on he said 'I once knew a mute my dears. My dears he was *beautiful*! oh! really beautiful my dears! He was always in the Golden Lion my dears. I adored him my dears. He was lovely . . . used to write everything down on paper!' C. said 'Such as: that'll be eighteen quid for the night?' 'Oh no my dears! Nothing like that! He was charming . . .' But the laugh had been established & we were all giggling. C. drove him home at 12.15 & I saw him in. He kept saying 'My dear I'm not drunk' but couldn't put the key in the lock.

Sunday, 20 February

We saw 'Scars on Sunday' with Gielgud reading bits from the Bible and a host of idiots singing silly songs and Eartha Kitt looking more mournful than any comparable occasion could demand. This programme is only describable in Ruth Pitter's poem about the Wreaths In The Factory Yard.[3] *That* says the truth about it.

Monday, 21 February

I walked to James Roose-Evans and we put down some biographical stuff on paper in order to start the sketching out of 'An Evening'. Got about four pages down. James said 'You just talk & I can type a lot of stuff down . . .' In the middle of it he lost the H key. It fell off. He rattled the machine to find it. I do like him I must say. He says we must go thro' the whole period & then weed out the deadwood or add gloss to stuff already noted. It is an exhausting task and not unlike psychoanalysis.

Tuesday, 22 February

Up at 7.30 with this filthy church bell crashing. Loathsome sound. It don't feel like a birthday to me. It feels like *doom*. At the [Equity] Council meeting in the afternoon, they all sang 'Happy Birthday To You' and I laughingly said 'Thank you for such a spontaneous outburst – it only confirms the enormous affection in which I'm held' and then rushed 'em into having coffee. Walked home feeling depressed, old, tired, and very near to tears. Isabel Dean gave me a marvellously funny birthday card. She is a dear person.

---

[3] 'Funeral Wreaths', collected in *Urania*, 1950. 'Mindless and pagan offering, wicked waste,/This is the efflorescence of godless toil,/Something that has no meaning, that has no taste,/Something that has no use but to cry aloud . . .' etc.

Thursday, 24 February
To James Roose-Evans. Told him I'd no stomach for the narcissism of the 'Evening With'. We talked about other ideas and I mentioned the trial of Charles the First and he was just as enthusiastic as I was.

Saturday, 26 February
Bills have arrived for the work done on the Hot Water Storage tanks. Got a cheque from Louie for her share; gone are the days when I easily handled *all* the bills. I went to Marylebone High Street and got waterproof bandages for Louie. An unshaven & dirty old man shouted at me: 'You ain't made any films lately 'ave you?' but I feigned deafness.

Friday, 4 March
Telephoned travel agent and he offered me 27 March to 12 April in Tenerife at 600 pounds. I owe it to Louie to take her away for a complete change of scene. She's been a prisoner in the flat since before Christmas & has endured awful pain and trouble.

Saturday, 5 March
Lunch with Louie. Very good oxtail. After, she said 'I must clean these chair covers & the settee, they're filthy!' so I got them off and did the bath bashing & she did the spin drying etc. We were both laughing & giggling a lot. Just the same as we did at 57 all those years ago! moving beds downstairs & laughing so much we were stuck helpless on the landing. Suddenly I think 'What if she's not there one day?' and everything goes utterly bleak & I start to cry.

Monday, 7 March
Talk about fortune in the descendant!! I think my star started waning in '72. It's really only recently started hitting me – the idea that I'm offered little or no employment in this country while, all around, the rubbish proliferates. Of course, I know that the Carry Ons used to be the mainstay: as long as they were there, I never had to worry about being unemployed. Ah well, if this situation persists, I will have to do either pantomime or summer season next year.

Friday, 11 March
Laurena rang: 'Will you go to Scotland for a TV show with Stanley B. & John S. & Peter Nichols?' I said yes. I must be mad. Later: I was. They telephoned to say that Baxter, Nichols and Schlesinger had backed out & I'm to go up there and do it on my own.

Sunday, 20 March

Tom rang at 10.30 saying 'Thought I'd better remind you to put your clocks forward' & I said I'd done that & was boiling the face flannel. He came over at 11.30 with *new car*!! Champagne coloured Chrysler. It is huge & richly upholstered: quite the grandest car! There was enough sun for drinks on the terrace where he casually dropped 'I'm having this police cadet . . . quite interesting' which intrigued me. As usual, T & C were attentive & kind to Louie.

Sunday, 27 March

Dreared about doing the packing & desperately trying to stave off the depression. Took off 45 minutes late. Plane was a huge roomy Tri Star with a super crew. At Tenerife we were put in a minibus, and told to wait while they collected the luggage. Just ten minutes later, a KLM jumbo crashed into a Pan Am jumbo and hundreds of people were killed.[4] All luggage handling stopped. We left with whatever *had* been collected & drove to Los Cristianos on the coast road. The courier said 'Don't worry, your luggage will come on afterwards by taxi.' I *knew* it was going to be disaster. Then we arrived. It's exactly as Stanley described it: 'Like the surface of the moon,' and what's more, the place is only half built. Everywhere is cement & building workers. I couldn't change or wash properly 'cos I've no bags. The stomach feels terrible & the head is banging with anger. Went up to bed feeling dirty, degraded & foul.

Tuesday, 29 March

Met Shirley and Ivor & we went for a stroll in the town (wind blew sand in our eyes & it was all rather nasty) where I found a hat for 2 pounds. We learned that the death toll at the airport is over 500 and that people are still dying from burns in hospital.

Friday, 1 April

We talked to some new arrivals, Neville and his chum, and several children. Louie saying 'Oh! we don't want all these kids round us' but I adore their company. Children never cease to fascinate & intrigue me.

Saturday, 2 April

Sat with Dot – Grandma to Michael & Tanya. They brought over Darren & his two sisters Susannah & Simone. Their mother is Ursula. They live at Golders Green. Simone said 'Mummy was from Germany

---

[4] The worst disaster in the history of civil aviation: 574 people were killed. The KLM Jumbo had not been cleared for take-off.

& worked as Daddy's secretary but then they started kissing after the day's work was done, you see . . .' Sat at the local bar with the children & gave them all tea. O! the joy of children! They are sheer bliss. Alas, all I ever do is spoil them.

Tuesday, 5 April

In the afternoon, played football with many children. One boy, Jens (from Denmark) was Captain on our side, and the other, Andrew (Scotland) Captain for the other side. Jens was superb. After, he even joined Tennis Elbow & was a sight more lively than the rest, except for a *tiny* little Scot called Nicholas, who was superb.

Wednesday, 6 April

Took the girls down to the town to get elastic for Tanya's hat. Returned to the hotel. Was lying in the bath when Louie banged & banged on my door & I thought it was an emergency so I rushed out of the bath to answer & slipped on wet tiled floor & hit the foot, cutting the toe (Big) and bruising the third toe. The pain was awful. Louie called me again! Would I take the telephone. It was a drunken woman: 'Hallo! It's Trish here! I was ten years on the Daily Mail so I'm not impressed by you . . .' It went on and on. Eventually I said 'If this is what you wanted to tell me, you needn't have bothered' & I put the receiver down. I limped down to dinner.

Friday, 8 April

Letter of apology from Trish about the phone call; but it's all basically resentful. She makes too much of everything.

Wednesday, 13 April

Disappointed to find nobody to meet me at Gatwick. Back in the flat by 6.30. What a stinking holiday! What a rotten, cheap and sordid affair it all was!

Thursday, 14 April

Eade on the phone: 'I do think you should do this "Night of 100 Stars" . . . I've had Delfont on the telephone about it . . . it is important that you should be *seen* . . . I can't keep telling people you're writing for Tatler . . .' Looks as if I'm lumbered. I received the letter inviting me to take part in this crap about 25 March. I chucked it in the waste paper basket. I suppose I'll have to retrieve it.

Saturday, 16 April

Suicide is caring about what other people think and is to do with pride. Suicide is about other people and self-pride. Suicide is caring about what other people think. Suicide is about caring. The 'not carers' go on living: badly.

Tuesday, 19 April
Attended the Equity meeting at Harley St. The voting results were given apropos the next Council. I am again in the top five. Gratifying. I was glad to know that Isabel Dean is in still.

Wednesday, 20 April
Letter from Equity asking if I wish to stand for the Executive. Tried writing a bit for this Jubilee show in May. Telephoned Stanley to ask if he was going to be in it. 'Certainly not,' he said shortly & told me 'You should stand for the Executive' so I wrote my decision & posted it.

Sunday, 24 April
Equity AGM at the Victoria Palace. Every motion of the Left was won. The majorities were averagely two to one and sometimes larger. At 5.30 I could stand no more of the long hair & dirty jeans brigade sprawling in the auditorium with their feet on the seats. I left.

Monday, 25 April
Denis Goacher Party. The place was packed. All literati. I met Peter Ackroyd[5] (Lit. Ed. Spectator) who said repeatedly 'You must come & lunch with us at the Spectator . . . it's great fun . . . why don't you write for us?' The persistence was so forceful that I wrote down the telephone number & said I would ring him. He kept saying 'Cross your heart! Let me see it . . .'

Sunday, 1 May
Tom came & they gave me lunch. We went into Priory Park and were talking when a boy approached us and Tom greeted him with affection & said 'Go round to Clive and have coffee with him . . . we'll be back later . . .' Afterwards I asked 'Why invite someone I don't know . . . I don't want to cope with strangers today . . . I thought I was invited to spend the day with you . . .' He said 'I don't wish to pursue this conversation. It is my house. I can do what I like in it . . . you've got a nerve . . . when I think of the number of times we've put up with Louie . . .' And then something snapped in me. Whatever my mother's shortcomings, I don't want to hear her spoken of as something you have to tolerate. I said aloud 'I

---

[5] b.1949. Novelist, biographer and critic.

wondered when *that* was coming' and after a silence I told him 'I think it's best if I shove off.' He said 'Oh! I knew you'd do that . . . I simply want to invite Albie to my house . . .' I said 'Well you can have him . . . I'll see you . . .' And walked away. Just past the clock tower I got a taxi. The driver said 'I thought you people spent your holidays in the South of France.' I thought 'I wish that's where I was right now.'

Monday, 2 May

B. rang. He said 'I understand you and Tom had words.' I told him I'd written apologising, but only in the cause of social harmony. I won't take Louie to that house again.

Thursday, 5 May

Walked to B.H. for the John Browell party. Con Mahoney[6] made a v.g. speech and J.B. was on form with a witty reply: 'Difficult following a comic . . .' I talked with Roy Hudd: 'Codron asked me to take over from you in *Fat Friend* . . . I told him no way . . .'

Saturday, 7 May

I feel quite peaceful and unworried. It is odd. One minute I'm thinking I'll never act again, and then I don't bother about it at all – I have faith in my ability & think that something will turn up – the entire thing changes. Sad to read in the papers about Maureen Pryor dying. She was a warm impulsive girl & very talented. It said that she was in great pain towards the end.

Sunday, 8 May

To N. Acton. We went thro' all the songs.[7] The real work is on Roy Castle who copes v. well! Lance, David Wood, me & Toni do the rest. Toni Arthur is sweet, and Sally Gilpin v. kind but O! these bloody steps! Roy told us a v. funny account of Tommy Cooper who was doing a routine with a walking stick which inadvertently dropped thro' a hole in the stage: he was left with nothing to finish the act! He told Roy 'But I did a brilliant ad-lib!' & Roy asked 'What was that?' Tommy said 'I pissed off.' It's marvellous how Roy casts himself for the feed in his stories. He has a lovely ingenuousness which is most endearing.

---

[6] Then Head of Light Entertainment, Radio.

[7] The (BBC TV) show was 'Let's Make a Musical', starring Roy Castle, with Toni Arthur, Joe Brown, Lance Percival, KW, David Wood. 'Roy and the team tell the story and sing some of the songs from the musical *Pickwick*.'

Friday, 13 May

I'm still amazed at the comparative unreadiness of the cast. I enjoy the rehearsals v. much and love the chats over lunch.

Sunday, 15 May

It was a day of dreary tedium. The Pickwickian Quartet went wrong *every time*. Eventually they accepted a take containing errors or fluffs. Every one of the foursome went wrong somewhere. Roy was quietly cheerful & gentle throughout. No question but that it was a lovely team. Yet, to this day, I don't understand why I was cast in it! As a production it didn't need me. At the end, I couldn't face seeing any of them & I quickly disappeared.

Monday, 16 May

Tom phoned. 'Nothing to say really . . . it's all v. dreary . . . people's morale is low . . . voices trail away into silence . . .' I agreed. The mind is now preoccupied with the 'spot' for the 100 Stars rubbish on Sunday. Peter E. rang. 'Would you like to go to Hampstead to see a girl in a play whom Helen M. thinks is another Maggie?' & I said yes. It was called *Abigail's Party*.[8] I saw only one half. It was one of those pieces put together with impromptu dialogue & depicted the empty vacuous nature of suburban life. All very 'lifelike' but alas, one goes to the theatre to see an artist's *vision of life* not the actual mess. The audience was frightful. Hampstead sophisticates knowingly laughing at all the bad taste lines 'Oh! a bottle of Beaujolais! How lovely! I'll just pop it in the fridge . . .' and they fell about, loving their superiority. The girl (à la Maggie) was v. good.

Saturday, 21 May

At 8 o'c. I walked to the National Theatre – it's like a terrible municipal housing estate & is nothing to do with *theatre*. The 'Rustics'[9] rehearsed v. badly. After the stagger thro' on the stage, we found a rehearsal room where precious time was lost with Ron Moody arguing about how Wall (Brian Rix) should put the fingers out. That Inman creature said to me 'We'd all better learn the words of "Hello Dolly".' Richard Goolden you can't hear, Charlie Drake you can't hear, Bernard Bresslaw was absent! Oh dear! it augurs ill for the night.

Sunday, 22 May

I'm going over the lines in my head all the time. When it came to the show, I got thro' the Shakespearean bit fairly; but my own spot,

---

[8] By Mike Leigh, b.1943. His wife Alison Steadman played the lead role.
[9] From *A Midsummer Night's Dream*.

after a shaky start, got a few laughs, and I wasn't left omelette sur le visage. I had a quick drink with Helen Ryan & Patrick Allen & then left. When I told them I thought our stuff would be cut out of the [televised] show, Patrick said 'Not with all those *names* old boy! It's a v. good line-up for the TV Times; they won't waste that.'

Thursday, 26 May

To the Savile Club where I met John Curtis of Weidenfeld & Nicolson. He wants me to have a go at an account of the career in light hearted fashion, and suggests I send him a chapter as a sample. I think it's a daunting task but I suppose I should attempt it. To bed at 10.40. This book is v. much on my mind. I think the reproof about irresponsibility undermining authority from Basil Hodges should be the starting point. He was trying to teach me a lesson I have never learned.

Wednesday, 1 June

The letters include one from CHE, the homosexual group for Equality: asking me to talk to them! Heaven knows what about!

Thursday, 2 June

Peter Eade at 10.30. He's been sent a film script for me,[10] written by Peter Cook and Dudley Moore, offering me the part of Sir Henry. It made me laugh out loud: some of it is v. funny.

Sunday, 5 June

In the evening I watched 'Night Of A Hundred Stars' with Louie. The entire 'Rustics' episode was *cut*, and so was my compere bit. The whole thing *gone*. They must have thought it was terrible. Of course my first reaction was disappointed hurt, and then I reflected that I should have obeyed my first instinct and not taken part in the spurious rubbish. Ah well, it's an insult I'll just have to swallow.

Monday, 6 June

Sat & sat for hours, staring into space, and smoking cigarettes, desperately trying to think what to write about the period after Bicester. Read the '42 diary but little of it was any help to me.

Tuesday, 7 June

Everything seems utterly bleak to me and all these Jubilee celebrations malapropos; in a time of economic recession, the Queen should have set an example of austerity: thousands of pounds wasted on processions and bonfires, which could have been used for better purposes.

---

[10] *The Hound of the Baskervilles*, very freely adapted from the Conan Doyle original.

Went in to Louie at 10.30 to see the impressive State procession from the palace to St Paul's. It was superbly stage-managed and the crowds ecstatically enthusiastic for the Queen. She did a walk-about afterwards, thro' the City to Guildhall and her good-humoured composure & painstaking consideration for the spectators was extraordinarily moving. We opened a bottle of champagne & had lunch, watching the glittering spectacle on television.

Friday, 10 June
Typed the rest of what I'd pencilled out & it comes to 12 pages, so I've got much further to go before I reach the 20. Trouble is, I've no objectivity. Once the stuff is set down I think it's wonderful. I went to John Wood studios to do v/o for the chimpanzees in PG Tips commercials. The director said 'I wanted you ages ago: I had a sequence especially arranged for you but they said you'd never do a chimp's voice.' I told him 'What nonsense! I've always found these commercials funny!'

Saturday, 11 June
I should get on with the writing but I sit full of erotic thoughts instead: heaven knows what starts this off. I fancy all kinds of ludicrous situations with disciplinary strictures. Cut this excerpt from a piece in the TLS, about Havelock Ellis.[11] I remember being impressed, years ago, by his analysis of the homosexual problem, and his 3 cycles explanation of the developing periods in the growing male. I don't think I've ever come upon anything better than this latter, in terms of a reasonable account of what is apparently abnormal. But then I suppose I'm bound to be pleased with it. This excerpt about 'the best results' states a position which I've consciously adopted all my life. I wonder if 'the best result' is really the right phraseology? Perhaps it should read 'the most convenient compromise.'

Monday, 13 June
John Wood Studio. The director (Bernard) of the PG Tips had me doing a 'David Frost' type voice & an amended version of Friday's work. Dubbing the chimps is a dreadful task because their mouth formations are totally at variance with human speech patterns. One can only hit it occasionally & it's largely by accident. If I were rich I'd say no to this work. Kenneth Connor does them, and Hugh Paddick and Irene Handl. Today, there was Miriam Margolyes!

---

[11] Henry Havelock Ellis (1859–1939), sexologist. In a 1913 article, 'Sexual Problems, Their Nervous and Mental Relations', Ellis had written: 'Much the best result seems to be attained for the Congenital invert, as modern society is constituted, when,

Tuesday, 14 June
Writing about Dehra Dun,[12] I was surprised, by my record of the dates, to find that I arrived in Bombay on V.E. Day and was in Dehra Dun for V.J. Day.

Friday, 17 June
To Lime Grove for 'Tonight' programme. A panel of Anti-Smokers with me as the odd man out. Brian Rix (him again!) was nastily abusive about my 'stinking rooms out with your tobacco fumes' & M. Karlin did her 'You're talking rubbish' bit. I shouldn't have appeared on the thing at all.

Monday, 20 June
Eade telephoned and said 'They want you to play Sir Henry after all, they can't get Hawtrey. Will you leave me to do the deal? They are trying it on at the moment with Carry On salaries. I think we should try to get them to fix transport.' I said a fervent yes to that.

Tuesday, 21 June
Peter E. phoned and said: 'I've fixed your contract for the film. I've got you 7½ and a car!' and I admitted it was better than anything I'd got before. The first bit of good news for a long long time.

Thursday, 23 June
I did the letters and went to the chemist, where the owner was serving me with shampoo when I railed against the inefficient post office nearby: 'They're all crooks and wogs in there!' and turned to find a huge negro behind me. So much for National Front sympathisers.

Sunday, 26 June
Walked to the Paris in the evening to do 'Quote Unquote' for John Lloyd. The team was Peter Cook, Irene Handl, Richard Ingrams and me. Irene Handl told me 'I'm very frightened of you because you *know everything*' and Peter Cook on the way to the pub: 'I was frightened of you during the revue days! Let's face it, I still am.' Goodness knows why anyone should think me formidable! John Lloyd said 'Irene told

---

while retaining his own ideas, or inner instincts, he resolves to forgo alike the attempt to become normal and the attempt to secure the grosser gratification of his abnormal desires.'

[12] In the Himalayan foothills.

me she found your nostrils daunting.' Yes well, I can't help the physiognomy.

Monday, 27 June

Michael came & drove me to the Chepstow for this talk to CHE. The room was packed. There was a lot of sniping from a journalist called Robin something about me stereotyping 'limp queens' & giving the public an erroneous image etc. etc. and a dreadful boy who got v. emotional & said 'It's people like you that get queers spat on!' I said 'People spat on Oscar Wilde before I was born' whereupon his friend cried out 'Oh! you change the subject very cleverly! You always skirt the real issues!' Somebody then shouted 'Why don't you give us your support at the forthcoming trial at the Old Bailey when Gay News is being prosecuted by Mary Whitehouse?' I said 'I need notice of that question. I know nothing about this case' as indeed I don't.*

*Apparently a Professor Kirkup[13] has written a homosexual poem about a centurion and Christ. It sounds banal & pathetic.

Wednesday, 29 June

To Wig Specialities. Peter Cook & Dudley and Paul Morrissey[14] were there. All v. friendly. Dudley seemed subdued. 'You've heard I'm playing Watson Welsh?' & I said 'Yes, it sounds great fun.' I'd forgotten he was so tiny. Paul M. said 'If you can think of any funny lines, let me know.' Then they fitted me for the bald wig & then the other wig.

Sunday, 3 July

I finished typing the piece for Punch. I don't think it is what William Davis really wants, so I've sent a letter saying: 'If you find this unsuitable, just post it back to me.'

Monday, 4 July

Script conference with Peter C., Dudley M., Irene Handl, Max Wall, and Paul Morrissey. Peter Cook reiterated: 'Sir Henry must be very mild and vulnerable . . . be careful you don't get that *edge* into your voice . . .' It's ludicrous the way he and Dudley talk about *truth in characterisation* the whole time, 'cos the script contains a mass of inconsistencies. They object to 'law enforcement' and 'twit' because 'it's not right for the period' but they've written a line: 'Good evening &

---

[13] James Kirkup, b.1923. Recreation in *Who's Who*: 'standing in shafts of moonlight'. *Gay News* was fined £1000 on 11 July, in the last blaspheny trial (at the time of writing) to be held in the United Kingdom.

[14] b.1939. American director in 'underground' idiom, e.g. with Andy Warhol, engaged to direct *Hound of the Baskervilles*.

welcome & piss off' which isn't right for Baskerville Hall either. The seriousness with which everyone sits around discussing the merit of this word or that word for inclusion in this hotch-potch of rubbish is the sort of thing Cook would have ridiculed in his undergraduate days.

Thursday, 7 July

I went to Dr Wilkinson who did the medical check-up for the film *Hound of the Baskervilles*. He said 'I last saw you in '61 for *One Over The Eight*' and I remembered him. When I told him *then* about my suicidal thoughts he said 'You are a bad risk.'

Saturday, 9 July

A rejection from Punch who've returned my piece. I shall have nothing more to do with them.

Monday, 11 July

I tried to learn some of the Carry On linking material which arrived this afternoon but Oh! it is dismal stuff.

Tuesday, 12 July

Left at 8 o'c. for Pinewood. Barbara was looking v. fit and was full of good spirits: she's lovely to work with. We altered a lot of the script and made it much more workable. The work was gruelling because there was no let-up – since we're the only ones in it, we're on camera all the time – and the endless set-ups continually demand your presence.

Wednesday, 13 July

I was surprised watching the rushes today. I looked very good, the light blue summer suit photographed well, the lighting was excellent, and the projection room looked very good. The whole thing looked stylish and smart. Of course the dialogue is lousy a lot of the time, but the look and the manner are OK. Critics will say 'tired, laboured, unfunny' etc. but it don't matter, and I do need the money.

Monday, 18 July

Car at 9 o'c. and we were at Bray in 40 minutes. It is a rambling & derelict house with dirt, decay & cobwebs everywhere. I talked with Paul Morrissey & John Goldstone[15] & then Peter & Dudley came up. Peter cried 'Hello, you camp Ada!' which completely threw me, but

---

[15] Producer of *Baskervilles*, and of later British film comedies, e.g. *Carry On Columbus* (1992).

I repeated it gaily adding 'Yes!' Then I went to make-up and they fashioned the bald wig, the alopecia wig & then the toupee. I was home by 3.30.

Tuesday, 19 July
We picked up Irene Handl at 7 o'c. She chattered away to me and to Beulah (the chihuahua) all the time. Boundless energy. We started off with the scene where Mrs Barrymore shows us into the attic room. Irene was rather halting & her work didn't have great flow (as I'd expected) & Paul went again and again. I find Dudley's Welsh accent hilarious & I'm doing it myself!! all the time. I must stop it 'cos it can be v. irritating for him. Don't care for Peter's voice – curiously muted Jewish – don't know *why* he's saddled himself with such a rotten sound.

Thursday, 21 July
Peter Cook said on the phone: 'John Goldstone & Dudley & I agree that Paul has made you do things which are over the top and bogus & we must put it right . . . I want this picture to be really good . . . Dudley & I have had a row with Paul about it . . . but he was the only one at the rushes who was laughing at your stuff . . .' He certainly threw me for six.

Friday, 22 July
All of it seemed to go well. Talked with Peter most of the day. Dudley joined us in a discussion about Faith & he said 'I've always felt that the world was a threatening place' & when I said 'Most people feel that,' he replied 'No! I know some people who've had quite a happy childhood & they've grown up with tremendous generosity & are naturally affectionate, giving people . . . I don't go with the argument about talent accompanying neurosis . . .' At the end of the day Peter asked me to rushes. I saw myself for the first time. The character looks *other* than me. It's a good wig and the alopecia is convincing. The moments when I stay in character are good . . . the odd bits (snorting etc.) when I don't, are bogus. The whole film looks lavish & expensive. P.C. gave me drinks & brought me home in his car. His conversation is infectiously good humoured & enthusiastic. Lovely fellow.

Monday, 25 July
I talked to Peter a lot in the morning & he was funny about the Sitwells – 'That was all they could do: sit well. That Sir Several told Edith to stay stationery. They used her for stationery. They actually wrote on her . . . wonderful woman . . . she could rhyme anything! When they gave her *Sitting here upon my bottom* she straightway replied

with *Always wondering how I got 'em* & she brought the house down. They left her in the rubble. She couldn't get out. She was stationery you see . . .'[16]

Tuesday, 26 July

None of it was quick work. Max Wall put in 'fish & chips' instead of 'fried potatoes' & we had to go all over again. Dudley came on as Mrs Holmes and was v. funny indeed. He suddenly bashed me with his handbag & said 'I saw you looking at my breasts!' & I could hardly keep a straight face. There was an interview with Owen from the E. Standard – 'Is this another Carry On?' O! the questions they ask.

Wednesday, 27 July

I met Terry-Thomas (whose scene was next) and thought 'Hallo! this one ain't going to know a line.' He was shaking visibly & someone said it was Parkinson's Disease[17] but it looks like a touch of your geriatrics as well. Rather frightening. The more I see of John Goldstone the more I like him. I like him so much it's almost unhealthy. Love it when I can make him laugh. I do, quite often. *And* Paul. He laughs at me. Today he was crying when I demonstrated Charlie and the rejection of the request for blow waves in the shop.[18] Peter E. phoned: 'Are you enjoying the film?' I told him: 'It is marvellous – everyone is lovely and I have never been treated better in my life' and he said 'Well, I've never heard you speak so enthusiastically before!'

Tuesday, 2 August

I talked to P.C. most of the time. 'Edith Sitwell became an enormous *cult*. The papers built her up. She wasn't aware of the size of her cult 'cos she was absorbed by her Art. She didn't notice the cult at all. It was the same with Sir Several Sitwell. He was a huge cult . . .' etc. etc. Joan Greenwood is a delightful person & a great sport. I like her very much I must say. About 10.10 the telephone rang: 'This is John Goldstone, we are not shooting tomorrow because Paul Morrissey has got hepatitis and he must rest for a few days . . .'

Wednesday, 3 August

Rang hairdressing (Henry Watts) and they said 'We have closed that department down for good . . .' So that is the end of *over 20 years* of

---

16 The real Sitwells behind this fantasy were Dame Edith (1887–1964) and Sir Sacheverell (1897–1988).

17 It was.

18 KW's father 'did their hair *his* way', resisting particularly any change of colour: 'You can't improve on nature. You ought to know that. You're old enough and ugly enough' (*Just Williams*).

a relationship and I wasn't even informed! Went to the Blood Donor Centre and donated at 10 o'c.

Friday, 5 August
To Audley Square, where everyone gathered to watch 63 minutes of what has been shot so far on *Hound of the Baskervilles*. It was all rather depressing. Again & again in this script, I've thought 'That is hilarious' yet the fact remains, there is nothing hilarious in any of the stuff I saw in the cinema today. It looked as if cues weren't being taken up with enough expertise & there are certain bits (the sex-talk between Holmes & Watson, and the one-legged man) which don't really belong to the story at all. Tried writing more of the biog. Extraordinary to read in the '52 journal about the desire to die: it occurs quite a lot.

Tuesday, 9 August
My mind is full of travel ideas; must try to book something for Louie & me, at Christmas. It would be good to get away from all that holiday rubbish. To Peter Eade. Met a man there about Brooke Bond coffee TV commercial. Have to do a v/o for client approval. P.E. said Helen Montagu is leaving Tennent's!

Saturday, 13 August
The news was all about riots in Lewisham where the Left attacked the National Front March & the police were overwhelmed as in the Grunwick dispute, with several men in hospital after vicious attacks. The Left always finds the thugs.

Saturday, 20 August
A postcard from T & C. They're in Barcelona. I replied in friendly fashion, but don't want to get too involved up there any more.

Monday, 5 September
Paul Morrissey is *very lucky* to be able to complete under good conditions the scene he left August 2nd!!! It was great good fortune.

Wednesday, 7 September
P. Eade phoned with yet another 'big television commercial . . . I'm asking 25 thousand . . .' There have been a couple of these for the last 5 years. He has mentioned not only Brooke Bond, Rumbelow's & Creda, but also Timex watches, the Post Office and Cinzano. All of them came to nothing. Since I don't want to be linked (in the public mind) with any commercial (visual) I don't care, but I am sick of the continual overtures which begin with such rosy heraldings and then come to nothing.

Monday, 12 September
I talked with P.C. & he was hilarious as a French director with an appalling accent discussing the filming. O! he does make me laugh. Apropos Dudley Moore living in California he said 'It's the space you see . . . he loves the space . . . Californians have a lot of space . . . most of it's between their ears . . .' and I fell about.

Wednesday, 14 September
Letter from John Curtis of Weidenfeld saying that the writing is OK!!! and they want me to continue with it!! I am v. pleased I must say.

Friday, 16 September
At the studios we did the falling in the Marsh Pool. I was relieved to find I was excluded! Joan Greenwood, Denholm Elliott & Lucy Griffiths & Hugh Griffith & Dana (& eventually Terry-Thomas) were all put in. H.G. so pissed that he kept reeling over & floating & crying out 'Oh! for fuck's sake shoot the bloody thing!' The heat was atrocious.

Tuesday, 20 September
Denholm Elliott told me 'Peter Cook paid you a great compliment . . . he said today that you were a great raconteur . . . better than Ustinov . . .' I brushed it all aside with 'Yes, well one is always in the mood with Peter' 'cos I simply can't take praise at all. Apart from being alone with a written compliment.

Friday, 23 September
P.C. said stay for lunch at the Crown in Bray. I had far too much to drink & we drove back to the Old House and suddenly P.C. started this 'You're wanted on the set for another shot of you & the dog' stuff, and he and Charles Knode pushed me into some stables & pulled my clothes off. It was like some daft sort of public schoolboy cruelty and had a curiously sinister undertone. I was shoved in front of the camera and Paul kept giving me directions about kissing the dog, but it was all rather perfunctory & I could see a lot of people giggling expectantly & I suddenly realised they were hoping I would make a drunken exhibition of myself. Eventually I was released & got the car home. At the flat he woke me up & said 'You've been asleep & snoring all the way!'

Saturday, 8 October
Saw Louie for a meal & we waited up to see 'Parkinson' till 11.30. Desmond Morris was boring & Diana Dors was like some barmaid, and

I looked like an imitation of Lord Clark.[19] It was badly photographed & the lack of flow in conversation plus fearful interruptions & upstaging from D.D. made it all fragmentary. No marks for a very bad try.

Thursday, 20 October
I went to De Lane Lea to do *one line* in a Heineken lager ad. I did about 50 takes. Producer Roy Collins said 'Write something philosophical for my book' so I penned the Lytton quote from Richelieu. Walked home reflecting that a year which began horribly is turning out v. well.

Monday, 24 October
B. mentioned T & C on the telephone & I suddenly realised how much they'd receded from my thoughts! It's true that I'm not really a gregarious creature at all. On some occasions I'm stimulated & delighted by company but nowadays I *never* feel I *need* it. Years ago I would telephone someone out of sheer loneliness but I haven't done that for about ten years. I'm content to be solitary.

Friday, 28 October
The news announces that this Baader-Meinhof gang[20] have again started more thuggery: they've kidnapped a Dutch millionaire. So the mess goes on. All the warnings have been in vain. Some of my earliest diaries have got entries about the terrors that would be unleashed as a result of disbelief. The world of the agnostics/atheists is a cruel and comfortless one. Not only are the neighbour's goods coveted, they're actually stolen: and the neighbour is murdered. And all without passion. It's done coldly, sickeningly . . . as mindless as the Manson horrors.[21]

Sunday, 6 November
Equity SGM. The moderates defeated the reds on every issue except the creation of a [voting] box for 2 Councillors representing Fringe Theatre (whatever that means) and I spoke against this. My speech ended with 'Specialisation means that everyone becomes better & better at less and less and eventually someone will be superb at fuck-all.' The intemperate language was dreadful & I felt rather – no – very ashamed.

---

[19] Desmond Morris, b.1928, observer of animal and human behaviour. Diana Dors (1931–84), actress. Kenneth Clark (1903–83), art historian.
[20] German terrorists. Andreas Baader had been jailed for life in April.
[21] Charles Manson, American multiple murderer jailed indefinitely in March 1971.

Tuesday, 8 November

It is amazing now to look back at an entry like January 10th in this volume & realise the extent of my former depression, and *low fortune*. What you've got to do in England is *wait*. Most of the time it's essential to wait and do nothing while you're waiting, apart from pretending that you're not waiting.

Saturday, 12 November

Got to B.H. at 10 o'c. for rehearsal of 'The Inquest',[22] a theological piece about Heaven in which I'm playing Azrael, the angel of death. Rest of the cast were extraordinarily mediocre. Saw the British Legion service at the Albert Hall, attended by the Queen. The display of all the Services was impressive & curiously moving . . . the sight (in the community singing) of young servicemen sitting on the floor with their song sheets . . . all looking relaxed as children at a party & unselfconscious . . . made me want to cry. The bishops & the priests trooped in with their awful *intoning* and put paid to *that*. One isn't moved by prayers spoken like railway platform announcements.

Sunday, 13 November

To B.H. I heard a bit of my own stuff, on the playback, & it was embarrassingly pedantic delivery lacking in spontaneity & truth.

Monday, 21 November

Central line to N. Acton. I don't know anyone in the cast,[23] apart from a girl called Julie (who was in *Carry On Cleo!*) but they're all helpful. Sally Gilpin is doing the movement & of course I'm dreadful at it.

Thursday, 24 November

We did a run-thro' of everything. Saw dear Ronnie Barker up there & congratulated him on his v. funny 'letter from prison' to Richard Beckinsale which was on TV last night. It ended 'Good luck & good fortune in all that you do. And those you have done . . .'

Saturday, 26 November

At one point in the dressing room I thought 'What am I doing here? I am virtually acting as a crowd artist in some scenes! And as set-dressing in others!' Johnny Morris[24] told me he felt much the same thing: 'One agrees to do these things for friends but one begins to wonder what the professional limits *are*!' I agree with him. If Alan

---

[22] By Stuart Jackman. Broadcast under the title 'Post Mortem'.

[23] Of 'The All-Star Record Breakers', a children's TV show compered by Roy Castle.

[24] b.1916. Naturalist, traveller and broadcaster.

Russell asks me to do any of this kind of thing again, I shall stipulate that the 'join in the team' stuff is *out* as far as I'm concerned: for the simple reason that I'm *not* part of a team. I'm something better. Roy (Castle) said 'Thanks for being in it and for all the laughs' and *he* makes everything worth while.

Sunday, 4 December
Geoffrey Cannon has written saying he doesn't want me to write for R.T. any more 'cos he's getting a new list of writers: I feel indignation tempered with relief. It was always a chore.

Thursday, 8 December
Peter rang me. 'Gerald is sending the script of *Carry On Emmanuelle* to see if there's anything you want to play . . .'

Monday, 12 December
I started watching 'Panorama' (it was about Prisoners of Conscience) and I suddenly felt I couldn't face any more of this documentary moralising. Switched to Beryl Reid who was superbly entertaining throughout. She's got all the requirements for stand-up comedy *and* she can be a comedienne as well. I was laughing out loud several times, and I can't remember that happening since Alan King at the Palladium. It's the daring element in them both (perilously near to desperation) which I'm drawn to & which I admire.

Monday, 19 December
Gerald Thomas gave me lunch. He talked to me about the *Carry On Emmanuelle* script; it sounds pretty dirty. 'We really miss old Sid James,' he said, 'he was cuddly & warm' (you could have fooled me) 'and there are so few like him.' Then he saw Jimmy Tarbuck at another table and said 'He's got that quality!' & I said 'Yes! he *is* cuddly & warm & I think he's smashing . . .'

Tuesday, 20 December
Went in to see Louie. It was dreadfully remiss of me, but I completely forgot that it was her *birthday* today!! But as I told her 'The Tenerife holiday is my present to you' so I'd thought ahead.

Wednesday, 21 December
The take off was at 10.30. While we were having the drinks Louie said 'It is all going beautifully isn't it? I do think Laker's are good!' and then the pilot said 'I'm having to put down at Faro 'cos there isn't enough fuel.' Got to Tenerife at about 4.45. The air here is balmy & the temperature in the 80's.

Saturday, 24 December

Louie brought a great crowd with her, including Alan (B'ham jeweller) & his mother & wife & friends, and Mark and Bobbie. I actually found myself stupidly saying to Alan's wife 'Your Birmingham accent is *awful* . . . such ugly sounds . . .' and she said to Mark: 'You look very Jewish, don't you?' which he smilingly ignored, thank goodness. It was all rather weird with moments of sheer amiability interspliced with inane rudeness.

Sunday, 25 December

Went down to dinner prepared to sneer at their 'Gala Dinner' and was utterly confounded. They laid on a superb evening and in the end, with paper hats & silly disguises, everyone became absurdly & childishly happy. I sat with the Swedish family for a bit, & with a Welsh family, and with a mad pop group manager. I became fearfully drunk, I was dancing with all kinds of people . . . eventually *fell* into bed.

Tuesday, 27 December

We went for a coffee to a café on the front: there were six of us. We sat chatting & (since it seemed imminent) I said 'I hate being told stories because I tell them better than anyone else & I dislike it when people try to *top* me . . .' After that, there was no competition. Ken's Joan said 'Of course you hate yourself, don't you?' & everybody laughed. Strolled back by 12 o'c. and went up to the room for traditional activity.

Wednesday, 28 December

There's no doubt about it, I'm ever conscious about tradiola: it's either positive desire or vague undercurrents but it's always there. One tries to rise above it, but Nature is disinterested in rationalisation & tranquil life styles. O! what a bane it all is. Cleaned my teeth, used the Oraldene & went to bed full of hope for the ludicrous & unlikely event.

Saturday, 31 December

In a way, holidays reveal the worst side of human vanity & I'm suicidal today. Lunch with Vojtek & Margaret & Joan & Ken & after, we went back to terrace where the wind was blowing over iron chairs, tables & goodness knows what. Joan told us that she'd been told that the wig lady & son are really husband & wife, adding 'Now I've heard everything!' and Ken said 'Well now it can come out! Joan's my mother!' & we all fell about but Joan threw a shoe at him. Dinner at 7.30. I was pestered for autographs, photographs, dances, & heaven knows what not. At about 1.30 I thought 'I can't stand another minute of it!' and fled.

1978

Sunday, 1 January
We left Tenerife in blazing sunshine, in London it is cooler, but not freezing. My flat smelled of *dustiness.* Tomorrow I must get up early and clean it.

Sunday, 8 January
We saw the *Carry On Abroad* film which was made in '72 & I noticed that there were quite a few cuts! It wasn't at all bad considering the circumstances but the cast reminded one how unlovely the actors were. Not a dish to be seen. Kenny Connor was wonderfully diverting: he always has something singular to offer & this performance was delightful. Nobody else was v. good, apart from Joan Sims in the bed sequence and the pub, both v. authentic. I was all faces & jerks and *old* looking. The only thing (ironically) I did that was funny was manipulate the exploding switchboard.

Friday, 27 January
Watched Gordon in 'The Professionals'.[1] Now, he's my friend & I've never seen him do anything that wasn't truthful but this role doesn't work for him. Usually his work seems effortless but this part makes him look laborious: he seems to be *working* at it. The writing is the sort of stuff which is banal enough to require great bravura delivery (à la Kojak or Stratford Johns) and the nearest Gordon gets to that is to shout. No wonder he told me he was unhappy in the series.

Saturday, 28 January
So sick of worrying about this *book* that I've written to John Curtis saying I'm going to drop the idea. The task is daunting and I can't see any intrinsic *worth* in it. There are loads of readable books about actors: who wants another?

---

[1] Paramilitary crime-busting LWT series in which Jackson played the supposedly hard-nosed taskmaster of the action men, Bodie and Doyle.

Monday, 30 January
Oh! I don't know, everything conspires against me! No work, the awful weather, the threat of strikes (latest is the oil-men delivering), my failing eyesight . . . I've an appointment with oculist Dr Green at Curry & Paxton on Wednesday. When I consider suicide I think 'How would Louie manage?' and that stops me, but I remember James Mossman and he chose that way after his mother had gone. I went in to Louie at about 5.30. I was so downhearted I could hardly speak.

Wednesday, 1 February
Dr Green tested my eyes. He said 'Your long vision is good, 6 out of 6, you could drive Concorde . . . but for reading you need glasses.'

Monday, 6 February
Peter [Eade] took me to Lariana. Peter talked about the anathema of the night-club in the basement of his flats. All flats provide aggravation of some kind or other. Then the subject comes round to the S/M scene . . . Oh! I've heard it all before. The despair was *welling* up inside me & I kept thinking of Eliot's 'Find a face to meet the face . . .' Just about managed it. To the flat at 11.15. There was a fantasy session but largely for therapy: no real hunger. And it was enormously successful.

Saturday, 18 February
I walked with Louie to the Paris for 'J.A.M.' There was a crowd at the studio and I was amazed! It was a *filthy* night. The show was: Clement, June Whitfield, Peter Jones. I did the usual shouting & bawling. On 'Paper Tearing' I said 'I know nothing about this apart from doing it in the lavatory . . .' & there was a big laugh. Oh! what one will stoop to, in order to make them giggle! Got to the block at 7.30 & noticed a man in a camel hair coat, dark, about 35/40 leaving the block & smoking a cigar. Something clicked in my brain. The cigar in the passageway I found some weeks back. I went & looked there. Carefully placed in the corner were 3 bottles of drugs! Including Mandrax. Told Dunthorne.[2] He took them to the police.

Sunday, 19 February
Louie told me: 'The police came . . . a very nice Sergeant . . . he told me that the woman in 14 said those pills belonged to her! She was hiding them from her husband . . . he's had a nervous breakdown & tries to take more than he should.' Apparently she went to Dunthorne & he told her that I'd reported the drug find to the police & she went to the station & got them back again!

---

[2] Head Porter.

Tuesday, 14 March

Read the *Carry On Emmanuelle* script. It's all about a nymphomaniac who does it with all kinds of people in all kinds of situations & keeps taking the pill. The dénouement is that her one genuine lover switches placebos for the pill & she conceives. You begin with her wanking a Steward on the Concorde. I found it monotonous and unfunny. When you get to her having the PM, the Judge, the Commissioner of Police etc. etc. with no variations whatsoever, the credibility is gone & there's nothing *funny* to redeem it. It's so far away from the sort of story which a Carry On used to have. All this seems to do is to attempt to shock, whereas that element (as in *Nurse* etc.) was incidental to the story. Sadly, I'll have to turn it down: it's a sad business, 'cos Gerald & Peter have been good to me, but with a script like this, I've no option.

Wednesday, 15 March

Laurena telephoned: 'Peter Rogers rang & said that the script shouldn't have been sent to you . . . it's got to be amended & cut . . . you are not to judge it' & she said 'Gerald rang as well, and said that the nymphomania of the girl is really innocent & charming . . . & also that the money would be better than before . . .' Both reasons are specious.

Thursday, 30 March

Went to Eade to read the revised Carry On script. If anything, it's worse than before & the dialogue clumsy, inept and not a good joke anywhere. Peter said 'They are willing to pay you six thousand but if you want a car they will dock it from your salary.' I said no thanks, and told him 'Better settle for 5,750 and have *them* do the car at their expense.' I'm not having my money whittled away in such an unforeseeable fashion.

Sunday, 2 April

Walked to Gordon & Rona. We had tea & I told them about the artist who's done such a clever job on the huge advert in Gt. Portland Street of the baby holding Softex lavatory paper. A bubble has been added to the mouth, with the dialogue: 'Fuck this for a game of marbles: I'm joining the Anarchists.'

Monday, 10 April

Car came promptly & I was made up by Robin (who did *Baskervilles*) and on the set by 8.30. In the bedroom sequence, Gerald said to Suzanne Danielle 'Clutch one of the pillows to you . . . as if it were your lover!' & she did; it *made* her bit that much more assured & right

. . . just like the time he told Hattie (as Matron in *Doctor*) 'Run your hand along the rail to check for dust . . . as you are passing . . .' It's these seemingly small touches which are the bricks & mortar to a solid performance. I suggested several amendments to the script to Gerald, and he accepted them all. Even P. Rogers said 'Keep that in!' when I ad libbed 'How can I feel myself if I'm completely bent?'

Tuesday, 11 April
This girl, Suzanne Danielle, is very good. She came to my d/room & said 'Thank you for all the help you gave me on my first day of the film . . .' She is a kind & considerate girl.

Wednesday, 19 April
Got the papers. Saw the headlines 'Barbara Windsor says Carry On without Me' & realised that she's withdrawn from the film. At 8.25 the phone rang: 'This is the Evening News . . . could you comment on Barbara leaving your film? She says it is just pornography . . .' I thought 'Yes! so do I' but I said 'I've only just got out of bed! Ring me later!'

Wednesday, 26 April
Filthy letter from one of the investors: 'We came on the set and heard a repugnant sequence describing ways of having intercourse . . .' and asking *me* for assurances that it would not be pornographic 'as Miss Barbara Windsor alleges.' Thankfully, I handed it over to Peter Rogers & he dealt with it in a letter that was both firm and polite. What was horrid was the implicit accusation of hypocrisy: 'We have seen you talking about religion on television . . .' I'm amazed at Gerald passing some of the otiose dialogue we have to contend with. I keep thinking 'It wasn't as bad as this in the old days' & then I think again and admit 'Oh yes it was!'

Tuesday, 2 May
Another letter about the film being dirty! I replied 'I've been working on it for 3 weeks & I've not seen anything erotic yet!'

Wednesday, 3 May
Got to Pinewood to find Richard Burton in the D/room opposite!! plus his enormous Rolls-Royce outside. The assistant on his picture (*The Absolution*) told me: 'Richard wants to see you' but I had to go on the set.

Thursday, 4 May
Richard Burton came into my dressing room & I greeted him warmly.

He looked at me & said 'You're looking very fit . . . keeping yourself very *spare* . . .' I was in the PT kit & said 'Yes! it's ironic! I'm playing a keep-fit enthusiast & I've spent 52 years avoiding any kind of exercise.' He said 'Come into my room' & I met his wife & we sat talking. We went back over the years to Swansea, The Grand, *The Seagull*, my understudying him etc. and he told me about Hollywood and 'all these charity do's I have to attend . . . organised by stalwart matrons covered in rhinestones . . . no wonder I wanted a *drink*!' I said 'But you always played games & that compensates . . . you use a lot of energy playing games . . .' He smiled 'Oh yes, I went on playing games . . . I just played them *badly* . . .' He has a grave and urbane air now . . . like a man who is doing penance: there were lots of references to 'the Good Lord' and 'Heaven help us' in a quite serious vein. Couldn't stay with him long 'cos I was called on to the set.

Friday, 19 May

Peter E. left me a film script to read!! starts in July apparently!! It's called *Arabian Adventure* & I'm offered Khasim (a sort of sidekick to the Caliph).

Saturday, 20 May

I walked to Senate House in Malet St for 'Quote Unquote'. Met Kingsley Amis (delightful: kind & warm & generous) and Benny Green (effervescent & v. fluent) and Celia Haddon (author, journalist & charming) and when we filed into the hall we found the audience was in evening dress! We (in casual gear) looked incongruous! I knew none of the questions. The only source I got right was Gray! (They asked where 'Ignorance is bliss' came from, & I knew it was 'On A Distant Prospect of Eton College.'[3])

Monday, 29 May

I met Paul Richardson in the Rose Garden & we sat talking. A grey-haired sixty-year-old stripped to the waist told a mildly amusing story about a man coping with a plastic inflatable dummy lady (made by the Japanese for intercourse) 'I was just biting her neck when she suddenly farted & flew out of the window . . .' We laughed obligingly & there followed *another* . . . not so good . . . rather trying.

Sunday, 4 June

Left at 9.30 for the Shaftesbury and the SGM for the Branch & Delegate, New Rule Book Debate. It was acrimonious and nasty. There was the usual repeated accusation about 'this corrupt council,' and

---

[3] By Thomas Gray (1716–71).

cries of 'West End stars & elitism.' Dear Laurence Olivier sat there *throughout* and was a model of politeness & patience in spite of a nasty snide reference to him from the platform when John L. said 'Sitting here today is a man who was once my employer . . . a very noble man . . . but why has he never attended our meetings before? Why is he turning up only on this crucial day?' as if it were a crime not to be a busy little Union bureaucrat, instead of being one of the greatest actors of the era.

Monday, 5 June

I spoke to Laurence Olivier: 'I think it's splendid of you to come & sit thro' all this obscenity with such stoical patience' & he told me 'I wish my son, who wants to be an actor, could come and witness the spectacle for himself! Actually *see* what he wants to be a part of!' Eade telephoned at 4 o'c. asking me to *reconsider* the Arabian film!! 'The Carry Ons are finishing and these people will go on making films . . .' In other words: one employer is vanishing so grab a new one quickly: nothing to do with whether the work is right for me. I said no again. The idea of a turban wound right round my head drives me up the wall.

Tuesday, 6 June

Council Meeting of Equity. The Election Results came in & there was the effect of a bombshell when it was realised that the Right was *in*! I lunched at the club with Isabel Dean and Chris Melville (both in) and all agreed it was a surprising victory. I think it was helped by the Levin articles in the Times (he printed the A[ct] F[or] E[quity] list) and by the fear aroused by the Left with their awful B. & D. structure & their daft rule book.

Friday, 9 June

Went to the post at about 3.45. As I came out of my door, one man was hurriedly descending the stairs & another following him – a rather seedy looking creature with receding hair – when he saw me he called to the other man: 'You got the pliers Bill?' & went after him. I saw that No. 9 flat had the front door opened & thought 'Chantal is having some wiring done . . .' Later on, Victor Orlov from flat 10 called & said 'Have you been in all the afternoon?' and I said yes & he said 'Burglars have broken in to No. 9 and they tried to smash my door as well but only succeeded in splitting the wood.' When Chantal returned, she said they hadn't taken anything, just upset the place, and that they'd obviously been disturbed: that was *me* coming out into the corridor.

Sunday, 18 June

C. picked up Louie & me, and took us to a restaurant called Bodegon in Chelsea. We had lunch in a garden there and it was superb. We were joined there by Peter who'd been to All Saints for communion. He admitted: 'I can't take communion in my own (R.C.) church because I'm homosexual' and that astounded me; I had no idea such proscription existed in the Catholic Church. It seems monstrous to me & it is certainly an idiotic & senseless persecution in P.'s case because he's serious about his theology & is the sort of young man whom the Priest should welcome.

Monday, 19 June

We saw 'Panorama' on Chile, blatant anti-junta propaganda & a holier than thou attitude which British documentaries delight in. It was deplorable to see this film which denigrated General Pinochet and slandered & libelled his regime & never produced any proof: the patronising rudeness handed out to his Foreign Minister was contemptible. The BBC news reported Pardoe (Liberal)[4] as saying that Mrs Thatcher's promise to Ulster of U.K. status was 'the most despicable thing since Chamberlain flew to Munich.' Chamberlain did nothing dishonourable at Munich: he signed an agreement with a totalitarian leader just as Callaghan has recently done with the Rumanian thug.[5]

Wednesday, 21 June

There was a re-showing of the Morecambe & Wise Show in December which I watched because of Gordon appearing in it. His was a funny sequence & all its effects worked. The opening revolved round a device whereby M. & W. tried to reject the services of a singer – Des O'Connor. It's interesting to watch this kind of thing 'cos it's a hangover from the great days of American Vaudeville & movies & Pro jokes which certainly worked for Jack Benny & Bob Hope etc. because they were international names and because their characters were well established. These conditions didn't apply here. The endless denigration of this singer would only have been funny *if he'd been a good singer*: in the event, he was as bad as M. & W. had been saying he was.

---

[4] MP for Cornwall North, 1966–79.

[5] Nicolae Ceausescu, the Romanian dictator, had visited England earlier in the month. He was received by the Queen and signed a joint statement on economic and cultural cooperation with Prime Minister James Callaghan. He was to be stripped of the honorary knighthood he received during this visit on the day he was ousted by the Romanian people – 23 December 1989. Two days later he and his wife Elena were shot, by decision of an emergency court.

Saturday, 24 June

Lunch with Louie and then we went to the Rose Garden. I remonstrated with the ticket collectors 'Why are you allowing these children to wreck the deckchairs? They're standing on them!' & one said 'They're rather sweet . . . they told us they were bored.' 'They should return to the Caribbean & ruin their own furniture.' 'Don't you like black kids?' 'No. If you cleared all the Negroes out of London we'd have an hour's more daylight.'[6] They moved away disgusted. I went over to the little hooligans & said 'Clear off! Or I'll get the Park Police!' & they grudgingly departed, leaving one ruined chair lying on the grass.

Tuesday, 27 June

I walked thro' the drizzling rain to the Haymarket to see Ingrid. There were lots of cracks about my *not* going to see her play: 'You've saved me five pounds on tickets' etc. Ingrid admitted the play was tiring: 'I'm getting older . . . I've decided to buy this apartment in Cheyne Walk . . . I'm sick of other people's things around me . . . I want to have something of my own . . . you must come & see it . . . I leave on Saturday . . . I've missed you . . . my little *mascot*!' Considering I was told to arrive at 10.50 & she ordered her car for 12 o'c. she wasn't missing me *that* much!

Friday, 7 July

I've got to go to RADA this afternoon to make a speech apparently!! Hugh Cruttwell greeted me on my arrival & gave me tea & then introduced me on the stage of the Vanbrugh Theatre. There was quite a good house. I took Entry Into the Profession as my theme. The student audience was very much on my side & I couldn't really do wrong. Fabia Drake cornered me: 'You could have been a very good straight actor if you'd really wanted to . . .' and Lydia Sherwood: 'Do you remember our antics on the Gower coast? All those years ago, & I come here today to find you doing the *same old act* . . .'[7]

Monday, 10 July

Walked to Richard Williams and took him to dinner at Lariana: it was Harry Packers. Richard talked about *The Thief* [*and the Cobbler*]: 'If all goes well we could do it in two years & if it goes badly it will take *ten*

---

[6] This crack was not of recent invention. KW had cited it as long ago as 1962, in his interview with David Bruxner of *Topic* (see entry for 2 August 1962, p. 195). On that occasion he remarked: 'That sort of thing is so evil just because it's humorous. It's a purely destructive kind of humour. It sounds funny, but it's basically very wicked' (*Topic*, 1 September 1962).

[7] See entry for 3 September 1950, p. 55.

. . . but it's going to be a very big venture . . .' When I said Margaret Thatcher would win the next election, he said surprisedly 'Do you really think so?'

Monday, 17 July

John Wood Studios to do v/o for animation of cars for Dunlop Tyres, with Bill Oddie and Deryck Guyler. We were all v. good. Bill is ebullient & his good humour is infectious. After one take he said to Deryck & me 'You were both marvellous! I was terrible' and on every playback, it kept coming round again, till he said deprecatingly 'Well we all need a bit of encouragement!' I went to the loo at Tott. Ct. Rd. ('cos I'd called on Floella Benjamin & drunk loads of tea!) and then to Littlewoods for my fags. Not as cheap as Woolies.

Monday, 31 July

Gave George dinner. George told me of his reunion with Gracie Fields in Sorrento, after twenty years. 'Do you remember me?' he asked, and G.F. replied 'No' with delightful candour. 'But we were introduced by Beryl & George Formby!' 'Were we love? I can't even remember what happened yesterday!' George said to me 'Of course she's over 80 you know . . . but I told her that she was just as beautiful as ever . . .' and was waxing sentimental & maudlin over this extraordinary non-recognition. He told me 'She sang "Send In The Clowns"[8] . . . and it was marvellous . . . of course the voice isn't what it was . . . more talk than music . . .' & I felt like saying 'So is the song' but merely smiled & nodded. I told him about Golda Meir[9] expostulating at the cinema box office about paying 1.50 for *Dr Zhivago*. 'One fifty! What is he? Some sort of specialist?' and he roared with laughter.

Thursday, 10 August

Walked via Hyde Park to B & G. Took them to dinner at El Bodegon. When we got to Cathcart Road I said to G 'Let's go to that pub over the road!' & he said 'No! It's full of crooks' but B said 'No, it's all right! Come on, we'll have a quick one.' It was a *fatal mistake*. I got v. sloshed (changing to beer shandy after wine) and was shouting obscenities & singing bawdy songs etc. Next to me at the bar was a tough young lad who whispered 'Come through to the toilet with me . . . just for a lark . . . & come out doing your flies up like we done something . . .' & I said 'Oh no! I would get much too excited' & he replied unbelievingly 'Leave off! I only mean for a joke . . . come on . . .' but I said 'Alas, it would not be a joke for me. I'm a raver . . .'

---

[8] By Stephen Sondheim, from *A Little Night Music*.
[9] 1898–1978 (née Mabovich). Prime Minister of Israel 1969–74.

& he said 'Are you serious?' Then a woman came in with a dog & attacked him 'I've been waiting & waiting for you . . . I've had your boss on the phone rucking me!' and there was quite the scene. B & G drove me home. Then I went out again. Followed one piece in Euston Rd. but it turned out to be seeking a taxi. All the sublimated desire for sex arose & I wandered round the block but eventually the headache forced me home & I took Codis & went to bed feeling quite dreadful.

Saturday, 2 September

Postman delivered the Lahr book on Joe Orton:[10] it looks interesting & there is a sweet note from John Lahr to me. In the afternoon I made telephone enquiries & found that Stanley was in St Thomas's Hospital. Got a taxi and was in his private room by 2 o'c. He told me that the accident occurred on Thursday! It seems he was rehearsing a scene, and a flat fell forward on him. It has caused a pelvic fracture. He has to lie flat. His room was jam-packed with fruit, flowers, gifts etc. I stayed until 4 o'c. & I asked 'It is Sunday tomorrow so you'll want to take it easy with the papers . . . so I won't come' & he asked 'Why not? Reading the papers won't take all day!' so I said 'All right! I'll come same time tomorrow.'

Sunday, 3 September

Walked all the way to St Thomas's Hospital. The nurse said (after going into Stanley's room) 'He doesn't think it is a *good afternoon* . . .' I said 'Oh! Well I will push off then . . . he can always get in touch if he wants me for anything . . .' and I left hurriedly. No matter how ill I felt, I could never administer such a rebuff! I felt utterly humiliated.

Tuesday, 5 September

Stanley rang: 'I want to explain about not seeing you on Sunday . . . It was because they were trying to remove the tube from the bladder . . .' I said 'Oh my dear! I quite understand!'

Friday, 8 September

I am greatly pleased with my pens! The desk one (Sheaffer) and the pocket one (Mont Blanc) are excellent, and I've the Waterman in reserve as well as the Sheaffer, for the pocket. I have had the Mont Blanc since 1956 – tho' it's been repaired a couple of times – and it is in excellent working order.

---

[10] *Prick Up Your Ears.*

Friday, 15 September
To Bristol & taken to a Quaker Meeting Hall for the LP of Parlour Poetry.[11] My reading was several times impaired by bad vision & I should really have taken the spectacles. Reading some of those 'poems' I was aware of my failing powers . . . the breathing wasn't always adequate for some of the metrical continuity & the Hiawatha send-up was diabolically difficult.

Wednesday, 20 September
Reflecting on the number of otiose 'game' shows I've been doing lately (all because I'm offered little else!) I thought to myself: 'It's really tatsville . . . you're doing all the things which you once avoided . . .'

Monday, 25 September
Reading the different accounts, in the Lahr book, of the same events, is disquieting; of course one knows that people say contradictory things the moment one's back is turned, but it's still a shock to have real evidence of it. People are mercurial and changeful but the fact is that we *think* of them as constant & consistent, and when we find they're nothing of the kind we're put off, sometimes even offended & hurt. We always expect too much, we're always disappointed: it is the nature of humanity; that's why we need Faith so much! The unaltering, the eternal, and the endlessly forgiving . . . this is what the spirit craves. Always I come back to Schopenhauer's 'I would willingly exchange all this for a never having been . . .' and though I *know* the ridiculous paradox involved (how can you consign to the unconscious without having first been conscious?) I am utterly empathetic to the sentiment. The mind that can revolve contented thought is just as capable of harbouring hateful discontent & deathly despair. I know that the contemplative & cerebral creature is saved by the therapy of work etc.: but in a sense, that's only a palliative . . . a putting-off . . . like a drug . . . sooner or later you're back to the same questions.

Wednesday, 27 September
Walked to Punch & Alan Coren was v. nice to me, and so was Miles Kington . . . and I was pleased to see Joan Bakewell.[12] William Davis (ex-editor of Punch) was scathing about the 'liberal' ineffectiveness both in South Africa & in England but there is an element of hypocrisy in a lot of people wining & dining in luxury while they discuss human

---

[11] Issued by the Saydisc company.
[12] b.1933. Billed by the *Radio Times* in 1966 as 'The beauty plus brains girl'.

misery of vast proportions; and none of them will lose a night's sleep over any of it.* Walked home in a bemused state, smiling at strangers.

*of course, neither will I.

Friday, 29 September

Taxi to Lime Grove and Diana Millward was doing a 10 minute spot on the Orton Biography. Mike Billington was interviewer. John Lahr came later and confessed to feeling apprehensive. He needn't have bothered. On the take, he was fluent & enlightening. On the bits I had, I was at pains to make the book sound as funny as it was. John Lahr told me after that Peggy Ramsay had tried to get veto rights over the entire project!! and that the general hassle had been irksome in the extreme. Diana Millward seemed anxious to assert herself; at one point she said 'Orton had no compassion' & J.L. challenged that 'The output alone provides the compassion . . . it represents a plea for a mass of inarticulate sufferers' & she replied 'No, I don't accept that . . . not the *work* you see . . . in the *life* there was no compassion . . .' whereas the relationship with K.H. represents a saga of compassion.

Wednesday, 4 October

I left on foot for John Lahr's house, arriving at 4 o'c. Alan Bennett came as well – for tea – and we talked about the Orton book. John's had the idea of Alan doing a screenplay of the life. Alan said 'It is impossible to write a treatment with all real people in it . . . the identities would restrict the imaginative impulse horribly . . .' Walked home over Primrose Hill & the city looked beautiful with lights in the gathering dusk. I sang songs like 'Sing Joyous Bird' and 'Deep in my Heart'[13] & was v. buoyant.

Wednesday, 11 October

C. came at 7 o'c. We went to his flat for drinks. On to Peter H.'s birthday party. I turned on P.B. screaming 'You dirty ingrate! Sitting there on your fat arse!' & he left in tears. C. drove the car & we caught up with him. When we got to Piccadilly he [C.] said 'I'm very angry with you!' & I told him 'Yes you're right 'cos I behaved very badly . . . I say these things for effect half the time . . . there's a colossal streak of malicious nastiness . . .' Walked out of the flat & got a taxi. I was so drunk, all the basic desires were roused . . . walked the streets till about 2 o'c. Madness of alcohol, or simply the uninhibited natural behaviour of an invert?

---

[13] Songs by Phillips and Usher, and Sigmund Romberg respectively.

Thursday, 12 October

The guilt of last night hangs over me like a pall. The process is endless with me. 'Expecting perfection, but just muddling through/Can't expect miracles? . . . most of us do.'

Monday, 16 October

The news is that their new Pope in Rome is a Polish Cardinal who seems to be rather more intellectually lively than most of the Conclave. The Greenpeace movement has successfully stopped the killing of the seal-pups in the Orkneys! I'm glad I sent my cheque to the movement. I can't believe that the shooting of young animals in this systematic fashion is right or proper. Don't believe all that rubbish about them eating too much fish . . . nature doesn't arrange things like that . . . she always finds a natural balance . . . it's *man* who does the ecological ruination.

Wednesday, 18 October

To John Wood Studios to do *Wind in the Willows*[14] script for Graham Goodwin (EMI–Music For Pleasure) & he was very easy and cooperative. When I began narrating, Graham asked 'Is that your own voice you are using?' & mystified, I said 'Er – yes . . . ?' & he went on 'I only ask because, if it's an assumed voice, you're in trouble because you'll have to use it throughout the script.' I found myself maintaining stoutly 'It's all right! It *is* my voice' but I thought after 'Who else's voice could it be?' After an hour of work he flung open the windows crying out 'Peggy Ashcroft always opened the windows wide, after a session!' & I said coldly 'I don't share her proclivities' & closed them.

Sunday, 22 October

We saw a bit of television; that series about Lily Langtry is full of the old tats doing their costume bit – utter rubbish & badly cast. *All* of them were saying PORTRAIT instead of portrait & there were loads of solecisms.

Sunday, 29 October

I am tired. I'm tired of the endless round, I'm tired of every cliché I have to listen to. Sometimes when they begin their lying tributes: 'I've always admired you very much . . .' I want to scream 'Piss off & shut up!' & then I think again & realise they're only voicing a kind of diplomacy . . . it's just a way of oiling the wheels of sociability; trouble is, I'm not social. I've a capacity for entertaining people, not

---

[14] By Kenneth Grahame (1859–1932).

for loving them . . . only sometimes when I see a face preoccupied, unaware of spectators, & I see that it could come from a renaissance canvas . . . then I realise the great beauty of men . . . & I feel a surge of great love.

Monday, 30 October

Lime Grove at 11 o'c. We did two run-thro's[15] and had lunch. It was all over by ten to three. Jeremy [Swan] told a glorious story of Bobby Helpmann on tour having to make up in the Umpires' Room in a huge sports stadium they were forced to play in. The call boy doing the half found him standing (dressed as Oberon) high on a trestle table doing elaborate eye make-up by *one* naked light bulb & asked 'Are you all right?' & Bobby replied 'Yes I'm all right, but I don't know how these Umpires manage!'

Thursday, 2 November

Walked to Rosary Gdns. to see Denis Goacher & Annie. They have this wee flat. Denis gave me a drink & said 'I've been drunk for about 6 days! The hand shaking you know?' & then Annie came in and started on the whisky. Eventually I said 'We must *eat*' & she produced this cottage pie & Denis had to go out & buy bread & butter . . . oh dear . . . Then walked to Alan Bennett, past the lady tramp who was undressing in her van & smiling invitingly![16] I rang the bell pretending not to notice. Peter Cook came 'I'll just have a tonic water' & sat smoking fags & gleefully relating the worst notices he'd read for *Baskervilles*. Alan deprecated my censure of BBC announcers eliding their words, Doctor Rowing instead of Doctor Owen: 'Oh! it's too pedantic of you!' Peter was v. funny about the Boothby book[17] saying Churchill had a 'cruel streak' & started endless fantasies 'It's been revealed in these hitherto unknown letters that Hitler had a cruel streak . . .' Then it was Princess Margaret 'It's been revealed she has a cruel streak . . .' Alan didn't offer much: he made it obvious that we should go, by pointedly collecting all the crockery & glasses into the kitchen sink at about 11.15.

Thursday, 9 November

We saw '[The] Sweeney'[18] & the morality was appalling. *Three* policemen slept with the same tart, who asked one: 'Would you wear

---

[15] Of 'The Dribblesome Teapots', by Norman Hunter. A 'Jackanory'.

[16] An uninvited 'lodger' who parked herself, permanently, on Bennett's doorstep. He immortalised her in *The Lady in the Van* (1990).

[17] *Boothby: Recollections of a Rebel* (1978), by (Baron) Robert Boothby, 1900–86.

[18] TV series about the Flying Squad (1974–78).

your helmet?' Heaven knows what sort of image they wish to present for our police.

Thursday, 16 November

Walked to Spectator. I sat with Alexander Chancellor on right & Peter Ackroyd on the other, and facing this dish Geoffrey Wheatcroft.[19] The meal began with a fish paté in which most of the bones had been left & went on to Irish stew: not a meal you'd *ask* a man to.[20] Conversation was lively & I got into a great argument with G.W. apropos the disassociation twixt Faith & philosophy. Stayed far too long drinking too much wine, smoking too many fags & being vulnerable to rudeness.

Thursday, 23 November

The team for 'J.A.M.' was Clement Freud, Peter Jones & Derek Nimmo. Everyone saying how loyally Clement was behaving towards Jeremy Thorpe who is contending with all the assorted lies of Bessell at the Minehead trial;[21] this latter has now named 5 ministers in governments as 'knowing Jeremy was homosexual.' O dear! What other irrelevancies are to come out in this particular bagwash?

Tuesday, 28 November

Equity Council Meeting. The business was largely about re-drafting of Rules and there was all the usual nit picking. I wrote rude limericks to Clare Trevor & made faces at Isabel Dean & larked about all the time. At coffee break, as I took my cup, the President (John Barron) asked Peter Plouviez[22] 'Have you put cyanide in his?' & inferred that my behaviour warranted it. Lunch at the BBC Club with Isabel.

Wednesday, 29 November

John Wood Studios for v/o and talked to Charlie Hawtrey: what a difference retirement has made for him!! He's relaxed, amusing, rather urbane & quite without the irritating desire to score or be intriguing which used to be so annoying. Barbara & Ronnie were there & Bar said 'You must come out to dinner . . .' I did my stuff in about 8

---

[19] Chancellor, b.1940, journalist, latterly at the *New Yorker*. Wheatcroft, columnist.

[20] 'This was a good dinner enough, to be sure; but it was not a dinner to *ask a man to.*' Boswell's *Life of Johnson* (5 August 1763).

[21] Jeremy Thorpe, b.1929. Leader of Liberal Party 1967–76. Accused of conspiracy to murder Norman Scott (né Josiffe), a former male model, who said he had been a homosexual partner of Thorpe's. Bessell, Liberal MP for Bodmin 1964–70, was the chief prosecution witness. He claimed that Thorpe, in his presence, had incited a third party to murder Scott.

[22] b.1931, then General Secretary, British Actors' Equity Association.

minutes (six versions) & they settled for the one with a voice change on the tag 'feel quite chunky!'

Sunday, 3 December

Louie gave us lunch at Cosmo. Pat said she'd been seconded to Brussels & would be commuting weekly. We had a rather pissy lunch & the Grand Marniers were fast & furious with the coffee.

Monday, 4 December

Got to Lime Grove on time & did the recording in fragments.[23] I was adequate. Got the tube back & was surrounded by giggling negro children who shouted 'It's that cunt from the Carry Ons!' and I talked to a young trainee railway guard. 'We have to learn all about the Signal System . . . there's a lot of drawing & theory involved . . .' A very pleasant lad. Saw Louie at 5.30. She complained about her washing machine going wrong *again*! Inside I was thinking 'Oh! stop moaning for heaven's sake! I've got my own troubles!' but out loud I burst into 'It happened on the beach at Bali-Bali'[24] & danced up & down. At the end, she said 'I wonder you didn't take up comedy!'

Thursday, 7 December

Walked to Nick Spargo's office and did the pilot script for his animation series with 'Willo the Wisp' voice. He said 'The BBC people said it would be wrong to have your voice just before the news' which is so mad it must be a garbled version of another explanation.

Friday, 8 December

The Spectator has printed my letter about the mistakes in their journal.[25] I do like seeing myself in print & that's a fact. At 4 o'c. Peter Eade phoned: 'Have you anything to say to the newspapers about zip fasteners?' and I said no & put the phone down. I don't know why he bothers me with this kind of rubbish.

---

[23] Possibly 'Jackanory Writing Competition', broadcast 19 December. 'Kenneth Williams with special guests Vivian Pickles and Martin Jarvis.'

[24] 'On the Beach at Bali Bali', by Sherman and Silver.

[25] 'The *Spectator* should pronounce against solecisms and uphold standards. When I heard someone recently pronouncing Syndrome with a long O sound, I told him: "The O is short and the final E pronounced as it is in epitome or Penelope." A few weeks later he gleefully told me about his holiday flight to Italy: "We landed at Pisa where they've got a lovely aerodromy!" and he added triumphantly: "Your ruling is faulty!" I kept my countenance, retorting with some asperity: "One bad doctor does not invalidate medicine" and departed in a flurry of talcum powder.'

Saturday, 9 December
Walked to B.H. for the 'Carols With Kenneth' programme.[26] I had one or two fluffs but wasn't too bad. It wasn't easy to read some of the Bible stories because some of the language was rather gauche.

Friday, 15 December
Arrived at about 5 o'c. at Tenerife. Coach to the Atlantis. It looks rather tat & everyone admits that the sun goes from the terrace after midday. I will probably have to see Wings about a change, 'cos you must have a place where you can sit in the sun. Louie looked v. peaky. At the Irish Harp all bedlam reigned! Reeled back to the hotel at about 1 o'c. or 1.30. Took Alka, Paracetamol, and 3 Bile Beans 'cos I don't want to risk the bum in any way. The neck is still agony.

Saturday, 16 December
A loudspeaker van in the street announced a *strike* of all hotel staff on the 21 December. Funny, 'cos I said to Louie last night 'I've got a feeling we're going to be in the shit' & it appears I'm right. Dinner at table alone (after Maria had instructed the staff 'Mr Williams is a famous actor who must have privacy.')

Monday, 18 December
Dinnner at 7.15 and when we came into the Hall after, we met Ken & Joan!! They were looking splendid, unchanged since last year.

Wednesday, 20 December
Went down to dinner & was informed 'This is the last meal . . . all the waiters and hotel staff are on strike tomorrow . . . the strike is indefinite.' We've had rain since we've been here, lousy accommodation, not *one* deck chair to be seen, and rain every day, and now a strike. I've got bumps all over the head, a tongue that is numb, earache, the farmers,[27] backache, neckache & I will never risk this sort of thing ever again. Next year I must sort out something else.

Thursday, 21 December
Made my own bed. Got coffee & milk powder from the supermarket. Back to Atlantis for lunch. It was a carrier bag picnic meal; they're all taking it with the apathetic calm which many mistake for British phlegm.

---

[26] Broadcast Christmas morning at 7.03 a.m. 'Carols sung by the Midget Choir, conductor Alec Rush.'
[27] Rhyming slang: Farmer Giles = piles.

Friday, 22 December
O! if I'd been on my own (without Louie to contend with) I'd have got a plane out yesterday. Loads of idiots came up to me 'May I say how much pleasure you have given me?' & one mutters 'Too kind' but longs to say 'May I say how much utter tedium you've given me?'

Sunday, 24 December
Colin (Glamorgan) told us about about a supermarket that was *open* so we shot up there & I spent 1,200 pts. on food & drink in case we are beleaguered. Returned to find the hotel running a hot lunch!! *and* doing a dinner tonight! Went to the kitchens & met the clerical staff who were doing all the work! They gave us champagne & were charming: a book-keeper is the chef! Dinner in the evening was passable. Joan & Louie went to kitchen after to wash up. Then there was dancing & drinking etc. Then I went up with Ken to take his tray & drinks etc. When I returned I saw that Louie was terribly drunk – heaven knows who gave her the stuff – & I got her in the lift somehow & into her room. In trying to undress her I had terrible trouble & she fell over several times & I picked her up. Then suddenly there was *blood* everywhere – the bed, the floor, on her dress, on the sheets . . . I rushed to my room & got the antiseptic & found that she had cut her lip open! Found myself praying for deliverance from this ghastly holiday – will I ever be back to normal?

Monday, 25 December
I was right. She bit her own mouth and lost a centre tooth in the process. There is now a gap in the mouth. I realised I'd got a migraine and I went to bed: the nose running all the while and the sneezing intermittent. Joan & Louie went to the Orotava 'Oh! it was wonderful! We were treated like two Duchesses!'

Tuesday, 26 December
Telephoned Wings Office and Matt (manager) said 'I will reserve 2 seats for you on the Friday flight, 29 December.' Joan kept reproaching me 'You'll ruin it for us if you go!' but 2 weeks will have been enough of this.

Wednesday, 27 December
Penelope P. came for the interview: obviously a wet twit. Every time I said *fuck* she coloured & looked away. Went for a walk with Louie, Ken & Joan, dodging the rain etc., and they announced the strike was settled.

Friday, 29 December
Landed at about 8.45. There is an enormous pile of mail to be dealt with, but it looks as if it mainly consists of Christmas cards & I am not going to acknowledge them. Oh! I am so disappointed and jaded with *travel*!

Sunday, 31 December
The streets are thick with snow & everything has a muted air of disquiet. Well it was the lousiest Christmas I can remember for ages. Certainly I shan't bother with the Canary Islands again. Went in to Louie in the evening. Put an electric one-bar fire in the kitchen for her 'cos it is absolutely freezing in there. Every time I do *anything* (like clearing up, cleaning etc.) she complains 'Oh leave it alone! I can do it! Anyone would think I was a bloody invalid.' Heaven knows how *husbands* manage to look after women but certainly I'm getting fed up with it. Returned to my flat at about 10.45 after fixing Louie's electric blanket & giving her Benylin for a chesty cough she's got.

1979

Monday, 1 January
G came & drove Louie & me to B's. Everything was warm and cosy there & they gave us a superb lunch. As usual, they both showed solicitude over Louie & were marvellous company. Both these chums are the *best in adversity* because they *act* whereas most people mouth their sympathy. G poured hot water all over his car and it then *froze* completely!

Wednesday, 3 January
T & C arrived at 8.45. They looked and sounded no different than when I last saw them both & there was something truly sad about it all. The same old chatter about *camp*, the same old 'female' appellations, the same aimless search for fulfilment in all the wrong places. I know they're well-intentioned, but the company eventually palls to a point of exasperation. At my hint, they left at 11.30. I went to bed at about 1 o'c. after v. erotic experiments.

Thursday, 4 January
Up at 7.30 to get the papers: all the talk at the bookstall was about the utter hatred of unions and strikes etc.: one day, I think this loathing will be channelled into action. We saw the TV and it was *Carry On Henry* . . . amazing how well this was made! Everyone in it was competent and the sheer *look* of the thing was very professional. We turned it off after that because it was the RSC production of *Macbeth* and we can do without *that* sort of rubbish.

Sunday, 7 January
Tom came and drove me & Louie. The house has been considerably improved. It was a pleasant day and both T & C were kind & considerate, by any standards, but the sheer glamour of these two has strangely dimmed . . . it's all very domestic & suburban I suppose . . .

Wednesday, 10 January
Saw the news. Callaghan arrived back from Guadeloupe saying 'There is no chaos' which is a euphemistic way of talking about the lorry drivers ruining *all production* & work in the entire country, but one admires his phlegm.

Sunday, 14 January
Taxi for TV Centre where I did 'Star Turn'. I was with a team including Leonard Sachs who said 'I worked with you years ago in a radio show & you told me about the Shop of A Thousand Tiles . . . d'you remember?' & I smiled confidently & nodded, but I have never met him anywhere. The other side was headed by Billy Dainty, whom John Law used to refer to as 'a terrible provincial comic.' The only persons I liked were Billy Dainty and Brian Cant: the set-up is awfully BBC rep tat.

Thursday, 18 January
O this comfortless month! these spiritless times! Up at 7.30 & got papers: they're greatly diminished 'cos of the lorry strike & no newsprint etc. Peter Butterworth has died (heart attack, 59) so must send a note to Janet Brown 'cos it will be an awful blow.

Sunday, 21 January
Equity SGM. I had to speak against a Madhav Sharma motion. I was heckled and eventually laughed at. There is no way of properly expressing the deep humiliation inflicted and the wound which cuts deep & leaves a scar that renders you vulnerable for the future. Of course I wasn't the only one; they shouted down & heckled every Right wing speaker, and one heard their screaming obscenities & their insults coming from a tight group of Activists in the auditorium. Isabel was enchanting and she told me 'Don't worry – you were very good & completely authentic' but my great mistake was departing from the motion subject (I deviated, saying that the Council shouldn't be sneered at & that I joined out of altruism . . . then I said the fatal thing 'for the same reason that I'm a blood donor.' *That* produced howls of derisive laughter! and from then on, I lost the atmosphere completely.) If someone offered me membership of the Actors' Guild I would join it!

Monday, 5 February
The TV news was all about strikes galore & the mounting refuse has caused the authorities to set rat bait down & spray the stuff with disinfectant!

Monday, 19 February
Laurena Dewar rang *twice* about the TV programme on 22!! 'Don't for goodness' sake tell anyone you're doing it because it's got to be kept secret . . . you are put in this box and the Fortune Tellers & graphologists have to guess who you are . . .' She says the BBC are sending the car on Thursday & I am to be called Mr Guest. It's like some daft intrigue!

Thursday, 22 February
John (postman) knocked on door to say 'Happy Birthday' & give me the letters: they included a handsome Colibri lighter from Joan & Ken! Post Office rang & said 'Your new number is 388 0249!! so I'm delighted that all those people with my number whom I don't want to know will not be able to bother me. Cab at 5.45 to TV Centre for this Astrology Game. The astrologers guessed the identity of both of us (me & Susan George). My bit of filming included testament from Andrew Ray! He said some very kind things about me . . . and at one point he smiled 'Kenneth is a bit of a hypochondriac . . .' There was a ghastly party after, & they produced a *huge* birthday cake! & Michael Aspel (who chairs the show) made a speech & I had to reply! Alas! it was very lame 'cos I wasn't expecting it at all! Chris Powell (researcher) told me after 'It was very good of you to enter into the spirit of the thing at that party . . . it just *made* it for everyone there . . . you must surely realise how very popular you are?'

Friday, 23 February
Went with Louie to Norman Mills. Norman told her 'You're a very good patient, Louisa!' & it is true 'cos she's totally uncomplaining. We walked back together & returned to the flat to see me in 'Star Signs' – this Astrology game. I certainly *looked* full of sinus & sounded it! And the total effect was of immense intellectual grandeur. I sound like some fastidious university don who's somehow got involved in a children's panel game.

Tuesday, 27 February
To John Musgrove. He said there was an infection: he prescribed pills, linctus & gave me some drops for the nose. Came home to the noise of workmen doing the Entryphone! They fitted mine by 4.30 & had done Louie's as well! One of the Engineers told me: 'Burglary is becoming common nowadays . . . one of our biggest jobs is fitting Entryphones for Westminster City Council on their flats . . .'

Friday, 2 March
Oh! I hope that today sees the Scots & the Welsh saying No to these

daft devolution plans! The TV news announced that Wales said no, and Scotland only got 32% for!! So that should effectively put an end to the whole stupid charade. Louie & I opened a bottle of champagne and drank the lot, celebrating the devolution defeat & the Conservative by-election victories.

Saturday, 3 March

I saw Edward Heath being interviewed by young people: it wasn't adroit. The usual clichés from a left wing youngster: 'I don't have job satisfaction . . . I just do it for the money . . .' What does he think accountants do it for? A love of poring over figures? Socialism has propounded so many myths! – Utopia, Egalitarianism, *job satisfaction*, welfare states – all of it illusory, all of it lies. I have never worked because I *liked* working & I have rarely felt any satisfaction about anything I've been paid for doing. I *have* felt satisfaction about work done for *myself* – making my own blind, cleaning my own flat . . .

Monday, 5 March

We saw Maggie in *Jean Brodie*; curiously, it wasn't so effective as a whole, but Mags was as marvellous as ever! Her scenes with the Headmistress were superb! She is the only actress in the world who can give you the *whole* coin: pathos & comedy together, sometimes teetering on the brink of lunacy; it is brilliant. Gordon was v. good but fundamentally too intelligent for such a daft role, and the girls were all rotten.

Tuesday, 6 March

Equity Meeting (Council). Nothing momentous. I had lunch at BBC Club with Isabel Dean. She is the most attractive, most elegant and most intelligent woman in England. She never ceases to delight me. Geoffrey Edwards joined us for coffee. We talked about religious issues. At 2.45 they went back to Equity & Isabel said 'Well you don't *have* to return 'cos you have been ill' & I fled up Portland Place.

Thursday, 8 March

To John Musgrove. He said the chest pain is due to an inflamed nerve which goes under rib cage & that it's the sort of nerve inflammation which could last a month.

Tuesday, 13 March

My Nomination for Council Form came today, so I'll get someone to propose me at the meeting today. Went in the pouring rain to Equity for the Exec. Meeting. I got Isabel to propose me & Derek Bond to second me. On several issues at the meeting, I voted against the conservative position. On the BBC television news I saw Gordon, Rona & the boys at Buckingham Palace, after receiving the O.B.E. Gordon was in the top hat & the tail coat & looked very smart I must say!

Thursday, 15 March

Saw in the paper that British Leyland are down to 20p so I rang Webber & he suggested 500 pounds in them & 500 in Charterhouse. I agreed. I felt quite elated afterwards!

Looking at men's faces in the street (I seldom remark women since they've never attracted me very much) I frequently find myself thinking they're like works of Art: lovely to look at but not to be handled.

Sunday, 18 March

Michael came & we got to Windsor at 9.30. Went to a hotel for coffee: 'I'm sorry, it is residents only . . .' so drove to Roger Royle's[1] house at Eton. He gave us coffee & introduced us to Timothy & Luke – the latter boy did the interviewing when I got to the Hall to do the 'chat' show. It was well attended (about 400) & I had competition from the Bishop of Lincoln who was taking the service in Eton Chapel. At the end of the talk, one boy in the auditorium asked 'How do you manage to look so *young*?' It must be the most delightful compliment I've ever been paid in *any* place but it is particularly delightful coming from a schoolboy. All the Etonians I met were charming & their manner seems a superb blend of courtesy & confidence. Roger got Luke & Tim to show M. their chapel organ & he played it superbly! Marvellous sound!

Saturday, 7 April

Ever since I moved here in '72 I've become closer & closer to Louie: my life more or less revolves about her & I have no absorbing interest in anyone else. I feel I wouldn't care if I didn't see anyone else. All my worries & obsessions are about her. I breathe a sigh of relief at not hearing from T & C & desperately hope they've got the message: an acquaintanceship that bears the odd meeting but nothing more.

Monday, 9 April

The mail came & I found a letter from Who's Who!! Well! I suppose this means I've arrived! Oh! what an honour! I find myself swooning. Went to give blood at Margaret Street.

---

[1] b.1939. Senior Chaplain at Eton, later broadcaster of popular religious programmes.

Tuesday, 10 April
I walked to Molinaire [sound recording studios]. Gary Watson was doing the straight voice & we chatted. Stanley arrived late. First version I played Father & Stanley son in a rhyming piece about Sealink, then we reversed it & I did the kid & Stanley did the Father & he made the tag very funny indeed. I gave Stanley dinner at Lariana. We saw a stooped figure hurrying by, eating fish out of paper & S. said 'Oh! it's Richard the Third with Chips.' I said 'Oh! that's a marvellous title!' & we fell to conjecturing all kinds of show formats from the idea.

Thursday, 12 April
FAST DAY. P. Eade rang to say that a magazine wanted to do an article on me but 'I got you out of it' & said he was off to the country for the Easter holiday. I asked Louie if she'd eaten anything all day & she said 'Only a Welsh rabbit' so I think my fasting influences her!

Friday, 20 April
Of course I'm a prisoner in the economic sense – not enough money to buy privacy – and so well known that I *need* privacy. I can't walk down a street in London without the nudges, the staring, the following, the requests for autographs & all the shouting (abuse & praise) which accompanies my every excursion. I loathe all of it. I would willingly exchange it all for anonymity and a steady uninspiring job which required diligence & integrity. Heaven knows what I'm doing as an *actor*. I am not really interested in acting at all! I never go near a theatre if I can help it. I suppose I entered the profession 'cos it was the only one which required no qualifications: only talent.

Thursday, 26 April
Laurena telephoned at 9.55 in a terrible state: 'Peter died last night . . . a sudden heart attack . . .' & I mouthed some sympathetic platitudes but the enormity of his loss hasn't really hit me yet . . . Peter dead! the only & the best agent I ever had . . . dear God . . . it is appalling. Laurena asked me to tell the chums I knew, so I rang George B. who was shattered & then Norman Mills ('cos Peter was a patient of his) Oh! I can hardly write 'cos I'm crying. Rang Annette, & the Codron office and Eleanor at Bianchi restaurant which P. used a lot, and Peggy Ramsay. Told Louie I couldn't eat anything. Washed my hair for something to do. I feel utterly disorientated. At 12.50 Laurena told me the circumstances: 'He said he'd got a pain in the chest . . . I went out of the office about 4 o'c. to get him some paracetamols which his doctor had suggested . . . by the time I came back . . . it was all over . . . ambulance took him to the Middlesex . . .' Walked

to Laurena at 2.30. She told me privately that P. had left her the agency for at least six months if she wanted it. She looks shaken & ill but is coping with every kind of difficulty. I left after putting my arms round her & expressing my affection & concern for her. I keep thinking of Peter. Last time I saw him he said 'You look so young!' & cheered me up enormously. I can see him now – laughing uproariously at my jokes – making wry remarks about our business . . . the nights we used to sit & talk about the loneliness of bachelor existence – his worries over his mother's death & his father's failing sight . . . his going with Louie to Charlie's inquest . . . helping us with all the legal difficulties . . . it's the end of the chapter for me & a blow from which I'll never really recover.

Friday, 27 April

Arrived Bristol at 11.47. Left bags at Unicorn & went to BBC. Pamela [Howe] met me with 'I'm so sorry about Peter' and that started all over again. Lunch at canteen & Pamela left me to talk to her boss. I sat like a lemon: then the lovely Amanda [Theunissen] came & conversation was animated. O! but I'm tired! And my heart isn't in this radio thing[2] . . . I simply don't believe it comes alive . . . it's essentially a literary joke . . . on the page. Laurena phoned: 'Would you read the speech at the memorial Service for Peter in Ropley?' and I said yes. It will be the last tribute and it is obviously right that I should make it: of all his clients, I knew him better than anyone else.

Saturday, 28 April

Two episodes done by lunchtime. Two more by about 4.30. Now I've got to go thro' *four* scripts in readiness for tomorrow. How awful it must be, to be an actor who must continually accept work in strange places.

Sunday, 29 April

Just made the 6 o'c. train to London. I unpacked the bag & foolishly put my thumb (left hand) against the razor and blood spurted everywhere. I felt like screaming with vexation & then, like crying. Put a bandage on it & went in to see Louie.

Tuesday, 1 May

Exec. Meeting. They broke at 2 o'c. and said 'Back at 3.15' but I returned to the flat to try writing something for the Peter Eade mem-

---

[2] *Augustus Carp, Esq., by Himself, Being the Autobiography of a Really Good Man.* The unadmitted author of this burlesque was Sir Henry Bashford (1886–1961), ex-honorary physician to King George VI.

orial service on the 4th. Didn't get very far. Kept crying. I *must* get all this weeping done before the occasion or I'll be inarticulate & foolish.

Friday, 4 May

It looks like a Tory victory!! But it's not yet clear if the majority is decisive. Annette came & we drove to Alresford for lunch at the Swan and then to the church at Ropley for the memorial service for Peter. The service was intimate and well conducted. I spoke from the pulpit – mostly ad lib and only made one real slip when I missed out a sentence or two, but kept going all right. Annette told me 'You spoke very well and you said all the things one wanted to hear said about Peter' so that was reward enough. Mr E. told me 'I never heard a word you said . . . I never hear anybody' (he is 97) and he added 'It should have been *me* that died, not Peter. I am too old to be living any more.' Annette drove me home & came to see Louie for a cup of tea and a chat. She doesn't change one iota & she was the one person I would have wanted to go with to Ropley on this kind of day. It was utterly appropriate. Saw the news on TV and found that Margaret Thatcher has got a good overall majority (43) which is excellent. Maggie has seen the Queen and is now the first woman PM in Europe and it's the first time since Macmillan that we've had a leader with style and dignity.

Friday, 11 May

Saw Louie in the evening & again there was all this 'I don't want to watch *that*!' as soon as I spoke of a serious programme. Having sat thro' her awful quiz games, and 'Hawaii 5–0' etc. she then said she wanted to see *another* load of crap on ITV (I wanted to see the BBC news) so I said 'Oh well, I'm going to bed' & I left. There are remarks like 'It's my flat! I live here! I can watch what I like . . .' but basically it's a desire to avoid serious subjects because of her dislike of bad news (murder, N. Ireland bombs etc.) and her indifference to all intellectual discussion: 'I don't know what they're talking about.'

Saturday, 12 May

Saw Louie at about 5 o'c. & all that football muck was on TV. Oh! what yobs they all are! but there was some comfort in the fact that Arsenal (London) beat the Manchester idiots.

Friday, 18 May

Of course I am as aware of insecurity as I always am but nowadays the feeling seems to be ever-present. There is this endless question 'Will I be able to remain solvent? Will I last out until '86 when I'm able to retire?' and even: 'Will there be enough money to retire on?'

With inflation rising steadily every year this last point becomes increasingly difficult to answer. Obviously during the next few years I must make the contributions to the Pension fund as large as possible.

Friday, 1 June

Walked with Louie to do 'Quote Unquote' at the Paris at 6.45. I got a big laugh with the Evita story ('I've just got back from Evita.' 'Really? You don't look very brown!') & with the lovely creature in Scarlet.[3]

Saturday, 2 June

To National Hospital at Queen Sq. to see Robert Bolt. He was looking spare & fit, with a gigantic scar down the chest indicating the heart operation. His eyes were bright & twinkling & he laughed a lot at some of my sallies. His speech has been impaired by the coronary but I understood most of it.

Sunday, 3 June

We saw *Kaleidoscope* with Warren Beatty which was repeated *yet again*!! Strange to see Michael Balfour, now dead*, looking so permanent. So many people have died – people who looked indestructible. Still can't get over Peter and I remember him saying how odd it was about a young man like Beckinsale dying. I was surprised at the indecent speed with which his wife came on television hawking for moneys towards some Heart Foundation.[4] It is unnatural, the way we have proscribed mourning: we have dammed the flow of proper grief. Years ago (when I was young) it was considered right to wear black and if one couldn't afford to buy mourning clothes, one wore a black armband. Now, such apparel is never seen. One learns with a shock that someone has lost their nearest & dearest & stammers 'I'm terribly sorry . . . I didn't know' without also saying there was no way one *could* know . . . Oh! it's getting a more barbaric world in every way, compared with the world I knew in my youth.

*not dead at all

---

[3] In December 1970, Gordon Jackson had given KW a cutting from the *Sunday Times* retailing stories about the accident-prone George Brown (1914–85), Chancellor and Foreign Minister under Harold Wilson. 'The one I liked best,' said the writer, 'concerned a diplomatic party where George kept jigging up to a group in the corner saying "I must dance with this gorgeous creature in scarlet." Each time his offer was politely rejected. At last, it is told, he asked: "Gorgeous creature in scarlet, why won't you dance with me?" To which the creature replied: "First because I don't think you are quite in condition for more dancing. Secondly, because I am the Apostolic Delegate."'

[4] Judy Loe, b.1947, actress, widow of actor Richard Beckinsale (1945–79), Ronnie Barker's co-star in the series 'Porridge'.

Friday, 15 June
Walked to Cork Street in the afternoon to read a play by Trevor Baxter in which I've been offered the part of the Undertaker.[5] It's very good – not a lead but it can be very telling. Means travelling all the way to Greenwich which is a great bore but will have to surmount that difficulty when it comes.

Sunday, 17 June
The day is overcast and humid; everywhere you see these aimless wogs. In the park loads of 'em with scruffy families adding to an air of dereliction and desuetude. Powell was right, they should have stopped immigration years ago – all it's done has [*sic*] imported alien cultures and poverty. O! how dreary these days are! I am conscious of ennui and a great pall of depression. Louie walks more slowly than ever and the dialogue gets barmier & barmier: when we passed a Lebanese restaurant she said 'Oh! they're opening a lesbian restaurant there!' I replied 'It is Lebanese' & she went on 'Yes . . . they're all over the place now, aren't they?'

Thursday, 21 June
At 3 o'c. I talked to Ken Tynan about Maggie Smith 'cos he's doing a profile on her for the New Yorker. He said 'One of my lungs seems to have packed up' and used an oxygen capsule.[6] I tried to recollect all the things I'd known about Mags and at the end he said 'You've been enormously helpful' but I think he knows her well enough to write an article without my help.

Friday, 22 June
Went to Eade Office where Radio Times did the interview (Trevor Fishlock). 'Why did you want to read this Augustus Carp story on radio?' and one longed to cry 'Because I wanted the work, you daft 'aporth!' but instead one searches for aesthetic literary reasons.[7] On the news they announced that Jeremy Thorpe had been acquitted!! so that lying crook Scott has not succeeded in his vindictive quest!! They were cheering Jeremy outside the Old Bailey & he rather spoiled it by making a sanctimonious speech about Justice etc. whereas he should have just expressed satisfaction & breezed away!

Tuesday, 26 June
Equity Council Meeting. When at 4.45 the election results were circu-

---

[5] *The Undertaking*. Trevor Baxter, b.1932. Actor and writer.
[6] Tynan died the following year.
[7] 'Kenneth Williams was delighted with the script,' says the article.

lated, I found I was second in the Poll! Nigel Davenport first & then me! so I've got more votes than the President (Barron!) Well, I've always felt I should serve Equity as long as the membership gives me a good endorsement! so I shall serve another year!

Friday, 29 June

'Petrocelli'[8] was diabolical: this series makes no pretence now to be anything but ethnic-minority orientated! Every week it is some Greek or Indian or Mexican who is wrongly accused! And every week, a WASP is shown to be a pig-headed fascist. It is utter rubbish.

Sunday, 8 July

To George by 6 o'c. and Michael came at 6.10. We went to Cantina for dinner & G. got quite sentimental about the past 'Oh! those were the days! when we used to go to the Grill & Cheese & have dinner for 30 shillings!' etc. A group of lads came in with a *vision* & I asked Peppi who he was and was told 'He's with his affaire' so I said 'Then forget it!' but it didn't stop me dreaming. Wonder how Louie and Jean are faring in Barbados.

Monday, 9 July

Went to see Gyles Brandreth[9] and he told me about the idea of the book of 'acid drops' which he would collate & have me sponsor: the foreword which they want from me can be done with tape recording & I don't have to write a spiel. I found him very engaging & because of this I became more and more forthcoming & was eventually talking in terms of the confessional: 'My sexual indulgence is all masturbatory . . .' etc. He said that he could arrange for the publishers (Dent) to pay for my endorsement of the book over 3 years.

Monday, 23 July

Listened to 'Carp' on the radio: awful lot of narration & the dialogue not so hot: the vicar's speech overlong & not pointed enough; altogether v. disappointing. Louie told me more about Barbados. I have not heard her enthuse about a resort so enthusiastically ever before. She & Jean want to book up for same time next year!

---

[8] American series about a lawyer of Italian descent at work in the south-western states.

[9] b.1948. Writer, broadcaster, book packager. Elected Conservative MP for Chester in 1992.

Monday, 30 July

I got the script out & started to learn lines and didn't go to bed till about 12 o'c.!! It is unusual for me to learn like this! Most of the time I've always refused to learn till the rehearsal period but sheer boredom & idleness has ensured that I do this preparatory work.

Thursday, 2 August

Laurena rang to say 'You'll be rehearsing at the Cornwallis in Marchmont Street for first week of the play . . .' I said 'Well, I have had to apply for the season ticket in advance (for Greenwich) so I told them 6 weeks . . . I will have wasted a week's fare money but it's too late now . . . I have to collect it at Warren Street on Sunday.'

Monday, 6 August

Walked to the Cornwallis in Marchmont St (where I grew up at No. 57) to rehearse *The Undertaking*. There wasn't one reading which impressed me. John Barron was nearer than anyone else & the moments he hit accurately were very impressive, but there was no sign of *homework* from anyone. Back at 2.30 & I dropped the book – everyone in the cast commenting* – & Donald McKechnie said 'You and Laurence Olivier are the only ones I know who do *that*.' Miriam K[arlin] said 'you're making me feel v. guilty doing it all without the book.'

*It is such a small part that it is not difficult: if it were all typed in one section, it would be only about six pages.

Tuesday, 7 August

I told John Barron how exhausted I felt on the way home: when I said 'I'm sick of all this rubbishy *analysis* of roles that goes on with actors & producers . . . it's all embroidery about nothing . . . why don't they *get on with it*!' and he said mildly 'Oh! it's not been too bad has it? I don't think there's been a *lot* of that?' I said 'Oh you were out of the room for masses of it.'

Wednesday, 8 August

When it came to my long speeches D.M. started nit picking: 'You're not getting enough colour into it . . . these lines should sound as enthusiastic as your conversation about Swinburne which I heard in the lunch break.' The comparison is ludicrous, since involuntary speech and formal dialogue each demand a different delivery.

Thursday, 9 August

Sat whispering to the Company Manager rude comments about D.M.'s direction. Afterwards D.M. said 'After I'd given the note to Miriam I noticed you making a disapproving remark about it.' I told D.M. that in fact I'd said of him 'More fucking *theorising*!' and added 'You must understand: I am someone who wants to get on with learning the steps, not hearing a lecture about how the waltz evolved.' It all seemed to pass off amicably enough, but this morning I rang Trevor and moaned about D.M.'s pedestrian production so I feel a worse traitor. Home by 4.30. Suddenly I feel: to hell with it! You have tried, got little thanks for it, now leave them to stew in their own juice – fuck the lot of 'em, and their production! If I dropped dead from anxiety over it, they'd only be concerned with re-casting.

Friday, 10 August

There is endless talk but really very little work done. D.M. allows misreading after misreading in other members of the cast but not *me*. Again & again one hears lines delivered senselessly but he doesn't stop them. Miriam is averagely good & occasionally stunning. The conversation is all horribly polite and if anyone's got a malicious humour they're taking bloody good care to hide it. I sally up with 'I've got this huge knob you know' & they smile embarrassedly and walk away.

Wednesday, 15 August

After McKechnie had picked me up on textual mistakes for the umpteenth time, I said 'Everyone else in this cast gives senseless renderings which are never questioned but I'm picked on *every time*!' & he replied 'They are slower than you: you've got it all there & you can take the corrections . . . don't worry I'll get round to them later . . .' *If he'd said something like this days ago it would have allayed all the anguish.*[10]

Thursday, 16 August

Walked to Cornwallis. Again they were all theorising about the probable & possible motivation . . . ugh! I am sick of it. I was larking about at the back & D.M. said 'If the company get put off by Kenneth miming masturbation, will they please tell me & I shall slap his wrist and stop it!' I protested 'I wasn't wanking' & he said 'Well you were doing Parkinson *and* the disease.' I had lunch with Lorraine[11] & her boyfriend John at the Russell Hotel and the manager said 'Would you have a

---

[10] Written, for effect, in black ink instead of blue.

[11] Lorraine Chase. Former fashion model (b.1941) of distinguished appearance and broad London accent, a combination of attributes which made her famous in a series of filmed advertisements for vermouth.

bottle of wine on me?' & I said a delighted thank you. I feared I would be *dead* in the afternoon but it was all right!

Saturday, 18 August
With Louie to Old Vic to see *Romeo & Juliet*, with Michael Thomas. He was a fine young Romeo and had the poetry, the passion, the looks, and that unselfishness in playing which is the mark of generous confidence: the rest were all good, but he stole it all. I have never had such a moving & rewarding evening at the Vic ever before. I wrote a letter telling Michael Thomas that his performance had won my unbounded admiration.

Monday, 20 August
We did the whole of the play in the afternoon & I must say, everyone is proving v. interesting. Steven Grives really does his homework, Gerald Flood is getting better & better and Miriam is super: J. Barron good when he pulls his finger out.

Tuesday, 21 August
At lunch time I had a drink downstairs and drank too many white wines! Started giggling during the run-thro' and wasn't very good. In fact the whole way thro' everyone was flat. It was an utterly dreary run-through and one felt that D.M. was keenly disappointed. I am so depressed about this play: what irony that I was the one complaining to the author about the standard of performance and production! It's *me* that ends up being bad! D.M.'s geography has got better & better & his instructions have tautened everything, and actors have responded by performing that much better. They've all gone ahead: I've just stood still.

Wednesday, 22 August
Oh! I was rotten! & after, when I said so, D.M. said 'You were a bit down, that's all . . . but you're all right . . . trust me.' Earlier Annette Crosbie had said 'You're someone who needs to be surrounded by affection.' Not once have I got thro' this play correctly! Always I make mistakes, always I'm inhibited, never do I enjoy it. At 7 o'c. there was a phone call from Donald McKechnie which was at once perceptive and solicitous and kind. Glad I'd been on the telephone to Trevor Baxter (saying he was all of these things) five minutes earlier. D.M. told me 'Don't be downcast – only with you in that play, doing what you are doing, makes all the rest possible.' He couldn't have said anything more encouraging to me.

Monday, 27 August
Up at 6.30 on this momentous day. After 3 weeks' rehearsal we actually perform it tonight, and who knows whether audiences will find it enthralling? All the men are in a communal dressing room so there is no privacy. The D/rehearsal went OK. Notes after in Green Room & D.M. told me 'Don't lose the *drive* on those big speeches . . .' I only really understand quick or slow. I think this means quick. The news on radio was that Lord Mountbatten had been assassinated by the IRA. John Barron changed the play ref. to Royal Family: he made it 'the ambassadors' instead, but references to the Queen got laughs, so death didn't affect the auditorium. The opening got lots of laughs & I really wished I'd been part of the comedy but I had to go on and do the 'voice of authority' which can only invoke silence in a theatre. The second half I was about 25% off the text and unsure, relying on technique & enduring one ghastly dry, which they took for a pause, then I carried on. Bill K[enwright],[12] Trevor B. came round & were very kind.

Tuesday, 28 August
The laughter was nowhere near the 1st night level!! and some of 'em were thrown by it. Suited me 'cos I don't get any! so I wasn't as jealous. Well at least tonight I was more in command with my little bits but obviously I didn't please everyone! Mim & I were both anxiously querying them 'We were better tonight weren't we? Didn't you think?'

Wednesday, 29 August
We had notes from D.M. and another run-thro'. The play started at 7 o'c. (actually about 7.10!) and the reception was fair. I heard Lorraine Chase say her cue to Miriam ('Don't you like being raped?') right thro' a laugh! And yet Mim's reply 'Strange as it may seem I have never been taken by force' still got the laugh! She is a super pro! There was a crowd after! Rona & Fred Carpenter came! lovely, and Fenella!! and B & G brought Louie & we all had a party downstairs given by Bill Kenwright which was lavish.

Thursday, 30 August
In the D/room Bill Kenwright said 'In spite of those notices I still have faith in this piece' and told us that if the cast was willing he would like to tour it at a few dates before trying a London theatre. 'I'd like to do a week in Brighton & say the Arts Centre at Poole . . . so that

---

[12] Actor turned producer, b.1945.

we could live down these notices . . .' and asked us to think about it. So it's rewrites time!

Friday, 31 August

In the interval D.M. came round: 'You're far too self-indulgent and it's dragging the pace back . . .' That put me off for the 2nd Act & I ruined a couple of things and got my final speech messed up completely. Trevor B. came in, and Bill Kenwright. Trevor said 'You mustn't leave the play or you'll jeopardise the production . . . I've got to fight for my play . . . otherwise there'll be no London production . . . no French's Acting Edition . . .' I said 'It's a lonely part & I will get frustrated in a run . . . and I was told originally that I was to act with Prunella Scales and Carol Hawkins . . . that was changed and nobody told me . . .' B.K. said indignantly 'I don't want to stay here and listen to this: I am not going to hear my company disparaged.' There was quite a row with me calling him 'pompous', but in the end I told T.B. 'If you really believe I'm essential to your production, I will not let you down.' I was seething with anger.

Saturday, 1 September

In between the two houses, I went with Steven Grives to a nearby restaurant & after that we strolled up to the Observatory. Some negro lads from Shoreditch talked to us & one let me ride his bicycle which was v. thrilling 'cos I got up quite a speed. One of them (George) told me he'd fallen, hit his face, and lost the sight of one eye: he was extraordinarily matter of fact about it and was a handsome boy with a twinkling good humour.

Wednesday, 5 September

Ned Sherrin rang at 3.10! 'I'd just like to go over the points of our conversation tonight . . .'[13] Oh dear! Got the 6.11 train to Greenwich which was packed with people & v. unpleasant. The show went badly for me 'cos I had to put in a new line to replace reference to the Abbey (where the Mountbatten funeral takes place today) and I ruined the rhythm. BBC car drove me to Quaglino's and I sat at a table in the night club with Ned Sherrin and Charles Aznavour and Nigel Dempster – there was hardly any talk of the play. Ned said 'We mustn't sound as tho' we're plugging the play . . .' Car home by 12.30. Thought of George Shoreditch and erotic fantasies . . . oh! I must get this out of my system!

---

[13] On 'Medium Dry Sherrin' (Radio 2), 'a late night cocktail of conversation, music and mirth, live from Quaglino's Restaurant in the heart of London.'

Sunday, 9 September

I played the guitar recording which Bill [Kenwright] has given me. It is superb! On the second side, there is a version of *Jeux Interdits* (Yepes)[14] which is entitled 'Romance' & labelled 'traditional'. I will always remember the film & Gordon Jackson with this. The former when the children climbed to the owl's perch & hung the pendant round its neck & said 'Keep it for a thousand years . . .' and the latter playing the melody on guitar in the D/room at Hackney Empire when we were doing Orson's film of *Moby Dick*. Realised with a jolt today that I like this company, this management, this play (not the part) more than anything else I've ever experienced! I have been greatly fortunate in my career. Only *wish* dear Peter – who shaped so much of it – had been here to see this.

Friday, 21 September

I recall Bill K. saying last night, apropos the play not getting a theatre: 'Well, actors have all got to *live* . . . so if it comes off after the tour . . . well we'll have tried anyway . . .' & Trevor said 'Yes, & I will have to write another play . . .' The tone was one of sad resignation. In the afternoon I went to see Laurena & she gave me a superb photograph! I nearly cried when I saw Peter's face! It was suddenly as if I could see him again, and all the old grief came rushing back in waves of the past. O what a dear friend I lost there!

Monday, 24 September

Caught the 11.35 to Poole. Curtain is 7.45. The audience was terrific! And the reception of the play was superb. Rather like the first preview (Monday) at Greenwich. Trevor Baxter came round after & said 'Well done' but he should have said 'You were wonderful' 'cos I was. I told him frankly that the rewrites represented a threat to me and would ruin my sense of rehearsed rhythm. He said 'I've watched you all grow in the play without interfering, now you must let the play grow too . . .'

Wednesday, 26 September

Rehearsal at 3 o'c. At about 5 o'c. we (Donald, J.B., Gerald Flood) were taken by Jonathan (a chum of Gerald's) for a walk round the harbour & the church & the old Customs House (beautiful Georgian structure) & he told us 'That pub called The Angel is the haunt of all the local homosexuals' saying the word with two O's like the sound in Bow. When I expressed surprise he told me 'Oh yes! there are loads round here!' like a Leigh fisherman talking about cockles.

---

[14] Narciso Yepes (guitar). *Les Jeux Interdits*, 1952, film by René Clément.

Thursday, 27 September

Audience very good. At the end, Bill & Trevor walked in! There was recrimination from Trevor: 'At least I would have liked to see my cuts and rewrites *tried* . . .' etc. but both admitted it had been a v. good performance.

Monday, 1 October

Reached Brighton at 5 to 2 o'c. There was a brief run-thro' for feel of the stage. Coffee in a Wimpy with Trevor, Lorraine, Annette & J.B. Trevor said 'We're all in his diary you know! He's recorded that I hit him after a dinner at Overton's!' & when Lorraine says 'Oh! it's awful to think what's been written about us all in his diary!' Trevor replied 'No dear, it's awful if you're *not* mentioned in the diary!' The company was addressed by Bill Kenwright: 'I'm offering you a week out, then Wilmslow & then if I still can't get a theatre, I'll put you into the Mayfair (which I don't want to do 'cos I'll have to take my show there off) so that you come to London with this play.'

Tuesday, 2 October

Rang Bill & told him to name his own price, rang Laurena & said I'd do the dates he wanted. Then went to sit in a deck chair on [the] front till a collector woke me 'If you haven't the exact sum for payment you must leave the chair!' so I left: this resort is full of old world charm.

Wednesday, 3 October

Charles Laurence came! The performance was OK but the house rather rowdy with lots of clapping on certain laugh lines. After the show Charles told me: 'It is very good indeed: an ensemble piece, very well cast & played, with a lovely production & it *works* when there's every reason to believe that it shouldn't!' Got away at about 11 o'c. Went straight up to my room for a fantasy apropos George Greenwich.

Wednesday, 10 October

Laurena told me that the papers announced the death on the 9th Oct. of John Musgrove. Another dear chum gone. I saw him on two occasions this year (see 27 Feb. & 8 March) and he got me thro' that terrible flu infection: he was a miracle-worker as far as the voice was concerned.

Friday, 12 October

Bill Kenwright phoned: 'Don't tell anyone but we've got the Fortune! It is just right for our play! Oh! my stomach's been going over and over all week . . . but I settled this deal an hour ago & it's starting to settle down now . . .'

Saturday, 13 October

Parkinson Show. It was Kevin Keegan[15] (excellent & dishy) then Lorraine (elegant & poised & v. human & funny) then me. Talked about nose kicked at football, sinus congestion, rep days, u/s Richard Burton, playing Tonevale, getting 'H[ancock's] H[alf] H[our]' through *St Joan*, *Moby Dick* entrée to Sandy Wilson, my audition singing etc., Joe Orton, Edna Welthorpe, diarrhoea (Lorraine chipped in there about my alibi for her being *off* – 'She's got dreadful diarrhoea') and a bit about Charlie & theatre – 'all pansies & whores' & finished with 'Crepe Suzette' which Harry Stoneham set for me marvellously & I paid tribute to Gordon (for inspiring the idea of the tune).[16] O! it was a lovely evening.

Sunday, 14 October

Set out for Gordon & Rona. Gordon showed the recorded TV show on their set. It was quite a shock to see my face on that screen! It looked scraggy & baggy-eyed & the voice sounded like something twixt a bad cold and a foghorn. And the speech mannerisms! O dear. You could hear all the peculiarities you didn't want to hear, and essential words (*Ritz* hotel in the Orton bit) weren't heard at all! Nevertheless, the persona oozed self-confidence & sang-froid & with a face like that, it was just as well.

Monday, 15 October. Wilmslow

Evening perf. was not good. The cast were tentative & lacking the precision & poise this play needs. We repaired to the De Trafford Arms for drinks. Trevor was v. amusing & told us about playing Robert Burns in an ill-fated production where his opening line was 'You'll excuse my crutch, Miss Maclehose?'

Wednesday, 17 October

Went to theatre & was informed by Branwell[17] 'The play is to go to the Campus theatre at Welwyn Garden City next week . . .' Apparently the date's been fixed with 3 days' notice! It's all v. extraordinary.

Friday, 19 October

The cast all feel now (rightly or wrongly) that the production is bewil-

---

[15] Captain of the England football team 1976–82.

[16] A variation on 'Auld Lang Syne'.

[17] Michael Branwell, Company Manager; later an Equity Council member.

dering to the audiences, and this is eating like a cancer at their essential strength: confidence & pride in performance. It needs a producer/ director – someone in authority to *right* this situation.

Monday, 22 October

4.20 from King's X to Welwyn. The performances were enhanced by the small auditorium & it was packed!! and they did it all with 3 days' notice!! Bill & Trevor, after seeing it tonight, are unanimous about the need for some radical rehearsing to bring what B. calls 'that extra 20% to the staging of the piece.'

Wednesday, 24 October

To Campus 5 Theatre. The resentment of the cast gradually eroded as they listened to Trevor & started getting enlightenment they'd never had from McKechnie. Grives later described the speech as 'Churchillian' & it was certainly good oratory: pellucid & fascinating. When Grives questioned one of his positions D.M. sneered 'You suggested it baby . . .' We had the tea break & then, when it came to rehearsal time, D.M. disappeared. Gene (SM) said 'I'm afraid he's left the building' & a search failed to find him in the complex. I said 'Well we must get on with Trevor doing it' and then we got on & did it. Evening perf. was greatly improved.

Saturday, 27 October

Caught the 3.20 to Welwyn, for the Notes from D.M. He'd assembled a circle of chairs & each one had a picture card on it, with a message . . . a sort of apology about Wednesday. Then he gave his notes (none of them were radical) & then we gave the 1st house perf. The Welwyn Theatre management gave us champagne & a buffet meal between the houses & were truly welcoming. The 2nd perf. went well & after that the management gave the ladies splendid bouquets with charming ceremony & it gave a v. fine theatrical ending to our week at Welwyn. The entire episode restored company morale & put the production back into proper perspective.

Monday, 29 October

Walked to Fortune for rehearsal at 2.15. The company in apprehensive mood – all vaguely discontented both with dressing rooms (up endless flights of stairs) or with set conditions . . . With this company, one should have public D/rehearsals, not paid Previews. Curtain up at 8 o'c. The start was fair; there was reciprocity from out front, and then, with the 'women's scene' onwards, it fell away. There was a little rally in the 2nd half but it couldn't repair the damage & the curtain descended on a shaken & demoralised company.

Wednesday, 31 October
The Opening Night[18] is tonight, and it's the first West End opening I've known with no press invited! Lorraine came at 1.40: 'What a nice little house you've got here! Going to give me a cup of coffee? Ah! you are a dear little soul!' and we went to Capital Radio for the radio interview, then she went home: 'I've got to do my presents for the cast!' & I shot round to Lewis's and bought 6 Royal Doulton ashtrays in separate boxes for everyone in the company! First time I've ever given gifts in my life on an opening!! Wrote notes for each person & for Miriam I said

'Thc dialogue's tricky, not easy to say,
The "changes" like doing revue!
But all my misgivings just faded away
When they said I was playing with you'

'cos she is the one for whom I have that special affection which goes right back to the Globe where I received one of the most generous & encouraging letters from her in 1963. A very late curtain eventually went up on the piece with all the house lights left on!!! Instead of the 75% of the play last night actually working, this was about 60%. I rushed my party to Lariana where Giovanni coped with us brilliantly.

Friday, 9 November
To Paris for 'J.A.M.' I lost my temper with idiot Parsons who said (after a sally of mine had no response) 'Well the audience didn't think that was very funny did they?' & I retorted 'And with what relish you greet the failure! You obviously delight in the defeat of a fellow performer! And proceed to rub his nose in it don't you?' and he quickly passed on to another subject.

Saturday, 10 November
In the interval, Lorraine in tears saying 'When you told me Sara was so good in my part & that she made me look like amateur night in the provinces, that really upset me! & I thought you were my friend! I'm intelligent you know! I know bloody well I've only been cast to bring in a few punters off the streets . . . but you were really cruel!' I loftily told her 'For heaven's sake try to recognise a joke when you hear one! Do you imagine I would ask for you to be in a radio programme ('J.A.M.') with me, if I didn't think you had talent?' & she seemed mollified.

---

[18] At the Fortune Theatre.

RIGHT: Publicity time: KW, Louie and Sid James, launching *Carry On Up the Khyber*. 'It was very good indeed. Almost a *Cowboy* in quality. After, to the reception for the critics at the Ivy and made a great fool of myself with various people, and told them they were a load of shit as indeed all critics are.' 26 November 1968.

BELOW: 'Taken by Dennis at a café in the main square at Larache on 25 February. Larache was very sleepy and Spanish. We sat in the burning sun till about 3.35 pm when we set out for home and Hassan piled a box of oranges into the boot of the car as a gift!' 25 February 1970.

LEFT: 'Ingrid came into the wings and was very affectionate, put her arms around me, and said "So, at last my dear! To think I stood here and wished you luck half a year ago!"' 31 July 1971.

Photograph of KW and Ingrid Bergman from the early rehearsal period of *Captain Brassbound's Conversion*, January 1971. (*Hulton Deutsch*)

BELOW: 'Tom had brought his new Polaroid camera down with him and took this photograph of Pat and myself sitting in the drawing room. Tom said "You would never know you'd got such a stinking cold from looking at that photograph..." which is true.' 10 January 1971.

LEFT: A measure of success: 'I rushed to the St James Church Hall Piccadilly for the first rehearsal of *My Fat Friend*. There were press photographers there & all that hoohah.' KW and Jennie Linden, 16 October 1972. (*Hulton Deutsch*)

RIGHT: 'At 7.30 to the Meridian Room where we joined the queue to meet the captain. It was absurd. He whispered to me "I want to have a word with you later" and asked me to the surgeon's cabin. This turned out to be a crowded drinks party and I only just made it to dinner at 9 o'clock.' 15 December 1974, with Louie on board the *Canberra*.

LEFT: 'Louie and me with the girls from the film and Peter Rogers in the bar at the Odeon Marble Arch for the showing of *Carry On Behind* and reception after for the London cinema managers. The man from the Elephant Odeon said "We haven't seen you lately!" So it's nice to be remembered.' 18 December 1975.

Evening Standard, 29 July 1977: 'Enter Hamish, an amiable Irish wolfhound the size of a donkey... Williams: "Very well, I'll tell you how we are doing it. It is being played for absolute reality. It's not a Carry On. Everything has to be sincere and every reaction has to be honest. That's what makes it so screamingly funny. See?"' Peter Cook, KW, Hamish and Dudley Moore in *The Hound of the Baskervilles*. (*Hulton Deutsch*)

ABOVE: Last of the true Carry Ons: (from left) Joan Sims, Kenneth Connor, Suzanne Danielle, KW, Jack Douglas and Peter Butterworth at table, in *Carry On Emmanuelle*, 17 April 1978. 'I had to be photographed with the group and chat with a girl from the *Evening Standard*. All useless. You want publicity when the film's released, not *now*.' (*Hulton Deutsch*)

LEFT: 'In the afternoon, I went to see Laurena & she gave me a superb photograph! I nearly cried when I saw Peter's face! It was suddenly as if I could see him again, and all the old grief came rushing back in waves of the past. O what a dear friend I lost there!' 21 September 1979. Peter Eade (on telephone) with clients KW, Joan Sims and Ronnie Barker, and Laurena Dewar.

LEFT: *The Undertaking*: KW and Miriam Karlin advertise themselves and (second left) Annette Crosbie. 'MK said "Well, they weren't over the moon!" and I said "Mondays are very bad nights" and she replied "No excuses please! They didn't *like it*..."' 29 October 1979. (*Hulton Deutsch*)

BELOW: 'Walked to St Paul's Covent Garden. Into the vestry where I roughed out some notes for my speech. The choir sang Hattie's favourite songs. I was frozen. The church was bitterly cold.' 10 November 1980. Barbara Windsor and KW after the memorial service for Hattie Jacques. (*Hulton Deutsch*)

'Changed into a suit & went to this dinner at the Lancaster Hotel for the Film & Cinema Veterans. It was death. When I got up to make the speech I felt utterly doomed and I got thro' it (for the most part in silence) pretty quickly! Percy Livingstone (President) sent me photographs and said it was all a great success so perhaps I've no judgment in these matters.' 22 April 1981.

ABOVE: 'Lunch at the Griffin in Kingston and then a signing session at Smith's there. Managed only about fifty or sixty and it wasn't exactly a *hit*. I had forgotten how gruelling these sessions are!' 13 November 1981.

LEFT: 'Michael took this photograph of me and Lou outside the block.' 21 September 1986.

Monday, 12 November

The company was addressed by Bill on stage & he said 'I'm not getting the performances I want & which I was getting on the Tuesday before we opened here . . .' He talked about the lack of engagement in the playing & repeated 'There isn't a line that can be thrown away in this piece . . . you can't sit back & relax in it . . .' In the event, the performances from the rest of the company were wildly fluctuating. Bill came up in the interval & told G.F. 'You're all over the place! just gabbling . . . nobody appears to be *listening* to what other people are saying . . .' I interrupted 'Yes! he should agonise more . . . like Gielgud would in the role . . . it is ideal for Gielgud, and Ralph R. should play Barron's part . . .' Bill said 'You're awful!' & I mused 'I suppose I'm not greatly liked.' 'Liked?' he exclaimed, 'You're not likeABLE!' He said that the audience (including a party of Americans) didn't know what it was all about. Walked home. In Drury Lane, an old man walking his dropsy-ridden dog said 'How's your show Ken? Is it picking up yet?' & I muttered 'Yes thank you' & fled.

Tuesday, 13 November

Miriam told me last night 'You're dropping the line "I have power" . . .' so tonight I gave it more projection & she looked approvingly at me. O! would that everyone had her perceptiveness & integrity in the play. G.F. came up grandly! the vowels being given proper care & so my remarks apropos Gielgud were not futile at all!

Wednesday, 14 November

Had the Times yesterday (back after nearly a year's absence) but went back to Telegraph today 'cos I prefer the lay-out. Hate the idea of going to Teddington for this TV rubbish 'Give Us A Clue'![19] After a lot of standing about and v. tiresome schoolboy jokes from Spike Milligan, we got under way & I was out by 5 o'c. The performance from company was good. One of the obelisks fell as J.B. kicked it on leaving & I had to stand holding it up. Miriam said 'Looked as if you were having a pee up the back there . . .'

Sunday, 18 November

Ate some toast etc. before going to Bill for the lunch. I was ragged by them all about being too loud, my conversation obscene & my persona abrasive etc. etc. Since all the raillery contains some hidden truth I sometimes wonder why I'm invited in the first place! Bill told Louie (about me) 'I never know when he is serious and when he is joking.' I think he *does*, but he chooses to misinterpret & avoid a challenge.

---

[19] Long-running charades game played between a male and a female team.

Monday, 19 November

The evening was made for me by a letter from dear Ron Hayden![20] He is a cousin of mine, and was apprenticed at Stanford's at the same time as me! We used to cycle to work together & we joined the sea-cadets together. Oh! he used to be so dishy! He was Dolly Kiff's son & she was daughter of Grandma Williams' sister so we're related.

Thursday, 29 November

I went out early and went to Drake's & found a salver which can bear an engraved inscription 'To Bill from the cast' etc. Sitting in the flat after lunching with Louie at 12 o'c., she came in & said 'Haven't you got a matinée?' & I suddenly realised I had forgotten it!! Got to theatre in time for the half. To 'J.A.M.' after. I bawled & shouted dreadfully: quite disgraceful. It's desperation stakes. Guests were Tim Rice & John Junkin, both non-starters. The former said when I spoke 'Can one challenge for *boredom*?' & the latter 'I am dropping off when he starts' and they didn't get any laughs. Back to the Fortune.

Saturday, 1 December

I said to Steven 'I may drop dead one of these nights' & he replied 'Yes, it's a good way to go – in the middle of the play – Ronnie Radd went like that . . .' and I suddenly realised that so many of the cast of *Paradiso* whom I worked with are now dead.

Tuesday, 4 December

Walked to theatre. The house was dreadful. Looked full of paper, and the Upper Circle closed!! I suppose they put the cheap seats people down in the stalls & circle! They sat mute for most of the evening, and the effect is hysteria-making: one longs to start laughing. Once or twice, I looked at Miriam and it was all I could do to control myself. Playing this to empty houses, as we're all forced to do, is becoming *purgatory*. In a sense, I wanted to do this play because I felt I owed something of a debt to the theatre; by the time I get out, I will have paid that off!

Saturday, 8 December

In between houses, Lorraine gave a champagne party & after I'd had a few, the second house perf. was dulled for me & went a bit haywire. In the interval, Miriam said 'We had a touch of the revue Kenneth Williams tonight didn't we? We lost the integrity of the performance I used to admire . . .' There was no answer to the rebuke. I said 'I never have been a consistent actor . . . I'm not made of that quality

---

[20] An instance of mellowing. See entry for 23 February 1948, p. 23.

of steadfastness that befits a star . . .' & she said 'Rubbish! you *are* a star . . . you were just *pissed* dear . . . too much champagne.'

Monday, 10 December
Rehearsed the play with Carol Hawkins who opens tonight. Played to an empty house: there were about fifty people in the stalls and the rest of the theatre was closed!

Tuesday, 11 December
Laurena phoned: 'I am thinking of giving up the business . . . so I'm going to get people to make other arrangements & give it a year to run down . . . I want to have some married life of my own . . . anyway I want you to think about it . . .'

Friday, 14 December
Some of our performance variations are *mad*. Last night I suddenly went into an 'Olivier' voice! And when I went to J.B. for 'material witness' I farted as I spoke & *knew* that he was aware of the dreadful odour that ensued. Everyone now is talking about when it will come off and somehow I don't think the issue of my handing in the notice is going to be relevant.

Sunday, 16 December
Terry B. gave a party. It was distinctly uncomfortable: an uneasy mix of sexes & ages. One dreary matron carried on about 'a humane society which should care for victims of thalidomide' & all sorts of maladjusted misfits, and I said 'Rubbish! they should all be painlessly disposed of' & she produced the would-be trump card 'Who would you get to do the killing?' I observed that we never used to find it difficult to recruit hangmen & after that she pointedly ignored me.

Wednesday, 19 December
There was an embarrassed gathering of the cast in the wardrobe & Bill stood huddled in his lumberjacket like an uneasy stage-hand surrounded by aesthetes. Steven presented the salver to Bill. Bill said 'In all the years of presenting shows, this is the first time a company has ever given me a present!' & kissed the tray & thanked everyone. He said 'I can tell you all that you'll be here till January' & when M.K. said 'And after that?' he adroitly sidestepped to save my face. Carol gave me a lift home.

Thursday, 20 December
Laurena rang: 'I delivered your notice to the Kenwright office . . . did he say anything about it last night?' I told her no, she said 'Well

that's done with now & I've told him you are leaving on Feb. 2, 1980.'

Monday, 24 December
We had about a hundred or so out there & they didn't make a sound. When I got to the line 'Living proof of death' M.K. got hysterical & told me after 'That's us!' & fell about laughing. Everyone was given useless presents & silly tokens. Everyone now openly admitting it's purgatory & longing to get away from the prison sentence.

Tuesday, 25 December
Went for drinks to Paul, then on to St George for lunch. I had the lie down till about 7 o'c. Went in to see Louie at 7.15. I told her: 'This is certainly a better Christmas for you than last year! When you cut your lip and had all that injury & dentistry to cope with!' & she said 'Yes! don't remind me of all that thank you!'

Thursday, 27 December
I walked to the theatre & on the way I dumped the American (Webster) dictionary which B.K. gave me in the basket of a student nurse's bicycle; she will probably think it's a prank! But I don't want a dictionary that spells honour *honor* . . . the whole thing is a rotten production. Performance delayed 'cos a man suffered a heart attack in the D/circle & they tried the kiss of life unsuccessfully. Curtain rose at 8.18 on the line 'We have buried Maud . . .' which was appropriate.

Saturday, 29 December
Up at 7 o'c. to the clashing noise of dustbin lids as the refuse men clear the White House rubbish: went over there for papers & a man standing by the desk said 'You ain't all that on "Give Us A Clue" are you Ken?' & I felt like replying 'You aren't all that in a hotel lobby either' but instead I kept my back to the offensive creature & thanked the Porter effusively.

Monday, 31 December
At the curtain Carol said 'I can't give you a lift home tonight' & I replied 'I hope you have a lousy evening & I hope you get done for drunken driving.' When she asked 'Will you come & meet my sister?' I said 'No!' and went upstairs & tripped up & hurt my foot. Grives said 'Are you celebrating tonight?' & I cried out 'Mind your own fucking business!' and went home on foot thro' freezing streets. Every moron I passed recognised me & shouted 'Carry On Kenny' or similar rubbishy slogans. Joined Louie for supper & we saw the *Sunset Boulevard* film. When I first saw it I thought it was good but now you see how rotten it was.

1980

Thursday, 3 January
D.M. turned up at the Fortune & in the interval he said 'I must tell you what a splendid performance you are giving in this play . . . it is really stunning . . .' & I murmured 'How kind' feeling like a dying Florence Nightingale hearing the compliments of Victoria. The house was about a third full downstairs. Carol gave me a lift home: her perf. came right up tonight & I told her so!

Friday, 4 January
Mike Murray (Company Manager) is taking over from J.B., so we have to rehearse this fucking play *yet again*!!! I am utterly sick of performing it now & I am truly *delighted* I handed my notice in!!

Saturday, 5 January
2nd House half empty. J.B. said 'That is terrible business for a Saturday!' & M.K. replied 'We don't need you to tell us that! We're aware it's Zimbabwe out there! No need for you to stand gesturing like Moses leading us to the Promised Land . . .' Grives furious about rehearsing on Friday 'I've made arrangements & everything.' I said 'You'll have to cancel them!' & he muttered 'You malignant little creep' & I laughed 'Oh! don't try to ingratiate yourself with *me*!'

Monday, 7 January
Telephone call from Rod[1] (Kenwright office) saying 'We have to take the play off on the 28 January because the business has collapsed & there is no advance now . . .' Walked to theatre. Nobody there, so they shoved the few into the stalls & the embarrassing charade continued. Grives was excessively polite: 'I want to be recorded in your diary as a pleasant & complaisant juvenile 'cos you're a very good leading man.' All this with the great smile. Hm. One or two of the actors have made cracks about 'Fine draw you turned out to be!' and whilst I used to laugh it off, I'm now getting irritated by it.

---

[1] Rod H. Coton, Kenwright's General Manager.

Friday, 11 January
At the theatre, they told me 'The Box Office rang the Kenwright office & told them there were only 7 seats booked so could they cancel the matinée, but they refused & said the actors must perform it to the empty auditorium.'

Monday, 14 January
Tonight was easily the most appalling performance of the play that has ever been given. One kept wondering why the few spectators were staying to watch such halting phlegmatic rubbish. I certainly have *never* been so glad to get off a stage! Taking the one curtain call was excruciatingly embarrassing.

Wednesday, 16 January
It's in the papers that David Whitfield has died in Australia! aged 53 . . . our liaison in H.K. seems light years away! So does his snubbing me at that Olivelli's restaurant in Store St . . . ah well, it's all water under the bridge now.

Friday, 18 January
Well, I began this chore by saying it was a punishment for my walking out of shows like *Platinum* and *Fat Friend*, so I'm certainly being made to serve my sentence to the full. M.K. muttering 'Only ten to go!'

Tuesday, 22 January
I heard M.K. on the stairs saying 'There were no seats booked so they had to ring round the hospitals & offer comps to nurses . . .' The auditorium was dotted with a pathetic few who either didn't understand it, or didn't like it. They sat mute throughout. M.K. cried out in the interval: 'Oh! this is rock bottom! You can't go any lower than this! It's all a bloody nightmare!' and she is right. For this was a horrendous evening. Carol gave me a lift home, and I nearly broke down. Started crying. Then pulled myself together. You'll just have to get through these horrific days . . . it can't last for ever.

Thursday, 24 January
Loads of letters to answer. Mostly children who are seeing 'The Dribblesome Teapots' on 'Jackanory' this week. Met Ronnie Waters & told him 'I spoke with Michael Anderson about going to him as my new agent' and he said 'Yes, it's a very good idea & you must get a clear date & understanding about it with Laurena . . .' so I'd better drop her a line about it.

Saturday, 26 January
2nd house fair in numbers. McKechnie came round: 'I could see you doing all your little tricks! Putting new moves in, and talking to the others surreptitiously . . .' I could hardly believe it, since I'd performed it *scrupulously*. I just gave up. M.K. came & gave us drinks & we stood in embarrassed knots on the landing, sipping wine . . . And I suddenly thought 'To hell with all this false bonhomie', got my coat and left. I struggled along with the two bulging plastic bags containing all my belongings & reflected that *nothing about this show had been easy*! Relieved to get in by 11.30. The prison sentence is over.

Wednesday, 30 January
Started work with Gyles Brandreth at 11 o'c. and we did not stop till about 6.30 when he said he'd got other things to do. It was profitable work because it really meant putting all the linking material into shape & making it sound like me and not some researcher.

Friday, 1 February
Walked to the office & saw Laurena & read a play she'd found *Fourth Girl Sharing* which had comedy dialogue but very little plot and really didn't go anywhere. She said she'd been asked if I would do a week of chat-shows on Australian TV if they could tie it in with the film dates and I said all right.

Tuesday, 5 February
We saw a profile of Arthur Askey & he was incredibly brave. He's playing Dame in panto at the Alexandra in Birmingham & we saw a funny excerpt & then he was interviewed. He said, apropos Communists and Liberals, 'I'd put 'em up against a wall and shoot them! I would!' and spoke of their undermining a decent society.

Friday, 8 February
Was at Paddington by 9 o'c. Met by Michael (manager of Nimbus) 1 and a half hours later & he drove me to Wyastone Leys. It's a magnificent country house in wooded grounds & the recording studio is a lovingly restored ballroom with a ceiling that is pure delight. Met all the people I'm working with – Numa[2] seems to be the prime entrepreneur – and after coffee we did a test recording of Chapter One[3] which seemed successful & may well be kept. Worked till about 6 o'c. Then drinks & dinner & coffee in the drawing room and lots of

---

[2] Numa Libin.
[3] Of *Monkey*, 1942 translation by Arthur Waley (1889–1966) of a sixteenth-century Chinese novel.

chat & I lost all sense of discipline and they were too polite to exert it, so I didn't get up to the room till gone 11 o'c.!! Must be *mad*. Well, one has to learn that's all: can't work properly if it's all going to be fun, and they encourage me! Tell me 'Your anecdotes are very good' and it's like letting an alcoholic loose in a brewery.

Sunday, 10 February

I think we're all going to be very tired of Arthur Waley ere long. Went on till 6.45 when, in the midst of the start of a new story, I realised that I was making errors thro' tiredness and concentration was ebbing. We had drinks & talked and I launched into a great saga about Singapore & the Hank Marriott scandal. It's still remarkable to me *now* that it all actually *happened*. Talking of Lieder I mentioned *Vier Ernste Gesänge* & Numa said 'Would you like to hear it now?' & of course I said yes & I heard that *and* two other songs but sung as I've never heard before by a German singer who is exclusive to Nimbus: a voice of extraordinary range & singular quality.[4] Life always brings me back to the safe circle of spiritual kinfolk. Nothing is really coincidental, but only another piece of mosaic finding its place in the design.

Monday, 11 February

After breakfast we did the last 30 pages & then I re-recorded Chapter One so that they can compare first with last. When I heard the playback, it was gratifying to hear that the first recording was the best. Eugene Beer, their PRO, came over & we all had a chat. Gerald said to me 'Shall we say that this session is the equivalent of ten LP's?' I shall tell Laurena to keep the fee down to a minimum. Mike drove me to the station and told me 'Sometimes Numa will suddenly put that Persian cat down on my desk just as I'm trying to get on with something . . . then I realise he's right! There isn't any need to bust a gut! And I relax and take my time . . . They're a very special lot here & their only real concern is with quality.' He is right. Before I left, I heard a bit of a piano recording they've made by this young 19-year-old Belgian: it is Opus 18, Brahms transcription from Sextet, and it was simply stunning.[5] A pellucid harvesting of tonal riches. I feel quite exhausted after working in such concentrated fashion for four days.

---

[4] A gentle (though risky) joke was being played on KW here, since the recording must have been the one made not long before by Shura Gehrman – alias Numa Libin.

[5] Usually known as 'Theme and Variations in D minor, for piano'. The issued Nimbus recording of the piece by Luc Devos bears a recording date of 3/4 July 1980.

Thursday, 14 February
To Heathrow where we were given the VIP treatment by Chris of Cyprus Airways. Plane packed & full of idiots. Taxi at airport took us to Apollonia Hotel. Everyone looks dubious when you talk about the weather here, so obviously we've come at the wrong time I should think.

Saturday, 16 February
Alas! the weather isn't good! The only consolation for me is watching the idiots deprived of their sunbathing and swimming: that is a great delight I must say!

Tuesday, 19 February
I went with Louie to the bank in Limassol (by taxi), then we went for a walk along the byways & she fell over on the pavement. I think she escaped with broken skin on the knee. One's reaction nowadays is 'Oh no! not again!' 'cos one remembers how much trouble all these wounds are. Suddenly I scream with irritation inside & ask 'Why didn't you go somewhere on your own?' With Louie everything is helplessness on holiday 'What do I do?' 'How shall I dress?' 'How does *this* work?' It's like going around with a mental defective. Moved into the bar for coffee where we met Ian & Sue. They run a restaurant in Surrey, and he was bumptious & boring: 'My children remarked on your *age* . . . must be awful to see your old movies with the younger face.'

Thursday, 21 February
Chatted with Roger & Anne from Gants Hill: he said 'I am Jewish but I'm not orthodox.' His children are gorgeous. Down to dinner at 8 o'c. and the usual banalities exchanged & then coffee in the bar with Louie yawning & bored till I said 'You should go to bed' & the flare-up 'I'm going! Don't worry!' And the sulky exit. Oh! I am so conscious of age now! So aware that I'm getting old, getting tired . . . impatient where I should be solicitous, unkind where I should be compassionate, fed up with the endless pretence & the unfulfilled existence. I must learn from this 'holiday' nightmare: there is no recuperative element in it for me, I am really required to work. And the more I work, the more thankless it is. There were three or four references to my *conceitedness* today from both Carol & John – ostensibly jokey but fundamentally serious.

Friday, 22 February
Louie pushed under the door a card from B & G, but I don't want to be reminded of birthdays! I want to forget them. I hope to heaven

none of them start all that rubbish in the hotel. Some fat Cypriots tried to interest me in buying property here!! Good night!

Saturday, 23 February
They were all sitting stupefied in the lounge, while the muzak blared Merry Widow tunes for the umpteenth time. This isn't a holiday: it's a *living nightmare*. In the street today, an unshaven & dirty man smelling of BO cried 'I met you in Pinewood with Charlie Hawtrey!' & I recognised the aging bit of rent.

Monday, 25 February
Message from Nicosia: 'You must report 2 hours before flight tomorrow, leave hotel at 7 o'c. Your plane is going via Paris . . . they expect 2 hours' delay . . .' It is all fitting for this nightmare of a trip. How I wish I'd never come to this accursed muckheap.

Tuesday, 26 February
The President of Cyprus & entourage took over the plane and we left for Paris at about 10.45. Eventually, after sitting in the plane for 2 hours at Orly, we took off for London, arriving at 6.45 so we had been cooped up in that Boeing for *nine hours*. Dear Michael was there, having been waiting since 1.30 when it was supposed to arrive! I have never been so glad to see his face!

Wednesday, 27 February
Laurena rang: 'The Australian film is off now, 'cos they can't get the money . . .'[6] I'm glad I ain't got to go there!! Walked to the John Wood Studios for the v/o for Spam with Kenny Connor. It all went smoothly & they were very encouraging but I was a bit irked when they made me do a speech for their delegate conference in Harrogate!! Gratis! Saw the start of 'This Is Your Life' with Emlyn Hughes & his good looks and winning smile utterly sickened me & I switched it off and returned to my flat.

Friday, 29 February
In the mail today is a Jury Summons for April 21st!!! I wrote a letter to the Jury Summoning Officer saying that I was an actor comedian doing send-ups of Judges etc. and not suitable for Jury Service. It is worth a try-on and if they don't accept it, then I'll have to do the dreary task.

---

[6] Probably a long-projected *Carry On Down Under*.

Saturday, 1 March
Quite a few letters to answer. One man says I advised him to seek a more stable career than acting & that he suffered a nervous breakdown as a result! & this was all in 1966! He asks: 'What should I do now?'

Tuesday, 4 March
I got to Ealing Studios at ten to 10. Finished the first one at about 12.20. We started the second one at about 2.45. Break for tea & then back to complete the third! In spite of the sound going out of synch. & having to run it *all over again*! I screamed at the sound man 'You should be wearing sackcloth and ashes!' & seeing his dismay, I added 'Just because you're good-looking you can get away with it, but wait till you're *old* like me!' and then he smiled.

Friday, 7 March
Delightful letters in post! 1) saying I'm excused Jury Service! and 2) charming note from Steven Grives, with his new Hampstead address. Louie played me her L.P. of 'Beyond Our Ken' and it was marvellous to hear such comedy again! One still had the odd laugh and continuous giggle at the fun of the scripts. All that cast was good & K.H. superb! Paddick did some v. subtle & brilliant things! In comparison, my stuff was very crude.

Monday, 31 March
I have to go to the second day of this [Equity] AGM, and listen to more rubbish. When I got there I was voted into the Chair 'cos President was absent. I rushed business as fast as I could and four motions were withdrawn by left wingers so that Vanessa Redgrave could put her motion which was to veto all our productions in Israel. There were some v. nasty moments with Kempinski tearful about forebears suffering under Nazism. She lost the vote & there was a demand for a recount but we had to vacate the Astoria by 3 o'c. & I closed the meeting having forgotten to ask for a vote on acceptance of Annual Report!! As a Chairman this behaviour was ludicrously inept.

Tuesday, 1 April
I am secretly dreading all the publicity fuss over the forthcoming book. Went to Equity Council meeting at 10.30. All the rubbish of the AGM was discussed & possible revoking explored. I fancy most of the damage was repaired.

Sunday, 13 April
Lately, I find it increasingly tedious to cope with Louie. Always the childish questions, always the desire to be entertained, and always a

closed mind. Nothing is any different year in and year out: I am still explaining the same things over & over again.

Friday, 25 April
It is significant that the entries here have been sparse of late: it's 'cos I'm depressed. Walked to Robert Bolt's new home and took Bob to Hungry Horse for dinner. Bob told me that Willman is acting in N.Y. with K. Hepburn! O! they all fall with their arse in the marmalade.

Wednesday, 30 April
At 2.30 went to Molinaire to do 4 more scripts for 'Willo the Wisp'. Must say, I admire Nick Spargo's industry & inventiveness! His ideas are charming.

Thursday, 1 May
To Maidstone for STV programme 'Opinions Unlimited' with Sir David Napley, Sarah Hogg and me. In the middle of one of my bits I got cut off 'I'm sorry we must move on to another question . . .' and the question? 'Should men wear underpants which are coloured, or wear white ones . . . ?' and for that sort of frivolous rubbish I was cut off in midstream.

Monday, 12 May
My membership of the Society of Authors came through today! I've been accepted.

Tuesday, 20 May
Elsie telephoned me: 'It's funny that you should have been telling me on Monday that you'd like to direct a play because I've had David Porter on the line asking if you would direct *Loot* at their Studio theatre at Hammersmith Aug. 18 to 11 Sept . . .' I said yes I would be interested. Re-read the copy of the play which Joe gave me. Can't help wishing it had a better tag line, but certainly I think the final moment should have Dennis & Hal exchanging conspiratorial nod and wink when Fay kneels in reverence.

Thursday, 22 May
Feeling that I should be dead by now. I have actually reached the stage where I take work to avoid boredom. Went to Mowbray's and got a detective story ([P.D.] James) to read and that took me thro' the day.

Friday, 30 May
Long telephone call from Peggy Ramsay: 'Do you really want to do

Loot? When I told Michael Codron he said he thought it was a very good idea . . . as long as it's not gimmicky with them selling all those paperbacks[7] that have just come out in the foyer . . . of course I haven't read it . . . I get *loads* of letters about it . . .'

Saturday, 31 May
Went to Selfridges in the afternoon and I saw a woman take shampoo & steal it, a child take bits of jewellery, and a student walk with a sweater to the hall of foyer, take off his jacket, don the sweater & then put the jacket over it! I have never seen such blatant theft before. I felt disgusted & then thought 'That store deserves it . . . the place *invites* thieves . . .'

Wednesday, 4 June
Went to Bush House walking slowly 'cos of the very hot weather. In the studio, the producer Anne Theroux said 'Thank goodness it's cool in here' and it was. I had to talk about Calligraphy. I talked about Trajan Roman and subsequent effect of Goths, Gothic script, then the clear uncluttered nature of the script introduced by Alcuin of York[8] (Charlemagne) and subsequent resurgency of engrossing lettering in Victorian time & the effect of Eric Gill[9] (sans serif) but there was a lot of wandering & it will need considerable editing. Saw Louie before she went to her club. She weighs 7st 3lb on the scales: suppose she should be about 3lb lighter than that. I weigh about 9 stone (with summer clothes on) at the moment, but I'd prefer to be less than that.

Tuesday, 17 June
Went to Molinaire at 3.30. Met Pat Hayes & greeted her warmly: she is smashing. It was a radio commercial for Ford, Godfrey Davis & Eve. Standard & we did it in about five different characterisations. There was a sexy one sounding like two people in bed which was very funny. Saw Louie at 5.45. We watched 'Q9', the Spike Milligan Show & it was a great tonic to see something that was funny and bright. What a change from most of the rubbish! Here was infectious humour & I should think they had congratulations flooding in.

Wednesday, 18 June
Got tube to Hammersmith. We interviewed several people for parts of Hal, Dennis & the Nurse & found all three. Harold: Rory Edwards,

---

7 Of *Prick Up Your Ears*.
8 Alcuin (735–804), also known as Albinus, or Ealhwine. Theologian and educator. Befriended Charlemagne in 780.
9 1882–1940. Stonemason, engraver, typographer, inventor of typefaces.

Dennis: Philip Martin Brown, Nurse: Joan Blackham. Now we're left with McLeavy and Truscott and David Porter is trying to get a meeting arranged with actors for these parts at Cork Street so it's more convenient for me. Joan Blackham has brown hair & I asked if she could change the colour. 'Daily!' she replied blandly. V. confident lady. When I said to Rory 'You've been sent for Dennis,' he said smiling 'It's ridiculous . . . I'm Hal . . .' & of course he is.

Friday, 20 June

At 10.30 to Dent's to sign hundreds of book plates for OXFAM. Peter gave me 12 copies of the book[10] & it looks v. handsome! They've done it very well indeed. Seems slimmer than I'd envisaged but that's all right.

Monday, 23 June

Rehearsed at Cottage Place, Brompton Road for 'Whizz Kids'. The script is full of corny gags which actually made me laugh! These days are becoming more and more unreal . . . I do jobs (like this Southern TV one) not because I want to, but because I'm frightened of the boredom of idleness . . . like that last venture in the theatre . . . you think 'Well there is nothing else in the offing, so I might as well do this . . .' and you land up in tatsville & the only consolation is that you're surrounded by pros.

Tuesday, 24 June

I parcelled up two copies of my book to send to Mags and to Jacksons, went to Post Office. Tube to S. Ken. and walked to rehearsal. Arthur Mullard is the most diligent (as far as lines are concerned), Sheila White gets it all wrong & giggles tiresomely, Rita Webb does the same & says 'Oh! I fucked that up!'

Thursday, 26 June

The mail included the statement from Laurena for St Ivel . . . it's over 5000! More than I ever earned in a Carry On! Rehearsed at Brompton Rd. Sheila White got irked when I said of her handwriting 'It looks like the work of a mentally retarded child' & retorted 'I was good enough to play a leading role in "I Claudius"!' I told her 'It's only me being malicious . . . take no notice . . .' Arthur Mullard told me in the loo 'We're too old for all this buggering about . . . we should just go on and *do it* . . . I'm fed up with all these rehearsals . . .' & I know what he means.

---

[10] *Acid Drops.*

Saturday, 28 June

To BBC at Pebble Mill.[11] They told me 'The star of the show, Douglas Fairbanks, can't come . . . so the arrangements & running order are all chaotic at the moment . . . Miss Collins the book writer will interview you . . .' I quickly interjected 'No thank you!' & after my firm rebuttal of that idea, I got Bob [Langley] (who's done it before & is very good) & we ran thro' a few ideas & roughed out some headings. It was, then, endless sitting about till 11.30 when it started! I came on about 12.10! The applause was deafening & the audience so much on my side that I could do no wrong. Talked about: French song, German song, Rambling Syd song, then Army audition S'pore, then Flagship incident Hong Kong, then training period at Carlisle, P[hysical] D[evelopment] C[entre] etc. and at the end Bob produced a copy of *Acid Drops* and we did a couple of quotes. On way out, a picket of striking musicians (who'd been playing outside building in order to create a sound disturbance) hectored me: ''ere! Is Kenny Ball[12] in there? Come on! As an Equity member, tell us the truth!' and I replied 'I don't know', got in the car and left.

Sunday, 29 June

I walked to Peter & Thelma [Nichols]. Their guests were Stephen Sondheim and Hal Prince and Barry Humphries! Peter waxed lyrical over the latter: 'His performance on stage is magical' and said of Sondheim 'The lyrics are brilliant.' Both the Americans were so loud you had to shout in order to converse. Sondheim said of America 'It is an illiterate society . . . the laugh of the week on TV was a state school teacher saying "I teaches English."' Their show *Sweeney* [*Todd*] opens on Wednesday at Drury Lane.

Wednesday, 2 July

With Rita Webb and Arthur Mullard to Southampton, taxi to hotel. We all sat on the terrace having drinks. I had the Camparis. On an empty stomach it is always trouble, but I always feel like a holiday when I'm in an hotel. Everyone sat telling the anecdotes etc. It is odd that a group of pros reveals its insecurity in this fashion. Every new job is a trial & as Wilde said 'They're all trials for one's life . . .'[13]

Thursday, 3 July

Sheila White's admonishments leave one numb: 'You must be careful

---

[11] For 'Saturday Night at the Mill', presented by Bob Langley, with guest presenter Jackie Collins. With Kenny Ball and his Jazzmen.

[12] Trumpeter and bandleader, b.1931.

[13] 'All trials are trials for one's life.' *Selected Letters of Oscar Wilde*, ed. Rupert Hart-Davis, 1979, p.509.

not to anticipate my laugh lines . . .' I said 'Thank you for your advice about playing comedy . . . I have so much to learn . . .' I buggered up several takes over the counting of the chalks 'cos I had to do it upside down & it wasn't easy.

Wednesday, 9 July

Tube to S. Ken & rehearsed till 2.15. The tedium is ghastly. Michael came at 7.15 and we went to the Cosmo. A note came over 'Will you join Phyllida & me for coffee? Eric' & I had an awful shock (thinking it was Sadie Thompson) but then I saw Charles Laurence and Jack grinning at another table & realised it was their joke!

Friday, 11 July

Rehearsed from 10 o'c. Bill Blezard came to play the piano for the school song but the musical element will be so erased by the cacophonous mess we make of it that he can only be an unwarranted expense for Southern TV. A day of appalling tedium. At one point, an exasperated Rita Webb complained 'I *am* acting you know!' & I replied 'You could have fooled me!' whereupon she walked out in a tantrum! Arthur Mullard said 'She's wild 'cos she's found out that her part was first offered to Hattie Jacques yer see!' & Sheila White asked him 'Who told her *that*?' & he said 'I did.' Louise Dogherty (of Dents) told me: 'You ought to know we've a pre-publication sale of ten thousand on your book! and that is very good indeed . . .'

Monday, 14 July

Suddenly remembered! No travellers' cheques for Morocco! Wrote a note & went to bank with it: on the way I spoke to P.O. Engineers working outside our block, they said 'We'll be at work for hours yet . . .' & I suggested coffee & tea & they said they'd like that, so I made up thermos flasks of both and took it all down at about 8.30. One of them said 'People would never believe this!' as though it were all miraculous or something.

Thursday, 17 July. Southampton

At the tea break I was using a knife to butter a biscuit & Rita Webb said 'Give me that knife' & I said 'No, I'm using it' whereupon she screamed abuse for several minutes with remarkable fluency! With cast, producer, S.M.'s etc. she shouted 'I'll knock his fucking head off! He's a cunt spelled with a K the dirty little bastard! And you should hear what he calls the rest of you! On the train he said you were all cunts . . .' It went on and on. It was quite nauseating to watch the exudation of so much malignity & spite. I left the room. I suppose she must be a very unhappy creature.

Friday, 18 July
I was treated like a pariah and (apart from Patrick Newell who was sweet) they all ignored me. I didn't mind. I stayed in the dressing room, and at meal times I went in the canteen & queued with wardrobe people. Nevertheless, the atmosphere was horrible & their ostracising me achieved exactly what they wanted. Never has a television job proved so unpleasant, thankless & boring.

Tuesday, 22 July. Tangier
Found C. lying by the pool and we had coffee there and walked down to Ibn Touta. It was all as if nothing had altered since the Windmill! 'My dear, I took these two sailors in there! One on each arm' etc. etc. No tag lines anywhere. Coffee by the market and Abdulatif came & sat down and bored the arse off us both. A Moroccan father with his enchanting daughter was at the next table & she bade us a dignified & grave farewell when she departed . . . lovely face.

Thursday, 24 July
One had thought so many things would be different but they aren't . . . the same slowing down of one's tempo . . . the baking heat . . . the Byzantine tat . . . any of these back streets could be Turkey . . . and the endless evidence of poverty but not spiritual vacuity such as Europe is full of . . . they all have a zest & vitality & are not vandals.

Friday, 25 July
We wandered into the Socco & I saw this poor lad with rubber shoes – ugh! – so I took him to a shop & got him sandals & a shirt & then some knowing urchins started ragging him & shouting to me 'You want to fuck him!' & all the altruism went out of the window in their eyes. V. sad.

Sunday, 27 July
To Market & I met Mustafa!!!! after all these years! It was marvellous! We embraced warmly & he led C. and me thro' all the labyrinths of the Medina. Then we went to the Captain Simba café & Mustafa told me the usual despairing story about no work . . . no money & so on. He said his brother had died suffering from a duodenal ulceration. 'In the next bed was a little boy . . . he take him in his arms to play with the child & next minute . . . he died . . .' There were tears in his eyes: that is the last of his family gone. I put 150D into a guide book surreptitiously & handed it to him.

Monday, 28 July
I was home by 3 o'c. our time. Read the paper. Shah of Persia dead,

Peter Sellers dead, and tonight, Kenneth Tynan dead. Took one mog. and went to bed.

Thursday, 31 July
Taxi to Selfridges where I signed copies of the book for purchasers. It was only fair . . . no great crowd but I signed for about an hour . . . and astoundingly John Reid[14] came!! 'Sign one for me & one for Elton please . . .' I couldn't believe it!

Friday, 1 August
All that is happening this year seems to be something arranged by someone else . . . as tho' there was a choreographer mesmerising me in the dance . . . what am I doing signing books at stores & writing ludicrous messages to people I don't know?

Saturday, 2 August
To Leicester where I signed in Hudson's Bookshop. Doing the book promotion is like appearing in a provincial tour that's a flop in every town.

Monday, 4 August
To B.H. at 8.30 for 'Start The Week' with Kenneth Robinson: he was v. complimentary about the book. Radio London at 12 for an interview and a phone-in!! One woman upbraided me for snubbing her daughter: 'She only wanted an autograph & you stuck your nose in the air and walked away.' I said 'Yes well I hope you will forgive me . . .' & promised to send an autograph to the wretched creature. Car to Lime Grove for interview on 'Nationwide' with a Sue someone. Appointment with designer Saul [Radomsky] at Eade office. Saul came with the model. It is superb: as soon as one looked at it one knew: 'Here is that rare creature, the artist who faithfully interprets the playwright.' I told him how delighted I was with it.

Saturday, 9 August
Liz Newlands drove me to Barker's and *another bloody journalist* was shoved in! Oh! if anyone else asks me 'What is your favourite quotation?' I shall scream! Then by car to Brent Cross. Before we arrived I said 'This is going to be death' and it was.

Monday, 11 August
Got to Bristol and did the radio interview & then went to George's bookshop. Nobody there. Coped with two bloody reporters: 'Which

---

[14] Manager of the pop star Elton John.

is your favourite story in your book?' etc. and the Harlech TV news cameras in the shop! So one's humiliation (piles of unsold books . . . nothing to sign) is actually filmed! But you dance like a dancing bear.[15] On from there to an exhibition of *unsold* Bratby canvases and I'm hanging alongside the Queen Mother: she's listed at £200, me at £500 & both are ignored by the buyers. On to Harlech TV studios. Eventually appear in front of cameras with Faith Brown. She's v. kind about the book and does one or two of the best women's cracks. Rush for the 5.10 train. 'British Rail regret to announce . . .' It is late. Liz Newlands sitting opposite me looking like a funeral attendant. I'm taking Alka Seltzer 'cos the bowels are in uproar from unnecessary hurried eating. I talk too much to cover the appalling reality of a day filled with horror. Back in the flat with distended belly & wonder how I'm living through the entire stupid con trick.

Saturday, 16 August
Thank God this is the Last Day of Book Signings! & may I never get involved in such tedium ever again. Got the 8.55 to Manchester. The manager entertained us in a freezing underground cellar which had been whitewashed. I did a bit of signing but there was only a few customers interested. Caught the 2.12 getting in at 4.45.

Monday, 18 August
Went to Lyric & met cast[16] over coffee. It was a depressing reading. The only good note was struck by Neil [McCarthy]. The only person to start the theorising crap – 'Do I really believe this?' etc. was Joan! I pointed out as tactfully as possible that analysis in this piece was disaster: 'Your world is entirely *real* to you. That's all that matters.'

Friday, 29 August
Ran thro' the play and it is running quite well. They're still a bit sticky on lines & there are one or two bits of geography which will have to be seen to, but it's in reasonable rep state at the moment. Letter from Dent's saying that *Acid Drops* has gone up to No. 2 in the Best Sellers List!

Friday, 5 September
Got papers at 6.45. The front page carries news of the O'Toole debacle in *Macbeth*!! The savaging by the critics is iterated. Suppose it will help the box office. Went to Hammersmith to rehearse.

---

[15] 'And I must borrow every changing shape/To find expression . . . dance, dance/ Like a dancing bear': from T.S. Eliot's 'Portrait of a Lady'.
[16] Of Orton's *Loot*.

Tuesday, 9 September
Had a technical run-thro' at 2.30 and it was atrocious. The cast all inhibited & nervous in the new set and making endless errors and none of them had made out a personal prop list so everything was awry. Exits & entrances muffed and all the body business with the coffin, screens, cupboards etc. quite dreadful. Kept my temper & went through all the tricky bits of business, finishing at 8.30. Home by 9 o'c. Very depressed. At one point J[ohn] M[alcolm] asked for door chimes to herald the line 'Who'd have thought she'd be back so soon' and to expedite proceedings I said yes, but I will have them taken out tomorrow: it is a spurious device & I'm not having my direction marred by J.M.'s diktat.*

*left it in, in the event.

Thursday, 11 September
Went to B.H. at 10 o'c. to do this b'cast for 'P.M.' D/rehearse at 2.30. Since it was the first time I'd seen it run properly (without stops for some reason) I was pleasantly surprised by the whole thing. David Porter told me that he thought they were doing splendidly & that 'the first week is sold out which hasn't happened before . . .' The performance was good & the cast responded well to a house of rotten laughers who became more receptive in the 2nd half. I could say 'You were all splendid!' with honesty when I went b'stage. Michael drove me to Wigmore Rest. where I gave him dinner & then we drove to B.H. where I talked more about *Loot* on Radio 2 with Pete Dunn. M. said 'Well it's been *three* triumphs for you today' & I was glad glad glad of his company.

Friday, 12 September
Head full of the feelings of last night! Sitting there, watching them struggle manfully against such odds! The tiny room, the heat (I was sweating horribly!), the inhibited audience sitting on hard benches, an idiot getting up walking through line of vision to another seat, then sitting in a gangway, then leaving through the pros. arch!! & banging thro' Emergency Exit . . . Oh! what they had to cope with! Lunch Louie at 12 o'c. Phoned by Lyric Ham: 'John Malcolm has been attacked & has had 16 stitches inserted in the face . . . he may not be able to appear . . .' so I started learning his part. Then another message: 'I've seen him and the stitching is mainly inside his lip so you can't see much & he sounds OK . . . the Doctor says he can go on.' Went with Paul by tube to Hammersmith where I was told 'John Malcolm can't go on!' and they said his face had swollen badly & his diction was impaired. I told J.M. to go home and I went on stage for

him, reading it all from the book. Paul said 'After a while one accepted the convention & the audience really enjoyed it!' They gave us a rousing reception at the end & I made a short speech of thanks. David Porter came b/stage: 'It was terrific . . . you should have seen the surge of excitement as that audience trooped out of the Studio! It was electric! You've made history here . . . no director has ever gone on stage and read the part . . .'[17] Joan Blackham was v. nice to me & I sat in her room after. Tube home with Paul & we had a meal at the Lanterns. A boy walked past the window with no trousers or pants on followed by friends who smacked the bare behind as they walked!

Saturday, 13 September

Got tube to Hammersmith reading script and memorising dialogue on the way. Got there and found that John Malcolm had announced that he *was going on*!! J.M. remonstrated 'I've only had *one* night (Thurs.) with an audience & I must have another opportunity before opening in front of critics!' It was a valid argument & I assented. All my learning of lines had been a waste of time! The cast were inhibited with fear about J.M.'s stilted delivery: the stitches make it impossible for him to enunciate clearly, but he got thro' it fairly.

Monday, 15 September

To Dent's to collect six copies of the book to give members of the cast tonight. Noticed that Mowbray's isn't displaying my book. It's number one in the Best Sellers list this week!! Amazing really. The opening went fair and the cast was obviously nervous & dry mouthed. The second act went v. well. I went b/stage & told them 'You did v. well . . . they were a rotten but typical first night load of shit.' John Lahr (reviewing it for BBC) gave me the thumbs up sign & said 'I've seen it in London & New York & this is the best!' & I could have hugged him!

Tuesday, 16 September

The Times is good for the play and so is the Guardian, so that is encouraging. Telegraph is nasty but that's to be expected. Now the horrible wait for the Sundays!! phew! it's like being on the stage myself!

Wednesday, 17 September

Jill (Press & Publicity) told me 'We are sold out for the entire run' and Helen said 'There are quite a few managements seeing it this week . . .' I affected interest, but would rather it finished at Hammer-

---

[17] This was KW's last appearance on the 'legitimate' stage.

smith. Michael Blakemore spoke to me in the foyer tonight & he said 'They should have done it in the big auditorium . . . they seriously miscalculated there!' That's what I've thought all along!

Thursday, 18 September

Got the 8.50 train from King's Cross for Leeds and cab to the University Refectory: two radio interviews & then the Yorkshire Post Literary Luncheon. Speakers were: Peter Scott (wildlife), Mrs Monserrat (Thackeray biog.), Jean Metcalfe (radio) and then me. P.S. was awful! Strung together a load of funnies and couldn't deliver them. By the time I got up I realised I'd not been facing any competition! I strung a speech round the idea of specialisation v. amateurishness & used a few anecdotes apropos eccentricity in the theatre & finished with a passage about Britain flourishing from her ability to embrace all kinds of oddities & quoted the Clemence Dane 'Welcoming Land'[18] at the end. It went v. well & people commented after 'You *worked* on that speech!' but of course I'd done no work on it at all, but simply relied on the retentive memory. Train home arrived at 7.15. While I was at Louie's I saw a bit of the Benny Hill rubbish on television: it looked like amateurs staging a stag night with stealthy prurience & no honest healthy vulgarity. Rita Webb doing her 'I'm really a very good actress' number & failing miserably. It's a show of which any network can be ashamed.

Sunday, 21 September

The S. Times gives a fair notice, but the Telegraph is viciously nasty & the Observer ignores it. Hope the cast is not depressed by these shits! Thank heavens it's sold out. Wrote to Michael Anderson to say that Laurena is pulling out by February '81 and asking about the new name in Spotlight for the next edition. When I mentioned changing to Gordon on Saturday he told me 'Oh yes, they will be very keen to have you . . . quite a distinguished name for their list' & I replied 'Hm . . . but I shouldn't think the money will impress them . . . I don't make a lot . . . they'll think it's peanuts.'

Monday, 29 September

I went to see Michael Anderson at I.C.M. I was v. frank & told him the sort of money I earned etc. We agreed that I should join I.C.M. as from the new year.

---

[18] (Winifred Ashton) 1888–1965. KW's quotation included the lines 'Then came exiles who fled from death,/Hunted Huguenots, Jews from Spain,/To the wise island; drew sobbing breath/In the easy air and smelled the may,/Sweet as a kiss on a summer day.'

Tuesday, 30 September
Laurena rang: 'The Lyric Hammersmith want you to do *Mr Sloane* in their big theatre . . . in February . . .' and I was furious that she was interested in arranging work for a period she knows I shall be under another agency. I said 'I will have to think about it.' Went to the Dentist at 6 o'c. When Norman started about me smoking too much I said 'Yes I know it shortens life . . . frankly the shorter mine is, the better' & he said 'I think that is rather sad' & I replied 'So is the human condition.'

Wednesday, 1 October
Went to see Bill Kenwright and had coffee and a chat with him: 'Your Hammersmith production won't go anywhere . . . no name you see . . .' And I agreed.

Thursday, 2 October
Bill Kenwright telephoned: 'Listen, I'm trying to arrange transfer of *Loot* from Ham'smith to the Phoenix . . . are you for it?' & I said yes of course. Then I had a call from Bill Thomley saying it would be dicey 'cos Neil McCarthy has got TV engagements during October.

Friday, 3 October
Bill rang: 'I've got the Arts Theatre and I'll store the scenery for 2 weeks and then open there . . . that gives Neil McCarthy time to do his television & for us to prepare an understudy . . .'

Saturday, 4 October
TV Centre at 1 o'c. and talked with Chris (researcher) and Mike Parkinson and John Fisher. I was complacent and confident till I saw the monitor and watched Tom Lehrer[19] singing his own song at the piano! It was superb. The tune, the lyric & the delivery . . . everything was cabaret par excellence & I thought 'Follow *that*??' My entrance was marred by my tripping up on the bottom step, the opening dialogue was stilted & unfunny & four or five minutes of turgid rubbish constituted the chat till I got off the play and on to the book! Telling stories – the Helpmann at the umpires' room, Maggie Smith teeth fillings & the bra story, Edith Evans and the Crescent Hotel, syndrome and aerodrome, Stanley Baxter, and finally Charles Laurence's Mae West line. By that time I'd started climbing and by the end it was OK, but only just! Why? – well, the competition was fierce, I'd been lazy, and I've done the best of the Orton (last year!) on this show and couldn't repeat it. Altogether a salutary experience. Tom Lehrer was marvel-

---

[19] b.1928. Satirical songster-pianist and university lecturer.

lous to me! quoting the Rambling Syd lyrics: 'I've got all your records . . .' and being v. complimentary.

Monday, 6 October

Elsie rang: 'Hattie Jacques has died . . . will you go on Radio London to talk about her?' & I said no. Curiously, I'd always thought of Hat as living for a long long time . . . oh! it's like Peter E . . . the blow will really hit me later on.

Wednesday, 8 October

Gyles rang: 'Peter Shellard wants you to do a book . . . he says the stories you told on the Parkinson show are not in the *Acid Drops* collection & that you should compile some of these anecdotes . . .' We arranged to meet in a few weeks' time to talk.

Saturday, 11 October

Quite a few letters to answer! One from Bob Bolt almost reproachful about not telling him about the book! One doesn't draw the attention of the distinguished to superficial stuff like that! Reading about Thomas Mann I found that he worried about his being attracted in middle age to young boys – no, young men – tho' it never seems to have gone v. far. I've always been attracted to men & always known that indulgence would be disastrous. Truly staggered to find this *lengthy* notice for me in the TLS today![20]

Sunday, 12 October

To Birmingham, went to the ATV studios at 3 o'c. We did our bit – a talk on racialism in humour – after seeing a particularly vulgar pub act with blasphemous references and snide cracks about Pakistani people. It was me, Gita Mehta & some northern comedian. I said we'd watched something which was unfunny & tasteless & that we'd seen the half-educated talking to the uneducated, and this northern comedian did the 'I think he's good & we've all got to earn a living' act.

Monday, 13 October

Went to Dent's to get some more books 'cos I've run out. Saw Peter Shellard: 'We're going to reprint eight thousand instead of three . . . we've had so many orders come in . . . the buyers are all reporting very good reactions to your book . . .' Gita Mehta told me that Gladwyn Jebb had reproved Krishna Menon[21] for archaic English usage

---

[20] By Peter Keating, *TLS* 10 October 1980: 'amusing and entertaining anthology'.

[21] Baron Gladwyn (b.1900), diplomat and civil servant; Vengalil Krishnan Krishna Menon (1896–1974), Indian statesman and lawyer; Gita Mehta, author.

& the latter retorted 'I had to *learn* English . . . you just picked it up.'

Wednesday, 15 October
Bill rang & we're to rehearse on Monday in a hall somewhere & I'm still not told who's to play Meadows!

Thursday, 16 October
I've always been irritated by the odd number of shares (987) I have in Universal Energy so I telephoned Britannia Trust Management & contracted to buy 513 units making my total 1500 altogether.

Sunday, 19 October
Did the hair with Restoria and washed shirts & socks. The news is all about Isobel Barnett being convicted of theft (she stole a couple of items from a village store) & instead of a summary hearing by magistrate she *elected* to go for trial with a jury, and was convicted & fined 75 pounds. It's all so footling & unnecessary. She's an elderly lady who wants psychological help not humiliation. No good will come of it & I don't envy the shopkeeper who reported her to the police . . .

Monday, 20 October
To the Arts for Dress rehearsal. The set has been cut down to fit the new proscenium & sight lines ruined in the process. I had to re-stage loads of things & heaven knows if cast will remember. The carpet got rucked & several near-accidents, sound effects were non-existent or wrong, no door bell, doors that simply won't work making the actors' attempts fruitless. It was misery and TAT. I've not seen anything like it since Newquay rep. News has been announced of Isobel Barnett's death[22] . . . Oh! it's all so sad . . .

Tuesday, 21 October
The preview began at 8 o'c. and you'd never have known from the front that this wasn't a well-rehearsed & organised production. The company performed with energy & panache & J.M. was a tower of strength . . . when the new boy (as Meadows) dried momentarily he was altruism itself & stepped in so deftly with a cue that it was covered: such generosity was heartwarming. I went b/stage after and told them all how splendidly they'd performed.

---

[22] She was found in the bath; drink, drugs, and a portable electric fire had all reportedly played a part in her demise.

Sunday, 26 October

I found a pound note lying in Devonshire Street just past the mews. First time in my life I've ever found paper money.

For years I have been using my own material in chat shows or panel games, and I feel now that I have become drained of all the old ad-lib inventiveness. I am nearly 55 years old and I am tired . . . mentally tired of the entire broiling. One has been round the same old Mulberry Bush so many times! All the chums have died: Kenneth Horne, Peter Butterworth, Hattie Jacques . . . one is left marooned on the shore . . . the tide is receding and leaving some incongruous wrecks exposed . . . I fear I am one of them.

Tuesday, 28 October

B.K. asked me (obliquely) to direct David Blake Kelly in the play & I said yes: I suddenly realised how diligently *theatrical* he is. He told me: 'Of course they all think you're a cunt . . . you walked out of *Fat Friend* when it was a huge success . . . everyone says you are difficult . . . Rod says you can turn in an angle of 300 degrees in five minutes . . . I get on with you 'cos I love you . . . but they all say you are difficult . . . the cast were all railing about the direction at Hammersmith! J.M. saying "This cunt won't give us any room to manoeuvre . . . it's got to be all *his* way" . . .'

Thursday, 30 October

I realise that this cast were OK when they were *trying* in the Studio at Hammersmith, but here in a theatre flushed with past success their meagre ability was shown up in embarrassing proportions. Oh dear! If we'd been relying on reviews last night! Oh! we'd be sunk. At 5 o'c. with Paul to Paris Studio for 'J.A.M.' During the games, Parsons got all his announcements wrong & I cried out to the audience 'He don't want a desk chair, he wants a bath chair . . . they carry him in here you know! . . . Oh yes . . . they have to inject him before he goes on . . . they pump all this Queen's Royal Jelly into him . . . poor old thing . . . he needs the adrenalin you see . . . stupid great nit!'

Friday, 31 October

Went to Freemason's Arms in Long Acre to rehearse David Blake Kelly (McLeavy) and Charles Rae (Truscott) to take over at the Arts as from Nov. 10th. They're both right-looking and will make a good stab at the roles.

Friday, 7 November

Codron is taking off the new Alan Bennett (*Enjoy*) and it's only just opened! Leonard Rossiter (*Make or Break* at Haymarket) has nose dived too! If our little enterprise can totter along a bit longer, it will be a victory and a half! Especially since we've no names in it!

Saturday, 8 November

In the speech for Hattie's Memorial Service I must use that story about the Leukaemia Fund event at Chelsea Town Hall when we had to gather round an ice-cream stall & the photographer said 'Let's have shot of you all licking your cornets & then turn & lick each other's . . .' & I said to Hattie 'I don't fancy licking other people's cornets! They may have germs and I don't even *know* them . . .' She told me 'Don't worry, if you catch anything I'll introduce you' which had a sort of mad logic & made me laugh.

Monday, 10 November

Walked to St Paul's Covent Garden. It was v. full. The choir (from the Players') sang Hattie's favourite songs, then John Le Mesurier talked about Hat & her varied activities (she was a welder in a factory during the war!) and then after a hymn, I spoke about my work with her mentioning the ice cream cornets incident (they laughed) and finished mentioning the line 'Sweet as a kiss on a winter day'[23] from the record she gave me, and the George Eliot quote about 'the comfort of feeling safe with a person . . .'[24]

Thursday, 13 November

Posted a reply to Rita Webb because she's written a very kind letter to me apropos the Memorial Service for Hattie & obviously wants to let bygones be bygones: I'll accept that. I replied warmly & sympathetically. I noticed that I got tired when I reached the Old Bailey today, whereas this was one of my favourite walks and never used to tire me when I used to walk there *and back!*

Friday, 14 November

The two 'J.A.M.'s were with Clement, P. Jones, Aimi Macdonald & me. At one point I said 'I've been using witchhazel cream for ten years' and P.J. remarked 'And to no effect whatever.'

---

[23] Or 'summer day'? See 18 September 1980, note, p. 616.

[24] 'Oh, the comfort, the inexpressible comfort, of feeling safe with a person; having neither to weigh thoughts, nor measure words, but pour them all out, just as they are, chaff and grain together, knowing that a faithful hand will take and sift them, keep what is worth keeping, and then, with a breath of kindness, blow the rest away.' Not by George Eliot at all, but by Dinah Maria Mulock (Mrs Craik, 1826–87) in her 1859 novel *A Life for a Life*.

Saturday, 15 November

Alexander Herold rang: 'Philip Martin Brown is ill and we need a young actor to read the part tonight . . . do you know of anyone?' Within minutes, B. found me Kerry Shale and he was in the Arts rehearsing with me by 2 o'c.!! He was just super! I've never known anyone give such a specially intelligent first reading & he was composed & diligent throughout. Kerry had about 10 minutes in which to familiarise himself with props, stage, costume, coffin, dummy . . . Oh! heaven knows how he managed it. He acquitted himself on that stage incredibly well.

Sunday, 16 November

Michael came & drove us to his flat. We didn't leave till 5 o'c.!! with Louie saying 'Why can't we stay? I'm enjoying myself!' & quite high on the wine & liqueurs . . . oh dear! there was all that excruciatingly embarrassing gush about 'I love my Ken & I don't care who knows it . . . I'd do anything for my Ken . . . there is nobody in the world like my Ken . . . my Charlie was jealous when I had him! He used to say I was spoiling him but I didn't care!' etc. etc. Went to bed after reading some of my 1970 journal. Oh! what an unpleasant creature I sound like! & the interminable wranglings with the friends!! It seems light years away now . . . I am much less social than in those days!

Wednesday, 26 November

Rachel Roberts has taken her life . . . she was found in the garden of her home in Hollywood. Apparently her last job was in Schlesinger's film *Yanks* and that didn't enjoy much success. It all seems a far cry from the days when I introduced her to Peter Eade (who became her agent) and to Baxter (and Moira) at that dinner in Percy Street where (in a talk about sex & promiscuity) Moira said of the indulgers 'At least they *do* it, whereas your abstention denies you any knowledge of relationships.'

Wednesday, 3 December

Today I went to BBC TV Centre for 'Tomorrow's World', and it was a hell of a day: beginning with exercises in track suits on apparatus, then the Dinner Table scene & the eating of synthetic foods, and then me demonstrating the watch which gets its energy from body heat on the wrist. Taxi at 10.30. The driver of the radio cab was chatting on the intercom with the telephonist 'Is Geoff there?' 'No he ain't . . . d'you want to give him a message?' 'No, nothing special . . . just tell him what a lovely body I've got . . .' I told him afterwards 'Your dialogue is a lot better than anything on LBC . . .' & I certainly meant it.

Friday, 12 December

Car to Teddington for 'Does The Team Think' pilot show. There were two programmes and I was in the first, with Eamonn [Andrews] in the chair, and team was: Jimmy Edwards, Mike Reid, me & Roy Kinnear & our show went v. well. The second was Jimmy Edwards in the chair, and team: Frankie Howerd, Alfred Marks, Bernie Winters, Ray Alan. Hope they didn't do as well as us 'cos I'd like to do more of these. It is a format well suited to me & could provide exactly the sort of series I'd be good in. I felt quite elated afterwards!

Tuesday, 16 December

Got tube to Lyric Ham. and with David Porter I met Dave King to talk about the play & Orton's writing. He looks & sounds dead right for the part[25] & I told him I was delighted to have got him in the role. The TV was all rubbish. Apart from News the television isn't worth the licence money & I'm v. glad I haven't got a set.

Saturday, 20 December

Oddly enough, even though the economic gloom is all round one & the long range forecasts are dire for Britain, I feel quite buoyant lately! The personal blows, like the exterior repair expense and the colossal rate rises, will mean that the holiday in winter is out of the question I should think.

Monday, 22 December

The newsvendor (Bill) said 'All this fuss about John Lennon![26] It's all you read about!' & I said 'Yes, ludicrous! Even I would not deserve such eulogies!'

Tuesday, 23 December

Saw Louie & we watched the 'Les Dawson Show'. The format is wrong but he continually triumphs. There are endless repetitions of the same joke on TV this year. Son to father (apropos Christmas present) 'I've got my eye on this bike!' and the father replies 'Well keep your eye on it 'cos you ain't getting your arse on it.' Then there is 'Why do they have to have Christmas in December when all the shops are so crowded?' The only thing that did make me laugh was when the Ghost of Christmas asked Dawson 'What about the Cratchits?' & he replied 'They're fine . . . I think that ointment's done the trick.'

---

25 Of Ed in *Entertaining Mr Sloane*.

26 Lennon had been shot dead in New York on 8 December.

Tuesday, 30 December
Gordon came & we went to the Arts to see the play. It went at a cracking pace & they were all good! Went round after & congratulated them. Joan Blackham said 'It's the first time we've had a house! It hasn't been like this since Hammersmith!' Gordon looked tired & is looking forward to Madeira. He told me 'You've directed it beautifully . . . those moves are marvellous & they focus the action pointedly . . .' and was truly enthusiastic and encouraging.

1981[1]

Thursday, 1 January
Louie & I watched *Zhivago* on TV in the evening and it was extraordinary to see so much expense and time taken over such tedious rubbish. If there was one close-up of Omar Sharif looking dewy-eyed there was two: he looked about as Russian as my arse.

Sunday, 4 January
Still feel a bit guilty about not answering the last letter from Tom: the guilt is apropos correspondence, nothing else; I always feel 'a letter should be answered.' The reason I can't reply to this is because it suggests a meeting & I know there's no point in that, but can't bring myself to write 'cos it's too hurtful. I really wanted the whole thing to simply wither and die a natural death.

Tuesday, 6 January
Every year one is worried by rising costs and the everlasting question 'Will I be able to continue to meet them?' because my entire existence – built upon this con trick of entertainment – is so precarious. I'm always amazed, looking back on it, to think of what I've got away with for so long! So little real ability, no proper qualifications, & an inherent laziness . . . yet still managing to survive.

Friday, 9 January
Find myself increasingly wondering 'When was the last really *low* period?' 'cos so often, that is the consolation of history; the knowledge that one lived through (and in spite of) it. I think of Caligula being

---

[1] When KW came to assemble his mock-diary *Back Drops* in 1982, he used some of the events of 1981 as a nominal structure. The book, however, departed so frequently from the real order of events (using dates for the most part simply as paragraph headings, and dipping at will into previous years' diaries for anecdotes) that I have not felt it worthwhile to point out those occasions when *Back Drops* coincided with reality.

stabbed & stabbed crying out: 'I'm still *here*!' in that marvellous last scene by Camus.[2]

Sunday, 11 January

Barbara Windsor rang 'I haven't actually looked at the play yet . . .' and I told her 'No . . . don't bother' & she told me she'd got 3 weeks' more panto in Newcastle & that business was marvellous: 'They all come to look at the notorious woman, don't they?'

Wednesday, 14 January

I watched the Max Bygraves show & it was v. interesting 'cos there were moments that were excellent and moments that were excruciatingly bad. Arthur English was superb doing his old 'Open The Cage' routine, and then Yootha Joyce (now dead) appeared & she was paired with Max to sing 'For All We Know'. When it came to the line for Yootha to sing 'Tomorrow may never come' it had an extraordinary poignancy & it looked as if she were crying . . . at the end of the number she got up and said to Max 'Thanks . . . it was good of you . . .' and walked off the stage . . . one had the feeling that she never intended to return. We know, from the inquest, that she had a drink problem but all I know is that I worked with her and found her totally professional & very lovable, and she gave no sign of either the drink problem or the inner turmoil that caused it. Louie came in: 'I had to hold on to the railings outside the Post Office or I'd have been blown away . . . what a terrible night!' I reminded her about singing 'Bali Bali' in 1978[3] and she laughed . . . tho' it's a lot later now, nothing has altered very much.

Thursday, 15 January

I had a rest and then walked to St James, the Embankment, City, Fleet St., Clifford's Inn to Gray's Inn, bus from there to Gt. Portland St & walked home. The day was cold but not dauntingly so, and the sun shone bravely over Waterloo Bridge . . . St Paul's gleaming in the afternoon's glow . . . oh! it looked beautiful . . . it looked as if nothing could ever go wrong . . . utterly stable, tranquil & permanent.

Wednesday, 21 January

Gordon told me on the telephone that he'd been hailed by a TV fan in Madeira: 'Nice to see you without turning the knob!' & G. replied 'And considerably less painful!' which I thought was very quick! So

---

[2] *Caligula* (1944), translated 1948.

[3] See entry for 4 December 1978, p. 570.

I will use it in the radio interview tomorrow – it's a good side light on the celebrity/performer relationship.

Thursday, 22 January
Went to Radio London for the interview & phone-in with Lorraine Chase: she handled it all with great aplomb, and she gave me a lift home afterwards. To Molinaire for Spargo's film 'Willo the Wisp' & I did two scripts: there is one to go before finish.

Sunday, 25 January
Said goodnight to Louie who seemed preoccupied & resigned & returned to the flat & considered my desolation. Jotted down the lines

> Determined to hide it and not give a sign
> Of the desperate ego and id that is mine.
> Never to speak of my love for a man:
> Hope that God loves me, for no one else can.

It seems a reasonable description of my dilemma: pride forbids my admitting vulnerability and knowledge foredooms any real relationship, yet I'm conscious that without the aspiration and constructive endeavour life becomes increasingly pointless.

Monday, 2 February
Letter from John Lahr quoting Orton on casting Sloane 'Someone – 15 to 17 – you'd like to fuck silly' so I've done the right thing I'm sure. Walked to Ken. Ho. in Shepherd's Bush to talk to Nigel Williams[4] about the *Arena* programme on Joe Orton. Problem is how to talk on Orton without repetition 'cos I've done a lot of that with the *Loot* production.

Tuesday, 3 February
Letter from Coronet Books about launching *Acid Drops* in paperback. Replied saying I ain't doing all that touring etc. which Dent's forced me into.

We got the bus to the Haymarket to see Maggie at 8 o'c. The piece starring Mags[5] is a collection of memorabilia apropos Virginia Woolf and the burden of the evening rests entirely upon her. It must be a gruelling task: she has to range from comedy to tragedy & requires all the energy & technical resource she can muster. In the event she is superb, but the fundamental fault remains: a bundle of speeches

---

[4] b.1948. Novelist, playwright, TV producer.
[5] *Virginia*, by Edna O'Brien. Patricia Conolly as Vita Sackville-West.

doesn't constitute a play. Mags greeted us warmly & gave us champagne. The actress playing Vita came in & we talked endlessly before I realised it was her! & then I congratulated her. She was superb. Mags said it was essentially a piece for the Bloomsbury aficionados & I said yes. She gave me her number & hugged me: 'I make a lot of noise . . . empty vessels always do, don't they?'

Tuesday, 10 February

Don't know why – don't know why – but I looked at the Obituary column in the paper & found Philip Dudley had died!! Only 45, on location near Norwich. Oh! it is sad 'cos I liked him; we worked together at Birmingham Rep and I gave him my tape recorder.

Monday, 16 February

To Hammersmith to the Lyric to meet the company. Usual waste of time read thro' in the foyer & then plotted up to page 24 in the church hall. David Blake Kelly is his usual brilliant self, the rest . . . I ain't seen much sign of anything.

Tuesday, 24 February

We saw the TV news which devoted loads of time to the engagement of the Prince of Wales to Diana Spencer: there was a ludicrous interview with such foolish questions & silly answers you thought 'What are they going on and on about?'

INT: 'Are you both in love?'
DIANA: 'Oh yes very'
PRINCE: 'What is being *in love*? A state of mind? You put your own interpretation on it . . .'
INT: 'You're both very happy?'
PRINCE: 'Oh yes'

I thought they should have shut up.

Saturday, 28 February

Peter Eade Ltd. is to cease trading as from today and I am apprehensive about the smooth transference to I.C.M. I've got a feeling that firms will continue to send stuff to Eade's office.

Monday, 2 March

Coffee at Lyric where I talked to Jonathan Miller and Bob Hoskins & Peter Wilson. Rehearsed at 10.30 with Barbara & Glyn [Grimstead]; the improvements are gradual. The entire cast came and we did Acts 2 & 3. D[ave] K[ing] was wonderfully helpful with fight technique.

Thursday, 5 March
Rehearsed right thro' play & dealt with certain bits which needed colour & variety. Barbara responds to this method more than any other . . . When, apropos one line, I complimented her on the reading, she replied 'Yeah! All these wonderful moments . . . but what for? A four week run & it's all over . . .' Every now & then (like all comedians) she's in the throes of pessimism and despair. I left for the work at Molinaire. Met Nick Spargo and the rest and we did the last 'Willo' script: it was an amusing one too, apropos Christmas & Mavis Cruet hanging up *both* her stockings. Nick produced a bottle of champagne & we all had a celebration drink for the occasion of the 26th and final script.

Thursday, 12 March
The preview began at 7.30. The opening was marred by lack of projection from B.W., and when D.K. appeared it picked up. M. gave me a lift home; he praised D.K. as being the most effective Eddy he could imagine, and the Boy. Qualified about B.W. and praised D.B. Kelly.

Friday, 13 March
The audience was indulgent and gave them a v. good reception they didn't deserve. I couldn't go to see the actors 'cos I fear I'd have said such lousy things they'd have had a depressing night & day tomorrow. If necessary I'll rehearse Monday and I'll rehearse Tuesday as well. I'm not having this kind of rep tat go on in my name.

Saturday, 14 March
6 o'c. rehearsal. Thank heavens it worked! Barbara played it v. well indeed! M[ichael] said 'Before, it was D.K. who stood out, but now the others have come into their own . . . and Barbara has found a vocal level that is right.'

Sunday, 15 March
All the problems reverberating in the mind. Unlike the *Loot* production, I have never once felt this was real: always, it looks to me like actors exchanging lines. I never feel they're involved with each other & consequently I don't feel involved either. I have pointed out the errors of addressing the fourth wall (a trick they all seem to enjoy) and underlined the importance of making *points* rather than trotting out dialogue . . . but in the end you're left with a v. ordinary bunch of actors giving the ordinary performance which is all they're capable of. I suppose it is all my fault, but the Lyric management said they wanted a commercially viable production.

Tuesday, 17 March
Went b/stage after to see them but no one about except D.B.K. & I asked 'Where are they?' & he said 'They're all on stage . . . they have inquests after the show every night . . .' This is the real problem. D[ave] K[ing] is trying to direct the thing himself and is losing his own role in the process. D.K. is another John Malcolm, both are frustrated directors.

Wednesday, 18 March
Went round to see the cast and wish them well. An *extraordinary* thing happened b/stage!: the SM's and staff presented me with a filthy phallic object & I laughingly refused to accept it, saying 'I'll just take the wrapper if you don't mind' – it was utterly disgusting & I felt unclean as I left the room. The performances in the play were all fairly good. Dave King was fair: at least, he didn't slow it down quite so much.

Thursday, 19 March
Thank goodness there's a good notice in the Times! This isn't the first time Ned Chaillet[6] has saved me! He did it before with Barillon in *Signed and Sealed*. The Financial Times is reasonable too. I never dreamed, when Joe Orton gave me the inscribed copy of *Sloane* that I would one day be directing the play! I actually took that copy to the Lyric recently & used it for the rehearsal session & notes: weird to think that a present in 1965 becomes the tool for my trade in 1981.

Sunday, 22 March
Glad to see reasonable mentions in two of the papers; they carp and carp, but there is grudging praise somehow. Mags came over. She said the Virginia Woolf role was exhausting & depressing & she was looking forward to its ending in four weeks' time. She reminded me of Mrs Patrick Campbell examining a vase she'd been sent as a present 'Made in Czechoslovakia . . . dropped in Belgravia' (as she smashed it) and made me laugh. She said Bev was working on a script. The bill at Drones was £31.15 and far too expensive.

Wednesday, 25 March
On the front of the Mirror it says that Barbara collapsed on stage last night! So the show at the Lyric Hammersmith was cancelled. Rang the Lyric: they said Barbara has been given the night off . . . 'She's got a sore throat . . . it sounds like a bad cold . . .' so that is two shows that have been cancelled!

---

[6] American-born critic, later a script-editor and producer in radio drama.

Thursday, 26 March
Watched a programme about the birth today of the Social Democratic Party with David Owen & Roy Jenkins and Shirley Williams[7] . . . they're all *worthy* one feels, but terribly *dull*. If they pick up any support in an election I fancy it will be the Orpington kind of success.

Sunday, 29 March
Cab to TV Centre. It was all run-throughs until 4.15 when we started the VTR. We finished at about 5.45 and I chatted to Freddie Treves and Jean before taxi came to take me home. Fred asked after Louisa & remembered Tin Lizzie's[8] funeral & everything!

Monday, 30 March
I told Edward Pugh (directing) 'The artist here is secondary to drawings, captions and sound effects . . . it should be the reverse!' and he didn't like it. No, I certainly wasn't popular. So often, I've commented on the actor's life as 'easy' but it was truly brought home to me today that the concentration and mental energy required to sustain performances is enormous.

Saturday, 4 April
After the TV game tomorrow, I have got nothing in the way of future employment. The future looks very bleak indeed. I don't want to get involved with acting in the theatre (which is the only thing I could actually engineer) 'cos the thought of it is dispiriting, so I can only hope that alternative employment will come along in some form or other.

Sunday, 5 April
I had forgotten the utter boredom of this programme 'Give Us A Clue'. Got thro' it all right but only *fairly* all right. M. drove us home and Louie gave us dinner at the Tent Restaurant. There were two traditional pieces who smiled from a nearby table & we chatted. Louisa started to tell them the bus conductor story but I was impatient with her embroidery so I took it over & told it more succinctly. She sulked 'It wasn't like that at all!' I should've let her tell her own anecdote

---

[7] (Lord) Owen, b.1938, Foreign Secretary 1977–79, leader of SDP 1983–87, etc.; (Lord) Jenkins, b.1920, Chancellor of the Exchequer 1967–70, President of European Community 1977–81, leader of SDP 1982–83, etc.; (Dame Shirley) Williams, b.1930, Secretary of State for Education and Science 1976–79, President of SDP 1982–88, etc. Together with William Rodgers, another former Labour Cabinet Minister, they made up the 'Gang of Four', who founded the Social Democratic Party.

[8] Ellen (or Eliza) Cod, Louisa Williams's stepmother.

but I scream inwardly at a badly recounted story & the performer in me *must* rescue the attempt.

Monday, 6 April

Michael came and we went to the Lyric. The performances were all v. different. Only Glyn stayed true to the production. D.K. was all tricks and self-indulgence, Barbara with a new found bravura doing all sorts of trills & frills, and Blake Kelly curiously muted. I felt bitterly ashamed of the whole affair, and the sparse house didn't help either! There was only a handful in the stalls, tho' the cheap seats were full. Barbara iterating endlessly 'You must come on Saturday! It is our last night' and me muttering excuses. I really don't want to see it any more. I don't want to visit the Lyric Hammersmith any more. I don't want to direct any more.

Wednesday, 8 April

C. came and we drove to this Manor Hall in Streatham. The place smelled of milk & geriatrics. The secretary didn't turn up to greet me. I wasn't offered a drink or a chair. One sat on the edge of a bench feeling like a spare prick at a wedding. Eventually an unlovely collection gathered & I spoke from about 8.30 to 10 o'c. Not an offer of a cup of tea, not a mention of travel expenses or a smack in the eye with a wet cod fish. One approached me after: 'Remember me? I asked you a question at the Monday Club? I told you that people like you stopped me coming out 'cos I was afraid people would think all queers were like you.' 'Yes I remember,' I replied with distaste & he went on, 'Oh, it's OK, I've got over it now!' & I thought 'I wish I could say the same.' There was a moment of redemption when a bearded 60-year-old told me 'What a pity it can't be you every Wednesday here! You make it all such fun.' C. told me after: 'I watched them all quite carefully during your talk & you didn't lose their interest once; it all held throughout.' I replied 'Yes but I think this has got to be the last time . . . it is not good for me, it's unrewarding, and they're really not the sort of people I want to meet. The sad truth is that I actually prefer normals.'

Wednesday, 15 April

I went to the Rose Garden and a man called 'Hello Kenneth!' and it was John Stonehouse:[9] he said 'I wrote a very good notice for your

---

[9] 1925–88. Former Labour Cabinet Minister, disgraced in 1974 after a business scandal and subsequent attempt to fake his suicide. Stonehouse died a few hours before KW.

play (*Undertaking*) in the Standard . . .' I mouthed some conversational pleasantries.

Wednesday, 22 April

Lunch with Pan Books about this advertisement they want me to write: it entails reading four books. Changed into a suit & went to this dinner at the Lancaster Hotel for the Film & Cinema Veterans. It was death. When I got up to make the speech I felt utterly doomed and I got thro' it (for the most part in silence) pretty quickly! They'd asked for 10 minutes but I only did about 5 or 6 I fancy. I rushed for my coat & heard one old fart saying to the friend 'Kenneth Williams was a disaster wasn't he?' which I thought was a pretty succinct summation.

Later: Percy Livingstone (President) sent me photographs of the event and said it was all a great success so perhaps I've no judgment in these matters.

Saturday, 25 April

I typed out the copy for the review of the 4 books. I flatter myself I've done it all rather well: nothing in it I feel ashamed of & *at last* I got something written conversationally without wearing heavy erudition in the process.[10]

Monday, 18 May

Michael Anderson rang: 'They've telephoned me from Australia & said they'd like you to go out on the 17 June and do two Parkinsons on the 20th, they'll guarantee two thousand and provide fare & accommodation . . . that all right?' & I said yes. I don't seem to have anything else to do.

Saturday, 23 May

Lunched with Louie at 12 o'c. She went off to meet Edith & they are going to see Alice in the home. Louie came back at 5.30 and I'd got some prawns for her tea. She said 'I told Edna that I thought Alice would go in the evening or in the early hours of tomorrow . . . there is nothing of her . . . you'd never recognise her . . .' During the evening at about 9.45 they phoned & told her that Alice had died, and she telephoned other people who had to be informed. I didn't say anything. I knew she was feeling miserable about her sister's death

---

[10] The three books eventually reviewed were *Unreliable Memoirs* by Clive James, *The Paladin* by Brian Garfield and *Platinum Logic* by Tony Parsons. KW may have been influenced in his approach by James, of whom he wrote: 'It has always been his gift to wear the learning lightly.'

but the fact is that Alice is better off 'cos she had no consciousness of the world & it was hardly a life at all, in the end . . . she was a vegetable.

Tuesday, 9 June
Louie was doing her 'I am bored' act; continually getting up and doing something . . . eating biscuits & cheese noisily . . . looking out of the window . . . Couldn't stand it eventually & at 9.15 I said I was going to bed. She said 'You went to bed early last night' as if *that* was wrong. This is the period when Louie needs a holiday, a change of scene, something . . . I don't know. I can't cope with these changing moods all the time; it's enough of a problem for me to keep going year in & year out without giving way to that insistent little voice crying 'What's the use? Give it up!'

Wednesday, 10 June
Up at about 7 o'c. & got papers. First time I've sat perusing them without the fags! Walked to Radio London & rudely asked the producer: 'Why do I have to be here an *hour* before the show?' & he said 'To familiarise yourself with the studio' & I replied 'I've seen it loads of fucking times.' Then there was a pause: they obviously thought 'Here's a shit' so after that, I was v. cooperative. It was phone-in stuff. When I was walking home, I thought 'Once I'd have had at least 10 fags by now!' Today, I've had none.

Sunday, 14 June
Went for 15 minutes' jogging round the park. Dreading this ghastly journey & this mad trek into the unknown.

Monday, 15 June
Michael took me to the airport. I said goodbye to him at Terminal 3 and then felt utterly desolate & alone. Sat in the First Class lounge feeling stared-at and alien. Took off about 8 o'c. I refused all food because I knew it was going to be an endless round of eating . . . all across the world. Plane landed at Muscat on the Gulf. The first class on BA is superbly luxurious.

Tuesday, 16 June
Plane arrived in Singapore, and went on to Brunei in Borneo. More eating. In the evening they showed *The Mirror Crack'd* and it was a v. curious film! Rock Hudson amazingly badly dressed! Oh! I'm so conscious of decay & the sadness of old age creeping on!

Wednesday, 17 June
The plane arrived at Sydney about 6 o'c. in the morning and I got a taxi to the Town House Hotel. I got postcards to send to the chums. Had the fags! So my resolution to give up smoking has gone bust! The surprise has been the weather! Sunny and bright . . . not unlike April or May in England.

Thursday, 18 June
With Michael P. to the Yellow Room Restaurant. He's v. likeable & patient & I'm afraid I went on a bit but he bore it all with sympathy. I know why I'm on edge: I feel I've got to prove myself and that can only be done by doing a good show with him; in the back of my mind lurks the horrible suspicion that (out here) I may not work in the same way as I do in London.

Friday, 19 June
Walked round the area in the morning and was accosted by prostitutes & saw a drunken old loon peeing into a rubbish bin . . . 10.30 in the morning in a busy street!!

Saturday, 20 June
Car to the studios. Met Marti Caine and Colleen McCullough who are on the show. Did a run-through etc. & got made up, then there was that awful wait while you watch the others doing their stuff & I went on eventually. We talked about joining the army (medical etc), audition in Singapore, Barri Chatt (never got to the Serg. Major & suicide bit) & then on to Carry Ons & then to Orson Welles & *Moby Dick* & finished singing 'Ballad of the Woggler's Moolie'. Everyone was v. kind afterwards & said it was good but I wasn't over the moon about it. The audience was good tho' I felt their energy ebbed after Marti Caine (who went v. well indeed) and the author (who was fair). Still, at least I didn't die the death . . . but I noticed that the Australian audience reacted quite differently to an English one . . . the laughs are in different places.

Sunday, 21 June
We were taken on board Sir James Hardy's[11] yacht *Nerida* and sailed round the harbour & islands sipping champagne & eating a delightful cold lunch. I got v. high! From the time I boarded the aircraft for this trip, there has been a feeling of unreality: the continual question 'What on earth am I doing?' Of course there's an economic explanation, and a sheer 'something to do' explanation but neither of them

---

[11] Businessman, b.1932. Australian Yachtsman of the Year for 1981.

have been paramount. In a way, it's the result of lethargy and allowing events & other people to control the life which has been the decisive factor. Every time one avoids responsibility, someone else takes it over *for* one & the result is victimisation.

Monday, 22 June

Nobody has really endorsed a verdict (no pro I mean) on the TV show. One desperately wants someone to say 'You were good' & know they can be trusted.

Tuesday, 23 June

Richard [Lyle] came & took me to Butler's for lunch & an English lady who owned it said 'Your Parkinson Show was fine for the English there, but the Australians didn't get a lot of it . . .' Walked right into Bill Kerr!! who embraced me warmly & we did some taped interviews for David Hawkes of Perth W.A. radio.

Wednesday, 24 June

John Vermeer came with a woman called Robin & we went to Bondi Beach but their timing was bad & they had to journey back too quickly & forced me to a hurried lunch in a dirty Italian trattoria which reeked of Parozone. Did the ABC int. at Upper Forbes St and then walked round the Rocks – sort of rehabilitated Cov. Garden Piazza place & in the café I was asked to sign autographs. Back to Hotel. The TV crew arrived to film me doing bits for 'Ratbags' – a sort of TV revue show. I did a couple of things & they seemed satisfied. Made me sign a form about copyright.

Thursday, 25 June

1st interview at 10 o'c. ABC. Then a lady came 'I'm doing a series called "Travellers' Tales"' so I talked about tarts in King's X, & men urinating in rubbish bins. Then another man came called Tony & I had to talk to him for 30 minutes about the book and about my career. At the end he said 'How much longer d'you give yourself?' & I felt horribly *old*. Rita Spencer & John Vermeer took me to David Jones [department store] & we did the signing session & they said I signed over 300 books but it sounds a bit incredible to me. Since I didn't wear glasses I could hardly see what I was doing.

Friday, 26 June

Phone rang & it was Paul [F.]!! & he told me he's back in Sydney after all the wandering & so I walked into town & met him at the Victoria Statue in Queen's Square & he took me to the Westbury & we had drinks & a chat. He hasn't altered. Walked back to the hotel by 3 o'c., my head abuzz with meeting him 'cos the old excitement never abates. Car came & drove me to TV studios. I went on first this time & I think it was better. The only longueur was during the Hancock thing but then the subject (his death out here etc.) was sombre. Then there was a singer called Tom English, then Jack Absalom who is a painter and authority on the bush country. M.P. gave me the microphone & I chatted (after the show) to the audience & thanked them for creating such a pleasant atmosphere. They paid to get me out here & I feel I've acquitted myself creditably but it's all been a bit too easy.

Saturday, 27 June
Went down to b'fast where Jack Absalom buttonholed me & went on & on! 'What Mike needs on his show is not a load of Pommies but a few real characters from the bush country: I could introduce him to dozens of wonderful characters . . . people who say of their kids "I grood him" and so forth – it'd be wonderful! That's what people want to hear!'

Sunday, 28 June
Dinner with Paul & after, he took me to a friend's flat. He was called Brian & he helped dig the Jubilee Line. He opened the door and there were two men naked on the bed with a boy sitting by the door watching TV and Brian asked 'Won't you join us . . . have a joint?' & offered Marijuana. I said I'd prefer a cup of tea & we left after hasty apologies. Paul took me to a homosexual haunt called Signal where pornographic films were shown round the bar & a boy called Peter chatted amiably about schoolboy experiences & told me how he'd met Louisa on the train to Gatwick. 'She was with two other ladies & they couldn't wait to tell me who she was!' Goodbye to Paul who got a bit emotional. Just sat in the car & wouldn't drive off. I went into the hotel.

Monday, 29 June
The plane left at 4.10 and the endless journey began. I'd had brandy at the hotel, brandy at airport & I drank brandy on the plane 'cos I didn't want the B[owel] M[ovement] condition of this morning to continue. When I woke up after falling asleep on the aircraft I felt an awful pain in my neck. I asked the steward for an osteopath to fix it & he told me 'We don't carry one I'm afraid.' Lousy service; don't suppose they've got a doctor either.

Tuesday, 30 June
The nightmare plane journey finished at Heathrow at 7 o'c. this morning (and Air Traffic Control strike begins there at 7.30!!) Louisa came

in & told me the news & I started coping with a stack of mail straightway. Oh! it is such a relief to be back from that ludicrous adventure.

Saturday, 4 July

At 4 o'c. I went in to Louie's to watch my adorable John McEnroe beat that insufferable Scandinavian![12] Oh! what joy it was to see John win the title and take the Gold cup. It was a hard fought battle but the best man won & takes 21 thousand pounds in the process.

Wednesday, 8 July

Met Paul [Richardson] at 9.15, got tickets to Brighton. We walked to the Royal Crescent. Had a drink in the bar and met Simon Gray and Harold Pinter & we chatted amiably. They've got a play on at the theatre here.[13] Walked to Hove and then to the station. Sat in a 1st class carriage going back 'cos the train was full of idiots. The ticket collector said 'Well you don't want me to go to all the trouble of writing out a ticket do you? Just give me a pound for the two of you . . .' Then he sat down and told us of his tattoos and asked 'Who's got the fags then?' and Paul obligingly produced a packet.

Thursday, 9 July

Looking back on the trip to Australia, it all seems like some insane nightmare. The consolation of it all was Paul [F.]. Without him, that last two days would have been horrible. Of course I've always known that to be alone in an alien place is horrible but it seemed even worse that time. At my age, the truth begins to dawn: look in the mirror and see an old face and the grey hair & know that you're no longer dreaming of adventure . . . just desperately trying to provide for the old-age pension.

Monday, 13 July

Watched 'Panorama' on Negro society in England. It concentrated solely on unemployed black youths, Soul music & reggae. Never was a cultivated black man seen. It was totally biased against whites with endless sneering references to this country & complaints about harassment and unemployment: the film didn't show any of the black people who are content & working: not *one*. The BBC TV is one of the great stirrers of trouble in our midst. For all the black grumbles about inactivity & poverty, you could have found hundreds of whites with the *same moans*, but it was all presented as peculiarly negroid. Specious rubbish & dangerous.

---

12 McEnroe beat Bjorn Borg 4–6 7–6 7–6 6–4.

13 *Quartermaine's Terms*.

Wednesday, 15 July
Went out to get batteries for calculator & on the way home I directed a Nigerian to the Regent Centre & we talked of bureaucracy in our countries. I told him 'One computer strike and our entire system is ruined' & he said 'At least the response here is good . . . in my country the incompetence of government officials is appalling . . . it takes ages to even get a reply!'

Monday, 27 July
Watched the 'Panorama' programme about Iraq and it was the usual pious rubbish about Saddam Hussein being a tyrant & a torturer. When such a leader is removed, the ensuing chaos is deplored by the *same censurers.*

Tuesday, 28 July
Went to Equity for the Exec. and a Council Meeting. At one point,the President (John Barron) said 'We need people for the various committees . . . what about you Kenneth?' & I said 'I'd find them just as boring as *this*' and there was embarrassed laughter. The more I see of Unionism the more I resent its parasitic growth in societies like ours: it lines the pockets of more & more bureaucrats and none of them are remotely connected with the work done by those they purport to represent.

Wednesday, 29 July
Went in to see Louie and she was glued to the television. The Royals left the Palace en route to St Paul's and from there on, it was cheering all the way: a blaze of colourful pageantry glittering in the London sunshine. When the much heralded dress of the bride was revealed, one saw a badly designed gown full of silly flounces & totally lacking the sort of simplicity & elegance demanded for the persona of Diana & the nature of the occasion. At the altar, the Prince muffed his lines and so did she, the music was rotten and the speakers of prayers & addresses all very bad indeed.

Thursday, 27 August
Went to Radio London early. Did the interview with Morecambe & Wise (their new book *There's No Answer To That* comes out shortly) and it flowed all right: there is little doubt about the fundamental honesty & goodness of both of them. No wonder they're so universally popular. They've enjoyed a partnership of 41 years.

Monday, 31 August
Saw Louisa in the evening & we saw some rubbish on TV. At 8.30 I

could stand no more of it: 'I'm going to have an early night' I said. Louie retorted 'Well what about tomorrow?' & then came the endless refrain 'I don't know what to get to eat . . .' I have heard this cry ever since I came to Marlborough. Then there was the complaining 'I can't go to bed at this hour . . . I won't sleep anyway . . .' I returned to the flat with the despair welling up inside. Oh heavens! It can't be right that the elderly should be such a snaffle on those younger than themselves!

Tuesday, 1 September

Equity Council meeting: so boring I fell asleep & had to be woken by a cry of 'Kenneth!' from the President. Everyone laughed.

Wednesday, 2 September

Oh! these days that have to be lived through! All those illusions one had about serene twilights and autumnal decay! It is an endless slog against adversity & all dear names men use to cheat despair don't help in the heat and dust.[14]

Friday, 4 September

Met Paul & we sat in the park. In front of us, a man lay sleeping with his head crooked in the curve of his arm . . . he was shirtless & one could see the surgical scar from an operation running in a curve across his tanned skin . . . his inert vulnerability & childlike slumber was incredibly touching . . . one wanted to weep. Then we were joined by Paul The Sailor (which is what Paul Richardson calls him) and he came & chatted. He'd been to the Eastman-Dental & is in for a lot more dental work as a result of a mugging: three of them set about him from behind with an iron bar. He is Welsh & has a miraculously sunny personality. We returned to the block together.

Thursday, 17 September

Watched the 'Fame' programme on Barbara Windsor . . . it was all a bit 'gutter journalism' in flavour. The bit showing me rehearsing & talking of Barbara's qualities as an actress was all right, but I looked

---

[14] I have been so great a lover: filled my days
So proudly with the splendour of Love's praise,
The pain, the calm, and the astonishment,
Desire illimitable, and still content,
And all dear names men use, to cheat despair,
For the perplexed and viewless streams that bear
Our hearts at random down the dark of life.

Opening of 'The Great Lover', by Rupert Brooke.

very like the dried-up & prune-like poof: not at all lovely, I'm afraid, & the morale took a great nose dive.

Wednesday, 23 September
Watched 'Willo The Wisp' & one's heart sank 'cos one realised that it's 1) technically indifferent with recording levels wrong 2) it lacks drive & energy 3) there's nothing with which the young can identify 4) the jokes aren't good enough. Oh! one could go on and on.

Monday, 28 September
Michael came at 2.55 & drove us to Roger St where Terry Donovan photographed Louisa in her W.V.S. uniform & then said 'Why not one of you as well?' & I agreed but I think my hair was in disarray so I'm secretly disappointed that I didn't check the appearance first. Louie's dress was so badly stained that Terry said 'Get a damp cloth & rub those stains' & I got most of them out, but really, you'd think Louie would turn up looking better than that. I was inwardly fed up with the whole thing. M. drove us back & we could hardly enter the block for the procession of wogs coming out.

Thursday, 1 October
So this is my first visual commercial![15] Going to a film studio to do something which I'd have despised years ago! I was made up with devil's horns stuck on the forehead. The cloak of scarlet velvet weighed a ton. This director Howard Guard had me jumping up & down *huge* steps & everything was an encumbrance. *Nothing was easy.* Everything was made laborious & exhausting, lines said so often that eventually they lost any spontaneity. By six o'clock I was exhausted and at 9 o'c. I told the producer 'Look here, I'm going to leave at 10 o'c. whether it's completed or not, because I have to work tomorrow & when I took this job of *three lines* I never thought it would take a 12 hour day to film . . .' Eventually I was released about 9.45. Ironic to think that I'll get 4,500 for this work today whereas the most I ever got from a Carry On film was 5,000 and *that* wasn't a day's work! It took at least 4 weeks, & often more.

Tuesday, 6 October
The TV news announced the assassination of that noble man President Sadat of Egypt:[16] apparently the streets are full of screaming & delighted crowds in Libya . . . I've no doubt that Gaddafi is behind it

---

[15] For BP fuel.
[16] Mohamed Anwar el-Sadat, President of Egypt from 1970.

. . . it is the sort of appalling deed which is committed by the warped mind. Went to bed early feeling utterly cast down.

Saturday, 10 October

I was in good spirits & I set out in the raincoat, walking to Selfridges where I got prawns for Louie. Back by 3 o'c. marvellously cheerful & that insidious voice inside began: 'Careful! Something will occur! Something will destroy all that elation before long!' Then I went in to see Louie & the TV news showed the horrible results of an IRA bomb outside Chelsea Barracks . . . a surgeon at the Westminster says the injuries are the worst he has ever seen. These heinous crimes – in the name of *politics*! – go on, year in & year out . . . invalids live on, mutilated, blind, limbless . . . and the news shifts from this to the funeral today of the murdered Sadat of Egypt, and then: 'and now news of football . . .' etc. The misery welled up inside me & the spirits sank to zero.

Wednesday, 14 October

To Pebble Mill where I did this omelette cooking & talked of Edith, Ingrid & Mags' little boy & the potato. Drinks after & then taxi to station with a Doctor David Delvin[17] & we travelled back together. During a conversation on the train with him, I spoke about [Q.] asking if she could come up to the Endsleigh Court flat and my making that ludicrous excuse 'I've no lavatory' & this Doctor said: 'At the risk of sounding rude – don't answer if you don't want to – why on earth did a *woman* think you'd be interested?' I replied lamely 'Lots of women found Novello[18] attractive . . .' and he conceded 'Yes . . . there is that . . .' but it was the first time a cultivated man & a stranger to me had said openly that I was an obvious homosexual. It wasn't earth shattering but it wasn't pleasing.

Saturday, 17 October

Went to TV Centre at 1 o'c. for the 'Parkinson Show'. It was Windsor Davies, then me, then Douglas Bader,[19] then Vera Lynn. It started well with W.D. being warm & funny, I went on and told the Nee Soon story of Hank Marriott & Leo Wilson in the monsoon ditch[20] and after that, it went steadily down hill. Got home by about 4 o'c. Saw Louisa at about 5 o'c. We watched the Stanley Baxter show on ITV and again

---

[17] b.1939. Television doctor and medical columnist.

[18] Ivor Novello (Davies), 1893–1951. Composer and actor.

[19] Group Captain (1910–82). World War II fighter pilot who operated in spite of the loss of both legs in a flying accident. Subject of film biography *Reach for the Sky*.

[20] The story of the burial of the suicide Marriott, which took place in a rainstorm. See entry for 24 June 1947, p. 13.

I was struck by Stanley's obsession with the past; it was all about old films, film directors, film stories re-jigged, film personalities (Jimmy Durante etc.) & so was fine for the middle-aged but had nothing for the young.

Tuesday, 20 October

Teddington at 4 o'c. for 'Give Us A Clue'. Nanette Newman said to me 'D'you remember when we travelled up to Manchester and this man in the carriage was reading The Times & you pulled it down from his face & said "Oh! leave that! Our conversation will be much more interesting!"' I didn't remember it at all. It's extraordinary how we all have different mental portraits of each other.

Tuesday, 27 October

Oh! the letters that pour in apropos 'Lady of Shallot' on Parkinson! And they send me their own ill-constructed efforts! All so sad. One woman writes: 'I send you this, like a dog dropping a bone at your feet . . .' We saw Russell Harty interviewing Dirk Bogarde & v. squirmy it was! The anecdotes were tag-less and badly told & the appearance discouraging! – awful black-dyed hair which threw the lined face into relief & the mannerisms were extraordinarily camp but *not* funny. D.B. said he deplored the deterioration in 'English manners' and went on about the decline of moral standards, but since he's living abroad (in France) I don't think he's much of an authority on English standards anyway. It was all rather tatty and sad.

Thursday, 29 October

I walked to Hodder's at Bedford Square & went thro' the itinerary for the signing sessions. It's the Blackpool trip that's going to be murder. Walked home thro' the clear autumnal air (the dead leaves smell fragrantly in the breeze) and thought of the events that led me here . . . I little dreamed when I was a boy walking thro' this area, that one day I'd be calling on the publishers of my book & hearing them say 'the sales are marvellous . . .'

Friday, 6 November

There was a dish returning from running in the park & we shared the lift: think it's on the fifth floor, ain't seen it before. In the evening I walked to Michael's flat. Met his guests, Christopher and Anne. Since the two guests offered nothing in way of conversation I found myself desiring to shock the pair of them & got more and more provocative, telling stories with such obscene remarks that they fell shocked & silent. M. endeavoured to change the subject but it was disaster. Got home feeling quite ashamed.

Tuesday, 10 November

Got the train to Preston & changed there for Blackpool. It was a luncheon given by the Lancs. Literary Club. Mainly ladies. Just got away with it. Car from there to Manchester for the TV interview at Granada TV. Motored to Preston. Interviewed for radio there, and for a magazine. I did a different speech entirely (apropos Donal Brooks & the operation) and went like a bomb. Signing session after & over a hundred books sold. At 12.45 I returned to the hotel room. Horrified to find duvet instead of proper bedding & the awful smell of fruit (they left a bowlful in the room!) which I got rid of by shoving everything in the loo.

Saturday, 14 November

Flight to Dublin. Taken from airport to Bloom's Hotel. Left for the TV studios. There, all was chaos. Reception room crowded with idiots, including a load of Frenchmen who were there to blow trumpets. After them, I went on for the chat with Gay Byrne.[21] It went *fair* & then I realised the audience was the same as in '69 – stodgy staid drears. After me, Ilie Nastase came on, saying to me 'You make me nervous' and proceeded to put the whole show on the floor. Then James Burke[22] came on . . . babbling incoherently . . . audience bemused. Then a procession of undertakers & a vicar to discuss the costs of burial. Only in Ireland could you have found such an incongruous & unfunny mixture.

Thursday, 26 November

Went to Paris for 'J.A.M.' Peter Atkin[23] is new producer. I said (on first game) to Tim [Rice]: 'It's an all male panel!' & he looked at me witheringly saying 'Well all . . . most' and I told the audience; they fell about!

Thursday, 10 December

Went to Paris studio for 'J.A.M.' H.S. came to the show: 'Don't you remember me? Christmas '73 . . . you made love to me . . .' I said 'You must be mistaken. We've never met' & he handed me three photographs showing me kissing his cheek. 'It was at Belgrave St . . . if you've got a diary look it up!' I did when I got home. He was right. It was 15.12.73 & we'd gone on after a party given by Desmond, but if it hadn't been for the evidence, I'd have said it was all made up. I remember (from diary entries) that I'd had a lot to drink.

---

[21] Perennial presenter of 'The Late Late Show'.

[22] b.1936. Television presenter, science documentarist and author (*Connections*, etc.).

[23] b.1945. Later Head of BBC Network Radio South and West.

Tuesday, 22 December

Letter from George Borwick confirms that he has married Lady Ellerman – he says they were secretly engaged last August, and that it was high time he settled down! He's going to get rid of the mews flat and move into her flat in the Baker Street area. Louisa went to the doctor at 5 o'c. When I complained to her that the cuts on the thumb should have been tackled before they'd become open wounds, Louie began to cry, and she said 'All you do these days is find fault with me . . . there is nothing I can do right' and of course I felt a pig, but all energy was gone from me & I was utterly dispirited, unable to make the sort of cheering effort required. After a dolorous silence I said 'Yes, well I'm going to bed' and left. All of life is putting on an act of some kind or another & now I'm beginning to find it almost impossible.

Wednesday, 23 December

It is interesting that this year I've not been asked to take part in *one single Christmas event!!* Usually I've done something in radio, or on the box, but this time: nothing.*

*With the exception of Michael Parkinson! He's included me in his chat show compilation . . . oh yes & there is a Carry On showing . . . & I am on LBC . . . no! Capital Radio, and on the BBC TV Children's hour doing v/o in 'Willo The Wisp'.

Sunday, 27 December

I walked to Euston thro' driving wind & snow & found all the papers had gone . . . Staggered home thro' the slush & thought that this must be the most miserable period I've experienced since 1976.

Thursday, 31 December

Went to bed at 11 o'c. with the French idiot blaring thro' the wall. So that's it, the end of a year . . . and not a v. profitable one either . . . a year which has brought home to me the appallingly high taxation we're enduring – VAT, Inc. Tax, Ins. Tax, Rates, Water, Higher Earnings Tax . . . we're well on the way to Italian corruption and decadence.

1982

Sunday, 10 January
The news was all about the dire state of the country in the grip of the freeze, with cattle dying and travellers stranded . . . Oh! it is unrelieved gloom! In desperation one begins to lose caution . . . I sat drinking sherry and eating crisps and chocolate . . . in fact, doing all the things I should normally avoid!

Tuesday, 12 January
Went to Equity Executive Meeting. It was all piddling rubbish & I foolishly rejected taking the Chair! Lost patience by 12.30 & left. Staggered home thro' the snow-laden & filthy streets, my body trembling with cold – Oh God! this is one of the most miserable periods I've ever known! And there seems to be no let-up! This, plus the endless worry of not getting any work and the flat costs rising every year! It's horrible to contemplate. The paper says Ronald Lewis has taken an overdose! He was declared bankrupt last year! Obviously nobody offered him work & he was driven to despair. I remember Ronnie . . . and that drinking session at the White Horse all those years ago . . . he was a kind boy & people used him. He was 54.[1]

Thursday, 14 January
I saw the TV 'Does The Team Think'. This is the result of the pilot I did last year! There were two pilots done: I was in the first with Eamonn, the second one was under Tim Brooke-Taylor. The second one was the success as far as transmission & ours was scrubbed. At the time I thought ours was the better by far & felt rather sorry for the other lot! What irony! It's interesting that, in all the TV pilots I've done, *not one* has been a success.

Saturday, 16 January
Letter from Bill Kenwright suggesting I star in a double bill – *Black Comedy* (Shaffer) and [*The Real*] *Inspector Hound* (Stoppard) but I don't

---

[1] They had appeared together in *Twice Round the Daffodils.*

like either of them. A letter also from a film man who says he wants to make a documentary about me & would like 'to follow you about for a few days . . .' Don't fancy that either.

Wednesday, 3 February
I walked to Film House in Wardour Street to do the v/o for BP Heatsave: it was voice over a picture showing a hand reaching for the red telephone in Hell. It was an arresting idea. Those writers were there: again reeking of garlic. The loquacious one told me that the market results of the film had been good & that they'd start running the campaign in earnest in 1983. I watched the Variety Club awards at the Hilton with Wogan mouthing some bad taste gags & a succession of performers professing modesty & looking justified. The only bright spot was from Les Dawson who said of Wogan on radio 'He's given a new meaning to the word drab' and he also said 'The recession hasn't affected me: I was a flop when there was a boom.' Oh! he was a delight. There is enormous comedy potential in satirising these ludicrous affairs. It is the sort of hypocrisy that could certainly take a few knocks.

Sunday, 7 February
I walked to Gordon & Rona at Hampstead. Gordon looked thinner and tired, he said 'I must admit I don't enjoy going to the theatre every night.' He made me laugh when he said that Dorothy Tutin had spoken to him about the way some people shortened their names (Ethel Murmanski changed to Merman)[2] & he told her 'like you knocked the Khamun bit off yours!' He said 'She didn't laugh . . . just looked bewildered.' Gordon said that they'd been chatting to Katie Boyle[3] & that she'd said 'Kenneth Williams frightens me . . . I worked with him once & he gave me such a *look* . . .' I said I didn't remember the occasion, but it's odd how these echoes recur; several other people have voiced comparable sentiments, yet I'm a vulnerable creature who feels no malice towards anyone in the profession.

Monday, 8 February
Walked to The Barge in Little Venice to do three v/os for radio commercial & wasn't pleased to find I was doing them with Bill Franklyn – I remember the idiot who directed the film saying 'He'll be ideal to play the God figure' and of course he is not. He's got that brash hearty exterior which I can't stand & then I thought 'Well, a lot of people

---

[2] 1909–88. Her original name was actually Zimmermann (see entry for 4 December, p. 667).
[3] Caterina Imperiali di Francavilla, b.1929. Broadcaster and columnist.

can't stand your kind of arrogant rudeness' & I suddenly realised how we're all taken in by facades! Bill is a kind fellow & probably a lot better natured than I am. Walked back & noticed lots of buds burgeoning in the park! It was mild and balmy & I thought 'My career had just begun when I was only twenty-one.' I've been earning a living as an actor for 35 years!

Tuesday, 9 February

I went with Cyril Smith[4] to Leeds. He was v. amusing about after-dinner speeches – the fielder who let the ball go through his legs telling an irate Freddie Trueman[5] 'Sorry, I should have kept my legs closed' getting the reply 'Nay lad, thee Mother should!' The talk I did on 'Sunday Best' was about the Subadhar at Kurunegala & my having to apologise etc. Donald Swann[6] told me 'That story was marvellous & very moving! I felt almost choked with emotion! You told it beautifully!' In so far as I told a narrative rather than enter into theological discussion I think I was successful but there's little one can do in a 5 minute spot.

Friday, 12 February

M. came at 7.15 and drove to Savoy Hill where we parked & then went to the Vaudeville. The play *Cards On The Table*[7] is quite unbelievable. Creaking nonsense produced in a stilted bogus manner & rendered lifeless by a lot of posing & hapless performers. Gordon does what he can with 'Inspector Battle' & a battle it must be nightly!! He is the only one with pace or truthfulness. Went round to see him after & he said 'Why d'you come to see this rubbish?' & I told him 'You have no objectivity about it 'cos you've been in it too long . . . you have the look of great confidence & ease . . . & your clothes are superb . . . the sets are very stylish . . .' All true, thank heavens! M. drove me home saying 'You've done your duty.'

Saturday, 13 February

TV programme at Teddington. On the show, Denis [Norden] introduced me as 'The John McEnroe of panel games' & the audience fell about!

---

[4] Liberal MP for Rochdale 1972–92.

[5] Frederick Sewards Trueman (b.1931), belligerent Yorkshire and England fast bowler, later a commentator and raconteur.

[6] Songwriter, singer and pianist, b.1923, formerly of the duo Flanders and Swann.

[7] Adapted by Leslie Darbon from Agatha Christie's detective story. Poirot, amazingly, was removed from the story and his deductions distributed between two other characters, one of them Jackson's (Superintendent Battle).

Monday, 22 February
A man stopped me in the street: 'Kenneth! A Happy Birthday to you!' & I stammered a surprised 'Thank you!' A bouquet of flowers arrived from Bill Kenwright! I wrote my thanks. With Paul at 5.30 to Leic. Sq. Cinema where we saw *Death Wish II* with Charles Bronson. It's really pornographic titillation plus fascism as content & appeals to reactionaries I suppose.

Thursday, 4 March
I went to post and to Dent's. Peter Shellard gave me & Gyles lunch at Langan's. I said 'How does the idea of a fictitious funny diary attract you?' and both were enthusiastic. Peter said 'We'll give you a better advance than last time 'cos of your track record' & I said 'I don't want an advance' & he told me 'Gyles does!' It's all so complicated. I've had a letter from Peter Rogers saying that Sir Joseph Lockwood[8] wanted a compere for a charity show at Sadler's Wells in October and he'd suggested me. He enclosed a patronising note from Lockwood saying 'Kenneth Williams would be a suitable choice.' I'll bet I would! I replied to Rogers saying 'Alas I don't do compering any more' and said I'll be busy with book promotion. I've done all the favours for the Carry On crowd that I need to do *and* more!

Saturday, 13 March
When I went in to Louisa at 4 o'c. she had the TV on and was watching *Twice Round The Daffodils*! I looked about eighteen in it, and Lance like a youth! Sinden had none of the mannerisms he's acquired since, Andrew was truthful & vulnerable, Ronnie Lewis attractively surly . . . oh! it was extraordinarily fascinating to see them all again and to realise what a talented bunch they'd collected in those films!

Monday, 15 March
C. took me to CHE at the Chepstow. I talked about Holiday Incidents & tried to keep it all amusing & light. Met a charming taxi driver called David and a dentist called John who knows Paul very well! Last time I was here was 1st Dec. '80. My subject then was Biography and I talked about the Knoblock saga and Johnny Vere.[9]

Thursday, 18 March
I went to see Jonathan [James-Moore] at about 10.30 & his secretary

---

[8] 1904–91. Chairman of EMI 1954–74. Formerly Treasurer, British Empire Cancer Campaign.
[9] John Vere (Biggar) had at one time been the secretary of Edward Knoblock (1874–1945), American-born playwright, a specialist in dramatising novels.

Carol [Smith] has typed the script for Saturday quite marvellously! Don't know how she read my writing! When I told her she said 'You should see some of the scripts I get!' Walked home thro' the cold streets.

Saturday, 20 March

Shocked to read in the paper about the death of Alan Badel. Lovely actor. He was superb in *Stranger Left No Card* & was never given proper recognition in this country. V. much in the same tradition as Eric Portman – both superb romantic actors, yet both capable of an extraordinary tour de force and character ability (Portman in *Playbill* for instancc) and Badel in *Kean*. Lunch with Louie at 12 o'c. feeling utterly depressed. Alan was only 58. At 2.30 to the Paris for 'One Man's Variety'. Various run-thro's & all the boredom of having to wait about. Lance was super & smashing to have on the show – his spot went v. well. Stanley Unwin was marvellous, Cantabile terrific, and Elaine Del Mar sang beautifully. The audience was terrible: a cross between old folks' outing and foreign holiday makers. The only consolation is that one didn't have to break a leg or anything . . . once I realised they were a lousy house I didn't bother . . . just go thro' it professionally. Smiling & unconcerned.

Monday, 22 March

Got the tube to Notting Hill. Gyles met me at the house, with Clive,[10] and I worked with the latter till about 4.30. It was mainly taken up with skimming thro' '81 diary & finding stuff that one could cull. At one point Clive cheered me greatly when he said of one piece: 'I'd be proud to have that in a book I'd produced . . . it's a good piece of writing . . . you must include that . . .' He's very encouraging.

Wednesday, 24 March

Clive came at 11 o'c. and we worked on material for the book. I said it would have to be set in '81 because otherwise it would have no credibility. Not the year '81 in the title: in the preface it should be stated[11] & all the entries simply bearing day & month. Finished about 6 o'c. and I suggested we meet again when I had found some more material.

Friday, 26 March

In the evening we saw a film starring William Holden. He was found dead in his apartment, apparently he'd fallen over in a drunken

---

[10] Clive Dickinson, of Victorama Ltd, Gyles Brandreth's company.

[11] No year is given in the Foreword of *Back Drops*.

stupor: hardly surprising after some of the scripts he'd had to cope with.

Monday, 29 March

I went to Molinaire to do a v/o with Arthur Mullard for Leicester B. Society: only one line each. Ludicrous waste of time. Arthur told me: 'I don't do much nowadays, 'course I'm always being asked to go into the theatre but I don't fancy that.' 'Neither do I,' I replied, 'who wants to be a prisoner 6 nights every week?' The news was all rubbish apart from a scurry in the Falkland Islands where some impertinent Argentinians are pinching scrap metal or something.

Wednesday, 31 March

BMW car ad with Edward Judd. I was supposed to do it à la Arthur Negus[12] but I wasn't very good. At 4.20 there was no car. Rang the Parkinson office at TV Centre and told them. Got to the Centre. Rehearsed with the guitarist. Talked with Michael P. and with Jimmy Tarbuck, Billy Connolly, Adam Faith. On the show, J.T. opened with M.P. and there was talk of getting pissed, the word bollocks, and etc. It all got v. vulgar *without* ambiguity. B.C. did a cooking send-up which was v. funny but untidy, Spike Milligan came on then, and was practically incoherent. Then a woman sang, then Sammy Cahn[13] appeared & sang a musical tribute to M.P. Then it was me. I did the 'Joe he was a young cordwangler,' talked about Australia & the Bill Kerr Story, and about Louie on the 30 bus, then M.P. asked me to tell the Edith story & the porter farting. Then there was a birthday cake & everyone had a farewell drink for the last 'Parkinson' show. In the make up room M.P. asked what I was doing & I said 'Very little' and he told me 'You are ridiculously under used! You're miles better than most of the performers you see nowadays' and it was rather embarrassing as I stuttered on about getting bits here and there.

Friday, 2 April

The TV news was full of the Falkland Islands invasion & there have been angry accusations about Government tardiness. They certainly seemed to have no intelligence about the deteriorating situation & to have learned nothing from the landing of 'scrap merchants' in South Georgia. For the first time since the Suez Crisis, there is to be a debate in the Commons tomorrow!

---

[12] Antiques expert and broadcaster, 1903–85.

[13] 1913–93. Songwriter.

Sunday, 4 April

Taxi to Royalty, Kingsway, where about 300 turned up for the [Equity] AGM. We sat on the stage freezing in draughts, while Barron bored everyone with droning tedium. The Obituary[14] was read by him with appalling slowness and after that there was the hypocrisy of 2 minutes' silence. I found myself thinking 'My name will be read out to this rabble one day!' and on the whole I think I'd prefer 'em to sit. I went up to the circle & sat there till lunch time 'cos at least it was warm.

Thursday, 8 April

I went to Campden Hill to work with Clive. I suggested *Devious Diary* or *Diary of a Deviant* as title for the book: certainly items written in my journal tend to go off at a tangent at the drop of a hat.

Friday, 9 April

I went through the '75 diary in an effort to cull more material but nothing was forthcoming. Reading what I wrote in that period was enlightening! The depression evinced amazed me, 'cos I was certainly being more sociable in that period & it's solitude that's supposed to induce melancholy! Well, that isn't true of me – I am by nature melancholic. I always have been.

Sunday, 11 April

Got papers at 8 o'c. Jock said to me 'Will you be going to entertain the troops in the Falklands campaign?' There have been quite a few remarks like this lately.

Friday, 23 April

Charming card from Gyles!! He says that Clive is typing the stuff: 'It's *War & Peace* with laughs!' I'm going to suggest *Back Drops* as a title, 'cos the diary is dropping a backward look & the back drop in a theatre denotes changes of scene & mood.

Sunday, 25 April

I walked to Gordon & Rona. He was funny about David Lean making a film with Greta Gynt. In a desperate effort to find film footage on which she'd looked ecstatic, he went thro' all the over-takes & found one where the second assistant had called 'Tea up!' & her face lit up, so he used that. Having made her a star he tried to greet her at the

---

[14] An annual reading out of the names of Equity members who have died during the preceding year.

premiere but the burly boyfriend elbowed him into the gutter. No thanks for the film Svengali.

Monday, 26 April

Went to Greenwood Theatre for 'Choices'. I was on the panel with Phillip Whitehead & Mary Whitehouse.[15] It was a lousy format for an entertaining half hour because the diffusion rendered everything bland. At one point, after I'd spoken, Whitehead said 'If I can get a word in, after this Megastar . . .' The audience didn't laugh. At the end of the show, I rounded on him: 'What did you mean by making sneering cracks about me? Why did you call me a megastar? How would you like it if I gratuitously refer to you in the same way? What if I'd said "If I can get a word in after this Great MP?"' He muttered something about being sorry & I ranted on 'It is disgraceful to make such derisive & cheap cracks on a programme which is supposed to be concerned with moral truths! I'm glad the audience didn't find your remark amusing! You didn't get a single laugh . . .' Oh I went on & on. After, the guilt was all-enveloping. When I got home I wrote a note apologising for the outburst: not for the complaint, but for the form it took. I shouted so much at the man, he was quite shaken: my anger was appalling.

Tuesday, 4 May

Tube to Gyles and we worked on the book. He said 'We might need to add a few amusing touches, here and there' but privately I feel I've nothing more to add: this book will contain some of my best anecdotes, and it's a sadness in a way 'cos they're gone from me, once they're published.

Tuesday, 11 May

Went to park for an hour & then got tube to Waterloo & met Chris for lunch at County Hall with Illtyd Harrington. I was introduced to Ken Livingstone[16] and his mother by Illtyd & they were both charming. I think Ken is v. attractive I must say. It was interesting to see the interior of County Hall again: haven't been there since my childhood! The vast corridors, the marble pillars & general air of solidity & luxury is an extraordinary reminder of the L.C.C. mentality of the 30's.

---

[15] Whitehead, b.1937; Labour MP for Derby North 1970–83, TV producer and specialist in broadcasting policy. Mary Whitehouse, b.1910; founder of National Viewers' and Listeners' Association, campaigner for cleaner media.

[16] b.1945. Leader of Greater London Council and Labour Group 1981–86, MP for Brent East from 1987. Harrington, b.1931. Deputy Leader of GLC 1981–84, etc.

Thursday, 13 May
Went to Silksound to do the Jeyes Bloo chat for the sales conference, with Sue Bethell & a script that was chronically unfunny. It was about the commission likely for successful salesmen & I put in 'There's no remuneration but they'll give you something in loo' & Sue said 'We'd better do a straight version if you don't mind . . .' & put the tin lid on that.

Wednesday, 19 May
Walked to Peter Nichols in the afternoon. He was looking well – so was Thelma, and Dan. Peter showed me the photographs of Nee Soon and it was amazing how little had changed! The New London was still there! And the house in Cameron Highlands where we were all billeted! Peter told me: 'Weidenfeld have asked me to write a memoir . . . I said I'd call it *Peter Who?* and Dan said "Why d'you always run yourself down, Dad?"' He added that he'd wanted to give up playwriting for some time.

Thursday, 20 May
Went to Liverpool St where I met Johnny Morris. At the Swan Hotel at Southwold, we met Percy Edwards[17] and Roger (sound) and Vanessa (producer) and we were told that we would all meet at 4 o'c. tomorrow morning to drive to a spot where we'd hear the dawn chorus. It's absurd to journey all this way to ad lib a few daft comments, eat a lot of unnecessary food, get constipation & tongue ulcers . . . for what? About fifty quid, at the end of the day! And probably 25 after tax.

Friday, 21 May
Up at 3.30 in this Swan Hotel at Southwold. Car came at 4 o'c. & we went to the forest at Minsmere, then to Dunwich and then to the Bell at Walberswick. The whole thing was ludicrous 'cos birdsong could be heard all over the place at 7 o'c. and 8 o'c. so one need never have risen at such an ungodly hour. Johnny Morris and me boarded the train for London. At Colchester, Mary Whitehouse got in. 'I could hear your voice right down the corridor of the train.' I'm incensed by a patronising letter from this Bowen man at European Business School. He actually asked 'Have you done this before?' apropos talking about comedy!! I wrote a letter cancelling the 11th and saying I'm not coming. There are loads of letters to answer. Gordon & Rona have sent me a book with extracts from Johnson's dictionary! They know I'm mad about Sam: it is a sweet thought.

---

[17] b.1908. Countryman, broadcaster, specialising in imitations of birds and animals.

Sunday, 23 May
Did the Restoria & went for the papers. They say that the Task Force is dug-in round San Carlos Bay & will take the heights overlooking Port Stanley. Much is made of the fact that our flag flies over the Falklands once again. I've no doubt our troops are superior to the Argentine rabble but I hate the idea of lives lost.

Friday, 28 May
Tube to Gyles. We went thro' the rest of the material. Curiously it all seems old hat & jaded to me now. We did some re-writes & corrections.

Saturday, 29 May
Lunch with Louisa & then walked to park to meet Paul. There was a curious boy shouting at people! 'Don't stare at me! You are obnoxious!' & then he came and presented me with an ice cream! 'Here you are Kenny!' and insisted on my meeting his father: 'He had an affair with Margaret Duchess of Argyll, you know![18] *And* the Duke of Windsor!' His conversation was v. fanciful.

Tuesday, 1 June
Now the preoccupation is with the aftermath of the Falklands conquest! With arguments about why we need the cooperation of Argentina! Oh! they are fools! We needed their cooperation all along! Walked to Foyle's to get *The Living and the Dead* by the much-praised Patrick White.[19] It's like reading something between T.S. Eliot and Henry James with an awful lot of Virginia Woolf thrown in. A rambling messy sort of writing with all the story impetus lost in 'philosophical' musings.

Sunday, 6 June
We drove, with Irene Handl, to Cambridge, Irene rhapsodising over the countryside 'Oh! isn't it lovely! All that barley in the fields!' & we were ensconced at the Garden House Hotel where the arse sticks to PVC chairs. Met Mavis Nicholson – lovely girl who astonished me by saying she'd 3 sons!! 21, 19 and 18!! When I left for bed, Irene protested 'Say goodnight properly' so I had to go back & do it dutifully & kiss the cheek.

---

[18] Margaret Whigham, third wife of the 11th Duke of Argyll.
[19] (1912–90) English-born Australian novelist, winner of 1973 Nobel Prize for Literature.

Monday, 7 June

There was a queue at the [Arts Theatre] & Richard Baker[20] introduced everyone including the musician & conductor Antony Hopkins. The show went v. well. Irene, discussing a plan to paint her dog with phosphor, said 'I thought, over my dead arse!' & the laughter was immediate. I thought she'd said 'Over my dead aunts' but she hadn't.

Wednesday, 9 June

Walked to Noel St where I met Peter Bayliss to do the message to the Falklands troops & found it wasn't radio but video!! I wasn't made-up, hair-combed or anything! I did a couple of spots – talking of the C.S.E. audition & the dysentery story in Rangoon, and another spot with a verse (life is a glorious cycle of song) and the 'blew his hat off' story.

Saturday, 12 June

Peter Nichols phoned & invited Louie & me to lunch on Sunday & I assented. He talked sense apropos Falklands crisis & said 'I think it's finished the Labour Party.'

Tuesday, 15 June

Headlines are all about the Argentine surrender on the Falklands. We saw a special programme 'Falkland Special'. David Dimbleby interviewed Defence Minister John Nott with appallingly embarrassing questions about inadequate armaments for our forces in the South Atlantic – this on the Day of Victory! – and questions like 'Are you now going to resign?' I wonder Nott didn't leave the studio.[21]

Sunday, 20 June

Walked with Louisa to Peter & Thelma. Other guests were Eileen Atkins & Bill and Terry Hands.[22] I was v. taken with T.H., such an attractive & interesting personality. When I spoke of Extras & Walk-ons getting paid for residuals [Peter] said 'That is ludicrous' & I pointed out that socialist arguments for egalitarianism had produced it. 'You're a supporter of equality . . . they're saying they contribute *equally* to a show's success & deserve a share in the profits' & he said 'Then it's a misuse of the egalitarian argument.' But alas, all socialists fall into

---

[20] b.1925. Newsreader turned general broadcaster, here chairing 'Start the Week'.

[21] A prescient remark. (Sir) John Nott, b.1932, Secretary of State for Defence, did walk out of a television interview on 5 October 1982, when Sir Robin Day in the course of framing a question called him 'a here today and, if I may say so, gone tomorrow politician'. Nott resigned in January 1983 and was replaced by Michael Heseltine.

[22] b.1941. Then Joint Artistic Director, latterly Director Emeritus, Royal Shakespeare Company.

this trap! They promulgate a dogma which then produces a backlash, nonsense is made of real ability & talent – hospital porters dictate medical terms to a surgeon – and then they find their organisation split by extremism. I notice this about Peter: he's always attentive to Louie – so is Thelma – and both of them totally lack pretension.

Wednesday, 30 June

We saw a bit of TV but it was dire. Benny Hill looks more and more like a desperate adipose decrepit. When I told Louie that old age would curtail her activities in time, she replied 'Well, when that happens I'll just lie down and die. I'm not afraid to die.' I kept my countenance but quaked inwardly.

Monday, 5 July

Read Anthony Powell.[23] This writer is praised by critics for his learning & his wit. His writing is full of literary pretension and the narrative line endlessly interrupted by authorial conceits. Tedious, rotten stuff.

Wednesday, 7 July

Motored to Birmingham. At Pebble Mill I met the other people on the '6.55 Special' programme, George Melly and Sinead Cusack. I saw the dishy David Soul & cried out 'I thought you had the day off?' & he said he 'liked to be around' and came & talked. I started showing off about semantics & he told me 'You are a natural teacher! I could listen to you all night!' We got a taxi back together to the Albany & when, in the lift, I said I was tired, he said 'Yeah . . . no doubt about it . . . you've really *faded* . . .'

Thursday, 8 July

Taxi came and took me to Pebble Mill. I introduced the various items in the Children's festival and ran from studio to studio, acting as a general enthuser for the project. 15 minutes' lunch break & then I was back at it. I was in & out of six studios working on one thing or another.

Friday, 16 July

Got to Leeds at about 8.50. Hung about till Shirley Williams's late plane arrived & then we did the programme. She was her usual warm & amiable self & the conversation flowed OK in the first half, bit stilted in the second, but fair throughout. Then I had to meet Frank Smith who showed me a videotape of a panel game about words,

---

[23] b.1905. Novelist.

'Countdown',[24] and asked if I'd like to play the Judge With Dictionary role. I said yes.

Sunday, 18 July

We saw the LWT 'National Salute' – this concert for the Falklands campaign. In a 'walk-down' at the end, various celebrities trotted embarrassedly past the cameras & at the tail end was Stanley! He stopped and reached out a hand for Dame Anna Neagle, and in the finale he was heavily featured standing next to Vera Lynn singing 'Land of Hope & Glory'. Stanley sang it gazing towards the gods, and kept his countenance. 'Thank goodness I didn't get mixed up in *that*!' I thought to myself. It was excruciating: the sort of patriotic jingoism and amateur theatricals which leave you squirming.

Monday, 19 July

I walked to Molinaire for this TV books programme. I was kept hanging around till 3.30 and by that time, all the impetus had drained away & I was terrible. When I faced the camera I felt inhibited & unconfident & the incoherent rambling was unacceptable. They settled for a 'fits & starts' recording which they hope will edit all right. The endless waiting made me spiritless & the end result was incompetence. Never before have I *ever* experienced such horror. It was as if a voice inside was saying 'Forget it! You are no good at all.' Walked home marvelling that I was able to *face* the world at all . . . all the way, people were greeting me . . . a lorry driver called 'Hallo Ken!' & I smiled acknowledgment.

Tuesday, 27 July

Went to the Equity Council Meeting. There's no doubt but the new political complexion has wrought no improvements. They're all on the ugly pill, Manning is back in the Presidency, & the bores chunter on. I had a giggle with Leonard Rossiter and left at 11.45.

Monday, 9 August

Packed a bag & said goodbye to Louisa & left with M. at about 10 o'c. We motored to Peterborough – quick look at the Cathedral – then to Stamford. It's marvellous but ruined by traffic. Had lunch there in a hostelry. The menu said chicken was speciality of the day. I said to the barmaid 'What's special about chicken? You can have it any day of the week' & she said 'It's about as special as you'll get here!' Motored thro' flat Lincolnshire to the Humber Bridge. It is a poetic

---

[24] The first programme to be shown on Channel 4, on 2 November 1982, and still running ten years later.

triumph of engineering, beautiful in its simplicity & frugality. The toll was £1. Alas, there was hardly anyone about. M. said 'It's an expensive White Elephant.' Then we motored thro' various depressing places. The Peak District National Park (hiding various quarries) was all v. Wagnerian & rain began to fall. As the light waned I became increasingly hungry & impatient. At Buxton we found St Katharine's Hotel where the receptionist asked 'Name?' when I enquired for a room.

Tuesday, 10 August
We were away by 8.30. Driving thro' the Yorkshire dales in brilliant sunshine. Picked up a cricketer who was going to Kettering 'I teach at the Christian University at Fort Worth . . .' We got to London at about 3.30.

Thursday, 12 August
I went to the BBC and talked to Jonathan James-Moore.[25] He said 'My paper on your show got lost and had to be resubmitted . . . they've now accepted the idea, but want a variety format . . . four half-hour shows . . . with your monologues providing the links . . .' Then we talked about casting & the ideas seem to be compatible. Now, I have to go away & rough out the dialogue for four shows. Rona came and drove me to Joe Allen's, we met Gordon there. G. told me he'd seen Stanley at the Falklands concert & he'd said of me 'I think he still likes me 'cos he mentions me on chat shows' & G. said the concert had been unmitigated disaster.

Friday, 13 August
Barbara (Windsor) rang me & said they've done a TV compilation of Carry Ons for Thames TV!! Joanne rang 'They want you to publicise it . . . they'll pay for a car!' I told her to tell 'em to stick it. It's incredible that Gerald & Peter can behave with such stupid lack of feeling. A series for TV and we are not even *informed*, and then we're asked to do publicity for nothing!! Well, now, I'm certainly not going to Gerald's party in September & I've chucked the invitation in the WPB.

Friday, 20 August
Walked to Meridiana for lunch with Robert Bolt. He is speaking more easily. When I spoke about looking after Louie he said earnestly 'You are a good man . . . you are very *good* . . .' which was a bit embarrassing. Every now & then he's rather vicar-like.

---

[25] Latterly Head of Light Entertainment, Radio.

Thursday, 26 August
Walked to Dent's for the photography session: they wanted head lower half of design with wording above, I wanted head top (looking over shoulder) with the lettering on my back – *Back Drops* – they did some of each, but I think they will accept my idea. I was a little shocked to see the cartoons which P. Shellard has arranged to head certain sections . . . bit undignified . . . but he & Gyles are v. keen so I said OK. Peter S. took me & Gyles & Liz [Newlands] to Langan's for lunch where we waited over an hour!! Liz rudely said, apropos 'J.A.M.' 'You get nastier and nastier on that programme . . .' While it may be true, I didn't want to hear about it on this kind of occasion.

Monday, 30 August
Did a bit of writing for the radio scripts – oh! it's an uphill task. I got prawns for Louisa. Went in to see her for meal at 5.30 and she told me 'Poor Ingrid Bergman is dead' & there was an item about her on the TV news, and a shot of her talking about *Casablanca*. She looked very altered from the '71 days when I worked with her. She died of cancer. Lars Schmidt was with her, at the end.

Wednesday, 1 September
We saw the television tribute to Ingrid Bergman. It was staggering to see clips of her early films when she looked so radiantly beautiful, and then the later shots of her (during the illness) when the face aged so rapidly. The interviewer asked her 'Were you frightened when you found you'd got cancer?' and for a tiny moment Ingrid's patience broke. 'Of course . . . wouldn't you be frightened if you found that out about yourself?' Then the smile was resumed. I remember that dinner with her at the Garden in '71. I wrote in that diary how I'd said at the end of the evening 'You're the best person I ever worked with' & she replied 'Oh my dear! There will be lots of others . . .' There were not.

Wednesday, 8 September
To BBC at 12.30 to do the Gloria Hunniford show. I followed James Mason who said 'It's Kenny Williams!' as he emerged from the studio, and his wife revealed 'We've got your record "Willo The Wisp" 'cos we love Evil Edna . . .' and when I reminded James about our meeting at Pembroke Square with the De Rosso's he said 'But I came backstage when you were in *Cinderella* at the Coliseum' which I'd practically forgotten!

Saturday, 11 September
Ralph Thomas & Joy picked me up and we drove to Gerald & Barbara

at Burnham. It was a huge party! over 70 and a great marquee had been erected for the supper. Champagne was flowing & the food was superb. Sat next to my adorable Jill Purdom. Her husband Dick fell about telling us of the doomed pair of romantic lovers who endeavour to commit suicide only to find no pills but suppositories.

Sunday, 12 September

These days are proving to be full of depression and bane. There isn't a glimmer of hope on the horizon . . . on every side you hear nothing but depressing news; bankruptcies, strikes, murder, war . . . Oh yes, you need fortitude all right! And for this modern world you need Herculean strength as well. I ain't got it.

Friday, 17 September

To the St George Hotel to meet George. He doesn't change at all. After the meal he showed me the flat he shares with Esther. It's a mixture of Versailles and Golders Green. Opulence fighting taste & winning the battle. Everything splendidly uncomfortable.

Friday, 24 September

Met Peter B. at Joe Allen's: 'My hands were sweating with nerves when I phoned you.' Can't understand why anyone should find me formidable. He said 'People like Benn and Scargill have reinvigorated the Labour Movement & Labour will win at the next election.' Apropos deviation he said 'When I was once supposed to meet T. at the airport I'd come from a session where I'd been tied up & chained & spanked . . . he tore my jeans & shirt in the process . . . T. looked at me & said *you slut* as we wheeled the baggage out . . . we didn't speak for 3 days . . .' I said 'In five years' time you'll wonder what on earth you saw in all of it.' Left him at Covent Gdn. buying a biog. of Attlee!! He's a curious boy.

Wednesday, 29 September

Went for a walk in afternoon – wandered round the city & thought 'All your life you've done this . . . walking the streets full of misery.' I was looking in Clement's window on the return & suddenly a voice cried 'Hallo!' making me jump with fear, as a negress in traffic warden's uniform stood leering at me.

Tuesday, 12 October

I arrived in Leeds at 1.10 & went to the studio. They gave me a drink and then I had to get made up for a photograph with Ted Moult[26]

---

[26] 1926–86. Farmer, broadcaster, actor.

(who's doing the same job I'm doing for the first programmes) and after that I hung about doing nothing till 5 o'c.!!! I was sitting with Frank Smith in his office watching the stuff being videoed . . . one's arse fell off with boredom. I'm furious 'cos I needn't have come here at all today! I wasn't used, I've already seen the show and know what's wanted of me.

Wednesday, 13 October

We did 4 shows in the afternoon. Frank Smith & John Mearn busily scripting yet another show & the earphone bawling 'Say something funny Kenneth' with minutes to spare . . . no! seconds!

Thursday, 14 October

Oh! the tension . . . the scrabbling after any shred of comedy one can muster, with a handful of spectators & no laughter to encourage one at all. Frank Smith wants to do a show 'Talking Pictures': the pictures can be anything which spark an interest in one. I thought of 1) *Hulot's Holiday* & the wreath blowing up. 2) Gordon's statue 3) Guercino's 'Doubting Thomas' 4) Duke of Vendôme Audience in St-Simon[27] 5) Ernest Thesiger, kitchen scene, *Last Holiday* – 'I'm a ballet dancer' 6) Letter scene in *12 Night* – rude bit, Malvolio. 7) Nightingale House, Harley St 8) Sam Johnson statue, Fleet St 9) Coward, clip film.

Friday, 15 October

We did 2 shows in the morning. In the afternoon we did 4 shows. I was only supposed to do 2 but Frank Smith said 'Benny Green[28] can't come 'cos he's got 'flu . . . would you do his shows?' so I was at it till about 5.30. 4 on Wednesday, 6 on Thurs., 6 today, means I did 16.

Sunday, 17 October

Walked to the Paris for the Paul Daniels Game at 5 o'c. Paul is a thoroughly likeable man with an unerring sense of comedy. He kept everything going v. well.

Tuesday, 19 October

Car to Seaco House on the South Bank where I talked to David Bell and Richard Drewett about 'An Evening With'[29] for LWT. We're going

---

[27] The Duc de Vendôme received visitors while seated on a *chaise percée*, or commode. KW had read of this in *Saint-Simon at Versailles* by Lucy Norton.

[28] b.1927. Author, critic, broadcaster, jazz musician.

[29] The show, one of an occasional series of solo celebrity performances, was called 'An Audience with Kenneth Williams', the title punningly emphasising the contribution of a celebrity audience who were primed to ask questions.

to have to chart the show by talking to researchers who will develop a plan on which we can build the thing in terms of shape & colour.

Sunday, 24 October

Went to bed at 9.20. Phone rang! It was this Libby someone (BBC producer) to talk about my appearance on 'Blue Peter'. Just got back to bed when Kenneth Robinson rang!! & I'd taken the pill! 'What is it?' 'Perhaps I shouldn't bother to talk at all.' 'I've got people here.' 'Aren't you *ever* telephoned?' 'Well what *is it*?' 'Oh! perhaps we shouldn't meet . . . let's scrub tomorrow.' 'Yes! all right' & I put down the receiver. The man is a pain in the arse. He rang & asked me originally to be interviewed by him for the Express. I said I wasn't keen. He phoned again repeating the request so I agreed to meet him tomorrow, and tonight he cancels it. Just as well.

Wednesday, 27 October

I had a session with Richard Drewett and Alasdair [Macmillan] (producer & director) and some research girls & we went thro' some of the subjects which are usable on the show. R. told me that after the Parkinson Show where I confronted Jimmy Reid 'I had Paul Fox[30] on the phone saying never again . . . keep the format as it is . . . don't attempt that sort of abrasive argument ever again . . .' and it certainly shows the BBC in its mediocre light! Bland Bland Bland . . . and 'Blankety Blank' . . .

Saturday, 30 October

To S. He had quite a throng! Toby, Ronald, Colin & Jeffrey, and Denis Lemon.[31] That old wrangle apropos the blasphemy trial was raked up again and D.L. being very pontifical. I tried to tell a story about Johnny Vere/Edward Knoblock, but all to no avail. S. said 'What a waste! That's a brilliant anecdote and none of these buggers is even listening!' and I said 'Yes well, I must go home' & rose from the table. Said to T. outside, 'You were heavily engaged with that Ronald' & he said 'He was touching me up under the table, but I went off it when I realised he was Irish.' 'Yes,' I said, 'there's always an element of danger with them . . . the allure which leads one on to doom.'

Friday, 5 November

When I was walking down Bolsover St some men were digging in the road & they cried out 'Here's old Willo The Wisp!' as I came along

---

[30] Sir Paul Fox, b.1925, had been Controller of BBC1 1967–73.

[31] Editor of *Gay News* at the time of its prosecution over the James Kirkup poem.

& shouted 'Hallo Kenny!' I'd never have thought navvies would watch 'Willo'! It's extraordinary the audience television attracts.

Wednesday, 10 November

I was telephoned by Peter Adams (Mike Walsh Show) in Sydney 'Is it all right to put you in the Seibel Town House?' Yes. 'We'd like to do bits about your career, the theatre, the films, the people you've worked with, and perhaps you could perform a piece . . . a monologue of some sort . . . ?' Yes. He said he'd phone again, nearer the time.

Thursday, 11 November

Death of Brezhnev of USSR but that won't rouse much sympathy anywhere I shouldn't think. We saw Charles Laughton in *Hobson's Choice* & it was astonishing how *reppy* everybody was! Including him! Prunella Scales looking no different than she does today! Brenda de Bongo[32] being v. good and John Mills competent & the rest, mostly pretty dreary.

Friday, 12 November

Read some more of these books for 'Kaleidoscope'. The Coward Diaries[33] are really a means of money-making for the Coward Estate – like someone getting the appointments book of Alexander: it's chock full of names but these entries read like a guest list & there's precious little about what anybody said. Overall, there is a yearning and a sadness. Oh! you don't need to go to the so-called diaries – so called, 'cos the preface admits they began as engagement books – the lyrics say it all: 'Tho' we still feel a glow from the embers, love cannot be what we hoped it would be . . . Pity the lover who fails to discover the peace of a heart that is free . . .'[34]

Sunday, 14 November

Read more of these 'Kaleidoscope' books. The Lahr one on Coward[35] is all damning with faint praise except *Blithe Spirit.* Where Lahr *is* percipient is in his observation about everyone running away at the end, in Coward plays. It's in the lyrics too . . . 'Let's creep away from the fray for the party's over now . . .'[36]

---

32 Brenda de Banzie.

33 *The Noël Coward Diaries*, edited by Graham Payn and Sheridan Morley.

34 Conclusion of 'Light is the Heart', from *After the Ball.*

35 *Coward the Playwright.*

36 Actually 'Let's creep away from the day . . .' Song 'The Party's Over Now' from *Words and Music.*

Tuesday, 16 November
Richard Drewett suggested taking a rehearsal room & having a try-out but I rejected the idea. The thing will either work as a spontaneous exercise or it won't . . . no amount of rehearsing will make it any better. Already, there is the danger of over-analysis . . . I'm beginning to feel the first stirrings of misgiving . . . what if it all grinds to a miserable halt? Watched myself in 'Countdown'. It was *terrible*. I looked awful & because there was no audience reaction to any of the lines I looked like Cyril Fletcher smiling at his own inanity. *And* I wasted the marvellous Eliot story on it![37] Told it to no reaction at all. Waste waste waste.

Friday, 19 November
Michael Anderson rang to say 'They want you for another 16 "Countdowns"' but I said to try & get me out of it 'cos I can't think of new material which it will require. Found a replacement address book for £5 in Smith's at Bourne's which is a bargain price! Spent the rest of the time writing addresses in the new book! It's amazing the number of people who have died or who've been dropped.

Thursday, 25 November
7.50 to Leeds. Nothing happened till about 12 o'c. when we did a show. And they wanted me to stay overnight yesterday!! In the afternoon we did 3 shows. Finished at 4.15. Frank Smith is an idiot. He said, in front of Richard Whiteley,[38] 'You said he was no good on the show . . .' whereas I'd said he lacked sex-appeal which is quite another matter. Ugh! I don't care. Don't want to go back anyway.

Friday, 26 November
I walked to the Paris for these two radio shows. The sheer amount of *work* is unbelievable. Cantabile had a dirge-like version of 'Strawberry Fair' & I got that changed. My stuff had moments but went only fairly well. It's really a pointless exercise – doing all that *work* & using all that material for tuppence ha'penny.

---

[37] A special favourite of KW's. Its basis was a letter to *The Times* (7 February 1970) written by Valerie Eliot, widow of the poet T.S. Eliot. Her original text ran: 'My husband, T.S. Eliot, loved to recount how late one evening he stopped a taxi. As he got in, the driver said: "You're T.S. Eliot." When asked how he knew, he replied: "Ah, I've got an eye for a celebrity. Only the other evening I picked up Bertrand Russell, and I said to him: Well, Lord Russell, what's it all about?, and, do you know, he couldn't tell me."' KW embellished the tale a little, his chief addition being to the punchline: 'Do you know, the twit couldn't tell me?' He had included the story in *Acid Drops*, and was about to use it again, to excellent effect, on the LWT 'Audience with Kenneth Williams'.

[38] b.1943. The 'Countdown' presenter.

Monday, 29 November

On the news it said that a new variety of venereal disease – herpes – is reaching epidemic proportions! And there is no cure! When one hears this sort of thing one thinks 'Thank heavens I'm celibate.'

Tuesday, 30 November

Walked thro' freezing cold streets to Silksound for a session on PIP printing: they were a load of old Mary Anns forever hair-splitting & fault-finding & the idiot who wrote the rhymes (v. bad ones) was holding forth about emphasis etc. as tho' he was literate or something. At 4 o'c. to Silksound again, to do the Temik v/o with Pat Coombs and Arthur Mullard. I got taxi from there to Seaco House where I had a conference with Alasdair Macmillan and Richard Drewett & Helen Wright & we finalised plans for tomorrow. At one point R.D. said 'We're in danger of over-discussing this . . .' and I know what he means.

Wednesday, 1 December

Went on about 8 o'c. Lovely house . . . v. partisan. No terrible hitches. The tempo was kept *fairly* well . . . nothing extraordinary . . . but it never plummeted. Messed up the final French song but Richard Drewett let me do it again. At the Party after, the world & his wife appeared! I've never been surrounded by so many celebrities. I was especially delighted to see some of the 'Coronation Street' company 'cos I was able to tell them about my enthusiastic loyalty to this series. Went to bed with the mind performing a post mortem . . . Oh! the extempore act is such a tightrope! & after, there are a thousand recriminations in my head . . . should I have said that? Was I too risqué in places?[39]

Thursday, 2 December

Back Drops is printed & bound & v. handsome it looks! Phone rang & rang with complimentary calls! Gordon: 'You were marvellous last night Kenneth! I'd not heard about Siobhan and the Bishop.'[40]

Saturday, 4 December

I wrote a note to Peter Shellard saying I'd made a mistake in the

---

[39] An edited version of the performance eventually found its way on to a video, probably the best record we have of KW's stage and storytelling manner.

[40] The story of a monumental 'dry' perpetrated in *Saint Joan* by the veteran actor Frank Royde, as the Archbishop of Rheims. Having made a hilarious attempt at a paraphrase of the required speech, he wandered over to the wings to receive a prompt, assuring the audience as he went that 'This is a very difficult piece, you know.'

book (Ethel Merman shortened her name from Zimmermann) & it is irksome 'cos it will be seized upon, I know.

M. came and we got to Oxford by 7 o'c. It took us over an hour to find St Edward's School. I walked up on to the stage for the talk. It was a rambling discourse but went v. well considering. I stopped at about 9.30 and then signed autographs for the boys. One of them said 'I've been waiting for ages but I don't mind 'cos I've been admiring your spun gold hair . . .' This is the line I've used on radio so often!! Oh! it made me laugh. Before we departed, a cherub ran up to give me a handful of his sweets. 'Something for your return journey' he cried & I was v. touched.

Monday, 6 December

I went to Samuel's & found a pair of cuff links for M. Then to chemist for expectorant. I have felt *happy* today and, as usual with me, that is immediately followed by guilt. Saw Louie for a meal. She was watching 'Countdown' and again I noticed how dreary it is . . . the endless mechanical pauses, the contrived look of my comedy efforts, the safe smugness of Richard Whiteley and the unattractive contestants.

Wednesday, 8 December

BBC TV Centre for the 'Paul Daniels Show'. It was *horrendous*. Sat with dear Jill Gascoine & she was one of the consolations of the whole disastrous evening. We were kept hanging around with no knowledge of what we were supposed to be doing. Eventually we sat around on a set acting as stooges for P.D. to do conjuring tricks. It was truly awful. Degrading & nasty. I complained loudly & P.D. called out 'All you have done is moan ever since you came here' & I said 'That's right . . . if you'd engaged extras instead of actors you wouldn't have any trouble at all.' I would never work with this man again . . .

Friday, 24 December

Post came at 10.45!! Two statements!!! LWT show and the commercial film! I have never had so much money on statements in my *life* before!! It brings December month's total to over 22 thousand! And there's still 3 months of the financial year to go!

Saturday, 25 December

Duncan Dreary came & drove Louie & me to B and G. We didn't have lunch till gone 2 o'c. which put me in a bad mood. At the lunch table B. flared when I said 'You're always knocking other people . . . you said C's house was wrongly carpeted & had a lavatory lamp in the drawing room . . . you said his Piccadilly apartment was like a Holiday Inn . . . in Tangier they called you Poison Ivy . . .' Duncan said he didn't want to stay if the conversation continued. [B.] said 'You're a dreadful liar Kenneth' & the atmosphere was appalling. Of course, they'd poured champagne down me for nearly 2 hours & I'd had nothing to eat. After helping to wash up, I made tea. Some pale looking urchin came in and was introduced by B. as an 'interesting piece' & 'rather you'. It was about as alluring as a buff envelope. In the evening we were saved by Scrabble and all ended reasonably convivially.

Monday, 27 December

Joy [Kaufmann] telephoned: wanted to speak to me. 'My mother is unconscious in hospital & they think she may die . . . will you break it to Louie gently . . . she's an old lady & I don't want her to be shocked . . .' At 5.30 Michael Collyer rang. 'Edith died a short time ago . . . she went peacefully and comfortably . . .' I told Louie who began weeping. 'Our Ede was always close to me . . . we used to meet every week . . . Oh! I am going to miss her!'

Friday, 31 December

The Gyles Brandreth book[41] prints two stories from me with no acknowledgment! Yet he's written in it 'Yours are the best stories & I can't use them . . .' Went to bed at about 10 o'c. It has been one of my highest earning years but not a particularly happy one.

---

[41] Probably *Great Theatrical Disasters*.

1983

Thursday, 6 January

At 12 o'c. M. came, and drove Louie, Pat & me to Bedford Chapel at Golders Green Crematoria. The chapel was tiny & the service meagre. Nearly wept uncontrollably when they said 'Now lettest thou thy servant Edith depart . . .'

Sunday, 9 January

Walked to the Paris for 'Just A Minute' at 5.30. Parsons said: 'I was rather hurt that you didn't invite me to the LWT show . . .' I passed it off lightly & said 'Well I called you an idiot on the show & they probably thought it was a bit rude you see . . .'

Friday, 14 January

7.50 to Leeds. When I walked on to the set, Frank Smith and John Meade led the audience singing 'Hello Kenny!' to the 'Hello Dolly' music. They were all v. cordial. I again told J.M. how much I liked working with him. I asked about Gyles & F.S. said 'Well his face smiles but his eyes don't . . . you feel the mind is elsewhere . . . but he was v. good on the show & makes some witty observations . . . he used your pun about Syngman Rhee[1] . . . you must have told him . . .'

Tuesday, 25 January

Tenerife by 12.45. Warm but v. cloudy. The room was disgusting – iron bars on a glassless window! I went to the desk & it was changed but I don't like this one either. The spirits sink . . . the tat of the place is quite awful. Went with Louie to the town. We sat at a street café and had sausage & chips & coffee. All v. adventurous, but our spirits are v. low. Walked back to the hotel. Sat in one of those mournful Spanish lounges which look like a crematorium waiting room. A girl sang & an idiot played a Yamaha organ, oh dear. There was this boy Colin (on his own) who's nice but I think might be ivy league.

---

[1] 1875–1965. First President of the Korean Republic.

Wednesday, 26 January
Dinner at 8 o'c. with Ivy who talked till it was coming out of her ears & I foolishly let it come with us for coffee after & got landed with the bill. At the café where we had the coffee I ordered a Grand Marnier & Ivy kept taking & drinking it! Did it *three* times & it began as irksome & ended by being really annoying. Now I don't want to see it again *at all.*

Friday, 28 January
Lunched at the buffet. Ivy kept flitting by. Goodness, I do admire Louie! She walks round with us & keeps going in spite of age and fatigue & keeps v. good humoured. Saw Noel & Brian and the former told me he'd had an English girl 'It was a 15 minute job, she left yesterday' so he's not wasting any time! They've changed our rooms to the fifth floor & they're lighter & airier than the others.

Tuesday, 1 February
These fortnight's package holidays in the sun are all so *mad*. The only thing that is good about coming away is the idea of changing the routine & principally, the motive this time was to get Louisa away from London to new surroundings etc. to get her over the demise of Edith. Of course the irony is that she goes mad with drinks & late nights and ends up tiring herself.

Wednesday, 2 February
I find Louie is increasingly bad tempered, rude, forgetful, stupid & in most senses, a great bore. Mind you, so are most of the idiots staying in this hotel.

Saturday, 5 February
Dinner at 7.30. Then to the bar with Niavis (snowdrop) who is really rather sweet, but the friend Annette turned up. More Spanish than you can imagine but says 'I coom from Harrogate' & asks how I can get her into Equity. Came up at 11 o'c. for tradition . . . yet I was really much too tired to rouse any enthusiasm. It is ludicrous that I've lived my life so frugally . . . that I've never had an abode where there was quiet . . . or even a table at which to eat . . . or a companion with which to share the lonely mystery.

Monday, 7 February
The two Keep Fit boys Graham & John contrived a conversation with me. It was all 'you are so clever' & 'I wish I had your confidence' etc., and John became quite effusive towards me. When I visited the loo I said 'I'm in Room 538, what time can you come up?' & he said

'About 11.15.' I returned to the group & chatted till then. Flew back to the room & turned lights low & got into pyjamas etc. Then the waiting started. I tiptoed to the door several times. Nothing. Decided to go to bed. In the middle of chewing the Gaviscon, 11.50, there came a knock on the door. I rushed to open it & pulled a reluctant J. into the room. Should've known then that it was death. Lying fully clothed on the bed, he said 'I have misled you, I am really only ten per cent gay . . . I can't do anything . . . it would be different if Graham was here . . . I am sorry . . . I've led you astray . . .' Within two minutes I'd shown him out again. I suppose it's the story of my life really.

Tuesday, 8 February. London

I ate the bran & had the fags, aware that the smoking is giving me a ghastly cough & thinking that it would be far better to snuff it. Plane took off at 1.50. It is bitterly cold here.

Sunday, 13 February

Walked thro' the cold & bleak streets to Gordon & Rona taking with me a copy of *Back Drops* suitably inscribed. Gordon said 'It's extraordinary, isn't it? – the Lyric, Apollo and the Globe all dark . . . it's the worst possible period for the theatre . . . Codron says if the plays are good enough the public will come back . . .' I said I thought it was part & parcel of the decline of W/End. People don't want the hassle of parking, or the congestion, or the peremptory box office staff, or the rotten casts which are so endlessly assembled.

Monday, 21 February

Went to B.H. at 9 o'c. I talked about the book with Pattie Coldwell[2] who was v. aggressive: 'You don't reveal the *real* you' etc. Phone went endlessly – Michael Anderson: 'There's been an awful row with "Nationwide" saying they don't want you because you're doing the TV-am show . . . they say it's a rival network . . . if you do go on it, they say they will drop you from their show . . .' I said I wasn't submitting to blackmail & that I wasn't doing the TV-am show apropos the book but about my birthday, and that I couldn't let them down at a moment's notice 'cos of threats from the BBC.

Tuesday, 22 February

TV-am in Camden Town. Interviewed by David Frost about the Birthday and chatted to Anna Ford & Angela Rippon. They were all very pleasant to me. Rang Dent's & went round to collect 12 books: Liz

---

[2] b.1952. Journalist and interviewer.

Newlands cross about losing "Nationwide" & she said this morning's programme was a 'shambles'. V. encouraging. Michael came & he drove Louisa and me to the Tent where we had dinner. All was going well until the coffee was served (tea made for Louie) when Louisa became strangely quiet and when I asked her 'Are you all right?' she said 'Yes' but the voice was so low & the energy so lacking that I knew something was amiss. Then she tried to express some words but they were fragmented & so sotto voce I couldn't understand. Then she appeared to drift off to sleep. I had to hold the head lest it fall forward on to the table. That Scots boy Alastair carried an inert Louie to the car. As we drove off M. said 'I'll make for hospital' but within minutes Louie was asking 'Where is my tea?' & 'I don't remember leaving that hotel!' Got her back to the flat & she was OK. M. was visibly shaken. 'I thought she was going to die . . . on your birthday . . .'

Wednesday, 23 February
I walked to LBC arriving at 2.55. Eventually at 3.15 I was told 'The man who's supposed to interview you hasn't turned up' and at 3.20 he appeared, saying his car got jammed at Hyde Pk. Corner. I refused to shake hands and ranted on about my loathing for unpunctuality and the interview was lousy. All the omens are bad for this book. The 'Nationwide' fiasco, and this occurrence, all point to a flop.

Thursday, 24 February
Awful notice for the book in the Telegraph. I have a feeling that this volume is going to die a death. I walked to B.H. to do the John Dunn Show. Already I feel tired of talking about this book – it's always the same sort of question one is asked & the self-advertising performance is very wearing. I understand exactly why star performers rebel, or have breakdowns: they're in a dreadful dilemma 'cos they're asked to show so much of themselves and the vulnerability leaves them feeling naked.

Tuesday, 1 March
Train to Kingston for Benthall's Store. It wasn't an overwhelmingly successful signing session. I only did 35 & when one passing shopper remarked 'That's Kenneth Williams' to her friend, the reply was 'There isn't much of him is there?'

Thursday, 3 March
1st interview with man from C[entral] O[ffice of] I[nformation] for recording to go overseas. 2nd interview with lady from women's magazine. 3rd interview with Gay News by which time I was tired &

became indiscreet. 'Why do you describe yourself as asexual?' I told them 'I have masturbatory fantasies which nothing in *life* could ever match' & burbled on about auto-eroticism. Stupid, 'cos it will all rebound on me with horrid results.

Thursday, 10 March
I loathe all this rushing about on trains & in cars, attending these daft junketings . . . out of over a hundred people attending, only a small number of people actually buy a book and incessantly one hears the refrain 'I'll wait for the paperback to come out . . .'

Saturday, 26 March
We saw *Carry On Jack* and my incisive performance was hardly in accord with the dithering idiot I was supposed to portray.

Thursday, 31 March
To Tape Gallery to do v/o for Bounce with Peter Hawkins. It was OK. P.H. has changed incredibly over the years! From the dishy young American in *The Hasty Heart* at High Wycombe Rep. to the stooped & donnish droop-faced man I saw today.

Monday, 4 April
Saw Louisa at 3.30 to watch *Showboat* with Irene Dunne and Alan Jones: it was v. good. Extraordinary how much better the negroes came over then! So gloriously jovial!

Tuesday, 12 April
In the afternoon I went to John Lewis for toilet bags and then to Mowbray's for thrillers for the journey tomorrow. Started learning the Asp sketch 'cos they want me to do a turn of some sort on the M[ike] W[alsh] Show in Sydney. Oh! heavens! here I am re-learning stuff I performed originally in 1959!! Extraordinary how it hasn't dated at all!

Wednesday, 13 April
On boarding the plane I was stuck next to this Leena woman who asked: 'They all call you Mister Williams . . . are you famous? Should I know you?' I told her 'No – I'm nobody dear . . . just got a yard & a half in *Who's Who*, that's all.' She is from Finland.

Thursday, 14 April
The journey continued thro' the day with Leena babbling ceaselessly about her possessions & her way of life & her disapproval of my modus vivendi: 'You are very selfish.' Tell me something I don't know.

Stopped at Singapore. Back on the plane at 8.40. Leena telling me what I should do with my life: 'You don't *have* to be sexually attracted to the girl, that can come later . . . it's important to like each other . . . you must have someone in your life . . . otherwise you end up lonely . . .' I nod & look understanding but think 'She's lonely anyway . . . with husband & 3 children . . . that's why she keeps nattering to me . . .'

Saturday, 16 April. Sydney

No one knows, except the sufferer, what agony these sort of journeys are!! One thing is certain. I must *never* do this again. I look ill & tired, the eyes are bagged heavily, the complexion is blotchy, the intestines are in uproar, I'm in totally alien surroundings and of course, the room has been changed, and of course, I walk into plumbing trouble!!!

Monday, 18 April

I left with Peter Adams for studios. Met Mike Walsh (great charmer) and went on (2nd spot) and all went well. He is a disciplined interviewer, kept everything in control and steered me thro' it brilliantly. One couldn't have asked for a better audience: they were superb, rose to everything & were on one's wavelength throughout. Up to the room where P.A. worked with me on the format for tomorrow. At the conclusion he said 'You're a pleasure to work with' & of course I'm too embarrassed to say how sweet I think he is – a veritable life-saver in this sort of situation.

Wednesday, 20 April

Went to the studios with P.A. and met Malcolm Fraser[3] there – delightful man. I went on about 1 o'c. They showed me a playback & it all looked infectiously jovial. Got a quiche at an open-air restaurant where we sat – undisturbed – working out the format for tomorrow in the afternoon sunlight. The air was balmy – oh! on days like this, Sydney is truly beautiful. I've got the sketch (Asp) *and* two spots tomorrow!

Thursday, 21 April

Up at 8.20 with idiot woman on phone 'I was with you in *High & Low*, do you remember Albert Arlen? I'd like to take you to the American Club' – 'I'm very tired' I said & rang off. We went to the studios & I did the 4th show which went OK. Went on the 5th show at about 4.10, and again, it went well & I finished with the verse 'Far away

---

[3] Prime Minister of Australia 1975–March 1983.

land, on the other side of the world . . .'[4] & said 'Barbara Windsor was right about the programme! She told me: you won't (on the Mike Walsh Show) be down under, you'll be up top!' Walked in a park with P.A. for an hour & then back for office party with the crew. They were *all* complimentary to me & it gave the morale a Great Boost. I have never had better support or felt such genuine friendliness – there was a moment at the end when I v. nearly became emotional.

Friday, 22 April

To David Jones [store]. Signed solidly for over an hour!! All went well, tho' there were quite a few *Acid Drops* as well as *Back Drops*.

Saturday, 23 April

Did the fan letters & went down to foyer & posted everything. To Grace Brothers at Chatswood where Adrian (Book Dept.) gave us coffee. There was another queue already formed and I signed solidly for an hour or more. Car back to Town House where I lunched with journalist Ben Mitchell & hard work it was. Apropos Hancock saying 'What if it's all a joke?' my reply ('Make it a good one') was ignored & he asked 'What was your reaction to his suicide?' Oh dear! Paul came at 5.45 and of course embarrassed me with the expensive gift – opal for Louisa – & I had to stutter my admiration & thanks. Why do people do this???

Monday, 25 April

Got plane to Melbourne. Met by Ian and Janine Day & driven to the Regent Hotel which is pure fantasy!! You need a map to find your way round! And a chart for number of light switches in the room!! It is Marie Antoinette opulence & tortures my Puritan Conscience. My room is on 48 floor!!

Tuesday, 26 April

Met Janine Day & Ron and we went to 3UZ for radio interview with Philip someone and then on to ABC for Alan Stokes, then coffee, then to Myer store for the signing session. Then interview (journalist, Tom Duggan) then to Radio 3AW, interview with Muriel Cooper and then back to hotel for interview with a lady from TV Week. Had a ziz for 15 minutes. Ian & Janine came at 7.30 for champagne & then we joined Steve & Cathleen at the Big Australian Bite – a pretentious little restaurant in a converted house in the suburbs. Commenting on the narrow gauge toilet paper in Australia, Steve asked why I didn't like it & I said 'It's too meagre for me' & he said 'That must be why

---

[4] Third refrain from Coward's 'Faraway Land', from *After the Ball*.

so many Englishmen are fat-arsed.' I suppose I asked for that. Read in the paper today that Gay News is finished!! I did that interview with them on March 3 and I said then that they were heading for disaster!

Wednesday, 27 April

I had to talk to Radio Stations from the hotel. Brisbane, Adelaide, Perth . . . it just went on & on. It's a horrid way to do things because there isn't the variety of going to studios & you haven't got good sound. I sit here marooned in my 48th floor eyrie in the sky, utterly alone, trying to sound amusing on the air every time a telephone rings.

Thursday, 28 April

We took off at 12.15 for Sydney and then it was the horrendous crawl to Singapore. Walk round, meet the jockey etc. I don't know how I've lived through this past 15 days. Beset with apprehension over work and over the publicity etc. for the book & whether the signing sessions would be an awful fiasco. In the event, my fears have all been unfounded. But what does linger in the mind is the conviction *now* that the book is not very good. *That's* what I will have to bear in mind when it comes to the paperback.

Saturday, 30 April

Did the month's accounts for VAT. I've earned £33,095.61 since April 6!! It amounts to over a thousand a day! It has certainly never happened in my life before. I met Paul and I gave him lunch & thanked him for being so solicitous to Louisa while I was away in Australia.

Sunday, 8 May

I don't have to worry about doing any work till April '84. I have certainly never been in that position before. Of course the danger is that one starts to feel one is rich: of course one isn't, 'cos there's the VAT to be paid and the Tax to be paid, and the Pension money, to say nothing of the cost of running these 2 flats!

Friday, 13 May

Saw Louie at 5 o'c. When I talked about Grandma Williams speaking of the old girls in the Regent 'holding the old men's dicks for a tanner . . . watching out for the usherette shining the torch . . .' she burst out 'You are a *liar*! Grandma Williams never said anything of the sort!' and was vehement & angry. Extraordinary outburst! In fact it is true. My mind isn't capable of *that* kind of fantasising!

Tuesday, 17 May
Saw Michael and we went to the Ecu in Chelsea. We talked about the paradox of Western freedom encouraging the sort of materialism which Solzhenitsyn warns will be our undoing. The democratic bestowal of individual freedom includes the freedom to opt out of civic responsibility . . . that leads to a weakening of society which is welcomed by the communists. M. pointed out that the sort of religious resurgence called for by Solzhenitsyn is unlikely with our present set of prelates. They're mostly dull conservatives or trendy lefties who confuse Christianity with Socialism. We both agreed that this Election will prove a turning point in British history.

Thursday, 26 May
I went to Vecchia Milano and met Liz Newlands for lunch. We were joined by Peter Shellard later. He & Liz admitted that the latest book wasn't going to be the success which *Acid Drops* was but P.S. said 'We shall get our money back because of selling the paperback rights profitably' and he said he thought this latter project would do very well, in 1985 when they will start marketing it. I told them about the events in Australia.

Wednesday, 1 June
Loads of letters & the dreaded BBC contract for 'Comic Roots' arrived! Oh!I shall be glad when next week is over. Half the time, with contracts, I feel I'm signing my life away. We saw the news. Healey has made a dreadful speech about Mrs Thatcher 'glorying in slaughter' apropos the Falklands. This must take the biscuit for sheer nastiness & cheap contumely. Oh! what a contemptible rogue he is!

Tuesday, 7 June
Today is the start of this awful filming job. Walked to Cromer St. We did shots outside the block. In the afternoon we did the stuff in Sandwich Street – dirty bloomers – and then on to Duke St Drill Hall, shots in Woburn Walk & Euston Road & St Pancras Church and then to the school in Camden St. Shots in the playground with children which I didn't know they were taking! I was just chatting away to the children.

Wednesday, 8 June
At 7.30 to Boot pub where we filmed the 'Signora'[5] & 'Hawkin' me greens.' The pub was full of undesirables . . . and a gaggle of queens who made several esoteric remarks while cameras were rolling!

---

[5] By Merson, O'Connor, Ross.

Thursday, 9 June
Collected Louie & went to vote for the Conservatives. Got the tube to Acton & made a little 'scene' with Peter Lee Wright. 'I don't want to do *anything* in this bloody awful place!' & he did one shot of the drawing office & we got away quickly. Then to Lyric Ham'smith where we did the concluding shot – 'If life is a joke . . . make it a good one . . .' and after to the remnants of Collins Music Hall, Islington.

Friday, 10 June
To Leather Lane, Barber Shop scene . . . then to Marchmont St. Lunch. Then shot from window at 57 and then on to grating – Charlie getting peed on etc. Then Long Acre shots of Stanford's which I wasn't in. Released. The Conservatives have a majority of over 150!! Talk about a turning point in our history! And it's 90% due to Maggie Thatcher: there's no doubt of that!

Saturday, 11 June
Met the crew in Marchmont St. Had to cycle past camera. Same at Guilford St and Russell Square. Then stand (end of Montague St.) and talk about Johnny Vere. Then cycle into Floral St by Stanford's. Then back to Manchester St school for shot, walking out of playground. Oh! it is a wonderful relief today to know that it is over!! that this ghastly self-devouring project is behind me! This year seems to have been endless excoriation, & I'm amazed to find I've any skin left.

Thursday, 23 June
John McEnroe beat a nasty looking Rumanian,[6] and when he hit the ball into the net in irritation over a mistake, the Umpire called it a violation!! and gave him a penalty point!! When the poor boy protested, the Referee rescinded it, quite rightly. It is this sort of petty nastiness which makes a player feel persecuted & unhappy. Makes me sick. All these commentators were damning J.M. with remarks about his behaviour etc. None of them understand what an asset the boy is, to tennis and to their *jobs*. Ugh! their sanctimonious cant is sickening.

Sunday, 26 June
I like these sort of days because there is a *bit* of work to do, but not a lot and I don't have anything to preoccupy me & fill me with apprehension. My life is really rather like the 18th Century's man

---

[6] Florin Segarceanu, at Wimbledon, 4–6, 6–2, 6–3, 6–3.

of leisure, a bit of writing occasionally, meeting friends and making occasional sallies into the countryside.

Thursday, 7 July

Went to Peter Mario & gave John M. lunch. He told me he'd been shocked to read the Gay News article!! (see March 3) so all my misgivings at the time were justified. He said 'I was surprised you weren't punished for it! I felt sure the national dailies would pick it up and cause a scandal . . . I thought you must have been mad to talk like that in print . . .' I kept saying 'Have another' and we got v. pissed indeed. Practically fell on the bed when I got home.

Saturday, 9 July

Papers are full of the Hanging issue and politicians are holding forth with their usual hypocritical cant about civilised societies rejecting the idea of Capital Punishment. Their rubbishy talk about civilised society is ludicrous! Ours is a most uncivil society, full of wickedness and evil behaviour. Of course the Government won't legislate for Hanging; they'll all pretend that the concept is horrible, unchristian etc., whereas they're really dodging their responsibility – they should be executing all terrorists, murderers & assassins: it is scandalous that the diligent citizen has to pay to keep the Moors Murderers alive . . . and this filthy Yorkshire Ripper idiot . . . they should go the same way as the terrorists & the anarchists. These women who lie on the ground at Greenham Common should be shot too! It's unbelievable to watch! Police & troops having to move their dirty forms from the roads while they keep up a cacophony of shouting & screaming. They say they're against the Bomb. One wishes one would drop on them.

Tuesday, 12 July

Got the 11.11 to Beckenham. Richard Pearson met me at the station. Pat greeted me warmly & we sat having coffee & talking. We talked about our youthful illusions, how we thought that progress & maturity would lead to consorting only with the competent, when in fact, one faces the same incompetence at 60 as one did at 16. Nothing changes.

Wednesday, 13 July

In Devonshire Street, a swarthy young man fell into step beside me 'I really admire you, you know? I watch your films & your facial expressions are wonderful! I would like to arrange to meet you again somewhere; can we arrange that?' I told him wearily, 'I've got enough friends as it is.' 'Yes, I suppose you have, but I would really like to see you, you know . . .' Then he began a diatribe about women! 'When they don't want you, you haven't got a chance, but when they fancy you, they always get you . . . you know!' 'Ah yes! indeed,' I agreed. Then he said he was sorry to have bored me, told me his name was Zag, and left. I think it was trade but in this weather, it's as much as I can do to walk to the shops and back. Saw Louisa and had some cold meat & tomatoes with her. We sat baking in the front room, wiping sweat from the brows & I fear this awful weather gets us both down & we were neither of us seized with joy.

Thursday, 21 July
At 6 o'c. I went to the Blood Donor Centre for the drinks & presentation party. I was staggered when my name was called for the 50th Gold Badge!! Chatted with other donors and it was all v. convivial.

Friday, 29 July
They announced the death of David Niven & showed a clip from his Parkinson interview: 'This director said go back to your dressing room & get the script & I said you fucking go & get it yourself.' Hardly suitable obituary material . . . but then the BBC standards are sinking lower and lower. Walked to Rona at 7 o'c. Jean Marsh was there. Rona told us both she'd been burgled!! Gordon came in at 8.45 (from Leeds where he'd been doing TV) and I told him what had happened. His TV job had been about burglar alarms!!

Sunday, 31 July
M. came and took Louisa & me to the Tent. Home by 10 o'c. Woken at 12 o'c. by a group of youths serenading a woman in Regency 'Hallo Senorita!' etc. She threw a bucket of water over them. Then they saw me looking & I had to quickly withdraw! The whole thing was curiously exciting . . . Couldn't get off to sleep. Sweating profusely.

Tuesday, 2 August
They announced the murder of Peter Arne[7] in his flat behind Harrod's: met him once & liked him.

Friday, 5 August
Went to the window & saw Louie walking slowly to the bus stop & I was suddenly overwhelmed by the sheer vulnerability of this tiny figure . . . grabbed my coat and went after her. Joined her at the bus stop & accompanied her on the 27 to Bishop's stores & carried her shopping for her.

---

[7] (Albrecht) b.1922. An actor specialising in smooth foreign villains. He was clubbed to death.

Sunday, 7 August
I know that my other diaries record suicidal desires: it is an iterated echo throughout my life, but the ghastly pointlessness of my existence seems to be worse as the years roll on. An endless waiting for death. Every day a walk in the street is impossible without the greeting & the staring from well-intentioned idiots ('May I say how much I admire you?' etc.) and every day I have to cope with some example of Louie's failing powers. Some of her questions are so childish one could scream with vexation.

Saturday, 13 August
This morning Louie showed me the blue dress I tackled for her and incredibly it looks fine! Saw Louie at about 5 o'c. and she'd ironed the dress and scorched it! So having managed to eradicate the stains after all my efforts, she's succeeded in ruining the results. She told me 'The iron wasn't even hot – they are not scorch marks' but of course they are. Then I noticed a high-pitched buzzing noise in the room and found she'd left the deaf-aid on inside its case. Oh! I suppose it's all signs of age and the incompetence that goes with forgetfulness but it is screamingly irritating. Now I'm full of apprehension about all this new furniture she's buying because it may well turn out that she can't sit for long in that either! These days I'm feeling more & more like an Old People's Warden or something. It is so depressing.

Tuesday, 23 August
Had a vivid dream. Peter Eade came into the room with a case! Greeted me cheerily & said 'I hear you've been feeling rather low' & I was too stunned to speak! I asked people with him 'What about the burial?' & they told me 'It was all arranged . . . he never died at all you know . . . just wanted everybody to *think* that he had . . .' It was all so amazingly vivid.

Monday, 29 August
In the evening we saw a v. stupid film *Wilderness Family* about some town dwellers who go to live in the mountains: utter rubbish . . . yet the fact remains that the flickering screen in the room is a barrier against the silences & the embarrassment of mute interludes when conversation peters out . . . like occasions during hospital visits. That is really why television is so valuable socially; esp. for the elderly: it provides the illusory link with a hundred events the body can no longer attend.

Sunday, 4 September
Thought, on reflection, that the reviews for the TV programme were

really v. good. I hadn't expected such coverage, nor such praise. Richard Last talks about meeting me years ago in Peter E.'s office . . . I don't remember, and I would certainly never have wailed about my career going wrong! Certainly not to a journalist! I expect his memory has played him tricks.

Monday, 5 September
Decided not to go to the Blood Donor Centre. I will let them *ask me* in future, after all this nastiness about homosexuals.[8]

Wednesday, 7 September
I have been told by Joanna that the KW Audience-with Show is being shown on the Channel 4 network in November! So LWT didn't really want it after all! I know why. It's too pro-ey and esoteric for them *and* it goes outside their conventional time slot.

Friday, 9 September
Looking up a diary entry in '74 I came upon a funny incident in *C.O. Dick* & it prompted me to write a letter to Gerald & tell him how much joy he'd made possible. It's right to keep loyalties young.

Sunday, 11 September
Saw Louisa for the News and a daft film about helicopter pilots. In the variety programme which followed, I saw Roy Castle and marvelled again at his artistry: musician, dancer, comedian with a delightful personality and yet he has *never* been accorded proper recognition for his talent: it's positively protean.

Wednesday, 14 September
Went to I.C.M. to talk to Alexander Walker about his book on Rachel Roberts & I recalled the vivid incidents which stayed in my mind about her – including the sitting naked as supper was served with R.W[est] horrified & her saying 'I'm a Methodist Minister's daughter! & I don't come easy!' Alex told me 'There were no financial worries for her . . . she killed herself because she could see no way of getting out of the alcoholic circle . . . all the analysis & the clinics and the solace of friends had been in vain.' He also said that Rex H. had been a comforting influence right up to the last.

---

[8] AIDS had been identified in America towards the end of 1981, and early publicity concentrated on its prevalence among homosexuals. A scheme for testing British blood donors for the virus was not announced until March 1985.

Monday, 19 September

Stanley came & took me to Lariana. He said 'I saw your "Comic Roots" at Bruce's . . . he had it on tape . . . you do too much of that leering into the camera with the funny voice . . . you are much better when you're relaxed. That bit at the end on the stage at the Lyric was excellent! You had the highest ratings of the whole series!' Then Giovanni brought my book to be signed & Stanley said 'You actually have me telling *jokes* in it! Terrible joeys which I wouldn't use!' & I said 'I do not' and he said 'Well I agree with the Telegraph! There are too many references to me throughout the book . . . makes me sound like a latter day Oscar Wilde of the trattoria!'

Tuesday, 20 September

Walked to Terrazza in Romilly St to meet Gerald Thomas & forgot to take the book I promised to give him! He talked about a Christmas Carry On Compilation with Barbara & me doing the linking & it sounds like it could be great fun.

Friday, 30 September

Cleaned walls & ceiling of the bathroom. At 12.30 dear Henry [Gess] arrived with the renovated chairs and he's done a superb job of all three! Did more cleaning after that, and cleaned some of the front room carpet & the rest will have to wait for a bit. It's curious how my modus vivendi has altered lately: all the activity in the flat, clearing away the years of dirt, and the renovation of furniture etc., the sorting out of possessions & coming upon an inscription in a book given me by a dear friend now gone . . . And the sleeplessness. I used to get off reasonably well, but now it's not so: the afternoon snooze has gone . . . even when I try it, it doesn't work.

Saturday, 1 October

Did the month's accounts – first time I've had to put 'Unemployed' on an expense sheet for a long time.

Tuesday, 4 October

We watched 'Jackanory'. It was OK but I've not got the warm friendly face of a children's presenter.

Friday, 7 October

There is still a lot of speculation about the ex-Party Chairman of the Tories (Cecil Parkinson) having a child by his secretary & admitting being unfaithful to his wife. There is talk about 'It is a private matter' etc. but of course it isn't. He is Minister of Trade & Industry, therefore a public figure & should lead a proper public life, not go round indulging in adultery. He should be sacked, and Mrs Thatcher should be ashamed of herself for keeping him on all this time, when she's known of the scandal since April.

Monday, 10 October

We saw the TV news and they announced the death of Ralph Richardson saying fulsome compliments about his work and calling him *great* on lots of occasions. John Mills appeared saying he would be 'quite irreplaceable' several times.

Wednesday, 12 October

Richard Drewett sent car to take me to Seaco House where he showed me the 'Audience with KW' on the television screen in his office. It is marvellous! I look good, the house looks good & the direction (Alasdair) is superb! He's carefully pruned it here & there, to make a marvellously entertaining whole. I was more pleased than I ever dreamed I would be. It's the first time in my life I've been presented so beautifully. I could only stammer thanks to all concerned but I *felt* like having a party!! Had meal with Louie at about 5.30. Told her I'd seen my show at LWT & that she was in it, looking v. good in the audience with the furs etc. & she said 'What show?' 'The one we did in December last year.' 'Oh! . . . I don't remember.'

Tuesday, 1 November

I noticed that the News is relentlessly depressing. Cheerful items are either ignored or given sceptical delivery and the accent is forever on some alleged wrong. Either a sob story about the socially deprived, or the handicapped or the mentally retarded . . . oh . . . any unfortunate they can focus upon for sensational purposes. Last night (apropos Government cuts) they showed a woman crying 'cos her dead husband had been denied a kidney transplant . . . cut from her to the funeral . . . stuff that doesn't even *belong* to a news item! It is bogus moral flag flying which is insidiously creeping into everything nowadays.

Thursday, 3 November

BBC had a strike of A[ssociation of] B[roadcasting] S[taff] so a cancelled OB was replaced by a programme called 'Spotlight' (the BBC's answer to 'Audience With') with Jimmy Edwards reminiscing about his life. Oh! it was so sad. The lousy photography, the tatty auditorium of a hired theatre, the sparse & ancient audience, and the tired performance of a man who endeavours to hide his real nature under a bluff & hearty exterior.[9] It's the paradox of a man who masks his cry for affection with an air of arrogant indifference: the result is a fundamentally estranged house, where the only thing they can do is clap the items which are adept & skilful. He did quite well consequently with the trombone & other instrumental items.

Monday, 14 November
We saw the News and it was all Cruise Missiles. Oh! it went on & on till it was coming out of their ears. What is the truth about this situation? It is that modern states (like USA, USSR, & UK & Nato allies) have become trapped in their complex technology; they've gone so far into their labyrinths that they can't find any way out. The fact is that Atomic Bombs are useless. Every time this is questioned, experts are consulted. It's like asking a gunsmith if guns are necessary. Governments increasingly resort to esoteric argument over nuclear weapons & have handed the case for Anti-Atomic Weapons to the chanting weirdies of CND – so ironically the fools outside Greenham have been *given* all the right weapons by default.

Thursday, 17 November
Car at 6 o'c. to Lime Grove where I culled 8 items from the papers for the newspaper spot and took portrait of Louisa in discussion about coping with the elder parent. It all went well – I fluffed on one good Jasper Carrott quote – and Selina Scott looking stunningly lovely – Frank Bough said 'Thank you! You're a Prince.' Must say, they're a smashing team on that show. Talked to Francis [Wilson] (weather) & he asked 'Who wrote that "Infamy" line in *Cleo*?' Gerald Thomas rang & asked me to think up another link for the Carry On Xmas prog. The News showed Chancellor (Nigel Lawson) warning of Inc. Tax rises in the Spring!! and a rise now in the NHS subscription!! The Tories have craftily put up *all* the hidden taxes!! Health, VAT, Water Rate, Elec., Gas, Rates, ever since they've been in office.

Saturday, 19 November
With Paul to Selfridges where he got crystal glasses. Then to Woolworth's where I got several things and walked out with 3 ties on my arm!! Had a shock half way down Mary. High St.!! Walked all the way back to pay & the manageress said 'It was good of you to return . . . most of 'em don't bother.' (£5.07).

---

9 Edwards (1920–88) had long been a purveyor of aggressively heterosexual humour, but it was revealed (by the columnist William Hickey) that he had been living for some years with an Australian female impersonator.

Thursday, 24 November
To Teddington at about 9 o'c. only to find Barbara in the make-up room saying 'We're not wanted till 10.30.' They took till lunch time to do a few links! And then, after that, we did the fairy bit with me dressing up in a tutu skirt & waving a wand to make snow! Gerald was there (lovely influence) and Peter Rogers turned up! It might have been years before to hear his opening remarks! 'Where'd you get that terrible suit?' and 'You're looking too thin and haggard' etc. etc. Nothing changes at all. I was back at the flat by 5 o'c. There was a feeling of enormous relief when the TV stuff was finished today! The fact is that I don't enjoy acting any more. It was good to see Barbara though, and her indomitable spirit is an example to everyone. The irrepressible humour and the implacable determination to rise above adversity – oh! it's all so admirable.

Sunday, 27 November
Had a look at the '82 diary before going to bed. Interesting to see I was gripped by the same despair in that period as well. I'm a living corpse. I feel I am dead & am surprised when I find I can actually walk and even run!

Monday, 28 November
Louie wanted to see 'Coronation Street' and then Thora Hird in some rubbish about a funeral parlour[10] & I sat there thinking 'I am watching my life ebbing away.'

Friday, 2 December
Went out to get *Required Writing* by Philip Larkin. He must be one of the best writers in this country. Went to Thames TV at Euston and did the interview with Mavis Nicholson. It was useless as a coherent discussion about Censorship. My bit was OK but Mavis forgot what her initial gambit was to be! She told me she knew P. Larkin! 'He used to stay at our flat in a big double bed & I remember him saying to me one morning "You know Mavis, sex is too beautiful to be shared" & he used to have all these Muscle Men magazines! He would comment on how one model was getting fatter or leaner as the case may be . . . it really seemed important to him . . .'[11]

---

[10] 'In Loving Memory' by Dick Sharples (YTV).

[11] A gross misconstruction of the story. KW seems to have reassembled it from some authentic component parts in order to make Larkin's sexuality appear to resemble his own. Mavis Nicholson says (11 February 1993) that Larkin stayed only once, when he missed his last train. He did make the remark about sex, but it was apropos the 'girlie' magazines which, as has been made clear by *The Selected Letters of Philip Larkin* (1992), he collected and discussed with enthusiasm. It was the girls pictured in these

Monday, 12 December
The misery of No Heat continues. The block is freezing cold and it is miserable. Obviously the Engineers didn't turn up. Oh! the utter dolour of this period is horrible! And I suggested to Louie *long* ago, 'Let's go away for a few days.' Walking along with her today, aware of the fact that she is limping with a bad leg, my spirits were at zero – I'm spending all my days now with someone who is getting old and frail, increasingly forgetful & more & more of a burden . . . yet someone who (in her own inimitable way) has sustained me in my most despairing moments.

Thursday, 15 December
My show 'Audience with KW' is billed for 10.30 at night on Channel 4 on the 23 December. So it certainly isn't getting a good showing! Heigh ho! I don't care. The fewer viewers the better 'cos then I can use the material again.

Monday, 19 December
I walked to B.H. for the David Hatch party. He gave me a book about theatre which contains a photograph of me! Talked to the Editor of The Listener,[12] and to Jock Gallagher. Clement Freud being enigmatic & avuncular at the same time . . . Just as I was leaving, I saw Miles Kington[13] & David said 'Do you know each other?' & I said 'Oh! yes! I like him so much it is unhealthy' and I meant it. He looked tired, dishevelled & incredibly attractive. Weird how a fundamental likeableness overcomes everything else. We worry about appearances but the facade has v. little to do with basic charisma.

Sunday, 25 December
Duncan came at 12.45 and drove us to B. & G. It was all v. convivial. At lunch, Duncan was quite waspish & when I commented (apropos disease) 'I'm a blood donor & I can't risk any contagion,' he said 'As the Oldest Virgin here, you should know!' And I did the mock exit 'I'm not staying here to be insulted' & everyone laughed. I developed a chronic headache & had forgotten to bring Gaviscon.

Saturday, 31 December
Went to bed at 10.30 with a Supponeryl. I suppose, on the whole,

---

whose names he knew and whose varying forms he studied. In an effort to make things fair, Larkin did bring along for Mavis Nicholson one solitary muscle-man magazine, which he handed over with a defeated air: 'It won't appeal to you, and it doesn't appeal to me.'

[12] Russell Twisk, editor of the *Listener* 1981–87.

[13] b.1941. Columnist and broadcaster.

it's been an uneventful year, tho' several things came to roost! My '82 show actually got shown! Louisa ain't been in bad health, the money has been good . . . can't grumble at all really.

1984

Friday, 6 January
M. came at 7.20. I gave him dinner at Vecchia Milano. At one point, he said 'Don't ever hesitate to say if you've had enough of me . . .' & I told him 'I can't think of one occasion when that's occurred.' Indeed I can't. We agreed on our similarities: low boredom threshold & impatience and great selfishness apropos lifestyle.

Monday, 16 January
The 'Benny Hill Show' must mark a watershed in the otiose. It was as if they'd given an overfed cretin unlimited opportunities in a TV studio. There aren't words to describe the tedium, the jaded banality . . . the overwhelming *tat*.

Friday, 20 January
Taxi at 5.45 to Greenwood Theatre for 'Private Lives' [chat show] with Maria Aitken and Germaine Greer.[1] It went all right but M.A. puts in the odd crack which isn't flattering & that don't help one's morale. Germaine is a lovely creature: a beautiful woman with a charming presence & full of good humour, but she's *not* a performer & while the programme (for her) would have been OK in a studio, with a live house in a theatre it was in sharp contrast to mine 'cos she didn't project.

Tuesday, 24 January
After the TV news, we watched a documentary about the policeman P.C. Olds who was wickedly shot by a felon & is crippled. He was interviewed by Desmond Wilcox.[2] Now, this latter may be well-meaning but as an interviewer he is patently inept. He continually attempts to put words into the mouths of others 'Wouldn't you describe yourself as *brave*?' etc. etc. and this technique obviously embarrassed Olds. At one point he burst out 'Look! I'm an ordinary

---

[1] Feminist, author and lecturer, b.1939.
[2] Producer and presenter, b.1931.

bloke . . . I want to be like I used to be . . . a fornicating, urinating, defecating copper . . .' Then we saw him going thro' the ghastly treatment in America where electrodes administer shocks to the atrophied muscles & make them function again. It is brought home to one how appalling it is for a fit & normal man to be suddenly rendered impotent & when Olds said he wished he had been killed & not 'cheated of death' I understood what he meant. He wants to live in the only way he knows how to live, and he can't, and all the placatory talk about love & friendship & compassion is, in the end, otiose.[3]

Sunday, 5 February

Wanted to watch the Secombe show[4] 'cos I'm to be in it (27 Feb.) & found it was very much a mish-mash & some of his interviews so perfunctory as to be derisive! One poor cow who was weaving in Paisley got out all of two sentences. It seems to be unable (as a programme) to make up its mind whether it's about religion or urban history. Saw Richard Briers in 'Ever Decreasing Circles'[5] & thought 'Why on earth does he accept this sort of crap?' He is a v. good actor & he plays with real authenticity but the writing is vacuous and full of despair. And Richard looks ill. Oh . . . the fact is that the sit com is death . . . the only time it works is when it's filmed. The BBC TV method of video/static set is so tatty it's like watching home movies. When the dreaded lurgy Esther Rantzen came on I thought 'Goodnight Ada!' and left.

Friday, 10 February

We saw a Margaret Rutherford film *Murder At The Gallop* which was charmingly old-fashioned: some of the casting was ludicrous, but the old girl's charm won in the end. She was a unique blend of grave decency & twinkling humour. Her father *in real life* was a murderer . . . ending up insane . . . and at one point she was a voice-off for Edith Evans!

Sunday, 12 February

In the evening we saw my bit in 'Sunday Sunday' and I thought 'Oh! how *old* you look!', the hair very much whiter and the face lined & shrivelled. Hastily switched off when my bit was over.

---

[3] The death of Philip Olds, after 'a huge overdose of drugs and alcohol', was reported on 2 October 1986.

[4] 'Highway', a 'God-slot' programme, 1983–92.

[5] TV sitcom by Esmonde and Larbey.

Monday, 13 February

Gordon & Rona picked me up in their car and I took them to Peter Mario for dinner. Henry Cooper came over for a chat. 'We've been to see *Dolly* . . . it was only half full' & G. said 'If you'd played it, it would've been *packed*' and everyone (including Henry) fell about laughing.

Wednesday, 22 February

Car at 8 o'c. & Penelope McNeile was waiting below. We drove to Heathrow: shuttle to Edinburgh. Interview at the hotel with John, a journalist snivelling with the 'flu and v. unprepossessing. Train to Glasgow. There we went to the revolting Holiday Inn for a disgusting meal & interview with another journalist. Idiot called Max who gave me his joke book . . . oh dear. A photographer (who'd been drinking liberally) suggested I sit on a railing in the middle of the road: 'It would make a funny shot!' I think some of these people are demented. I refused. Then to BBC for radio interview. Then cab to STV. I was mumbling & bumbling thro' it. Taxi to airport & we had to run like mad to make the flight! I wasn't best pleased with all the hassle & was stroppy with Penelope who got quite bolshy herself. I'll be glad when it's all over.

Thursday, 23 February

To the BBC at 11 o'c. for this hook-up to Radio Derby. Cab to British Forces radio in Smith Square. Cab to Savoy where we had lunch in the Grill room with a journalist. After that, reporters and photographers in another room from 3 till 4 o'c. and when I thought *that* was over, an idiot with a Uher[6] turned up from Radio Victory & I had to record 3 interviews by 5.15!! I resent this kind of thing bitterly. In the end, I was barely polite and I walked out of the Savoy saying nothing. One thing I'm sure of: I'm not going to take on any more chores for this book after the schedule that's been arranged.

Sunday, 26 February

Car to Thames TV at Teddington for the 'Looks Familiar' show with Denis Norden. I met Farley Granger who said 'People often mix me up with other actors . . . they frequently say I was good in a part which was actually played by Monty Clift!' I said 'I can't see how *anyone* could confuse you with another! *Strangers On A Train* might have been specially written for you! It's one of the classics of the cinema.'

---

[6] A German-made portable reel-to-reel tape-recorder, standard issue for the radio reporter until recently.

Monday, 27 February
Caught the 1.13 to Luton, sat in the Strathmore Hotel with Harry Secombe & Bill Ward talking till about 3.15 when we went to the High Street & did about 2 minutes of filming. Ward told the story of Churchill in the wartime bunker & the aide coming to knock on the door of the loo to tell him that Rab Butler[7] (whom he didn't like) was there – 'Prime Minister! The Lord Privy Seal is waiting!' & the reply 'Tell him I'm already sealed in the Privy & I can only deal with one shit at a time.' Home by 5.10. Altogether a waste of time but I feel a tremendous loyalty towards Harry.

Saturday, 3 March
Up at 6.15. Shaved & got ready for this TV appearance. Car came at 7.30 & I was there in 5 minutes. I was on with Henry Kelly & Toni Arthur & a bit with Rustie [Lee] doing the Caribbean cooking. Other guest was Dora Bryan and I burbled on about the book.

Monday, 5 March
I walked to B.H. and did one of those earphone talks for Radio Oxford with some idiot disc-jockey. Had a meal with Louisa. She'd done the laundering & was sitting sewing her WVS apron . . . carefully repairing the damaged hem . . . there was something very touching about the head patiently bowed over the task. Walked to B.H. again. Did the talk for Radio 2. It was the usual rambling mess. I'm truly *sick* of talking about myself. I know I've said it for years but it really has got to stop.

Thursday, 8 March
I walked to Bush House to do the talk on Philip Larkin: the interviewer was Derek Parker and he was v. good. Better reader of poetry than I am. If anyone was ever glad to be in his company it was me today.

Friday, 9 March
With Louisa on the bus to 'J.A.M.' The shows were fair. The team was P. Jones, Derek, Freud & me. Some of it was irksome & my bad temper showed.

Monday, 12 March
Loathe the idea of going to Plymouth – oh! this must be the last bloody chat show surely? Met Joe Steeples and Nina Myskow on the train. Drinks with producer & the team in a nasty little room where

---

[7] R.A. Butler (1902–82), Chancellor of the Exchequer 1951–55, Home Secretary 1957–62, etc.

everyone was glued to a TV screen (watching 'Coronation Street') till I asked the producer to turn it off so that one could converse. At 8.15 they asked me to do a warm-up for the audience. Two rows of hard chairs to accommodate about forty elderly Plymouth residents who looked vaguely discomforted. Eventually we did the show & it was v. hard work trying to raise a titter. At the end, the producer's PA said 'Don't make any arrangements for tonight because we're taking you all out to a Chinese Restaurant.' I said 'I can't eat that sort of rubbish. I'm going back to the hotel' and I did.

Wednesday, 14 March

'J.A.M.' Derek got away with the 'bugger Bognor' quote which surprised me: I didn't think that Pete Atkin would allow it.

Friday, 16 March

When I was signing autographs at the Paris tonight a woman said 'Funny! I always thought you wore a toupee.' I said 'Yes, one's hair sometimes looks like a wig' & curiously I wasn't in the least perturbed! Once, I'd have been furious.

Monday, 19 March

I went to Tape Gallery to do v/o for Dreft playing a distraught sweater. Met dear Julian Holloway there. I was working with a v. nice man – moustached – but I can't remember his name. During the evening I realised that every now & again with Louie the conversation borders on madness. The gulf between our outlooks provokes irritation or anger & the resulting altercations arouse nastiness & rancour. Thank heavens it is quickly dispelled 'cos the fundamental affection remains unaffected but it is dangerous 'cos I often forget how much Louie remembers. Oh! it's only one of the perils bred of monotony & inertia. I need a holiday.

Friday, 23 March

Having read A.N. Wilson in Spectator & thinking how witty he was, I looked for a book by him. Found a paperback *Oswald Fish*[8] so I bought it. It is a tedious, humourless load of crap. 'Would-be shocking' & would-be satirical etc. but no story to grip one: no exciting sequence of events . . . nothing. Just a lot of stereotyped characters 'Liberal MP' 'Queer' 'Emancipated woman' 'enfants terribles' etc. etc. Utter shit.

Monday, 26 March

Saw the News. Then there was 'Panorama' devoted to the argument

---

[8] *Who was Oswald Fish?* (1981), by Andrew N. Wilson, b.1950.

for making smoking illegal. The doctors all saying it kills people, industry saying they employ people and sponsor everything from sports to Glyndebourne. It's all hypocrisy. If it is killing they object to, why don't they campaign against sending our troops to die in Ulster? Why don't they campaign against the road accidents which cause death by the hour? Why don't they campaign against alcohol & the pubs which supply the source of liver damage daily? Why is nothing done about lead pollution from all the traffic on the roads? Ah! they're all mouthing their righteousness to justify their jobs.

Saturday, 31 March

I reflected today that I was born in 1926 the year of the General Strike & was evacuated by the school from London 13 years later because of the war, served in the army till I was 21, lived thro' the misery of austerity, knew the brief prosperity of the Macmillan era before the Oil crisis plunged us all into the sort of monetary chaos which has been present ever since! What a time to live through! Whenever death comes, it can't be untimely.

Wednesday, 4 April

Stanley came at 7 o'c. & took me to Osteria Lariana. His capacity for enjoyment & his relish for the ludicrous is infectious. Nowadays, with him, I feel like a languid moon to his ebullient sun. Even when he does mention depression it is funny. He told me about meeting Hugh Paddick & how he'd asked after me. H.P. is a v. kind man.

Tuesday, 10 April. Manchester

To rehearse at 11 o'c.[9] All piddling stuff. At a run-thro', the producer Geoff Moore said I was too slow. 'The stuff should be delivered more slickly . . .' It would be nice if there was some material to deliver! I said 'You're called Moore and most of this material seems to have come from your Almanac . . .'

Wednesday, 11 April

The show went like a damp squib. Most of my stuff *just* got by . . . several items (as I predicted) died a death . . . Oh! I knew it! I've been sold a pup.

Thursday, 12 April

2 o'c. back to rehearse, and at 4 o'c. they all watched some of the show on a TV monitor . . . it all looked frightful. Shots of me bug

---

[9] The Granada TV series 'Some You Win'.

eyed & unattractive. 6 o'c. drinks in the bar again. Johnny Briggs[10] came over. Big kiss. V. embarrassing. One mouthed pleasantries. Think I am going mad.

Friday, 13 April

Press again. Photos with streaker Erica Roe.[11] Frankie Howerd came to D/room. Long talk about us working together . . . mind elsewhere . . . Show. Nice audience & my stuff went a bit better . . . not so much egg on the face.

Friday, 20 April. London

The streets are silent & there is the pall of another holiday for the great unwashed hanging over everything. Pat came at 11.30. Louisa joined us in the Park & we got chairs etc. Then a gang of youths with beer & transistor radio came along & began shouting abuse 'You're a shit actor! On the fuckin' dole!' etc. A man remonstrated with them but they shouted obscenities at him, so he fetched two policemen. They spoke with them. As soon as the police had gone, the insults began again. Their nastiness was (I'm sure) apropos boredom.

Sunday, 22 April

I had a rest. Then read more of the Raymond Williams book *Culture & Society*: what a muddled lot of rubbish! He criticises Orwell for wanton generalisations about the Working Class and proceeds to make the same sort of generalisations himself. He says that the society in which he grew up consisted of Masters & Servants and that he sympathised with the servants ('cos they were exploited by their masters) because servitude isn't good for men etc. 'They're too much in awe of authority', tho' the [Admirable] Crichton story would seem to contradict *that*. He concludes with exhortations for a radical reappraisal in the intellectual approach based on 'working in community' & 'caring for the neighbour' . . . but can offer no imperative for such behaviour. He's left Faith out of the equation. We end up with a 'learned' quote from Milton[12] which echoes the Biblical prophet 'O earth . . . etc.?'

---

[10] b.1935. Mike Baldwin in 'Coronation Street'.

[11] Streaked (from the waist up) at a rugby international at Twickenham on 4 January 1982.

[12] 'What I have spoken is the language of that which is not called amiss the good Old Cause . . . Thus much I should perhap[s] have said, though I were sure I should have spoken only to Trees and Stones, and had none to cry to, but with the Prophet, O *earth earth earth* . . .' From 'The Ready and Easy Way to Establish a Free Commonwealth' (1660) by John Milton. Concludes the 1963 postscript to Williams's 1958 book.

which is about as relevant to our problems as a fart in a wet blancmange.

Tuesday, 1 May
Spent the afternoon working on the Biog. 'cos Gyles Brandreth says that Dent wants to do it, and despite my misgivings, I think I ought to finish it.[13] Only did a couple of pages.

Wednesday, 2 May
M. came & gave me the dinner at Vecchia. I told him P. Nichols' book had arrived & that the description of me (as a raver) wasn't the sort of picture I'd like to be given to the public. It's full of faint praise – an anecdote is praised & then someone quoted saying 'It is all untrue.' Like his plays, the book can't be straightforward & simply tell a story, it's got to have leaps back & forward in time, and literary digressions apropos a fundamental inferiority.

Saturday, 5 May
We drove to Teddington for 'Whose Baby?' & I was delighted to find that it was presented by Bernie Winters!! & that I was on with Barbara Windsor & Nanette Newman. In the second show, it was Barbara & George Best! G.B. looks v. good. No drink, 'I've had this surgical implant,' and an infectiously charming manner. Curious I should meet him now because ten years ago ('74) I was with Marty Feldman on 'What's My Line?' and M.F. was coping with G.B.'s drinking bouts in Manchester!*

*This was short lived: G.B. was arrested for drunken driving and for assaulting a policeman by the time I did this show again on November 6th.

Sunday, 13 May
We watched 'Mastermind' and then 'Dynasty': the latter is really funny with pretentious music swelling all the time & a ludicrous picture of large families all living in Maples' window.

Tuesday, 29 May
Train from Euston to Manchester. Went to Midland, unpacked, and walked to the office at Granada. It was as if one had never been away & I felt a surge of affection for them all. It may be a lousy show as far as material is concerned but the team is one of the most charming, caring & attractive ones I've ever met with. 4 o'c. Photos. Every bleedin' day there's another photo session.

---

[13] The text he had begun for Weidenfeld.

Monday, 4 June
I am desperately sorry I ever got mixed up with this . . . I feel *alien* . . . the truth is, I don't really belong at all . . . it wants someone young-looking & energetic . . . and someone who wants to hear pop music: I don't. I think it's barbaric cacophonous sub-cultural rubbish & I think it is responsible for some of the most degrading aspects of youth.

Wednesday, 6 June
We were supposed to do the Coward song 'Bad Times'[14] & I made a scene 'cos the others were late. Then, during the rehearsal, Lulu said it was too high & I agreed & asked the pianist to take it down to another note & he said he couldn't do it!! So we had to struggle along accommodating *him*! I said it was incompetent etc. We got thro' it & I returned to my room & Geoff Moore came in and said I'd upset everyone! 'Peter doesn't have to take that kind of thing from you, he's the best F[loor] M[anager] there is . . . and how dare you say such rude things about the pianist . . .' It went on & on. The FM & the pianist are obviously v. high on the estimation list. I said 'Yes well I'm afraid I'm a shit you see' & privately thought 'Oh just let me get *away* from it all!' It ruined me for the show 'cos I was spiritless and the confidence ebbed away. Just about managed to keep my professional countenance. The audience was good. No. 7 [in the series].

Thursday, 7 June
Arrived Euston at 9.05. Got cab home. Louie came to the door at 9.30. 'I've had a fall.' The face is bruised and the voice is different. It's as tho' there had been some traumatic shock . . . the speech is slowed & indistinct. The face is bruised. Apparently it happened on Tuesday. One's spirits sink & the fear grows that this marks a dreadful turning point.

Friday, 8 June
At 2 o'c. Pat rang my bell! 'I've had an awful shock! I met Louie in the street & she said "'Scuse me . . . I know your face but what is your name?"' I said she'd had a fall and it might have made her forgetful . . . oh! I don't know. Took her into Louie's flat & they had a chat & Louie seemed normal enough, but tired . . . nowadays she looks so *tired*.

Saturday, 9 June
Went in to see Louisa. She'd been ironing dresses 'I'm going away

---

14 'There are Bad Times Just Around the Corner'.

this week.' I said 'No, it's not till 19 June' and there was a lot of confused talk about dates etc. The mind seems to be wandering. For this to have happened so quickly is worrying. I think I'm now getting frightened. No reasoned arguments apply. At the end of a garbled sentence she says 'Oh! I don't know what I'm doing. I'm sorry. You must get very annoyed with me but I can't help myself . . .' and then I'm so near to useless tears I can hardly keep my countenance.

Monday, 11 June
Suggested to Louisa that we should get her a stick because of bad balance. She pooh poohed it. 'They're for old people.' 'Eighty-four is old.' 'I'm not eighty-four.' 'You will be in December.' 'Yes, well it's not December yet! The trouble with a stick is that it's something you can get to rely upon & then you stop *trying* . . .'

Tuesday, 12 June
I took her to Peter Mario for lunch. Louie said v. little and I knew she found the stairs tiring. I ordered lobster for her and she said it was enjoyable. I was v. near to tears. It was the saddest lunch of my life. She made her way unsteadily downstairs after, holding my arm & told Gloria 'I'm getting old I'm afraid' and in the street she told me 'I am so depressed because I know I can't do any of the things I used to do . . .' I can't concentrate on anything . . . it is Louie who dominates my thoughts.

Thursday, 14 June
We watched the news and I looked across & saw that she was sitting askew & realised she'd become unconscious. I got hold of her & lifted her from the chair & laid her flat with the head propped with a blanket. After about 5 minutes her eyes flickered open & she asked what I'd been doing etc. She drew long tired breaths & seemed to be exhausted. After the 9 o'c. news I said goodnight & she repeated the sentiments 'I'm so grateful to you, I don't know what I'd do without you . . . I hate being a nuisance.' I told her 'That's what I'm here for' but it makes no difference, she just shakes her head ruefully & says 'I don't know why I've gone downhill so suddenly . . .' She is simply fighting the shadows that are closing in round her.

Friday, 15 June
I must say, Louisa has improved enormously today: much brighter & like her old self! When I said as much she told me 'Well you may think this is daft but I think it's because I started smoking again! I felt better straight away!'

Monday, 18 June

Stanley came at 7.45 and gave me dinner at Peter Mario. Stanley was riotously funny about a Chinese woman reproving a hippy who took a comb to wave his hair & then replaced it on a rack in the shop . . . the dialogue & the Chinese intonation plus the cockney laid-back replies of the hippy made me laugh out loud.

Tuesday, 19 June

I rang the hotel and spoke to Louie and to Jean. They both said the flight was fine, the hotel fine & the weather OK. I was greatly relieved! I hope this is a portent for the rest of the year. Walked to Granada for the Press Show of 'Some You Win'. I must say it looks v. smart & stylish & has been edited cleverly & speedily. I look baggy-eyed and old but that's nobody's fault. Altogether, I feel unusually at peace with myself this evening. Better than I've felt for a long time.

Wednesday, 20 June

Did a bit more writing on the biog. Must say, I'd forgotten that 1958 was such an auspicious year! I did 'B[eyond] O[ur] K[en]', the two Carry Ons (first two!) and the revue (*Lettuce*) and TV and the pantomime at the Coliseum!

Sunday, 24 June

I walked in the afternoon sun to Gordon & Rona. A Rolls-Royce stopped & Tom Conti got out & shook my hand & chatted. Oh! he has immense charm & such a graceful presence. I asked 'Are you a guest at the same house as me?' & he said 'No, but do give them my love' & I went on. Gordon looked rather tense I thought & there is a curious downward twist of the mouth towards the right side: at times it's so much in evidence you think it's the result of some trauma but then he smiles & it disappears. Rona in a white track-suit looking marvellous! like a teenager & v. buoyant. Gordon is filming next week. R. gave me champagne! and she served a marvellous dinner.

Wednesday, 27 June

Went in to Louie's flat to see the TV news. All about striking miners marching thro' London & bringing transport chaos. Oh! this dispute has been handled No! *bungled* by both sides in the most pig-headed fashion. Thatcher deserves to lose popularity over it: I'm not surprised she's down in the polls. Governments are supposed to be competent not obdurately stupid. This ludicrous idea of a showdown with one side seen to be a winner is fatuous. Any victory will be pyrrhic!

Monday, 2 July
Did a bit of writing but it is making me depressed to read about the events of '62 & it is extraordinary how much depression was evinced: in those days my despair seems only just about controllable.

Wednesday, 4 July
Letter from Equity came today telling me I have been voted on to the Council *again*. I've been voted for ever since '76 & this is the Council for 84–86 so I will have been in for ten years! Apparently the left wing has been beaten & we moderates are in a majority, thank goodness.

Saturday, 7 July
Letter from Isabel Dean asking me if I would object to being nominated for the Equity Presidency: I said no but I didn't think it would get a majority of votes.

Sunday, 8 July
The temperature soared to over 100° today. It is insufferable! We saw some TV. My beloved John McEnroe won the [Wimbledon] Championship for the *third time*! In this heat! The extraordinary energy & genius that's stored in that delicate frame!

Tuesday, 17 July
To Equity, & being early, I got a seat. The result of a ballot for Vice President went in [Nigel] Davenport's favour & I was proved right. I'd told Helen [Lambert] & Isabel that it would split the vote, so I got 30 & he got 33 & I was left with egg on my face. Next time I shan't be persuaded. Loads of 'em came up commiserating! It's a joke 'cos I didn't want the job anyway.

Tuesday, 24 July
Went to Equity at 10 o'c. Theme of the morning was a motion from the Left asking [Derek] Bond to resign as President since he was going to perform in S.A. I spoke against Bond and said he should go as an individual not as President of Equity. The situation is ludicrous. But the A[ct] F[or] E[quity] gang stood solidly behind Bond and we couldn't shift him. I felt disgusted.

Friday, 27 July
The BBC TV news announced the death of James Mason. He was always kind to me & his individual & distinctive vocal style was v. impressive. A nice man. Thankfully it sounds as if he died peacefully.

Saturday, 28 July
We saw 'S[ome] Y[ou] W[in]' & I was relieved to find that I didn't gabble as much in this one! But the appearance ain't good: the face has been badly lit & I appear baggy-eyed & horribly lined. The content remains inept & unsatisfying: the Rock Hudson interview was a waste of time: he was determined to say nothing.

Sunday, 5 August
On the TV news we heard [of] the death of Richard Burton at 58 & I suddenly remembered those days in 1950 when I worked with him at Swansea. All that hope! And his saying about America 'I shall go to Hollywood but it won't corrupt *me* . . . Sybil and I come from these valleys and that's where our values are . . . when I make money it will be to bring it back here & it will be jobs for the boys . . .'

Monday, 6 August
The papers all headline the death of Richard Burton which is proof that all the faint praise meted out to him was erroneous: one of the greatest voices in the history of the 20th Century.

Tuesday, 7 August
With Stanley to Vecchia for a meal on me. He said 'You're right about the Nichols book: he's got it all wrong. You didn't talk like *that* in Singapore. You weren't using polari then. His picture of you is one of the camp chorus-boy type & you were not like that.' He said he'd talked to P.N. on the phone & that the latter remarked 'As soon as you start an autobiography you embark on an act of fiction.' He means of course that nothing can ever come out on paper *quite* as it originally occurred; that is true, so I suppose one can't be cross but I hope I don't paint such a shabby picture of my friends.

Friday, 10 August
Walked to Rona & Gordon. Just passing the cemetery at Highgate when Jean Marsh came by in her car & offered me a lift! Sat waiting for Michael Lindsay-Hogg till gone 9.30 so of course we ate v. late. M.L.H. talks shop till it's coming out of his ears, but he's so attractive he gets away with it. When I related S.B.'s story of the Chinese lady remonstrating about the hippy using the comb, M.L.H. said 'That is a complete sketch! It's marvellous. Your humour is merciless . . .' I pointed out that it was S.B.'s story.

Friday, 17 August
Arrived at Gyles's house. We worked till 6 o'c. He showed me the typed MS which has been compiled from the dictated stuff and we

are already over 200 pages! I expressed misgivings about the length, & he said 'Try aiming for a finish on the 50th birthday year . . . it won't be easy to go beyond that because the events are so much more recent . . .'

Sunday, 19 August

M. came and I read him a bit from the biog. & he said 'It reads like a Johnson letter to Mrs Thrale' which wasn't a comment I'd expected to hear. I found my bathroom bulb has given out! I got this in 1960! from Heal's! It is Finnish and cost about 15/- all those years ago!

Friday, 24 August

Phone rang: 'This is Annette Burgess. I am at Pat's flat. She's had a heart attack. The doctor says I should stay with her.' Then the front door buzzer went & Harvey Proctor[15] appeared. 'I'm Pat's boss & I think you should know that she is ill.' I said we knew. At about 6.30 Louisa rang the door ceaselessly 'I can't get the key to work!' & I let her in. She brought Annette Burgess with her for a cup of tea. They'd been waiting ages for an ambulance & saw Pat into U.C.H. I did a bit more work on the biog. Must say, it is coming along quite well.

Sunday, 26 August

I walked with Louie to U.C.H. and saw Pat in Ward 44 on 4 Floor. It's a communal ward & there is that weird indefinable odour . . . vaguely unpleasant . . . the place depressed my spirits horribly. P. was very cheerful & laughed loudly over descriptions of Joy Kaufmann placing hands round her face & saying 'Never forget you are loved very much.' She fell about.

Saturday, 1 September

Did a bit more writing & found myself practically at the end of '72 with the opening at the Globe & reunion with Mags. Became *convinced* that this is the place to stop with the book. I am sure that there is enough material now to comprise a substantial volume & there's no reason why it shouldn't finish with me at the age of 46. Nor is there any reason why I should not use *Scene Drops* as the title: that's what the book is: drops from the whole scene & they're all scenes from my life. I am conscious that these days are rather *pleasant* . . . I'm more relaxed & contented than I've been for years . . . unemployment suits me . . . I am pleased with my writing . . . it's all a bit too good to be true. So I'm probably about to get a kick up the arse.

---

[15] Pat's boss at the computer firm where she worked evidently resembled Harvey Proctor, then a Member of Parliament (for Basildon, 1979–83; Billericay, 1983–87).

Saturday, 8 September
Washed the hair etc. and went thro' my stuff for the David Frost papers spot on TV-am. The show went OK. David told me about a man given suppos. & telling doctor 'I did what you told me, put them in the back passage every night under the mat but for all the good they did I might as well have stuck 'em up my arse.' Can't get on with this writing at all. I think it's because I've come to a period of such dolour that there's little to say that isn't downbeat and dreary.

Saturday, 15 September
Saw the TV news announcing the birth of a son to Princess Diana & then watched Fred Hoyle[16] on 'Revelations'. It wasn't any good because he tried to make a sort of faith out of mathematical formulae but got into a mess about *why*. 'There must be a moral thread running thro' the intelligence in the Universe . . . we need something better than these religions of 3000 years ago & better than modern materialism if we're not to blow each other to pieces.' He rejected God because 'religionists say he is perfect whereas the world is full of imperfections which contradicts the idea that he could have created it.' Which seems to leave out the idea 'Who gave you the ability to envisage perfection?' entirely. The world isn't full of imperfections, it's full of mysteries we don't understand.

Monday, 17 September
At 10 o'c. I went to the Blood Donor Centre at Margaret St to give blood: they asked me to fill in a form testifying to abstention from promiscuity. That was an easy task for me.

Wednesday, 19 September
Wrote the concluding sentence for the book. 'There is not only one second chance, there are numberless second chances, just as long as we wonder at the sunset, marvel at the stars and eagerly await a new dawn.' If Gyles accepts this, it means the end of all this work! It has lasted for the best part of year, and has made me v. miserable at times.

Saturday, 22 September
Letter from P. Nichols says he is v. proud of his book!! And that he's been shocked by the critical reaction to it. Should have thought he'd been hardened by adversity by now.

Wednesday, 26 September
Met Paul at Joe Allen's. We sat next to Rock Hudson & I foolishly

---

16 Professor Sir Fred Hoyle, b.1915. Astronomer, author.

talked to him about the Lulu interview!![17] I said 'We wanted to know less about the fame & more about the obscurity' and he was very pleasant but I realised I was falling into the trap I deplore when people do it to me.

Friday, 28 September

This miners' strike seems to be on for the duration![18] None of them seem to be bothered about not earning any money and none of them seem to be facing any real hardship. Even if they are, Mr Scargill ain't, 'cos his salary goes on being paid. When asked on TV 'Why don't you condemn violence?' he said 'Oh I do! I condemn police violence!' And it is that side of him that reveals how devious he is. I don't think he gives tuppence about the miners; I think he is after the sort of anarchism which brings about the collapse of a society he hates. The man is consumed with self-loathing and inferiority.

Wednesday, 3 October

The entertainment offered on both channels was dire. You have a sit-com 'Home Sweet Home' which is totally banal: it could only be saved by a Leonard Rossiter & alas, it's got rep casting.

Saturday, 6 October

Got papers at Warren St where the lady told me of the death of Leonard Rossiter! Apparently he died after a heart attack in the D/room at the Lyric!![19] It is astonishing because he wasn't old & nor was he overweight: I can only guess that the nervous energy he expended made for a tremendous strain. He was unique & he will be sorely missed: a rare talent now lost to us. In the evening, I saw 'Revelations' with me talking about Ceylon. The appearance was shocking. An old & lined face and look of aestheticism & the sound of a Mary Ann. O! dear! I should really *stop* performing altogether. It is a depressing & debilitating spectacle.

Wednesday, 10 October

Saw Louisa in the evening. She looks white & strained and tired. While I was watching a programme about the Parthenon she noisily turned the newspaper pages because she wasn't interested. The elderly become more & more like children.

---

[17] On 28 July 1984.
[18] The strike lasted officially from March 1984 to 3 March 1985.
[19] He was playing Truscott in *Loot*.

Friday, 12 October
We got a paper and saw the horrifying reports of a bomb outrage at the Grand Hotel in Brighton. Norman Tebbit[20] has been injured! This marvellous man has been subjected to an appalling ordeal: I pray for his complete recovery. The entire evening was clouded by this awful event.

Thursday, 18 October
Went to see Richard Peel at 11 o'c. and he is going to draw up a new will for me. It will name Michael [Whittaker] as my sole beneficiary. In the event of his demise, everything goes to Michael Anderson. M.A. rang about a job on 5 November. He never mentioned the Australian commercial so I should think he's displeased with my refusal.

Friday, 26 October
The BBC TV news was again about Ethiopia. If I see another emaciated famine victim I think I'll throw up. Turned it off. The BBC are in another of their bogus virtuous moral moods & it has about as much interest for the British as a typhoon in Ulan Bator.

Saturday, 27 October
Looked in mirror & saw this grey-haired, bug-eyed old man & thought 'Who on earth would find *you* funny?' & then realised the answer was 'I would.'

Monday, 29 October
NS. I shall put NS when the non-smoking rule is observed. I didn't smoke at all yesterday. Just hope that I am going to experience all those improvements the abolitionists speak of. The turntable on the gramophone broke & I got a new one but the amplifier has to be changed too! Oh! the expense and trouble! Went back on the fags by 2 o'c. so all the above about NS is a lot of wishful thinking. Went to LWT for 'All Star Secrets'. The entire evening was disaster. I said to Anthony Booth 'That Derek Jameson is *awful* isn't he? The way he mouths everything! So amateur' & after a pause he said 'This lady is his wife' to a woman standing with him. She did all the 'You should be careful what you say' stuff & reproved me for speaking ill of a man trying to repay the costs of a law suit.[21]

---

[20] Baron Tebbit of Chingford, b.1931. Conservative MP for Chingford 1974–92, etc.
[21] He had sued the BBC in 1980 over a John Langdon sketch for 'Week Ending' which jocularly claimed, *inter alia*, that Jameson was 'a man who still believes that erudite is a glue'. The script was found to be defamatory but not malicious, and Jameson faced costs of £75,000.

Thursday, 1 November

Went out to post & then to B.H.S. for socks. All the way it was shouting from people 'Hello Kenny!' and drivers calling 'Carry On Kenny!' till you wanted to scream 'Piss off.' In the event, I just kept walking: the truth is, I live in a zoo.

Saturday, 3 November

In 'The A-Team' there was a superb vignette from the dish in the team, playing a cod-vicar . . . a scene with a nurse that was a tiny little acting essay: quite enchanting. 'Dynasty' was divertingly daft and then came 'Wogan' with Rabbi Blue[22] who was delightful and funny, Gore Vidal who was neither, & then Beryl Reid who is a typical English example of 'If you've been around long enough you are adored' 'cos she got claps and laughs over nothing at all.

Monday, 5 November

U.S. election: it was amazing to see some of the moments in the Reagan campaign when he obviously *dried*! One saw the wife Nancy prompt him on one occasion. On this kind of evidence it is obvious that the man should not be President but the tide of opinion seems overwhelmingly in his favour! It's an extraordinary state of affairs, and the sort of thing one would expect in Russia where these old dodderers get re-elected because of an inexorable grinding bureaucracy . . . makes one realise that these cumbersome empires are v. comparable.

Thursday, 8 November

M. came and we went to Vecchia. I'm afraid my depression hung over me like a pall, yet M. was wonderfully loath to fall in with it & he talked animatedly about his plans. More & more now, I understand the feeling of hopelessness that assails the addict . . . the man addicted to anything is a prisoner & the bleak walls of his cell offer no comfort.

Thursday, 22 November

I am now uninterested in work: the idea of having to do something is increasingly irksome. And I'm less & less interested in the Diary. I used to want to preserve so much that I'd heard or seen but nowadays I couldn't care less. The material has been used up I suppose and after the preparation of the *third* book, I don't think I shall ever bother with another.

---

22 Lionel Blue, b.1930.

Friday, 30 November

We saw 'Blankety Blank' 'cos I have to discuss it on the 9th. Les Dawson told the losing contestant 'You didn't win but don't think it hasn't been fun. It hasn't.' And at the end he said to camera 'To all you people out there I would like to say thank you for sleeping thro' the programme.' The format of the programme, the replies of the contestants & the prizes are openly derided & since L.D. is in charge it is all right: his comedy redeems the banality & puts flesh on a scarecrow.

Wednesday, 5 December

As I was struggling up Gt. Portland St with the shopping there were endless cries of 'Hallo Kenny!' etc. etc. I thought 'I am *sick* of greetings & good wishes . . .' & I jotted down the results when I got home & stuck them in this diary under the heading *Greetings*. It all flowed quite naturally & I was pleased with the result.

I'm tired of all the nods
All the nudges and the winks
I'm tired of all conjecture
As to what the public thinks
But I must go on playing
At this game of let's-pretend
Getting precious comfort from
The knowledge: it must end
And send me to that other place
Where all the spent ones come
Where vanity is silent
And all the pop groups dumb
Peace is there in plenty
And there's innocence again
Shelter for the good folk
And the bad left in the rain
I'm sure there will be justice
Though the wicked will not burn
They'll be forced to entertain us
With an everlasting turn
Hitler and Napoleon and even Genghis Khan
Made to do a tap-dance
Or to tell a funny yarn
The audience sitting comfortably
No heckling and no chaff
And the poor benighted beggars
Getting not a single laugh.

Friday, 7 December

I know I have been unemployed & depressed in the past so the experience isn't new for me but this year there has been the consciousness of *death* all the while . . . the knowledge that it is drawing ever nearer & that every day should involve preparation for it. The advantage of regular work is that one's mind is occupied with other things.

Sunday, 9 December

Car at 12.45 took me to TV Centre where I did 'Did You See?' with Ludovic Kennedy:[23] in life he looks like a shambling derelict but on screen he comes over attractive & benign. I had to talk about 'Blankety' and I thought I'd steered very adroitly till he said 'Would you like to be in it?' Nearly stumped me but I wriggled out of it 'Oh no, I don't like being part of a jury . . . don't mind appearing on my own but not as part of a team . . .'

Sunday, 16 December

Lately I have noticed a desire on the part of various performers to destroy studio illusions. Wogan said (after applause) 'Thanks for that totally *spurious* welcome.' Les Dawson told the audience 'This is a load of rubbish' and Christopher Timothy last night said 'That applause which greeted my entrance was signalled by a studio manager . . .' and mimed the latter arm-waving to the spectators. It's as though they're anxious to dissociate themselves from what is staged: if so, they are committing a fundamental error because once in an artificial setting it's best to accept the convention or you run the risk of invalidating the whole purpose of the enterprise. It is as silly as man rising to make a speech and prefacing it all with the warning 'Don't listen to any of this,' implicitly telling his listeners that it's not worth their attention. Tell them that often enough & they'll believe it.

Wednesday, 19 December. Madeira

Arrived in Funchal at 12.45. Coach to Savoy Hotel & M. found champagne from his travel people so we sat on his balcony and drank it. The 3 rooms are all alongside each other and are OK.

Friday, 21 December

Never again I tell myself. Never again. Guiding Louisa everywhere 'I can't find my way around this place' till you begin to feel like an invalid yourself.

---

[23] Writer and broadcaster, b.1919.

Tuesday, 25 December

Rainy morning & windy & cold. Santa Claus and children knocking on all the doors. Happy Xmas and here is a Madeira cake. Up to the Christmas Dinner at 7.30. Louisa in the georgette. The meal was revolting & I think the insolent queen serving us was drunk. 'Go on eat it! You have paid for it!' he cried out, as he plonked unwanted plates of rubbish in front of us. They said waiters will bear in the pudding flambé at 10.30. I couldn't be bothered. Left M. & L. at 9.45 and went to bed.

Saturday, 29 December

At 7.15 to Louisa where she cried because her dress was too tight. I made her change into another & told her 'Give that old dress to the maid' & took her up to dinner. Got through that all right.

Monday, 31 December

Invitation from the Consul. Drinks on Tues.! I'll be gone. Wrote my regrets etc.

1985

Tuesday, 1 January
Coffee in the Morgue lounge with hysteria bubbling up inside. M. keeps bursting into mirthless laughter. Last dinner at the Crematorium and we've never had such quick service!! The idea of home tomorrow is marvellous.

Thursday, 3 January
Paul F. came & I took him to Vecchia Milano for lunch and v. luckily Paul R. was able to join us. He's been taking Paul F. out for me while I've been in Funchal & arranged for him to see several ballets.

Thursday, 10 January
I got the tube to Gyles. We worked on revisions to the book (which I *hate*: most of the Shellard suggestions alter the style of the writing, and in some cases he simply misunderstands what I am saying). I left at about 3.45 feigning tiredness but in truth, I dislike the work and the venue now that Gyles and Michèle have shown their patent antipathy to my smoking.

Saturday, 12 January
With Paul to Camden Town where I got 2 prs. of slippers and a woman pestered me & I said 'Get away!' and she said 'I'm your Aunt Phyllis!' and I apologised.

Tuesday, 22 January
Sometimes, when I run across a road, I am amazed that I have the capacity to do it. It is continually surprising that (at nearly 59) I am still here at all! I don't feel this apropos Louisa 'cos there's something phenomenal in her zest for life. She has always had enthusiasm for it: I never have. Providing there is no *pain* I shall be happy to go when the time comes; nothing here has really delighted me except Art, the life-experience itself has no fascination for me and the very sight of active humanity invariably fills me with nausea.

Wednesday, 23 January

Worked with Gyles on revisions to the book. We were at it until 4 o'c. when it was finished & we made several cuts including the entire philosophical section which Shellard found so tedious. He asked for 40 pages to go & I don't think this has been accomplished. His requests are paradoxical 'cos again & again he asks 'Can't you tell us *more* about this . . . ?' etc. I told G. I was fed-up with the entire business and that if they made any more trouble, I would throw it all in. I'm not keen on any more literary efforts, and I couldn't care less about the ballyhoo circuit that goes with publication.

Saturday, 26 January

I am feeling reasonably calm at this period. Not really keen on doing this film (starting on the 4th) at all, but I said yes because I know that it is wrong to be so lazy & to be indifferent to M.A.'s efforts. But next year is my 60th one and then I am certainly not going to take on anything that doesn't really attract me. That means imaginatively inviting and involving no physical exertion.

Tuesday, 29 January

To Equity but didn't stay long. Rang the D.T.I. about EEC & armed with information I went to Thames TV to take part in the EEC debate. Had quite a few facts to counter some of the crap from a Labour Euro MP. Tried learning lines in the afternoon but it is a dreadful task.

Monday, 4 February

To Studios at Shepperton.[1] I was used for a line-up before lunch so I needn't have gone there till 12.30. The atmosphere is friendly but I really don't know what I'm doing: just stabbing in the dark and hoping it is OK. James Cellan-Jones says 'A bit over the top there' occasionally & so I bring it down & he seems satisfied. The stand-in was supposed to do all the 'Hand in shot' stuff but *now* they've discovered his fingers are unsuitable! The organisation certainly ain't brilliant. Wardrobe & make up girls are marvellous. I went to lunch with them. Rodney Bewes keeps up the humour & makes everybody laugh. He is very good in the role, there's no doubt of that: remarkably good in fact. Very real. By 5.30 I was feeling utterly worn out & the foot (big toe nail right) was being troublesome. Oh there's no mistaking: I'm too old for this sort of thing. It is the last time I will take on this sort of work.

---

[1] For a commercial training film.

Tuesday, 5 February

There's no let up in the pace. I get a bit annoyed at times when Bewes is doing the jokes in the middle of a sequence where I have to concentrate and today when he did it I loudly started running my lines & drowned his conversation. He doesn't do it maliciously 'cos he's not ill-natured, he is unthinking: that's the problem. James Cellan-Jones told me again to take it down a bit & I did: there's no doubt about it, I overact as far as the camera is concerned. One doesn't *need* to labour & point lines in the way I tend to do.

Wednesday, 6 February

I got v. tetchy during the rehearsals & shooting scenes because of the endless banter & funny sallies from Bewes & the director & several times I said 'Can we got on?' and stopped it. I know it is not conducive to a good atmosphere etc. but when one is supposed to be concentrating on a scene, I find it intolerable. It is the sort of thing I used to do myself 'cos I remember other actors complaining about *me* larking about when they were trying to concentrate so I know what it stems from. It's nothing to do with reverence for work, it's everything to do with waning confidence and a desire to *get the work over with*, get it finished so I can *get away*.

Friday, 8 February

A script has arrived from BBC offering me a part in the K[enny] E[verett] Show but it is too small and the writing is in v. bad taste. I am certainly not interested in this kind of rubbish.

Tuesday, 12 February

A letter from Gyles Brandreth tells me that the sales on *Back Drops* were lousy! Several thousand remain unsold in the paperbacks! Only hope they're not remaindered 'cos that would be the final indignity. Don't think Dent have lost out on the deal tho' because they sold the pb. rights at a v. good price at auction.

Tuesday, 19 February

To the studios. I did nothing till after lunch. Then the humiliating experience of standing round the shop as an extra while Nerys [Hughes] & Bewes bumbled their way thro' endless bum takes. Eventually my stuff got done at the end of the day and I had to do the narration stuff in the sound studios as well. They gave us champagne in paper cups after & Cawston[2] (producer) said 'You have been

---

[2] Richard Cawston (1923–86). Head of Documentary Programmes, BBC, 1965–79, then freelance.

very good on this picture . . . all the waiting round you've had to endure . . . and you've been good humoured throughout . . .' Then James Cellan-Jones said 'Will you come back to my house for drinks' and I said yes. Arrived at his Edwardian villa in Kew and sat with him and his son (dish) Simon and Nerys and Bewes. I got home at about 11 o'c. and went to bed full of relief that the whole experience has ended. The fact is I don't enjoy work any more, and I want to do it less & less. It all involves cooperation and ensemble effort: competence on both sides, and it is never forthcoming. Always the actor who knows his job suffers from working with some idiot who doesn't.

Friday, 22 February

Loads of birthday cards & rubbish in the post, but a lovely letter from Mags & a beautiful drawing from Jeremy. Went to M & S for shopping & at the butcher's, he cried 'Happy Birthday' which was kind. With Paul & Louie by cab to Peter Mario and Louie gave us lunch. I'd ordered a lobster for her & she enjoyed that. Saw the News, more panic about the pound at near parity with the dollar, more panic about Aids, more panic about N.U.M. thugs . . .

Wednesday, 6 March

More rubbish on TV. Harry Andrews on 'This Is Your Life' and Gielgud coming on clasping his hands in front of him like an amateur playing a clergyman & a host of other idiots mouthing compliments while H.A. sat looking embarrassed throughout. Why on earth do people submit to this sort of charade? It was worse than BAFTA.

Tuesday, 26 March

Letter from Pamela Howe says she wants to do my biog. on radio! She ain't even read it yet! She wants 10 episodes of 19 minutes (that's 3 hrs. 10 minutes! Don't think it will last that long!) Then I went to Equity for Executive Meeting: the Vice President of U.S. Equity was there & a great trick! Not enough to relieve the tedium tho'. With M. to Vecchia & I gave him dinner. When we talked about Death he said 'You can take comfort from the fact that you've made a lot of people happy . . . there are not many like you' & I said 'That isn't very *dramatic* tho' . . . not like leading all the blacks to the legislature in Pretoria & getting shot in the process . . .'

Thursday, 28 March

Oliver Hatch came at 10 o'c. and he took some polaroids to begin with: I suggested I sit on the floor beside the diaries & we did these, and then some on the gramophone table writing. I prefer the first ones.[3]

Sunday, 31 March

Started reading the Fitzgerald biography[4] & finding it interesting, but the writer lays it on v. thickly about sexual innocence. He would have us believe that all the male friendships were devoid of sex & points to the reticence of the Victorians but I *knew* about such desires when I was a boy (even if I couldn't articulate them) & I can't see why F. didn't.

Friday, 5 April

I make the total for year: £69,599. A higher figure than I have ever earned before; when I told Louisa she said incredulously 'But you haven't *done* anything . . . have you?' & I had to admit, I haven't done much.

Saturday, 6 April

Up at 6.30. Went to Warren St but the news stand was closed so I walked to Euston instead & the vendor who sold me the papers said 'You're not on the box any more are you?' & I said gaily 'No!' and left. At 10 o'c. car came to take me to television studios of TV-am & I did the papers spot with David Frost.

Thursday, 18 April

The 'Lenny Henry Show'[5] could be good if it were not so rushed and restless. There is an underlying lack of confidence which dictates speed all the time, whereas playing with relish and the savouring of moments would give a different performance. Shame 'cos L.H. is one of the few decent talents around at the moment. Looking at what I write these days, I'm conscious of repetition & the uneventful nature of my existence.

Thursday, 25 April

Went to Foyle's. In one dept. I was looking at shelves when a customer passed me & sneered 'I s'pose you're trying to make us believe you can *read*!' but I affected deafness.

---

[3] One of which was used on the cover of *Just Williams*.

[4] *With Friends Possessed: A Biography of Edward FitzGerald* by Robert Bernard Martin (1985).

[5] Actor-comedian, b.1958. A discovery of the 'New Faces' television talent show, he made his mark in a young people's comedy series, 'Three of a Kind', and graduated to his own projects in 1984.

Monday, 29 April

I set out for Richard Williams's studio. I met his editor, Ian, & he showed me some of *The Thief* [*and the Cobbler*].[6] Oh! it is breathtaking: animation at its finest & a story of such truth & humour! It was extraordinary to hear the voice of Felix Aylmer . . . alas, he's now dead. Some of the Baxter stuff is superb. I walked home being stopped by people: 'May I saw how much pleasure you've given me?' etc. etc. At the conclusion of one such incident, a bearded man told me 'It's been a pleasure Mister Hawtrey! Or may I call you Charles?' I thought 'Either would be wrong' but simply smiled & departed.

Wednesday, 1 May

To Dent where I collected the proofs of the biography. I read the proofs and there are several errors which have to be corrected, but again & again I found myself thinking 'I actually *wrote* this!' and I think it is very good. It gives a true picture of myself & creates the right atmosphere for the various events.

Sunday, 5 May

Several times in conversation recently, I've heard the line 'It isn't the world I grew up in' and it prompted me to gather some of the sentiments expressed & put them into verse.[7]

Wednesday, 8 May

The TV was all about celebrations re 40 years after VE Day with old farts remembering this & that & endless trivia & rubbish . . . people dressing up and processing in Westminster Abbey & prating about the

---

[6] A long-running, large-scale project, as yet uncompleted.

[7] Entitled 'Spinster's Lament', the verse begins:

> It isn't the world I grew up in
> People no longer believe
> In things that I was taught sacred
> I shan't be sorry to leave
>
> It isn't the world I grew up in
> Manners aren't nearly the same
> It's all 'the world owes me a living'
> No concept of praise or of blame . . .

and closes:

> With millions in Africa starving
> Here, pet food groans on the shelf
> Everything's gone to the dogs now
> In fact, I am going myself.

blessings of peace etc. If they spent some money on the wounded & the lame of the *last* war (Falklands) it would be better than all their silly parades and parties.

Friday, 10 May

To see Peter Shellard at Dent's about the various revisions he wants. It was stuff like 'I don't think people will understand the reference to Sacher-Masoch . . .'[8] so I had to put in extra stuff.

Tuesday, 14 May

Got a taxi with Paul to Covent Garden where we had superb seats in the Grand Tier at the Opera House for *Swan Lake* with Roland Price getting the biggest ovation from the house for his superbly danced Prince Siegfried. He looks a boy on stage, pity the Swan didn't look like a girl. As it was, you felt he was with a *woman* all the time & it took away some of the magic.

Titans of verse would not be there
If it were not for some of the small
Talents that thrive upon being
Better than nothing at all.

Thursday, 16 May

You can hear the rooks cawing in Regent's Park
The tits warbling by the zoo
Ducklings quacking round the lake
Where greylags swim two by two
Bird cries have echoed since time began
They'll sing on no matter what
Ptarmigan, ousel and ortolan
I'd happily shoot the lot

I read the poem (above) to Gordon & Rona . . . and both of them practically smiled it aside.

Saturday, 18 May

The box was all crap so I went back to the flat to continue with the

---

[8] Leopold von Sacher-Masoch (1835–95), Austrian lawyer and writer who described sexual pleasure derived from pain.

book on Auden:[9] in a way I wish I wasn't consuming it so quickly! There is so much in it that I warm to . . . his way of life, the discipline, the affection . . . the long search for a *home* . . . all these are the things which attract me. I can see just where the trap of 'love' led him. Interesting that he cut the line 'We must love one another or die . . .'[10] from the revised edition of his poetry! It is a superb line. He rejected it because 'It's nonsense . . . we are going to die anyway . . .' It shows how after-analysis can destroy a creative idea. The line does work insofar as, without love, the human being is (as far as the poet is concerned) living a dead life.

Thursday, 23 May

M. came at 6.50. Drove me to Bernie Winters & Ziggy at Arkley. The drawing room was like a film set! Enormous opulence. Talked to Jess Conrad & wife, to Maurice (producer Thames), Lionel Blair, Rolf Harris, Bob Wilson[11] . . . Uncle Tom's Cobblers & all. I must have been daft to go really, but when Bernie asked me, I could not do anything that might be hurtful to him. He's one of the most warmhearted & kind people I've known & has always treated me with consideration.

Saturday, 1 June

Liz Newlands came & we drove to Clarke's bookshop in Chelmsford. I said to Liz 'Don't expect a crowd because it is a lovely day so they'll all be out in the sunshine.' In the event, I had a terrific crowd! Signed a lot of books and hundreds of autographs. After, I had to go out into the street & launch a load of balloons: I did it with great panache. I was almost tongue tied at the end when I got an unexpected present!! They gave me the new Drabble Oxford Lit. Companion! I managed to stammer my sincere thanks. Liz said 'It was a very successful day' & I said I hoped it was a portent for the biography launch in September.

Monday, 3 June

Read more of the [Anthony] Powell book.[12] He expiates [*sic*] endlessly on how to write well but never achieves it himself . . . there is no narrative line at all. It seems to fall between anecdotes (with rotten tags, or non-existent ones) and literary criticism, with character analy-

---

[9] Either *W.H. Auden: A Biography* by Humphrey Carpenter (1981) or *W.H. Auden: The Life of a Poet* by Charles Osborne (1980). KW's output of verse squibs (pasted into the diary) became noticeably heavy during the reading of whichever it was.

[10] From Auden's 'September 1, 1939'; but persistently misquoted by KW as 'we must love each other or die'. Auden revised the line to read: 'We must love one another and die'.

[11] Former Arsenal and Scotland goalkeeper turned broadcaster, b.1941.

[12] *To Keep the Ball Rolling*, four-volume autobiography, abridged in one, 1983.

sis thrown in for good measure. He comes over as fairly pompous & the French terms abound 'He was a faux-naïf creature . . .' etc. etc. Oh dear oh dear . . . I shall be glad when I've finished it.

Tuesday, 11 June

Saddened by the news, tucked away in a small paragraph, of the death of my old chum Clifford Evans. He was responsible for so much that was made possible in my career.

Saturday, 15 June

Saw TV news . . . then there was 'Dynasty' . . . Oh dear, it is such unutterable crap. At first it was rubbish but engaging . . . now it is just degenerating into total banality. Last night we saw an extraordinarily emaciated Rock Hudson playing a few lines: the poor man looks terribly ill.[13]

Tuesday, 18 June

Went to Equity. It was all rubbish, except for an item about Geoff Capes[14] wanting to join & appear in Panto which Francis Batsoni opposed!! I spoke *for* and I won! Capes is a splendid man who should be welcomed in the same way that we embraced John Curry the ice skater who brought great distinction, internationally & otherwise, to our work.

Wednesday, 19 June

Liz rang to tell me that they're going to remainder *Back Drops*! 'If you want any beforehand, they will let you have them for 10p each.' Well I would like quite a lot but I've got no room for 'em in the flat. The bad news comes, oddly enough, after a Councillor said to me at Equity yesterday 'There are bad signs for us in the stars . . .' It was Peter Honri & we're both Pisces.

Thursday, 20 June

A note from Isabel Dean says 'I don't think you realise how many people wanted you as President of Equity & not Derek Bond . . .' She said my reason for losing so closely was 'cos of A.F.E. scheming & I think this is true but I can still see that the establishment figure (Bond) would appeal to a wide spectrum of the membership.

Friday, 21 June

To dinner with Gyles Brandreth and Michèle. It was a big party!

---

[13] He went into hospital on 25 July to be treated for AIDS, and died on 2 October.
[14] Shot-put champion and professional strongman, b.1949.

With Joanna Lumley, Juliet, Roddy & Tanya Llewellyn, and Stefan Bedenarczyk. Roddy told a story about a man going into the home of two spinsters to view a Ming vase & seeing a french letter lying on the piano stool. The old lady explained 'We found it lying in the grass on the common & it said *Place on organ to avoid infection* and we haven't got an organ so we put it on the piano & do you know we've neither of us had *any colds* this year!' He's one of the few people I've ever come upon who knows how to tell a story.

Friday, 28 June
I asked John Wolfenden to arrange for a will to be drawn up. I want to leave stuff for Michael, for Paul Richardson, and for godson Robert [Chidell], and I want the Midland Bank to be executors.

Monday, 1 July
Returned to my flat to do the accounts. I had to write Unemployed on two Expense Sheets: that is something I've not had to do for years! I suppose it is a reflection of the market in one sense & my own slothfulness in another.

Thursday, 4 July
Oh! the rubbish that comes thro' the post! Today there is a letter about a Japanese Bonsai tree alleging that it *farts* and imagining anyone cares! Ludicrous rubbish.

Friday, 5 July
I purchased Fauré & Scriabin piano music for £15!! Mad extravagance, but no one achieves the loudness of Scriabin with *his* justification, and Fauré . . . oh well . . . he's like some drug for me. Went to bed at 10.30. Couldn't sleep. I am tired but not at the times when I should be.

Monday, 8 July
Went to Dent and met Peter Shellard & Liz Newlands & we walked to the Clifton Ford Hotel for the reception apropos the book. I chatted with Cilla Black (they're publishing her as well!) and spent the rest of the time with the reps. Ernie saying 'You must *never* retire! There are only a few people like you! You are always entertaining . . .' Peter gave me an uncorrected proof copy of the book and reproductions of all the photographs. They look *splendid*. Type setting is vaguely disappointing: the pages look crammed. Everyone was v. nice to me at Dent I must say. You are made to feel important & the good things about the book are just as thrilling to them. Trouble is, at £8.95 people have got to fork out quite a lot! I think a fiver is a reasonable price.

Thursday, 11 July

Took up the Forster biography again.[15] It is good: there is so much about him that I admire but the liberalism that he champions is something I see as eroding much that he loved. He talks about wanting to preserve the order of things in this country, yet organisations he helped to foster (NCCL etc.) have turned out to be, very often, nests of troublemakers & communists.[16] He said people should not go to the Royal Tournament because it 'glorified war' but he was frequently attracted by soldiers, sailors & policemen. Oh! what the hell? Of course it's paradoxical, we all are . . . it's human.

Sunday, 14 July

M. came & drove us to Joe Allen's where he gave us lunch. After, M. drove us to St James's Park and we walked round the lake. One girl, lying on the grass with a group of others, shouted as I passed 'Oh! at last I've seen a famous person! Thank Goodness!' & I replied 'Goodness had nothing to do with it' & they all laughed.

Monday, 15 July

I set out for Angell Sound in Floral St and found I was doing the v/o with Hugh Paddick & Bill Pertwee! I felt a great surge of affection for them both and we chatted affectionately about the past. Walked with Hugh to the end of Long Acre 'cos he was getting the tube to Camden Town 'Too far to walk at my age!' He is over seventy!! but looks about 52. I said I'd like to see him 'but of course you're in the theatre every night . . .' He's doing *Noises Off* by Frayn at the Savoy. I don't know how he finds the energy!

Thursday, 18 July

We saw me in 'Whose Baby?' looking old but . . . sort of jaded posh . . . then me in *Carry On Abroad* looking reasonably young! Oh! the sadness of watching Hattie & Peter Butterworth & Sid . . . all gone . . . but, as usual, Kenny Connor made me laugh! What a lovely actor!

Monday, 22 July

The news was all about the violent events in South Africa. The world is getting utterly sick of the whole apartheid saga & its endless stupidities. The country should either go Nazi completely or create a prosper-

---

[15] Presumably *E.M. Forster: A Life* by P.N. Furbank (1979).

[16] Forster was the first President of the National Council for Civil Liberties. He campaigned in 1928 against the banning of Radclyffe Hall's lesbian novel *The Well of Loneliness*, and appeared as a defence witness in the *Lady Chatterley's Lover* trial of 1960.

ous black middle class. All this havering is a headlong rush to disaster. No it isn't – it's a crawl to disaster.

Thursday, 25 July

Wonder of wonders! a good programme on TV!! 'From The Face Of The Earth', on Channel 4. A documentary about a medical mission trying to wipe out a disease spread by a snail worm, on St Lucia. The sight of villagers helping to build a water system & singing together in their church was heartwarming. So was the easy & trusting relationship twixt black man & white man in their determination to tackle the problem. It was a superb example of love triumphing over adversity: sadly it seems, men need adversity before they can ever realise their altruism.

Thursday, 1 August

In the afternoon to Mowbrays to get [*An*] *Orderly Man* by Dirk Bogarde:[17] he writes very well & there are moments of extraordinary poignance. Not a vein of comedy but lots of ironies & a good feel for atmosphere. There is quite a lot devoted to belittling the early film work & a dismissal of chat shows as rubbish etc. but the former brought him fame & the latter brought him a publisher.

Friday, 2 August

Read the rest of the Bogarde book. There are some passages I don't understand. 'They say I dye my hair' occurs. Well why not admit it? Certainly (with his knowledge of the camera) it seems ludicrous to deny it. Men of 60 don't have jet black hair: his looks as if it's covered in boot polish. I suppose vanity forbids that he says it. He's certainly frank about all the later pictures being commercial flops. That's the real truth I suppose: he worked profitably in superficial stuff but wanted to be in 'great artistic' pieces. Why? A sort of snobbery really & an inability to accept certain fundamental truths.

Tuesday, 6 August

Cab came at 6 o'c. & took me to Lime Grove for Breakfast TV. The subject was the bombing of Hiroshima etc. I talked of justifying its use & of the hatred which the Japanese had evoked over their cruelty & treachery (Pearl Harbour etc.) & they paraded Jap survivors who cried about their misfortunes. Frank Bough[18] said lots of people had telephoned to say I was right and several men came up to me saying 'Your arguments were sound!' Saw Louisa for a meal. She said she

---

17 The third part of his autobiography.

18 TV linkman, b.1933.

was enjoying the Dirk Bogarde book 'but it's not as good as Peter Nichols' . . . I s'pose that's 'cos I know him . . .'

Wednesday, 7 August
In the mail is the finished production of *Just Williams* which Peter Shellard has sent to me! Must say, it looks very good! As far as I can see, the corrections have been dealt with, but I expect there is something we've missed.

Thursday, 8 August
Rang Liz Newlands & said I'd discovered *more* mistakes in the book and she said it would be best to forget them. 'There's not much we can do about them now.' At 12 o'c. a great box of books was delivered from Victorama! A fourth (or a sixth?) of the thousand *Back Drops* I've ordered. Heaven knows how long they will take to shift.

Monday, 12 August
I was awake at 6 o'c. & thinking how in a life of nearly 60 years I have never really wanted for anything & never really had to work hard. Tried again with the Kipling book but it remains leaden stuff. Angus Wilson is a dull writer and that's a fact. Dull as ditchwater. If you want a lousy biography you send for Angus Wilson.

Tuesday, 13 August
To Liz Newlands to collect 10 copies of my biog: *Just Williams.* Would have stayed to talk but she had people to see. It suddenly hit me . . . what a delightful woman she is! Walked home with my two carrier bags laden . . . Oh! the weight of books!

Monday, 19 August
Boarded the Bristol train. No one to meet me, but I got a cab to BBC and paid my own way. The abridgements are awful! At first I was furious & then I thought 'Oh! what the hell? It's too late now to do anything about it.' Apart from certain rewrites I *had* to do 'cos the new version sometimes didn't make sense, I just made the best of a bad job.

Monday, 2 September
I had a rest before departing to LWT for Aspel's 'Child's Play'. They've asked me at such short notice I'm obviously a stand-by 'cos someone's fallen out. It started going horribly wrong for me from the start. I walked into the contestant room where they were gathered & started showing off & talking indiscreetly ('wank & a Mars bar' etc.) Then, on stage with audience I started more shouting & bawling & when I

asked Aspel 'When does this show start?' he said 'When you shut your mouth' which got a huge laugh & left me with egg all over the face. He has never been rude to me before. I thought he liked me. That shoved the ego round the ankles. I lost the game, couldn't even *understand* some of the questions. Left full of dudgeon at 8.50.

Thursday, 5 September
To Wardour St with Liz to do a tape interview about the book. Then to Vecchia for lunch. Then Jane Kelly interview for Mail on Sunday, then photographer in Welbeck St. The Kelly girl said 'The book is amusing, but it doesn't tell us anything about *you*' which is what loads of people said about *Backdrops*. I think she's talking rubbish of course: you can't write anything without saying something about yourself.

Wednesday, 11 September
Taxi to TV Centre where I recorded Episode IV of 'Galloping Galaxies'[19] for Jeremy: had to do the voice of my son in it! He is a small computer!

Friday, 13 September
Car came & took me to Shepherd's Bush for 'Wogan'. The driver (a young lad) said 'They get to be a bag of nerves on this show, no matter how much acting they've done, they get into a terrible state 'cos it's a chat show & anything can happen . . .' When we arrived I told Mark Giorgiou (researcher) and Roger Ordish about his dire predictions . . . laughingly I thought . . . then, on the journey back, he revealed that he'd been ticked off for talking like that to me! So it had all been reported! Which I never intended! Oh! infuriating. My stuff seemed to go all right with the house, but I thought it was all a bit vulgar for the box. At the conclusion I said 'I've blown the gaff on the Carry Ons . . . revealed the truth and told stories about what really went on . . .' & Wogan said 'Save it for next time . . . will you come back on the show?' & I said OK.

Sunday, 15 September
There's a feeling of impending doom, some ghastly nemesis awaiting me. Heaven knows I've lived life in the same fashion for years but just lately I seem to have come upon a period of yawning gaping boredom.

Monday, 16 September
Went out at 2 o'c. & got a Ruth Rendell[20] story, then walked home.

---

[19] By Bob Block. 'Sid's voice and son of Sid's voice' by KW.
[20] Crime novelist, b.1930.

A lorry driver called out 'Hello Ken!' & I waved. He smiled back at me. It was a delightful gesture on his part and made my day. At 4.40 I listened to the first part of my book on the radio. It held all right in spite of the appalling abridgment & I read it well.

Friday, 20 September

Leadenhall City Bookshop. The signing session went like a bomb! Loads of people & everything went swimmingly. Then tube to Knightsbridge. Signing in Harrod's. Rush from there in a taxi to Welbeck St for interview for magazine. Walked home from there by 5.15, thinking 'Why should anyone want to know about poor tired old me?' I honestly don't know.

Saturday, 21 September

To P[ost] O[ffice] with Charles Laurence play. Certainly there is no point in criticising it, since I'm not going to do it, but someone should tell him, you can't put on a play *today* which endlessly discusses promiscuous sex, without mentioning Aids. To Hatchard's in King's Road. I started signing straightway & did about 86 to 90 books. Quite a few G-plan people with embarrassing requests: 'Put something witty in it for me!' Saw a bit of TV but it was dire! That Russell Davies doing a tat Melvyn Bragg act.[21] Sounds like amateur recitals.

Saturday, 28 September

Signing session at Claude Gill. There was quite a crowd to greet me & all went well. Then came the nightmare! On the way to the tube, three young thugs recognised me & pursued us all the way on to the train & began a harangue about a mother dying of cancer: 'Please write a letter to her . . . she is dying.' I said 'We all are' & certainly felt it! Eventually they left, spitting at me. I thought the public transport idea was wrong from the beginning. I should have gone by car.

Tuesday, 1 October

Met Paul at 2 o'c. and went to the park. We were sitting in deck chairs when a voice said 'Hallo Kenneth!' and it was Lionel Bart! It seemed incredible that this sad, disillusioned pale invalid was the dynamic host of those Moroccan days. He admitted 'I got through millions of pounds in a few short years.' We walked home by 5 o'c. past an Irish boy working at the White House: 'I never dreamed I'd be talking to Kenneth Williams!' I said 'You'd better believe it honey!' & felt quite buoyant.

---

[21] Presenting the arts programme 'Saturday Review'.

Wednesday, 2 October

I met Bob G. & gave him lunch. He showed me a script he'd written for me. It is a good idea, but I don't want to do it 'cos the *acting* would all be hard work and I don't want any hard work. I saw him out of a sense of loyalty (I knew him years ago when I worked with John Law at TV Centre) & I wasn't altogether taken with his didactic nature . . . he was very disparaging about Swinburne & Tommy Steele. Extraordinary the way people attack talent.

Saturday, 5 October

We had some chicken. Then we saw the TV News and some documentary stuff. It was all pretty terrible. That Russell Davies was on with a load of intellectuals manqué who blethered on about some play about a drag queen:[22] it was all v. silly. One member of the panel said it was ironic that people should be invited to applaud the sort of phenomenon which resulted in Aids and that was the only sane & reasonable voice one heard. I see that no papers have reviewed my book, yet loads of others (including biog.) which were published *after* mine are in the critical columns. It happened before, with the other two. I think it's a desire to wound by ignoring one. Probably bound up with the literary prejudice about actors should stick to acting.

Sunday, 6 October

There was that ghastly Whicker basket interviewing Jim Dale in New York. Jim said all the reasonably tactful things about living abroad etc. The Basket said 'But after your success in *Barnum* you haven't had any role that is comparable, have you?' & J.D. said 'No, I don't suppose I ever will.' He looked as if he'd aged a bit & the figure has thickened out. The old boyish charm has gone. The Basket looked quite abstracted & seemed to be paying attention only to his own questions & not even listening to the replies. When the Carry On films were mentioned, J.D. said that he had learned a lot from the comedy talents assembled in them.

Monday, 7 October

The News was all about negroes rioting in Tottenham with petrol bombs, guns, murder & mayhem. A policeman was killed and many others injured. We had the usual line-up of Black apologists saying that these people were deprived and that this was a White Society which discriminates against them etc. etc. Oh dear. We've heard it all before. Now, if you're unemployed, your crimes are somehow excusable! On BBC2 there was a mass of crap put together by Glasgow

---

[22] *Torch Song Trilogy* by Harvey Fierstein.

University saying that our News was dominated by right wing propagandists. It didn't seem to realise that *it* was dominated by left wing anarchism.

Tuesday, 8 October

A taxi to Maggie. She was looking very good indeed, lovely hair style. She greeted me warmly & I took her to dinner at Wheeler's. She admitted she evaded the chat show when the play wanted publicity 'I just run away and hide! I think the TV advertisement signifies that no one is coming to see the show.' She talked about the appalling nature of the media 'It's an invasion of privacy' but of course M. enjoys gossip as much as the rest of us. M. said of Louisa '84!! my goodness that's marvellous! But of course she's only reached it through *you* . . .' which is exactly what Michael always says.

Wednesday, 9 October

Teddington for 'Whose Baby?'. Nanette [Newman] said 'We've been on these game shows, you & I, for years & years, haven't we?' I said 'Yes! & one day you'll come & say "Where is Kenneth?" & they'll say "He is dead" & you'll have to do it with someone else.' She quickly replied 'You don't look sixty to me' & was very sweet: she is a kind woman as well as a pretty one & it was a stupid thing for me to say. I am conscious all the time now of the imminence of Death.

Thursday, 10 October

The death of Yul Brynner was announced at 6 o'c. and on the 9 o'c. news they announced the death of Orson Welles!! Talk about the end of an era! I felt quite a pang about O.W. 'cos he was v. good to me & I always felt he was a presence, there in Paris. Surprised to learn that he died at 'his home in Hollywood' so he must have gone back, knowing it was final. Our business has lost some big figures this year.

Saturday, 12 October

C. came & we went to Roy's where he gave me dinner. C. said of the clientele 'Bit off-putting seeing such a gathering of clones' & I agreed. Society *needs* women because it wants the leavening only they can provide. There is something very unhealthy about the homosexual world: no wonder they arouse such antagonism.

Thursday, 17 October

9.10 to Sheffield. The dinner was at Cutlers' Hall & the first speaker was Merlyn Rees.[23] V. good. I was last. It went down like cold custard.

---

[23] b.1920. Home Secretary 1976–79.

We caught the 4 o'c. train back & I was indoors by 6.50. At the Sheffield do, one writer said she married a Persian & I said to another woman 'Wonder if she had a carpet?' She replied 'Should think she had kittens' which I thought was v. good for Sheffield.

Wednesday, 23 October

11 o'c. train to Newcastle. Went to the studios and did the interview with Nick (what a trick!) & it was OK but awfully scrappy. Liz Newlands handed me some proofs at the end of the journey and told me that the illustrations were fine but the dialogue was lousy. She asked me to write some verses to go with them. I said 'I don't think it is me . . .' and she said 'Well keep the pictures with you over the weekend & see if you think of something.'

Thursday, 24 October

Returned to the flat to write the verses for the children's book Liz Newlands gave me. I have done about half of it! Thought of some more verses when I was in bed, so got up & wrote them down & then went back again.

Tuesday, 29 October

Call from Vanessa (Editor at Dent of Children's Books) saying she liked the verses I'd written for the illustrated book, but that she was worried about the Underground one where the creatures didn't look like moles. I wrote an alternative & took it round to her at Dent at 2.15. She said she is going to issue a contract for me!![24]

Stanley gave me dinner at Peter Mario's. Simon Gray came in. Stanley told me of his fears about having to appear as himself at the Greenwood to introduce his TV showing & we designed a speech full of characters which he could perform. I told him 'I never thought I'd ever sit helping you to work out an after-dinner speech!'

Thursday, 31 October

Got up at about 7 o'c. For a moment I thought I was at home! Then I realised I was in the Station Hotel, Newcastle, with a lousy headache! And *no* paracetamol in the case!! Did a taped b'cast for local radio, then interview with reporter, then to bookshop for signing session (50 books). On the train Liz produced the verses for the book 'cos she wanted an extra one written, and after that, I rewrote the garden one & made an improvement.

---

[24] The book became *I Only Have to Close My Eyes*.

Friday, 1 November

To the studio for 'Wogan'. I went on after the Duchess of Argyll had primped thro' an interview of astounding banality. I did the Orson on vowels, Guinness on flies and Siobhan & the bishop & Edith Evans and basting. Seemed OK but I gabbled. Drinks after in a tiny room full of noisy sycophants. Went to bed full of recrimination – oh! the fact is (on these chat shows) that I've been eating at myself for years . . . just living off body fat . . . & people say 'All he does now is go on & tell those *old* stories we've all heard before with his usual lavatory gags and his camp blether . . .' Pathetic. And I'm increasingly conscious now of people not bothering to ring me any more! Gordon ain't been in touch for ages! I've seen him about once this year!

Saturday, 2 November

Woke with a dream fresh in my mind! A scene at the Jacksons' house with Rona being needling & I walked out! Gordon followed & said 'Look you must understand, it's a parting of the ways 'cos it is time we moved on . . .' & I said 'Thanks for everything . . . I'll never be able to repay the debt . . . goodbye . . .' & then I was with Joy Kaufmann who was saying 'It *had* to happen . . . they've outgrown your company.' Up at 7.30 and got papers at Warren St. I am feeling suicidally depressed.

Sunday, 3 November

We walked to Hart's. On the way, Louie suddenly gripped my arm & said 'I don't know what I'd do without you' & I was v. moved. So near to tears that I quickly turned the subject to other things. Apart from balance she is OK but the fear of vertigo means that she becomes tentative in movement & that invariably results in wobbling.

Wednesday, 6 November

Detective[25] Geoff Watts collected me & took me to Kentish Town Police Station for this lunch. Never dreamed I was going to *speak*!! But Geoff did the speech of invitation so I had to reply. I burbled on in a very desultory fashion. They were all v. nice to me but several reproved me for speaking in a rude way (apropos the odd 'fuck' & 'shit' etc.) I found them all curiously mundane, unimaginative people.

Thursday, 7 November

On the first game with Bernie, the team was me, Nanette and Gary Wilmot (dish) and after, it was me, Nanette & Henry Cooper. Henry told me that Peter Mario was finishing! I said 'It's the end of an era!'

---

[25] Actually Chief Inspector.

He said the Chinese wanted the whole street . . . but I think the restaurant has been going downhill for ages.

Friday, 8 November

I had to do more work on the Dent children's verses. It is turning into quite a chore. I cleaned up the scansion in several places & rewrote some of the verses. I really hope this is the end of it, 'cos there comes a point at which all the tinkering leads to a loss of any spontaneity.

Friday, 15 November

I had to do rewrites on the children's book for Dent! That Vanessa Hamilton keeps sending the stuff back for revision. Rang Liz Newlands & asked why. She said 'Well, some of the rhymes are a bit contrived.' I felt like saying piss off but just put receiver down on a curt goodbye.

Saturday, 23 November

10.18 to Portsmouth. A gang of youths started causing trouble on the train. Two of them got into our carriage & I asked 'Are you first class ticket holders?' When they said yes I asked to see the tickets & they left shouting rude remarks about 'fucking film stars', then they gathered with four others outside the carriage shouting rude remarks from the corridor into the window of our door. I got the Guard and, to my surprise, he put them all off the train at Havant! Then he told me 'This is why BR is stupid to get rid of guards on trains' and I totally concurred. Book signing at Theatre Royal foyer; then to Smith's to do more signing. I *must* remember to say no to all this ludicrous travelling round when Fontana start on me in '87! I must find the resolution to say No.

Sunday, 24 November

We saw that Walden[26] creature mouthing his platitudes to camera: it's like someone addressing the educationally subnormal. In the interview section he made his subjects sound like doorbells: 'Now, I'd like to press you on that' and 'Can I press you further' and 'I must press you again.' Oh dear, the man is an ass.

Tuesday, 26 November

Got the tube to Chalk Farm & walked to John Lahr. He showed me the Orton diary excerpts concerning me. I was appalled at the picture it paints of me! I sound like a foul-mouthed frustrated queer! I suppose it's authentic enough: certainly I used to move in circles which

---

[26] b.1932. Labour MP 1964–77, then TV interviewer.

encouraged that sort of thing . . . oh I have changed since then . . . it is years & years ago. John asked me to sign my agreement to the excerpts being made publishable & I did. Perceptive critics will seize on these mentions as being at variance with my account in the biog. Saw the start of Des O'Connor's show. He told everyone 'Go out and do something wild! Write *Widdle* on the wall! Tie the knockers on people's front doors to another one! Jump up & down naked in front of the bathroom mirror . . . you'll see something to make you smile.' This was greeted with gales of inane laughter. We turned to another channel. I telephoned John Lahr and asked if I could see the Orton pages again. 'No Kenneth, I can't let them out of my hands . . . it is against the law.' I said 'Well bring them in your hands to my flat then' and he agreed to do this tomorrow. I think I must ask for certain cuts to be made because the indiscretions could result in appalling publicity.

Wednesday, 27 November

John Lahr came and we went over the Orton letters and he excised the offensive stuff. He said 'Don't worry, I don't want to hurt you in any way' & said he'd let me see the amended typescript. I gave him the photographs of Joe in the Favier flat & pointed out it was the same apartment where Tennessee Williams wrote *Suddenly Last Summer*: he agreed it was an extraordinary coincidence. I went with M. to Vecchia. He gave me dinner. I mentioned I was stuck for a tag line to the story about stereos being put in coffins in Rio de Janeiro & he said 'They've got an awful lot of coffins in Brazil' which was perfect!!

Thursday, 28 November

Ever since I saw the Orton diary excerpts I've been cast down. They reveal an astonishingly unattractive picture of myself. I know that *if* I come to think it is an utterly truthful representation, I shall be *finished*. There was a disastrous element in Joe & it spilled over on to a lot of his acquaintances.

Sunday, 1 December

We watched the Royal Variety Show from Drury Lane. I never thought I'd live to see it! A good Command performance! It was a show with lots of good things, melody, rhythm, verve, talent, nostalgia . . . oh! terrific. Marvellous to see Alice Faye after all these years! & Elizabeth Welch! The highlights for me were: Gary Wilmot and Iris Williams, the former delightfully inventive & funny & Iris singing superbly with that incredible distinction & superb diction. Could have done with a little cutting . . . Norman Wisdom a bit too long. Ron Moody in excellent form & getting an immediate response from the house. One was left feeling that the world & the times one grew up with was a much better set-up than the present.

Monday, 2 December

Day clouded for me with the news of death of Philip Larkin: he was a lovely person. The wonderful poetry will live on but I suppose one must be glad that that his suffering, after the throat operation, is over. For me, '1914' and 'Whitsun Weddings' are among the loveliest things he's written.[27]

Monday, 9 December

Porter told me that Norman (in the ground floor flat) had died on Saturday. Apparently he'd suffered from Parkinson's disease. He was a sweet person & helped me when Louisa was ill & couldn't go to the post office . . . he used to countersign the Pension form. He wasn't very old . . . a bit over sixty, if that. Now his brother Joe will be left alone. When I first came here, they were brothers three, now there is one left. The barmy one who used to walk out in the nightdress has died. Lydia Pickering has moved away up Albany St., and Rose Taylor hardly goes out now . . . it won't be long before there will be more empty flats in this block.

Tuesday, 10 December

Cab to Festival Hall. Signed books in foyer, then went up to meet Charles Osborne. In the Waterloo Room, I walked on & introduced the proceedings & then brought him on. Peter Shellard turned up as well! I said 'That Conrad book[28] is lousy' again! & I don't know why the impulse to be rude is so strong . . . he said it would sell '2 or 3 thousand copies' & admitted it was more expensive to produce than mine (which will go to over 30 thousand copies.)

Thursday, 12 December

On BBC2 there was a superb jazz pianist illustrating the various keyboard styles . . . only marred by that fat slob Russell Davies who stood by the piano & made fatuous interruptions.[29] Told off Louisa for fidgeting during the programme & then felt awful after 'cos she fidgets when she's not interested in the TV and the programmes I enjoy generally bore her. I suggested at the end, 'Would you like a brandy?' and she assented, so that made up for it somewhat.

---

[27] In his own *Oxford Book of Twentieth Century Verse*, Larkin included 'The Whitsun Weddings' but not 'MCMXIV'.

[28] Probably *The Everyman History of English Literature* by Peter Conrad (Dent, 1985).

[29] 'The Honky Tonk Professor', featuring Dick Hyman at the piano.

Thursday, 19 December
To see Liz Newlands at Dent. I signed another lot of books. She gave me the Motley (*Dutch Republic*) and a 4th Reprint copy with more errors corrected. I also saw Vanessa who gave me proofs of my verses for the children's book.

Saturday, 21 December
We were reduced to watching *Carry On Camel* with me being remarkably good as the German Commandant and Jim Dale remarkably attractive as Beau. It was v. well written & actually had a tag line! Angela Douglas was super! Really attractive & effectively ironic. Oh! this girl has been endlessly underrated. It's weird how this country rewards the mediocre & ignores excellence. Alan Badel is a case in point (straight actor) & there are others in variety – Ken Dodd – who have to steer a lonely path.

Wednesday, 25 December
We had the duck for lunch & Louie made mince pies. Had a rest after, then we watched the Queen's Speech on TV.

Friday, 27 December
I've been aware all thro' this *holiday*!!! that I'm reaching some sort of crisis. A feeling of inadequacy and of coming to an end. Plus the fact that I'm endlessly with an old lady who is increasingly senile . . . there is screaming irritation . . . she sits smoking endlessly & the breathing is now an audible wheeze . . . the toothbrush is clogged with paste after *one* day . .. Oh! it is hopeless.

Sunday, 29 December
Quite a shock to realise that this volume will soon be finished!! All gone! Another year of desperation got through!

Tuesday, 31 December
Car came at 10.30 and took me to Shepherd's Bush for 'Wogan'. I went on about 11.30 and did the bit about speech making for Cadbury, Jeyes, Bloo Loo etc. Bone in throat, oysters aphrodisiac etc. Finished lamely & with little response from a bemused audience dressed in paper hats. The rest of the show was shapeless and ragged. At the end, we all stood with glasses of ginger ale (pretending it was champagne) and toasted the New Year. Only bright spot for me was talking to Julie Walters, my dear old chum David Jason and meeting Bob Lindsay. First time I've ever 'performed' on a Christmas New Year show.

1986

Wednesday, 1 January
Spent most of the day reading Motley. Saw Louisa at 5 o'c. Returned to the flat at about 9 o'c and enjoyed the traditional bath. I haven't been eating because I've had pains after all meals since Christmas.

Thursday, 2 January
I noticed awful pain behind the ribs – seemed the alimentary tract was afire. Went to chemist & got antacid tablets. By the time I'd reached Oxford Circus they hadn't worked & I went to the Regent Chemist who gave me some other stuff (another antacid) and returned home. The feeling is of a clamp under heart & there is sweating & incipient headache. I'd taken doses of Unigest, Asilone, Gaviscon and still the pain (now gone from breast to stomach) persisted, so I took K&M in desperation at 5.45.

Monday, 6 January
I went to Dr Clarke, told him of the events & he gave me some new medicine Tagamet. He said to try them for 2 days & if no improvement, he gave me letters for the gastroscopy etc. Hope it won't come to this.

Saturday, 11 January
To Devonshire Place to see Iain Murray-Lyon. He examined me. Said he didn't think there was any need for hospitalisation!! Sent me to Harley St for blood test, & is going to arrange Barium X-ray next week. Told me to eat bland mushy food & chew well. He is a v. likeable man. At 6 o'c. I took 2 paracetamol and Bisodol 'cos I don't want to do the show feeling lousy. Car came at 6.15 to take me to TV Centre for the 'Joan Rivers Show'. Saw Peter Cook & Dudley Moore in the make-up room. When P.C. was out of the way I told Dudley 'I find one always gets an *act* from Peter & therefore I'm obliged to act back, but there isn't the fundamental ease in the relationship which I used to know . . .' When I got on to do the interview it was all frenetic. I did the farting stories & some rubbish about being celibate. Still, it didn't actually die the death.

Tuesday, 14 January
Got taxi to the St John & E. Hospital. I had the Barium Meal X-ray. Went on till 11.45. Taxi back. By 10 o'c. there were no ill effects! & I went to bed.

Wednesday, 15 January
Pain kept nagging at me & I became so cast down that I made my way home again after an attempt to walk it off. By 9 o'c. the pain was acute and I became hot and the incipient headache came on. That plus agony in abdomen and heartburn meant I hardly knew what to do while watching the news.

Friday, 17 January
Dr Murray-Lyon phoned! I told him of my symptoms. He now suggests a Sound-wave test, & I've to collect a prescription from his secretary today. He admits it is very mysterious. At 3 o'c. like a time bomb just above navel pain started. That area suffused & when you touch it you can feel extraordinary *throbbing*.

Sunday, 19 January
M. came at 12.15. He took Louisa & me to Joe Allen and we had a v. good lunch. I had paté & bread & pickled cucumber & halibut & potato in jacket, and brownie cake & ice cream. I had red martini to begin & wine with meal. I had two Unigest tablets and on getting home I took Asilone. By 4.45 there was no attack!!

Monday, 20 January
I went to Harley St for this sonic scan. There were no stones in the abdomen. So that's another test for nothing. He said 'Your kidneys are a funny shape but you've probably been like that since birth.'

Wednesday, 22 January
Went to see Iain Murray-Lyon. He said there are several diverticula in the upper & smaller intestine. Most unusual. Said there are cysts on the kidneys & 'tho' they're nothing to do with your trouble I think you should see a specialist.' He gave me prescription for Tetracycline 'in case there's any infection.'

Saturday, 25 January
Car at 10 o'c. took me to TV-am. I felt marvellous. Chatted to everyone and did the David Frost spot with John Wells, OK, and had about 3 cups of coffee. What is it about today? I'm singing, running, joking . . . feeling like I haven't felt in weeks! If you said I was on a high with some drug, it wouldn't surprise me! Saw Rod Steiger at TV-am

& said 'Your line "That doesn't make me a bad person" in the film *No Way To Treat A Lady* was a comedy classic' & he told me 'I got that ad lib from a waiter in a restaurant; after I'd heard it, I asked him what was his favourite wine & when he told me I said "You've got it!"' By 10 o'c. aware that painful release was occurring in lower triangle & just above groin an enormous swelling . . . heaven knows what it all means.

Tuesday, 28 January

Went to Grant Williams who admitted the kidneys were not the trouble: 'but I think someone is going to have to open you up & look inside.' Came home with the inside a churning mess. Went to Murray-Lyon at 4 o'c, and he said he'd try & get me in to a hospital where they could do more tests. Told him how suicidally depressed this is making me.

Wednesday, 29 January

At 11 o'c. Murray-Lyon's secretary rang & said I was to go into Charing X Hospital at 2 o'c. Went in to see Louie – played the hospital down. 'I'll only be away a few days.' Told M.A. & M.W. and got a cab to hospital.

Thursday, 30 January

Nothing to eat or drink this morning. At 10 o'c. they wheeled me down to Floor 1 for this Gastroscopy. They said I was sedated but I was conscious throughout. Got a cup of tea at 12.15. A doctor called & said 'You've got a big ulcer there . . . it is smoking that causes it . . .' Must've dropped off for a bit. At about 3.30 they wheeled me down to ground floor for the scan. Needle in my arm & dye put in there, the nausea rises in the throat. Then an endless series of orders 'Breathe in, hold it, breathe out' etc. etc. ad infinitum ad nauseam. Then wheeled back up to 15th floor. Idiot porters asking questions 'What's your next job, Ken?' & 'What about another Carry On?' One finds a face to meet the face. A Doctor Chen called. 'Are you feeling OK?' & I said yes. I told him 'I've got an ulcer' as if I'd struck oil & he said 'I know. The medicine will reduce the amount of gas produced in the stomach & the body [will be] kept stable, so the discomfort can end.'

Friday, 31 January

Mr Reynolds came. He said the ulcer would be treated medicinally & that if it didn't respond 'You'll have to see me again & it'll be an arsehole to b'fast time & no laughing after I can tell you.' But he said he thought they'd let me go home soon! M.W. came at 3.30 & took me out of this Hell Hole & I was home by 4 o'c. & spirits sank when

I found Louisa still beset with backache! Oh! nothing is easy in this life . . . they design it *difficultly*.

Saturday, 1 February

Took Louisa to Dr Johnson. He did some manipulation & was wonderfully encouraging & helpful. Louie threw up at osteopathy & again at home: stomach upset. She's shifting all the while in pain, endlessly coughing, endlessly sniffing, endlessly breathing loud sighs. One feels 'For heaven's sake shut up!' 'cos one's own pain starts to drive one mad! We saw a bit of a programme on Sondheim. Everything he wrote sounds like the middle eight of a song. Came back to flat & there was traditional activity. Superbly realised.

Sunday, 2 February

Looked in on Louisa. She was sleeping. Woke her & gave her some chicken soup but she hardly touched it. Went round to Surgery & put a letter in their box saying someone must come to see her. Cleared up in her flat & saw she was in bed OK. I could hear her saying prayers. I called on Paul upstairs. Came down. Looked in on Lou. She was saying to herself in bed 'Go there on Friday . . . that's what you must do . . .' This rambling incoherence indicates her stress.

Monday, 3 February

I was resting when a floral delivery man brought flowers from Rona & Gordon & I had to let the man in. Ah well! people *mean* well. Dr Pickard came at 3.50. She said Louie was fundamentally OK but she'd damaged the sciatic nerve & would have to rest. I think she's been unsettled in her mind. She told Doctor she fell in the street after getting off a bus, she told Ann she fell getting out of bed & she told me she failed to grasp the headboard. I think it's all fundamentally anxiety about *me*. When I'm away & she hasn't a settled routine, she goes haywire.

Wednesday, 5 February

Had to open the door for more bloody flower deliveries! It was the fireman from the theatre where I did *Undertaking*!! He was nice. Pat sent the flowers.

Thursday, 6 February

Out to Baldwin's to get electric heater 'cos my kitchen is freezing. I am wearing pyjamas under trousers for insulation! Became aware that I've strained my back!! I vaguely remember feeling it when I turned Louie's mattress and remade the bed on Tuesday! Oh dear I'm so sick of everything . . . my illness, Louie's illness, filthy weather . . . approaching Death *forever* beckoning & flirting with me.

Friday, 7 February
Went in to see Louie at about 9 o'c. & found chaos! She couldn't get to loo in time. Had to strip bed & clean sheets etc. etc. Went to post and then to Smee [accountants]. Got home about 1.30 to find chaos again. For a second time, she couldn't get to the loo! So, I started washing and carpet cleaning etc. all *over again*. She was bleating 'I'm so sorry, but I couldn't get there in time' & I stayed polite, but I was inwardly furious. I ran a bath and got her into it. All movement is agony for her, so she was brave & I washed her legs etc. She has a fearful bruise on the bum where she fell. At quarter to four I had bread & butter & marmalade. The porter told me Rose Taylor died last night! 'I found her this morning.' She was a dear sweet woman!

Sunday, 9 February
Car came & I got to Teddington in 30 minutes. For the *first time in my life I really needed make-up*! On the run thro' (without it) I looked like death on the monitor! It was with Richard Baker & Sally Ann Howes. I'm not 60 till the 22 Feb. but I looked about 70 today! A prune-like face on a decrepit frame.

Wednesday, 12 February
I got abdominal, right, pain at 4.30. Took Sucralfate & Zantac. Ate at about 5.30 & the pain lingered . . . this course doesn't seem to be working . . . & I so wanted to avoid an operation!

Sunday, 16 February
M. came & I gave him lunch at Joe Allen. This place is full of Kangas:[1] never known a Sunday joint like it! They're all over the place with their offspring as well. Wrote a verse about dying . . . it has been in my mind for a day or two . . . says what I feel about ending it.

Give me a hand
On the way to death
The hand of a friend
Not a love
Gentle and light

---

[1] Rhyming slang: kangaroo = Jew. Contrast this usage with the sentiments of 13 April, p. 742.

As that long last breath
A comforting hand
Not a shove

Monday, 17 February

Suddenly realised: I'm doing all the things I dreaded . . . looking after someone who is losing ability to do anything for herself. Everything gets dafter and dafter 'What day is it?' 'What time is it?' When newspapers and clocks are touchable . . . it's driving me barmy too. I got so preoccupied I forgot my own medicine!

Friday, 21 February

Went in to Lou at 9.30. Found her on the floor!! Both legs cut & bleeding! She was shivering! She had the deaf-aid on & blaring! Cleaned the wounds, applied bandages, got her back to bed. Rang Pat & rushed to St Anne's Court for this v/o with Miriam Margolyes for B. Telecom. We were a couple of pigs. Rushed back. Pat had made tea for Lou. Of course it wasn't drunk. We talked about the hopeless nature of it all. Wrote a letter to Dr Pickard and took it to Surgery saying I couldn't cope any more & Louie should be in hospital. Went to Dent & Peter & Liz took me to Vecchia for lunch. My mind was elsewhere. Walked home full of trepidation about what I'd find . . . went in to Lou and she was still asleep. Went round to Doctor again, with a letter. Returned home. Rang Bloomsbury Health Authority asking *how* do I get someone to do something about Louie. They told me to get hold of U[niversity] C[ollege] H[ospital] so I rang & a secretary answered & then the doorbell rang! & it was Dr Pickard!! She said 'I think it was wrong of you to suggest that your mother hadn't received proper attention . . .' so I had to apologise. She examined Lou & then rang 999 and by 4.50 an ambulance came & took Lou. Lou asked 'Where are my teeth?' but I couldn't find them anywhere. Quickly changed into a suit and left for LWT to do the '6 o'c. Show' with Mike Aspel, Danny, & Gary Wilmot. It went OK. Home by 7.10. Got things for Lou (found her denture under the bed) and walked to U.C.H. She was in a casualty cubicle. A Sister Hammond told me she would spend some time in hospital to be assessed.

Saturday, 22 February

The bathroom was so cold I got extension lead & put fan heater on in there so I could undress! Loads of bloody birthday cards! Went to U.C.H. Louie in the Geriatric Ward 4/4. Pat was there. We saw a Dr Ibrahim (from Iraq). He said Lou had a bowel obstruction. I told him I'd have to talk to the Welfare Social Worker about getting Lou into

Nursing Home. 'That's if she agrees,' he said. 'I'll make her agree,' I said & P. agreed.

Sunday, 23 February

Thro' the bitterly cold streets to U.C.H. Louie lying there looking drained & tired. I kept on about finding a Nursing Home for her when they send her out of hospital. The opposition wasn't as fierce as I'd anticipated. When I said 'There are some homes where they let you take a piece of furniture you like,' she replied 'Sod the furniture . . . if the room was all right I wouldn't want my own furniture . . .' I can't see any answer *except* nursing care in the future, 'cos even without the back pain, Louie can't safely get about. Spent evening alone.

Wednesday, 26 February

Stanley rang!! 'Come out to dinner with me tonight.' I could have cried in gratitude. Stanley came with a bottle of champagne, and gave me dinner at Vecchia. I told him: 'In moments of crisis for me, you always turn up trumps!' It was a joy to see him. He said the panto had gone well but that it was hard work.

Thursday, 27 February

I went to see Kathleen in the Social Department. She's going to make enquiries about homes that would take Louie but there's a waiting list etc. etc. Sounds like Lou will come back to her flat. Yesterday Stanley said 'You can write another book' & I said 'I'm not a writer' & he replied 'Did it make money? The last one?' 'Yes.' 'Then you're a writer!' He did not say I *could* write, which is what I would have liked to hear. Oh! I suppose we all say the wrong thing when we least suspect it.

Friday, 28 February

One day I think it's fine & I'm on the mend & then, next day, I'm plunged back in the same bloody fearful state. And there is the knowledge that soon I'm going to be back in the old prisoner/jailer relationship which is going to totter into eternity. O! it is bloody horrible to contemplate.

Saturday, 1 March

There was a letter in the ward for me from the Social Worker. It says that there is a vacancy in one of the Hampstead O.P. Homes Housing Trust at about £150 a week. Talked to Louie about it & she was perfectly amenable 'Just want to get the whole thing *settled* . . . know where I am . . . it is so *boring* in here . . . I just lie in bed counting the lights on the ceiling . . .' So she is agreeable . . . but there is the nagging doubt in my own mind . . . How would I feel myself? In her position? Would I want to lose the ability to do what I like when I like? But then, what quality of life does she have now? She's more or less confined to the flat. Oh I don't know . . . there are so many imponderables. I'm miserable & cast down. The terrible truth is: no matter how tiresome & troublesome she is Louie is a part of me, and a part which I *need*. Came home thro' cold streets crying all the way. The tears of a failed & a lonely old man.

Monday, 3 March
Saw Dr Francis. He said that Louie wasn't bad enough for a home yet: 'She's v. bright & enjoys getting round on her own' & thought if she could return to her flat it would be better for her. Lou was looking fair, but the foot is up on a stool 'cos of fluid & swelling. Dr Francis said he was treating Louisa for Thyroid deficiency.

Wednesday, 5 March
Went to U.C.H. at 10.30 and got Louisa out of there. Never so glad to see the last of a hospital! Louisa told me 'Oh! I'm so glad to be back in my own flat again!' We had ham salad for lunch with the vintage champagne from Stanley. Wrote a note of thanks to him.

Thursday, 6 March
Since she's been home again, her delight in her old surroundings has been obvious & I'm glad I stuck to my own convictions about coping! This is where she belongs & if my own life becomes circumscribed in the process, so be it. I don't want Lou in one of these institutional places – no matter how nicely they're arranged, there is a continual reminder of decay, and the notion of 'putting the old away . . . out of sight out of mind . . .' is fundamentally wrong.

Tuesday, 18 March
We queued for Lou's pension. With her, everything is so *slow* it is maddening & of course she said she'd signed but she hadn't, so that held things up even more. I was barely civil by the time we got back. She let go a fart in the P.O. which made those in the queue behind us wilt visibly. Went to Equity Council Meeting at 10.15.

Wednesday, 19 March
The announcement of the engagement twixt Prince Andrew and Sarah Ferguson took up most of the News with endless interviews & pictures. She looks like one of those Roedean girls with an inferiority complex and heavily capped teeth & the conversation with both of 'em was unbelievably banal. Curiously they neither have what Charles

& Diana had (at this stage). There is no aura. They look like any couple of Chelsea yobs who belong to that Hooray Henry set.

Thursday, 20 March
Looked at the 1966 journal and was amazed how the situation was more or less exactly the same as today! The endless staring in the streets, star status but no star money, nowhere decent (or *quiet*!) to live, the same family problems . . . altogether I suppose it's always been a mess of a life.

Friday, 21 March
Played the Grieg songs sung by Flagstad: they never lose their appeal for me . . . must've bought them in '56! The recording still plays well.

Saturday, 22 March
Saw Dr Murray-Lyon. He did the Gastroscopy. He said the ulcer was receding!!! He will see me next week to decide on the new medicine to take. Great Relief I must say!

Monday, 24 March
Haircut at 3.15. Nick cut it short 'cos it's easier that way. When he asked if I was working I said no & he replied 'Well of course, so many of your friends are dead now aren't they?' Which was tactless but true. Louie wanted to see me in the 'Joan Rivers Show'. I was last on and phew! it looked *old*!! Every bit of sixty! Prune like and saggy. But urbane and rather grand. V. aesthetic.

Tuesday, 25 March
Went in to Lou and found she'd been to the P.O. for pension on her own! 'I had my stick and I took my time. I was all right.' I was amazed!

Wednesday, 26 March
Went to John Wood to do v/o for Fiesta Towels. It was voice to picture, which I hate and I fear that they weren't pleased with the result. Heigh ho. I met Robert Morley on the way & he was v. affectionate but trod on my nicely polished shoes which didn't please me. 'Dallas' gets barmier and barmier: you're asked to believe that Oil Tycoons do business walking about piazzas eating ice cream.

Monday, 31 March
M. came over and drove Lou & me to his flat in Chelsea. M.'s sister came with her sons & husband. They're an extraordinarily prudish family. When I mentioned a man farting in M&S they all looked

shocked, reddened & became mute. It was ludicrous. In the next breath, they asked me to sing Rambling Syd songs!!

Tuesday, 1 April
Phoned by Peter Estall.[2] 'Would you do the "Wogan" show on 21, 23, 25 April?' & I said yes.

Wednesday, 2 April
Peter Estall phoned 'Would you be a guest on "Wogan" on the 11 April?' & I said yes.

Thursday, 10 April
Car took me to the TV Centre. In the foyer I met Ernie Wise. We were joined by Peter Estall. After we'd said goodbye to E. Peter asked 'Why didn't you ask him on the show?' & I said 'It's a bit old hat' little thinking it was a perfect description of *me*. It was all very constructive. They said there was a chance of getting Frank Bruno.[3] Good. I said I'd like someone who worked down the sewers. I ran thro' my opening preamble . . . they seemed amused . . . but the hypnosis song didn't get laughs. Heigh Ho. I'm still going to do it. We roughed out the spot with Terry – I have to appear at the beginning & chat at a whelk stall . . .

Saturday, 12 April
Paul said 'You were good last night on TV' and in Hart's shop, two women told me 'You were smashing on TV last night!' So perhaps I'm enjoying a vogue.

Sunday, 13 April
We went to Royal Garden Hotel for the Book Fair to raise funds for a University in the Negev Desert. All the people were friendly and the number of truly beautiful children was astonishing. No wonder Israel is full of dishes.

Monday, 14 April
Saw Sue Lawley starting off her stint on 'Wogan' & she got in a good joke (wearing a striped dress) about looking like a zebra crossing but when she went on to interview an old fart from 'The Archers' it sank to zero.

---

[2] Producer. Transferred from radio where he had produced 'Start the Week'.
[3] Franklin Bruno, b.1961. Heavyweight boxer and pantomime artiste.

Tuesday, 15 April
To TV Centre. Peter Estall met me in foyer with a list of guests for the dummy run on Thurs. Nicholas Parsons is on it!! One wonders: does he know it's a dummy run? It all seems v. cavalier I must say.

Thursday, 17 April
Eventually did the run before about 20 people. Waste of time all round.

Monday, 21 April
Did more writing for tonight's show. O dear! I'm 60 & still trying to be funny! Did run through. Then did the show. The preamble went fair – not fab, but OK, then the bit with Derek Nimmo, fair, then the song Elaine Paige:[4] Dreary, then the bit with Janet Brown,[5] v. good, then the limericks . . . OK, then Norman Parkinson.[6] Ramble . . . Quick out. Everyone said it was OK after, but there was the feeling of something that hadn't quite come off.

Wednesday, 23 April
Car at 2.30. When I got there they said that one of the guests had dropped out!! Could I write more material to fill in!!! Car back to flat . . . collected old scripts . . . back to theatre to write it all out . . . I've never worked in such confusion.!! Barbara Windsor went OK, Stephen Fry OK, the music group OK, then the spot with Michael Palin. We started OK & the thing went fine till I bade him Goodnight too early and then asked him to fill in with more limericks. Had to say goodbye again to him, & go centre for closing speech. The FM signalled *Hang it out* . . . got thro' it somehow & people said it was OK but I was conscious that I'd messed up the Palin 'spot' and that started the rot.

Thursday, 24 April
It will take me today to get over last night: extraordinary how much I *care* about doing a job properly! One voice says 'Forget it! It doesn't matter that much' & another voice says 'Oh yes it does! Don't erode standards!' Peter Estall came at 8 with research stuff: 'The sewer men are proving difficult . . .' I said 'Oh well, drop them & get someone else . . .' Always the same with these shy performers: we'd do better with an actor in waders.

---

[4] Actress and singer from 1968.
[5] Impressionist (especially, at the time, of Mrs Thatcher) and widow of Peter Butterworth.
[6] 1913–90. Photographer.

Friday, 25 April
The show was fair. My opening went fair. Nick Parsons interview OK, then Bertice Reading, fine, then music, then Fay Masterson and then Denise Coffey (very good on sewers) then Rambling Syd (apropos 'Wogan' take-over) the audience singing Bring Back Bring Back etc. & finished with me congratulating them. Everyone seemed pleased.

Sunday, 27 April
Peter Estall rang & said I'd done well on the Wogan show. 'Is there any book you'd like?' I said yes, the new biog. of Rilke.[7]

Wednesday, 30 April
Dinner at the Tent, but tho' the meal was good, I fear Lou was suffering from back pain too much to really enjoy it. Significantly, there's been oblique talk of suicide: 'I read in the paper that people who are in pain should be allowed to go quietly . . . with a few pills . . .'

Tuesday, 6 May
TV-am for the Jimmy Greaves[8] programme. It was me & Anne Shelton waxing lyrical about the 50's . . . hogwash. Saw Barbara & her husband. Dish.

Wednesday, 7 May
Stanley came & we went to Il Barbino where I gave him dinner. There was a gauche young German waiter & Stanley foolishly asked him how long he'd been working in London & then there was a torrent of garrulity which quite floored him. His is a v. low boredom threshold & when the boy was ranting on about 'Mother is in Switzerland, brother in New York, Grandma in Germany,' Stanley muttered 'Dad's in the Elephant & Castle . . .' He asked me about the flats & I said the lease will be finished when I'm 74 and he said 'Yes, well we'll be finished by then I hope! Nobody wants to go on *that* long' & I agreed fervently.

Monday, 12 May
Went to meet Eva & Bob (Block)[9] at the Westbury and they were v. sweet. Eva says she met Bob and they talked about comedians, 'found we had you in common and we got married.' Age has been kind to both of them & they were charming. It is years since I met them, during *Pieces of Eight* (59/60) and I wrote in the biog. for them.

---

[7] *A Ringing Glass: The Life of Rainer Maria Rilke* by Donald Prater (Oxford).
[8] b.1940. International footballer and TV entertainer.
[9] Comedy scriptwriter.

Tuesday, 20 May

A woman has written from Calgary, Alberta: 'Tho' you call yourself Kenneth Williams now, I know you are the John Redford I used to know . . .' I've sent a copy of my book & a note saying 'I've had this name since birth & will certainly have it when I die.' Postage was over 2 pounds.

Friday, 23 May

Went to Dr Dow at Harley St. The barium was injected & the X-rays taken. It was agony and seemed to go on & on. Eventually he showed me negatives & said they depicted a spastic colon. He said 'One can't see any reason for it, but it would give you pain, but Murray-Lyon will know what to do . . . he's very good you know . . .' Came away with enormous feeling of relief. Took Lou to Vecchia. Her back was painful & she said 'If this is to go on all the time, then I wish I was out of it altogether.' I told her 'I shan't be sorry to go at any time: it's never been a joyful place to me . . . always a place of suffering . . . we have become a couple of old crocks . . .'

Sunday, 25 May

In the paper, Francis King reviews the Coward biog.[10] & there is the usual crap about 'this unhappy man.' It's as though a zoologist was to write 'This was a monkey who *liked nuts* . . .'

Thursday, 29 May

To Murray-Lyon & he said it was a spastic colon 'like having the cramp in your leg.' He also said that I shouldn't be having the worry of Louisa but you can't explain to a relative stranger the peculiar bond that binds us.

Tuesday, 10 June

Saw Murray-Lyon. He suggested starting a new treatment with Libraxin & seeing how that turned out. I pointed out the swelling by the navel but he wasn't perturbed by it 'You've put on a bit of weight . . . that looks like fat tissue to me . . .' Whatever it is I'm suffering from, my moods are up & down like a yo-yo. Sometimes I feel that none of it matters & on other occasions I just want to die. But *quietly*.

---

[10] Francis King, novelist and critic, b.1923. The book reviewed was Coward's *Autobiography*, consisting of *Present Indicative, Future Indefinite* and *Past Conditional*. King wrote: 'Lacking any inner life and pursuing an outer life extraordinarily narrow in its range, Coward regarded worldly success as the final criterion of merit' (*Sunday Times*, 25 May 1986).

Wednesday, 11 June
Reading J.S. Mill:[11] he's the first man I've read to make the point that religion actually asks man to halt his intellectual inquiries. It seems to question the very ability to think, let alone form moral judgments. What are we to make of divine injunctions in the bible to slaughter people? It is a weird mess, Christianity, & it is even weirder that it *worked* after a fashion for a time! Of course it's now as creaky as Byzantium before the onslaught of Mehmet.

Friday, 13 June
Peter Estall rang: 'Will you come on the "Wogan" show and be interviewed by Anna Ford[12] who is standing in for Wogan on Monday?' I said yes. Peter Estall is the only one who's offered me work this year! Apart from dear loyal Jeremy.

Monday, 16 June
'Wogan' hosted by Anna Ford. I was on first. Talk a lot of blether, but mentioned the book. Got away early, but No! the bloody fans were waiting in that alley. Oh! they're such a pain in the arse. Refused to sign etc. & drove away quickly.

Sunday, 22 June
The Eliot biog. is a continually intriguing book. Don't think I've ever come upon such an absorbing affair! I've written to Peter Ackroyd congratulating him on such a superb piece of detective work and literary analysis. It is years since I had dinner with him in Chelsea all those years ago!

Sunday, 29 June
M. took Lou & me to Tent for lunch. Whether it was 'cos she hadn't slept properly or what, Lou got v. aggressive & loud 'That Jean has never written to me! People think they can treat me like dirt! Well I'm not bothered about any of 'em! As long as my Ken is next door I don't care what happens!' And a lot more in that defiant vein of inferiority.

Tuesday, 1 July
M.A. rang: 'The "Joan Rivers Show" want to know if you'd go to America . . .' I said no.

---

[11] Philosopher and reformer, 1806–73.
[12] Television journalist and newscaster, b.1943.

Sunday, 6 July
M. drove us round the City & we saw the new development proceeding at Broad Street and the hideous new building Rogers[13] has designed for Lloyd's. Looks like a gasworks or a chemical plant: a revolting sight.

Monday, 14 July
Car at 6.15 to Lime Grove to talk about the Children's Book: I had to read bits of it while the camera dwelled on the pictures. I was interviewed by Selina Scott. Car took me to John Lahr & he showed me the proofs of the Orton diaries. The whole idea of this book is unpleasant to me: suggesting a regurgitation without any real enlightenment. It is so full of prurient details & so pointless.

Monday, 21 July
Went to B.H. to do 'Start The Week' with Richard Baker. Car came & took me to Covent Garden where I found Joan Rivers. Did the interview and then the girl and I walked round trying to find the car but we failed, so I walked home. At 3.45 taxi came & took me to TV Centre where, with Jeremy, I did the v/o for 'Galloping Galaxies'. Reflected that it is a weird life! I'm either doing nothing or I'm suddenly (like today) plunged into 3 jobs at once! And for what? Nothing. Joan Rivers' producer went on & on at me to go to America on her show. 'Come on Concorde . . . it's only 2 hours' and 'You've got a big following in the States . . .' I said I'd got a spastic colon. He said 'You should worry! I've had a heart by-pass operation.'

Wednesday, 23 July
While doing the crossword I suddenly felt so unutterably depressed & suicidal it practically stopped me in my tracks. We had lunch & saw the Wedding. The bride fluffed her husband's name, Andrew Albert Charles Edward, after telling us on TV last night 'I shan't fluff because after Andrew it's "ACE" so I'll remember.' Well, she didn't.

Sunday, 27 July
Amazing that every year I return to reading about religion, in some form or another. The point Erich Heller makes about the inherent contradiction in Christianity is echoed by Passmore in *Perfectibility of Man.*[14] Heller begins with Jesus–v.–Pharisees & overruling their laws whereas Passmore begins with the Sermon on the Mount 'Be ye perfect as your Father in heaven is perfect' – an impossible command

---

[13] Italian-born architect, b.1933.
[14] By John Passmore (1970).

which apologists have been trying to interpret ever since. The trouble with all faith is when it becomes institutionalised & there seems to be no way round that, unless one accepts the flux and the endless succession of revolutionaries . . . be they Jesus or Luther . . . ironically they both talk about eternal & unchanging values.

Wednesday, 30 July
Reading Iris Murdoch's book *Black Prince* is an irritating experience: for any entertainment to succeed we must find it credible, or its incredibility possible. Here, the ground is continually cut away under our feet, with various versions of the story . . . there are several authors at work apparently . . . eventually one cares nothing for any of them. None are real, it's all curiously Shavian, the ideas flood in & the people disappear. Some of the scurrilousness reminded me of [Anthony] Burgess – a lot of her writing reminds me of him.

Monday, 4 August
Did 'Galloping Galaxies' for Jeremy Swan. Quite a shock to look at the engagement list & see that, after the next two of these, I've got no work at all!! Of course I know the future has looked just as bleak in the past, but it certainly ain't cheery.

Thursday, 14 August
Saw Lou going to bus stop leaning on her stick . . . she now walks so *slowly*! Oh! my heart goes out to her! I know she's got that back pain all the time but she *tries* to overcome the depression, oh how she *tries*.

Saturday, 16 August
Read the rest of the Berryman biog.[15] Towards the end, he obviously mellowed & every now & again one finds oneself warming to him & then Bang! he does something so inordinately selfish & crass that one feels revulsion. In the end, he jumped off a bridge & killed himself: seems an odd way to go for someone who all his life had taken drugs of all kinds . . . certainly he had enough knowledge of toxics to have chosen something tidier than this. One searches his work for something poetic . . . something lyrical . . . but it is mostly confessional prose.

Sunday, 24 August
The News was about yet another lot of Africans starving . . . Oh dear! we're getting this till it's coming out of our ears. Not once do these news agencies speak about the incompetent & corrupt governments

---

[15] *The Life of John Berryman* by John Haffenden (1982).

which allow their people to go without food . . . it's all presented as something tragic and inevitable with undertones of reproach for the West. I don't have to give to charity 'cos with the amount of Tax I'm paying I'm paying well over the nose!

Wednesday, 27 August

We saw 'Dallas' and the news . . . more killing of blacks in Soweto . . . these people seem intent on destroying what little they've got! They must be the most mentally retarded outside Friern Barnet.

Wednesday, 3 September

Ted Moult has taken his own life. He was 60. I should think he was suffering from something very serious to have been driven to this.[16] He was a dear, good, affectionate man & on the few occasions I talked with him, I found his amiability charming.

Wednesday, 10 September

Saw Moore & mentioned that fat woman who's moved into the empty flat. I saw her putting stickers up on the telephone kiosk. He said 'I'm going to find out from the agents who she is!' I said 'What are those stickers about?' & he said 'They give a number to ring for Massage!! I think she's on the game!'

Tuesday, 16 September

We saw a programme commemorating Tommy Cooper and some of his stuff was very funny indeed but the 'tributes' from friends were mostly embarrassing, apart from Mike Yarwood who told a delightful anecdote about a florin being lost on a pub counter & Tommy saying 'It's not the principle, Mike . . . it's the money.'

Friday, 3 October

We saw the removal men taking all the stuff for the tart in that flat who was moving out! Lou said 'Heaven knows who we will get next!' She took a lot of stuff with her, including mirrors.

Thursday, 9 October

Car for LWT. Did the critic spot with Joanna Munroe & it went off OK. Patrick Lichfield was on it: he is a charming man & told us ruefully about losing two teeth in a boxing match where he (Guards officer) was fighting an Army cook with the crowd baying for his defeat & crying out to the cook 'Mash him like your potatoes!' There was an

---

[16] According to obituaries, the amiable Moult had been seized by an unaccountable depressive panic over his career.

Irish comedian Frank Carson who told a story 'This man bought a bullet-proof vest 'cos of all the troubles in Northern Ireland, then he went out & got shot up the arse.' It hardly seemed appropriate for a show called 'Sunday Sunday'. Perhaps they'll cut it.

Friday, 17 October
Lou upset 'Ann Lowe phoned & said Charlie Trigger had died.' All her chums are steadily disappearing. Then to Donor Centre to give blood. I was v. loud & aggressive & kept saying it was high time I was excused this 'agonising process' but at least they've devised a new method of sampling from the finger so there was no pain.

Monday, 27 October
Went to B.H. to do 'Start The Week', producer Victor Lewis-Smith. They had Dave Allen on & the interviewer with him went on & on & on and I was amazed that Richard Baker didn't cut it down. I eventually talked to John Lahr about the Orton Diaries and we got in some reasonable stuff. John Lahr gave me a signed copy after with a sweet message! He really is a kind person.

Thursday, 30 October
Gyles Brandreth writes about the 4 boxes of books which he's been keeping for me & can't any longer. I don't know where they can go! Gyles sent taxi with boxes! Tom (porter) helped me put them in the front room. Now I'm lumbered with five of 'em. I covered the boxes with white paper. Looks like a huge fridge stuck in the lounge!

Saturday, 1 November
We saw a programme celebration: 50 years of BBC TV. I actually appeared in a clip from Hancock!! The Alpine Yodelling Competition! That was all you saw of me. What was interesting was the sheer quality of the performers! Miles better than anything about today.

Tuesday, 4 November
Read some of the Heller essays *In The Age of Prose*: he must be the only writer to whom I continually return.

Thursday, 6 November
Met Nick Hern (Methuen) and John Lahr & we got train to Cambridge where we were shown into a hall belonging to the Catholic Chaplaincy[17] which smelled of incense. Here, before a sparse audience we rambled on about the Orton Diaries using (perforce) language and

---

[17] Fisher Hall.

gestures which were horribly inappropriate in such surroundings. It was bizarre. Very Ortonesque! Nick Hern said 'The difficulty is presenting a book without an author . . . it's like a wedding without the bridegroom.' I thought it was more like a burial without the body.

Friday, 7 November
Les Dawson in 'Blankety Blank' is amazingly flamboyant with despair. You can see how he is driven to the desperate gestures & dialogue! He's like a tightrope walker . . . & always retrieves himself even when you think the teetering will end in a fall: it doesn't. To Jan Leeming[18] he said 'You're looking lovely . . . I'll pop round tonight if you've got nothing on.' When she grinned he said 'What a smile! . . . it is like a delta!'

Monday, 10 November
There is drilling from Gas people at White House & the porter is busy sawing & hammering . . . everything Eden-like. Telephoned Michael and he told me the Doctor says he's got shingles.

Wednesday, 12 November
With Paul to the shops. We looked at a revamped Woolworth's in Edgware Rd., terrible: and at a new BHS in Oxford St., terrible: & at Debenham's, terrible. They're all going in for the jumble-bazaar look. No straight lines, everything twisting & turning so the customer is made to look at things he wouldn't ordinarily bother with. It is all the result of design-marketmen and it *stinks*.

Thursday, 13 November
Feeling suicidally depressed. More & more I am glad I've got my supply of pills to finish it all off when the crunch comes. Don't think it is *that* far away.

Sunday, 16 November
Got the papers. Out of sheer nerves I started chattering to Adonis about Enid Bagnold[19] & 'loyalty died with Queen Victoria.' He looked bemused & obviously didn't know what I was talking about. Michael came & took us to Joe Allen. I had to put my cap on Lou's head when we left 'cos the rain was coming down as we walked to M.'s car.

Wednesday, 19 November
Train to Leeds. The show 'Thro' The Keyhole' started at 7 o'c. You're

---

[18] Newscaster and presenter, b.1942.
[19] 1889–1981 (Lady Jones). Novelist and dramatist.

shown house interiors & have to guess the occupants. One was Spike Milligan (with mask of P.M. in his house!) & I asked 'What was Mrs Thatcher doing in your cellar?' & he said 'Getting pissed I suppose.' Whereupon the audience roared with laughter.

Friday, 21 November

I sometimes think I'm going mad sitting with this deaf old lady & watching rubbish I don't want to see just to keep her company. I'm even reproached obliquely for *working*! On my return from Leeds it was all 'I missed you not being there on Wednesday evening.' So, to keep her happy I have to be with her every evening.

Sunday, 23 November

Turned the page of engagement pad & saw with horror that on Saturday (yesterday) I should have gone to the Paris to do a BBC programme! Felt that ghastly sickness in the stomach . . . then realised it was too late for any remedy. Wrote to producer, rang Duty Office at BBC desperate to get the number of the producer . . . all to no avail. M. drove me & Lou to Joe Allen. Found Lou more & more irritating as you have to keep repeating *everything*. The fact is, my life is so circumscribed by her that it actually ruins my work – it was going in to her flat last night that ruined the job – if I had stayed in my own place, the phone would have rung with them asking where I was – I could have been there in 10 minutes! But no! I go in there, see that she has something to eat, takes the pills, put on her electric blanket . . . and in the process, fuck up my own agenda. I was barely polite thro' the meal.

Monday, 24 November

Rang David Hatch who told me 'Don't worry about it . . . I'll write on your behalf.' Got thro' to [the producer, Dan] Patterson & apologised. He was v. kind about it. Still feel sick inside about my failure. Read in the paper that dear Billy Dainty had died – oh! it caused quite a pang! He was such a delight. A warm & kind-hearted man, with humour and such an extraordinary gift for the delicate & the deft touch in comedy. Siobhan McKenna is gone too – both of them dead & neither of them really old.

Tuesday, 25 November

To Leeds.[20] Shared cab with Eve Pollard to studio where we met Chris Tarrant. That was the panel. I guessed Janet Brown from the Thatcher

---

[20] For 'Through the Keyhole'.

mugs etc. Talked to her after in hospitality and to Harvey Smith – lovely fellow – and to the producer.

Wednesday, 26 November
To M&S for food. On the way back the chauffeur of a huge Rolls-Royce called out 'Remember me?' and gave me a lift to Albany Street. He said 'I've left the scene now . . . met my wife at a gay club. She had two kids, one lesbian & one gay . . . the boy died of Aids last week . . . I'm glad I've left the scene . . .'

Sunday, 30 November
The unbelievable pathos of Harry Secombe! As a member of the Goons he'd send up everything from religion to royalty! & here he is parading up & down church yards singing about 'the old rustic cross' and talking to mediocrities & bores about their 'Faith.'

Tuesday, 2 December
It is most uncharacteristic 'cos my mood is habitual scepticism but lately I notice that cheerfulness keeps breaking thro' – no, not cheerfulness but a contented resignation – perhaps it is to do with acceptance of Death . . . the idea is growing on me.

Saturday, 20 December
Gave Lou her perfume and stockings. At 12 o'c. Paul came & we went in to Lou. She'd got Anne & Nora there & we got a cab to Joe Allen where we found Pat waiting! Michael came and we had a v. good lunch. P. was on form!! Very funny & Paul was roaring with laughter over her accounts of my childish blackmail when we were kids. Altogether, the most successful birthday Lou's ever had!

Monday, 22 December
Gordon came & took me to the Palladium show *Cage Aux Folles* which was dire sentimental slush about two old queens. The sight of these portly gentlemen singing their love for each other was risible and the antics of the cast were energetic & deplorable. Gordon went round after & Phyllida Law was bravely bawling endearments. The cast were all furious 'cos they'd received notice that it was finishing on Jan. 31. In the auditorium I'd refused to sign autographs but Gordon obliged. We went to Joe Allen's. Apropos the autographs, I told Gordon 'You are always doing that sweet act and signing for those idiots . . . I refuse to do it.' He said 'Yes you are willing to hurt them and that is sick . . . that is sick . . . I'm sorry but I find that *sick*.' I secretly began to wonder why my company had been sought at all! Rona agreed with me 'Well I'd never be as *rude* as Kenneth, but Gordon does overdo it

with the fans . . . he will not keep them at arm's length . . .' I said 'Well I'm sorry if I hurt your feelings' & he told me 'You didn't hurt my feelings, you hurt the feelings of that poor woman in the theatre.' I said I couldn't care less about the bloody woman, that their (fans') enthusiasm was bogus & their adulation worthless, but it certainly caused an atmosphere. When Rona said I could take Louie up there for Christmas dinner I firmly rejected it 'Oh no! Lou has to rest after a meal . . . and she doesn't hear properly . . . it would be best if we were on our own.'

Wednesday, 24 December

That idiot porter again knocked on my door! He brought a letter from an anonymous German girl who has visited England, found out my address and given him flowers & chocolates to give *me* – she doesn't sign the letter, but she quotes the entire passage in my biography about contemplating suicide. The entire incident succeeds in embarrassing & annoying one.

Friday, 26 December

Realised with a jolt that the only verse I've written this year (Feb. 16) is about Death. Well of course I've written about *him* before, but the *only* thing I've written this year! O that ain't good.

Wednesday, 31 December

Even while reading the paper I was thinking 'What would be the most efficient way to kill oneself.' If they told me tomorrow I was for the elbow, I could only view it with relief. It has been a horrible year. One in which I *just* got by . . . in spite of all the medical high-tech stuff, the digestive problem remains, & the geriatric problem remains . . . & there is no health in us . . .

1987

Wednesday, 7 January
Statement from PLR tells me that over 11 thousand people took my biog. from public libraries!! & it has earned me about 140 pounds![1] Quite extraordinary! Went to bed. Gaviscon no good. Up again at 12 o'c. to take K&M & Lactulose . . . Oh! to go to bed & *never wake again* . . . what utter bliss!

Thursday, 8 January
It is a good job I am going to get the E[quity] & L[aw] money in February! There is a [tax] free sum of 9 thousand and that will be useful with the extra expense of the flat and the chance of adding some money to the house-fund – this dream I have of actually getting a place of my own somewhere!

No, I don't suppose it will ever come true. What do we, any of us, live for, but our illusions, & what do we ask of others but that we be allowed to keep them.[2] I expect I'll end up in another little flat – depends how long Louisa lives – can't move her out of here & upset her equilibrium.

Monday, 12 January
I found Lou has no cold water to bathroom! Something is frozen in the pipe . . . Well, it is the first time it has happened in 21 years! I have never known such cold as this! It makes the ears sing with pain.

Wednesday, 14 January
Taxi to Greenwood Theatre for 'Arena', with David Frost, Russell Harty & Gus Macdonald.[3] The clips they showed were marvellous! In a couple of 'em, I looked quite boyish & the contrast with today's

---

[1] Public Lending Right arranges for the payment of authors, pro rata, according to the demand for their work in public libraries. It was secured by Act of Parliament in 1979, and payments began in 1984.

[2] Somerset Maugham, *op. cit.* Spoken by Mrs Tabret in the last act of *The Sacred Flame*.

[3] Angus Macdonald, b.1940. Director of Programmes, Granada TV, 1985–90, etc.

prune-like greyness was remarkable! The three of us blethered on but don't think any of it really got anywhere 'cos the subject Chat Shows is something we've all got a vested interest in, & therefore we have no objectivity. Taxi back home and the driver said 'I'm going to watch your show on Saturday' and knew all about the details of my career. When I got out, he said 'Don't leave the entertainment scene for a long time yet . . . we'd all miss you . . .' I was so touched that I could barely stammer a reply.

Thursday, 15 January
To Silksound to do v/o for Plants and Flowers. They showed me my original & said they wanted something better. I had to record 5 different voices & do them more attractively than last time. I hated it. Didn't like the job when I first did it. The news was all about the disastrous results of the Siberian conditions all over the country. One good thing is that lots of *birds* have died in the freeze.

Saturday, 17 January
We waited up till 11 o'c. to see my TV show repeat. It was a chastening experience! Time makes one objective & I saw *all* the faults. It was a self-indulgent parade of vanity. Unbelievable to see someone going on and on & imagining that it was all so fascinating. The sheer conceit of it was daunting to watch. 'Oh! it is time to go.' I thought, when it finished. A deeply depressing experience which highlighted the overweening arrogance in a persona fighting self-dislike to a point of absurd pathos.

Sunday, 18 January
Michael came at 12 o'c. He drove us to Joe Allen where Lou gave us lunch. He said 'Do you mind if I give it a miss Feb. 15 . . . I'm playing the organ in Norfolk.' I said we didn't have much option. I was secretly furious 'cos I depend on him so much for the Sunday outing which Lou enjoys.

Monday, 19 January
Wogan being blasphemous with Cliff Richard 'You've been young since God was a boy.'

Tuesday, 20 January
'J.A.M.' at the Paris. It was Peter Jones, Eleanor Summerfield, Freud & me, and in the 2nd team it was Stanley Unwin. Both games OK but Stanley was all over the place! Poor man! I fear that he is no longer able to cope with an audience. Taxi home with Lou who said of Eleanor 'Stuck-up bitch . . . she never said a word to me . . . she

don't half like herself . . .' In truth, Eleanor is a sweet person & this is the sort of inferiority in Lou which has infected me all my life.

Monday, 26 January

Letter came by afternoon post from Alan Spicer telling me Jack Lunniss had died suddenly. So that boy who walked in front of us at Bicester brilliantly imitating the big drums of a brass band, always amiable & endlessly laughing at our incongruities, has gone. Leaving us to wait our turn & think of how it all turned out . . . things endlessly gone awry . . . but the rueful fun of him stays with me. It was leukaemia, diagnosed 2 years ago.

Thursday, 5 February

Michael Anderson phoned 'Will you take over as guest on the Mike Aspel show . . . they've been let down at the last minute . . .' I said yes. I went on the show with Dennis Taylor (snooker) and an American girl called Hot Lips from 'M.A.S.H.'[4] The audience was super!! My spot went v. well but of course I felt all the self-loathing after over such appalling indulgence. With me it is verbal diarrhoea and while I'm gabbling on, another side of me is saying 'Oh! dear! what an exhibition you're making of yourself.'

Thursday, 19 February

To Teddington for 'Whose Baby?' The most beautiful children were [John] Conteh's – both incredibly lovely. When Nick Parsons' boy (Justin) appeared, I played stumm & whispered the name to Liza [Goddard]. Didn't want to spoil things. Went to bed at 10.30 with usual 2 Fybo & tradiola ensured I didn't think about the belly.

Friday, 20 February

Loads of daft birthday cards & rubbish. To Teddington for 2 o'c. There were no marvellous guests and we were hard put to it to actually *name* some of the old farts they produced. Went to bed about 10.30. Tradiola.[5] Taking 2 Fybogel before.

Sunday, 22 February

Forgot it was my birthday till Lou came to the door at 8.45 with a cheque for a hundred!! Michael came and took us to Joe Allen where Lou gave us lunch & all the waiters stood around singing 'Happy Birthday to you!' Very embarrassing.

---

[4] Loretta Swit, who played the character 'Hot Lips' Houlihan in the long-running television series.

[5] Now seemingly equivalent to 'barclays'.

Thursday, 26 February
Second post brought cheque from E & L for £9,335 so I took it to the bank & paid it in to the C/A before going to Vecchia to meet Gerald. It was a delight to see him again! Oh! the years that have rolled by since our association began! It was because of him that I was able to pay the premium on the policy that produced the cheque today! He said Thames had asked him about a Carry On Xmas panto – but I said I didn't fancy Buttons & perhaps there was some other part for me. Of course, I don't really want to get lumbered at all. Strolled home in the rain *singing* loudly & several people stared.

Sunday, 1 March
I went to chemist with Paul. We talked about article in the papers saying that Russell Harty had been shopped by a rent-boy called Dean who visited him several times in his basement flat. It sounded like a most sordid betrayal. It will be rotten for Russell 'cos there will be repercussions which won't enhance the career.[6]

Tuesday, 3 March
Turned back to reading Steiner's *Antigones*:[7] fascinating stuff. The more one reads about the nature of conflict in humanity, the more one marvels that there is any civility at all in the world: the violence that does occur is always just another symptom of the same old malaise. We're born diseased & every now & again, the malignancy gets the upper hand.

Wednesday, 4 March
They've announced the death of Joan Greenwood (with whom I worked on the Baskerville fiasco) and today, Danny Kaye. My earnings are up to 48 thousand & we're not at the end of the financial year yet! It's an improvement on last year (42) but of course I haven't really done any work . . . but then, I haven't done any work ever, in the professional sense. Nearest I've got to work is in the flat, cleaning etc.

Thursday, 5 March
Went to Silksound to do the Sony v/o with Geoffrey Palmer & Sheila Hancock. The v/o stuff was horribly technical with little or no relief anywhere: the one or two attempts at humour in the script were

---

[6] Alan Bennett asserted at Russell Harty's funeral service (1988) that his death had been hastened by overwork, occasioned by fear of the collapse of his reputation. He also took the opportunity to criticise the prurient intrusiveness of tabloid journalists.
[7] *Antigones* (1984) by George Steiner, b.1929, author, essayist and academic.

either dirty or feeble. For some reason Sheila kept stumbling over pronunciation of *innovative* & I corrected her. After, she said 'You are a didactic little sod.'

Monday, 9 March

Shep. Bush for 'Wogan'. Burl Ives first, then Teri Garr (actress from *Tootsie*), then me. They altered the format we'd planned 'cos they said 'We want to bring the others into the chat' & in the event, Ives pissed off & I got stuck with the girl who was about as loquacious as the Sphinx. We covered none of the ground we should have done but Terry was good 'cos he got the book mentioned. First time I've been with him & seen the *nerves* – he was in quite a state!

Sunday, 15 March

Stanley telephoned and we arranged to meet on Tuesday next. He said 'You were v. good on "Wogan" . . . less of the camp; now you're developing an elder statesman sort of comedy . . . very grand & urbane . . .' He has forgotten that he's told me this before & it doesn't matter. It is his way of encouraging one and it is valuable. It is a friend saying 'You're very good' at something & it's enormously comforting.

Monday, 16 March

We were forced to watch a 'Horizon' piece on Engineering. It was interesting apropos bridges – they've always been an abiding passion for me. Unfortunately the American commentator was an Engineer & not a broadcaster. No delivery & no ease in front of camera.

Tuesday, 17 March

To M&S for food. Back after directing a German to Boosey & Hawkes: I reeled off '*Hier lagen wir im hecken Dorn*' but he was totally unimpressed.[8] Saw Stanley and he gave me dinner at Campana. He went right off about the magical poetic delivery of J[ohn] G[ielgud] but I said I didn't think he could ever be *funny*.

Friday, 20 March

Car to Menzies bookshop at Broad St and the queue for my signing session was immense! I got there at 12.45 and I was still signing at 3 o'c.! Car collected me at 3.30 & I spent the last half hour having a cup of tea in the staff room. Everyone was v. nice to me . . . it is

---

[8] 'Hier lagern wir am Heckendorn in Gras und grünen Ranken', from 'Zieh, Schimmel, zieh!', one of the *Lieder eines fahrenden Gesellen* (1878) by Rudolf Baumbach (1840–1905), set to music by Gustav Mahler. The musically-minded visitor was presumably bewildered by KW's mistranscription: the original describes an encampment; KW's version suggests two people lying together in a hedge.

extraordinary that I'm so liked because I'm invariably rude & tetchy.

Monday, 23 March
Went to the BBC for b'cast down the line to Wales all about the book. I praised Clifford Evans & talked about understudying Richard Burton. Finished with *Cymru am byth*. When I got the Daily News (excellent new paper) for 10p at 3 o'c. I said to the boy at the newsagent's (tube) 'I expect you were looking forward to seeing me, weren't you?' 'Er . . . yes . . . I suppose . . .' 'That's right! It gives a tremendous lift to your life doesn't it?' Sailed off leaving him looking bewildered.

Thursday, 26 March
Somehow I have felt really serene today. Moments of calm contentment. Quite extraordinary. Nothing to do with optimism, more to do with recognising death as a proper release. I must make more plans for dying, and seeing that someone worthy gets some financial relief out of it.

Monday, 30 March
Went to BBC for interview about the book at 1 o'c and after that, I did 'Desert Island Discs' with Michael Parkinson. I told him truthfully 'What a difference doing it with you! That awful Plumb Leigh[9] was dreadful, so oleaginous!' I get on fine with M.P. 'cos he's direct and honest & lets you become uninhibited.

Tuesday, 31 March
Took the milk of magnesia last night. Ain't done nothing for the banging heart. Perhaps the pump is saying to me 'Finish it off!' Certainly that's how I feel. Saw Lou for the news and had roes on toast. The programmes were all dreadful. We switched off and sang old songs instead: 'Forty Seven Ginger Headed Sailors' and 'Marta' and other numbers from the Twenties.

Wednesday, 15 April
To John Wood Studios to do v/o for Electrolux 'Nothing sucks like an Electrolux' & tho' I said it was synonymous with a certain sexual activity everyone professed astonishment.* Did about 3 versions and the two men in charge didn't agree. Heigh ho.

*this was a test v/o and I was rejected.

---

[9] Roy Plomley (see entry for 2 May 1961, p. 172).

Saturday, 18 April
What a comment on a life! 61 and about a hundred thousand in the bank! Oh! Such a paltry result of so much hard saving! It wouldn't buy a house in London & in the places it would buy decent houses, I wouldn't want to live. I've been chasing my own tail all these years.

Friday, 24 April
Sad to read of the death of Dick Shawn[10] – he collapsed on stage in America – he was a delightful comedian and I remember him at the Palladium being a brilliantly funny and original actor, and he was good on my own programme 'International Cabaret'. An untimely death 'cos he was younger than I am.

Monday, 27 April
Looking back on the earlier entries in this diary I'm amazed at the turmoil caused by the digestion problem! It has certainly receded of its own accord. I take no medicine & follow no diet and I have no dreadful after-effects apart from the v. slow draining of the alimentary canal which was *always* a problem.

Wednesday, 29 April
Read *Brideshead* by Evelyn Waugh. Finished it. Whole chunks of boring writing. No story. More like a disjointed biographical account. Again & again, we are assured that Ryder *loves* Sebastian but there is precious little sign of any love. When Sebastian is in the greatest need Ryder doesn't seem to be around – or want to be. The BBC News prefaces everything with starvation in Mozambique – this is the ploy they used about Abyssinia. Their announcers mouth their disquiet about the world's hungry before going off to their 5 course dinners. Utter cant. We all know it is the incompetent governments which cause national starvation: remove *them* and you might get improvements. Throw money at it & corrupt officials will benefit.

Tuesday, 5 May
All the promise of serenity in one's declining years when retirement means no more having to work is false. Old age carries with it the ever-present pain of decay . . . all one's previous fears and apprehensions reappear in other forms . . . the endless bane of existence offers no respite.

Wednesday, 6 May
Several times today I was stopped in the street & greeted by strangers.

---

[10] 1924–87.

They all say much the same things 'You are a v. good performer' etc. and all of them *inevitably* ask 'What are you doing next?' as if there is a series lined up! They seem to think that all successful actors are offered work on some endless belt! I have certainly never been offered *much* . . . always bits & pieces here and there . . . it is amazing when I look back on it all! I think 'How on earth did I get away with it?' and how did I earn enough to keep me & Lou & provide a home for us! Astonishing.

Thursday, 14 May
TV was the usual crap but easily the *worst* programme was a dreadful compilation of Carry On excerpts. Sid James looked as bad as his acting. The scripts were schoolboy scatology . . . the most depressing sort of would-be funny rubbish. News was mostly about Election. I will be glad when it's all over.

Sunday, 17 May
I am torn by desire to get out of this awful block – just go – and simply give in & stay, doing the prison warder stuff. I may as well *stop* all this, and just resign myself to staying here. The sentence may be a long one.

Monday, 18 May
I called on Bill Kenwright in his office at Shaftesbury Avenue. Had coffee with him. Must say, he is v. likeable. Told him I didn't want to do the Moss Hart play. He said 'Well, what about a one man show? I'd love to put you on in the West End for 6 weeks!' Said I didn't think I had the right sort of material. I am *longing* to get out of this rut I'm in – just leave it all & go away & live quietly in some pleasant place. Peter C. has sent me property lists in Blackpool and the prices of houses are remarkably cheap compared with the South!

Thursday, 21 May
Car to Shepherd's Bush for this line-up of British Film Stars. They even produced Stewart Granger!! There was Bryan Forbes doing his important act 'Would you mind Kenneth? I've got to answer this researcher's questions' etc. Eventually Wogan brought on Barbara, Bernie, Kenny Connor & me & there was a bit of chat before a finale of montages & clips. It was more interesting in the dressing room. Barbara said 'They think, with all the Carry On repeats that we are *rich*' & Kenny Connor said 'I don't disabuse 'em, I even go to the Post Office in gold lamé slippers . . .' No, he actually said 'I even wear gold lamé slippers to the Post Office' which had all the connotations of an

old age pensioner. I realise why I rephrased it. I thought the slippers should be the tag but Kenny's version is more apt.

Friday, 22 May

At 9.30 to post & the M&S for food & to Littlewood for fags. Got home to find chimps in the foyer. Whole pack of 'em have gone into flat 10 – ugh! – and a bunch of wogs are looking at the flat adjoining Paul! This place certainly gets worse and worse.[11]

Sunday, 24 May

With Michael to Joe Allen for lunch. The clientele there is appalling – the riff-raff ranges from yuppie ad men to yiddisher mommas. We talked about alternatives but agreed that the prices elsewhere were ridiculous so we booked for tomorrow as well.

Monday, 25 May

M. came at 12 o'c. Oh! his patience is unbelievable. He took me & Lou to Joe Allen. There, because she wasn't helped with her coat she cried out 'If I'm not wanted, I'll go home!' etc. & made quite a scene. Despair is now something which daily afflicts me & threatens to overwhelm me. I'm virtually a prisoner . . . chained to this elderly derelict . . . forever reminded of geriatric problems . . . the stained mattress, the cigarette burns on carpets & chairs, the conversational repetition. Saw myself looking old on 'Wogan'. Our bit was cut drastically but loads of crap from crashing bores like John Mills was left intact.

Tuesday, 26 May

In thc aftcrnoon I postcd a lcttcr to Stanlcy saying I was an old Army friend & did he remember me? etc. etc.

Thursday, 28 May

In the afternoon I walked round the old haunts: there are flats going in Endsleigh Court & Russell Court . . . there's a 2 bedroomed flat going in Beaumont Street! Quite reasonable! And Clare Court has got several on offer as well.

Thursday, 4 June

Up at 7 o'c. after dreadful sleepless night & awful dreams. People saying 'Don't you see? Your face has *altered*! The eyes are quite sunken and the jawline has receded . . .' To LBC for a b'cast about one's political allegiances & I spoke for capitalism & private enterprise.

---

[11] See entry for 26 June, p. 765.

Saturday, 6 June
Went to bed reflecting on the difficulty age has in pretending. It's easier for youth & middle age to cheat despair, but after 60 life's utter futility becomes cruelly obvious. The whole con is exposed & you see that there is not going to be any happy ending, contentment, or fulfilment . . . just a waiting for death as the final, sole, and only relief.

Sunday, 7 June
I walked to Gordon & Rona. G. switched on TV 'Let's watch Laurence Olivipong reading poetry,' and we saw that Patrick Garland handing sheets of paper to the ancient Lord for him to read aloud. It was a dreadful exhibition of senility. He quavered his way thro' bits and pieces like some poor old sod being made to audition. It was depressing.

Monday, 8 June
Taxi to TV Centre and I appeared on the 1 o'c. News being interviewed by Martyn Lewis.[12] Eleanor Bron for Labour, and Robert Powell for Alliance & me for the Tories. Both of them did too much uming & ahing. I got on with it. The Editor told me after that I was the best & I smirked my thanks.

Wednesday, 10 June
The BBC TV showed three interviews with party leaders. Kinnock ranting on about 'this dirty government' etc. etc. Owen saying he thought the 'thoughtful voter' would help him, and Mrs T. being needled by Nimble Bee[13] into talking about people who whine & drool & then saying 'Sorry, I shouldn't have used those words.' She shouldn't have apologised at all, but you can see how all those accusations about 'not caring' have provoked her. This brave woman has been subjected to the nastiest personal abuse I've known in politics & if this election doesn't vindicate her, then this country will get the sort of divided & divisive gerrymandering rule it deserves.

Friday, 12 June
The headlines are all about Tory Victory. We have got over a hundred majority! All that Kinnock humbug has not worked! Even the weather has changed! It is sunny & warmer.

---

[12] b.1945. Later graduated to the 9 p.m. bulletin.
[13] David Dimbleby, on 'News and Election 87'.

Sunday, 14 June
M. came and drove Lou & me to Joe Allen. We had a drink and Michael Anderson arrived at about 12.45. I haven't seen M.A. socially for ages! Seemed extraordinary when he told Michael 'Kenneth was leading man & I was the ASM at Eastbourne Rep . . .'

Thursday, 18 June
I got an ironing board for 9 pounds. Never thought I'd be struggling through the streets with an ironing board at 61 years of age! I'd envisaged a decline into a life of ease.

Friday, 19 June
To Teddington. My team on 'Give Us A Clue' was Simon Williams & Martin Jarvis. No show could be more enjoyable 'cos the people are all delightful to be with. Michael Parkinson in the chair & he asked me (as he always does) 'What are you working at?' & I said fuck all.

Monday, 22 June
Wrote these verses[14] about the abortive week old affair with Oliver Ford all those years ago!! in '48. It certainly contains a truth. Who knows? Without the smell it might have worked.

Thursday, 25 June
Awful dream where I arrived at an apartment & found Charlie in bed with Lou & another Lou lying by the bed (on the floor) with blood on the face & me thinking 'I'll have to get her to a home' and neighbours telling me of Charles 'He wants to go to Albany.'

Friday, 26 June
Up at 7 o'c. & got papers. Joe Idudu was outside the block with his wife. Their taxi failed to turn up! I went over the road & got him a cab. Sorry to see him go, he's the best one who's ever occupied the furnished flat No. 10. Load of fan mail has arrived.

Monday, 6 July
Stock market is up again! I don't trust these endless rises! It has got to fall quite drastically soon. The world's economic state is parlous in view of the enormous budget deficit of the USA and the endless debts of South America and East Europe . . . sooner or later, these chickens will come home to roost.

---

[14] One stanza reads: 'Actions had made for the tension/The rest could be taken as read/I knew that I never could mention/The bodily smell in the bed.'

Tuesday, 7 July
I visited Peter C. in Marylebone St I took him to Vecchia to lunch and after, to the Guercino (Doubting Thomas) at the Nat. Gallery. Then I showed him the gravestone of the King of Sardinia[15] & a dreadful drunk accosted me & began to cry 'I'm so ashamed.' I said 'Oh! don't cry!' & handed him two pounds.

Wednesday, 8 July
Lou moaning 'Oh this heat is killing me . . .' 'Oh! I can't eat anything' 'Can you fix this deaf aid?' 'Can you pay this telephone bill?' O! how I wish I'd never come to live here! How I wish I'd been selfish with my life . . . just gone somewhere where I liked acting & ignored all the dependants . . .

Wednesday, 15 July
With Michael to Hertford and then Royston and eventually to Elmdon where we had lunch at the King's Head. The morning was o'cast but afternoon hot & humid. The countryside was looking beautiful & some of the villages we passed thro' on the minor roads were so lovely it was almost moving. It reminded me of Philip Larkin's poem '1914' with gardens better tended etc.

Friday, 17 July
To Murray-Lyon at 12.30 and he examined me & listened to the complaints. Said there was nothing wrong with me. Went in to Lou for meal. The rest of the evening was *purgatory* with the stomach like a churn of nauseating pain.

Friday, 24 July
Went to Harley Street for X-ray. Have to go back for another one on Monday.

Sunday, 26 July
Took the 12 capsules for the Test tomorrow at 9.30 feeling as if I was taking my own life as I did so! To bed with awful pain from the usual place – lower right side – shooting & piercing thro' my body. Lots of nausea & over-salivation – oh! horrible.

Monday, 27 July
Went to Harley Street at 9.30 for X-rays. The radiographer said there are *no stones*. Went to John Wood Studio for v/o for Jump-in-Choc.

---

[15] Almost certainly Theodore, King of Corsica (d.1756), whose memorial is to be found at St Anne's, Soho.

John W. was v. helpful to me with cue lights etc. Did 3 versions & they settled for the snide voice.

Wednesday, 29 July
I went to the Tenants' meeting at Flat 11 in Regency House. Mr Saxby spoke about the need for a committee, and the 20-odd people present elected a Residents' Committee. I promised to type a resumé of the proceedings and give it to the Chairman, & get copies to everyone else.

Sunday, 2 August
To bed with Gaviscon etc. but by 11.30 I was up again. In desperation I took K&M. About 12 o'c. youths shouted outside the building 'Kenny is a poof!' & kept that up for quite a bit. To Die would be a release from people as well as pain!

Wednesday, 5 August
While I was out, with the everlasting staring and 'Hello Kenny!' from passers-by, I felt utterly suicidal. Before I take the lethal dose I will have to write a letter to Michael. Certainly he has been the best friend a man could ever have. Typed brief report of Committee Meeting for Jacqueline to copy: must keep a record of things & show people that we are doing something!

Friday, 14 August
Saw Lou 'I thought you were cross with me . . . we seem to be drifting apart . . .' I said it was nonsense.

Monday, 17 August
Charming letter came from Philip Lowrie: he obviously feels guilty about playing *me* in *Diary of a Somebody*[16] at the Boulevard Theatre and writes to say that the audience enjoyment is derived from their affection for me. It is certainly a charming gesture.

Wednesday, 19 August
Michael came at 7 o'c. & drove me to Sadler's Wells where I met Paul & saw *Bless The Bride*. They cut the song 'What will I do without you, ducky' but the Nanny was played wrongly & I suppose she wasn't doing it well anyway. The children enchanting, Ruth Madoc superb, Una Stubbs lovely, Simon Williams as dishy as ever. Went round to see Una (and S.W. and Jeremy Sinden). Then we went to Joe Allen for supper. Paul paid.

---

[16] An adaptation for the stage of the diaries of Joe Orton.

Thursday, 20 August

Dreared about feeling lethargic in all this heat. Sheila rang 'Dr Murray-Lyon suggests you go into the Devonshire for another gastroscopy . . . he has heard that you're very unhappy.' When I asked how she knew, she said 'Through a colleague at the Charing X Hospital.' This is Ted Newlands! (Liz's husband!) Walked to Paris for pilot show 'Drop That Name' and the cast was Amanda Barrie, Claire Rayner,[17] Graeme Garden & me. There was a superb house! And it went very well indeed! Overran endlessly!

Saturday, 22 August

Dr Murray-Lyon did the gastroscopy. He said the ulcer was back again. 'We must start to treat it immediately' & he gave me a letter for Bertie Clarke.

Friday, 28 August

Paul came with me to the Tape Gallery where I did a v/o for second hand car sales. Met Tony Valentine coming down the stairs . . . this v/o business has become his territory! He does hundreds of voices for advertisements! It's a far cry from the eager young actor I once knew, who was so anxious to make himself a comedy actor.

Saturday, 29 August

Took Lou to Victoria. Her chums were all waiting on the station fore-court for her. Walked back with Paul afterwards. Did all the fan mail. There were loads of letters!

Sunday, 30 August

Another day yawns ahead of me. All that is in my mind now is the *way* to commit suicide: it has got to be efficient and it has got to be in a place where no one is inconvenienced. Cooked the chicken dinner and had that at 12.15. Never known a period when I felt so utterly *lonely*. In the evening went to Lou's flat and saw the Simon Callow piece on Charles Laughton. Callow's diction shifted from tentative hesitancy, to casual pronunciation, to agonising inarticulation. A good commentator he ain't. He didn't seem to know what to do with Laughton. I suspect he *meant* to show that homosexuality and unattractiveness can combine to achieve genius in the theatre. I think Callow sees that it is when apparent weakness is *harnessed* that it becomes strength. There was a veiled reference to his own inner turmoil . . . but the programme often neared the truth but never con-

---

[17] Amanda Barrie: actress, latterly well-known as 'Alma (Sedgwick) Baldwin' in 'Coronation Street'. Claire Rayner: writer, broadcaster and 'agony aunt', b.1931.

fronted it. The one moment which could have been fascinating (the appearance of a young man who had an affair with Laughton) was shot thro' a would-be poetic haze of birds on a beach and the real comments misted over . . .

Wednesday, 2 September
Saw Michael at 7 o'c. and we went to Vecchia Milano where I gave him dinner. Oh! but he is the most wondrous patient friend I've ever known.

Saturday, 5 September
Met Lou coming off the 12.10 from Margate. It is sad that the others had no one to meet them. I would have liked to take them all out to lunch, but luggage & their arrangements were an impediment.

Sunday, 6 September
Michael came at 12 o'c and drove me & Lou to Joe Allen. M. said he'd be away next weekend. I said 'I hope the weather is *lousy* for you.' It's too bad of him to desert us like this.

Sunday, 13 September
Looking back on the life I used to lead, and the monotonous existence I'm now reduced to, it seems amazing that I used to cram so much in! Thought nothing of going to parties – now I avoid 'em like the plague – harboured illusions about love & a partner – now, I regard such pipedreams as foolish – and worried endlessly about money and not being able to make ends meet. Well, that hasn't changed much, but it has changed. Now that I'm receiving pension money (even tho' it's heavily taxed) I feel a bit more secure, but I'm all too aware of the pension pitfalls . . . inflation can make nonsense of the sums provided . . . that is why I must have the Equity portfolio, and why I must keep a sum in reserve (Nat. Sav. Certs.) of 55 thousand to purchase an annuity when the age makes it profitable.

Monday, 21 September
Read the TLS and was struck by a review of a book *Cities On A Hill.*[18] I got the book at Claude Gill. It is an extraordinary account of the homosexual movement in San Francisco. I had *no idea* that it had such enormous sociological implications.

Wednesday, 23 September
Letter from BBC TV saying they're repeating 'Comic Roots' on Friday.

---

[18] Subtitled *A Journey Through Contemporary American Culture*, by Frances Fitzgerald.

It was first shown in Sept. '83 so it's on again in 4 years! They must be short of material.

Friday, 25 September
Emlyn Williams is dead! That lovely actor/playwright talent which this country practically ignored.

Saturday, 26 September
A film about plutonium-infection made by Mike Nichols[19] was so boring we turned it off. You could see the message: woman in atomic establishment gets infected & from lethargic drifter in society becomes a union activist in the fight for compensation for infected workers. The old old story; paint the employers villains, paint the workers gullible nice-guys . . . Oh! such tripe. The story of all political systems is the choice between responsibility & irresponsibility. Most citizens opt for the latter 'cos the former entails a lot of work which amounts to altruism & they'd much rather work for themselves: at least *they see it* as working for themselves, and (tho' it isn't) that's all that matters. They're only stirred into activity when they're threatened in some way. Then suddenly altruism & cooperation become attractive. By then, most of the time, it's too late.

Tuesday, 29 September
Stanley phoned. Said he'd not liked the Ionian Islands – 'mosquitos and all that scratching.' When he asked about the ulcer I told him 'Oh! I wish I was dead' & he said 'Oh no! not you!' He said he's going to do panto next year 'It does keep one fit doing twice nightly.'

Wednesday, 30 September
Michael came and we drove to Thame – lovely town, and had coffee there. Then to Bicester where we had a look round. Then to a pub at Kirtlington and in the bar I met a man who was nephew of old Mr Chisholm!! Extraordinary coincidence.

Thursday, 1 October
Caught the 7.20 to Norwich. Taxi met us & took us to Anglia TV for a ludicrous load of rubbish about hotels & shops . . . discussion was split among so many that it became fragmented & nonsensical. Sat with Derek Taylor[20] on train! He'd been in the show. He is Rose's son. Rose Taylor used to live here. Lovely lady.

---

[19] *Silkwood.*
[20] Journalist, author, publicist; in the sixties, the Beatles' publicity manager.

Friday, 2 October
The 2 Ronnies continued with their repeats and the formula was as sterile as ever: it's a peculiar English thing where everyone goes thro' the motions thoroughly professionally without making you laugh at all. A 'comedy formula' which produces no comedy. Like watching the Japanese immaculately performing a Morris Dance.

Monday, 5 October
There seems to be a dearth of mail. Counted my capsules of poison and I have got over 30 so there should be enough to kill me. Just have to work out the time and the place. Went to M&S, on the way I was hailed by window-cleaners, postmen, costermongers, etc. 'Hello Kenny!' all very cordial. Then to Mowbray's where I paid £15 for the Ellmann[21] biography of Wilde. I felt it was an extravagance I deserved.

Tuesday, 6 October
At 12 o'c. to B.H. to do the interview with Robert Booth on 'Three Wishes'. Chose 1) Audio cut-out 2) to be edentate 3) a polyglot.

Friday, 9 October
In Gt. Portland St., police were escorting the King's Troop & one of the soldiers called out 'It's Kenny Williams!' & they all turned & greeted me from their saddles! It was quite delightful.

Wednesday, 14 October
Went in to Lou & she'd put a fag butt (not out) in a packet & shoved it in D/gown pocket. Set it all alight. I have told her *dozens* of times not to do this. Told her off & she did the crying etc. Did v/o with Stanley!! For Vauxhall Senator car. One rustic & one Scots. At 4.30 I went in the rain to get a paper. Stood, waiting to cross the road by the church (Soane) & thought 'It *is* all lovely, the traffic, the rain, the crowded streets . . . I've lived here all my life & can't really envisage living anywhere else . . .'

Friday, 16 October
Up at all hours![22] Dreadful winds battering the windows! About to pack for Bristol when Pat phoned: 'There are no trains! 'cos of the hurricane in the night.' I phoned HTV and Cecil Korer told me 'The 11.25 will run from Paddington.' Streets were chaotic, so I struggled with my suitcase on foot to Paddington. Then it was announced 'The 11.25 is cancelled' so I went to the Area Manager's office. He told me

---

21 Professor Richard Ellmann, 1918–87.
22 The night of the 'storm of the century' in southern England and Wales.

to get the 12 o'c. to Bristol Parkway & said he'd ring HTV & tell them to send a car. That worked out OK. The day was taken up with endless rehearsing. Roy Hudd was chairman (v.g. too!) and all would have been fine but the show had the obligatory two dolly birds and they couldn't even speak properly. Taxi at 10.45 to the Dragonara Hotel. I was in pyjamas when a receptionist knocked on the door & handed me a glass of champagne. I said 'Thank you so much' & poured it down the sink.

Tuesday, 20 October

Headlines are Wall Street Crash! A fall of 25% (worse than the '29 crash) and our own S.E. hit almost as badly. They think there'll be more selling today. It seems to have been raining steadily since 9.15 this morning. There is something curiously *amiss* these days; these last few weeks it's seemed as if everything is awry . . . there is an odd feeling of *disjointedness*.

Thursday, 22 October

Saw Michael, and gave him dinner at Vecchia. He views the S.E. dive as a prelude to a recession caused by the U.S. deficit: 'People will get frightened and spend less & turnover will suffer . . .' If he is thinking that, so are a lot of other people. I said that the share market would recover once the U.S. deficit is *seen* to be tackled & that Capital Investment would remain the staple of the Western World. I don't see anything replacing it.

Friday, 23 October

Share prices have plummeted again! I've lost about 90 thousand. Read the rest of the Higham biography of Orson.[23] It reads more like a logistic/social report than anything else. He is certainly not equal to his subject. Orson was a paradoxical creature, a poetic visionary & a mendacious con-man magician. His mercurial nature oscillating between rancorous rudeness and humorous charm. You can't pin him down with Higham 'journalism', it needs an Ellmann or a Holroyd to do him justice.

Saturday, 24 October

Went in to Lou at 9 o'c. Did beds etc. Did the washing while she stood there full of ill-humour & niggling. When I tried to clear up dirt behind the oven it was all: 'Oh! you just look for work!' & I shouted fuck off. I'm just *sick* of the whole broiling. At 11 o'c. the telephone rang.

---

[23] *Orson Welles: The Rise and Fall of an American Genius*, by Charles Higham (1985).

The producer of the Shaffer play:[24] 'I wish you wouldn't come to the opening night: Maggie says if she hears *your* laugh it will finish her . . . you could come on another night.' I said I'd accepted the tickets, & the job of talking briefly about it, from the TV company & couldn't now let them down. At 3.30 a load of wogs started moving furniture into the block. The row they make is unbelievable. Above me the ancient poof has the blaring TV. Oh! it drives one mad. Think I will try to get out of the job on Monday. I will return the tickets, and say I've been asked not to attend.

Monday, 26 October

Handed the tickets back. Certainly I am glad I'm out of it! Rather like being invited to a party & then having the host telephone & say *don't come*: you're left feeling vaguely insulted.

Saturday, 31 October

Went to the Devonshire Hospital. Murray-Lyon said the ulcer had gone. 'I'm going to recommend a further course of pills.' Walked home in a euphoric daze feeling totally uninhibited, talking to everyone from street diggers to motorists. Lousy headache is result of gastroscopy, and sore throat.

Tuesday, 3 November

Car to TV Centre for 'Cover to Cover'. There was Jack Someone, Victoria Glendinning, Patricia Highsmith and me.[25] Patricia came right across the hospitality room to me with outstretched hand 'You *are* Kenneth Williams? I *so* wanted to meet you.' I could hardly believe it. Ever since I read the Ripley books I've been greatly in awe of her! I was amazed that she'd even *heard* of me: she's always lived in France or Switzerland. I spoke glowingly about the Ellmann biog. of Wilde and was rude about the Jacobson novel. Tried to be reasonable about Highsmith but made it clear I found it disappointing. She said 'Kenneth obviously thinks I've written a moral tract instead of the usual thriller' but I quickly interjected 'No, it is entertaining reading . . . just not what I expected . . .'

Thursday, 5 November

The death of Eamonn Andrews has occurred: he was the first chat-

---

[24] *Lettice and Lovage*. Produced by Robert Fox.

[25] A book programme chaired by Jill Neville. The actor Jack Klaff was the missing name. Under discussion were Richard Ellmann's biography *Oscar Wilde*, Dan Jacobson's novel *Her Story*, and Patricia Highsmith's *Tales of Natural and Unnatural Catastrophes*.

show man I ever appeared with, he was amiable and *always* kind to me.

Friday, 6 November

The Chancellor has now *lowered* interest rates by one point, pandering to the spenders in a Keynesian gesture which is quite misplaced. All these Credit users should be taught a lesson & it simply isn't happening. With the example of America it is hardly surprising. The biggest & most powerful economy in the Western world running a Budget & Trade Deficit which mounts every year! The fear is that if the brakes are slammed on, there will be a recession. It is *mad*. The brakes *should* be slammed on & there *should* be a recession. That way, people might learn some lessons.

Saturday, 7 November

One of the Peers in the Lords said in debate 'One of the ways to combat ragwort is to let sheep graze on the affected fields during the month of May' & Lady Trumpington[26] rose & replied: 'My noble Lord . . . a lot of things happen in the month of May . . .' & everyone fell about.

Wednesday, 11 November

When I was getting ready for bed at about 10.20 I saw a young Negro hurling bricks at the telephone kiosk opposite: after smashing 3 panes, he ran across the road in the rain towards Marylebone Rd. It looked like anger & frustration over the phone not working. First time I've ever actually seen vandalism.

Thursday, 19 November

Headlines are about a fire in tube at King's X where 30 people were killed. It sounds horrendous. I walked to Bridge Studio to do v/o Plants & Flowers – they've altered the original & I had to do a couple of new characters. This is a lovely commercial. Wish I'd been 20 years younger & I could have done much better.

Saturday, 21 November

The more I think about it, the more I wish I'd never agreed to do this sketch for the 'Wogan' show. It won't get rehearsed properly, the material ain't good, there is no tag line, and the subject of Homosexuality is now in great disfavour. When we were performing the Jule &

---

[26] Baroness Trumpington of Sandwich. Parliamentary Under-Secretary, Department of Health and Social Security, 1985–87, etc.

Sand stuff in the 60's the atmosphere was utterly different, and of course, nobody knew about Aids.

Sunday, 22 November

I went to Shepherd's Bush to rehearse 'Wogan' with Hugh Paddick. We rehearsed with Wogan perfunctorily, with Terry saying 'That's enough . . . let's keep it fresh . . .' Had a rest. Car came at 6.20 and we went back again to do the show. We were in the second half and the first didn't finish till gone 9 o'c.!! The theatre was full of deadbeats. Irene Handl in a wheelchair. Oh! it was ghastly. The tedium was unbelievable. The ghastly Munchausen[27] going on & on. Spike Milligan was asked about Peter Sellers in the Goons & Terry said 'Alas, he is no longer with us.' Spike said 'No, and he isn't with anybody else if it comes to that.' The audience laughed. We got away at about 10.45 and Hugh said 'Don't bother about make-up . . . let's go' so we got the car and I was home by about 11 o'c. Went in to Lou's flat quietly and took a tin of soup & 2 bits of bread. Had that before going to bed 'cos I'd not eaten properly all day. Heard the clock strike 12 o'c. Thought of Hugh saying at 3 o'c. 'I think this is all going to be a bit hairy . . .' Oh! he was so right.

Sunday, 29 November

On the News they announced the death of Irene Handl! It was a surprise to me – having only just worked with her – but it sounds as if she died peacefully. A lovely character actress. We won't see her like again.

Wednesday, 2 December

Watched some TV including a programme devoted to Rex Harrison. He was interviewed by the oleaginous Garland. There was not one story . . . it was all vague compliments and superlatives used about everybody. Not a word about the marriages. Apparently, he's over 80 and the walk was a bit wobbly. He referred several times to the *Fair Lady*[28] as 'my enormous personal success' & 'my biggest success' & is obviously very proud of his performance in that. You saw a clip from it: it was rotten. A clip from *Platonov* revealed (after all he'd said about making Chekhov funny) that his comic ability was nil. The whole point about the suicide speech is to sustain a vocal note right up to the choosing of the gun, pointing to the temple, and *then* it has to change with a total vocal volte face, on the line 'No! I haven't got the energy.' Nothing remotely like that happened. It was all on the same

---

27 Bob Monkhouse.

28 *My Fair Lady* by Lerner and Loewe, from Shaw's *Pygmalion*.

note. Utterly dreary & certainly not funny. A limited man, rather reppy, whose youthful good looks & some luck with the parts ensured a profitable career.

Thursday, 3 December

Terrible night. I was up at 2 o'c. in the morning taking Gaviscon . . . At 9 o'c. to Gresse Street for HMV v/o. 'Ho! Ho! Ho! It's no fun being Santa Claus . . .' etc. It went OK until I had to do *two pages* of different addresses, still keeping the same inflections used in the original! I almost gave up twice 'Oh! I can't do this! It's impossible!' The copywriter came thro' to the studio & was v. placatory. Oh! I'm too old for this, I really am.* The TV was dreadful. We were forced to watch '[Call My] Bluff' with all those old dodderers *still at it*! It is extraordinary. The BBC is full of deadbeats & ITV is full of Kangas.

*left the studios feeling they weren't best pleased with my temperamental outburst, but a few days later, Gillian rang from I.C.M.: 'The advertising people were so pleased with your work they've sent you champagne & a tape of all the voices you did!' I was astounded. Gillian sent me the tape, I told her to keep the champagne.

Saturday, 5 December

Walked to Paris Studio for the 'Law Game'. On the panel with me were Nerys Hughes & Ian McCaskill,[29] so I had good company. One of the actors in the playlets was called Stephen (dish) & producer made him re-record a terribly difficult bit of comedy patter! Agony! I told Lissa [Evans] (producer) 'It was wicked of you!' & she said 'Ah! but I'll keep most of his first reading' so I kissed her & said 'Oh! you're a cracker!' Shaw Taylor presided suavely over both programmes. I got in the bit about sheep grazing in the month of May & Lady Trumpington's reply – it got a v. good laugh.

Sunday, 6 December

A letter was delivered by hand from the BBC!! Asking me to appear on Breakfast TV to talk with Gerald Thomas about their making another Carry On!! I telephoned & said No. It is *extraordinary*! They issue statements about making films to the press & TV and without a *word* to me & then expect me to say I will act in it! I don't want to do any films, least of all a C.O. film! O it is amazing impertinence.

Tuesday, 8 December

With Paul to Selfridge's where he got paintbrush, then to M&S where

---

[29] Welsh actress and Scottish TV weatherman respectively.

I got food, & feigned crying. Calling out to Paul 'You swine! Leaving me *alone* at the bacon counter!' & people eyed us bemusedly.

Monday, 14 December

To M&S for food, then Boots for bandages etc. & then Littlewood for fags. Gave stuff to Lou who maundered over the change till I cried 'Oh! give it to me you dozy cow!' & flew into a huff. She wears you out at times. Met a security man from Plaza (ex-Horne & Bollocksworth) who said he'd lived in Deal! Next to Charlie Hawtrey. 'He's always pissed . . . several of the pubs barred him . . . he can get very nasty you know . . .' Stanley came at 7.30 & popped in to give Lou a box of chocolates. Then he took me to Venezia. When we walked thro' the cold streets after, I guided him to Mortimer Street. 'We're bound to see a cab soon . . . we will catch something round here.' 'Probably pneumonia,' he replied.

Wednesday, 16 December

Saw Lou and collected her old passport and sent it off to Petty France with application for new one. Wonder *why* I'm doing this? Is there a sentimental idea of taking her somewhere . . . even at this late date . . . for a holiday?

Sunday, 20 December

Michael came at 11.45. Eventually Nora, Cissie & Anne Lowe came. M. took them to Joe Allen & I went in a cab with Paul. Pat was there & Jeremy Swan, so it was nine of us altogether. At 6 o'c. Paul & Roland came to Lou for Scrabble. It was a v. good-humoured evening & everyone surprised when the time turned out to be 9.45! Lou was certainly ready for bed! But it was one of her most successful birthdays . . . seems incredible that she is 86! She will end up as the longest living of all the Morgans.[30]

Friday, 25 December

The streets are empty & everywhere has that muted hush & consequently *bird* song is there to irritate one. Did the turkey with sausages, roast potatoes & sprouts: Lou made gravy. It was simply superb & we had the Soave wine. Had a rest after. Saw Queen's Speech. It wasn't v. good. The script was dire. Whoever writes this drivel? Lou & me took a turn in the park . . . the sky was gold pink & the air was mild. V. pleasant . . . A girl with two dogs said 'Merry Christmas' as she went to park thro' Chester Terrace.

---

[30] She died in July 1991.

Thursday, 31 December
Loads of fan mail to answer – lots of 'em asking if there's to be another C.O. film. Ugh!

1988

Friday, 1 January
Took milk in for Lou at 8 o'c. Well, I wonder what *this* year will bring? The forecast from most economists is recession, we'll have to wait and see.

Saturday, 2 January
The papers full of 'Best of '87' lists and praise given to the usual mediocrities: it validates my belief that in England you just have to *endure* to score. The really talented seldom figure in any of the lists, it's always the rubbish that has been around for a long time. I suppose history will record it as the Year of the Market Crash. Thank goodness I only invested spare money on the Stock Exchange, and kept the important cash in the HICA and the DA for Tax, and the rest in NS Certificates. That means I've got realisable assets of about 180 thousand, but *that* is earmarked for a home when this flat proves invalid. The lease is up in 2000 and whatever happens I mustn't bank on staying here.

Tuesday, 5 January
Stayed indoors & read the rest of the Schumann biography.[1] It is obvious that his stay in the Mental Home was a dreadful mistake. What he really needed was some rich homosexual to take care of him, but the daft Clara put a stop to any chance of that. Ostwald reveals that Schubert was a homosexual!! & probably caught syphilis from a male prostitute! But he died of typhus. Saw Lou in the evening. The film was *Carry On Abroad* & I was featured doing all the old crap. Looking at this rubbish you realise that nothing has changed! British sit-coms all consist of the same routines, jokes, and dirt. Very depressing.

Sunday, 10 January
Lou suggested a walk. Conscious all the time of tooth pain moving to

---

[1] *Schumann: Music and Madness* by Peter F. Ostwald (1985).

the bridge tooth & back to mid tooth . . . I fear the Flagyl has not been of any use at all. Home by about 3.20. By which time the tooth next to mid one had become ultrasensitive! Pain on touching it or applying slight pressure! And the French idiot with TV blaring, the poof overhead banging about . . . oh! death would be marvellous.

Monday, 11 January
Took Lou in cab to Paris studio for 'J.A.M.' Producer said 'I think we should mention that Clement Freud has been made a knight' & I said 'I don't see why a game show should plug his honour' but it was done. Derek was good, Peter was good & so was I.

Thursday, 14 January
There is a statement from Norwich Union offering a Tax Free Cash sum of £24,204 and pension rising at 5% of £5,369 p.a. The 5% minimum would mean losing about 21,433 pounds till the 11th year (when I would be 74) after which you'd be over the 8000 mark and starting to show real profit.

Friday, 15 January
I went with Paul to John Lewis & then M&S and Marble Arch where we met M[ichael] A[nderson]! He said 'Who played the woman in *Browning Version*?'[2] & I said 'Jean Kent' straitway [*sic*].

Monday, 18 January
Ronnie Barker has announced his retirement at 58!! He must have made a fortune to be able to get out so quickly. Certainly don't blame him.

Tuesday, 19 January
Read some more of the Rock Hudson book.[3] I should think he was a pretty dull sort of man. There isn't one account of him reading a good book or knowing any poetry. ITV showed *Carry On Henry*. Oh dear! it was so bad in places . . . truly chronic dialogue . . . dreadful acting. Sid James had never been quite as bad as this. A collection of such rubbish you're amazed it could ever have been stuck together. Only an audience of illiterates could ever have found this tripe amusing.

Thursday, 21 January
In the post: one fan letter and a statement for tuppence ha'penny.

---

[2] The 1951 film of Terence Rattigan's play.
[3] *Rock Hudson: His Story* by Rock Hudson and Sara Davidson (1986).

What a year this is turning out to be! O! and there is a letter from Peter Shellard suggesting a Dent paperback of *Acid Drops*.

Tuesday, 26 January

Got papers. Wraith cleaner said to me 'Your filum is on tonight!' as if it were news of Nirvana. Went to Ian Wray. Discussed the Norwich Union offers and he said I should not take it at the moment. He said 'You've got enough coming in (apart from earnings) and any more would attract unnecessary tax.' Watched the TV news and then *Carry On Matron*. I was amazed 'cos there was actually a story/idea behind this one, as opposed to the usual stream of would-be jokes.

Wednesday, 27 January

More fan mail to answer. I think they imagine I look like the surgeon in *Carry On Matron* which was shown last night! I looked about 35! It was odd to watch – Bill Kenwright made a brief appearance! – and possibly, my bits were the best I've ever managed in that sort of crap. Went out to get refill for Edding pen. Met Mark (who wrote asking me to speak at the Theological College) and he walked with me to the pen shop & then to Ryman where I got envelopes. Asked him to have lunch with me at Vecchia tomorrow. After, I thought 'Why on earth am I doing this?'

Thursday, 28 January

Met Mark at Vecchia & gave him lunch: at the conclusion, he asked for Cointreau! A pleasant enough fellow: he loves Larkin, but seems strangely ambiguous about his real desires & vocation. There is a ready sense of humour. I suppose once I might have been flattered that the young were interested in my company (he is 19) but now, I don't really care about knowing anybody. Just nice to sit at a café table & watch the faces passing . . . nothing more.

Sunday, 31 January

Lou came in about 8.10 and called me into her flat. The bathroom window had been opened from outside & someone had got in!! She found her desk open! We checked everything & found nothing had been stolen! Jewellery and chequebook, cheque card etc. were all there. The only explanation is that someone got in, and then was disturbed & fled without stealing anything. She said she got up at 6 o'c. to go to the bathroom so I should think it was then (by turning the light on) that the burglar fled. Of course Lou was upset. I said that in future, we would lock everything – keep the window shut. We watched the Vet series: it was v. good: one scene where a farmer's much loved cow turned away from the slaughterhouse & returned home to a remorseful farmer was extraordinarily moving. Only the reciprocity of affection redeems this terrible life of ours, & men are just as predatory as animals: we tend to think of human beings as *all civilised* but they're not. Some remain savages to the end & prey on their fellows with unspeakable acts of horror, revealing our animal origins.

Wednesday, 3 February

Went shopping. I was feeling quite different from yesterday! Extraordinary how the mood can change! Suddenly quite optimistic!

Thursday, 4 February

Warned Lou that it was cold & windy. She went to her club at 11.45. I had fish cakes in her flat & saw the News: shares falling. Lou got back about 4.15: 'I'm so depressed . . . the idea of someone breaking into my flat is so horrible . . .' She obviously can't get it out of her mind!

Friday, 5 February

Switched from BBC to the other side 'cos *every* programme had idiots wearing plastic noses & behaving stupidly for some charity idea . . .[4] I have never been more sick of all this charity crap than in the last few years! It has become a mundane gimmick now & lost all the novelty value it once possessed: just an excuse for a lot of people to indulge themselves.

Saturday, 6 February

Letter from Jeff. He certainly has literary ability! The erotica is v. well expressed. Got me going! Saw Lords on TV debating the anti-homosexual clause in Local Govt. Bill . . . all dreary posturing . . . everyone pussyfooting round the uncomfortable truth that deviation is part of the human condition.

Sunday, 7 February

Changed into suit & went to Gordon & Rona at 7.15. Stood in rain & got soaked trying to find a taxi & then had premonition of disaster! I knew I didn't *want to go* & hated having to go. Eventually got cab and arrived there in the rain. We sat drinking till 9.45!! 'cos guests Roy & Carmel Kinnear were late. Barbara Murray (their other guest) was charming – unbelievably unaltered since I knew her at Margate in Rep!! She, intelligently, left at about 11.45. I stayed talking . . .

---

[4] 'Red Nose Day', for Comic Relief. A day-long charity fund-raising exercise dominated by comedians, clowns, and well-meaning exhibitionists.

eventually the Kinnears gave me a lift home & as their car drew away, I started searching my overcoat pocket for my keys! That is where I'd left them. In the taxi going to Hampstead, I'd taken out the key case & checked that it contained keys and a fiver (for cab or emergency) and *I know I put the key case back in the overcoat pocket.* Had to waken the Porter & he let me in. Rang Rona 'No there are no keys here . . .' So I will have to get new keys cut. The nervous system was given a horrible jolt. Lately, I've been losing so many things! – that watch (Rotary) inexplicably gone after the Gloria Hunniford radio prog. in December '87 and a few days ago, the newspaper cutting vanished, the nail scissors which were *always* in the bathroom gone . . . I s'pose it's old age . . . so unutterably depressing.

Monday, 8 February

The Porter came up & gave me a duplicate Front Door key. I must make it up to him for the awful intrusion of last night. Telephoned Roy Kinnear & he found my keys in *his car*!! (8.50am!) Got tube to Shep. Bush & met Roy & he gave me my keys. What a relief!! Oh! it will take me days to get over the horror of last night!! Sent note to Porter with a fiver.

Tuesday, 9 February

The PM spoke against televising the House of Commons, but in the event, the vote was for it! So she isn't in the mainstream of feeling on the issue. Of course it had to happen. The horrible inevitability of modernity means that much that was hallowed & private becomes public & mundane. There's nothing can be done about it. It's a pity the members can't get their act together & satisfy the public apropos capital punishment 'cos the return of hanging would be a v. good thing.

Thursday, 11 February

Tried to find a recording by Granados but the tune which Gordon played on Sunday – oh! exquisite – I couldn't remember the title – and the only recordings were on cassette not disc. Then I felt intense irritation that HMV play loud pretentious music when you're searching & need to concentrate. O! all these places are run by idiots.

Saturday, 13 February

Got fags at Littlewood & then fled up side streets away from the idiots & came home. An old queen was trying to get in to the block to see his Aunt Crookback. 'I left my umbrella behind!' she smiled. She never stopped smiling. Crookback was on the stairs 'I'm coming down with it!' so they sailed past each other. Turned off the later News 'cos it was only a rehash . . . *again* they picked on fighting by youths in Israel . . . how they love to disparage Jewry.

Sunday, 14 February

Up at 7.20 & got papers. It is a mild damp morning. I'm brimful with depression & suicidal theories . . . how quickly & easily could one make an end? Michael drove me & Lou to Joe Allen and Lou gave us lunch. M. dropped us at Chester Gate & I took Lou for a stroll in the park: it was a lovely afternoon with wintry sun thro' the cloud. In the evening we saw '[All] Creatures Great and Small'[5] which is excellent: the series gets better and better & the casting is little short of miraculous. Robert Hardy especially good! One of our finer actors with an extraordinary quality all his own.

Tuesday, 16 February

Michael Anderson rang: 'They're offering you 5000 for a week in Australia . . . you can do your own thing.' I said I couldn't leave Lou to fend for herself. Then he asked if I would talk about *Buccaneer* to HTV & I said yes.

Friday, 19 February

In the afternoon I got trousers at M&S & took 'em to Tony Philips for alteration: they're 34 waist 'cos I'm too fat for 32 now. Walked home without overcoat! There's no doubt, the weather is marvellous.

Saturday, 20 February

For one day, I leave off the Fybogel & of course this morning the B[owel] M[ovement] was awful. Had to use syringe. Did replies to letters & went to post at 11 o'c. I collected trousers from Tony & he's done the elasticated waist for me. Back by about 2 o'c. The queen above banging about . . . heaven knows what she gets up to. Had a bath. Spent a long time lying in it which is rare for me . . . thought to myself 'One day this poor old bag of flesh & bones will be lying on a mortuary slab . . . cold sterile hands will feel the flab . . .' Put on the Fauré record after: it is music full of regret & understanding. Received letter from Tim Rice in New York and I was greatly touched: it is such a generous gesture. I must ask Michael Anderson if there is an English address I can write to 'cos I'd like to express my thanks. Every time he's been on 'J.A.M.' I have liked Tim enormously.

---

[5] BBC TV series based on the veterinary stories of James Herriot (J.A. Wight), b.1916.

Monday, 22 February
Up at 8 o'c. after terrible night. Several letters but certainly no avalanche on my 62nd birthday! One sweet one from David in Melbourne, and one from Paul F. in Sydney. A very funny card from Jeremy! Got papers . . . Lou put 'Happy Birthday' note thro' my door. Saw Lou in the evening. She said 'It hasn't been much of a birthday for you . . .' I said 'Nowadays I don't care at all for celebrations . . .'

Wednesday, 24 February
After the cornflakes/muesli I had nausea and it went on & on! Lunch with Lou at 12 o'c. (stewed steak) and after that it was *awful*. Went to bed but row from the French cow went on & on. Took some Zantac 'cos I think the ulceration may be back!

Thursday, 25 February
Went to do v/o for Pallasades at 145 Wardour St. The girl made me go back on it loads of times to get timing exact. Three 30 second commercials. All the time the ulcer was playing up! Stabbing as far as the mid-breastbone! It is back with a vengeance. Rushed home to take the Zantac. Only had 1 piece of dry bread this morning 'cos I didn't want any trouble. Saw Lou at 5.15 for a meal. Haddock mornay. Afterwards there were chest pains and after about an hour, the mouth began filling with saliva & the head became hot. Eventually it passed but the nausea was horrible. I don't know why I should be getting such awful bouts of ailments *this year*! Repaired Lou's switch on her reading lamp on dressing table. The new switch cost me 1.40 and when Lou asked what she owed me I said 'Well, there is the cost of the switch, then there is labour costs, then there is VAT so call it 28 pounds' & she said 'Goodnight!' & we both laughed.

Friday, 26 February
The French cow has gone to France . . . leaving a mountain of rubbish in the hall. Lurgy said they're going to do the outside of the block next month!! That would be the time to take holiday! Gordon rang 'We went to see Maggie in her play![6] Oh! she is marvellous in it! She mentioned you afterwards in the dressing room, said you'd *never* go to the theatre . . . and she remembered it was your birthday recently . . .' We had quite a talk. He said 'You really *should* go & see the play' but I said I'd no interest in theatre. I really haven't . . . it's like a Pollock set[7] one has grown out of.

---

6 Peter Shaffer's *Lettice and Lovage*, at the Globe.
7 'Pollock's Toy Theatres', sold from a shop in Hoxton during KW's youth.

Saturday, 27 February

On '7 Days' that man Kee[8] went on & on about a British soldier whose regiment took him back after a court found him guilty of shooting an Irish civilian during a disturbance. He went on & on about the 18 yr. old being a murderer who should never have been allowed back in the Army, & quoting a Judge as saying the boy had told lies etc. This Robert Kee was using all the language of revenge & punishment. The whole evening was ruined with stomach pain. Oh! I hope this ghastly affliction passes!

Sunday, 28 February

Took Bisodol before going to Joe Allen with Michael and Louisa. Had soup and salmon. No wine. M. said he was going to Italy in a fortnight. 'Creatures Great & Small' was again superb! That boy I used in *Loot* was playing a compassionate father . . . a wee bit over the top, but then he always was.[9] Robert Hardy & all the others were super, but R.H. has got something special. This is a really *good* series & makes the others look like the rubbish they are.

Monday, 29 February

Read that the quarterly trade deficit is disastrous. It's the result of what I've deplored all along – cheap credit pulling in imports – the Bank rate should have gone up ages ago. Saw some TV: a programme about the failure rate in a cure for cancer in America & the sad testament of a patient who later died. By 8.40 the pain started and by 9.15 it was ghastly. The stomach feels like someone is squeezing a balloon. It's something between the pain of diarrhoea and hysteria with the blood pumping loud as a drum thro' the head & the body feeling feverish. Looking back over the diaries I see that the stomach trouble has really been with me, on and off, for years. It seems to be worse in the winter, but that's not an infallible rule. Trouble is, when the pain is at its height one just wants to die: as soon as it subsides, the spirits recover & there's an almost daft optimism.

Tuesday, 1 March

Consoled myself by looking up diaries for the last 2 years & finding all the symptoms much the same as before. The awfulness seems to come in bouts caused by heaven knows what, and then to subside after a while, before smiting one again with renewed malignance.

---

[8] Robert Kee, author and broadcaster, b.1919.

[9] Episode 7, 'Ace, King, Queen, Jack'. With Philip Martin Brown as Jack.

Wednesday, 2 March

Haven't had such a lousy night for ages! And the result of 3 bits of toast!! Rang Jeremy at 8 o'c. & cancelled Vecchia 'cos I couldn't risk pain of late eating. Replied to G. in Capetown & to Nick at Warwick University.[10] To post at 11 o'c. and then to look at frocks in M&S but couldn't find anything right for Lou. Did fillet steak for her & I had fish in parsley sauce. No awful after effects! Only the usual dyspepsia, but nothing horrific. Took Fybogel, but in afternoon, went to chemist's and got Isogel 'cos I think it's better. That comprised the day. What a life. Walking to shops & walking home again.

Thursday, 3 March

In the afternoon I went to John Fawcett Wilson taking the book of 'R.T.H.' to Room 105, so he can copy the songs I'm to do in the programme for him on Monday. Went to M&S at Marble Arch & found a size 10 dress. Red with brass buttons, for Lou. Came home & shortened it to 36″ overall. Then pressed it. I cooked the steak for her. I didn't have anything. Pain from abdomen was too much.

Friday, 4 March

Peter Shellard rang: 'Would you mind being photographed again for our re-issue of *Acid Drops*?' I said no & he said he'd fix a session & let me know. By 8 o'c. the diarrhoea-like pains began in the abdomen. I've been on the Zantac for days & days & it don't seem to make any difference. Only thing which *is* a rule is that the pain is usually worse at about 9 to 10 in the evening.

Saturday, 5 March

News showed more of the agit-prop groups marching to Hyde Park & screaming the odds about NHS . . . it said Nurses were shivering in the cold so let's hope they all get very ill indeed.

Sunday, 6 March

Michael came & took me & Lou to the Paris for 'J.A.M.' Both shows were awful. At the outset, I couldn't even get into the narration booth!! I stood around for ages & no one bothered so I went & sat in the foyer. The team was Nimmo, Percival, Freud, me and in the second Percival left & was replaced by Dickie Murdoch. The stuff was diabolical. Freud using extraordinary language . . . set quite the wrong tone! Apropos education in England, he said 'It is an entire W.C.' David Hatch would have stopped the show & started again. Flew out after & evaded autograph hunters.

---

[10] Nick Lewis, a student with whom KW had maintained an avuncular correspondence.

Monday, 7 March
I wish I didn't have to go the Paris tonight for this Spinners[11] show. Walked to the Paris studio with stomach churning. Met the Spinners in the narration booth & then rehearsed songs with Terry Walsh [guitarist] . . . oh! it was a delight to see him again. Alas! we have both grown old since the days of 'R.T.H.' Eventually I went on and did the spot in an enclosed space – they screened off the studio saying it made a good atmosphere but the truth was that it was a sparse audience.

Tuesday, 8 March
Michael has given me an anthology of diary entries; one notices that the modern ones are better than the old. The preoccupation with diary writing is caused by various things: the desire to keep a record which can be useful later, and committing to paper what can't be communicated to a mentor . . . oh! all kinds of reasons, but *fundamentally* it is about loneliness.

Wednesday, 9 March
With Paul to the bank where I deposited the endorsements for N[orwich] U[nion] policies. Then we walked to John Lewis where P. got spatula, then to M&S for food. By that time the stomach was like a vice of pain with nausea & contraction pains & I felt suicidal. Saw Lou at 5.45. I could barely speak 'cos the pain was starting up again. Saw the News and by the time 'Dallas' had finished, so was I.

Thursday, 10 March
Went to Boots & got an invalid liquid food, thinking that might be the answer. I had to sign autographs for a traffic warden. Michael came at 6.30. We drove to Sadler's Wells where Paul was looking out for us & Roland had the tickets for *Bitter Sweet*. The production was deft and immaculate & the singing excellent. The set was adroitly contrived so that transformation scenes practically glided by and when the last cycle was complete it was quite moving. A superb evening in the theatre only marred by a man coming on before the curtain to ask for money to rebuild the proscenium. After, with Paul and Roland & M. to Joe Allen where M. gave us supper. What a wonderful evening! The Master would have been proud of all of them in that cast tonight. I saw Bertice Reading[12] in J.A. and she kissed me affectionately. 'When are you coming to see *South Pacific?*'[13] I said 'Oh Bertice!

---

[11] Veteran Liverpool folk-music group, since disbanded.
[12] Rotund, energetic, big-eyed singer and star of musical comedy, d.1991.
[13] Revival of the Rodgers & Hammerstein musical at the Prince of Wales Theatre.

I've got a spastic colon!' & she said 'Oh!' in a tone of resignation. Pain in stomach all thro' the performance. It went off slightly during the meal. On arriving home, the belly was huge like a vast balloon. I couldn't pee properly. It was as if something was blocking the urinary tract. Ain't had *that* before. Took Gaviscon and put up a suppository. C. gave me the suppositories (Supponeryl) in 1970!!

Friday, 11 March

Stanley came and drove me to Upper St where we had dinner at a v. friendly restaurant. The soup was good but I couldn't eat the fish (it was too raw) and anyway, the stomach was agony *all the time*. Pain diminished a bit when I had a glass of wine, but it soon returned. I fear I was awful company: one is bifurcated by pain, the mind keeps wandering off on another tack. I think this is the worst period I've had since the onset of the trouble in early '86! No, it is worse because now it is ever present – night and day – an endless bane. I could hardly take in any of the conversation but tried to interject appropriately every now and again.

Saturday, 12 March

Went in to Lou to make bed & said I didn't really want to eat lunch. 'I feel so awful. Wish I was dead & out of it all.' 'But [what] about *me*?' was the reply. Nothing about my welfare, only 'What about me?' Walked to Boots at Marylebone & saw that marvellous manager. He gave me Carbellon and I took 2 tablets. The pain began to lessen. He also gave me a Boots magnesium mixture to try if the Carbellon didn't work. He said I must not stop taking the Zantac. Read TLS. By 6.30 I realised I'd been free from pain since returning from the chemist & heeding his advice. I shall go back to thank him *but* I'd like to do so much more for him.

Sunday, 13 March

I watched 'Money Programme' doing its forecast of the Budget on Tuesday: they don't know anything. Then it was 'Creatures Great & Small', brilliant as usual and then the dreadful Whicker Basket yacking away in Australia . . . then the News . . . people dead under avalanche of snow in St Anton . . . wish it was *me*. I could hardly sit & watch during the last half of the evening 'cos the pain was ever present and kept stabbing somewhere or other. I think about taking the overdose . . . where would I do it? Some place that would be safe & where one wouldn't be disturbed . . . and Lou would be left on her own, yes, it would be sad, but then I am sadder . . . the whole of life is sad . . . there is no compensation. Once the illusory fabric is shattered you face the fact that you're no different from the other animals in body

& reproduction, & that like them, there is a time to lie down & die. Took Supponeryl at about 10.45. Lay there for ages waiting for it to work while the pain needled me in groin, up breastbone, under right arm . . .

Monday, 14 March

Weird! how every day one *hopes* that the pain will stop! And how every respite finds the spirits raised ridiculously. Had cornflakes at 9 o'c. & by 10.30 there was no pain! I will stay on cornflakes I think & see how I fare on that sort of diet. Sat with Lou watching the TV rubbish. She has been v. down lately, I suppose there is something wrong but I am so low myself I can't really cope. I'd put a new battery in the deaf aid but tonight she complained 'I can't hear a thing even when it's full on . . .' 'O! really?' I replied & did nothing.

Tuesday, 15 March

Went to Doug at the chemist & he gave me a bottle of K&M & listened to more of my moaning. Pain returned at 4 o'c. with a vengeance. One wants to *die* now I'm practically doubling up with the agony. Tried to watch the 'Morse'[14] series but eventually fled back to flat hardly bidding goodnight to Lou. I'm reaching the point where I'm in danger of becoming unhinged. Today I forgot Equity meeting!! I'm putting shaving cream on the toothbrush . . . the abstraction is ghastly.

Thursday, 17 March

Got tube to Pimlico and saw Dr Newlands (Bertie away in Australia) who gave me prescript. for Zantac & advised different dosage & recommended something else. Tube back. London bathed in sunshine . . . quite mild & pleasant. By 8 o'c. the pain was back again. Could not face the news . . . tried to watch a bit of 'L.A. Law' and then I had to give up. Bade Lou a hasty goodnight and came back to flat. Oddly, the pain is more tolerable if one is alone. I had found Lou (noisily eating nuts all thro' the TV programme) terribly irritating.

Friday, 18 March

Found my tap wouldn't turn off in kitchen! Rang plumber & he came at 10.20. Fixed it for 13.70. Took all of five minutes. By 3 o'c. in Mowbray's the pain began, burning & stabbing right above navel. God! I practically fainted with the onslaught. Rushed back to flat. Nothing worked. Went in to Lou for the News at 6 o'c. Sat writhing in pain till 8 o'c. when I decided to have some toast. 4 slices. Then

---

[14] 'Inspector Morse', a series of two-hour detective dramas starring John Thaw. Discontinued in 1992.

coffee. The usual hiatus followed. Heard clock striking midnight & still the pain lurked up & down both sides of chest.

Saturday, 19 March

Horrible pictures of Irish murderers dragging two British soldiers from their car and stripping them & killing them.[15] Don't think I've ever seen anything so disgusting on television. These people are nothing to do with political activists or 'nationalism', they are sadists who get pleasure in this fashion; ignorant, evil scum.

Sunday, 20 March

After the cornflakes, pain started. When Michael came I said I couldn't face going out. He was v. patient and understanding. He said 'You really should see someone else about this endless pain.' Eventually, I took loads of hot water & Gaviscon. Then he took me & Lou to Joe Allen. I drank Fernet Branca. Seemed to ease things. Had soup & then fish. Ned Sherrin was at the next table & we chatted: he is a kind & courteous man. Got Lou settled in flat for her rest. Then I walked in the rain in the park 'cos there was no peace in the flat with the idiot above stomping about & having radio (or TV?) on at a ludicrous volume. Saw Lou in the evening. Watched the TV 'Creatures Great & Small'. It was, as usual, superb. Oh! it is the best thing one can see. The pain continued. Returned to the flat at about 8.45. Took more K&M & Bisodol. Thought of making an end of it tonight & then wondered whether things were left in proper order. Should I write a letter to Michael? best of people & best of my friends. Would it be fair to ask him to tell all the others? The dear chums like Stanley and Gordon & Paul? Oh, I don't suppose any of it would matter . . . once I'm gone, the Police are bound to be called in & they would find all the names in my address book of the people that would have to be informed. One only hopes that an autopsy would reveal the cause of all the pain: might help somebody else. Can't get the thought of those two soldiers in Belfast out of my mind. Hope the animals who killed them are caught. Went to bed at 10.30 but I was up again at 11.30 and up again at 12.30 taking Gaviscon. Took 2 I.F. tablets 'cos the constipation has been chronic. This, in spite of Isogel with the cornflakes. Oh! to be out of it for ever! To cease upon the midnight with no pain. Why do I linger? Not from love of life, I've always found it awful . . . no, it's rather from a sense of *curiosity* . . . not wanting to miss the third act.

---

[15] Corporals Wood and Howes of the Signals Regiment died after their car was attacked at a Republican funeral procession in West Belfast.

Monday, 21 March

Kept thinking 'I could have *gone* last night. Needn't have been here this morning to face another day of agony.' Went to M&S to get food for Lou. I'm not having any. Pain has started already (since 9 o'c.) & I don't want to add to the problem. Well, I think everything has been thought of. My will is deposited with the Midland Bank. Michael gets most of the stuff & I should think he could fix Lou in some retirement home. Dreared thro' the day. Went to have haircut: seems odd to bother about such things before dying. Had nothing to eat. Coffee at 4 o'c. & took Libraxin but it didn't kill the pain. The sun has come out – as if to say 'Stay! I'm beautiful' but I'm not deceived.

Went in to Lou for News and watched a programme about a nuclear physicist: Reynsford.[16]

Came back to flat & got out the Sodium Amytal[17] & then had cold feet. Took 2. Lay there waiting for the stuff to work for about 20 to 30 minutes.

Tuesday, 22 March

Woke with *dreadful head* at about 7 o'c. Up at 8 o'c. to get paper. Today I will *have* to do something about the stomach problem. Can't see any other way than to go back to Murray-Lyon. Rang & got appt. for 6.30 tonight ('but we'll ring if there's a cancellation'). Saw Lou: she'd been to P.O. for pension. Went out with Paul at 1.30 to M&S and Selfridge's. Had a Bounty & a choc. biscuit. No pain! but I feel as if the head is woozy. Went to Iain Murray-Lyon at 5.15. He saw me straightway. After examination he said I'd have to go to Hospital for more Tests and a gastroscopy. His secretary Sheila will find out when there's a bed available.

Wednesday, 23 March

Sheila rang about 10 o'c. I'm to go into Cromwell Hospital on Friday about 2 o'c. Nothing to eat from 8 o'c. on Friday morning. Rang M.A. & he cancelled 'J.A.M.' on 27th & HTV on 30th and I'm certainly pleased about that! Went to M&S & got fish. Had it with Lou at 12 o'c. Took a 300 Zantac before & there was awful pushing & squelching after as everything tried to get down. Went out to P.O. in afternoon to post letters. Walked around the block like a zombie. Toast. Pain intermittent & only slight.

---

[16] Richard Feynman. The programme was 'Horizon: The Pleasure of Finding Things Out'. Repeated from 1981, it was 'A celebration of the life of Richard Feynman, Nobel Laureate in Physics and renowned teacher, who died on 15 February, 1988.'

[17] A barbiturate.

Thursday, 24 March

Did letters. Sent cheque for £1000 to Camden for Estimated Rates & one from Lou for same. Letter from Isabel [Dean] asking me to sign her Proposal form for Equity. Posted everything in Fitzroy St. Walked to Angell Sound to do v/o with Brian Blessed. Told him how superb he'd been as Silver – marvellous actor. Second v/o was with Bryan Pringle: he looked curiously wasted. It was *lovely* being with actors again. Oh! I do enjoy their company. Walked home thro' windy streets conscious of pain coming up round heart. Saw Lou in the evening. Went to bed early.

Friday, 25 March

Up at 7 o'c. after lousy night. Went for papers. After I'd had coffee I realised I can't have anything to eat or drink till tomorrow! What a life! Now I have to drear about starving till I go to the Cromwell Hospital for these tests. Got cab at 1.20. Arrived on time. Waited in bedroom in the surgical gown for Sonic Scan scheduled for 2.30. Eventually I was done at 3.50!! 'So sorry, we thought you were coming as an out-patient & didn't know you were *in* the hospital.' One forgets the world is full of idiots. Murray-Lyon did the gastroscopy & said there was a huge ulcer in the same place. Then I was wheeled back to the room. I asked him 'Is there anything which exacerbates this condition' and he said 'Smoking' adding that there was *proof* that ulcers were the result of smoking. Had a meal at about 8 o'c. and everything tasted marvellous. Twinge of regret when it came to the coffee and one realised . . . no fags . . . shame. The habit of a lifetime taken away from one.

Saturday, 26 March

Murray-Lyon came in about 8 o'c. and said 'This is the third time you've had the ulcer so you will have to think about whether or not you can repeat the cycle. Talk to Keith Reynolds about the alternatives. No one wants to rush you into surgery, but you must consider your position . . .' Then he left. Then Reynolds came in. 'I used to smoke . . . 50 a day . . . I had to give it up. What you've got to decide is whether you can try going on & trusting to the Zantac, or whether you have the operation . . . you should come & talk to me when you get out and we can make a plan . . . you've got to remember the *timing* of the operation is important . . . you're no chicken . . .' After lunch I had a doze. Michael came in the afternoon & we were having the chat when in walked Stanley. He made us both laugh about the parvenu Princess Michael of Kent. He lent me a copy of a Spencer

Tracy biog.[18] Got the sleeping pills for rest at 10.15. Couldn't get off properly . . . A day of No Smoking.

Sunday, 27 March

Michael came at 8.45 and I got lift down to meet him in the foyer. He brought me home to the flat by about 5 to 9. He's going to take Lou out to lunch today & Paul is going too. I will think of some excuse to stay at home. While they were at Joe Allen's I took Lou's curtains down & washed them. Cleaned windows & ironed curtains & rehung them. Then I had Scotch broth out of a tin. Dropped off for a few minutes. Came to, thinking 'What on earth am I doing? What's it all for?' Went out & walked to Marylebone & back – for something to do. All the while the wind pain coming up to the chest . . . oh! the dolour is never ending. Saw Lou in the evening & it was all defiance: 'I'm going to have cigarettes if I want to' & 'I hardly smoke at all, anyway . . .' etc. Apropos the windows 'Yes, well, you needn't have bothered, I could have got someone in to do them . . .' I discovered the plastic cake box has been burned by a cigarette! Showed it to Lou 'Well I don't know how *that* happened.' But then she doesn't know how anything happens. Returned to my flat at about 9.15. Read before turning in. Another day of No Smoking. Stanley has given me a biography of Tracy and it is interesting to read that he was plagued by stomach ulcers!!

Monday, 28 March

Got papers. Did all letters etc. Went to post at 9.30 then to M&S for food. Came back, gave stuff to Lou. Then washed the ceiling & walls in the kitchen and the pails full of brown water had to be continually emptied down the sink. It was disgusting. Went to Lou at 12 o'c. & did grilled fish for lunch. She is being bad-tempered and unpleasant *all because I've said no smoking*! She doesn't want to give it up, but I've told her I'll leave if she smokes. The walls of her flat are dark brown with the stains. There was the usual pain after food, dyspeptic stabbing right side. It is still raining. At about 2.30 I walked to John Lewis to see if they had any decent cotton D/gowns but the only suitable one was too large. Did some more cleaning in the kitchen: it acts as a sort of therapy. Threw out all my stock of fags. Oh! it was such a daft & dirty habit to get into!! Third day of No Smoking. One doesn't feel any different. Not even *slightly* different. I feel exactly the same as before. I think the only difference will be a saving! 'cos I'll not be buying any fags.

---

[18] *Spencer Tracy* by Bill Davidson, 1987.

Tuesday, 29 March

Went to Equity. Council Meeting. Isabel thanked me for the Proposal Form. Nigel Davenport made reference to my indisposition. Stayed till 11.15 when I walked home in the drizzling rain. Lunch with Lou. She's still in a great sulk over the No Smoking. 'I don't see why I shouldn't have a cigarette if I fancy one! All the things that are supposed to be bad for us . . . Oh! you might as well lay down & die.' I said 'It is *lie* down, not lay down,' adding she could do as she pleased when I wasn't there. Saw Paul at 1.15 and we went to Selfridge's to look at D/gowns. The prices were ludicrous! Went to C&A where I got a nice one for £18. Gordon phoned earlier. Said I shouldn't go for surgery 'Keep taking the Zantac.' Rona asked me up there, but I said I didn't fancy being social & anyway couldn't risk eating without being able to escape quickly in case of pain. 'Oh you do sound *low* . . .' she said. Read the Tracy biography & finished it. G. said it was lousy & he is right. He told me 'Of course the real truth is that Spencer was gay, that's why the dykey tendency was OK for him: it provided perfect cover . . .' Seen that way, the paradoxical life all makes sense.

Saw Lou in the evening. Had some toast. Dyspepsia after. The television was awful. A dreadful musical revue thing with a juvenile introducing Dora Bryan with dialogue that must've come out of the Ark. Russell Harty in France talking about a woman feeling his legs under the table and then revealing that she was searching for a bell. That's his kind of prurience & the terrible thing is, it's mirthless.

Wednesday, 30 March

Lou gave all her fags to the Porter!! So she has definitely decided to give up smoking like me. This is my fifth day of No Smoking.

Thursday, 31 March

I continued cleaning the walls. I did the front room and the hall by 5.15. By 9.30 when I came back to flat, the pain was murder.

Friday, 1 April

Up at 7 o'c. (awake since 5 o'c.) Must've heard every quarter chime on the church clock. Walked to Cleveland St for papers. For lunch, did grilled pork chops for Lou & I had 3 lamb chops, chips & tomatoes. Tried to rest after, but Stanley telephoned, ostensibly to ask about the ulcer but really to talk because he's bored: 'I just don't know what to do, I thought about a walk across the Heath but it's a holiday so all the Nellies will be out . . . pointing at one . . .' At about 1.40 I walked to M&S at Marble Arch & found them open!! Wish I'd known that this morning! So I got food for tomorrow and for Monday.

By 6 o'c. I tried an enema. Bed at 9.30 but I was up again & again till 12 o'c. when I took K&M in desperation.

Saturday, 2 April

When I heard Lou go out (for her bus ride to Archway) I went in and cleaned the kitchen walls and ceiling. The water was utterly brown. Dark brown and I had to go over the job again & it's still not clean. But it's better than it was. At about 2 o'c. I had that awful blockage pain so I took 2 Fybogel. Seemed to ease it 'cos I did the work in kitchen without awful pain. Lou came back from Archway & uttered her usual cry 'Oh! Gawd 'elp us' when she saw me up the ladder & there were protests about 'You just want to *find* work.' Saw the 'Newsview' and then some dreadful crap about French collaborateurs.[19] What is there to say about *that*? Some people will submit to conquerors & some won't. Some believe in Nationalism & some don't. It's all one. They'll all die anyway. It was particularly irritating 'cos the translation was spoken over the French voices, giving one *two* lots of sound. Ugh . . . anyone who can produce such cacophonous crap should be shot (Ophuls). With this endless pain (it used to be 2 hours after eating, now it just goes on & on) I really don't know how I get thro' the days. It colours everything. Don't really want to see anyone.

Sunday, 3 April

M. came at 12.10. I rang Paul and asked him to lunch. He said 'I'm not dressed for it' but I said 'At Joe Allen's there's no dress.' We drove there & I got thro' soup & sole OK. Paul & Lou & me had a walk in the park. Sun was intermittent & there was a breeze, but I'd no overcoat! The News was all about various people going mad . . . one perfectly respectable mother in an Oxfordshire village suddenly murdered both her children and cut her throat & threw herself into a village pond & drowned . . . in another place a woman has been found in a river near Bridgwater dead for some time . . . police have arrested a spy in Friern Barnet . . .

9th day of No Smoking & I feel no benefit whatsoever, but I'll not go back to it – it's the sheer *dirt* of it that makes it so awful.

Monday, 4 April

Up at 7 o'c. & got paper. Met my hoarse friend again (same as yesterday) and we exchanged greetings & expressed doubt as to the sanity of the bishops.[20] Went for a walk with Paul. We had a look round

---

[19] *The Sorrow and the Pity* (*Le Chagrin et la pitié*), by Marcel Ophuls (final part).

[20] The Bishop of Durham, Rt. Rev. David Jenkins, had attacked Conservative government policies from the pulpit on 3 April, Easter Day.

Debenhams & I tried on a blouson but didn't like it. Lunch Lou. She's been grumpy & dreary ever since I came out of hospital. I'm too full of pain to care. Saw Paul at 1 o'c. & he drove me to Highgate Woods & we walked there for an hour or so. Had some toast about 6 o'c. and up to about 8.45 thought I'd got away with it, & then *bang*! the hopes were dashed as the same old pain returned & by 9.15 it was awful. O! these days are like living thro' some fiendishly designed Hell where the food is presented as it was to Tantalus & then as soon as the eating begins, the pain is assured.

Tuesday, 5 April

Went to M&S for food. Came back & gave stuff to Lou. Told her to grill the fish for herself 'I'm going out for lunch' & she said OK but it was all v. grumpy & resentful. To Vecchia at 12 o'c. Michael was there. Jean Jacques & Jeff came at 12.04. We had a pleasant time: M. kept things going v. well. After, I took them to John Lewis for sheets and to BHS and then, on foot, to Nat. Gallery where they wanted the Impressionists. Home by 3.30. No pain so far!!

By 8.30 the pain began. Returned to flat at 9.30 & took 3 Zantac. Pain took *ages* to subside.

Wednesday, 6 April

Up at 7.15. Got papers. Did letters & went to post. Then to Doug to get Lactulose – £4!! very expensive! Almost forgot! Yesterday was the end of the Financial Year! Made up the Ledger. So far, got nothing to show for this month at all! Lunch (lamb cass.) with Lou. Had a rest after. Must've dropped off for about 20 minutes. When I woke I was totally disorientated. 'Where am I?' 'What day is it?' 'What time is it?' Went out to M&S and got pork pie & salad for tonight. Served it at 6 o'c. and Lou said 'Oh! I feel bloated after that! My stomach feels as if it don't belong to me!' Saw the news. Same old rubbish. Hijacking of planes by Arab terrorists, murder of UDR man in Ulster, etc. etc. Year in, year out, nothing changes. Usual diarrhoea-like pains. Went to bed at about 10 o'c. Wish it was never to wake again.

12th day of No Smoking . . . odd that it was once such an *essential* part of my life! I see other people smoking & I think 'How sad' 'cos one knows that they've taken to it for the same reason I did – to cheat despair. But it's like taking aspirin: the effect is only temporary.

Thursday, 7 April

Up at 7 o'c. & got the papers. Had the coffee. That's the one time I miss the fags!! Did letters & went to the post. At 10 o'c. I went to M&S to get food. Then to cleaners to collect the corduroy trousers: hardly recognised the colour! They must have been filthy. By the time

I got home at 11.15 the dyspepsia was stabbing chest – O God! this pain never stops! There is atrocious *farting*, truly foul. Worse than anything I can remember. Went out at 2.15 to cleaners with grey suit & took the hand-made shoes back to Savva to have 'em stretched. Went to Mowbray but the idiot cashier loudly talking (as usual) sent me away: one simply can't concentrate while she rabbits on & on & on.

Read in the paper of the death of Myra De Groot at 51. It is extraordinary! She had written to me saying she was coming over, to do chat shows about her role in 'Neighbours'! Must have been something v. sudden to cause death . . . lucky old Myra! No lingering pain.[21] Watched TV with Lou. Longing to be out of it all.

Friday, 8 April

Got papers. After BM bent (as if to use suppos.) and there was dreadful pain from spine. Telephoned Johnson at 8.30 & luckily got a cancellation for 10 o'c. Walked to Marble Arch painfully. Johnny told me that his son had been murdered by black muggers (3 of them) in New York. Stabbed to death. This was in July last year. He said 'If there hadn't been bars on those windows . . . I'd have jumped out.' Here is a man who's saved thousands from pain and he gets the bitterest pill of all – he adored his son. Came home, still feeling twinges . . . Lunch with Lou at 12 o'c. Oh dear! she is a bad-tempered drear these days! I don't enjoy going in there at all. Had a lie down at 12.30. Dropped off. Woke with that awful 'Where am I?' feeling at 1.30. Had to turn on side to get up from bed. The pain is still there all right. Johnny told me that the swollen area is the Gall Bladder 'but the swelling is in the secum as well . . .' Went out to M&S for food. Walked home by 3.50. Pain in stomach – ate some cornflakes. Went in to Lou. Watched TV. More about hijacking of airliner by Arab terrorists: the filthy cowards have got over fifty Kuwaiti men & women & have now gone from Iran to Larnaca in Cyprus. Sat in pain all evening. Could hardly bear to speak to Lou who prattled on about various trivialities till I wanted to scream.

Saturday, 9 April

Up at 7.10 after terrible night. Can only turn over if I bend the knees. The back is agony. Can't stand & wash with both hands – have to use one hand to support self. O! these days are awful to live through. The stomach pain started about 8.30, in spite of Zantac. The idea of going to be photographed today is *loathsome*. Car at 12.30 for this photo

---

[21] She actually died of bone cancer. Her character in the Australian soap opera 'Neighbours', Eileen Clarke, did not die, but went to Brisbane.

session with Oliver Hatch. He was v. professional. Finished, as he'd predicted, at 1.30. Car waited & brought me home again. It was a photo with the Acid Drop. Had a lie-down on return home but noise of scaffolding put paid to that.

Went in to Lou and had some toast. She'd been all over the place trying to get a new glass for her bracelet watch – it's only a cheap wind-up I got for her in Ratner's – but she couldn't get a replacement. Saw some TV but the back pain now combines with the stomach pain to make everything awful. Don't know how I live thro' these days. What a joke to think I was posing for the photographs today!! Smiling & smirking into the camera with the inside crying out 'Die! Forget it!' and the pain ever present.

Can't get Yootha Joyce out of my head – and the time she sang 'For All We Know' . . . there was almost a break in the voice when she got to 'Tomorrow may never come . . .' but she carried on. She died shortly after. A lady who made so many people happy & a lady who never complained.

Sunday, 10 April

Back pain continues! I'll have to ring Johnny Johnson tomorrow. It is murder. Lousy night. Woke at 5 o'c. Up at 7 o'c. Got papers. My spirits are so low. Everything conspires to make life intolerable. Michael came at 12 o'c. & took Lou & me to Joe Allen; he gave us lunch & told Lou 'It's my turn! & don't forget I'm going away on Wednesday for a fortnight . . .' so we won't see him for two Sundays . . . mind you, it's just as well! He must get sick of the chore & us two crocks every week. Sixteenth day of No Smoking.

Saw Lou in the evening & we saw *Breaker Morant* about commando units in the Boer War. After watching it, you realise nothing has changed . . . the same old passing the buck, the same fools in in command & the same heroes below. A beautifully made picture but I can't stand the flash-back scenario. General Kitchener had a ludicrous role. It was written like a daft supernumerary.

Monday, 11 April

Rang Johnson and got appt. for 5.20. If I'd rung earlier I could have got cancellation at 8.40. Went to M&S for food at 9.40. Came back. Collected Lou's watch (Timex) and took it to shop in the tube at Oxford Circus: said they'd fix it by Wednesday. Walked home thro' sunny streets. Spoke to a navvy in the road 'You've not given up smoking?' 'I'll give up sex before I do that!' Back by 11 o'c. feeling v. tired – can't think why I should be so exhausted . . . ain't done anything. Lunch with Lou (fish) at 12 o'c. and after that I tried to rest but the builders in Follets ruined the peace – at 1.45 I walked to park & sat in a deck chair. So of course, an idiot nearby starts to load a lorry with grass cuttings, spade jarring on the asphalt, lorry engine being revved again & again . . . at least the sun came out for a bit & I got some colour. At 5.20 I went to Johnny Johnson: he was loath to do anything drastic. 'I think you should have an X-ray' but I said 'Only if it hasn't cleared up in two days.' I am not going to be rushed into these expenses any more unless I have to.

Back by about 6.30. Saw Lou. Had some toast. Saw the News. That hijacking at Larnaca is *still going on* with these animals killing more Kuwaiti hostages – oh! it's utterly foul. The rest of the TV was dire. Repeats and other rubbish.

Tuesday, 12 April

Back is a bit better! Hope this means it's on the mend! Up at 7 o'c. (awake since 5 o'c.) and got the papers. I have had nothing from I.C.M. for ages! Shows how bad the work situation has become! Good job I've got other money coming in, or I'd really be lost! Cancelled the appt. with Johnson on Wednesday 'cos I think the back is improving. Went to M&S at 10.30 and got shopping. Wearing only a raincoat 'cos the weather is milder! Lunch (steak pie & green beans) with Lou at 12 o'c. We sit eating like a couple of zombies. Even tho' she's given up the fags, her breath comes in wheezes & it really grates on one's nerves. O! the problems of the elderly! They're never-ending. Had to adjust lavatory *again* 'cos she can't pull the cistern handle properly!!

Went in to the Bank in the afternoon. Saw Mr Sparkes the manager. He said he'd arrange to close the D/A and open a HICA No.2 a/c. He said he'd inform Equity & Law about the new arrangements. Just hope it all goes smoothly. He said that the interest on the D/A was v. low and that I was losing money on the deal. I took the dividend mandate for Norton Opax which Ian Wray has sent me. Walked to Waterstone's & got a book. C. has sent me *The Swimming Pool Library*[22] & it is extraordinarily good!

Saw Lou at 5.30. Saw the TV News. This hijacking still drags on. Now, they've released *some* hostages and are flying from Larnaca to Algeria!! Ugh! they're unspeakable thugs . . . they murdered two Kuwaiti officers in Cyprus & threw the bodies on to the tarmac.

18th day of No Smoking and *nothing* to show for it! Not even a teeny weeny symptom.

Wednesday, 13 April

Up at 7.10. Got papers. Letter from I.C.M. saying I have to get train ticket for Swindon on Monday. O! how I dread all this! They say

---

[22] By Alan Hollinghurst.

'Bring wellingtons 'cos it's muddy.' I shall do nothing of the kind. Lou going to hairdresser. I went to Paddington to get ticket for Swindon where I have to go for this in-house video filming. Walked from Paddington to the park & sat with Sam & his wife & Sam Sugar, in the morning sun. Sat too long 'cos I got v. red. All the while, instead of usual right side stitch pain, it is now the left!! Pushing, stabbing, ebbing, then recurring. Returned to the flat about 2 o'c. and had branflakes & a rest after. Then I went to Tesco in Goodge Street. Got some bits & pieces. Ate Twiglets all the way home. Shifted the pain a bit but it returned doggedly. Had lamb casserole with Lou at 5.30. After that the stitch pain *left* stayed being a nuisance all the time. Saw TV news. The hijacked plane now in Algiers still has not given up the hostages!

Thursday, 14 April
Up at 7 o'c. and got papers. Back pain still continues to be a bane. Went to collect Lou's watch at the tube. Charge was £4 which was after I'd remonstrated about 4.95!! Walked to the bank & left documents for redemption of 3% Transport '88 (July) and thereafter I felt so weak I wanted to flake out. The pain (between hunger pangs & rats gnawing at your belly) got worse & worse. Dragged myself round Boots & M&S to do the shopping. Home by 11.30. Ate biscuits & the relief was pretty quick but the exhaustion *immense*. At 12.30 had fish cakes for lunch on my own in Lou's flat – she's gone to her club – and then had a lie down – oh! I'm so *tired* these days! No energy at all. *Pain* came back with vengeance! Nothing seems to allay it now. Rang Sheila at Murray-Lyon & rang agent & rang these video people. Sheila said she'd get on to Reynolds about an operation and we've said *some time after 25 April*. Even if the op. don't work, I can't be any *worse* off than I am at the moment.

Had meal with Lou at 5.30. Saw the News, watched the dreary saga of murder & mayhem. By 6.30 pain in the *back* was pulsating as it's never done before . . . so *this*, plus the stomach trouble combines to torture me – oh – what's the bloody point?

The diary ends. A sheet of blotting paper remains inserted at this page.

APPENDIX A

Addresses of Kenneth Williams

22 February 1926: Born Bingfield Street, London N1

Unknown date in infancy: Moved to 57 Marchmont Street, London WC1

Early 1940: Evacuated for several months to 19 Sheep Street, Bicester, Oxon

4 December 1947: Returned to Marchmont Street after war service abroad

24 March 1956: Moved to 817 Endsleigh Court, Upper Woburn Place, London WC1

7 October 1959: Moved to 66 Queen Alexandra Mansions, Hastings Street, London WC1 (room in John Hussey's flat)

24 February 1960: Moved to 76 Park West, Edgware Road, London W2

12 October 1963: Moved to 62 Farley Court, Allsop Place, London NW1

11 April 1970: Moved to 92 Queen Alexandra Mansions, Hastings Street, London WC1 (temporarily, during building work on 80 Queen Alexandra Mansions)

20 June 1970: Moved to 80 Queen Alexandra Mansions, Hastings Street, London WC1

3 August 1972: Moved to 8 Marlborough House, Osnaburgh Street, London NW1. Died there 14/15 April 1988

APPENDIX B

Films referred to in the diaries

Alamo, The: 1960, dir. John Wayne. With John Wayne, Richard Widmark

Anna Karenina: 1948, dir. Julien Duvivier. With Vivien Leigh, Kieron Moore

Arabian Adventure: 1979, dir. Kevin Connor. With Peter Cushing, Mickey Rooney

Bedtime Story: 1941, dir. Alexander Hall. With Fredric March, Loretta Young

Beggar's Opera, The: 1952, dir. Peter Brook. With Laurence Olivier, Dorothy Tutin

Bel-Ami: 1939, dir. Willi Forst. With Willi Forst, Olga Tschechowa

Ben-Hur: 1959, dir. William Wyler. With Charlton Heston, Haya Harareet

Bicycle Thieves (Ladri di Biciclette): 1948, dir. Vittorio De Sica. With Lamberto Maggiorani

Blow Out (La Grande Bouffe): 1973, dir. Marco Ferreri. With Marcello Mastroianni, Michel Piccoli

Bombay Clipper: 1941, dir. John Rawlins. With William Gargan, Maria Montez

Bonnie and Clyde: 1967, dir. Arthur Penn. With Warren Beatty, Faye Dunaway

Born Yesterday: 1950, dir. George Cukor. With Judy Holliday, Broderick Crawford

Boy from Barnardo's, The (aka *Lord Jeff*): 1938, dir. Sam Wood. With Charles Coburn

Boys in the Band, The: 1969, dir. William Friedkin. With Leonard Frey, Cliff Gorman

Breaker Morant: 1980, dir. Bruce Beresford. With Edward Woodward

Browning Version, The: 1951, dir. Anthony Asquith. With Michael Redgrave, Jean Kent

Cage aux Rossignols, La: 1947, dir. Jean Dréville. With Noël-Noël, René Wheeler

Captain Horatio Hornblower R.N.: 1951, dir. Raoul Walsh. With Gregory Peck

Carrie: 1952, dir. William Wyler. With Laurence Olivier, Jennifer Jones

Citizen Kane: 1941, dir. Orson Welles. With Orson Welles, Joseph Cotten

Connecting Rooms: 1969, dir. Franklin Gollings. With Bette Davis. Michael Redgrave

Cosh Boy (USA: *The Slasher*): 1953, dir. Lewis Gilbert. Cast incl. Sidney James

Cottage To Let: 1941, dir. Anthony Asquith. With Leslie Banks, Alastair Sim

Cruel Sea, The: 1952, dir. Charles Frend. With Jack Hawkins, Stanley Baker

Daddy's Gone A-Hunting: 1969, dir. Mark Robson. With Carol White, Scott Hylands

Dam Busters, The: 1954, dir. Michael Anderson. With Michael Redgrave, Richard Todd

Dirty Harry: 1971, dir. Don Siegel. With Clint Eastwood, John Vernon

Dr No: 1962, dir. Terence Young. With Sean Connery, Ursula Andress

East of Eden: 1954, dir. Nicholas Ray. With James Dean, Raymond Massey

Egg and I, The: 1947, dir. Chester Erskine. With Claudette Colbert, Fred MacMurray

End of the Affair, The: 1954, dir. Edward Dmytryk. With Deborah Kerr, Van Johnson

Flaming Star: 1960, dir. Don Siegel. With Elvis Presley, Dolores Del Rio

400 Blows, The (*Les Quatre Cents Coups*): 1959, dir. François Truffaut. With Jean-Paul Léaud

Gilda: 1946, dir. Charles Vidor. With Rita Hayworth, Glenn Ford
Great Escape, The: 1963, dir. John Sturges. With James Garner, Steve McQueen
Guinea Pig, The: (a.k.a. *The Outsider*), dir. Roy Boulting. With Richard Attenborough
Here Come the Co-Eds: 1945, dir. Jean Yarbrough. With Abbott & Costello
High Wind in Jamaica, A : 1965, dir. Alexander Mackendrick. With Anthony Quinn
Hombre: 1967, dir. Martin Ritt. With Paul Newman, Diane Cilento
Hound of the Baskervilles, The: 1977, dir. Paul Morrissey. With Peter Cook, Dudley Moore
Innocents in Paris: 1953, dir. Gordon Parry. With Alastair Sim, Margaret Rutherford
Intermezzo: 1939, dir. Gregory Ratoff. With Leslie Howard, Ingrid Bergman
It Started with Eve: 1941. dir. Henry Koster. With Deanna Durbin, Charles Laughton
Joe Kidd: 1972, dir. John Sturges. With Clint Eastwood, Robert Duvall
Kes: 1969, dir. Ken Loach. With Dai Bradley, Lynne Perrie
King Creole: 1958, dir. Michael Curtiz. With Elvis Presley, Carolyn Jones
Last Holiday, The: 1950, dir. Henry Gess. With Alec Guinness, Kay Walsh
Leopard, The: 1963, dir. Luchino Visconti. With Burt Lancaster, Claudia Cardinale
Love and Pain and the Whole Damn Thing: 1972, dir. Alan J. Pakula. With Maggie Smith, Timothy Bottoms
Maltese Falcon, The: 1941, dir, John Huston. With Humphrey Bogart, Mary Astor
Man Upstairs, The: 1958, dir. Don Chaffey. With Richard Attenborough, Bernard Lee
McQ: 1974, dir. John Sturges. With John Wayne, Eddie Albert
Mirror Crack'd, The: 1980, dir. Guy Hamilton. With Angela Lansbury
Monsieur Hulot's Holiday: 1951, dir. Jacques Tati. With Jacques Tati, Nathalie Pascaud
Murder at the Gallop: 1963, dir. George Pollock. With Margaret Rutherford
Mutiny on the Bounty: 1962, dir. Lewis Milestone. With Trevor Howard, Marlon Brando
Night at the Opera, A: 1935, dir. Sam Wood. With the Marx Brothers, Margaret Dumont
Notorious: 1946, dir. Alfred Hitchcock. With Ingrid Bergman, Cary Grant
No Way to Treat a Lady: 1968, dir. Jack Smight. With Rod Steiger, Lee Remick
Operation Pacific: 1951, dir. George Waggner. With John Wayne
Paisà: 1947, dir. Roberto Rossellini. With Carmela Sazio, Robert Van Loon
Pandora and the Flying Dutchman: 1950, dir. Albert Lewin. With Ava Gardner, James Mason
Passion of Joan of Arc, The: 1928, dir. Carl Dreyer. With Renée Falconetti
Passport to Pimlico: 1949, dir. Henry Cornelius. With Stanley Holloway, Margaret Rutherford
Pat and Mike: 1952, dir. George Cukor. With Spencer Tracy, Katharine Hepburn
Pierrot-le-Fou: 1965, dir. Jean-Luc Godard. With Jean-Paul Belmondo, Anna Karina
Pimpernel Smith: 1941, dir. Leslie Howard. With Leslie Howard, Mary Morris
Prime of Miss Jean Brodie, The: 1969, dir. Ronald Neame. With Maggie Smith, Robert Stephens
Punch and Judy Man, The: 1962, dir. Jeremy Summers. With Tony Hancock, Sylvia Syms
Quartet: 1949, dirs. Ken Annakin et al. With Mai Zetterling, Dirk Bogarde etc.
Random Harvest: 1942, dir. Mervyn Le Roy. With Ronald Colman, Greer Garson
Rebecca: 1940, dir. Alfred Hitchcock. With Laurence Olivier, Joan Fontaine
Rebel Without a Cause: 1954, dir. Elia Kazan. With James Dean, Natalie Wood
Ring of Bright Water: 1969, dir. Jack Couffer. With Bill Travers, Virginia McKenna
Roman Spring of Mrs Stone, The: 1961, dir. Jose Quintero. With Vivien Leigh, Warren Beatty.
Saigon: 1948, dir. Leslie Fenton. With Alan Ladd, Veronica Lake
Sapphire: 1958, dir. Basil Dearden. With Nigel Patrick, Yvonne Mitchell
Scarface Mob, The: 1958, dir. Phil Karlson. With Robert Stack, Neville Brand
Secret Agent of Japan: 1942, dir. Irving Pichel. With Preston Foster, Lynn Bari.
Seekers, The: 1954, dir. Ken Annakin. With Jack Hawkins, Glynis Johns
Sergeant, The: 1968, dir. John Flynn. With Rod Steiger, John Phillip Law
Shenandoah: 1965, dir. Andrew V. McLaglen. With James Stewart, Katherine Ross

Silkwood: 1983, dir. Mike Nichols. With Meryl Streep, Cher

Sodom and Gomorrah: 1962, dir. Robert Aldrich. With Stewart Granger, Stanley Baker

Some Like it Hot: 1959, dir. Billy Wilder. With Marilyn Monroe, Tony Curtis, Jack Lemmon

Sound of Fury, The: 1951, dir. Cyril Endfield. With Lloyd Bridges, Kathleen Ryan

Stars in my Crown: 1950, dir. Jacques Tourneur. With Joel McCrea, Ellen Drew

Stranger Left no Card, The: 1952, dir. Wendy Toye. With Alan Badel, Cameron Hall

Strangers on a Train: 1951, dir. Alfred Hitchcock. With Farley Granger, Robert Walker

Sunset Boulevard: 1950, dir. Billy Wilder. With Gloria Swanson, William Holden

Taste of Honey, A: 1961, dir. Tony Richardson. With Rita Tushingham, Dora Bryan

That Riviera Touch: 1966, dir. Cliff Owen. With Morecambe & Wise, Suzanne Lloyd

This Sporting Life: 1963, dir. Lindsay Anderson. With Richard Harris, Rachel Roberts

Touch of Evil: 1958, dir. Orson Welles. With Charlton Heston, Orson Welles

Trent's Last Case: 1952, dir. Herbert Wilcox. With Michael Wilding, Margaret Lockwood

Trio: 1950, dir. Ken Annakin, Harold French. With Nigel Patrick

Twice Round the Daffodils: 1962, dir. Gerald Thomas. With Juliet Mills, Donald Sinden

Victim: 1962, dir. Basil Dearden. With Dirk Bogarde, Sylvia Syms

VIPs, The: 1963, dir. Anthony Asquith. With Richard Burton, Elizabeth Taylor

Viridiana: 1961, dir. Luis Buñuel. With Silvia Rinal, Fernando Rey

Vote for Huggett: 1949, dir. Ken Annakin. With Jack Warner, Kathleen Harrison

Who's Afraid of Virginia Woolf: 1966, dir. Mike Nichols. With Richard Burton, Elizabeth Taylor

Wild and the Willing, The: 1962, dir. Ralph Thomas. With Virginia Maskell, Ian McShane

INDEX

Laurence Olivier

A Biography

Donald Spoto

'Rivetingly interesting, admirably researched and exquisitely written – an altogether wonderful book' Sir John Gielgud

'A work of subtle critical insight, warm, human, and always highly readable' *New Statesman*

In the first biography of Laurence Olivier to appear since his death, Donald Spoto reveals the man behind the mask of the flamboyant, heroic actor. Based on meticulous research and many previously unpublished documents, this is the first full portrait of our greatest man of the theatre.

Mae West: Empress of Sex

Maurice Leonard

In this no-holds barred account, Maurice Leonard brings the self-created myth of Mae West to life. He reveals how a mediocre vaudeville performer, who socialised with mobsters and boot-leggers, shot to stardom in the 1930s. As the Sex Queen of the Silver Screen, Mae West became the highest-paid woman in America, and almost single-handedly saved Paramount Studios from bankruptcy. Yet within a decade her fees had plummeted, and no one would give her a role. Down but not out, Mae fought back to make one of the most sensational comebacks in movie history.

Drawing on previously undisclosed material and unpublished photographs, Maurice Leonard brilliantly recreates Mae West's greatest – and worst – hours.

Chaplin

His Life and Art

David Robinson

'Unlikely ever to be surpassed.' *Spectator*

In just a few short years Charles Chaplin revolutionized the language of cinema and became the most universally loved performer of all time. But who was the man that dazzled and perplexed his adoring public? Perfectionist, playboy or workaholic? Spokesman for the poor or playmate of the international rich? Calculating or compassionate?

Only this definitive biography answers such contradictory and intriguing questions – the only one to be written with full access to the Chaplin archives – in which David Robinson provides a uniquely documented record of the working methods and extraordinary life of the mercurial genius of early cinema.

'An indispensable work for all concerned with the history of the cinema.' *Sunday Times*

'A classic piece of film biography which is also the fascinating story of a brilliant, perverse, courageous man, indisputably one of the great artists of the twentieth century.'
Lindsay Anderson, *Tatler*

ISBN 0 586 08544 0

An Autobiography

Part One – From Congregations to Audiences

David Frost

David Frost is probably the most diverse, long-lasting and consistently innovatory performer the television age has produced. From his earliest days on 'That Was The Week That Was' – the show which turned television in a completely new direction – to his recent interviews of presidents and prime ministers, he has never been far from the centre of events.

In the first part of his autobiography he gives his own account of his childhood as the son of a Methodist minister, his appearances with the Cambridge Footlights, and the foundation of London Weekend Television and the business interests that have made him, in the words of one commentator, a 'one-man conglomerate'. But it is by his interviewing that Frost has made his greatest mark. The encounters he presents here, with figures as diverse as Robert Kennedy, Muhammad Ali, Enoch Powell and the Prince of Wales, show him to be one of television's most incisive interviewers. They also illuminate some of the great questions of his time – drugs, racism, the decline of religious faith – and capture the moods of Britain and America in the 1960s.

Nobody who reads this wonderfully entertaining book can fail to be impressed by David Frost's energy and the impact he had on public life in the 1960s, on both sides of the Atlantic. There emerges from it a figure who was not only made by his times, but in part made them.

ISBN 0 00 638082 4

Hollywood vs. America

Popular Culture and the War on Traditional Values

Michael Medved

This book has struck a raw nerve. Film stars, commentators and politicians joined the fierce debate fuelled by Michael Medved's trenchant critique of the film industry – the most provocative study of the moral implications of popular culture ever written. His condemnation of sex, violence, bad language, and the seemingly consistent attack on traditional values, has given rise to feverish discussions on both sides of the Atlantic. Jane Fonda has accused Hollywood of immortality. Sir Anthony Hopkins may not now recreate the monstrous role of Hannibal Lecter.

Why do so many films attack religion, glorify violence and undermine the family? What is the cost of big-screen brutality? Have we become impervious to the increasingly grotesque violence erupting from our cinema screens and high-street video shops?

Greeted both with cheers of support and howls of enraged dissent, *Hollywood vs. America* confronts head on one of the most significant issues of our time.

'Real dynamite . . . The author says his book will make him the most hated man in Hollywood. On the other hand, it might save an industry that seems bent on self-destruction.' *Daily Mail*

ISBN 0 00 638235 5